ABEL JANSZOON TASMAN'S JOURNAL

EDITED BY
PROF. J.E. HEERES, LL. D.

AND

ABEL JANSZOON TASMAN: HIS LIFE AND LABOURS

BY
PROF. J.E. HEERES, LL. D.

ABEL JANSZOON TASMAN'S JOURNAL

EDITED BY

J E HEERES

CONTENTS

PREFACE...5
TRANSLATION OF THE JOURNAL. 9
AUGUST 1642 9
SEPTEMBER 1642 13
OCTOBER 1642 20
NOVEMBER 1642..27
DECEMBER 1642 45
JANUARY 1643 66
FEBRUARY 1643...85
MARCH 1643 100
APRIL 1643...109
MAY 1643..124
JUNE 1643 137

PREFACE

In laying before the reader the historic documents contained in the following pages, the Editors would beg leave briefly to set forth their motives in arranging for the bringing out of the work now submitted to the public.

For some years past numerous applications, in the first place from Australia, have been made to us for documents and works relating to Tasman and his discoveries. In the course of the investigations required on our part in order to comply with the wishes of such applicants, we soon became convinced that all existing works on the subject are either unreliable or sadly incomplete.

Even Jacob Swart's edition of Tasman's Journal in his Verhandelingen en Berigten beirekkelijk het Zeweezen [Papers and Reports relative to matters of navigation], Amsterdam 1854-60)[1], turned out to be untrustworthy, also as regards the annexed reproduction of the official chart of the voyages of 1642-44.

[1] Of these papers a very small number of copies appeared separately. The chart annexed to these copies had been slightly corrected.

This is not the place to point out the numerous mistakes to be found in Swart's edition. It must at the same time be admitted that his misreadings of the original MS. are for the greater part excusable, although it cannot be denied that his text shows a few errors of a very odd kind.

Still, however pardonable some of these slips may be, we are firmly persuaded that the documents relating to the discovery of the fifth part of the world deserve and require to be edited with the greatest possible care and accuracy, in the original text, with translations and elucidatory notes. Such notes are the more necessary since all that has been written and printed outside Holland on the subject of Tasman and his discoveries, from Thévenot in 1663 down to Rainaud in 1893, is either hopelessly wrong, or at all events disfigured by numerous errors as regards Tasman himself and the milieu in which his life requires to be studied, viz., the faits et gestes of the Dutch East India company of his day.

These traditionary misconceptions have long been an eyesore to us, and in order to put an end to them for good and all, we determined to have a facsimile reproduction made of the official Journal of the expedition of 1642/3, signed by Tasman himself, and preserved among the State Archives at The Hague; to subjoin to this reproduction an English translation of the text, as close as would be found compatible with intelligibility; to prefix to the whole work an elaborate introduction, and append a number of historical annotations, the introduction and notes to be written by the scholar on whom a task like this would almost naturally devolve, viz. Prof. J. E. Heeres, LL. D., since September 1897, Professor of Colonial History at the Colonial Institute, Delft, at the time one of the conservators of the invaluable Colonial Archives at The Hague.

Of course, only these Archives could in the last instance furnish the solution of all the questions that were sure to present themselves in the execution of the task proposed. It would be difficult to overestimate the amount of archival research which Prof. Heeres has been content to go through, especially during the last three years. It has not been his aim to write a précis for the use of the general reader: the learned author gives whatever he has deemed calculated to throw light on the subject in hand, and never fails to substantiate his views by references to the authentic sources entrusted to his care.

Of the literature of the subject he discusses or disproves only that which seemed to require discussion or disproval.

We must not omit to point out the historico-cartographic importance of the present undertaking. Our previous publication entitled Remarkable Maps. Parts II, III. The Geography of Australia as delineated by the Dutch cartographers of the XVII century, edited by C. H. Coote, of the British Museum, was in many respect a precursor of the work now issued. By consulting the maps there reproduced, readers will be enabled to follow step by step Prof. Heeres's elaborate investigations in this field, and at the same time become aware how his intimate knowledge of the Colonial Archives at The Hague has stood him in good stead for throwing frequent unexpected lights on many intricate problems of cartography.

Prof. Heeres's text together with Dr. Van Bemmelen's contribution to the work, take up about 150 folio pages more than we had estimated in our original prospectus to intending subscribers, while the number of charts appended to the work has been extended to five.

The translation of Tasman's Journal and of the documents forming the Appendices has been carefully supervised by Prof. Heeres; the preparation of the chart of the two voyages of 1642 and 1644 after the official chart of these expeditions, and the Englishing of the legends, has likewise taken place under his superintendence. It should, however, be noted that in reading the chart Prof. Heeres's introductory text should be consulted in cases in which he attempts to account for the corrections made by him. To avoid the appearance of overhasty conclusions, he often queries place-names in cases in which his presumption verges very closely on absolute conviction.

Next to Prof. Heeres, our best thanks are due to Dr. W. Van Bemmelen, assistant-director o the Royal Meteorological Institute, Utrecht, who has contributed the dissertation entitled: Ohservations made with the Compass on Tasman's voyage, etc.

We are also greatly indebted to Jhr. Th. H. F. Van Riemsdijk, LL. D., Keeper of the State Archives at the Hague, to the late Mr. F. D. 0. Obreen, Chief Director of the Government Museum at Amsterdam, and to his successor in office, Jhr, B. F. W. Van Riemsdijk, for the ready courtesy with which these gentlemen allowed us to use the hall of the Government Museum for the purpose of making photographic reproductions of the MS. and of the charts.

In the work of translating into English Prof. Heeres's text, the Journal, and the documents forming the Appendices, we have to acknowledge the good services of Mr. J. De Hoop Scheffer, of Amsterdam, and Mr. C. Stoffel, of Nijmegen.

The Editors:
FREDERIK MULLER and Co.
(F. ADAMA VAN SCHELTEMA and ANTON MENSINO
Amsterdam,
May, 1898

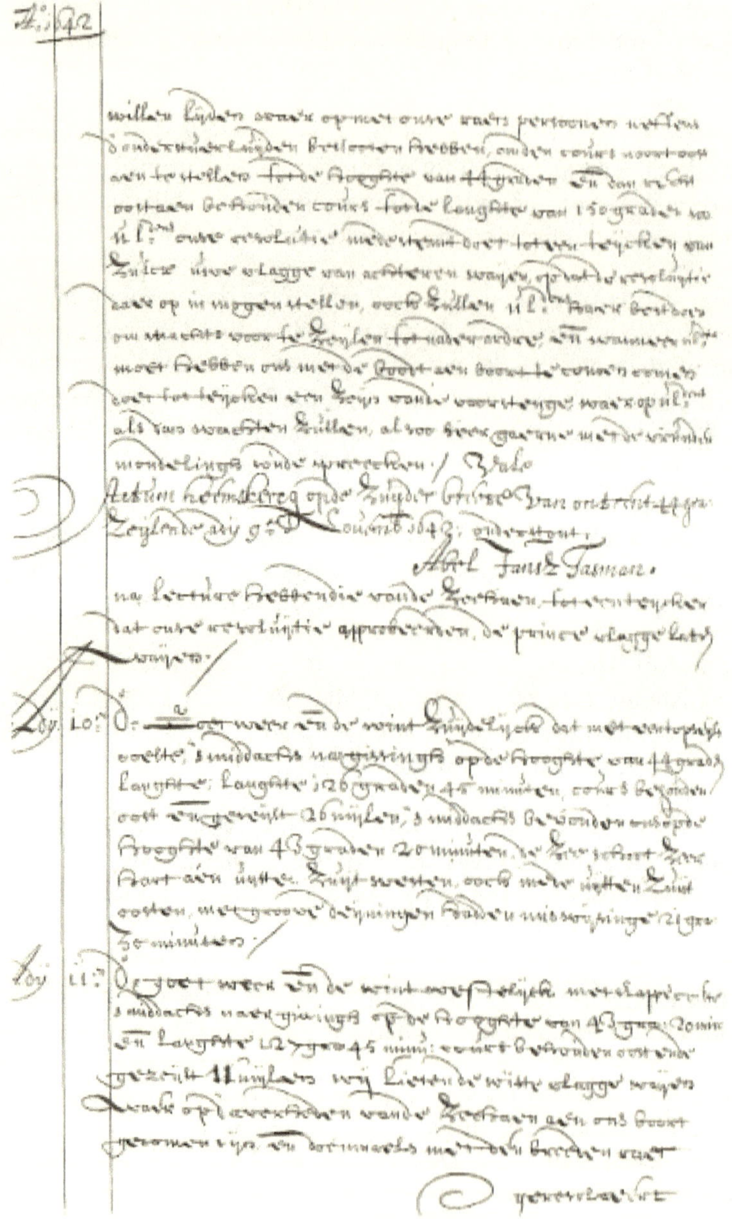

A page from Tasman's Journal

TRANSLATION OF THE JOURNAL

Journal or Description drawn up by me, Abel Jansz Tasman, of a voyage made from the town of Batavia in East India for the discovery of the unknown South land in the year of our Lord 1642, the 14th of August. May God Almighty vouchsafe His blessing on this work. Amen.

AUGUST 1642

This day August 14, A.D. 1642, we set sail from the roads of *Batavia*[1] with two ships, the Yacht Heemskerk and the Flute Zeehaan, the wind being north-east with good weather. On the same day in the evening the Zeehaan ran aground near the island of Rotterdam,[2] but got afloat again in the night without any notable damage, after which we continued our voyage to the Straits of Sunda.

Item the 15th.

Towards evening we went to Mr. Sweers, who was on board the Yacht Bredam, from whom we understand that at Bantam point there lay at anchor a quelpaert,[3] newly arrived from the Netherlands; at night we anchored off Anjer[4] in 22 fathom, where we refitted our ship which was disabled to such a degree that we could not possibly have put to sea in her.

Item the 16th.

The wind continuing east with a steady breeze, the current running fast from Sunda Strait; at night we weighed anchor with the wind blowing from the land, set sail and shaped our course so as to pass between the Prince Islands and Cracatouw.

Item the 17th.

In the morning we had the Prince Islands south-west and Cracatouw north-west by north of us, the wind being south-east, our course south-west by west; at noon we had the southernmost of the Prince Islands east-south-east of us at 5 miles distance, ourselves being in 6° 20' Southern Latitude and 124° Longitude;[5] in the afternoon we drifted in a calm; in the said afternoon it was resolved that from Sunda Strait we shall sail 200 miles to the south-west by west, as far as 14° South Latitude; from there to the west-south-west as far as 20° South Latitude, and from there due west as far as the island of Mauritius.

Item the 18th.

Latitude by estimation 6° 48', longitude 123° 20', the wind south-east with good weather, course kept south-west by west as resolved on in council on the 17th, sailed 13 miles; at night we had heavy rains with thunder and lightning.

Item the 19th.

At noon we found the latitude to be 8° 38', the longitude 120° 35'; we sailed 36 miles; course kept by estimation south-west by west, but we find we are more to the south; wind south-east by east, top-gallant gale; variation of the compass 3° north-westerly.

Item the 20th.

At noon Latitude observed 10°, Longitude 118° 30'; wind south-east by east, top-gallant gale, course kept south-west by west, sailed 36 miles, good weather and smooth water.

Item the 21st.

At noon Latitude observed 11° 12', Longitude 116° 42'; wind south-east, top-gallant gale, course kept south-west by west, sailed 32 miles; we saw numbers of birds and estimated ourselves to be in the longitude of the Coques Isles[6] variation 5° North-West.

Item the 22nd.

At noon Latitude observed 13° 31', Longitude 114° 40'; wind southeast, top-gallant gale, course kept south-west by west sailed 36 miles.

[1] The italicised names are found on Swart's reproduction of the Bonaparte chart.

[2] An island in the bight of Batavia.

[3] "Quelpaert," an old name for a galiot.

[4] On the north-west coast of Java, north of Tandjong Tjikoneng (Java's 4e Punt).

[5] The longitude is reckoned eastward from the Peak of Teneriffe, which is 16° 46' westward of the meridian of Greenwhich, and was nearly so estimated in Tasman's time. As regards the degrees of longitude and latitude, compare VAN BEMMELEN'S "Observations", and his book entitled De Isogonen in de XVIde en XVIIde eeuw. Utrecht, Van Druten, 1893. pp. 26 f.

[6] Or Keeling Isles.

Item the 23rd.

At noon Latitude observed 13° 57', Longitude 112° 23'; wind southeast with a steady breeze, course kept south-west by west, sailed 40 miles, the sea still running high from the south-west and south-south-west.

Item the 24th.

At noon Latitude observed 14° 29', Longitude 109° 41'; wind southeast with a steady breeze, course kept west by south, sailed 40 miles.

Item the 25th.

At noon Latitude observed 15° 13', Longitude 107° 20', the estimated Latitude being 15° 28'; wind south-east with a steady breeze, course kept west-south-west slightly westerly, sailed 38 miles; variation 8° 20' North-West.

Item the 26th.

At noon Latitude observed 16°, Longitude 105° 12', the estimated Latitude being 16° 7'; wind south-south-east, top-gallant gale, course kept west-south-west slightly westerly, sailed 36 miles; variation 11°.

Item the 27th.

At noon Latitude observed 16° 40', Longitude 103°; wind south-east but east in the evening, light top-gallant gale, course kept west-south-west, sailed 26 miles; variation 12° 30'.

Item the 28th.

At noon Latitude estimated 17° 7' south, Longitude 102° 22'; wind variable with a dark sky, course kept west-south-west sailed 18 miles.

Item the 29th.

At noon estimated Latitude 17° 50', Longitude 100° 34'; in the afternoon variable winds; at 3 glasses[1] in the first watch we again had the wind south-south-east, top-gallant gale, course kept west-south-west, sailed 28 miles.

Item the 30th.

At noon estimated Latitude 18° 51', Longitude 97° 58'; wind south-east with light showers, course kept west-south-west, sailed 40 miles; about noon the Zeehaan broke her spritsail yard.

Item the last.

At noon estimated Latitude 19° 55', Longitude 95° 14'; wind south-south-east, unsteady with drizzling rain, course kept west-south-west, sailed 42 miles, shortly after noon I compared notes with the skippers and steersmen, when we found the average latitude to be 19° 49' and the do. longitude 95° 24'; we continued to run west-south-west until the evening and then west, being in the longitude of the island of Mauritius.

SEPTEMBER 1642

Item the 1st of September.

At noon estimated Latitude 20° 28', Longitude 92° 19'; wind south-east with a steady breeze and drizzling rain, course kept west by south, sailed 42 miles.

Item the 2nd.

At noon estimated Latitude 20° 28', Longitude 89° 29'; wind east-south-east with a steady breeze, drizzling rains and high seas, course kept west, sailed 40 miles; variation of the compass needle 20° North-West.

Item the 3rd.

At noon observed Latitude 20° 36', Longitude 86° 56'; wind east-south-east, top-gallant gale with good weather, course kept west, sailed 36 miles.

Item the 4th.

At noon estimated Latitude 19° 55', Longitude 85° 13'; wind easterly, light top-gallant gale, course kept west-north-west, sailed 26 miles; variation 22° 30'; at night at the end of the first watch we saw land; we lay a-trying with clewed sails all night.

Item the 5th.

In the morning we saw that it was the island of Mauritius; we steered for it and came to anchor before it at about 9 o'clock, we being then in Latitude 20°, Longitude 83° 48'. When we saw the island of Mauritius we were by estimation still 50 miles east of it.

Item the 6th.

We sent 6 sailors, three belonging to the Zeehaan and three to our ship, together with one of our second mates, to the wood to assist the huntsmen there in capturing game and bring the same down to our ships. At noon we saw a ship outside the bay before the entrance, which ship came to anchor near us about 4 hours later, when we understood her to be the Arent, which had sailed from the Texel on the 23rd of April last in company with the ships Salmander and Zutphen, the Yacht Leuwerick and the galiot Visscher, the said ships and yachts having parted company with her at the Zoute islands[2] in order to continue their voyage to Batavia. The said Arent brought a quantity of provisions such as victuals and ammunition of war, together with a number of soldiers and sailors for the island of Mauritius. The officers of the said Yacht reported to Commander Van der Stel that on the 27th ultimo they had got to Diego Rodrigos, believing it to be Mauritius, seeing that it is in the same longitude as the latter island; that there they had found a French ship lying at anchor on the roadstead; that they could not clearly make out whence this ship had come, owing to the evasive answers they received from the crew, some saying they had come from Diepen, others from the Red Sea, and that they were bound for the Mascarinas or were going to call at Madagascar; that they had sailed from Diego Rodrigos at the same time with the French ship and had parted company with her on the 5th instant at noon; that they were still in sight of her in the evening, at which time they saw that she shaped her course west-south-west. On this report the Commander aforesaid straightways despatched some men to the north-west side of the island in order to ascertain whether the Frenchman could have gone thither, the Commander presuming that the Frenchman might have attempted to mislead our people to get an opportunity of cutting some ebony wood there, which we were bound to prevent him from doing.

[1] One glass is equal to half an hour.

[2] Salt Islands or Cabo Verde Islands.

Item the 7th.

We were engaged nearly all day repairing our ropes and tackle; considering that our rigging was old, weak and not much to be depended on we added three more large ropes to the rigging on both sides the main and foremast in order to steady the same; towards evening we got 8 head of goats and one pig from shore.

Item the 8th.

In the morning we sent to the Zeehaan four out of the 8 goats received yesterday; also sent for one more sailor in her whom, together with one of our own men, we despatched to shore to assist the huntsmen and the men who went ashore on the 6th instant.

Item the 9th.

We sent one of our carpenters together with 7 or 8 sailors from our ship and from the Zeehaan to the wood in order to cut down timber; in the afternoon we wrote an order to the officers of the Zeehaan, enjoining them to serve out to each of their men no more than half a mutchkin[1] of arrack as his daily ration. Then Worshipful Van der Stel informs us that he has got positive orders from the Honourable Governor-General and Councillors of India not to serve out more than one pympeltien[2] of arrack to each of his men, and this only to such as are cold, wet and dirty. In order to maintain peace among the men and prevent discontent, ill-will and envy as far as in us lies we have therefore deemed it best to serve out only half a small glass of arrack to our men while we are lying in this roadstead.

Item the 10th.

We sent our Skipper Ide Tjercxz to bring on board of us the Honourable Van der Stel with whom we discussed the question whether it would not be needed for our ships, and advantageous to the Company, before sailing from here to continue our destined voyage to appoint a place of rendezvous, the rather as the Honourable Governor-General and Councillors of India have expressly and instantly enjoined and recommended the appointing of such a place of rendezvous in our instructions; after due deliberation we summoned on board of us all our skippers, first and second mates, and informed them that we desired all persons present to give their advice in writing what place were best to fix upon for a rendezvous, in case we should get separated from each other by rough weather, storms or other accidents (which we hope will be spared us and God in his mercy advert) to the end that we may join company again; and that, after being made acquainted with each person's advice, we shall resolve upon such a line of action as shall be serviceable to the Company and to the furtherance of our voyage. In the evening we got from shore 8 goats and 2 hogs; our carpenter Jan

Joppen also returned on board, reporting that they had cut down a number of trees for timber but that no more fitting was to be had at that place.

Item the 11th.

In the morning our skipper, together with the carpenter aforesaid, went to the wood in the boat for the purpose of fetching thence the timber, and took the same to the fortress of Frederik Heyndrick, there to be sawn into boards of the most fitting dimensions. In the afternoon we sent 4 goats and one hog to those on board the Zeehaan.

Item the 12th.

In the morning our boat went to the wood a second time, and again took some logs to the fortress aforesaid. Towards the evening we again received 12 goats, half of which we sent to the Zeehaan. Our skipper reported that one of our sailors, Joris Claesen van Bahuys by name, had badly hurt himself in handling a log that was to be sawn ashore; on which we forthwith sent on shore our chief and assistant barbers to examine the patient and give him the requisite attendance.

[1] An old Dutch measure of capacity, equal to 1.056 imperial pint.

[2] An old Sutch name for a liqueur-glass.

Item the 13th.

Nothing worth mentioning occurred today except that we sent a bag of rice to our men in the wood and fished our main-yard.

Item the 14th.

We again received from shore 4 goats and 2 hogs, of each of which we sent half to the Zeehaan. In the evening the men despatched by the Honourable Van der Stel on the 6th instant returned, reporting that in none of the bays they had seen any sign of the French ship.

Item the 15th.

In the morning we sent ashore our chief boatswain and boatswain's mate with a number of sailors and a quantity of cordage in order to make ropes.

Item the 16th.

The Yacht Cleyn Mauritius sailed from here in order to fetch ebony from a spot about 10 miles to the eastward, to serve as cargo for the Arent; having got near the entrance of the bay she cast anchor because unable to beat out owing to strong wind. Towards noon the Honourable Van der Stel and Tasman convened on board the admiral the councils of the Fortress of Frederick Hendrik of the ships Heemskerk and Zeehaan and of the Yacht Arent, and submitted to the Council what was next resolved upon, as may be seen from this day's resolution. Towards the evening our second mate Chryn Hendricx, whom on the 6th instant we had dispatched to the huntsmen in the wood, returned on board bringing 10 head of goats; this day we ordered one of the second mates of the Zeehaan to go to the wood in our second mate's stead.

Item the 17th.

In the morning we sent our other second mate Carsten Jurriaens to the wood with six sailors to cut firewood; towards the evening we delivered 4 out of the 10 goats received yesterday to those on board the Zeehaan. This day by order of Commander Van der Stel and in pursuance of yesterday's resolution we took out of the Yacht Arent for the behoof of our ship and the Zeehaan the goods following, to wit:

```
6 ropes both large and small.
1 roll canvas. 20 pulleys, both large and small.
½ skin for pump-leather.
6 small clew-lines.
1 kedge-anchor.
A parcel of flat-headed nails.
4 pieces of horn for mending the lanterns.
```

Item the 18th.

Nothing occurred worth mentioning except that we fished our foremast at the back and got from shore 6 head of hogs, out of which at nightfall we gave three to the quartermaster of the Zeehaan.

Item the 19th.

The carpenters caulked the ship on the outside, stopped all the leaks they could find, and furthermore overhauled everything and duly pitched the seams.

Item the 20th.

I went shooting early in the morning in the west part of the island of Mauritius in company with Mr. Van der Maerzen, subcargo and second in command in the fortress of Fredrick Hendrick; we returned on board towards noon with 13 wild birds. This day we had a number of sawn boards brought from shore and a quantity of rope made ashore.

Item the 21st.

In the morning the Yacht Cleyn Mauritius got clear of the bay and set sail for her destination to fetch ebony for the cargo of the Arent; from the 16th instant when she left this roadstead she had been unable to beat out owing to the strong east-south-east trade-wind. This day we made a new main-top and fished the foremast near the top-yard on both sides; in the evening we received from shore 10 head of cattle to wit: 7 goats and 3 hogs.

Item the 22nd.

In the morning ourselves and Gerrit Jansz, Skipper in the Zeehaan, together with a number of sailors with axes, went ashore to the wood in order to procure fitting timber for top-yards, anchor-stocks and miz-zen-yards etc., for the purposes of our further voyage; we returned towards evening bringing a piece of round timber proper for fishing a top-yard, and also an anchor-stock for ourselves and two ditto for the Zeehaan.

Item the 23rd.

We fetched from the wood 3 anchor-stocks and a round piece of timber for

a top-yard with a quantity of firewood, and got a boatload of water from a watercourse east of the fortress of Fredrick Henrick.

Item the 24th.

We brought from shore a boatload of firewood and three ditto of water. Towards the evening we received in the huntsmen's boat 5 goats and three hogs, of which the same evening we handed three goats and one hog into the boat of the Zeehaan; during the night in the second watch we got on board another boat with 7 casks of water.

Item the 25th.

In the morning at daybreak there was a light breeze blowing from the land, at first from the north-north-east, afterwards somewhat fresher from north-west by west and west-north-west, which was the first land-breeze we had from the time we had come to anchor here. This day two pinnaces of firewood and two boatloads of water were fetched from shore; item our pilot-major Francoys Jacobsz and Mr. Gilsemans made a surveying of the coast.

Item the 26th.

We convened the council of the Heemskerk and the flute Zeehaan and resolved upon sailing from here on the 4th proximo, as may be more detailedly seen from today's resolution.

Item the 27th.

We sent our second mate Chryn Heyndrickse to the wood to cut firewood.

Item the 28th.

We sent our pinnace and boat to the wood to get firewood.

Item the 29th.

We still kept sending the pinnace and boat ashore for firewood; this day the Yacht Cleyn Mauritius returned, bringing one of the runaway Madagascar slaves.

Item the last.

We were still busy taking in firewood; towards the evening we got ten goats.

OCTOBER 1642

Item the 1st of October.

We were still engaged in taking in firewood with our pinnace and boat; towards the evening we got from shore 9 head of cattle, both he-goats and she-goats.

Item the 2nd.

Still busy taking in firewood and refilling the water-casks which were emptied day by day.

Item the 3rd.

Still kept the boat and pinnace at fetching water and firewood; at dusk we received on board 7 head of cattle, to wit 2 hogs, 4 he-goats and one she-goat.

Item the 4th.

This was the day we had fixed upon for putting to sea but owing to contrary winds we were unable to stand out to sea, so that we were forced to remain at anchor; we therefore despatched the pilot-major Francoys Jacobsz and the first mate of the Zeehaan, Heyndrick Pieter-sen, to take soundings in the eastern entrance, whence we were to set sail, where they sounded barely 13 feet at high-water at spring-tide.

Item the 5th.

The contrary wind still continuing, we were unable to beat out of the bay, and therefore sent our pinnace with the second mate Carsten Jurriaensz to catch fish with the dragnet, who returning brought a capital lot of fish for the whole of our crew.

Item the 6th.

We warped the kedge-anchor to get out at the south-east entrance and kedged a second time, but were compelled to give it up owing to the strong contrary wind. Towards the evening we learnt that the men sent out to seek the runaway Madagascar slaves had come back without having seen any of them; this day we again got a capital lot of fish for the whole crew.

Item the 7th.

The wind blowing from the east we were still busy with the kedge-anchor; in the evening we came to anchor under the islands in front of the bay in sixty fathom muddy bottom; this bay is very hard to get out of seeing that the south-east wind is continually blowing here; whoever has no urgent business here had better keep out of it.

Item the 8th.

In the morning the weather rainy with a light land-breeze and whirl-winds; we weighed our anchors but had to drop them again owing to contrary winds; about 8 o'clock the wind turned to the north-east by east, we weighed anchor and accordingly ran out to sea south-eastward, for which God be praised and thanked; the southern extremity of this island of Mauritius is in 20° 12'

South Latitude and 78° 47' Longitude. We shaped our course to the south-south-east, having the wind north-east, a weak top-gallant gale; at noon we turned our course to the south by east.

Item the 9th.

At noon Latitude observed 21° 5', Longitude 78° 47', course kept south, sailed 13 miles with good weather and a light breeze, the wind south-east. This day we drew up a resolution respecting the crew's meals as may be further seen from the same; in the evening we had the island of Mauritius still in sight.

Item the 10th.

At noon Latitude estimated 21° 54', Longitude 78° 11'; course kept south-west by south, sailed 15 miles, the wind being south-east with a light top-gallant gale; towards daybreak the sea began to run high from the south and we found our mizzen-mast to be quite broken at the partner so that we had to fish it on both sides.

Item the 11th.

At noon Latitude estimated 23° 28', Longitude 77° 51'; the wind easterly with a light top-gallant gale, course kept south by west, sailed 24 miles.

Item the 12th.

At noon Latitude observed 25° 18', Longitude 77° 51'; the wind northerly with a light top-gallant gale with good weather, a clear sky and smooth water; course kept south, sailed 28 miles; we again fished our mizzen-mast. Variation 23° 30' North-West.

Item the 13th.

At noon Latitude estimated 27° 26', Longitude 77° 51'; course kept south, sailed 32 miles, the wind from the north-west; in the morning rain and a top-gallant gale.

Item the 14th.

At noon Latitude observed 29° 20', Longitude 78° 45'; course kept south-south-east, sailed 29 miles, the wind west and west-south-west with a top-gallant gale; at night at the end of the first watch, the wind becoming south-south-east, we turned to the west. Variation 23° 30'.

Item the 15th.

The wind south-east and east-south-east with a dark sky and a stiff breeze; at noon Latitude estimated 29° 45', Longitude 78° 57'; course kept south-south-east, sailed 7 miles; towards the evening we got the wind east by south with a drizzling rain.

Item the 16th.

The wind south and south-south-east, at times south-east and east-south-east with a top-gallant gale; at noon we were in 31° 17' South Latitude, and Longitude 78° 13'; course kept south-south-west, sailed 25 miles. Variation 25° 15'.

Item the 17th.

A calm, the wind westerly; course kept south-south-east, sailed 9 miles; at noon Latitude observed 31° 51', Longitude 78° 26'. Towards noon we got a light top-gallant gale, wind as before. Variation 25° 30' North-West.

Item the 18th.

Good weather with a westerly wind and a top-gallant gale; at noon Latitude observed 33° 56'; course kept south by east, sailed 32 miles. Towards the evening the Zeehaan hove to leeward, whereupon we forthwith made towards her, she calling out to us that the wales to which her shroud-bolts are fixed had got disjoined so that they had to be fished. Variation 24°.

Item the 19th.

About 9 o'clock we got the wind south-south-west with drizzling rain and afterwards it fell a dead calm. At noon Latitude estimated 36° 2', Longitude 80°; course kept south-south-east, sailed 34 miles, with a top-gallant gale; in the afternoon the wind turned to the south-east and we tacked to the west.

Item the 20th.

Foggy weather with a drizzling rain. At noon Latitude estimated 36° 29', Longitude 79° 25'; course kept south-west with variable winds and the weather improving; sailed 10 miles; towards the evening the south-south-east wind fell almost to a calm.

Item the 21st.

Variable winds alternating with calms; at noon Latitude observed 36° 22', Longitude 79° 25', so that we found we had drifted two miles to northward. Towards evening we got a breeze from the north-west.

Item the 22nd.

Dark drizzly water with a westerly wind and a steady breeze; at noon Latitude estimated 38° 11', Longitude 78° 57'; course kept south by east, sailed 28 miles. Variation 24° 40' North-West.

Item the 23rd.

In the morning the wind began to blow stiffly from the west-south-west and south-west so that we had to take in our topsail. At noon Latitude estimated 40° 18', Longitude 80° 46', course kept south-east by south, sailed 40 miles; in the afternoon we turned our course to the south-east and had heavy showers of rain from time to time.

Item the 24th.

In the morning we took in our bonnets[1], lowered our foresail down to the stem, and ran on before the wind with our mainsail only; we dared not try to the wind because of the strong gale blowing. This gale was attended with hail and rain to such a degree that we feared the ship would not live through it, but at noon the storm somewhat abated so that we hauled to the wind; we could not see the Zeehaan, for which reason we hauled to the wind to stay for her. At noon Latitude estimated 40° 42', Longitude 83° 11'; course kept east by south, sailed 30 miles; the wind south-west and south with a violent storm; we kept a sharp lookout for the Zeehaan but could not get sight of her.

Item the 25th.

In the morning we sent a man to the masthead to look out for our partner whom he saw astern, of which we were full glad; the weather getting slightly better we again set our bonnets and drew up the foresail. Towards noon the Zeehaan again joined us. At noon our estimated latitude was 39° 58' and Longitude 84° 11; course kept north-north-east, sailed or drifted 12 miles; at noon we shaped our course to the south-east, with a south-west wind and a steady breeze.

Item the 26th.

Good weather, the wind south-west by west with a top-gallant gale; at noon Latitude observed 41° 34', Longitude 86° 10'; course kept south-east, sailed 32 miles; the sea still kept running high from the south-south-east; we changed our course to south-east by south and south-south-east; we spoke the Zeehaan and understood that this day a man died on board of her; as we were speaking the Zeehaan she broke her top-yard, which was forthwith replaced by another which they kept in stock. This day average Longitude 86° 14', Latitude 41° 40'.

Item the 27th.

In the morning before early breakfast we saw a good deal of rock-weed[2] and manna-grass[3] floating about; we therefore hoisted a flag, upon which the officers of the Zeehaan came to board of us; we convened the Council and submitted to their consideration the instructions of the Honourable Governor-General and Councillors of India in case we should see and observe land, shoals, sunken rocks, etc. We then submitted to the council the question whether, now that we observed these signs of land, it would not be best to keep a man at the masthead constantly and make him look out for land, shoals, sunken rocks and other dangers; also what sum had best be fixed upon as a reward to be given to him who should first see land, upon which the Council thought fit to keep a man on the lookout constantly, and to give three pieces-of-eight[4] and a can[5] of arrack to whoever shall first see and observe land, shoals, sunken rocks, etc.; all of which may in extenso be seen from this day's resolution. At noon our estimated latitude was 43°, and longitude 88° 6'; course kept south-east, sailed 30 miles, the wind being westerly with a top-gallant gale and a drizzling rain. Variation 26° 45'. At night we lay a-trying under reduced sail.

Item the 28th.

At daybreak we made sail again, turned our course south-south-eastward, in dark foggy weather; we still saw seaweeds floating about; at noon we estimated ourselves to be in Latitude 44° 47' South, and Longitude 89° 7'; course kept south-south-east, sailed 29 miles, in a north-westerly and westerly wind with a top-gallant gale; we also saw fragments of trees floating about resembling the leaves of wild bananas; at night we lay a-trying under reduced sail and dared not run on on account of the fog; gradually however the sea began to get smooth; we time after time fired a musket and now and then also a great gun.

Item the 29th.

In the morning we made sail again, held our course to the south-south-east, spoke the officers of the Zeehaan, because we thought it best to keep our course to eastward so long as the fog should last. Having hailed the friends of the Zeehaan we called out to them whether, seeing that in this fog and darkness it is hardly possible to survey known shores, let alone to discover unknown land, it would not be best and most advisable to shape our course to eastward until the advent of clearer weather and a better prospect; the which they deemed highly advisable; on which account we convened the ship's council with the second mates, and informed them of what the officers of the Zeehaan had said when we had spoken them, together with their opinion and advice; after which we asked all the persons assembled what they thought best to be done; whereupon a unanimous resolution was come to which may in extenso be gathered from this day's resolution and is fully accordant with the opinion of the officers of the Zeehaan. At noon we directed our course to eastward with a north-north-westerly wind and a top-gallant gale; our estimated latitude being 45° 47', and Longitude 89° 44'; course kept south-south-east sailed 17 miles.

[1] Bonnets are additional pieces of canvas laced to the foot of a sail to catch more wind.

[2] Rock-weed = Fucus giganteus.

[3] Glyceria maritima.

[4] "Reaal van achten," an old Spanish coin, peso de ocho = circa 4 shillings.

[5] "Canne", an old Dutch measure of capacity, equal to 1.760 imperial pint.

Item the 30th.

At daybreak we again made sail, shaped our course to eastward with a clear sky and a top-gallant gale from the west. At noon Latitude observed 45° 43', Longitude 91° 51'; course kept east, sailed 22 miles. Variation 26° 45'.

Item the last.

Towards noon a drizzling rain came on with fog, while the wind stiffened more and more, so that we took in our topsails; at noon we also took in our main-sail and ran on before the wind with our foresail, wind and sea running very high. At noon Latitude estimated 47° 4', Longitude 95° 19'; course kept east-south-east, sailed 50 miles; we then had a storm from the west and held our course to the east.

NOVEMBER 1642

Item the 1st of November.

In the morning the weather having somewhat improved we made more sail. At noon observed Latitude 46° 9', Longitude 99° 9'; we were greatly surprised at finding ourselves so far northward as we had estimated ourselves to be in 47°, and now found our latitude to be 46° 9'; course kept east but if we make allowance for the error in our estimation our course is east by north half a point more northerly, and we sailed 40 miles; in the afternoon the weather became foggy, the wind turning to the north-west with a light breeze; we saw a great quantity of rock-weed floating and shaped our course to the south-east, seeing that we were so far to northward; at night we lay a-trying under reduced sail. This day our master-gunner Eldert Luytiens departed this life in the Lord.

Item the 2nd.

In the morning we made sail again, shaping our course to the south-east; the wind north-west with a steady breeze; we sailed with the main-sail set, the weather being very foggy; course kept east-south-east, sailed 25 miles; estimated Latitude 46° 47', Longitude 101° 23'; we saw still a good deal of rock-weed floating about; at night we again lay a-trying with clewed sails as we dared not run on on account of the fog.

Item the 3rd.

The wind being south-west with a strong breeze we again made sail, held our course to south-eastward, and from time to time had heavy squalls of hail and snow with very cold weather. At noon Latitude observed 46° 47', Longitude 103° 58'; course kept east by south, sailed 27 miles; between the squalls we could keep a fair lookout so that we kept sailing during the night; we again saw quantities of rock-weed floating about from time to time, and found that we were driven to the north.

Item the 4th.

Wind and weather as before our course still being south-east; at noon we altered our course to eastward; Latitude estimated 48° 25', Longitude 107° 56'; course kept south-east by east, sailed 40 miles. In the afternoon we desired our skipper and mates to give in their average longitude and southern latitude which, after comparison with our own, we found to average 107° 25' Longitude and 48° 28' South Latitude. After this comparison of notes we convened the ship's council with the second mates, and submitted to their consideration what was subsequently unanimously resolved upon and is found duly specified in today's resolution, to which for briefness sake we refer. Towards evening we again saw various lots of rock-weed floating about, and observed large numbers of tunnies near and roundabout the ship; our boatswain's mate and one of the sailors also saw a seal, from which we surmise that there may be islands hereabouts, since these animals are not likely to go out far to sea; on this account we did not venture to run on full sail, but after supper held northward under reduced sail.

Item the 5th.

In the morning we had rather foggy, hazy and dirty weather with a dark grey sky; we made sail again and at first ran on east by south, seeing that last night we had been driven so far northward. At noon Latitude estimated 48° 25', Longitude 110° 55'; course kept east and sailed 30 miles.

Item the 6th.

We had a storm from the west with hail and snow, and ran on before the wind with our foresail barely halfway the mast; the sea ran very high and our men begin to suffer badly from the severe cold. At noon Latitude estimated 49° 4', Longitude 114° 56'; course kept east by south, sailed 49 miles. Variation 26°.

Item the 7th.

We received the notes following from our Pilot major.
Annotations drawn from the terrestrial globe and from the large
chart of the South Sea, and on the 7th of November A.D. 1642, handed
to the Honourable Commander Abel Jansz Tasman together with our
advice.

Imprimis:

The terrestrial globe shows us that the easternmost islands of the
Salomonis are in the longitude of fully 220°, reckoning said
longitude from the meridian of the islands of Corvo and Floris.

But they are in slightly short of 205°, according to the
longitude which starts from the island of Teneriffe, and which is
most generally used at present; and on the globe they extend from 7
to 14 to 15° Latitude south of the line equinoctial.

This being duly noted we shall follow the great chart of the South
Sea, using the longitude beginning from the Peak of Teneriffe, which
is generally used in our day.

First we have Batavia situated in Longitude   127° 5'.
And the south-west point of Celebes   11° 20'.

More to eastward, so that we get for the longitude of the
south-west point of Celebes   138° 25'.
now from the south-west point of Celebes to the easternmost
islands of the Salomonis, where the chart reads "Hoorensche
eylanden", we reckon   47° 20'.
So that we get for the longitude of the Hoorensche islands   185° 45'.

Now from the Hoorensche islands to the Cocos or Verraders islands,discovered by Willem Schouten, we reckon still more to
eastward8° 15'; so that for the longitude of Cocos and Verraders is-
landswe get 194°.

Should one wish to consider the Hoorensche islands, situated inLongi-
tude 185° 45', to be the easternmost of the Salomonis, thenthe charts
and globe would show a difference of about 19°; but ifone should look
upon the Cocos and Verraders island, situated in 194° Longitude and
17½° South Latitude, as the easternmost of the Salomonis islands, then
the difference between the charts and the globe would amount to no
more than 11°, the globe placing the islands 11° more eastward than
the charts; now to avoid all mistakes we think it best to disregard the
indications to eastward, both of the globe and of the charts.

Hence our advice is that we should stick to the 44th degree South Latitude until we shall have passed the 150th degree of Longitude, and
then run north as far as the 40th degree South Latitude, remaining
there with an easterly course until we shall have reached the 220th degree of Longitude, after which we should take a northerly course so as
to avail ourselves of the trade-wind to reach the Salomonis islands and
New Guinea by running from east to west. We cannot but think that, if
we find no land up to 150° Longitude, we shall then be in an open sea
again, unless we should meet with islands; all which time and experience, being the best of teachers, will no doubt bring to light.

Signed, Francoys Jacobsz.

In the morning, the wind still westerly with hail and snow so that we
had to run on with a furled foresail as before, and as we could not
make any progress in this way, we deemed it best to alter our course to
northward upon which, with our ship's council together with our
second mates, seeing that we could not speak the friends of the Zee-

haan, much less get them on board of us, we resolved first to our course north-eastward, running on to 45 or 44°; having reached the 45th or 44th degree, to direct our course due east until we shall have got to 150° Longitude; as will be found duly specified in today's resolution, to which we beg to refer. At noon Latitude estimated 47° 56', Longitude 119° 6'; course kept east-north-east, sailed 45 miles.

Item the 8th.

In the morning the weather was somewhat better so that we could set our topsails. At noon Latitude estimated 46° 26', Longitude 121° 19'; course kept north-east, sailed 32 miles, with unsettled weather and a westerly wind, which is very variable here. At night we ran on under reduced sail. Variation 25° 30'.

Item the 9th.

The wind southerly with a grey sky and a top-gallant gale; at noon Latitude estimated 44° 19' South, Longitude 124° 20'; course kept north-east, sailed 45 miles. At noon the latitude observed was 44°, which does not agree with our estimation as given above. We still saw rock-weed floating about the whole day. At noon we shaped our course east in accordance with the resolution of the 7th instant. Towards evening we dispatched to the officers of the Zeehaan the letter following, together with the Annotations of Pilot-major Francoys Jacobsz, the said papers being enclosed in a wooden canister-shot-case, duly waxed and closely wrapped up in tarred canvas, which case we sent adrift from the stern part of the poop; the letter duly reached its destination and ran as follows:
To the officers of the Zeehaan.

We should have greatly liked to have had your advice on the 7th instant but, time and opportunity being unpropitious, we resolved with the members of our council and our second mates to shape our course north-east as far as 44° South Latitude, and then keep a due east course as far as 150° Longitude; should you agree to this resolution then be pleased to hoist a flag at your stern as a sign of approval that we may duly ratify the resolution. We also request you to do your best to sail in during the night until further orders and, if you should think it possible to come alongside of us in the boat, be pleased to float a flag from the foretop by way of signal, in which case we shall stay for you, seeing that we are very desirous of communicating with you by word of mouth. Farewell. Actum Heemskerk sailing in about 44° South Latitude, this day November 9, 1642.

Signed,

ABEL JANSZ TASMAN.

After reading the above, those of the Zeehaan hoisted the Prince-flag in sign of approbation of our resolution.

Item the 10th.

Good weather with a southerly wind and a top-gallant gale. At noon Latitude estimated 44°; Longitude 126° 45'; course kept east, sailed 26 miles. At noon Latitude observed 43° 20', the sea running very high from the south-west, at times also from the south-east with heavy swells. Variation 21° 30'.

Item the 11th.

Good weather, the wind westerly with a light breeze. At noon Latitude estimated 43° 20', Longitude 127° 45'; course kept east, sailed 11 miles. We ran up the white flag, upon which the officers of the Zeehaan came on board of us, when we resolved in the plenary Council to run on in the parallel of about 44° South Latitude from our present longitude (averaging 123° 29') as far as 195° Longitude, being the meridian of the east side of New Guinea as delineated in the chart, all which may in extenso be seen from this day's resolution to which we beg leave to refer.

Item the 12th.

Good weather and smooth water, the wind westerly with a light top-gallant breeze. At noon Latitude observed 43° 50', Longitude 129° 17'; course kept east-south-east, sailed 18 miles. Variation 21°.

Item the 13th.

Dark, hazy, foggy weather with a steady breeze; we still see rock-weed floating about every day. At noon Latitude estimated 44° 16', Longitude 132° 17'; course kept east by south, sailed 33 miles; wind north-west; at noon we turned our course to eastward.

Item the 14th.

Still dark, hazy, drizzling weather, the wind west-north-west with a steady breeze. At noon Latitude estimated 44° 16' south, Longitude 136° 22'; course kept east and sailed 44 miles; the sea still running high from the south-west so that no mainland is yet to be surmised south of us.

Item the 15th.

Good weather and a steady breeze from the west-north-west. At noon Latitude observed 44° 3', Longitude 140° 31'; course kept east slightly northerly, sailed 45 miles. Variation decreasing 18° 50' North-West. We still saw rock-weed floating about every day.

Item the 16th.

In the morning it was very foggy but the weather cleared up towards noon. Latitude observed 44° 10', Longitude 144° 42'; course kept east, sailed 45 miles with a steady breeze from the west; in the evening we took the sun's azimuth. Variation 16°.

Item the 17th.

Good weather with a clear sky; we still saw a good deal of rock-weed floating about every day; the sea still running from the south-west. Though we observe rock-weed every day still it is not likely there should be any great mainland to the southward on account of the high seas that are still running from the south. At noon Latitude observed 44° 15', Longitude 147° 3'; course kept east, sailed 28 miles with a light top-gallant breeze from the west; we estimated that we had already passed the South land[1] known up to the present, or so far as Pieter Nuyts had run to eastward.

Item the 18th.

The wind north-westerly and afterwards northerly with a fog and drizzling rain, a top-gallant gale. At noon Latitude estimated 44° 16' South, Longitude 150° 6'; course kept east, sailed 33 miles. This day we saw a number of whales; at night during the dog-watch we lay a-trying under reduced sail. Variation 12°.

Item the 19th.

Good weather with the wind from the north and afterwards from the north-west, a top-gallant gale. At noon Latitude estimated 44° 45', Longitude 153° 34'; course kept east by south, sailed 38 miles. At noon Latitude observed 45° 5' so that we are farther to the south than I had estimated; in the morning variation decreasing, 8° North-West. Towards evening there came on a storm from the north and afterwards from the north-west, with hail and snow and very cold weather, so that we had to tack to leeward with our mainsail.

Item the 20th.

The wind west-north-west with a storm of hail and rain; in the morning we had to run on before the wind with a foresail halfway up the mast. At noon Latitude estimated 44° 43', Longitude 155° 58'; course kept east, sailed 26 miles; Latitude observed 44° 32'; during the night we lay a-trying with our mainsail set.

Item the 21st.

In the morning the weather somewhat better, we again set our topsails and slid out the bonnet of our foresail; turned our course to east-north-east, the wind being westerly and afterwards north-westerly with a top-gallant gale. At noon Latitude estimated 43° 53', Longitude 158° 12'; at noon Latitude observed 43° 40'; course kept east-north-east, sailed 26 miles. Variation 4° North-West, the sea running very high, both from the north-west and south-west; during the night we lay a-trying under reduced sail.

Item the 22nd.

At daybreak we made sail again, the wind being westerly with a top-gallant gale; there was a heavy swell from the south-west so that there is not likely to be any land to southward. At noon Latitude estimated 42° 58', Longitude 160° 34'; course kept east-north-east, sailed 28 miles; at noon Latitude observed 42° 49'; we found that our compasses were not so steady as they should be, and supposed that possibly there might be mines of loadstone about here, our compasses sometimes varying 8 points from one moment to another, so that there would always seem to be some cause that kept the needle in motion.

Item the 23rd.

Good weather with a south-westerly wind and a steady breeze; in the morning we found our rudder broken at top in the tiller-hole; we there hauled to windward under reduced sail and fitted a cross-beam to either side. At noon Latitude observed 42° 50', Longitude 162° 51'; course kept east, sailed 25 miles; we found the variation to the compass to be 1 degree North-West, so that the decrease is a very abrupt one here; by estimation the west side of New Guinea must be north of us.

Item the 24th.

Good weather and a clear sky. At noon Latitude observed 42° 25', Longitude 163° 31'; course kept east by north, sailed 30 miles; the wind south-westerly and afterwards from the south with a light top-gallant breeze. In the afternoon about 4 o'clock we saw land bearing east by north of us at about 10 miles distance from us by estimation; the land we sighted was very high; towards evening we also saw, east-south-east of us, three high mountains, and to the north-east two more mountains, but less high than those to southward; we found that here our compass pointed due north. In the evening in the first glass after the watch had been set, we convened our ship's council with the second mate's and represented to them whether it would not be advisable to run farther out to sea; we also asked their advice as to the time when it would be best to do so, upon which it was unanimously resolved to run out to sea at the expiration of three glasses, to keep doing so for the space of ten glasses, and after this to make for the land again; all of which may in extenso be seen from today's resolution to which we beg leave to refer. During the night when three glasses had run out the wind turned to the south-east; we held off from shore and sounded in 100 fathom, fine white sandy bottom with small shells; we sounded once more and found black coarse sand with pebbles; during the night we had a south-east wind with a light breeze.

[1] The portion of the south coast of New Holland which Pieter Nuyts discovered in 1627.

A page from Tasman's Journal--24 Nov. 1642

Item the 25th.

In the morning we had a calm; we floated the white flag and pendant from our stern, upon which the officers of the Zeehaan with their steersmen came on board of us; we then convened the Ship's council and resolved together upon what may in extenso be seen from today's resolution to which we beg leave to refer. Towards noon the wind turned to the south-east and afterwards to the south-south-east and the south, upon which we made for the shore; at about 5 o'clock in the evening we got near the coast; three miles off shore we sounded in 60 fathom coral bottom; one mile off the coast we had clean, fine, white sand; we found this coast to bear south by east and north by west; it was a level coast, our ship being 42° 30' South Latitude, and average Longitude 163° 50'. We then put off from shore again, the wind turning to the south-south-east with a top-gallant gale. If you came from the west and find your needle to show 4° north-westerly variation you had better look out for land, seeing that the variation is very abruptly decreasing here. If you should happen to be overtaken by rough weather from the westward you had best heave to and not run on. Near the coast here the needle points due north. We took the average of our several longitudes and found this land to be in 163° 50' Longitude.

This land being the first land we have met with in the South Sea and not known to any European nation we have conferred on it the name of Anthoony Van Diemenslandt[1] in honour of the Honourable Governor-General, our illustrious master, who sent us to make this discovery; the islands circumjacent, so far as known to us, we have named after the Honourable Councillors of India, as may be seen from the little chart which has been made of them.

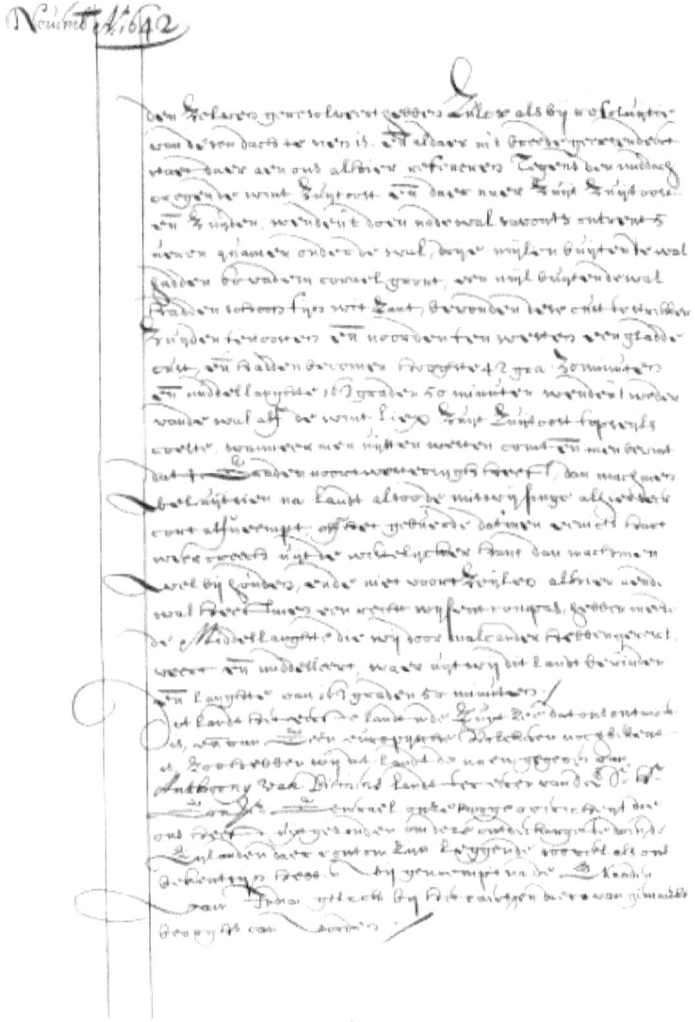

A page from Tasman's Journal--25 Nov. 1642

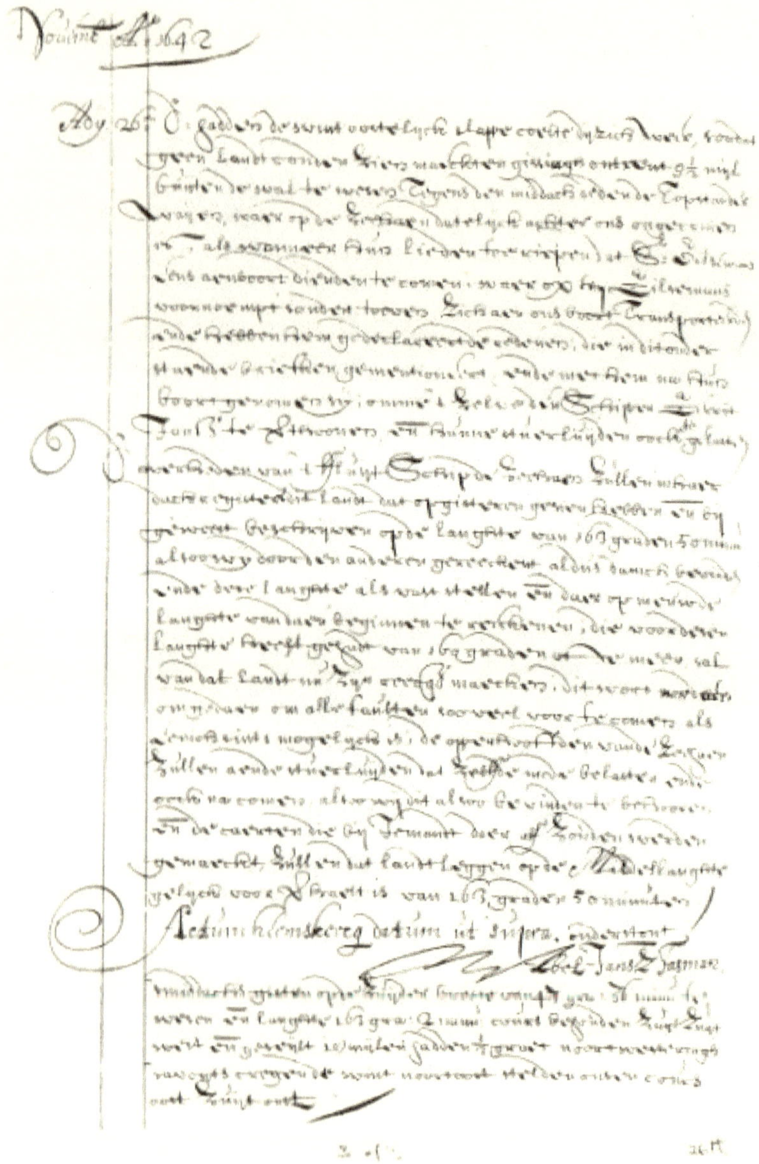

A page from Tasman's Journal--26 Nov. 1642

Item the 26th.

We had the wind from eastward with a light breeze and hazy weather so that we could see no land; according to our estimation we were at 9½ miles distance from shore. Towards noon we hoisted the top-pendant upon which the Zeehaan forthwith came astern of us; we called out to her men that we should like Mr. Gilsemans to come on board of us, upon which the said Mr. Gilsemans straightways came on board of us, to whom we imparted the reasons set forth in the sub-joined letter which we enjoined him to take with him on board the Zeehaan, to be shown to Skipper Gerrit Jansz, who is to give orders to her steersmen in accordance with its purport:

The officers of the Flute Zeehaan are hereby enjoined to set down in their daily journals this land which we saw and came near to yesterday in the longitude of 163° 50', seeing that we have found this to be its average longitude, and to lay down the said longitude as an established point of departure for their further reckonings; he who before this had got the longitude of 160° or more will henceforth have to take this land for his starting-point; we make the arrangement in order to prec-lude all errors as much as is at all possible. The officers of the Zeehaan are requested to give orders in conformity to her steersmen and to see them acted up to, because we opine this to be their duty; any charts that should be drawn up of this part will have to lay down this land in the average longitude of 163° 50' as hereinbefore stated.

Actum Heemskerk datum ut supra

(signed) ABEL JANSZ. TASMAN.

[1] Compare about "the localities mentioned in this journal", as regards Van Diemen's land or Tasmania, e.g. J. BACKHOUSE WALKER, The discovery of Van Diemen's land in 1642 (Tasmania, Strutt, 1891). The most curious corruptions of the name Van Diemen's land have taken place: e.g. Terre de Diamant (cp. RAINAUD, Continent Austral, p. 397); Demon's land (I. TAYLOR, Words and Places, London, Macmillan, 1875, p. 24).

A view of the coast when you are six miles from it.
A view of Anthonij van Diemens Landt, when you come from the west, and are in 42½° S. Latitude.

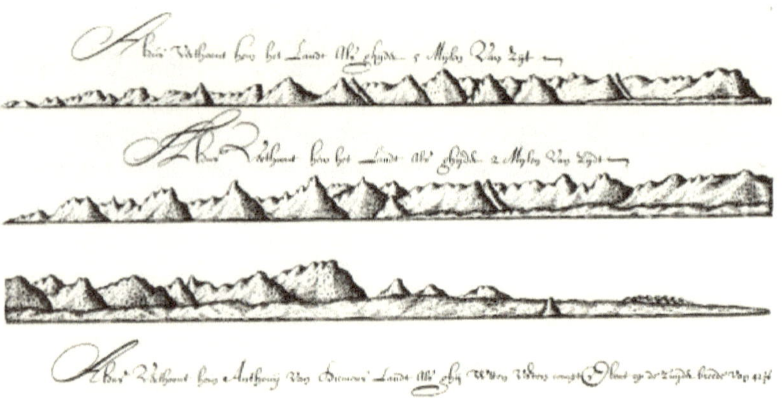

A view of the coast when you are 5 miles from it.
A view of the coast when you are 2 miles from it.
A view of Anthonij van Diemens Landt, when you come from the west, and are in 42½ S. Latitude.

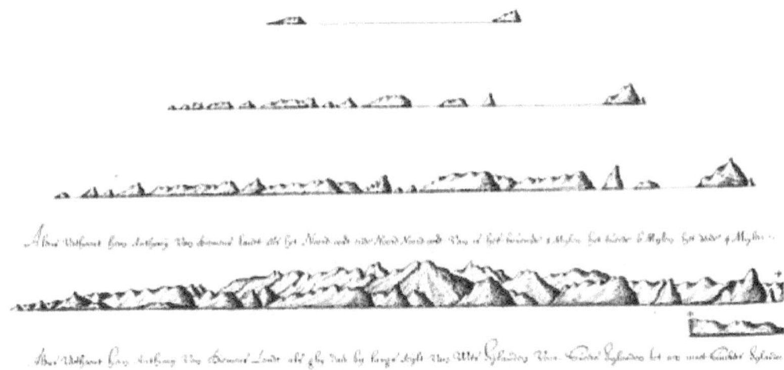

A view of the coast when you are 1 mile from it.
A view of Anthonij van Diemens Landt, when you come from the west, and are in 42½ S. Latitude.

At noon Latitude estimated 43° 36' South, Longitude 163° 2'; course kept south-south-west, sailed 18 miles. We had ½ degree North-West variation; in the evening the wind went round to the north-east, and we changed our course to east-south-east.

Item the 27th.

In the morning we again saw the coast, our course still being east-south-east. At noon Latitude estimated 44° 4' South, Longitude 164° 2'; course kept south-east by east, sailed 13 miles; the weather was drizzly, foggy, hazy and rainy, the wind north-east and north-north-east with a light breeze; at night when 7 glasses of the first watch had run out we began trying under reduced sail because we dared not run on owing to thick darkness.

Item the 28th.

In the morning, the weather still being dark, foggy and rainy, we again made sail, shaped our course to eastward and afterwards north-east by north; we saw land north-east and north-north-east of us and made straight for it; the coast here bears south-east by east and north-west by west; as far as I can see the land here falls off to eastward. At noon Latitude estimated 44° 12', Longitude 165° 2'; course kept west by south, sailed 11 miles with a north-westerly wind and a light breeze. In the evening we got near the coast; here near the shore there are a number of islets of which one in shape resembles a lion; this islet lies out into the sea at about 3 miles distance from the mainland; in the evening the wind turned to the east; during the night we lay a-trying under reduced sail.

Item the 29th.

In the morning we were still near the rock which is like a lion's head; we had a westerly wind with a top-gallant gale; we sailed along the coast which here bears east and west; towards noon we passed two rocks of which the westernmost was like Pedra Branca[1] off the coast of China; the easternmost was like a tall, obtuse, square tower, and is at about 4 miles distance from the mainland. We passed between these rocks and the mainland; at noon Latitude estimated 43° 53', Longitude 166° 3'; course kept east-north-east, sailed 12 miles; we were still running along the coast. In the evening about 5 o'clock we came before a bay which seemed likely to afford a good anchorage, upon which we resolved with our ship's council to run into it, as may be seen from today's resolution; we had nearly got into the bay when there arose so strong a gale that we were obliged to take in sail and to run out to sea again under reduced sail, seeing that it was impossible to come to anchor in such a storm; in the evening we resolved to stand out to sea during the night under reduced sail to avoid being thrown on a lee-shore by the violence of the wind; all which may in extenso be seen from the resolution aforesaid to which for briefness sake we beg to refer.

Item the last.

At daybreak we again made for shore, the wind and the current having driven us so far out to sea that we could barely see the land; we did our utmost to get near it again and at noon had the land north-west of us; we now turned the ship's head to westward with a northerly wind which prevented us from getting close to the land. At noon Latitude observed 43° 41', Longitude 168° 3'; course kept east by north, sailed 20 miles in a storm and with variable weather. The needle points due north here. Shortly after noon we turned our course to westward with a strong variable gale; we then turned to the north under reduced sail.

DECEMBER 1642

Item the 1st of December.

In the morning, the weather having become somewhat better, we set our topsails, the wind blowing from the west-south-west with a top-gallant gale; we now made for the coast. At noon Latitude observed 43° 10', Longitude 167° 55'; course kept north-north-west, sailed 8 miles, it having fallen a calm; in the afternoon we hoisted the white flag upon which our friends of the Zeehaan came on board of us, with whom we resolved that it would be best and most expedient, wind and weather permitting, to touch at the land the sooner the better, both to get better acquainted with its condition and to attempt to procure re-freshments for our own behoof, all which may be more amply seen from this day's resolution. We then got a breeze from eastward and made for the coast to ascertain whether it would afford a fitting an-chorage; about one hour after sunset we dropped anchor in a good harbour, in 22 fathom, white and grey fine sand, a naturally drying bottom; for all which it behoves us to thank God Almighty with grate-ful hearts.

[1] Tasman compares one of these rocks with a rock Pedra Branca off the coast of China, and accordingly this name is given to the western-most rock on his chart of Anthony Van Diemens landt (December 1, 2).

GEORGE COLLINGRIDGE, The discovery of Australia. Sydney, Hayes, 1895, p. 288, is therefore all at sea, where he says:

"The discoveries supposed to have been made during the Government of Speult in the Spice Islands, and bearing his name on some charts, are not recorded in Tasman's chart, neither do we notice the Portu-guese or Spanish inscription Pedra Branca which occurs in P. Goos' map, and is written also Piedra blanca in other maps.

"It is difficult to explain the presence of these words on maps sup-posed to be copies of Tasman's original chart. Other words, evidently of Portuguese or Spanish origin, appear also even on Tasman's chart in combination with his nomenclature. These names suggest an earlier discovery and the possession by the Dutch of maps relating to those discoveries (Cf. COLLINGRIDGE, pp. 80 f., 131 and note).

"Explorers and navigators who make discoveries give, as a rule, the reasons for naming the various places they discover. Tasman's journal makes no exception to this rule, and while he mentions Pedra Branca as resembling another Pedra Branca on the coast of China, he does not say that he named those rocks off the south coast of Tasmania."

Item the 2nd.

Early in the morning we sent our Pilot-major Francoys Jacobsz in command of our pinnace, manned with 4 musketeers and 6 rowers, all of them furnished with pikes and side-arms, together with the cock-boat of the Zeehaan with one of her second mates and 6 musketeers in it, to a bay situated north-west of us at upwards of a mile distance in order to ascertain what facilities (as regards fresh water, refreshments, timber and the like) may be available there. About three hours before nightfall the boats came back, bringing various samples of vegetables which they had seen growing there in great abundance, some of them in appearance not unlike a certain plant growing at the Cape of Good Hope and fit to be used as pot-herbs, and another species with long leaves and a brackish taste, strongly resembling persil de mer or samphire. The Pilot-major and the second mate of the Zeehaan made the following report, to wit:

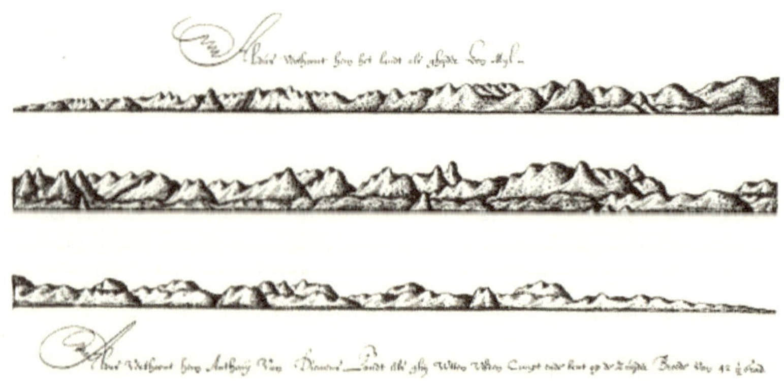

3 views of Anthonij van Diemens Landt, when it is north-east and north-north-east of you, first view at 8, the second at 6, the third at 4 miles' distance.

46

A view of Anthonij van Diemens Landt, as you sail along it from the Wits islands past Sueers islands as far as Maetsuickers islands.

A view of the land, when you are north-west of it at 5 miles' distance, the said land lying Latitude about 44°.
A view of the land, when you are south-west of it, at 4 miles' distance.
A view of Anthonij van Diemens Landt, as you sail along it from the Maetsuickers islands. far as the Boereels islands or Stormbay.

A view of this land, as you sail along it from the Zuyd Caep as far as the Maria's island.

A double-page chart showing the Boreels islands, Stormbay, the Zuyd Caep and Tasman's island

A view of this land, as you sail along it from Maria's island to Schoutens island.
A view of this land, as you sail along it from Schoutens island to Vanderlins island

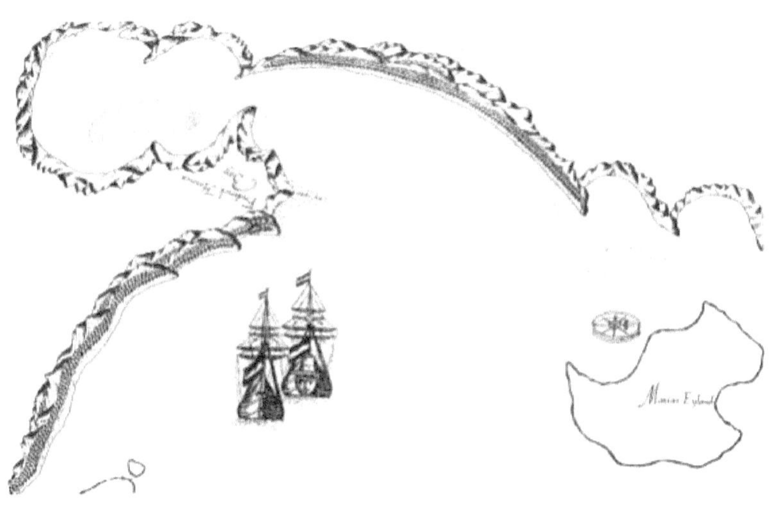

A chart of Frederick Henricx Bay with Maria's Island, with pictures of the two ships

That they had rowed the space of upwards of a mile round the said point, where they had found high but level land covered with vegetation (not cultivated, but growing naturally by the will of God) abundance of excellent timber, and a gently sloping watercourse in a barren valley, the said water, though of good quality, being difficult to procure because the watercourse was so shallow that the water could be dipped with bowls only.

That they had heard certain human sounds and also sounds nearly resembling the music of a trump or a small gong not far from them though they had seen no one.

That they had seen two trees about 2 or 2½ fathom in thickness measuring from 60 to 65 feet from the ground to the lowermost branches, which trees bore notches made with flint implements, the bark having been removed for the purpose; these notches, forming a kind of steps to enable persons to get up the trees and rob the birds' nests in their tops, were fully 5 feet apart so that our men concluded that the natives here must be of very tall stature, or must be in possession of some sort of artifice for getting up the said trees; in one of the trees these notched steps were so fresh and new that they seemed to have been cut less than four days ago.

That on the ground they had observed certain footprints of animals, not unlike those of a tiger's claws; they also brought on board certain specimens of animals excrements voided by quadrupeds, so far as they could surmise and observe, together with a small quantity of gum of a seemingly very fine quality which had exuded from trees and bore some resemblance to gum-lac.

That round the eastern point of this bay they had sounded 13 or 14 feet at high water, there being about 3 feet at low tide.

That at the extremity of the said point they had seen large numbers of gulls, wild ducks and geese, but had perceived none farther inward though they had heard their cries; and had found no fish except different kinds of mussels forming small clusters in several places.

That the land is pretty generally covered with trees standing so far apart that they allow a passage everywhere and a lookout to a great distance so that, when landing, our men could always get sight of natives or wild beasts, unhindered by dense shrubbery or underwood, which would prove a great advantage in exploring the country.

That in the interior they had in several places observed numerous trees which had deep holes burnt into them at the upper end of the foot, while the earth had here and there been dug out with the fist so as to form a fireplace, the surrounding soil having become as hard as flint through the action of the fire.

A short time before we got sight of our boats returning to the ships, we now and then saw clouds of dense smoke rising up from the land, which was nearly west by north of us, and surmised this might be a signal given by our men, because they were so long coming back, for we had ordered them to return speedily, partly in order to be made acquainted with what they had seen, and partly that we might be able to send them to other points if they should find no profit there, to the end that no precious time might be wasted. When our men had come on board again we inquired of them whether they had been there and made a fire, to which they returned a negative answer, adding however that at various times and points in the wood they also had seen clouds of smoke ascending. So there can be no doubt there must be men here of extraordinary stature. This day we had variable winds from the eastward, but for the greater part of the day a stiff, steady breeze from the south-east.

Item the 3rd.

We went to the south-east side of this bay in the same boats as yesterday with Supercargo Gilsemans and a number of musketeers, the oarsmen furnished with pikes and side-arms; here we found water, it is true, but the land is so low-lying that the fresh water was made salt and brackish by the surf, while the soil is too rocky to allow of wells being dug; we therefore returned on board and convened the councils of our two ships with which we have resolved and determined what is set forth in extenso in today's resolution, to which for briefness sake we refer. In the afternoon we went to the south-east side of this bay in the boats aforesaid, having with us Pilot-major Francoys Jacobsz, Skipper Gerrit Jansz, Isack Gilsemans, supercargo on board the Zeehaan, subcargo Abraham Coomans, and our master carpenter Pieter Jacobsz; we carried with us a pole with the Company's mark carved into it, and a Prince-flag to be set up there, that those who shall come after us may become aware that we have been here, and have taken possession of the said land as our lawful property. When we had rowed about half-way with our boats it began to blow very stiffly, and the sea ran so high that the cock-boat of the Zeehaan, in which were seated the Pilot-major and Mr. Gilsemans, was compelled to pull back to the ships, while we ran on with our pinnace. When we had come close inshore in a small inlet which bore west-south-west of the ships the surf ran so high that we could not get near the shore without running the risk of having our pinnace dashed to pieces. We then ordered the carpenter aforesaid to swim to the shore alone with the pole and the flag, and kept by the wind with our pinnace; we made him plant the said pole with the flag at top into the earth, about the centre of the bay near four tall trees easily recognisable and standing in the form of a crescent, exactly before the one standing lowest. This tree is burnt in just above the ground, and in reality taller than the other three, but it seems to be shorter because it stands lower on the sloping ground; at top, projecting from the crown, it shows two long dry branches, so symmetrically set with dry sprigs and twigs that they look like the large antlers of a stag; by the side of these dry branches, slightly lower down, there is another bough which is quite green and leaved all round, whose twigs, owing to their regular proportion, wonderfully embellish the said bough and make it look like the upper part of a larding-pin. Our master carpenter, having in the sight of myself, Abel Jansz Tasman, Skipper Gerrit Jansz, and Subcargo Abraham Coomans, performed the work entrusted to him, we pulled with our pinnace as near the shore as we ventured to do; the carpenter aforesaid thereupon swam back to the pinnace through the surf. This work having been duly executed we pulled back to the ships, leaving the above-mentioned as a memorial for those who shall come after us, and for the natives of this country, who did not show themselves, though we suspect some of them were at no great distance and closely watching our proceedings. We made no arrangements for gathering vegetables since the high seas prevented our men from getting ashore except by swimming, so that it was impossible to get anything into the pinnace. During the whole of the day the wind blew chiefly from the north; in the evening we took the sun's azimuth and found 3° north-easterly variation of the compass; at sunset we got a strong gale from the north which by and by rose to so violent a storm from the north-north-west that we were compelled to get both our yards in and drop our small bower-anchor.

Item the 4th.

At dawn the storm abated, the weather became less rough and, the land-wind blowing from the west by north, we hove our bower-anchor; when we had weighed the said anchor and got it above the water we found that both the flukes were broken off so far that we hauled home nothing but the shank; we then weighed the other anchor also and set sail forthwith in order to pass to north to landward of the northernmost islands and seek a better watering-place. Here we lay at anchor in 43° South Latitude, Longitude 167½°; in the forenoon the wind was westerly. At noon Latitude observed 42° 40', Longitude 168°, course kept north-east, sailed 8 miles; in the afternoon the wind turned to the north-west; we had very variable winds all day; in the evening the wind went round to west-north-west again with a strong gale, then to west by north and west-north-west again with a strong gale, then to west by north and west-north-west once more; we then tacked to northward and in the evening saw a round mountain bearing north-north-west of us at about 8 miles distance; course kept to northward very close to the wind. While sailing out of this bay and all through the day we saw several columns of smoke ascend along the coast. Here it would be meet to describe the trend of the coast and the islands lying off it but we request to be excused for briefness sake and beg leave to refer to the small chart drawn up of it which we have appended.

Item the 5th.

In the morning, the wind blowing from the north-west by west, we kept our previous course; the high round mountain which we had seen the day before now bore due west of us at 6 miles distance; at this point the land fell off to the north-west so that we could no longer steer near the coast here, seeing that the wind was almost ahead. We therefore convened the council and the second mates, with whom after due deliberation we resolved, and subsequently called out to the officers of the Zeehaan that, pursuant to the resolution of the 11th ultimo we should direct our course due east, and on the said course run on to the full longitude of 195° or the Salomonis islands, all which will be found set forth in extenso in this day's resolution. At noon Latitude estimated 41° 34', Longitude 169°, course kept north-east by north, sailed 20 miles; we then shaped our course due east for the purpose of making further discoveries and of avoiding the variable winds between the trade-wind and the anti-trade-wind; the wind from the north-west with a steady breeze; during the night the wind from the west, a brisk steady breeze and good clear weather.

Item the 6th.

In the morning the wind from the south-west with a light breeze; at noon we were in Latitude 41° 15', Longitude 172° 35'; course kept east, sailed 40 miles; the weather was quite calm and still all the afternoon, the sea running high from all quarters but especially from the south-west; in the evening when the watches were setting we got a steady breeze from the east-north-east and north-east.

Item the 7th.

The wind still continuing to blow from the north-east, the breeze quite as fresh as during the night. At noon Latitude estimated 42° 13', Longitude 174° 31'; course kept south-east by east, sailed 26 miles. Variation increasing 5° 45' North-West.

Item the 8th.

During the night we had a calm, the wind going round to the west and north-west. At noon Latitude estimated 42° 29', Longitude 176° 17'; course kept east by south, sailed 20 miles.

Item the 9th.

We drifted in a calm so that by estimation we were carried 3 miles to the south-eastward. At noon Latitude observed 42° 37', Longitude 176° 29'. Variation 5°. Towards evening we had a light breeze from the west-north-west.

Item the 10th.

Occasional squalls of rain mixed with hail, the wind being westerly with a top-gallant gale. At noon Latitude observed 42° 45', Longitude 178° 40'; course kept east, sailed 24 miles.

Item the 11th.

Good weather with a clear sky and a westerly wind with a top-gallant gale. At noon Latitude observed 42° 48', Longitude 181° 51'; course kept east, sailed 38 miles. Variation increasing 7° North-East.

Item the 12th.

Good weather, the wind blowing from the south-south-west and south-west with a steady breeze. At noon Latitude observed 42° 38', Longitude 185° 17'; course kept east, sailed 38 miles. The heavy swells continuing from the south-west, there is no mainland to be expected here to southward. Variation 7° North-East.

Item the 13th.

Latitude observed 42° 10', Longitude 188° 28'; course kept east by north, sailed 36 miles in a south-south-westerly wind with a top-gallant gale. Towards noon we saw a large, high-lying land, bearing south-east of us at about 15 miles distance; we turned our course to the south-east, making straight for this land, fired a gun and in the after-noon hoisted the white flag, upon which the officers of the Zeehaan came on board of us, with whom we resolved to touch at the said land as quickly as at all possible, for such reasons as are more amply set forth in this day's resolution. In the evening we deemed it best and gave orders accordingly to our steersmen to stick to the south-east course while the weather keeps quiet but, should the breeze freshen, to steer due east in order to avoid running on shore, and to preclude acci-dents as much as in us lies; since we opine that the land should not be touched at from this side on account of the high open sea running there in huge hollow waves and heavy swells, unless there should happen to be safe land-locked bays on this side. At the expiration of four glasses of the first watch we shaped our course due east. Variation 7° 30' North-East.

Item the 14th.

At noon Latitude observed 42° 10', Longitude 189° 3'; course kept east, sailed 12 miles. We were about 2 miles off the coast,[1] which showed as a very high double land, but we could not see the summits of the mountains owing to thick clouds. We shaped our course to northward along the coast, so near to it that we could constantly see the surf break on the shore. In the afternoon we took soundings at about 2 miles distance from the coast in 55 fathom, a sticky sandy soil, after which it fell a calm. Towards evening we saw a low-lying point north-east by north of us, at about 3 miles distance; the greater part of the time we were drifting in a calm towards the said point; in the middle of the afternoon we took soundings in 45 fathom, a sticky sandy bottom. The whole night we drifted in a calm, the sea running from the west-north-west, so that we got near the land in 28 fathom, good anchoring-ground, where, on account of the calm, and for fear of drifting nearer to the shore, we ran out our kedge-anchor during the day-watch, and we are now waiting for the land-wind.

Item the 15th.

In the morning with a light breeze blowing from the land we weighed anchor and did our best to run out to sea a little, our course being north-west by north; we then had the northernmost low-lying point of the day before, north-north-east and north-east by north of us. This land consists of a high double mountain-range, not lower than Ilha Formoza. At noon Latitude observed 41° 40', Longitude 189° 49'; course kept north-north-east, sailed 8 miles; the point we had seen the day before now lay south-east of us, at 2½ miles distance; northward from this point extends a large rocky reef; on this reef, projecting from the sea, there are a number of high steep cliffs resembling steeples or sails; one mile west of this point we could sound no bottom. As we still saw this high land extend to north-north-east of us we from here held our course due north with good, dry weather and smooth water. From the said low point with the cliffs, the land makes a large curve to the north-east, trending first due east, and afterwards due north again. The point aforesaid is in Latitude 41° 50' south. The wind was blowing from the west. It was easy to see here that in these parts the land must be very desolate; we saw no human beings nor any smoke rising; nor can the people here have any boats, since we did not see any signs of them; in the evening we found 8° North-East variation of the compass.

[1] As regards the localities in Statenland (New Zealand) touched at in this expedition, compare Dr. Hocken, Abel Tasman and his journal. A paper read before the Otago Institute, 1895, p. 7.

Item the 16th.

At six glasses before the day we took soundings in 60 fathom anchoring-ground. The northernmost point we had in sight then bore from us north-east by east, at three miles distance, and the nearest land lay south-east of us at 1½ miles distance. We drifted in a calm, with good weather and smooth water; at noon Latitude observed 40° 58', average Longitude 189° 54'; course kept north-north-east, sailed 11 miles; we drifted in a calm the whole afternoon; in the evening at sunset we had 9° 23' increasing North-East variation; the wind then went round to south-west with a freshening breeze; we found the furthest point of the land that we could see to bear from us east by north, the land falling off so abruptly there that we did not doubt that this was the farthest extremity. We now convened our council with the second mates, with whom we resolved to run north-east and east-north-east till the end of the first watch, and then to sail near the wind, wind and weather not changing, as may in extenso be seen from this day's resolution. During the night in the sixth glass it fell calm again so that we stuck to the east-north-east course; although in the fifth glass of the dog-watch, we had the point we had seen in the evening, south-east of us, we could not sail higher than east-north-east slightly easterly owing to the sharpness of the wind; in the first watch we took soundings once, and a second time in the dog-watch, in 60 fathom, clean, grey sand. In the second glass of the day-watch we got a breeze from the south-east, upon which we tacked for the shore again.

Item the 17th.

In the morning at sunrise we were about one mile from the shore; in various places we saw smoke ascending from fires made by the natives; the wind then being south and blowing from the land we again tacked to eastward. At noon Latitude estimated 40° 31', Longitude 190° 47'; course kept north-east by east, sailed 12 miles; in the afternoon the wind being west we held our course east by south along a low-lying shore with dunes in good dry weather; we sounded in 30 fathom, black sand, so that by night one had better approach this land aforesaid, sounding; we then made for this sandy point until we got in 17 fathom, where we cast anchor at sunset owing to a calm, when we had the northern extremity of this dry sandspit west by north of us; also high land extending to east by south; the point of the reef south-east of us; here inside this point or narrow sandspit we saw a large open bay upward of 3 or 4 miles wide; to eastward of this narrow sandspit there is a sandbank upwards of a mile in length with 6, 7, 8 and 9 feet of water above it, and projecting east-south-east from the said point. In the evening we had 9° North-East variation.

Item the 18th.

In the morning we weighed anchor in calm weather; at noon Latitude estimated 40° 49', Longitude 191° 41'; course kept east-south-east, sailed 11 miles. In the morning before weighing anchor, we had re-solved with the Officers of the Zeehaan that we should try to get ashore here and find a good harbour; and that as we neared it we should send out the pinnace to reconnoitre; all which may in extenso be seen from this day's resolution. In the afternoon our skipper Ide Tiercxz and our pilot-major Francoys Jacobsz, in the pinnace, and Su-percargo Gilsemans, with one of the second mates of the Zeehaan in the latter's cock-boat, went on before to seek a fitting anchorage and a good watering-place. At sunset when it fell a calm we dropped anchor in 15 fathom, good anchoring-ground in the evening, about an hour after sunset, we saw a number of lights on shore and four boats close inshore, two of which came towards us, upon which our own two boats returned on board; they reported that they had found no less than 13 fathom water and that, when the sun sank behind the high land, they were still about half a mile from shore. When our men had been on board for the space of about one glass the men in the two prows began to call out to us in the rough, hollow voice, but we could not understand a word of what they said. We however called out to them in answer, upon which they repeated their cries several times, but came no nearer than a stone shot; they also blew several times on an instrument of which the sound was like that of a Moorish trumpet; we then ordered one of our sailors (who had some knowledge of trumpet-blowing) to play them some tunes in answer. Those on board the Zee-haan ordered their second mate (who had come out to India as a trumpeter and had in the Mauritius been appointed second mate by the council of that fortress and the ships) to do the same; after this had been repeated several times on both sides, and as it was getting more and more dark, those in the native prows at last ceased and paddled off. For more security and to be on guard against all accidents we or-dered our men to keep double watches as we are wont to do when out at sea, and to keep in readiness all necessaries of war, such as muskets, pikes and cutlasses. We cleaned the guns on the upper-orlop, and placed them again, in order to prevent surprises, and be able to defend ourselves if these people should happen to attempt anything against us. Variation 9° North-East.

Item the 19th.

Early in the morning a boat manned with 13 natives approached to about a stone's cast from our ships; they called out several times but we did not understand them, their speech not bearing any resemblance to the vocabulary given us by the Honourable Governor-General and Councillors of India, which is hardly to be wondered at, seeing that it contains the language of the Salomonis islands, etc. As far as we could observe these people were of ordinary height; they had rough voices and strong bones, the colour of their skin being brown and yellow; they wore tufts of black hair right upon the top of their heads, tied fast in the manner of the Japanese at the back of their heads, but somewhat longer and thicker, and surmounted by a large, thick white feather. Their boats consisted of two long narrow prows side by side, over which a number of planks or other seats were placed in such a way that those above can look through the water underneath the vessel: their paddles are upwards of a fathom in length, narrow and pointed at the end; with these vessels they could make considerable speed. For clothing, as it seemed to us, some of them wore mats, others cotton stuffs; almost all of them were naked from the shoulders to the waist. We repeatedly made signs for them to come on board of us, showing them white linen and some knives that formed part of our cargo. They did not come nearer, however, but at last paddled back to shore. In the meanwhile, at our summons sent the previous evening, the officers of the Zeehaan came on board of us, upon which we convened a council and resolved to go as near the shore as we could, since there was good anchoring-ground here, and these people apparently sought our friend-ship. Shortly after we had drawn up this resolution we saw 7 more boats put off from the shore, one of which (high and pointed in front, manned with 17 natives) paddled round behind the Zeehaan while another, with 13 able-bodied men in her, approached to within half a stone's throw of our ship; the men in these two boats now and then called out to each other; we held up and showed them as before white linens, etc., but they remained where they were. The skipper of the Zeehaan now sent out to them his quartermaster with her cock-boat with six paddlers in it, with orders for the second mates that, if these people should offer to come alongside the Zeehaan, they should not allow too many of them on board of her, but use great caution and be well on their guard. While the cock-boat of the Zeehaan was paddling on its way to her those in the prow nearest to us called out to those who were lying behind the Zeehaan and waved their paddles to them, but we could not make out what they meant. Just as the cock-boat of the Zeehaan had put off from board again those in the prow before us, between the two ships, began to paddle so furiously towards it that, when they were about halfway slightly nearer to our ship, they struck the Zeehaan's cock-boat so violently alongside with the stem of their prow that it got a violent lurch, upon which the foremost man in this prow of villains with a long, blunt pike thrust the quartermaster Corne-lis Joppen in the neck several times with so much force that the poor man fell overboard. Upon this the other natives, with short thick clubs which we at first mistook for heavy blunt parangs,[1] and with their pad-dles, fell upon the men in the cock-boat and overcame them by main force, in which fray three of our men were killed and a fourth got mor-tally wounded through the heavy blows. The quartermaster and two sailors swam to our ship, whence we had sent our pinnace to pick them up, which they got into alive. After this outrageous and detestable crime the murderers sent the cock-boat adrift, having taken one of the dead bodies into their prow and thrown another into the sea.

[1] Knives used for cutting wood in certain parts of the East Indies.

Ourselves and those on board the Zeehaan seeing this, diligently fired our muskets and guns and, although we did not hit any of them, the two prows made haste to the shore, where they were out of the reach of shot. With our fore upper-deck and bow guns we now fired several shots in the direction of their prows, but none of them took effect. There upon our skipper Ide Tercxsen Holman, in command of our pin-nace well manned and armed, rowed towards the cock-boat of the Zeehaan (which fortunately for us these accursed villains had let adrift) and forthwith returned with it to our ships, having found in it one of the men killed and one mortally wounded. We now weighed anchor and set sail, since we could not hope to enter into any friendly relations with these people, or to be able to get water or refreshments here. Having weighed anchor and being under sail, we saw 22 prows near the shore, of which eleven, swarming with people, were making for our ships. We kept quiet until some of the foremost were within reach of our guns, and then fired 1 or 2 shots from the gun-room with our pieces, without however doing them any harm; those on board the

Zeehaan also fired, and in the largest prow hit a man who held a small white flag in his hand, and who fell down. We also heard the canister-shot strike the prows inside and outside, but could not make out what other damage it had done. As soon as they had got this volley they paddled back to shore with great speed, two of them hoisting a sort of tingang[1] sails. They remained lying near the shore without visiting us any further. About noon skipper Gerrit Jansz and Mr. Gilsemans again came on board of us; we also sent for their first mate and convened the council, with whom we drew up the resolution following, to wit: Seeing that the detestable deed of these natives against four men of the Zeehaan's crew, perpetrated this morning, must teach us to consider the inhabitants of this country as enemies; that therefore it will be best to sail eastward along the coast, following the trend of the land in order to ascertain whether there are any fitting places where refreshments and water would be obtainable; all of which will be found set forth in extenso in this day's resolution. In this murderous spot (to which we have accordingly given the name of Moordenaers-bay[2]) we lay at anchor on 40° 50' South Latitude, 191° 30' Longitude. From here we shaped our course east-north-east. At noon Latitude estimated 40° 57', Longitude 191° 41'; course kept south, sailed 2 miles. In the afternoon we got the wind from the west-north-west when, on the advice of our steersmen and with our own approval, we turned our course north-east by north. During the night we kept sailing as the weather was favourable, but about an hour after midnight we sounded in 25 or 26 fathom, a hard, sandy bottom. Soon after the wind went round to north-west, and we sounded in 15 fathom; we forthwith tacked to await the day, turning our course to westward, exactly contrary to the direction by which we had entered. Variation 9° 30' North-East.

This is the second land which we have sailed along and discovered. In honour of their High Mightinesses the States-General we gave Staten Landt[3], since we deemed it quite possible that this land is part of the great Staten Land, though this is not certain. This land seems to be a very fine country and we trust that this is the mainland coast of the unknown South land. To this course we have given the name of Abel Tasman passagie, because he has been the first to navigate it.

[1] Small boom-sails or yard-sails, as carried by tingangs (small Indian vessels).

[2] Murderer's Bay.

[3] Afterwards named New Zealand.

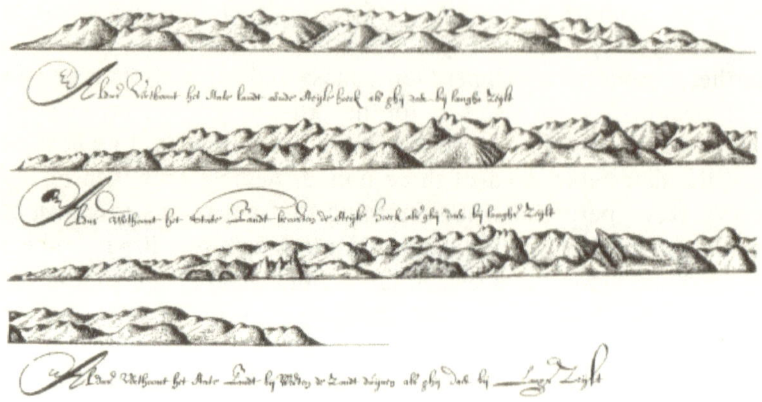

Coast-surveying. State Landt.

Item the 20th.

In the morning we saw land lying here on all sides of us, so that we must have sailed at least 30 miles into a bay. We had at first thought that the land off which we had anchored was an island, nothing doubting that we should here find a passage to the open South Sea[2]; but to our grievous disappointment it proved quite otherwise. The wind now being westerly we henceforth did our best by tacking to get out at the same passage through which we had come in. At noon Latitude observed 40° 51' South, Longitude 192° 55'; course kept east half a point northerly, sailed 14 miles. In the afternoon it fell calm. The sea ran very strong into this bay so that we would make no headway but drifted back into it with the tide. At noon we tacked to northward when we saw a round high islet west by south of us, at about 8 miles distance which we had passed the day before; the said island lying about 6 miles east of the place where we had been at anchor and in the same latitude. This bay[3] into which we had sailed so far by mistake showed us everywhere a fine good land: near the shore the land was mainly low and barren, the inland being moderately high. As you are approaching the land you have everywhere an anchoring-ground gradually rising from 50 or 60 fathom to 15 fathom when you are still fully

1½ or 2 miles from shore. At three o'clock in the afternoon we got a light breeze from the south-east but as the sea was very rough we made little or no progress. During the night we drifted in a calm; in the second watch, the wind being westerly, we tacked to northward.

Item the 21st.

During the night in the dog-watch we had a westerly wind with a strong breeze; we steered to the north, hoping that the land which we had had north-west of us the day before might fall away to northward, but after the cook had dished we again ran against it and found that it still extended to the north-west. We now tacked, turning from the land again and, as it began to blow fresh, we ran south-west over towards the south shore. At noon, Latitude observed 40° 31', Longitude 192° 55'; course kept north, sailed 5 miles. The weather was hazy so that we could not see land. Halfway through the afternoon we again saw the south coast; the island which the day before we had west of us at about 6 miles distance now lay south-west by south of us at about 4 miles distance. We made for it, running on until the said island was north-north-west of us, then dropped our anchor behind a number of cliffs in 33 fathom, sandy ground mixed with shells. There are many islands and cliffs all round here. We struck our sail-yards for it was blowing a storm from the north-west and west-north-west.

Item the 22nd.

The wind north-west by north and blowing so hard that there was no question of going under sail in order to make any progress; we found it difficult enough for the anchor to hold. We therefore set to refitting our ship. We are lying here in 40° 50' South Latitude and Longitude 192° 37'; course held south-west by south, sailed 6 miles. During the night we got the wind so hard from the north-west that we had to strike our tops and drop another anchor. The Zeehaan was almost forced from her anchor and therefore hove out another anchor likewise.

[1] On Swart's reproduction of the Bonaparte chart we find Abel Tasman's road (reede).

[2] Compare, however, December 24.

[3] Zeehaens bocht.

Item the 23rd.

The weather still dark, hazy and drizzling; the wind north-west and west-north-west with a storm so that to our great regret we could not make any headway.

Item the 24th.

Still rough, unsteady weather, the wind still north-west and stormy; in the morning when there was a short calm we hoisted the white flag and got the officers of the Zeehaan on board of us. We then represented to them that since the tide was running from the south-east there was likely to be a passage through[1], so that perhaps it would be best, as soon as wind and weather should permit, to investigate this point and see whether we could get fresh water there; all of which may in exten-so be seen from the resolution drawn up concerning this matter.

Item the 25th.

In the morning we reset our tops and sailyards, but out at sea things looked still so gloomy that we did not venture to weigh our anchor. Towards evening it fell a calm so that we took in part of our cable.

Item the 26th.

In the morning, two hours before day, we got the wind east-north-east with a light breeze. We weighed anchor and set sail, steered our course to northward, intending to sail northward round this land; at daybreak it began to drizzle, the wind went round to the south-east, and after-wards to the south as far as the south-west, with a stiff breeze. We had soundings in 60 fathom, and set our course by the wind to westward. At noon Latitude estimated 40° 13', Longitude 192° 7'; course kept north-north-west, sailed 20 miles. Variation 8° 40'. During the night we lay to with small sail.

Item the 27th.

In the morning at daybreak we made sail again, set our course to northward, the wind being south-west with a steady breeze; at noon Latitude observed 38° 38', Longitude 190° 15'; course kept north-west, sailed 26 miles. At noon we shaped our course north-east. During the night we lay to under small sail. Variation 8° 20'.

Item the 28th.

In the morning at daybreak we made sail again, set our course to eastward in order to ascertain whether the land we had previously seen in 40° extends still further northward, or whether it falls away to eastward. At noon we saw east by north of us a high mountain which we at first took to be an island; but afterwards we observed that it forms part of the mainland. We were then about 5 miles from shore and took soundings in 50 fathom, fine sand mixed with clay. This high mountain is in 38° South Latitude. So far as I could observe this coast extends south and north. It fell a calm, but when there came a light breeze from the north-north-east we tacked to the north-west. At noon Latitude estimated 38° 2', Longitude 192° 23'; course held north-east by east, sailed 16 miles. Towards the evening the wind went round to north-east and north-east by east, stiffening more and more, so that at the end of the first watch we had to take in our topsails. Variation 8° 30'.

Item the 29th.

In the morning at daybreak we took in our bonnets and had to lower our foresail down to the stem. At noon Latitude estimated 37° 17', Longitude 191° 26'; towards noon we again set our foresail and then tacked to westward, course kept north-west, sailed 16 miles.

Item the 30th.

In the morning, the weather having somewhat improved, we set our topsails and slid out our bonnets. We had the Zeehaan to lee of us, tacked and made towards her. We then had the wind west-north-west with a top-gallant gale. At noon Latitude observed 37°, Longitude 191° 55'; course held north-east, sailed 7 miles. Towards evening we again saw the land bearing from us north-east and north-north-east, on which account we steered north and north-east. Variation 8° 40' North-East.

Item the last.

At noon we tacked about to northward, the wind being west-north-west with a light breeze. At noon Latitude observed 36° 45', Longitude 191° 46'; course kept north-west, sailed 7 miles. In the evening we were about 3 miles from shore; at the expiration of 4 glasses in the first watch we again tacked to the north; during the night we threw the lead in 80 fathom. This coast here extends south-east and north-west; the land is high in some places and covered with dunes in others. Variation 8°.

JANUARY 1643

Item the 1st of January.

In the morning we drifted in a calm along the coast which here still stretches north-west and south-east. The coast here is level and even, without reefs or shoals. At noon we were in Latitude 36° 12', Longitude 191° 7'; course kept north-west, sailed 10 miles. About noon the wind came from the south-south-east and south-east; we now shaped our course west-north-west in order to keep off shore since there was a heavy surf running. Variation 8° 30' North-East.

[1] Compare Visscher's chart from the Huydecoper manuscript in my annexed Life of Tasman, chapter XIII.

Item the 2nd.

Calm weather. Halfway through the afternoon we got a breeze from the east; we directed our course to the north-north-west; at the end of the first watch, however, we turned our course to the north-west so as not to come too near the shore and prevent accidents, seeing that in the evening we had the land north-north-west of us. At noon we were in Latitude 35° 55', Longitude 190° 47'; course kept north-west by west, sailed 7 miles. Variation 9°.

Item the 3rd.

In the morning we saw the land east by north of us at about 6 miles distance and were surprised to find ourselves so far from shore. At noon Latitude observed 35° 20', Longitude 190° 17', course held north-west by north, sailed 11 miles. At noon the wind went round to the south-south-east, upon which we steered our course east-north-east to get near the shore again. In the evening we saw land north and east-south-east of us.

Item the 4th.

In the morning we found ourselves near a cape, and had an island north-west by north of us, upon which we hoisted the white flag for the Officers of the Zeehaan to come on board of us, with whom we resolved to touch at the island aforesaid to see if we could there get fresh water, vegetables, etc. At noon Latitude observed 34° 35', Longitude 191° 9'; course kept north-east, sailed 15 miles, with the wind south-east. Towards noon we drifted in a calm and found ourselves in the midst of a very heavy current which drove us to the westward. There was besides a heavy sea running from the north-east here, which gave us great hopes of finding a passage here. This cape which we had east-north-east of us is in 34° 30' South Latitude. The land here falls away to eastward. In the evening we sent to the Zeehaan the pilot-major with the secretary, as we were close to this island and, so far as we could see, were afraid there would be nothing there of what we were in want of; we therefore asked the opinion of the officers of the Zeehaan whether it would not be best to run on, if we should get a favourable wind during the night, which the officers of the Zeehaan fully agreed with. Variation 8° 40' North-East.

Item the 5th.

In the morning we still drifted in a calm, but about 9 o'clock we got a slight breeze from the south-east, whereupon with our friends of the Zeehaan we deemed it expedient to steer our course for the island before mentioned. About noon we sent to the said island our pinnace with the pilot-major, together with the cock-boat of the Zeehaan with Supercargo Gilsemans in it, in order to find out whether there was any fresh water to be obtained there[1]. Towards the evening they returned on board and reported that, having come near the land, they had paid close attention to everything and had taken due precautions against sudden surprises or assaults on the part of the natives; that they had entered a safe but small bay, where they had found good fresh water, coming in great plenty from a steep mountain, but that, owing to the heavy surf on the shore, it was highly dangerous, nay well-nigh impossible for us to get water there, that therefore they pulled farther round the said island, trying to find some other more convenient water-place elsewhere, that on the said land they saw in several places on the highest hills from 30 to 35 persons, men of tall stature, so far as they could see from a distance, armed with sticks or clubs, who called out to them in a very loud, rough voice, certain words which our men could not understand; that these persons, in walking on, took enormous steps or strides. As our men were rowing about some few in number now and then showed themselves on the hill-tops, from which our men very credibly concluded that these natives in this way generally keep in readiness their assegais, boats and small arms, after their wonted fashions; so that it may fairly be inferred that few, if any, more persons inhabit the said island than those who showed themselves; for in rowing round the island our men nowhere saw any dwellings or cultivated land except just by the fresh water above referred to, where higher up on both sides the running water they saw everywhere square beds looking green and pleasant, but owing to the great distance they could not discern what kind of vegetables they were. It is quite possible that all these persons had their dwellings near the said fresh water. In the bay aforesaid they also saw two prows hauled on shore, one of them seaworthy, the other broken, but they nowhere saw any other craft. Our men having returned on board with the pinnace, we forthwith did our best to get near the shore, and in the evening we anchored in 40 fathom, good bottom, at a small swivel-gun-shot distance from the coast. We forthwith made preparations for taking in water the next day. The said island is in 34° 25' South Latitude and 190° 40' average Longitude.

[1] The sailor's journal in the Sweers collection gives some more particulars, without great interest however.

Item the 6th.

Early in the morning we sent to the watering-place the two boats, to wit ours and the cock-boat of the Zeehaan, each furnished with two pederaroes, 6 musketeers, and the rowers with pikes and side-arms, together with our pinnace with the pilot-major Francoys Jacobsz and skipper Gerrit Jansz, with casks for getting fresh water. While rowing towards the shore they saw, in various places on the heights, a tall man standing with a long stick like a pike, apparently watching our men.

As they were rowing past he had called out to them in a very loud voice; when they had got about halfway to the watering-place, between a certain point and another large high rock or small island, they found the current to run so strongly against the wind that, with the empty boats, they had to do their utmost to hold their own; for which reason the pilot-major and Gerrit Jansz, skipper of the Zeehaan, agreed together to abstain from exposing the small craft and the men to such great peril, seeing that there was still a long voyage before them and the men and the small craft were greatly wanted by the ships. They therefore pulled back to the ships, the rather as a heavy surf was rolling on the shore near the watering-place. The breeze freshening, we could easily surmise that they had not been able to land, and now made a sign to them from our ship with the furled flag, and fired a gun to let them know that they were at liberty to return, but they were already on their way back before we signalled to them. The pilot-major, having come alongside our ship again with the boats, reported that owing to the wind the attempt to land there was too dangerous, seeing that the sea was everywhere near the shore full of hard rocks without any sandy ground, so that they would have greatly imperilled the men and run the risk of having the water-casks injured or stove in; we forthwith summoned the officers of the Zeehaan and the second mates on board of us, and convened a council in which it was resolved to weigh anchor directly and to run on an easterly course as far as 220° Longitude, in accordance with the preceding resolution; then to shape our course to northward, or eventually due north, as far as Latitude 17° South, after which we shall hold our course due west in order to run straight of the Cocos and Hoorense islands, where we shall take in fresh water and refreshments; or if we should meet with any other island before these we shall endeavour to touch at them, in order to ascertain what can be obtained there; all this being duly specified and set forth at length in this day's resolution, to which for briefness sake we beg leave to refer. About noon we set sail; at noon we had the island due south of us at about 3 miles distance; in the evening at sunset it was south-south-west of us at 6 or 7 miles distance, the island and the rocks lying south-west and north-east of each other. During the night it was pretty calm with an east-south-east wind, our course being north-north-east, very close to the wind, while the tide was running in from the north-east.

Item the 7th.

Good weather, the wind blowing from east by south and east-south-east with a topsail breeze; at noon Latitude observed 33° 25', Longitude 191° 9'; course kept north-east, sailed 16 miles. The sea is running very high from the eastward, so that in the direction there is not likely to be any mainland. Variation 8° 30'.

Item the 8th.

During the night we had good weather, in the forenoon fog and drizzling rain; during the whole of these twenty-four hours we had the wind from south-east, with a top-gallant gale. At noon Latitude observed 32° 25', Longitude 192° 20'; course kept north-east, sailed 21 miles. The great swells now come from the south-east. This passage from Batavia to Chili is in smooth water so that there is no objection to following it; we shall hereafter describe this passage in a series of sailing instructions, but at present must omit doing so for valid reasons. Variation 9° North-East.

Item the 9th.

We had variable easterly winds with a light breeze. At noon Latitude estimated 34° 4'[1], Longitude 192° 43'; course kept north-east, sailed 7 miles; at night we drifted in a calm.

Item the 10th.

In the forenoon it continued calm with a light breeze from the east; at noon Latitude observed 31° 28', Longitude 192° 43'; course held north, sailed 9 miles; in the afternoon the wind blew from the east-north-east with a light top-gallant breeze, our course still being over to northward close to the wind. In the evening at sunset the wind went round to north by east so that we had to tack to eastward. Variation 10° 20' North-East.

Item the 11th.

The wind still northerly with a light topsail breeze, seas running from the east-south-east and from the south-west at the same time against each other. At noon Latitude estimated 31° 10' south, Longitude 193°

35'; course kept east-north-east, sailed 12 miles. In the afternoon the wind turning to the north-north-west we changed our course to east-north-east; in the evening the wind went round again to west-south-west with a squall of rain, upon which we shaped our course north-eastward. Variation 10°.

Item the 12th.

The wind west-south-west with a topsail breeze, seas still running against each other, both from south-west and south-east. At noon Latitude observed 30° 5', Longitude 195° 27'; course kept north-east by east, sailed 29 miles; towards evening the wind turned to the west. Variation 9° 30'.

Item the 13th.

Good weather with a clear sky and a westerly wind with a light topsail breeze; at noon Latitude observed 29° 10', Longitude 196° 32'; course kept north-east, sailed 20 miles; the sea keeps running from the south-west and south-east; in the evening 9° North-East.

Item the 14th.

In the morning we had the wind from the south with a light breeze, the sea still running high both from the south-west and from the south-east as well. At noon Latitude observed 28° 40', Longitude 197° 5'; course kept north-east, sailed 10 miles; at noon the wind went round to the south-east with a slackening breeze. Up to now we have had westerly winds. Variation 8° 30' North-East.

Item the 15th.

Good weather, the sea running from the south-west is beginning to smooth, so that the swells from the south-west have abated a good deal, but the sea is still running strong from the south-east. At noon Latitude estimated 27° 43', Longitude 198° 9'; course kept north-east, sailed 20 miles; the wind being south-south-east with a light topsail breeze. According to my estimation we are now 105 miles east of the Salomonis islands but only 62 miles according to the average of our longitude. Variation 8° 15'.

Item the 16th.

Good weather with a clear sky and the wind blowing from the east-ward; the sea still running in from all sides; we had a light topsail breeze. At noon Latitude observed 26° 29', Longitude 199° 32'; course kept north-east, sailed 26 miles. In the evening the wind turned to the south-east.

Item the 17th.

Good weather, with the wind from the south-east, and trade-wind weather. At noon Latitude observed 25° 20', Longitude 200° 50'; course kept north-east, sailed 25 miles in smooth water. Variation 8° North-East.

Item the 18th.

Good weather with a grey sky and trade-wind weather, the wind blowing from the south with a light topsail breeze. At noon Latitude estimated 24° 18' South, Longitude 201° 45'; course kept north-east and north-east by north, sailed 20 miles with small showers now and then.

Item the 19th.

Good weather; the wind south-east with a steady trade-wind and smooth water. At noon Latitude observed 22° 46', Longitude 203° 27'; course kept north-east, sailed 33 miles. About two o'clock in the afternoon we saw land bearing from us east by north, at about 8 miles distance. We held our course towards it but could not make it owing to the sharpness of the wind. This island bears a resemblance to two women's breasts when it bears from you east by north at 6 miles distance, and is situated in 22° 35' South Latitude and 204° 15' Longitude. It is not large, about 2 or 3 miles in circumference, and to the view appears a high and barren island. We should have greatly liked to sail close along it in order to ascertain whether we should have any chance of getting fresh water or refreshments there, but we could not get nearer to it on account of the sharpness of the wind; we tacked close to the wind. Seeing that in the great chart of the South Sea there are 4 islands situated in this latitude, I am inclined to believe that this is one of them. Variation 7° 30'.

[1] Here the margin of the original manuscript has a note in a different hand: "a mistake, probably, for 31° 4'."

Item the 20th.

In the morning at sunrise we still saw the island which we had seen the day before; it now lay south-south-west of us at about 6 miles distance; to this island we have given the name of Hooge Pylstaerts island because there were so many pylstaerten (tropic-birds) about it. We had a south-east and south-east by south wind, with trade-wind weather and a topsail breeze. At noon Latitude observed 21° 50', Longitude 204° 45'; course kept north-east by east, sailed 24 miles. About one o'clock in the afternoon we saw land, bearing from us east at about 8 miles distance; we steered our course for it, and at night lay to with small sail. Variation 7° 15' North-East.

Item the 21st.

In the morning we had a calm; we had the southernmost island east by south of us at about five miles distance; we shaped our course for the northernmost island which is[1] in 21° 50' South Latitude, Longitude 205° 29', and sailed to the north-west of the island where we dropped anchor in 25 fathom, coral bottom. The place where we came to anchor is in 21° 20' South Latitude and Longitude 205° 29'. These two islands are nearly south-east and north-west of each other; we could see through between them, where there was a passage about 1½ mile in width. The one to the south-east was the highest, the northernmost one being a low-lying island, much like Holland. To the northernmost we gave the name of Amsterdam[2] because of the abundance of refreshments we got there, and the southernmost we christened Middleburch[3]. At noon a small prow with three men in it put off from land and came near our ship; these men were naked, of a brown colour and slightly above the ordinary stature; two of them had long, thick hair on their heads, the third wore his close cut; they had only their privities covered with a curious small bit of cloth; their prow was a very narrow one, covered in to a good distance in front and abaft; their paddles were of ordinary length, with blades broad in the middle; they called out to us several times, to which we responded in the same way, but we could not understand each other. We showed them white linen, throwing overboard a piece upwards of 1½ fathom in length, which they seeing paddled towards it, but as it had sunk to a considerable depth under the water the foremost man in the prow jumped out and dived for it. He remained under water for a very long time, but at last reappeared with the linen and got into the prow again, where he put it several times atop of his head, in sign of gratitude. They then gradually approached us with their prow, upon which we threw out to them a piece of wood to which we had fastened two large nails; we then handed out to them a small Chinese looking-glass with a string of Chinese beads, which they drew up into their prow by means of a long stick, to which they tied one of their fish-hooks with a small fishing-line, which they handed up to us to show their gratitude. This fish-hook was made of mother-of-pearl and shaped like a small anchovy. They repeatedly put the string of beads and the looking-glass on their heads; the middlemost man in the prow tied the nails round his neck, but as the looking-glass was closed with a slide they could not see themselves in it. We therefore handed down another to them which they looked into, and laid on their heads. We now showed them an old coconut and a fowl, and with aid of our vocabulary inquired after water, hogs, etc.; they did not understand us nor we them, but they constantly kept pointing to the shore. When we had made them a present of the objects aforementioned, and had shown them the coconut and the fowl, they at last paddled back to shore again and made signs to us, as if they were going to fetch the like from shore. At noon and in the afternoon we saw numbers of people walking along the shore, some of them with small white flags which we surmised to be signs of peace and amity. We therefore also hoisted our white flag astern, upon which there came alongside our ship a small prow with four persons in it; they were able-bodied men, having their bodies painted black from the waist to the thighs, their necks hung round with leaves; they carried a small white flag and a cloth made of the bark of trees. They fastened the said flag to the stem of our boat. The outriggers of their prow were trimmed with shells and conches. From these presents and from the embellishments of their prow, which seemed to be distinguished above the others, we concluded that this prow had been sent off by the king or chief of the country. We therefore presented these men with a small Chinese looking-glass, a knife, a piece of dungaree[1], and one or two nails. We filled a rummer of wine for them, from which we first drank ourselves lest they should think we were going to poison them or do them other harm; having taken the rummer they poured out the wine and took the rummer on shore with them. Shortly afterwards a great number of prows came alongside, some of them with 5 or 6, others with 10 or 12 coconuts, all of which we bartered against old nails; three or four coconuts against a double middle-sized nail. Some of them came swimming from the land with coconuts, all of which we bartered with them. After some time an aged man came on board of us to whom all the others paid honour, so that we concluded him to be one of their chiefs. We conducted him to the cabin; he did us reverence by inclining his head down to our feet; we paid our respects to him in return after our own fashion, and showed him a cup with fresh water which he showed us by signs to be obtainable on shore; we then presented him with a knife, a small looking-glass, and a piece of dungaree. As they were leaving the cabin one of the natives was caught in the act of stealing the skipper's pistol and a pair of slippers. We took these articles from him again without showing the least dissatisfaction. Many of these people had the lower part of the body painted black down to the knees, some had a mother-of-pearl shell hanging on the breast. Towards evening about 20 prows came close to our ships, which all stationed themselves side by side in regular order. Before coming alongside they made a good deal of noise, crying out repeatedly "Woo, woo, woo," etc., upon which those in our ship sat down. The said prows then came alongside, bringing a present from the king, consisting of a fine large hog, a number of coconuts, and some yams; the bearer of these presents being the same person who brought us the small white flag and the cloth of bark. We presented them in return with a common dish such as we use at meals, and a piece of copper-wire; we also bartered a few coconuts, baccovos[2], yams and a hog, etc., against nails and beads; about nightfall they all left our ship except one who remained to sleep on board of the Heemskerk.

[1] The Huydecoper copy of the journal has here: "because it was the larger of the two islands This southernmost island is in 21° 50' S. L., Longitude 205° 29'."--The sailor's journal has some more particulars about the dates from Jan. 21 to Jan. 23, without interest however. In MONTANUS, America en 't Zuid-land, pp. 579 ff. the naval surgeon Hendrik Haelbos gives some curious particulars.

[2] Or Tonga-tabu, the principal island of the group which Captain Cook named the Friendly Islands.

[3] Or Eavo-wee, also Eua.

Item the 22nd.

Early in the morning again a number of boats came alongside with coconuts, yams, baccovos, bananas, hogs and fowls, all of which we bartered with them; to wit, a young hog against a small fathom of dungaree, a fowl against a nail or a string of beads; coconuts, yams, bananas, etc., against old nails. Several women, both young and old, also came on board of us, the oldest of them having the little finger of both hands cut off, but not so the young women; what this meant we could not ascertain. About 8 o'clock the old man of the day before again came on board, bringing us 2 hogs in return for which we presented him with a silver-mounted knife and 8 or 9 nails. We conducted him below and went all over the ship with him, and caused one of our great guns to be fired, at which they were greatly frightened and ran away in amazement, but when they saw that no one was the worse for it they were soon set at ease again. We presented this old man with a piece of figured satin, a hat and a shirt, which we put on him. About noon 32 small and one large ditto, furnished with sails, and like those delineated in Jacob la Maire's journal No. [3] came alongside. From these prows 18 strong men and a few females stepped on board of our ship, bringing with them as a present a few bark-mats and fruits such as coconuts, yams and other roots which we had no knowledge of. We presented the leader of these persons with a shirt, a pair of drawers, a small looking-glass and a few beads; we put the shirt and the drawers on him, in which he thought himself very gallantly attired. Among these 18 persons there was a bony, corpulent man with a St. Thomas arm[1], and a woman who had a small natural beard growing about the mouth. We made the second mate of the Zeehaan come on board of us with his trumpet, and one of her sailors with a violin, and from time to time had them blow and play tunes together with our own trumpeter and one of our sailors who could play the German flute, at which music they were greatly astonished. Meanwhile we had a number of water-casks lowered into our boat and the Zeehaan's cock-boat that our men might together with these people go and see whether there was any fresh water to be obtained here, as had been determined in our resolution; we placed a first mate in command of each of the boats while our skipper Ide Tjercxz and Supercargo Gilsemans accompanied them in our pinnace, into which we also put the old man and the leader of the natives who had last come on board, these two undertaking to show the watering-place to our men. We also put a number of musketeers into our pinnace, for though these natives seem to be good-natured enough it is impossible to know what they hide in their hearts, for which reason we armed our people to be prepared for all accidents. When our boats had rowed a considerable distance along the north-east side of this land they were finally conducted to three small wells, from which water had to be dipped up by means of a coconut-shell. This water was quite unfit to be drunk, of a dirty greenish colour, and there was so little of it that it would have been of little use even if it had been good to drink. The people who had pointed out these wells to our men now led them inland to a kind of pleasance and to an elegant baleye[2] or raised and roofed platform, where our men were invited to sit down on handsome mats; but the natives brought them nothing but two coconut-shells filled with water, one for their chieftain and the other for our skipper. Towards the evening our men returned on board with a live hog and reported that there was no chance of getting water there. In the course of this day we obtained by barter upwards of 40 hogs, giving in exchange for each of them a double middle-sized nail and half a fathom of old canvas; and besides about 70 fowls, for each of which we gave a double middle-sized nail, etc., and a quantity of yams, coconuts and other fruit in exchange for beads. In the evening one of the chiefs had a roasted pig, some yams and other roots brought on board of us. The natives here have no knowledge of tobacco or of smoking of any kind; their women have the body covered from the waist to the knees with mats made of the leaves of trees, the rest of the body being naked; they wear their hair shorter than the men; the beards of the latter are as a rule the length of three or four finger's breadths, the hair on the upper lip being cut pretty short so that their mustachios are no longer than about two straw's breadths. We saw no arms worn by these people so that it was all peace and amity here. The current is not strong here, the flood runs south-west and the ebb north-east, which in our estimation makes it high-water with a south-westerly moon; the rise and fall of the tide is about 7 or 8 feet.

[1] A sort of cotton-cloth exported from the East Indies by the Company's ships.

[2] Baccovo or pacoba is the fruit of a species of Musa Paradisiaca; the English name of the fruit is "plantain."

[3] This No. left blank in the MS., refers to Plate G of the first editions (1618/19) of Le Maire's Voyage.

Item the 23rd.

In the morning we went to the shore with Skipper Gerrit Jansz and our two boats together with the pinnace for the purpose of digging wells to obtain fresh water; when coming ashore we forthwith went to the wells and made signs to the chief that the wells would have to be made larger, upon which he directly ordered his men to do this work for us. He then went with us to the baleye or platform, and caused a mat to be spread on which we seated ourselves. When we were seated he had refreshments brought in, such as fresh milk and cream, fresh fish and various kinds of fruit, of which there is great abundance here, and in every way showed us respect and friendship. They then asked us where we had come from and where were going, upon which we told them that we had been at sea for a hundred days and upwards, at which they were greatly astonished; we also told them that we had come there in search of fresh water, hogs, fowls, etc., to which they answered that they had plenty of them, as many as we wished. We then got 8 casks filled with water, and they presented us with four live hogs and a number of fowls, coconuts, bananas, etc. In return we offered them one fathom of linen, 6 nails and six strings of beads, for which they cordially thanked us. We then went up to the white flag with the three chiefs, signifying to them that we wished to leave the said flag near the platform in sign of peace and amity, at which they expressed great satisfaction and put the flag on their heads one after the other, thereby giving to understand that they desired nothing but our friendship. They next fastened the flag to the baleye as a sign that they had made a covenant with us. As the bottom here is steep and abruptly falling off our anchor lost its hold by the trade-wind in the afternoon, so that we drifted out to sea without our being able to prevent it; we did our best to haul our anchor on the bow but, as we had but few men on board, we could not secure it before midnight. In the course of this day we still got by barter a number of pigs and fowls, so that in all we have got for the two ships a hundred head of hogs, 150 fowls and a reasonable quantity of coconuts, yams and other fruit; we were compelled to stay on board the Zeehaan for the night since we could not get on board our own ship.

[1] "St. Thomas's arm." In WILLEM TEN RHIJNE, Verhandelinge van de Asiatise Melaatsheid. Amsterdam. 1687, p. 165, the author, referring to the sovereign virtues of certain Indian herbs, mentions "St. Thomas benen" [St. Thomas's legs] between "dikke kraambeenen" [swollen legs of women lying-in] and "geswollene beenen der Me-

laatse" [swollen legs of lepers].--This information has been kindly furnished by Dr. C. E. DANIELS, of Amsterdam.

[2] "Baleye"; a building open on four sides, where meetings were held, public affairs transacted, foreigners received in state, etc.

Item the 24th.

In the morning the Heemskerk had drifted fully 4 miles to leeward of this island; the flute Zeehaan having weighed anchor, we got near each other again on the forenoon so that we could get on board our own ship. We then ordered the steersmen of the Zeehaan to come on board of us, also whereupon we convened the council and submitted to the consideration of all persons assembled the points following: seeing that we have been forced to leave this island by an accident and against our will, seeing that there is small chance for us to come near it again except with great loss of time, seeing that there is hardly any water worth mentioning to be obtained there, whether it would not be best and most advisable to proceed on our voyage in accordance with the proceeding resolution, and in case we should meet with other islands to touch at the same, all which was approved by the council as may be seen from the resolution under this day's date. At the place where we had been at anchor there were two islets, high but small, about 1 or 1½ miles in circumference, bearing from us north by west at 7 or 8 miles distance. We now set our course north-eastward with a steady, south-easterly trade-wind. At noon we had the two islets aforesaid due east[1] of us at 4 miles distance.

[1] The margin of the MS. has a note here in a different hand: "This should be west."

These islets we estimated to lie in 20° 50' South Latitude, Longitude 206° 46'. About 3 o'clock in the afternoon, east-north-east of us at four or five miles distance, we again saw a low-lying island of pretty large extent. We steered straight for it. Shortly afterwards we saw east of us 3 small islets, likewise in the south-east 2 small islets, all of them low-lying; the farthest were at about 3 or 4 miles distance south-east of us. We now set our course due east-north-east, towards the largest of them, and anchored in 12 fathom, shelly bottom, at a swivel-gunshot distance from shore on the west side of the island; about an hour before sunset we had at the western extremity a large high island north-west by north of us at about 8 or 9 miles distance; and close to this, but more to eastward and north-west of us, still another island, round and a good deal higher still than the previous one, in height and size resembling Cracatouw in Zunda straits, at the same distance from us; furthermore from the north to the north-east by north we saw 7 more small islets at about 3 or 4 miles distance from us. All these islands are surrounded by a steep, abruptly descending ground so that it is impossible to approach them sounding; on which account one has to anchor by sight, close inshore; almost all of them are surrounded by coral reefs. Variation 7° North-East.

Item the 25th.

Early in the morning several prows came alongside with coconuts, yams, bananas, etc., to be bartered against nails of which their very desirous. There seemed to be few people living in the said island; some who seemed to be the most notable of them came on board of us and were by us presented with small pieces of linen, knives, small looking-glasses, etc. We then gave them to understand by signs that we were in want of fresh water, upon which they signified to us that this was to be obtained on shore in great plenty. We therefore resolved to send ashore the pilot-major Francoys Jacobsz and Skipper Gerrit Jansz with our pinnace together with the two boats, taking with them one of these natives to point out the watering-place to them. We handed into the pinnace a knife, a small looking-glass and a little flag in token of peace, and signified to them that we did not want to have their water without reward or payment. About two hours before sunset our pinnace returned with the Skipper and the pilot-major who reported that, on landing, they had seen from 60 to 70 persons seated on the beach, who, as they thought, formed the entire male population of the island; they had no arms but seemed to be a kind and peaceable sort of people; our men also saw many women and children; they conducted our men into the interior by a good path. These people proved to be exceedingly thievish for they stole whatever they could lay hands on, men and women alike. Our men followed them about 2/3 of a mile into the interior, where they came to a fresh inland piece of water, fully 1/4 mile in circumference, and no less than 1½ or 2 fathom above the level of the sea, but they did not know it was so near the shore; as they were going along the said piece of water they found it to be at the northern side of the island, at about a musket-shot distance from the sea, where there was a good sandy bay for landing with the boats, the water being conveniently smooth for embarking the casks; out at sea before the said sandy bay there was a coral reef on which the surf broke with great violence; and since the said coral reef has an opening on the west side it will be possible for our boats at low water to row along the shore and inside the coral reef into the smooth water. But in order to get to the sandy beach the water must first have risen about 1 1/2 or 2 feet higher. This bay was on the north side of the islet and, as our ships were lying on the north-west side, they had to row upwards of a mile along the shore. They were very glad to have found this fresh water. About three hours after sunset our two boats came alongside with filled water-casks, having been prevented from coming earlier by the falling of the water, which here rises and falls about 8 feet. In this fresh water aforesaid they had seen numbers of wild ducks swimming, which were not all shy or afraid of men. These natives brought on board several coconuts and gourds full of water; also some fruit and hogs, but not many; they had prows with sails, as well as smaller ones; their dress, appearance and manners are like those of the inhabitants of the other island, except that as a rule the men have shorter and thinner hair than the others; the women are, comparatively speaking, just as strong and able-bodied as the men. This island is in Latitude 20° 15', average Longitude 206° 19'; we gave to it the name of Rotterdam, seeing that here we got our casks filled with water. Variation 6° 20' North-East.

Item the 26th.

This day we fetched for each of the ships two more boatloads of water, each consisting of 10 or 11 casks, both great and small; we also bartered still a good many coconuts, bananas and other fruit against beads and old nails.

Item the 27th.

We still kept taking in water and bartering refreshments; before sunset we had again got on board two boatloads of water for each ship.

Item the 28th.

In the morning at early dawn myself with Skipper Gerrit Jansz again went to the watering-place with our two boats and the pinnace. Our main purpose was to shoot wild ducks but we could not get any. As we were engaged in putting off from shore with the loaded boats one of the natives approached with the intention of secretly carrying off a long pike, which he had actually snatched from the boat and hid under water; but one of our men saw him, upon which the thief, becoming aware of this, ran into the wood with the pike as quickly as his legs would carry him. The other natives seeing this ran after him with great speed, beckoning to our men to remain where they were because they were going to bring him back. They really did so, so that we had the pike returned to us. The natives here are excessively licentious, wanton and thievishly inclined, so that a man had need of Argus' hundred eyes to look about him. In the evening before sunset we again had got on board two boat-loads of water for each of the ships, so that up to now we already have 26 hogsheads quite filled, only about 10 hogsheads and casks being still empty; we also obtained by barter a considerable quantity of coconuts, bananas, baccovos and other fruit, so that at these islands we were well provided with refreshments and fresh water for which God be thanked.

Item the 29th.

We again sent ashore the pilot-major with our boats together with the pinnace to fetch water, but in the afternoon the wind began to blow so stiffly from the north that the men in the Zeehaan's boat had to let 5 casks of water run out at the bung-hole while rowing, and to throw the casks overboard; afterwards they had to let go 4 more casks, so that they got on board without any fresh water; our own boat managed to come alongside with 7 full casks, and to bring the empty casks with her, but they had had plenty of trouble in doing so.

Item the 30th.

We summoned our friends of the Zeehaan on board of us and, having convened the council, we read out to them our instructions, after which we requested every member of the council, if he should know of anything to the advantage and profit of the Honourable Company that might be unknown to ourselves, to inform us of the same and to assist us with all needful zeal and diligence. We likewise earnestly and kindly entreated each of the members assembled to act in every respect in such fashion as he intends to answer for on his return to Batavia before the Honourable Governor-General and Councillors of India. We likewise resolved if this wind should continue to set sail from here with our ships tomorrow; but if it should go round to eastward we shall directly make arrangements for getting all our casks filled with water; all of which may be seen set forth in extenso in this day's resolution, to which we beg leave to refer.

In this day's meeting of the council we also resolved upon the articles following, which shall be read to our men and posted up on the quarter-deck, that every man may comport himself accordingly:

Seeing that on the 27th instant at night we have found that some persons, even officers, do not properly stand their ordained watches, the which in many cases might cause hurt and peril to our ships and crews, in order to prevent such inconveniences and perils for the future the plenary council of the ships Heemskerk and Zeehaan has this day resolved and ordered that whoever shall, after now, be found sleeping or neglecting to keep a proper lookout, whether on watch or on the lookout, shall for the first offence be flogged by the partners of his watch; for the second offence, besides being flogged, he shall forfeit a month's pay; for the third offence he shall be deprived of six months' pay, and for the fourth offence he shall be deprived of his office and forfeit his pay or, if the offender should be a sailor, be forced to serve without pay.

[1] Namocka group.

According to the same articles all persons on board, none excepted, are strictly forbidden to use or carry about their persons any live matches, candles, or other lights of any sort, unless such matches, candles etc. shall be wanted in the discharge of office or for the requirements of the ship's service, and be used with the knowledge of the ship's officers; all this on pain of being put in irons for eight days in succession, and of forfeiting a month's pay over and above this.

Likewise after the watches have been set no one shall be permitted to make any noise whatever, but each person shall keep watch over such places as have been assigned to his care by the Commander, the skipper, the steersmen or the quartermasters; all this on pain of summary punishment.

The men on watch shall, whether by day or by night, not allow anyone to come on board except with the consent of the commander, the skipper, or the supercargo, on pain of corporal punishment.

Given on board the Heemskerk, at anchor in Latitude 20° 15', average Longitude 206° 19', south of the line equinoctial. This 30th day of January A.D. 1643.

Signed,
ABEL JANSZ. TASMAN.

Item the last.

In the morning we again set out the boats, together with our pinnace, to fetch water, but as the weather began to darken and to look variable. We made a signal for them to return, upon which they came back at once. At noon we, that is to say myself, our skipper, the pilot-major, the skipper and the supercargo of the Zeehaan and the secretary, went on shore with the two boats and the pinnace for the purpose of taking leave of the natives, since it was our intention to depart from here. As soon as we had landed a great multitude of people assembled. We asked two persons who seemed most notable of them after the chief of this district. They conducted us into the interior by narrow, cramped, dirty and miry paths (it having rained very hard for one or two days without interruption). We were first led to the south side of the island where a large number of coconut-trees stood side by side in regular order. Thence they went with us to the east side of the island where six large prows were lying at anchor, each two of them being fastened together by means of a floor of planks and carrying a mast. Here were also one or two small houses ornamented a little above the common, to wit, fenced all round with a bamboo enclosure. After leaving this place we came to a lake or piece of brackish inland water, about a mile in circumference. After staying here for some time we again asked after the Aisy or Latouw (which in their speech means king or chieftain). They then pointed to the far side of this water and, as the sun was close to the horizon already, we returned to our boats along a different path. Both in going and returning we saw many enclosures or gardens with plots elegantly squared and planted with all sorts of earth-fruit. In several places we saw bananas and other fruit-trees, most of them growing so straight that they were good to look at, on all sides emitting a most agreeable and gratifying smell and fragrance. From which we concluded that these people (who had the shape of men but inhuman manners and customs) were by no means destitute of human intelligence. About two hours before sunset we returned on board. These islands are in their average longitude 185 miles more to eastward than the Salomonis islands and, according to my estimation, are situated 230 miles east of the easternmost Salomonis islands. These natives know nothing of religion or the service of God, nor have they either idols, other relics, or priests. Still they are very superstitious for I have seen one of these persons take up a watersnake which came floating by his prow, lay it upon his head with great reverence, and then put it into the water again. They will never kill any of the flies which are very plentiful here and cause trouble enough, however many cover their bodies. While we were at anchor here our chief mate happened to kill a fly in the presence of one of the chieftains, who showed himself greatly incensed at this. The people of this island have no king or chief and are without any government. Still they have some knowledge of evil and punish evil-doers, but not through the arm of justice, all the non-culprits as a rule taking part in the execution of the punishment. We have seen the proof of this at a time when we were fetching water, and one of the natives had carried off one of our pikes, with which he ran off into the wood. We had seen him do it and signified to the others our anger. They seeing this, ran after him and, having taken the pike from him brought it back to us a great distance, and punished the thief or evil-doer like this: they took an old coconut and battered his back with it until the nut got cracked; we could not find out if this is their usual practice or was on this occasion done for our sake only.

FEBRUARY 1643

Item the 1st of February.

Seeing that at present we find ourselves provided with plenty of refreshments and that we have got nearly all our casks filled with water, for which the Ruler of all things be fervently thanked and praised, and that for some days past the wind has been continually blowing from the north, which makes the coast near the watering-place a lee-shore, so that we are unable to fill our remaining casks, therefore we have deemed it advisable to continue our voyage, for which reason early this morning we weighed anchor and set sail to northward with a favourable breeze from the east.

Item the 2nd.

At noon we had the southernmost of the high islands south-south-east and the northernmost south-east by south of us at about 6 or 7 miles distance. At noon Latitude observed 19° 20', Longitude 205° 55', course held from the island north-north-west, sailed 15 miles. These high islands are situated north-north-west slightly more to westward of the island where we got water at 7 or 8 miles distance. Halfway the afternoon we saw another island north-east by east of us at about 7 miles distance, also pretty high; the wind blowing from the east with a light breeze.

Item the 3rd.

In the morning we still saw the island which in the previous evening we had north-east by east of us; we now had it east-south-east of us at about 8 miles distance. At noon Latitude observed 18° 18', Longitude 205° 55'; course held north, sailed 15 miles; the wind blowing from the east-south-east and south-east with trade-wind weather, a clear sky and smooth water.

Item the 4th.

Good weather and a clear sky with smooth water; in the morning we estimated ourselves to have passed the 17th degree, on which account we turned our course to westward in accordance with the resolution. At noon Latitude estimated 16° 40', Longitude 205° 25'; course kept north by west, sailed 25 miles; the wind being east-south-east and south-east with a topsail breeze and trade-wind weather; towards the evening we had a few squalls with thunder and lightning.

Item the 5th.

We continued to have trade-wind weather with the wind as before, a topsail and smooth water. At noon Latitude observed 16° 30', Longitude 203° 12'; course held west, sailed 32 miles; at noon we set our course west by south in order to reach the 17th degree, and had a good lookout kept so as not to sail past the Cocos or Verraders islands; during the night when three glasses of the dog-watch had run out we saw land, upon which we immediately hauled aboard our larboard tacks and ran southward till seven glasses in the same watch were out, when we tacked to the north again.

Item the 6th.

In the morning we again saw land, to wit three small islets, on all sides surrounded by shoals and reefs; we tacked about to the south and saw a large reef to westward stretching as far as the south, which we sincerely regretted; this land is fully 8 or 9 miles in length; straight ahead there were also breakers which we were unable to pass. Seeing that we could clear neither the reef straight ahead nor another which lay north of us we observed to leeward a small space about two ship's lengths wide where there were no breakers; for this we made since there was no other way of escape; we passed between the rocks in 4 fathom, though not without great anxiety; all about here there are reefs and 18 or 19 islands, but the shoals which abound here and are very dangerous render it impossible for ships to pass between them. These islands are in 17½°[1] or thereabouts for we got no latitude. At noon we estimated ourselves to be in 17° 9' South Latitude, Longitude 201° 35', course held west-south-west, sailed 25 miles with a steady trade-wind from the east-south-east. We should have greatly liked to have come to anchor near one of these islands but could find no roadstead on account of the numberless shoals and reefs that run out to sea from all these islands. At noon we turned our course to northward in order if possible to get clear of all these shoals in the daytime. Towards the north too we saw numerous shoals everywhere, which it would be difficult to pass through. At length however we found an opening and sailed through between the reefs, but to our great regret had to leave these isles because we found no ground for anchoring. In the evening we saw three hills which we thought to be islands. During 5 glasses of the first watch we again made for the land in order to avoid the shoal ahead of us. The wind was blowing from the east and we sailed with our mainsail set. When 5 glasses of the first watch were out we tacked to northward and ran northward till daybreak, when we saw the island which on the previous evening we had seen north by west of us.

[1] The Huydecoper-copy has: "These islands are in 17 degrees S. L., the southernmost ones in 17½° or thereabouts."--The sailors's journal has some more particulars, without interest however.

Item the 7th.

We kept sailing to the north close to the wind with our mainsail set, the wind being north-east with a strong gale and showers of rain and a high sea running from the north. The Pilot-major thought that the islands which we had been near to on the 6th instant are the islands which in the large chart are found south-west of the Hoornsche islands; for which reason he was of the opinion that we ought to shape our course to northward close by the wind in order to keep clear of the coast of New Guinea, since this is a lee-shore and the season unfavourable so that it might prove impossible to put off from shore again. In the morning we came close upon an island, therefore tacked to the south until daybreak when we turned to the north again, the wind blowing a storm from the north-east; we therefore tacked to the north-west with small sail. At noon Latitude estimated 16°, Longitude 200° 48'; course kept north-west by north, sailed 21 miles.

Item the 8th.

The wind kept blowing very strong from the north-east and north-north-east with a great deal of rain. We still sailed close to the wind with small sail. Having called the Pilot-major aft we asked him whether he persisted in his opinion that these were the islands he had mentioned the day before. He answered in the affirmative and added that in his opinion we ought to steer northward directly if the wind should allow of it. Owing to the rough and stormy weather we could not get our friends of the Zeehaan on board of us nor even speak them; upon which we convened the council of the Heemskerk, together with the two second mates, and submitted to their consideration the opinion given by the Pilot-major; asking all of them to give us their own opinions in writing that from these collective advices we might draw up a resolution which we accordingly did in the afternoon. Wind and weather as before; at noon we estimated ourselves to be in 15° 29' South Latitude, Longitude 199° 31'; course kept west-north-west, sailed 20 miles, in accordance with the advices resolved upon this day.

We should have liked to have convened the councils of both ships, but were prevented from so doing by the turbulence of the weather with rain and wind; for which reason we summoned the council of the ship Heemskerk, together with the two second mates, and represented to them that for many days past we have had such weather that at times we could hardly see to a distance of two or three ship's lengths, and that on the 6th instant we had been entangled between islands and shoals to such a degree that we could only with difficulty get clear of the same. These islands are 18 or 20 in number so far as we could count them, though it is quite possible that there are more since, owing to the darkness of the weather, it was very difficult to count them. These islands are situated full in the course of Jacob la Maire, but since in this latitude he ran on for 430 miles due west and did not find any such islands there we might conclude that these islands do not lie in the line of the said course. But in the great chart of the South Sea certain islands are marked which agree with these as regards their latitude; but this would make a difference with our reckoning of more than 200 miles, the said islands being marked in the chart so many miles more to westward. Now during this long voyage we have almost continually been sailing eastward and westward, often with storms and tempests, for which reason the proverb which says that guesswork often shoots wide of the mark may well be applicable to us, and we be so far out in our reckoning.

[1] Named after Prince William of Orange. Fiji Group.

[2] Fiji Group.

For all which reasons it is our opinion that, wind and weather permitting, we should from here run due north as far as the 4th degree of Southern Latitude and then due west as far as the coast of New Guinea, seeing that the weather we now have is such that one might easily miss a known coast, let alone an unknown one; that there is no good anchorage there, and a lee-shore besides, so that we should run great risk of losing our ships and men alike, and that we are in the bad season here, when the south-east trade-wind and the northern monsoon meet each other, which cannot fail to cause much rain and rough weather.

Given on board the ship Heemskerk this day the 8th of February, A.D. 1643 in 15° 29' Southern Latitude and 199° 31' Longitude.

Signed,
ABEL JANSZ TASMAN.

* * *

This day the 8th of February A.D. 1643, our ships being in the estimated latitude of 15° 23', Longitude 198° 4', the Honourable Commander Abel Jansz Tasman has enjoined the council of the ship Heemskerk, each member to give his opinion in writing respecting the course to be held from here, whether to the west-north-west or more northerly, in order in the most convenient way to make the coast of New Guinea or the islands situated at the north-east point.

Therefore we, so far as regards ourselves, will give our opinion as follows: in the first place it is now the bad season and the period of rain in the Moluccas, and here we have every day rain and strong north-east winds which cause the east side of New Guinea to be a lee shore; also it is a rule all over the East Indies the nearer a lee shore the worse weather. If one wants to make the coast of New Guinea in the latitude of the Salomonis islands, partly in accordance with the directions and instructions given, though not constituting a positive command, this could not be done without incurring the risk of being cast into a bay from which it might be difficult or impossible to beat out again; and since the east side of New Guinea is still unknown it is quite possible that there may be plenty of small islands and shoals to eastward of the said Land of New Guinea, such as we have already met with before and, having no secure anchorage in such rough weather, in which it is impossible to keep a proper lookout, we might happen to be cast on the shore before we had become aware of the same.

For which reason we think that from here we should sail northward as close to the wind as shall be found practicable as far as 4 or 5° South Latitude; the object of our advice being to avoid all risks and prevent our being thrown on a lee-shore, seeing that the coast falls away there, whence we could run to the west in the first instance and next regulate ourselves by wind and weather.

Signed,
FRANCOYS JACOBSZ.

* * *

Whereas on the 8th instant we are now having a good deal of rough weather, both with rain and strong north winds, so that we can hardly carry mainsails and cannot see to a quarter of a mile distance, the

Commander had convened the council of the Heemskerk, together with the second mates, and desired each of them to give in his opinion in writing; I therefore state as my opinion that we ought to direct our course as far to northward as wind and weather shall permit, nay even due north or north by east, as far as 2 or 3° South Latitude, to avoid being cast on the lee-shore of New Guinea; seeing that we are in the bad season here and it is quite possible that we may have got farther to westward than our account makes it, since on the 6th instant we came across 20 or 21 islands lying in 17° 10' South Latitude, which were not seen by Jacob la Maire.

This day the 8th of February 1643 on board the Yacht Heemskerk, Latitude estimated 15° 43', Longitude 199° 7'.

Signed,
IDE TJERRXZ HOLMAN.

* * *

This day the 8th of February A.D. 1643. Whereas in my estimation we are now in Latitude 15° 47', Longitude 198° 10', the weather having been stormy for several days past and the Honourable

Commander having desired each of us to give his advice in writing regarding the course to be held and up to what latitude; it would be my advice that we ought to steer on a north-west course as far as 3° of Latitude south of the Equator and afterwards to westward.

Signed,
CARSTEN JURRIAENSZ.

* * *

To the Honourable Mr. Abel Jansz. Tasman.

It is my advice that from here, being the estimated southern latitude of 15° 44', and the longitude of 198° 19', we should steer our course as far to northward as shall be found practicable so as to avoid being cast on the land of New Guinea, as far as the southern latitude of 6 or 7°, since we are now getting on for the bad season here when the winds are blowing from the north-east and north-north-east, and there is much rain and a difficult lookout to be expected and, if we should happen to be thrown on a lee-shore with our ships, there would be small chance of getting them off again, owing to want of sailing wind, and we might easily fall into peril with our ships and cargoes; therefore in my opinion it is better to stick to the course aforesaid and, when we have got so far with the aid of God, to direct our course to westward and try to make the land of New Guinea, and afterwards to steer our course for the land of Gilolo. Given thus on board the Yacht Heemskerk, A.D. 1643, the 8th of February.

Signed by me,
CHRYN HENDRECXZ DE RATTE.

Item the 9th.

The wind blowing from the north with rain and a strong gale. We kept sailing with our mainsail set, the sea being very rough and running very high from the north and north-west. At noon Latitude estimated 15° 29', Longitude 198° 8'; course held west, sailed 20 miles. In the evening we tacked about to the east, hauled up our foresail, and in this way ran on close to the wind with our mainsail and mizzen-sail set until the end of the first watch; we then loosened our foresail again and tacked about to westward. In the day-watch we set our great topsail but before long had to take it in again.

Item the 10th.

We still had variable weather with rain and wind, the sea running from all directions, so that the water is very rough and we are experiencing very unfavourable weather for discovering anything, which is now quite impossible to all this dark, hazy, drizzling weather. At noon Latitude estimated 15° 19' South, Longitude 197° 20'; course held north-west by north, sailed 12 miles. For the last five days past we have been without seeing either sun, moon or stars. In the evening we lowered the foresail down to the stem and lay to with mainsail and mizzen-sail.

Item the 11th.

The storm still raging from the north, and the sea still running very high from all sides, with dark, foggy, drizzling, rainy weather and a good deal of lightning. At noon Latitude estimated 15° 5' South Latitude, Longitude 196° 6'; course held west by north, sailed and drifted 18 miles.

Item the 12th.

After breakfast it began to clear up to some extent, so that we set our great topsail; the sun broke through the clouds, and it seemed as if the weather was going to change; the sea is however still running very high, mainly from the west-south-west. At noon Latitude observed 15° 3', Longitude 195° 50'; course held west, sailed 18 miles; halfway the afternoon we again got the same rainy and stormy weather we had had before, so that we had to take in our great topsail and to sail with two mainsails without bonnets; the wind is mainly blowing from the north and north-north-west and is exceedingly variable. In the evening we steered to the east until midnight then tacked about to the west; during the night we had a pouring rain, so that the water seemed to come down in torrents, accompanied by thunder and lightning.

Item the 13th.

In the morning, the weather being somewhat better and the sea having calmed down to some extent, we set our topsails but without sliding out the bonnets. We continued to have occasional showers and the wind still blew from the north; during the last twenty-four hours we sailed and drifted 12 miles to west-south-west. At noon Latitude estimated 15° 21' south, the Latitude observed being 15° 38', Longitude 194° 4'; the sea is becoming a good deal smoother; during the night we lay to with small sail.

Item the 14th.

The wind north-west and north-north-west with good weather, though it was still thick, hazy and dark, so that it was difficult to keep a lookout. We sent the pilot-major with the secretary to the Zeehaan to require the opinions in writing of her officers. At noon Latitude observed 16° 20', Longitude 193° 35'; course held south-west, sailed 10 miles.

The following are the advices of our friends on board the Zeehaan: This day the 14th of February of the year 1643. Whereas the Commander had this day sent the pilot-major and his secretary on board of us to hear our advices as regards the shaping of our courses, and secondly in what latitude it would be best to touch at the land of New Guinea; my advice touching the point referred to is that we had best touch at the land aforesaid in 4 or 5° South Latitude. The reason why I would advise to touch at this land so far to northward is as follows: we have had very rough weather for 6 or 7 days past and been in fear of getting into a bay or being cast on a lee-shore; in the latitude aforesaid we should come upon the land in a known latitude; and if we have touched at the land in the said latitude it is likely we shall be able to get to the south if the time at our disposal shall permit us to do so. It is consequently my opinion that we should shape our course as far to northward as possible until we got to the latitude aforesaid and then steer due west until in the latitude aforesaid we come in sight of New Guinea. At this time of writing we were by account in Latitude 15° 49' south, Longitude 194° 37'.

Signed,
GERRIT JANSZ.

* * *

Advice or reasons why and for what cause we hold it most expedient to navigate to the north.

Whereas Your Worship has been pleased to ask us to give in our opinion or advice touching the question submitted to us in writing yesterday, my judgment in this matter is as follows: since we are at present in Latitude 15° 55' south, Longitude 194° 24', and the weather here about this time of the year would seem to be very variable, while in this region of the world we are as it were at the mercy of winds blowing from all the four quarters, and we do not know how near we have sailed to the land of New Guinea, except what in this respect we can gather from the terrestrial globe and the great chart of the South Sea, we trust that the islands made by the Honourable Commander are the Salomonis islands, seeing that in longitude and latitude we have found them to agree with the indications in the chart of the Portuguese; the said islands cannot have been seen by Schoutens and therefore they may be the land of New Guinea which, according to the Portuguese chart, we might also happen to fall in with.

For the reason above given it is therefore my opinion, regard being had to the roughness of the weather and to the possibility that we may be nearer to the said land than we suspect, to the fact that we do not know its trend in this latitude and what bays, inlets, bights, shoals and the like there may be in and about it, to the risk that with these northerly winds we may by storm or rough weather be cast and driven on a lee-shore, which would grievously endanger both ship and cargo; it is therefore, I repeat, my opinion that we ought to steer our course north-north-west to the known part of New Guinea about as far as 4 or 5° Southern Latitude, and by so doing avoid all perils as much as possible. Given on board the flute-ship the Zeehaan this 15th of February, 1643.

Signed,

Your devoted servant,
J. GILSEMANS.

* * *

My advice is that we ought to make the land of New Guinea in 5 or 6° South Latitude, seeing that for six days past we have had exceedingly rough weather; that if we should be driven into a bay we might get such weather that it would prove impossible for us to beat out of it; I think that we ought to shape our course as far to northward as the wind will allow us till we got to the latitude aforesaid, and then steer westward in order to make the land of New Guinea. We are at present in Latitude 16° 3', and Longitude 195° 27' on the 14th of February 1643.

Signed,
HENDRICK PIETERSZ.

* * *

This day the 14th of February, 1643. Whereas for 6 or 7 days past we have now had north wind with dark, rough and dirty weather, so that we may very well be nearer land than we suspect, and run the risk of being driven into a bay from which with a northerly wind and this un-settled weather it would be very difficult for us to get out again, therefore my advice is that we should run on as far as 5 or 6° South Latitude, so as to make the coast of New Guinea on the north side; and

I further think that we should shape our course as far northward as the wind will allow us until we arrive at the said latitude, and then steer to westward in order to touch at New Guinea. This day at noon we are in Latitude 15° 57' South, and Longitude 195° 49'.

Signed by me,
PIETER NANNINGHZ. DUYTS.

* * *

This day the 14th of the month of February, our ship being in 15° 57' South Latitude, and the middle longitude of 195° 10', and the Honourable Commander desiring to be informed of the reasons why we should set our course so far to northward as we had fixed upon, I give it as my opinion that, since we have now had a violent storm with rain and dark weather these 6 or 7 days past, and do not know whether we are still far from shore or near it, and whether we may not again be driven into some bay or be cast on shoals or reefs, as happened to us on the 6th instant, we ought to attempt to make New Guinea in 5 or 6° southern latitude to the end that we may be able to get off shore on a northerly course; it being further my advice that we should set our course as high to northward as shall be found possible, in order to reach that latitude aforesaid and then steer to westward until we get to the land of New Guinea.

Signed by me,
CORNELIS YSBRANTSZ ROOLOL.[1]

Item the 15th.

Still dark, foggy weather with rain and the wind from the north-west and west-north-west with a light breeze; we tacked this way and that so that we made no progress, having the wind almost flat against us. At noon Latitude estimated 16° 30' South, Longitude 193° 35'; course held south, drifted 2 miles. Towards the evening we got a violent squall of rain from south-west and set our course to northward. In the first watch it fell a calm so that we drifted in a calm the whole of the night.

Item the 16th.

In the morning we kept drifting in a calm. During the last 24 hours we made no progress owing to the dead calm.

Item the 17th.

We had a variable breeze alternating with dead calm so that again we failed to make any progress. Towards the evening the wind became south-west with rain, upon which we shaped our course to the north; after a short time however it fell a calm again so that we did not sail more than two miles to northward. Latitude estimated 16° 22', Longitude 193° 35'.

Item the 18th.

It continued calm until noon; we remained in the same latitude and longitude as before; at noon we got a light breeze from the south-east with occasional showers.

Item the 19th.

The wind still south-east with rain. At noon Latitude observed 15° 12', longitude 193° 35'; course kept north, sailed 18 miles. We still had dark, rainy weather every day, very unhealthy, and no chance of a look-out to discover land.

Item the 20th.

Still thick, dark, foggy, rainy weather with the sea running from all directions, and variable winds, now a calm, now a breeze. At noon Latitude observed 13° 45', Longitude 193° 35'; course held north, sailed 21 miles.

Item the 21st.

The wind still variable from the west and north-west going up to north; we set our course close by the wind to northward; the sea is still very rough with copious rains. At noon Latitude estimated 13° 21', Longitude 193° 35'; course held north, sailed 6 miles; in the afternoon we ran to northward. During the night we drifted in a calm for the space of

12 glasses, after which we got a breeze from the north, when we tacked to westward.

Item the 22nd.

In the morning the wind was still northerly with a good deal of rain, we still held our course to westward close by the wind, and had very heavy swells from the north-west. The weather was dark, drizzly, and foggy; now strong gales, now a sudden calm. At noon we made out by account to be in Latitude 13° 5' South, Longitude 192° 57'; course held west-north-west, sailed 10 miles. In the afternoon the wind went round to the north-east and east. Towards the evening the wind became south-east, and then south, with much rain and a strong gale. During the night we lay to with small sail; we also saw a number of logs floating about.

[1] The true name is Roobol, as shown in the Instructions of 1644. Thi family-name also occurs in other documents of the Dutch East India Company.

Item the 23rd.

A westerly wind with a storm, thick, dark weather and much rain; at times we could hardly see to a distance of two ship's lengths; the sea was very rough, running from all sides. At noon Latitude estimated 12° 10', Longitude 192° 57'; course held north, sailed 14 miles; during the night we sailed northward close to the wind.

Item the 24th.

In the morning we set our topsails. We had the wind from the west-north-west and north-west with a stiff gale and frequent showers, the sea being still very rough. At noon Latitude estimated 11° 2', Longitude 192° 28'; course held north-north-east, sailed 18 miles. In the afternoon we had to take in our topsails and ran over to northward close to the wind; during the night we lay to with one sail since we dared not sail on, there being no lookout, from fear we might come upon land or shoals.

Item the 25th.

In the morning we made sail again; when day broke we saw that the Zeehaan had her mizzen-mast broken; we then hoisted our foresail, hailed the Zeehaan, and asked her how she was getting on; they replied that they could help themselves until the weather should improve; her mizzen-mast is broken in such a way that she can still carry a small mizzen-sail. The wind was still blowing from the north-west and north-west by west with a storm, much rain, and dark weather; we went over to northward close to the wind; at noon Latitude estimated 10° 31' south, Longitude 193°; course held north-east, sailed 11 miles; during the night we again lay to with small sail.

Item the 26th.

The wind blowing pretty stiffly from the north-west, still with a good deal of rain and dark weather. I cannot understand how it is that such a steady westerly wind is blowing here so far into the South Sea unless it should be that the western monsoon is continually blowing over New Guinea and coming on stiffly, pressed on a good way into the South Sea with the trade-wind blowing lightly. For 21 days past now we have not had a single dry day. At noon Latitude estimated 9° 48' south, Longitude 193° 43'; course held north-east, sailed 15 miles; during the night we lay to with small sail.

Item the 27th.

In the morning we made sail again, set our course over to northward close to the wind with the wind blowing from the north-west and north-north-west, and thick, dark, drizzly, rainy weather, but the sea beginning to become smoother; at noon Latitude estimated 9° south, Longitude 194° 32'; course held north-east, sailed 17 miles; at night when 6 glasses in the first watch were out the wind went round to the north and we turned our course to westward.

Item the last.

The wind still blowing from the north and north-north-west with thick, foggy, drizzly, rainy weather, our course held westerly still. At noon Latitude estimated 8° 48' south, Longitude 194° 2'; course kept west-north-west, sailed 8 miles.

MARCH 1643

Item the 1st of March.

Good weather with smooth water and a northerly but variable wind; we turned our course to westward. At noon Latitude observed 9° 5', Longitude 193° 21'; course held west-south-west, sailed 11 miles. In the evening we got a squall of rain from the west and for the rest of the night drifted in a calm.

Item the 2nd.

Towards daybreak we got a light breeze from the north and set our course to westward. At noon Latitude observed 9° 11', Longitude 192° 46'; held our course west slightly southerly, east, west and west by south betweenwhiles, sailed 12 miles, with variable winds and weather. Variation of the compass 10° North-East.

Item the 3rd.

Wind and weather very unsettled, with much rain and very variable winds, alternating between a dead calm and gales so strong that we could hardly carry sail; we estimated that in the last 24 hours we had sailed 8 miles; course held west, Latitude estimated 9° 11' south, Longitude 192° 14'; in the evening we had very much rain again and drifted in a calm.

Item the 4th.

Wind and weather continued variable with much rain, the wind keeping however between the south-west and north. We are in hopes however that the weather will soon get better. At noon Latitude estimated 8° 55', Longitude 191° 57'; course held north-north-west, sailed 5 miles.

Item the 5th.

Wind and weather still variable with heavy rains. This variable weather has now lasted for a month past during which we have made little progress and have continually been holding our courses between the south-west and north but we hope things will soon mend. At noon

Latitude estimated 8° 32' south, Longitude 191° 42'; course held north-north-west, sailed 8 miles. Variation 10° 30' North-East.

Item the 6th.

Still variable winds with a good deal of rain, violent squalls alternating with sudden calms; a man who should wish to describe all these chops and changes of wind and weather might be kept doing nothing else but write. At noon Latitude estimated 8° 8' south, Longitude 191° 42'; course held north, sailed 6 miles.

Item the 7th.

Still thick, dark, drizzly, rainy weather with variable wind and weather and a very rough sea; the wind continues keeping between the west-south-west and north-west; we have the wind straight ahead. At noon Latitude estimated 8° 17' south, Longitude 191° 1 minute; course kept west by south, sailed 12 miles. This day we saw a great many birds.

Item the 8th.

Still thick, dark, drizzly, rainy weather with the wind as before; we therefore kept tacking about with the starboard forward in order to get as far to westward as possible; but we fear we shall get no good wind before the close of the western monsoon; we have heavy rains every day. At noon Latitude estimated 7° 46' south, Longitude 190° 47'; course held north-north-west and west, sailed 9 miles. Towards the evening the wind began to stiffen so that we had to take in our topsails and to sail with mainsails.

Item the 9th.

We kept sailing with our mainsails set with a storm from the north-west and north-north-west and in thick, dark, foggy, drizzling weather; we had a great deal of rain which is doing us a great deal of harm bo-dily, and the sea is very rough. At noon Latitude estimated 8° 33' south, Longitude 190° 1 minute; course held south-west, sailed 16 miles; during the night we lay to with small sail for the space of 16 glasses because we dared not sail full speed.

Item the 10th.

In the morning we again set our foresail and went over to westward; we had the wind from the north-north-west with very unsettled weather and heavy rains; we set our large topsail but had to take it in again directly on account of bad weather. At noon Latitude estimated 9° south, Longitude 189° 33'; course held south-west, sailed and drifted 10 miles; during the night we set our course to westward with small sail.

Item the 11th.

Still dark, foggy, drizzly, rainy weather, with a northerly wind but very unsteady; in the morning we had a north-north-east wind and set our course close to the wind. At noon Latitude estimated 9° 12' south, Longitude 188° 29'; course held west by south, sailed 17 miles. In the afternoon we saw that those on board the Zeehaan brailed up their mainsail and took in their foretopsail, upon which we forthwith let fall our foresail to stay for her and inquire whether she had broken anything. When she came near us we understood that her mainsail was torn to pieces and that they were engaged in repairing it.

Item the 12th.

Still unsettled weather; we had variable winds from the northern quarter. At noon Latitude estimated 8° 48' south, Longitude 187° 29'; course held west-north-west, sailed 16 miles; after midnight we drifted in a calm.

Item the 13th.

Still dark, thick weather; in the afternoon we drifted in a calm, the sea still running very high from the north-west; at noon Latitude estimated 8° 48' south, Longitude 186° 48'; course held west, sailed 10 miles. During the night we got a light breeze from the south and turned our course to the north-west.

Item the 14th.

The wind from the south but almost a calm; good dry weather and the sea still running from the north-west. We saw some boughs of trees floating but did not sight any land. During the night the wind went round to the south-east with a light breeze. At noon Latitude observed 10° 12', our estimation being 1 2/3 degree to northward than the latitude now got by observation. We had not been able to observe the latitude for 12 days past owing to the thick, dark, drizzly weather we had every day with heavy rains. According to our estimation our longitude was 186° 14'; course held north-west, sailed 13 miles. Variation 8° 45' North-East.

Item the 15th.

Good weather, the sea beginning to go down but the surges are still running against each other. The wind blew from the south-east with the weather improving; course held north-west, sailed 12 miles. At noon Latitude observed 9° 33', Longitude 185° 40'. Variation 8° North-East.

Item the 16th.

Good, quiet weather with a bright sun which we have not had for 6 weeks past. At noon Latitude observed 8° 46', Longitude 184° 51'; course held north-west, sailed 17 miles. Variation 9°.

Item the 17th.

Good weather and smooth water, the wind easterly with a light breeze. At noon Latitude observed 8° 7', Longitude 184° 11'; course held north-west, sailed 14 miles.

Item the 18th.

Good weather with an easterly wind and a light breeze with smooth water; at noon Latitude observed 7° 40', Longitude 183° 33'; course held north-west, sailed 12 miles. Variation 9°; in the afternoon the breeze began somewhat to stiffen.

Item the 19th.

Still good weather with a clear sky and a topsail breeze with the wind from the east. The sea begins to run from the east and north-east. At noon Latitude observed 6° 25', Longitude 182° 27'; course held north-west, sailed 23 miles.

Item the 20th.

Good weather and smooth water with occasional squalls of rain from the east and east-south-east, with a light topsail breeze; at noon Latitude found 5° 15', Longitude 181° 16'; course held north-west, sailed 25 miles. At noon we shaped our course to westward. Variation 9° North-East.

Item the 21st.

Still always good weather with a light breeze from the east and north-east with occasional showers and smooth water; the swells however are not running from the north-east. At noon Latitude observed 5° 25', Longitude 180° 20'; course kept west by south, sailed 14 miles.

Item the 22nd.

The weather continuing good with smooth water and a weak top-gallant breeze from the east and east-north-east trade-wind; at noon Latitude estimated 5° 2', Longitude 178° 32'; course held west, sailed 27 miles. At noon we saw land straight ahead of us at about 4 miles distance; in order to run north of it we set our course first west by north and then west-north-west; towards evening we sailed close along the land north-west. These islands are close upon thirty in number but very small, the largest of them being not more than 2 miles in length; the rest are all small fry, all of them being surrounded by a reef; to north-west there runs off from this another reef on which there are three coconut trees by which it is easily recognisable. These are the islands which Le Maire has laid down in the chart; they are at about 90 miles distance from the coast of New Guinea. In the evening we still saw land north-north-west of us; we therefore turned our course over to north-north-east close to the wind in order to steer north of all shoals, brailed up our foresail, and in this way drifted until daybreak.

To these isles we have given the name of Islands of Onthong Faua, because of the great resemblance they bear to the latter; they are also surrounded by reefs and appear as shown here when they are south-west of you at 2 miles distance.

Item the 23rd.

At daybreak we made sail again, set our course to westward, and then had the small islands we had passed the previous day south of us at about 3 miles distance. The wind blew from the east and north-east, with a dark grey sky and trade-wind weather. At noon Latitude estimated 4° 31' South, Longitude 177° 18'; course held west-north-west, sailed 20 miles. During the night at the end of the first watch we lay to and dared not run on from fear we might come upon the island to which Le Maire has given the name of Marcken.[1]

Item the 24th.

In the morning we made sail again, shaping our course to westward. Towards noon we saw land right ahead of us; this land was very low-lying and showed as two islands bearing south-west and north-west from each other; the northernmost bears some resemblance to the island of Marcken in the Zuyder Zee, as Jacob Le Maire says, for which reason he gave to it the name of Marcken. At noon Latitude observed 4° 55', Longitude 175° 30'; course held west as far as we could estimate but we find that there is a strong current setting to the south; we sailed 20 miles with a wind east and east-south-east, and trade-wind weather with a light topsail breeze. In the evening we brought our course round to north so as to run north of the island. During the night we drifted in a calm and stood for the island aforesaid.

[1] After the picturesque island of that name in the Zuider Zee (Netherlands).--On modern charts it is sometimes wrongly written "Marqueen." The name "Marks-islands" also occurs.

Item the 25th.

In the day-watch we heard the surf break on the shore; it being still quite calm we forthwith got out our pinnace and boat in order to tow us clear of the reef or shoal; the current and the sea however carried us some distance towards the reef. We found no anchorage here which we greatly regretted. About 9 o'clock a prow of the said island came alongside, containing 7 persons[1] and about 20 coconuts; we exchanged a dozen of these for 3 strings of beads and 4 double middle-sized nails; the said coconuts seemed to have grown wild and were of poor quality.

The people looked rough and savage with blacker skins than those in the islands where we took in refreshments; they were also less polite and went stark naked except that they wore before their privities a small covering, seemingly made of cotton, which was hardly large enough to conceal from view their yard and testicles. Some of them had their hair cut short, others wore it tied up like the villains of the Murderers Bay. One of them wore two feathers right on the top of his head just like horns; another wore a ring through his nose but we could not find out what the ring was made of; their prow was sharply pointed in front and behind like the wings of a seagull, but not elegantly shaped and rather the worse for wear and tear; they carried arrows and two bows and did not seem to set any store by the beads and nails, nay utterly to despise the same. We then got the wind from the south and fortunately got off the reef with the aid of it. The prow then paddled off to shore again. We saw another small prow approach us but it could not come near us in consequence of a sudden gust of wind. We now set our course to northward in order to get clear of the shoals and reefs. These islands are 15 or 16 in number, the largest of them being about a mile in length, and the other looking like houses; they all lie together surrounded by a reef. The said reef runs off from the islands to the north-west side; at about a swivel-gun shot distance from the islands there stands a group of trees, level with the water; two miles farther to the north-west there is another small islet like Toppershoetje (a small sailor's hat)[2] the reef extends another half mile farther into the sea so that the reef runs out to sea in a north-westerly direction fully 3 miles from the islands. At noon Latitude estimated 4° 34' South, Longitude 175° 10'; course held north-west, sailed 7 miles; about noon the wind went round to north-west and then to northward; we turned our course west, after which began to blow from the north-north-east with a light breeze, upon which we set our course to the north-west; during the night, the weather being quiet with a northerly wind, we turned more to westward.

Item the 26th.

Good weather and smooth water with a north-easterly wind and a light breeze. At noon Latitude observed 4° 33', Longitude 174° 30'; course held west, sailed 10 miles. We found that there was a strong current here setting southward, on which account we turned our course north-westward again. Variation 9° 30' North-East.

Item the 27th.

Wind and weather as before. At noon Latitude observed 4° 1', Longitude 173° 36'; course held north-west by west, sailed 16 miles; at noon we shaped our course to westward in order to run in sight of the islands lying eastward to the coast of New Guinea, and thence to cross to the mainland coast, which will thus become better known. Variation 9° 30' North-East.

Item the 28th.

Still good weather, the wind blowing from the east with a light breeze and smooth water. At noon Latitude observed 4° 11', Longitude 172° 32'; course held west, sailed 16 miles; towards noon we saw land straight ahead[3] and at noon we were still at about 4 miles distance from it. This island is in 4° 31' South Latitude and 172° 16' Longitude; it lies 46 miles to the west and west by north of the islands which Jacob Le Maire had named Marcken. During the night we drifted in a calm.

> To these islands Le Maire has given the name of Groene Eylanden [4] because they looked green and beautiful; they appear as shown here when the easternmost is south and the westernmost south-west of you at 2 miles distance.

> [1] The sailor's journal has some more particulars e.g. it says, that the bodies of the people were painted ("geschildert")--MONTANUS, America en 't Zuid-land, pp. 582 ff., also gives some more details concerning the part of the voyage still to be performed.

> [2] Poeloe Tampoeroeng or Toppershoedje, an islet in the north of Soenda Straits.

> [3] The Huydecoper copy has here: "and was very low land."

> [4] Or lage eylanden in Swart's reproduction.

Item the 29th.

In the morning we found that the current was setting us towards the islands. At noon Latitude observed 4° 20', Longitude 172° 17'. The whole of this day we drifted in a calm so that in the last twenty-four hours we have drifted 5 miles to the south-west. Halfway the afternoon two small prows came from shore alongside; they had two wings or outriggers, their paddles being small and thick in the blade, poorly made as it seemed to us; one of the prows had 6, the other 3 men in it. When they were about 2 ship's lengths from us one of the six men who were in the one prow broke one of his arrows in two, put one half into his hair and held the other half in his hand, apparently wishing thereby to show friendly feelings towards us; these men were stark naked, their bodies quite black, with curly hair like Caffres[1], but not so woolly as the hair of the latter, nor were their noses quite as flat. Some wore white bracelets, seemingly of bone, round their arms; others had their faces daubed with lime, and wore on the forehead a piece of tree-bark about the breadth of three fingers. They carried nothing but arrows, bows and calleweys[2]; we called out to them a few words from our vocabulary of the language of New Guinea but the only word they seemed to understand was Lamas, which means coconuts. They always kept pointing to the land. We presented them with two strings of beads and two large nails, together with an old napkin, in return for which they gave us an old coconut which was all they had with them, after which they paddled to shore again. Towards the evening it was still calm with a very light breeze from the north-east; we drifted quite close to the islands and had to get out the boats to keep us off the shore by towing. At the close of the dog-watch we at length got clear of these islands. There are two large islands and three small ones, the latter lying on the west side. To these islands Le Maire has given the name of the Green islands. West-north-west of us we still saw a high island with 2 or 3 very small ones, and to westward of us we besides saw some very high land which looked like a mainland coast. But the truth of this only time can show. Variation 9° North-East.

Item the 30th.

Weather improving with a light breeze from the north-east; still engaged in towing; we found that the current was setting us to the southward. At noon Latitude observed 4° 25', Longitude 172°; course held west, sailed or drifted 4 miles; in the evening we had St. Jans island north-west of us at about 6 miles distance.

Item the last.

Still good and quiet weather, with an easterly wind and smooth water. At noon Latitude observed 4° 28', Longitude 171° 42'; course held west, sailed 6 miles; at noon we hoisted the white flag and pendant, upon which our friends of the Zeehaan came on board of us, with whom we resolved upon what is in extenso set forth in this day's resolution.

APRIL 1643

Item the 1st of April, A.D. 1643.

We got the coast of New Guinea alongside in 4° 30' South Latitude, at a point which the Spaniards call Cabo Santa Maria[3]. At noon Latitude observed 4° 30', Longitude 171° 2'; course held west, sailed 10 miles. Variation 8° 45'.

Item the 2nd.

Still good, quiet weather, with a variable breeze. We did our best to sail along the coast which here bears from Sint Jans island north-west and south-east; north-west of this there is still another high island, somewhat larger than St. Jans island from which it is 10 miles distant; to this second island we have given the name of Anthony Caens island[4]. This is situated due north of Cabo Santa Maria. At noon Latitude observed 4° 9', Longitude 170° 41'; course held north-west, sailed 10 miles; we then had Cabo Santa Maria south of us so that the cabo aforesaid lies in longitude 170° 41', according to our estimation. In the evening we ran inshore in order to make better progress with the landwind. When four glasses in the first watch were out we got the wind from shore with a light breeze and shaped our course along the shore.

[1] "They had hair like the "Paepoes'" (Papoo's?), says the sailor's journal.

[2] "Calleweys," a sort of javelins or harpoons.

[3] The north-east point of New-Ireland (New-Mecklenburg).

[4] After a member of the Council of India.--On modern charts sometimes written "Kaan"-island.

Item the 3rd.

In the morning there was still a light land-breeze, our course still
north-west along the coast. About 9 o'clock we saw a vessel full of
men coming from shore; the said vessel was curved at both ends like
the corre-corre[2] of Tarnaten; she lay still a while beyond the reach of
our great guns and then returned to shore again. At noon Latitude estimated 3° 42' South, Longitude 170° 20'; course held north-west,
sailed 10 miles. Towards evening the wind began to blow from the
east-south-east with a light breeze; we kept steering north-west along
the coast. This land seems to be very pleasant but the worst of it was
that we could get no anchorage here. During the night we had thunder
and lightning, with rain and variable breezes.

Item the 4th.

We still kept sailing along the coast which here stretched north-west
by west and south-east by east. It is a beautiful coast with many bays.
We passed an island situated at 12 miles distance from Anthony Caens
island, the two bearing from each other north-west and south-east. To
this island we have given the name of Garde Neys island. At noon Latitude estimated 3° 22', Longitude 169° 50'; course held north-west by
west, sailed 9 miles; the wind still variable with light breezes and
calms; in the evening we got the land-wind, with rain, thunder and
lightning; we therefore did our best to sail along the shore.

Item the 5th.

In the morning we still had the land-wind with a light breeze. Towards
noon we came upon another island at 10 miles distance from Gardenys
island, the two bearing from each other west-north-west and east-
south-east. Inshore of this island we saw some prows lying, which we
supposed to be engaged in fishing, for which reason we have to this
island given the name of Visschers island[3]. Towards noon we saw 6
prows ahead of us, three of which came paddling so near our ship that
we let 2 or three pieces of old canvas, 2 strings of beads and two old
nails drift towards them; they did not seem to care for the canvas, and
the other things too hardly excited their attention; but they kept point-

110

ing to their heads, from which we concluded that they wanted turbans. These people seemed to be very shy, and by their gestures afraid of shot; they did not come near enough for us to discern whether they were armed. They were very black and stark naked, having only their privities covered with a few green leaves. Some of them had black hair, others hair of another colour. Their prows had outriggers and each of them carried 3 or 4 persons, but owing to the distance we could not discern any other details. When they had thus been pottering a long while near about the ships, and at times called out to us, to which we replied in the same way, though we did not understand each other, they paddled back to shore. At noon Latitude estimated 3°, Longitude 169° 17'; course held west-north-west, sailed 10 miles; in the afternoon we had the wind north-west with a light breeze.

Item the 6th.

In the morning it was calm. Halfway the forenoon we again saw 8 or 9 prows come from the said island, three of which paddled to the Zeehaan and 5 to our ship. Some of them contained 3, others 4, and some few 5 persons. When they were about two stones cast from us they left off paddling and called out to us; we could not understand them but made signs for them to come nearer, upon which they paddled round in front of our ship, and kept loitering ahead of us a long time without coming alongside. At length one of our quartermasters took off his belt and held it up to them from afar. Upon this one of these prows came alongside our ship; we gave them a string of beads and our quartermaster also handed his belt out to them, for which all we got in return was a piece of the pith of a sago-tree, which was the only commodity they had with them. Meanwhile the other prows, seeing that their comrades received no hurt, also came paddling alongside. None of these prows contained any arms or anything with which they could have done us harm. We at first suspected they might be villains who were intent on mischief and in search of booty since they affected such timidity. Had our suspicions proved true they would have been warmly received, for which we had made all due preparations, although the cook was not ready yet with the morning meal. We called out to them the words Anieuw, Oufi, Pouacka, etc. (meaning coconuts, yams, hogs, etc.) which they seemed to understand, for they pointed to the shore as if they wanted to say: they are there. Then they paddled to shore with great quickness and regularity but, since the breeze began to freshen, we did not see them again. These natives are dark brown, nay almost as black as the blackest Caffre; they have hair of various colours[1], owing to the lime with which they powder it; their faces are smeared with red paint except their foreheads. Some of them wore a thick bone through the lower part of the nose, about half the thickness of a little finger. For the rest they wore nothing on their bodies except some green leaves covering their privities. Their prows were new, trimly made up, and adorned with wood-carving in front and behind, with one outrigger each; their paddles were not long or broad, and pointed at the end, etc. At noon the wind went round to south-east with a fair breeze; we shaped our course west by north along the coast; Latitude observed 2° 53', Longitude 168° 59'; course held west-north-west, sailed 5 miles; in the afternoon we made good progress. During the night there was land-wind with a light breeze.

[1] Better, (Arend) Gardenijs (see infra April 4 and 5), after a member of the Council of India. In some maps wrongly named "Isle de Gardener" e.g. PRÈVOST (ed. Paris, Didot) XI, p 213.

[2] Vessels peculiar to some eastern parts of the Malay Archipelago.

[3] LEUPE, Tasman en Visscher, p. 132, says erroneously, that Tasman named this island after his pilot-major.

Item the 7th.

In the morning we continued drifting in a calm. In the forenoon there came again 20 prows hovering near and about the ships but, like those of the previous day, they kept out of reach of gun-shot. We repeatedly made signs to them upon which they at length made bold to paddle alongside of us. They had nothing in their prows except in one of them three coconuts, of which we got one in exchange for a string of beads. We thought we should have got all three of them for it, but they absolutely refused to part with the other two. Another man had a shark (which in their tongue they called Ilacxz) which we also bartered against three strings of beads; a third again had a dorado or dolphin, which one of our sailors exchanged for an old cap. Some of them had a number of small fishes which they threw to our men, but they proved not worth eating. Finally three or four of these people came on board of our ship, looked about them in great amazement, and walked about the ship as if they were intoxicated; a curious circumstance truly, for in their small prows they paddled about for miles out to sea without any signs of sea-sickness, but in a large ship like ours they seem to get intoxicated by the motion caused of the swell of the sea. They had no arms with them, or anything which they could have hurt us. They seemed to subsist by fishing for some of them carried wooden eel-spears. After they had been on board for a while they left together and paddled back to shore with a good deal of bustle and with loud shouts. We remained lying there during the afternoon or drifted in a calm. Farther to westward the land begins to be very low, but the coast stretched west by north and west-north-west as far as we could see. At noon Latitude estimated 2° 35', Longitude 168° 25'; course held west by north, sailed 9 miles. In the afternoon we still saw high land west by north and west of the cape aforesaid; this land we estimated to be fully 10 miles from us. We drifted in a calm but, soon getting a light breeze from the eastward, we endeavoured to get near the high land to westward. The current setting along this coast is steadily in our favour so that every day we made more progress to westward than we apparently proceeded over the water. In the course of the night we passed a large bay or inlet.

[1] "Red, blue, violet", says the sailor's journal, which gives some more particulars on these dates.

[2] In some modern charts, Cape Salomon-Sweert, the north-west point of New Hannover. All these names are quite wrongly spelt in the map [in A voyage to New-Holland, etc. in the year 1699. By Captain WILLIAM DAMPIER, III (Third edition, London, Knapton, MDCCXXIX)], called A View of the Course of Capt. William Dampiers voyage from Timor round Nova Brittania, etc. There, and in the title-page of A continuation of a voyage to New-Holland, are found the names Ant. Canes or Cave's; Ger. Denis or Garret Denis, Wisscharts I., C. Solomaswer. Can Dampier have used and copied the Sloane MS. no. 5222 art. 12 in the British Museum? (Compare my annexed Life of Tasman, chapter XI). The name Sweers hoeck seems to have been corrupted to Struijshoek in some maps, e.g. in De Nieuwe lichtende Zee-fakkel van JOHANNES VAN KEULEN--JAN VAN LOON--CLAES JANSZ. VOOGHT, 1706. I do not think, as does HAMY, Commentaires sur quelques cartes anciennes de la Nouvelle-Guinée (Paris, 1877) p. 15, that Struijs hoeck is a Dutch translation of some Spanish name.

Item the 8th.

In the morning, reaching the west side of the bay, we came upon four small low-lying islets along which we held our course; when we were past these islets we again came upon 3 small islets lying together west of the others which we had passed at noon. At noon Latitude estimated 2° 26', Longitude 167° 39', the wind blowing from the east-south-east but variable; course held west by north, sailed 12 miles. Variation 10° North-East. South-west by west of us we had a low-lying cape, north of which there were two low islets. From this point the land begins gradually to fall away to southward. About 6 o'clock in the evening we had these two islets south by west of us and the nearest land we saw, being level and low-lying[1], lay south-west by south of us at about 4 miles distance. We all the time held our course along the coast.

Item the 9th.

In the morning at sunrise we drifted in a calm; the point of the sou-thernmost land we saw lay south-east by east of us at about 2½ miles distance where the coast falls off very abruptly. We then had another low-lying small islet south-south-west of us at about 2 miles distance. We did our best to sail close along the said point but were prevented from so doing owing to the calm. At noon Latitude observed 2° 33', Longitude 167° 4'; course held west-south-west, sailed 7 miles. Varia-tion 10°. In the afternoon we steered for the point as before.

Item the 10th.

During the last twenty-four hours we made pretty good progress to southward. Owing to the calm and for other reasons we endeavoured to get to southward as quickly as possible, partly to explore the coasts and partly to find a passage southward. At noon we found the sou-thernmost point to bear from us east-north-east and the northernmost ditto north-north-east. At noon Latitude observed 3° 2', Longitude 167° 4'; course held south, sailed 12 miles. In the afternoon we kept steering south; towards evening the wind went round to north-north-west. In order to get near to the land again we shaped our course east-south-east and south-east, at times rough, light variable winds with rain greatly troubling us. After midnight we again drifted in a calm in smooth water.

Item the 11th.

At noon we drifted in a calm without being able to take the latitude. We still saw the land stretching north-east of us, to wit the most easterly point, the most westerly point bearing from us north-north-east and north by east. At noon Latitude estimated 3° 28', Longitude 166° 51'; course kept south-west by west, half a point westerly, sailed 7 miles. In the second watch we had a light breeze from the east-north-east; we turned our course over to south-east close by the wind but afterwards it fell a calm again.

Item the 12th.

Three glasses in the day-watch having run out we felt so violent a shock of earthquake that none of our men, however sound asleep, remained in his hammock, but all came running on deck in amazement, thinking the ship had struck on a rock. The feeling was as if the keel were dragging over coral rock but when we cast the lead we got no bottom. After this there were repeated slight shocks of earthquake, but none so strong as the first; at first with calm weather but shortly afterwards with heavy rains; the wind variable and sometimes a calm. We endeavoured to get as far to southward as possible. About 3 o'clock in the afternoon the wind was west with a light breeze. At noon Latitude observed 3° 45', Longitude 167° 1 minute; course held south-south-east, sailed 6 miles. Afterwards we turned our course due south-east and then saw a small, round, low-lying islet south by west of us at 4½ or 5 miles distance. During the night heavy rains with variable weather.

[1] Portland-Islands?

Item the 13th.

In the morning the wind came from the north-east with a light breeze; we saw high land with several mountains and low-lying land between them from the south-west by west to the east-south-east. As far as we could make out we were in a large bay. We kept doing our best to get southward. At noon Latitude estimated 4° 22', Longitude 167° 18'; course held south-south-east, sailed 10 miles. In the afternoon we drifted in a calm without being able to take soundings; the water here is as smooth as in a river without any motion, which made us the more believe we were in a large bay; but what the truth is we shall learn in time. During the night we had variable winds with now and then a calm. In the evening we had some mountains and hills south-south-west of us, towards which we shaped our course as much as possible.

Item the 14th.

In the morning we saw land from the east-north-east to the south-south-west and afterwards in the west-south-west. We hoped (although in vain) to find a passage between the two, but when we came nearer we found that it was a bay[1], and that the land all joined to westward. Therefore with a north-north-west wind we shaped our course west by south as high as we could sail, and about 3 or 4 o'clock in the afternoon came upon a reef which we judged to be usually level with the water, and which with the present sea-wind we could hardly sail clear of, the said reef lying 2 miles from shore as near as we could estimate. At noon Latitude observed 5° 27', Longitude 166° 57'; course held south-south-west, sailed 15 miles. Variation 9° 15' North-East. Towards evening we got a light breeze from the north-north-east. During the night we again drifted in a calm.

Item the 15th.

We continued to have variable winds and calms so that we made little progress. At noon Latitude estimated 5° 18', Longitude 166° 36'; course held west-north-west, sailed 6 miles. Variation 9° North-East. In the evening the high island[2] was due north-west of us at 6 miles distance.

Item the 16th.

We kept drifting in a calm and had the most westerly land we saw west by south and west-south-west of us. The land here from the one point to the other begins to extend mainly west by north, and shows from time to time high mountains with some pleasant, large, deep valleys. In the evening the high island was north-west by north of us at 2½ or 3 miles distance. At noon Latitude estimated 5° 5', Longitude 166° 27'; course held north-west, sailed 4 miles. Through the whole night we had calm weather.

Item the 17th.

In the morning we still drifted in a calm; about three hours before noon we had the high island north-east of us at 3 miles distance. We then got a light breeze from the south-east, upon which we set our course due west. We now had the two islands opposite each other. At noon Latitude observed 5° 8', Longitude 166°; course held west, half a point northerly, sailed 8 miles. Variation 8° 45' North-East. In the afternoon we again drifted in a calm; in the evening at sunset the high island was east by north of us at 6 or 7 miles distance, and the western extremity of a high range of mountains[3] in New Guinea south-west by south of us at 6 or 7 miles distance. During the night it was calm again.

Item the 18th.

In the morning at sunrise the high mountain aforesaid was south by west of us at 6 or 7 miles distance. In the forenoon we got a light breeze from the south-west, upon which we turned our course over to westward, as close to the wind as possible, in smooth water. At noon Latitude observed 5°, Longitude 165° 37'; course held west by north and west-north-west, sailed 5 miles with variable winds and a calm now and then. At noon the high mountain was south[4] of us; at about four o'clock in the afternoon it was south by east of us so that since noon we had drifted about 2 miles to westward. We next saw where the land extended to westward, another high mountain south-west by south of us. The wind being south-south-west, then but very light, we turned our course over to westward close by the wind; at night we had a fair breeze from the south-east but already at the end of the second watch it fell calm again.

Item the 19th.

In the forenoon we had a light breeze from the south, our course being west-south-west. At noon Latitude observed 5° 9', Longitude 164° 50'; course held west by south, sailed 12 miles. Variation 9° North-East. At noon we had a round high islet[1], situated three miles off the mainland coast of New Guinea, due south of us at 2½ miles distance. We set our course west-south-west, after which west by north of us we also saw land, which was supposed to be islands since we found the mainland coast of New Guinea to extend due west only. In the afternoon, the wind being south-east, we still stuck to our west-south-west course. At two o'clock in the afternoon we came upon a rocky reef which was only a fathom under water; from the masthead we saw, northward of the reef aforesaid, several more small reefs, between which the sea seemed to be deep; we ran round south of them and saw more reefs still, south of us. We accordingly passed between the two groups of reefs, and in quiet weather set our course west-south-west. We had the round high island which at noon was south of us, south-east of us now at a distance of about four miles, so that this reef aforesaid is north-west by west of the high round island at 4 miles distance. This reef is in 5° 10 or 12' South Latitude. The most northerly point of the mountains, which we had up to now taken to be islands, was west-north-west of us at about 7 miles distance, which indications will be sufficient to recognise these shoals by in future. In the evening the southern point of a high island[2] was west by north of us at about 5½ or 6 miles distance; we set our course as much due west as we could, with light variable winds.

[1] De bocht van Goede Hoop.--In this there are two islets: tolerably low and tolerably high. The translator of the Visscher map in the British-Museum (Sloane, no. 5222, art. 12) did not understand these expressions, and has spelt them wrong.

[2] The tolerably high island?

[3] Finisterre mountains.

[4] The Huydecoper M.S.: "south by east of us."

Item the 20th.

At noon we had the most southerly point of the island north-west by west of us at 2 or 2½ miles distance; in the evening the centre of the island was north-east of us at 1½ miles distance, and the south point of another and higher island west-north-west of us at 6 or 7 miles distance. We set our course west by north. At noon Latitude observed 5° 4', Longitude 164° 27'; course held west by north, sailed 6 miles with variable winds and an occasional calm. Variation 8° 30'. In the evening we again drifted in a calm, but shortly after the wind became east with a fair breeze. At night at the setting of the second watch we came close to the island and saw a large flame issue steadily from the top of the mountain. This is the volcano[3] which Willem Schouten refers to in his journal. In order to pass between the mainland of New Guinea and this island we drifted the night without sails set, and thus waited for the day. While drifting we constantly heard the heavy ripple of the current which carried us to westward, which was greatly in our favour. On the same island we saw many fires close to the water, and also halfway up the high mountains, so we concluded it to be a thickly peopled country; it lies in the latitude of ---- degrees ---- minutes. As we were here sailing along the coast of New Guinea we had frequent calms and constantly saw pieces of wood floating about, the size of small trees, also bamboos and other lumber from shore, coming down the rivers, which made us conclude that there must be many rivers, and that it must be a fine country. We held our course north-west along the coast.

Item the 21st.

In the morning the centre of the island was east of us at 3 miles distance, the south-east point being east-south-east and south-east by east, the northern point north-east by east of us; the nearest land on the mainland coast was south-west of us at 1½ or 1¾ miles distance[4]. We then saw one more island north-west of us at about 8 miles distance, which Willem Schouten had named the high island[5], and that justly since it is very high. At noon Latitude observed 4° 30', Longitude 163° 13'; course held west by north, sailed 20 miles with a variable wind. In the evening at sunset the wind became east with a light breeze. We had sailed to the north-west since noon, and now shaped our course north-west by west with a fair breeze, and afterwards west-north-west, so that in the evening the centre of the island was due north-west of us at 4 miles distance. At the close the 6th glass in the first watch, as we were in the narrowest part of the passage between the mainland and the island, we found that at this point of the mainland of New Guinea there begins a low-lying coast[6] which then trends west-north-west and north-west by west. Accordingly at the end of the first watch we took in all sails and let the ship drift with only the mizzen-sail set in order to await the day and avoid all perils; but since the current was setting here to the west we made more progress as measured by the land we passed than was apparent from our advance over the water. The mountain burnt with a steady flame issuing straight from the top.

[1] Krakar or Dampier Island.

[2] Tolerably high?

[3] Burning Island?

[4] The Huydecoper MS. has here: "This island by quess has a lenght of about 4½ miles.

[5] Vulcanus or burning island?

[6] Here ends the high land.

Item the 22nd.

In the morning in the day-watch we again made sail and set our course to west-north-west. At sunrise we got into very pale-coloured water and at first thought we had come upon a shoal, for which reason we forthwith turned our course to the north. At this time we had the high burning mountain east-south-east and south-east by east of us at 7 miles distance. At night the flames were very violent. We had another high[1] but small island north-north-east of us at 4 or 5 miles distance; the most westerly point of the mainland we saw being west-north-west of us at 4 miles distance, and a large river south-south-west of us at 2 miles distance. The north-north-west course lies between two high islets[2] situated close together. Westward of these we saw still more land, to wit, three more islands[3]. The mainland coast here extends chiefly to west-north-west. We took soundings here but found no bottom although we had sailed one mile from the low-lying land. We again set our course west-north-west along the coast, and this day passed six small islets, all of which we left on our starboard. At noon Latitude observed 3° 39', Longitude 161° 38', the wind being east and east-south-east, also at times east-north-east but variable; course held west-north-west, half a point northerly; sailed 27 miles. In the afternoon we got a fair breeze from the east-north-east; course held as before. We found here a low-lying land full of rivers, and saw many trunks of trees and other wood, together with a great quantity of green brush-wod, come floating from the rivers with a flow of whitish sandy water. This low land forms a cape here, and when you have passed this point the land trends away to westward, so that a large bay is formed here, the two points however bearing from each other west-north-west. In the evening the eastern extremity of the most westerly island of the six was north-east by north of us at 1½ miles distance. We had at that time another high island alongside west by north of us at 5 miles distance; we set our course west-north-west and north-west by west. At the end of the first watch we had the centre of the island south-west of us at one mile distance; we then set our course west-north-west with an easterly wind; at midnight a heavy shower of rain.

Item the 23rd.

In the morning the wind continued easterly; we kept our course west-north-west as before. In the forenoon we passed so much wood, pieces of tree-trunks, bamboo and other brushwood that it seemed as if we were sailing in a river, from all which we concluded that there must be a great river hereabouts and, since the current set us from the land, we shaped our course to westward and afterward west by south in order to get the coast alongside again. At noon Latitude estimated 3° 1 minute, Longitude 160° 3', the wind blowing from the east, course held west-north-west, sailed 26 miles. At two o'clock in the afternoon we again came near the mainland coast; in the evening we again set our course west-north-west, straight along the coast. In the afternoon a prow came to the Zeehaan from the mainland[4].

Item the 24th.

In the morning course and wind as before, with a fair breeze; at noon we took no latitude, though the weather was good; we estimated ourselves to be in Latitude 2° 22' South, Longitude 158° 36', the wind east; course held west-north-west, sailed 26 miles. Variation 8° North-East. In the afternoon we had rain, but at night at the end of the second watch we saw straight ahead low land with fires; we lay to with one sail close to the wind in order to await the day and drifted. During the night Latitude observed 2° 20'.

Item the 25th.

In the morning at daybreak we again made sail, and with an easterly wind shaped our course to westward towards the land we had seen during the night with the fires on the said land. We found it to consist of three low-lying islets, lying near to the mainland coast, about 5 miles to the eastward of the island of Moa, which we got sight of shortly afterwards. We then steered for the said island of Moa and made for the roadstead on the west side of the island, casting anchor in 12 fathom, good, grey, sandy bottom. This day we had much rain, the sea running fast from the north-west. When we had cast anchor a large number of small prows came swarming near and about our ships, loitering a long while before venturing to come alongside. We therefore tied a number of beads to pieces of firewood, which we threw out to them, on which almost all of them came on board of us, bringing with them no more than three coconuts. Making use of Jacob Le Maire's Vocabulary we gave them to understand that we wanted hogs, fowls, coconuts, bananas, and other refreshments, upon which they paddled to shore to fetch them, and returned towards noon, bringing with them, some four, others 5 or 6 coconuts, with a lot of unripe bananas, all of which we obtained of them by barter, 5 or 6 for an old nail or a string of beads, and 12 or 14 coconuts for a knife; they also brought us some fish both smoked and fresh. At noon Latitude observed 2° 11', Longitude 156° 47'; the wind east, course held west by north, sailed 28 miles. In the evening when all the prows had left us we sent our pinnace to fetch our friends of the Zeehaan on board of us, with whom we resolved upon what is in extenso set forth in this day's resolution to which we beg leave to refer.

[1] Tolerably high?

[2] Without names?

[3] High and tolerably high, and one island without a name?

[4] Some names on the chart are not referred to in the text of the journal.

Item the 26th.

Early in the morning again a large number of prows with coconuts and unripe bananas came alongside. It seemed that the natives here had nothing else to dispose of. This day we obtained by barter so many coconuts that each of the men of our crew got five of them, but the natives brought little else than coconuts and unripe bananas, together with some fish, both fresh and smoked, all of which commodities we obtained of them by barter. This day we had 2 low-lying islets west of us. About 4 o'clock in the afternoon we sighted the island of Arymoa, north-west by west of us at 8 or 9 miles distance according to our estimation. As we were lying off the island here we found the wind to blow north-east from the sea by day, and south-east from the land by night; we also found the current to set here steadily to westward at such a rate that in a calm we should be sure to drift 4, 5 or 6 miles in twenty-four hours. The prows of the natives here are very narrow, about a foot in breadth.

Item the 27th.

In the morning the wind was south-west. Latitude observed here 2° 10', Longitude 156° 47'. This day there came again a large number of prows alongside our ships, some of them from other islands in the neighbourhood and others from the mainland, bringing nothing but coconuts, unripe bananas and some fresh and smoked fish, almost all of which we obtained by barter. Among the said prows there were two large ones with 18 or 20 men in each of them, all of them armed with bows and arrows, and also with javelins and harpoons. These natives were almost quite black and went naked, having only a small covering to hide their privities from view. They could all of them exactly imitate whatever words they heard our men pronounce, a sure sign that their language is copious and difficult to pronounce, which we also infer from their using the letter R in so many of their words, some of them even containing as many as three R's. This day we got so many coconuts that we served out 6 coconuts and some bananas to each of our men. In the evening we again summoned our friends of the Zeehaan on board of us, and represented to them that we had come to the conclusion that we were lying not before Moa, but before Jamna, and asked them whether they did not think it best for us to weigh anchor tomorrow before daybreak and run for Moa, where we are likely to get more refreshments than here, which was assented to by the council, as may be seen from today's resolution.

Item the 28th.

In the morning at 4 glasses in the day-watch we weighed anchor and sailed with small sail to the island of Moa, where we dropped anchor at about noon in 10 fathom, stiff ground. As soon as we had dropped anchor numerous prows with coconuts and bananas came alongside. At noon Latitude estimated 2° 5', Longitude 156° 28'; course held west by north, sailed 5 miles. In the afternoon at the end of 6 glasses there came a large prow from the mainland with 19 men in her, bringing a number of coconuts, which those on board the Zeehaan obtained by barter. This day we got so many coconuts by exchange that we served out 6 of them to each of our men.

Item the 29th.

In the morning again a large number of small prows came alongside with coconuts, unripe bananas, etc., which we all obtained by giving in exchange old nails, beads and knives, so that this day we served out 4 coconuts to each of our men. Towards the evening a large number of prows came alongside among them one with 11 persons in her, bringing with them a large quantity of coconuts which we all obtained of them by barter. Towards the evening we summoned

on board of us our friends of the Zeehaan with whom we resolved to weigh anchor and proceed on our voyage as soon as wind and tide should serve.

Item the last.

In the morning a strong wind was blowing from the west-north-west, and the sea running very high, so that during all this day we could do nothing to give effect to our resolution of the previous day, to set sail from Moa and continue our voyage, but were compelled to remain at anchor. This day we again obtained by barter a number of coconuts, as many as the natives brought to our ships.

MAY 1643

Item the 1st of May.

As the wind still continued west-north-west we had to remain at anchor, since we had the current against us, so that we should have done no good by trying to tack; this day we got some more coconuts.

Item the 2nd.

We still remained at anchor because the west-north-west wind kept blowing with a stiff, steady breeze, and the current was setting steadily to eastward. We had rain now and then but most of the time dry weather. In the forenoon we got still a large number of coconuts, but in the afternoon no more prows came alongside owing to the stiff breeze. During the night we had pretty good weather and always west wind.

Item the 3rd.

In the morning several prows again came alongside. Our men being engaged in washing the deck, one of our sailors standing on the wales to hand up the bucket, was shot at with an arrow and hit in the thick part of the leg above the thigh; we immediately made some of our men fire among the prows with muskets, so that one of the natives was hit in the arm. Shortly after we weighed anchor, ran inwards to the spot where Jacob Le Maire had formerly been at anchor with the ship Eendracht, and dropped our anchor from the bows between the two islands in smooth water. The natives on shore, seeing that we came sailing inwards with both ships, waved with branches and seemed full of fear that we might come with hostile intentions. They immediately sent on board of us the man who had been discharging arrows against our ship to make his peace with us which was done. Then the other natives again came on board as before, but they did not venture to demand as much for their commodities as before, and were content to take what we offered them. This day we again got a few prows alongside with coconuts, which we all obtained of them by barter, so that we could serve out 9 coconuts to each of our men[1].

Item the 4th.

In the morning the wind kept always blowing from the west-north-west, so that we were forced to remain here; this day again numerous prows came alongside with coconuts, which we all obtained of them by exchange, so that we could serve out 7 coconuts to each of our men.

Item the 5th.

The west-north-west wind still continuing in the morning we remained lying at anchor. This day we got only a few coconuts on board, all of them very young ones, so that it would seem that most of the coconuts of this island had already been gathered.

Item the 6th.

About 8 o'clock in the morning there sprung up a light land-breeze, so that we weighed our anchors and set sail in order to continue our voyage. We were already under sail when some more prows with coconuts came alongside. From these islands, both Hamna and Moa, we have got 6000 coconuts for the two ships, and about 100 bunches of bananas, all which we obtained by barter for beads, old rusty nails, and pieces of iron hoops, which we ground on one side, and to which we fitted wooden handles so as to resemble knives, for which they were very eager. When we had got to a quarter of a mile distance outside the bay it fell calm so that we had to drop anchor in 9 fathom, stiff ground.

[1] The sailor's journal has some particulars not without interest: "The inhabitants of these islands had figures, resembling fishes, burnt or painted on their bodies," etc.

Item the 7th.

In the morning the wind went about slightly to landward but inclining to a calm; we continued trying to get a little more off the land. In the forenoon the wind was west by south with a fair breeze, course held north-north-west. In the afternoon the wind became north-north-west, on which we tacked about, steering west by south. In the evening at the setting of the first watch of the island Arymoa was north-west of us at about 3 miles distance; we then turned our course over to northward again and kept our course north by west without making much progress, since the sea ran very strong from the north-west. During the night the wind was west-south-west.

Item the 8th.

In the morning at sunrise we had the largest island of Arymoa due south-west of us at about 3 miles distance; the wind continued west by south and west-south-west; course still held north-north-west. In the afternoon we had good weather. Latitude observed 1 degree 30', Longitude 156° 22'; course held north by west, sailed 8 3/4 miles. Variation 8° North-East. We had the most north-westerly point of the island of Arymoa south-west and south-west by south of us at 5 or 6 miles distance. We then turned our course over to south-west with a west-north-west wind and a light breeze. In the evening at sunset we had the western point of the island of Arymoa south-west by south of us at about 3½ miles distance in calm weather with the wind west-north-west; we still tacked to south-west. During the first and second watch of the night we drifted in a calm, the sea still running from the west-north-west. At the end of the second watch we got a light breeze from the south-east upon which we set our course due west.

Item the 9th.

In the morning the wind was south by east inclining to a calm. At sunrise we had the island of Arymoa south by east of us at about 3 or 4 miles distance; we still continued to steer west. At noon we got a light breeze from the north. The island of Arymoa then lay south-east by east of us at 3 or 4 miles distance, our course being always west. At noon Latitude observed 1 degree 35', Longitude 155° 25'; course held west by south, sailed 7 miles. Variation 7° 30'. In the afternoon the wind became north-north-west with good weather. In the evening at sunset the north side of Arymoa lay east by south of us at 7 miles distance. We took soundings here in 67 fathom, at about 3 miles distance from the mainland, which was very low-lying here. The wind being north-west we made for the coast and got into gradually shallowing water, 50, 40, 30 and 35, all good bottom; when 6 glasses in the first watch were out we sounded in 24 fathom, upon which we tacked about, since the wind at times was blowing more from shore, so that when about midnight the wind had gone round to south-west we set our course north-west along the coast.

Item the 10th.

In the morning the wind was south, our course remaining as before. We continually sailed here in thick muddy water of green colour, along a low coast which, by reason of this discharge of water, we supposed to be full of rivers, but we remained so far from shore that we could not well discern any rivers. Before noon having set our course north-west we found that the current caused by the discharge of the rivers was steadily setting us off the land. At noon Latitude observed 1 degree 17', Longitude 155° 12'; course held west-north-west, sailed 12 miles with variable winds. In the afternoon the wind abated and in the evening in the first watch we drifted in a calm; in the second watch the wind was variable.

Item the 11th.

At noon the wind came from the south-east with a light breeze. We turned our course west by south in order to get the land alongside again since we did not see any. At noon Latitude observed 1 degree 3', Longitude 154° 28'; course held west, sailed 12 miles. Variation 6° 50' North-East.

In the evening with a south-south-east wind we set our course due west. All through the night we had a fair breeze with occasional calms. It seems however that the wind is getting to some extent influenced by the eastern monsoon. This day we had smooth water; the clouds which for some time past had been driving from the north-west were now at a standstill. We passed some low-lying land here.

Item the 12th.

In the morning the wind was east by north, our course being west. We again saw land, lying west by south of us, and set our course straight for it, when we found it to be Willem Schoutens island. At noon we had the northern point of it due west of us at about 6 miles distance in good weather. At noon Latitude observed 54°, Longitude 153° 17', with an east-south-east wind; course held west, sailed 18 miles. We continued sailing along it. About an hour before sunset 6 prows put off from Schoutens island to have a look at us, each prow containing 20, 24, or 25 men, but they were too shy to come alongside; these prows were about the length of the oranbays[1] of the Moluccus, but not so broad; the men were very expert paddlers, and seemed to be quick and intelligent; this land, about 18 or 19 miles in length, seems to be fairly well populated. In the evening at sunset we had the northern point of Willem Schoutens island west-south-west of us at about 1½ miles distance, so that we constantly saw the surf break on the shore. This day in the evening a heavy slow swell rose, coming from the north; what it means we shall learn in time. The wind still blowing from the east with a light breeze. In the evening we set our course west towards the most westerly point so that we sailed along the coast all night.

Item the 13th.

In the morning we were at about 2 miles distance from the western point of Willem Schoutens island, which was almost due south-west by south of us; another islet, lying north-west by north of the point just mentioned at about 3 or 4 miles distance, bore from us north-west. We kept sailing westward along the coast until the said point was east of us, and then, in order to get the mainland coast alongside again, we set

128

our course west-south-west. In the afternoon we got the wind from the south with a fair breeze. At noon Latitude estimated 54', Longitude 152° 6'; course held west, sailed 18 miles with an east wind. Variation 6° 30' North-East. In the afternoon the wind turned to the south-east with rainy weather. We then sighted land again, south-south-west of us; it was a low-lying coast, forming part of the mainland of New Guinea. From here we set our course due west; during the night we had a fair breeze.

Item the 14th.

In the morning we were again close to the mainland coast of New Guinea. Here the interior was very high like Il do Fermoza; but the foreland was almost everywhere low or level. We kept sailing to westward along the coast towards the cape of Good Hope. At noon Latitude observed 48', Longitude 150° 31'; course held west, sailed 24 miles with an east wind. In the afternoon there was a light breeze; in the evening it fell a calm; we saw the Cape de Goede Hoope[2] west and west by south of us at about 6 miles distance. Eastward of the cape of Good Hope the land begins to be very high until quite close to the shore, without having any low foreland; the land is somewhat higher than the island of Fermoza. We continued on our west by north course to the cape of Hope, the sea now running from the north-east. During the night we had dark weather with a drizzling rain, the wind being very variable; afterwards we drifted in a calm.

Item the 15th.

At noon we had the cape of Good Hope south of us at 3 miles distance[3]; Latitude estimated 41', Longitude 149° 53'; course held west by north, sailed 12 miles. Variation 6° North-East; the wind variable. In the afternoon the wind was east-north-east with calm weather. We set our course to westward to the west side of the bay which Willem Schoutens had sailed into, but had to return from[4]. During the night we drifted in a calm and made little progress.

Item the 16th.

In the morning we were still drifting in a calm, and saw the western point of the land at the west side of the bay aforesaid; this western point lay west of us at about 7 miles distance. At noon it was calm and we had the western point of the bay south-south-west of us; we set our course west by north. At noon Latitude observed 16', Longitude 149° 9'; course held west-north-west, sailed 12 miles. Variation 5° 50'; the weather calm; in the afternoon it was calm too, but since the current was carrying us to westward our progress was greater as measured by the land we passed than by our advance over the water. This day we saw several small islands near the western point; we steered our course towards them west by south. In the evening at sunset the westernmost point of the mainland we saw bore from us west slightly southerly, at 3 or 4 miles distance, and a small islet lying off the said point, west slightly northerly, at 3 or 4 miles distance. Between the mainland and[1] New Guinea and the island last mentioned we saw the open sea due west of us. We drifted in a calm; at midnight the land-breeze sprung up and we set our course west by north in order to run outside the said islet; during the night we had variable winds alternating with calms.

[1] East-Indian vessels. "The people seem to be 'Poepoes'" (Papoo's?), says the sailor's journal.

[2] Tandjong Jamoeseba (Jermoer Sba). But cf. Robidé van der Aa, on the places referred to in this note. Here Tasman makes a mistake. Schouten named Cape of Good Hope the north-westpoint of Schouten's island. But if we compare maps that have only the discoveries anterior to Tasman's (e.g. Remarkable Maps, II, 14) we also sometimes find this mistake, which is perpetuated in maps posterior to Tasman's journal. But compare also the note of ROBIDÉ VAN DER AA on p. 108 of C. B. H. Van Rosenberg, Reistochten naar de Geelvinkbaai in de jaren 1869 en 1870. 's-Gravenhage, Nijhoff, 1875. and ROBIDÉ VAN DER AA, Reizen Nieuw-Guinea, p. 60, note *)-- BURNEY, III, p. 107, note.

[3] Compare for this date and the following, Tasman's chart of Sept. 8, 1644, reproduced in this work, and discussed in my annexed Life of Tasman.

[4] Dampier-Strait, mistaken for a bay.

Item the 17th.

Early in the morning we were close under this island aforesaid at about one mile distance; we then came upon a shoal and, when sailing over it, we sounded in the shallowest part 9 fathom, rocky bottom. When we were past the shoal just mentioned we got deeper water again; but shortly after, when we had the island south by east of us, we could see the bottom, the sea being only 7 fathom deep here, bottom as before; this shoal runs off to north-west from the land aforesaid. We kept holding our course west by south, and saw still more islands ahead, west of us 5 or 6 of them. At noon the island we had passed bore from us east at about 3 miles distance. During these twenty-four hours we had advanced 9 miles on a west slightly southerly course. Latitude estimated 20' south of the equator, Longitude 148° 34'; course held west one third of a point southerly, sailed 9 miles. In the evening at sunset there lay west-north-west and north-west by west of us 7 or 8 small islands in a row, bearing from each other west by north and east by south. We then passed a number of rocks all overgrown with brushwood; these we left on our starboard, and four more small islands to larboard, the latter lying near the mainland coast. The coast of Noua Guinea[2] here is full of small bays and projecting points; but there is almost everywhere deep water so that we run on a mile only from shore; about 4 glasses in the first watch, off a pretty large bay, we were about 2/3 mile from shore. We took soundings here in forty fathom, sandy bottom, where we forthwith anchored. Here we had a large island west by south of us at about 6 miles distance where in the evening we had seen a passage through between the mainland coast and the said island.

Item the 18th.

Early in the morning with the landwind we weighed anchor and set sail for the narrows between the mainland coast and the islands in order to pass through. Shortly afterward we drifted in a calm; about noon a light breeze from the west and the current were against us, so that we were carried back, and at length came to anchor in 16 fathom between an island and a rock which lay level with the water, the bottom being small coral. At noon Latitude estimated 26', Longitude (not recorded)[3] sailed 6 miles. As we lay here the current began to run much stronger in the afternoon; we are here in 26' South Latitude; variation 5½° North-East. About four o'clock in the afternoon the current began to change, the ebb-tide running here to west and the flood to east, so that a west-south-west moon makes high-water here; but since we cannot be far from the western extremity of New Guinea, as the coast begins to trend southward here, it is quite possible that the two tides meet here at the extremity of Noua Guinea[4], since before we had the flood

from the east everywhere along the coast of New Guinea. As there was
no moon we remained at anchor during the night for safety. This afternoon several prows came close to our ship; the men in them said they
were Ternatans and spoke the language of Ternate, spoke with them a
long time, and with kind words tried to get them on board of us, but
they pretended to be timid and afraid; from which we concluded that
these men must have been Tydorese. They returned to the shore with
their prows[5], the wind being west with good weather. During the night
we had a violent current to westward and frequent whirling currents so
that, our anchor quitting its hold, we had to pay out more cable. For
the rest it was calm all through the night.

[1] Qy. of? The Huydecoper copy has "the mainland of Nova Guinea
and the island."

[2] Of the islands of Waigeoe, which they mistook for New-Guinea, because they took Strait Dampier to be a bay.

[3] From the 18th to the 27th of May inclusive the longitudes are left
blank in the MS.

[4] Waigeoe.

[5] The sailor's journal gives some more particulars.

Item the 19th.

In the morning the current again began to westward; we weighed anchor and went under sail, the wind being south by west with good
weather; we set our course south-east by east over to landward, with
good dry weather. In the passage we generally sounded from 25 to 45
and 50 fathom. At this point there was a good deal of broken land as
may be seen in our chart of the same. At noon Latitude observed 35',
Longitude (not recorded); course held west-south-west, sailed 7 miles,
the wind being south by west and variable; we tacked about to landward since the wind became south with occasional calms. In the
forenoon, the current setting from the south-south-west, we anchored
in 35 fathom, good sandy bottom. In the afternoon it fell a dead calm.
During the night we had variable currents.

Item the 20th.

In the morning the current ran slightly to south-west and was variable, the wind blowing from the south-east with a light breeze. We did our best to tack to the south and pass through between the islands. But a contrary wind and calms prevented us from making any considerable progress. We sailed here over a shoal where we sounded 5 fathom, sandy bottom mixed with shingle, but soon afterwards 25, 30, and 40 fathom, same bottom. In the forenoon the wind blew from the south so that we went over to eastward; shortly after noon, the wind being south-south-west, we again came upon the shoal aforesaid and, as the current was setting strong to the north-east, we cast anchor in 5 fathom. At this point here the current runs very strangely, so that in my opinion no certain information can be given concerning it. Who comes here immediately see it, and must shape his course accordingly. This point aforesaid of New Guinea mainly consists of broken land which would take more time in mapping out than we think necessary to bestow on it. We are satisfied with having discovered a good passage through, which in future may be of great use to the Company's ships coming from Peru or Chili at the time of the eastern monsoon. During the night the wind was southerly with a strong current setting to the south-west and we remained at anchor.

Item the 21st.

In the morning before daybreak, with the current setting to the south-west and the wind blowing from the south-east, we weighed anchor and went under sail with a steady gale and our course set to the south-west. In the forenoon the wind went about to south by east so that we made no progress by tacking. About noon we therefore cast anchor under a small island in 25 fathom, pretty good bottom, in Latitude 38' South, Longitude (not recorded) course held south, sailed one mile with a south by east wind; it being our intention, with the first favourable wind and current that should offer on the coast of New Guinea or near it, to steer our course for the south until we shall have passed the latitude of Cape Wedda in the island of Gilolo, from where we can cross as far north as possible. We sailed close to shore here in order to get some firewood, of which there was great plenty here. When arrived on the said island we certainly observed signs of men but did not see any natives. It would seem that the only persons landing on this island are fishermen who dry their fish here at certain seasons of the year and then carry the same to other places to be sold there. Near this islet and round the whole point along and between the islands there are everywhere currents as strong (as the old saw has it) as the tide before Flushing pier-head. In these parts the flood runs northward and the ebb southward, but almost everywhere here the tides follow the direction of the coast, of the islands and passages, narrows and straits. In the evening at the end of the first watch, the wind being south-south-east, we set sail, endeavouring by tacking to run to the south with a steady breeze.

Item the 22nd.

In the morning, the wind continuing southerly, we kept endeavouring to run to the south as before, but about noon were again forced to come to anchor in 35 fathom, sandy bottom, near a small island about 2 miles south-east by east of the island where we had previously been at anchor, so that in these twenty-four hours we advanced no more than 2 miles south-east by east. At noon Latitude observed 40', Longitude (not recorded) course held south-east by east, sailed 12 miles.

Item the 23rd.

In the morning, the wind being south-east but inclining to a calm, we set sail and endeavoured to run to the south. In the forenoon the wind was variable so that at noon we had progressed about 4 miles to the south by east. At noon Latitude estimated 55', Longitude (not recorded) course held south by east, sailed 4 miles, with variable winds. Variation 4° 30'. Here we again came close under a number of islands but at first found no anchorage. The coast of Noua Guinea in these

parts is continually running in and out, with so many windings and so many large and small islands that there is no counting them. During the greater part of the night we drifted in a calm; in the evening we had had soundings in 50 fathom.

Item the 24th.

In the morning we drifted in a calm as before; in the forenoon, the wind blowing from the south by east, we did our best by tacking to run to the south, but we made little progress. At noon Latitude observed 1 degree 6', Longitude (not recorded) course held south-west by west, sailed 3 miles, the wind being south inclining to a calm. We convened the council with the second mates of the ships Heemskerk and Zeehaan, in which meeting it was resolved and determined that we should shape our course above the point of Wedde and towards Ceram, and further navigate to Batavia, seeing that at this season of the year there is no other course possible owing to contrary winds and counter-currents; all which is in extenso set forth in the resolution this day drawn up touching this matter. In the course of the night we came close to a small islet which we could not weather, so that we were obliged to anchor there for some time in 11 fathom, coarse sandy bottom; as we were lying at anchor we found that the current was setting pretty strong to westward.

Item the 25th.

In the morning, the wind being east-south-east, we weighed anchor and set sail; we passed through between the two islets. This day we had many variable winds alternating with calms and rains; we kept doing our best to run to the south. At noon Latitude observed 1 degree 15', Longitude (not recorded) course held south-west by west, sailed 4 miles with variable winds. During the night we set our course due south by west and passed a large island to larboard of us.

Item the 26th.

At noon we took no latitude. Latitude estimated 1 degree 38', Longitude (not recorded) course held south by west, sailed 11 miles with variable winds. South-east of us we again saw a large island about 8 miles in length. It extended mainly east-north-east and west-south-west with many small islands lying off it on the north-west side. We then set our course south-south-west to run to westward of all these small islands. In the evening before sunset we still saw 2 high islets north-west by west of us at about 7 or 8 miles distance, for which we set our course. We then saw south-south-west of us the whole extent of the coast of Ceram; we steered straight for it in good calm weather, the wind then being north-west. During the first and second quarter of the night we drifted in a calm; in the day-watch we got the wind from the north with rain.

Item the 27th.

In the morning the wind was chiefly west; the point of the large island which we had passed the previous evening now bore from us north-east by north at about 5 miles distance; the wind being westerly with good calm weather we turned our course over to southward close by the wind towards the coast of Ceram, from which at noon we were still 5 miles distant, to wit from the centre of Ceram. At noon Latitude observed 2° 40', Longitude (not recorded) course held south-south-west, sailed 11 miles with variable winds alternating with calms. At sunset we were still 2 or 2½ miles off the land; the wind continuing westerly, we endeavoured to run westward, northward of Ceram. During the night we advanced about 5 or 6 miles with variable winds; in the day-watch it was mostly calm.

Item the 28th.

In the morning variable winds with rain, thunder and lightning. Since the landwind was partly blowing from the south we tacked about to westward. We were now right off the small islands which lie, 6 together, close to the coast of Ceram, and had the middle of the said coast south-south-west of us at about 3 miles distance. At noon the westernmost of the said small islands were south-south-east of us at about 3 or 2½ miles distance. Today in the forenoon we had had rain. At noon Latitude estimated 2° 48' South, middle longitude 146° 15'; course held west by south, sailed 10 miles; in the afternoon we had dry weather, the wind being south-south-east with a light variable breeze.

Item the 29th.

At noon we had the island of Boona west-south-west of us at about 5 miles distance; we set our course close along the coast with the intention of running southward through the straits of Nassouw; at noon Latitude estimated 2° 52' South, Longitude 145° 15'; course held west a quarter of a point southerly, sailed 15 miles with the wind southerly but variable. In the afternoon it was calm, and then the wind went round to westward of the south with a fair breeze, so that in the night we were forced to run northward of Boona; during the night the wind blew from the south; we set our course for the island of Boure as close to the wind as possible.

Item the 30th.

In the morning we were close under the mainland coast of Boure, along the north side of which we sailed with good weather and a fair breeze from the south. At noon we had the north-western point of Boure, known by the name of Tannewary, south by east of us at 1½ miles distance. At noon Latitude estimated 3° 8' South, Longitude 143° 52'; course held west by south, sailed 21 miles; in the afternoon we drifted in a calm under wind going round to westward; we tacked about to the south in order to be near the land in the evening as we expected the landwind; during the night we got a light land-breeze; course held west by south along the land.

Item the 31st.

In the forenoon we had variable winds alternating with calms. At noon we had the western point of Boure, known by the name of Tamahoo, south of us about 3 miles distance. About one o'clock in the afternoon, the wind becoming south with a steady breeze, we set our course over to westward. At noon Latitude estimated 3° 15', Longitude 147° 17'; course held west by south. Towards evening the wind went round to the south-east; we shaped our course to south-west with a steady breeze and good dry weather. During the night, at the end of the first watch, the wind became east-south-east and we set our course south-west by west for the entrance of the strait of Botton, because we intended to pursue our course through the said strait and then to the Booqueroenis.

JUNE 1643

Item the 1st of June.

In the morning the wind kept blowing from the east-south-east with good dry weather and a fair breeze; we set our course west-south-west for the northern point of the island of Botton. At noon Latitude observed 4° 13', Longitude 141° 5'; course held south-west by west, sailed 26 miles with an east-south-east wind. In the afternoon we sighted the strait of Botton. We sailed in the strait in the evening and during the night with variable winds alternating with calms, and endeavoured to continue our voyage through the strait to the south.

Item the 2nd.

In the morning at sunrise we had advanced into the strait a distance of about 3 miles. In the afternoon we drifted in a calm, the current being against us. We cast anchor close to the coast of Boutton in 26 fathom, stiff ground; here we found two junks at anchor, of which the Super-cargo forthwith came on board of us and showed us their passports which they had obtained from the Honourable Governor Gerrit Demmer, with which passports they were going to Byma to return afterwards to Amboyna or to Batavia. The names of the Anachgoddes[1] of the junks were Mouna and Jurregan Wanga, besides there was still a free black, Hendrick Jansz of Solor, ensign of the Groene Geuszen[2]. From them we learned that the Honourable Anthony Caen had arrived at Amboyna with a number of vessels with destination for Ternate. They also told us that the ship Hollandia was reported to have been lost on her way from Batavia to Amboyna, but whether this is true we shall learn in time. At noon Latitude estimated 4° 32', Longitude 141° 3'; course held west-south-west, sailed 13 miles with variable winds. During the night when 4 glasses in the first watch had run out and the current began to set southwards we set sail; all through the night the wind was very variable but chiefly south; we did what we could by tacking.

Item the 3rd.

We kept tacking as before, the wind being southerly. At noon we were full in the first narrows, with the wind northerly but with frequent calms. At noon Latitude estimated 4° 54' South, Longitude 140° 59'; course kept south by west, sailed 6 miles. In the afternoon we had heavy rains; shortly before the evening we anchored in a calm one mile past the first narrows in 30 fathom, good stiff ground, the current setting to northward. About midnight with still water we weighed anchor and set sail but there was hardly any breeze, so that we made little progress.

Item the 4th.

In the morning we still drifted in a calm. At noon Latitude estimated 5° 10' South, Longitude 140° 56'; course kept south by west, sailed 4 miles with variable winds. At 4 o'clock in the afternoon we got the wind from the south-east and set our course south-south-west straight for the narrows lying close to Boutton; this is the narrowest part of the strait of Boutton, where we cast anchor after midnight close to the island in 12 fathom, stiff ground.

Item the 5th.

Early in the morning we weighed anchor in a calm but, as the ebb-tide had nearly run out, two hours before noon we anchored in the middle of the narrows with our kedge-anchor in 45 fathom, hard bottom. At noon Latitude estimated 5° 5' South, Longitude 140° 52'; course kept south by west, sailed 3½ miles with variable winds and rain. In the afternoon at early ebbtide and in a calm, being engaged in weighing our kedge-anchor, we found that it had got under a rock and were forced to let it go, continuing our voyage to Boutton, so as in the evening to get clear of the straits south of Boutton, with a south wind alternating with calms. In the evening after the setting of the first watch the steward's mate Jan Pietersz of Meldrop, whom we had put on board the flute-ship until such time as we should arrive at Batavia, on account of certain charges that had been brought against him, and of misdemeanours of which he was suspected, let himself overboard into the sea by means of rope and swam to shore at Botton. During the night the wind was northerly with a light breeze; course held west-south-west.

[1] Anachgodde, Anachoda or Nachoda; the supercargo in a junk.

[2] "Groene Geuszen", are Green Beggars, the name by which the Company's native allies of the island of Solor were designated.

Item the 6th.

In the morning the middle of the island of Camboona was north-west of us at about 2½ miles distance; the wind being easterly and our course held west by south. At noon we had the western point of Camboona north by west of us at 3 miles distance. At noon Latitude estimated 5° 43', Longitude 140° 11'; course held west-south-west, sailed 11 miles. In the afternoon we had a steady breeze from the east by south. During the night at the end of the second watch we passed the islet known as the Booquernoenis in good, clear, dry weather.

Item the 7th.

At noon we had the western point of the high land of Turatte north-north-east of us at about 3 miles distance; course held west-north-west along the coast in dry weather and with a steady east wind. At noon Latitude estimated 6° South, Longitude 138° 1 minute; course held west half a point southerly, the wind being east with a steady breeze. In the evening at sunset we set our course west by south, straight for the great shoal which we passed over at midnight in 13 fathom, rocky bottom.

Item the 8th.

In the morning we had a steady south-east wind. About 3 hours before noon we passed over a large rocky reef, sounding 6 fathom in the shallowest part. We quite distinctly saw the bottom which was strewn with large stones. At noon Latitude observed 6° 2', Longitude 135° 21'; course held west, sailed 40 miles with a south-east wind; afterwards we set our course west by south in good weather.

Item the 9th.

South-east monsoon with good, dry weather. At noon the island of Maduere was by estimation at 8 miles distance, south-south-west of us. At noon Latitude observed 6° 15'; course held west by south, sailed 26 miles; Longitude 133° 49'.

Item the 10th.

Good dry weather; we took soundings in 35 fathom. At noon Latitude observed 6° 26', Longitude 132° 29'; course held west by south, sailed 20 miles; in the evening we had the western extremity of the island of Lubock[1] north by west of us at 4 miles distance.

Item the 11th.

In the morning the wind kept blowing from the south-east; we saw the line of the coast of Java, near Lubuan; at noon it fell a calm; Latitude estimated 6° 26', Longitude 131° 23'; course held west, sailed 16½ miles. We had here both sea and landwind; a light mild breeze; in the afternoon the wind became south with a fair breeze. We set our course

west; in the evening the mountain of Lubuan was due south of us; then
we also saw the high mountain of Japare, and the islet of Mandelycke,
which bore from us due west by south, at about 6 miles distance.

Item the 12th.

In the morning we drifted in a calm; towards noon the sea-wind sprang
up from the north-east; course held west by south. At noon we had the
islet of Mandelycke east by south of us at 4 miles distance, and the
central land of Crymon Java north-north-west of us at 6 miles distance.
At noon Latitude observed 6° 27', Longitude 130° 33'; course held
west by south half a point westerly, sailed 12 miles with land and sea-
wind. In the afternoon, the wind becoming north-east with a fair
breeze, we set our course west by north. In the evening at sunset the
island of Crymon Java lay north-east by north north-north-east of us;
we continued sailing on a west by north course as before.

Item the 13th.

In the morning the wind was south-east; at noon we had the mountain
of Cerebon south-east by south of us, and the Boomtjes island west of
us at 10 miles distance by estimation; course held as before in calm
weather. At noon Latitude observed 6°, Longitude 129° 3'; course held
west by north, sailed 23 miles with land and sea-wind. We then shaped
our course west by south in order to make Poulo Rakit and the coast of
Java; in the evening at sunset we had Poulo Rakit west by north of us
at about 5 miles distance, the wind being east-south-east with calm
weather, the mountain of Cerabon bearing from us south by west. During the night we kept sailing along the coast with the landwind in 20 or
21 fathom, stiff ground.

[1] Bawean.

Item the 14th.

In the morning we passed the point with the grove of trees; we had the
landwind with a fair breeze and thus sailed along the land in depths of
from 18 to 15 fathom, until we got near the shallows of the Schadelycken Hoek[1]. At noon Latitude estimated 6° 3' South, Longitude 127°
59'; course held west, sailed 21 miles. At noon we came upon the shallows of the Schadelycken Hoek which we rounded sounding in 7 or 8

fathom. At the end of the shoal we saw an English ship lying with flags from her main and mizzen-tops; on our approach she weighed anchor and sailed eastward, but for what port we do not know. In the evening at sunset we had the point of Carauan south-west of us at about 4 miles distance. We set our course along the coast, having the wind still along shore; during the night we passed through between the islands of Leyden and Enckhuyzen; when we had advanced a quarter of a mile between these islands we dropped anchor in 11 fathom, stiff ground; Latitude estimated 6° 12', Longitude 127° 18'; course held west by north and west-north-west, sailed 11 miles.

Item the 15th.

In the morning at daybreak I went to Batavia in the pinnace. God be praised and thanked for this happy voyage. Amen.

Done in the ship Heemskercq, date as above.

Your Worships' obedient and ever obliged servant,

ABEL JANSZ TASMAN.

[1] "Schadelijke Hoek" = Dangerous Point; Point of Krawang.

Abel Janszoon Tasman: His Life and Labours

BY

Prof. J.E. Heeres, LL. D.

CONTENTS

I 5
II 12
III 16
IV 19
V 28
VI 33
VII 77
VIII 97
IX 104
X 110
XI 119
XII 177
XIII 211
XIV 241
APPENDICES 260
Appendix A 260
Appendix B...260
Appendix C...261
Appendix D. 261
Appendix E...263
Appendix F. 274
Appendix G. 277
Appendix H. 280
Appendix I. 283
Appendix J..284
Appendix K. 286
Appendix L..288
Appendix M...290
Appendix N. 303
Appendix O. 305
Appendix P. 307
Appendix Q. 308
Appendix R..308

Appendix S..310
Appendix T. 313
Appendix U. 314
Appendix V. 314

I

INTRODUCTION.--THE DUTCH CHARTERED EAST INDIA COMPANY.

Just as a person's external circumstances at his birth greatly, often decisively, influence his subsequent career, so the destinies of a nation are to a great extent conditioned by the surroundings amidst which it first appears in history, by the physical and geographical condition of the country which it inhabits. The part played in the world's history by the inhabitants of the Low Countries, is intimately connected with the successful progress of trade and industry within their boundaries, and this progress in its turn depended on the place which the Netherlands occupied on the map of Europe, and on the nature of the products which their soil and their waters yielded to the inhabitants. Situated as they were, between England and Germany with the regions further east, between the Baltic countries and the south-west and south of Europe, the Low Countries, at an early period, became an emporium to which foreign commodities from all parts, as well as native products, flowed in profusion. Under these circumstances the possession of products for which there was a demand abroad, and the home demand for articles produced in other countries, naturally gave birth in the Netherlands to a desire, both to fetch these articles from foreign parts, and to carry the home products to foreign markets.

Again, the geographical position of the Low Countries naturally led their northernmost provinces to look upon the sea as their most convenient trade-route; so that, when once the North-Netherlanders had learned to use the sea-way, they no longer restricted their dealings to the traffic in home-made articles, or to the supplying of home wants, but extended their operations to such foreign products as were required by other nations than themselves. Especially from the beginning of the sixteenth century, they became the carriers of Europe.

The southern Netherlands, on the other hand, saw merchants from all parts of the known world come to their markets, by road and river, as well as across the ocean. In the southern provinces, Bruges was the chief seat of the world's trade in the thirteenth and fourteenth centuries. Later on, when the times became troublous, and the Zwin, the estuary by which Bruges communicated with the sea, got silted up, its commercial prosperity rapidly ebbed, and its place was taken by the city of Antwerp, situated on the Scheldt, the broad water-way to the German Ocean.

In the northern Netherlands the first place was held by Holland and Zealand, whose trade centred in Amsterdam, the city which, as early as the middle of the fifteenth century, was the most important mercantile town of the northern Netherlands, and, towards the middle of the sixteenth, had become the centre of the flourishing Baltic corn-trade, and the granary of Europe. Ships belonging to the port of Amsterdam, navigated the German Ocean and the Baltic, and bent their course to the south of Europe as well. It was especially after the discovery of America and of the route to the East Indies round the Cape of Good Hope, that this traffic increased in extent and importance; for the Spaniards and Portuguese, in the first place engaged in the trade with their own colonies, gradually gave up to the inhabitants of the Netherlands the navigation between their own ports and these more northern regions.

Nor were other causes wanting to promote this increase of maritime business: the Hanseatic League, once the keenest competitor of the Dutch merchants in the Baltic trade, had been defeated in the contest that had been going on during nearly the whole of the fifteenth century; and the circumstance of one ruler reigning over both Spain and the Netherlands, materially strengthened the mercantile connections between the inhabitants of his different dominions. Thus at the breaking out of the Eighty Years' war, Amsterdam was so important a trading city, that often some five hundred ships, most of them carrying Dutch colours, constituting half the mercantile shipping of Holland, were seen at anchor in its road-stead.

Among the commodities which these vessels brought from the south of Europe, the spices of India held a foremost place. Whereas during the Middle Ages eastern products came to the Low Countries only via the Mediterranean cities, via Venice and Genoa, the trade in these articles underwent a complete change after the Portuguese had discovered the route to the East Indies round the Cape of Good Hope. At first, it is true, they were brought to these parts by the vessels of the Iberian peninsula, but when, since the close of the fifteenth and the opening years of the sixteenth century, Dutch vessels had found their way to Spanish and Portuguese ports, and the inhabitants of these southern countries began more and more to engage in maritime commerce with their own colonies exclusively, thus leaving the navigation from Spain and Portugal to the Low Countries almost entirely to Dutch ships, the case got completely altered. Dutch vessels now began to fetch themselves the spices from south-western Europe, which in return they supplied with such Dutch and Baltic products as were in request there[1].

No perceptible alterations took place in the commercial situation above described in the first years of the revolt against Spain. Both parties continued to be aware how strongly they were interested in the maintenance of the mercantile status quo: the Spaniards fully understood that they could not do without the commodities supplied to them by the rebels; the authorities of the revolted provinces knew but too well that the well-being of the districts under their care was indissolubly bound up with the question, whether the said provinces could continue to be one of the leading European markets, where the products of the North and South, of the East and West were brought together, and whether the inhabitants of the Low Countries could go on enjoying the great profits which they derived from their steadily increasing carrying-trade between the different parts of Europe. Nor, in the opening years of the struggle against Spain, did the persons in power in Holland and Zealand swerve from this principle of action. Even when less shrewd and less far-sighted zealots branded all such commercial intercourse with the enemy as high-treason, the authorities very rarely yielded to the pressure thus brought to bear on them, and for a time only, affected to give in to a delusion of the day. It was only when a foreigner, the Earl of Leicester, was at the head of affairs, that for a short time a change for the worse was introduced into the commercial system of the Netherlands.

But after the lapse of some years Spain, which in 1580 had annexed Portugal, began to enter upon a series of measures which could only have been taken in moments when her rulers were stricken with total blindness. About the year 1585, especially, they hampered the movements of Dutch vessels to such an extent, that the trade to Spanish ports became attended with serious dangers.

The blow was acutely felt in the Dutch provinces. But the Netherlanders of those days would not have been themselves, had they received it with mute resignation, in hopes of better times to come. They were prevented from fetching the spices of India from Spain, it is true, but what then? The way to the wonderland itself, which was open to their adversaries, was it not equally accessible to themselves? The Spanish monarch himself suggested to his rebellious subjects the idea of becoming his rivals in the commercial markets of Asia.

Holland together with Zealand had now become the mainsprings of the revolt: thither flocked numerous malcontents from the southern provinces, bringing with them their capital, their intelligence, their energy, all of which they placed at the disposal of the commerce and industry of the northern Netherlands. And since, after the first trying years of the war, the seat of the hostilities was more and more transferred to the southern Netherlands, the trade and industry of the latter increasingly withdrew to the north, thus largely benefiting the commerce of Holland and Zealand. Thus strengthened, the Dutch merchants formed the resolution of extending their operations to the Indies themselves, and letting the red-white-and-blue flag float from their mast-heads in the eastern seas[2].

[1] Cf. R. Faun, Tien jaren uit den tachtigjarigen Oorlog, 1588-1598, Ch. XIII, 4th Ed. 's-Gravenhage, Nijhoff, 1889, pp. 181-192; P. J. BLOK, Geschiedenis van het Nederlandsche Volk, I, H. Groningen, Wolters, 1892-3. Especially II, pp. 482-504.]

[2] With regard to the red-white-and-blue tricolore, cf. D. G. MULLER, De oorsprong der Nederlandsche Vlag op nieuw geschiedkundig onderiocht en opgespoord (Verhandelingen en berigten betrekkelijk het zeewesen, for 1862, second section, pp. 81-181, and the literature there cited); R. FFRUIN. Nog een woord over den oorsprong der Nederlandsche Vlag (De Nederlandsche Spectator, 1864, pp. 81-83); W. J. D'ABLAING VAN GIESSENBURG, De Nederlandsche Driekleur (Nederl. Heraut, 1887, pp. 198-211).]

But they did not enter upon their expeditions across the great ocean without due preparation, and several years elapsed before they ventured to undertake the long voyage to India. One of the reasons for this hesitation was probably the fearful respect still entertained in the Netherland provinces for the Spanish-Portuguese power in the East. Hence also, that the Dutch ships were at first shy of using the customary route of their enemies for trying to reach Asia, and that they attempted to find another way round the northern coast of Russia in order to get to the wonderland, which latter attempts are well-known to have utterly miscarried.

But if there was hesitation, inaction there was not. By and by a part of the route to India had been reconnoitred by Dutch vessels, gradually feeling their way and steadily pressing forward. The way to Brazil had been known to Dutch skippers for some time past; the west coast of Africa was soon reached, and a few years later, in 1595, the

Compagnie van Verre of Amsterdam, the oldest East India Company of the Netherlands, fitted out the first Dutch vessels that were to navigate to Asia. Jan Huygen Van Linschoten, who mapped out the route to India, and wrote an itinerary based on personal observation, having, like many of his countrymen, made a voyage to the East himself; Petrus Plancius, a minister of religion at Amsterdam, and a well-known geographer and cartographer, who studied Spanish and Portuguese charts, and imparted to navigators the results of his scholarly researches; Cornelis De Houtman, who collected nautical data at Lisbon, who succeeded in inspiring Amsterdam merchants with the desire to extend their operations to the East, and to whom, along with certain others, the command of the first expedition was entrusted; it is to them, together with enterprising Amsterdam merchants and the daring Dutch sailors, that posterity is indebted for the blessed consequences resulting from the establishment of their colonial empire in Asia.

The first voyage to India by no means produced brilliant financial results, but on the other hand it taught two useful lessons: in the first place it was made evident that the route to India was as accessible to the Dutch as it had for some time been to the Portuguese and English; and secondly it became clear that the dreaded power of their former European competitors was by no means so formidable as it had been thought to be. Before long in various cities of Holland and Zealand new companies were formed for the trade to the East Indies, ships were fitted out, and crews enlisted; all being done under the auspices and with the aid of the authorities of the Republic. As early as 1598 some five and twenty Indiamen had sailed from Dutch ports, and at the time when the celebrated chartered company was established, this number had gone up to about sixty, a fact strongly characteristic of the energy and the spirit of enterprise prevailing at the period. But this spirit of enterprise was not without its dangers: the mutual competition sometimes stooped to unfair means, and thus threatened to nip the East India trade of the Netherlands in the bud. The keen rivalry thus born sent up the prices of Indian products to an exorbitant extent, and thereby exercised a fatal influence on the commercial advantages that were the object of the trade in question. The public authorities of the Netherlands were not slow to perceive this imminent danger, and in order to secure the India trade against decay even before it had begun to prosper, and at the same time to be able to attack successfully the Spanish-Portuguese enemy in its chief stronghold, India, they endeavoured to put an effectual stop to this internecine rivalry, by consolidating into one company the various competing shipping associations. They succeeded after using much persuasion and taking a good deal of trouble; and at last on the ever memorable twentieth day of March, 1602 the renowned General Dutch Chartered East India Company was actually established[1].

The company was established under a charter granted by the States-General of the United Netherlands, which charter specified the Company's rights and powers, and broadly outlined its mode of management. The management was confided to a board of directors, Bewindhebbers being their official title, to be chosen from the great shareholders. These Bewindhebbers or managers, often styled Heeren Majores or "Our Masters" in documents of the time emanating from the India authorities, were distributed over the various cities, in which the Company had established offices, or so-called "Chambers": Amsterdam, Middleburgh, Delft, Rotterdam, Hoorn, and Enkhuizen. The general management of affairs was entrusted to seventeen Deputed Managers, who usually held meetings twice a year. The Amsterdam chamber returned as Deputed Managers eight of its directors, Zealand four, and each of the other smaller Chambers, one; the seventeenth dignitary being appointed by one of the Chambers in its turn, with the exception of Amsterdam. Among the powers vested in the "Heeren XVII" was that of appointing the superior functionaries who had to represent the Company in the East Indies. From the year 1610 the general head-management in India was confided to a Governor-General, assisted by Councillors. In the various territories of which the Company had taken possession, or with which it kept up commercial connections, the conduct of affairs was in the hands of Deputy-Governors or other officials. Speaking generally, the Company was quite free in regulating its internal affairs; the control which the States-General had reserved to themselves as to certain points, got relaxed at an early period of the Company's existence, and in the time which is chiefly going to occupy us, had dwindled to next to nothing.

[1] Cf. FRUIN, l. c. pp. 193-236; R. FRUIN, Een onuitgegeven werk van Hugo de Groot (De Gids, 1868, IV, pp. 7-13); J. A. VAN DER CHIJS, Geschiedenis der stichting van de Vereenigde 0. I. Compagnie. Second Ed. Leyden, Engels, 1857; J. K. J. DE JONGE, De opkomst van het Nederlandsch gezag in Oost-India, I and II. 's Gravenhage and Amsterdam, 1862-1864; P. A. TIELE, De Europeërs in den Maleischen Archipel, V, VI (Bijdragen tot de taal-, land- en volkenkunde van Nederlandsch Indië, vierde volgreeks, 6e en 8e deel, 1882 and 1884); H. C. ROGGE, De eerste Nederlandsche handelsonderneming op Oost-Indië en Cornelis De Houtman (Tijdschrift van het Kon. Nederlandsch Aardrijkskundig Genootschap, Tweede Serie, XII, 1895, pp. 399 ff.).]

This is not the place to enter into the causes which led to this state of things; suffice it to say that during the period above referred to, the East India Company held a very independent position in the republic of the United Provinces. Nor could we go into detail as regards the nature of its charter. We need refer to two clauses of it only, which in the outset were most conducive to the rise and prosperity of the Company, but ultimately led to its decline and fall. The first of these clauses, contained in Article XXXIV, granted to the Company a monopoly of the navigation to the East Indies, to the exclusion of all such of its fellow-citizens as had failed to subscribe capitals at the time of its establishment, when the subscription was open to all Netherlanders, or had not succeeded in procuring shares at a subsequent time. This monopoly gave the Company great strength in the East, since in its endeavours to form and extend its business connections, it need not reckon with the rivalry of its countrymen. The second of the clauses referred to, enacted in Article XXXV, empowered the Company to conclude treaties and contracts with native princes and peoples, and to erect and garrison fortresses on the other side of the Ocean. The powers thus granted strengthened the association against the hostile rivalry of its competitors and enemies in Europe, and enabled the Company, where necessary, to secure its eventual rights against the natives, and create for itself a monopoly against both Europeans and Asiatics in various parts of the East. In these powers lay the germ of the suzerain rights of the Company and of the colonial empire which the Dutch have founded in the East Indies. It was especially during the first decades of its existence, when the Company's power and influence were still in posse, and had often to be conquered sword in hand; and in subsequent years, when this power and influence could only be maintained by means of the most arduous exertions; it was in the course of these periods especially that the great advantages of the powers above referred to were shown in the clearest light. It was not until a later time, when the results obtained were deemed sufficient to justify a cessation of further action, that these rights and powers began to exercise a fatal influence, because they gave rise to a relaxation of the old energy, dried up the marrow in the Company's bones, and sadly used up the strength of its body. During the period of which we are going to treat, only the advantages of the charter were clearly shown, while its drawbacks continued only to be rather feared than actually felt[1].

II

TASMAN'S BIRTHPLACE.

About a year after the formation of the celebrated East India
Company the man was born who carried the Dutch flag farther than
any of its servants, before or after him.

When, in 1844, the late professor G. Lauts brought out the
first biography of Abel Tasman[2], he was quite in the dark as regards
the year of his celebrated countryman's birth, and he soon turned out to
be on a false track as respects Tasman's birthplace.

[1] On the above points cf. 0. VAN REES, Geschiedenis der Staathu-
ishoudkunde in Nederland tot het einde der achttiende eeuw, II. Utrecht,
Kemink,1x868. Especially pp. 224 ff.; G. C. KLERK DE REUS,
Geschichtlicher Ueberblick der administrativen, rechtlichen and finanziel-
len Entwicklung der Niederländisch-Ostindischen Compagnie. Batavia &
's Hage, 1894; J. E. HEERES, Bouwstoffen voor de geschiedenis der
Nederlanders in den Maleischen Archipel, III. 's-Gravenhage, Nijhoff,
1895.]

[2] Verhandelingen en berigten betrekkelijk het Zeewezen en de
Zeevaartkunde. Nieuwe Volgorde, IV. Amsterdam, 1844. pp. 275 ff.]

Apparently without any basis of likelihood beyond the fact of
persons of the same name still living on the spot, the West-Frisian
town of Hoorn had had conferred on it the honour of having given
birth to our hero[1].

The unsatisfactory nature of the evidence, however, soon
caused doubt as to the correctness of the hypothesis. Whereas as late
as 1839 one of the local historians of Hoorn, Dr. C. A. Abbing, head-
master of the Hoorn grammar-school, continued to claim for the town
the honour of having been Tasman's native place[2], the same writer was
two years later compelled honestly to admit that he had found no evidence of the truth of his assertion[3]. And soon after, the man to whom
we owe so many important data respecting Tasman's life and work, the
Amsterdam bookseller Jacob Swart, senior partner of the publishing

firm of Hulst van Keulen, duly set forth the doubtful nature of the claims of Hoorn in the periodical of which he was editor[4].

Prof. Lauts, in the biography above referred to, shared this doubt, but admitted the equally groundless possibility, previously advanced by Dr. Abbing also, that the famous navigator might have first seen the light in one of the West-Frisian villages in the vicinity of Hoorn.

This uncertainty induced the then keeper of the Old Colonial Archives, Mr. P. L. De Munnick, who felt a profound interest in all attempts made to throw light on Tasman's career, to set on foot a fresh investigation of the documentary treasures entrusted to his care. Nor was he disappointed. As early as 1845 he had the satisfaction of being able to print a number of authentic documents that removed all doubt on the subject in question[5]. Certain expressions in Tasman's will, which had about this time been found back at Batavia, had meanwhile brought also Prof. Lauts to a conviction[6] which now became absolute certainty, thanks to Mr. De Munnick's fortunate find: Hoorn had to give up its claim in favour of the village of Lutjegast[7].

None of the documents unearthed in the course of those years, however, mentioned the year of Tasman's birth, and it was not until the year 1887 that the Leyden archivist, Mr. Ch. M. Dozy, adduced a piece of evidence[8] which, if it did not establish the point with absolute certainty, still rendered it possible to fix the discoverer's natal year with sufficient exactitude. In an official document, dated 27 December 1631, Tasman states his age to be 28, so that it is safe to assume that he was born about 1603.

Few at all interesting particulars can be given regarding the surroundings in which the great Dutchman who achieved such fame in his subsequent career, first drew the breath of life. Lutjegast was then, and still continues to be, a small Protestant church village, and numbers some two hundred inhabitants at the present time. It now forms part of the province of Groningen, and is situated near the Friesland boundary, west of the city of Groningen, in a country in which agriculture and cattle-rearing are the chief means of subsistence, while inland navigation on a small scale also contributes to support the inhabitants. The documents which furnished Mr. De Munnick with evidence that Tasman's cradle had stood here, allude to Lutjegast "in Vriesland," thereby reminding us of the old name of the region surrounding the powerful city of Groningen, viz. the so-called Friesche Ommelanden between the Ems and the Lauwers.

[1) G. NIEUWENHUIS, Algemeen Woordenboek van Kunsten en Weten- schappen. Zutphen, Thieme, 1822, i. v: Hoorn; MATTHIJS SIEGENBEEK, Over de verdiensten der Nederlanderen, in het ontdekken en bekend maken van onbekende of schaars bezochte werelddeelen en gewesten (Magazijn voor wetenschappen, kunsten en letteren. Verzameld door N.G. Van Kampen. Tweede deel. Tweede stuk, 1823, p. 247); G. MOLL, Verhandeling over eenige vroegere zeetochten der Nederlanders. Amsterdam, Van der Hey, 1825. p. 179; N. G. VAN KAMPEN, Geschiedenis der Nederlanders buiten Europa, I. Haarlem, Bohn. 1831, p. 378.]

[2] Beknopte Geschiedenis der stad Hoorn. Hoorn, Vermande. p. 16.]

[3] Geschiedenis der stad Hoorn. Hoorn, Vermande, 1841. p. 127 of the "Notes."]

[4] Cook en Columbus, naar het Engelsch, uit het Colonial Magazine, door R. M. MARTIN, met bijvoeging van den Nederlandschen ontdekker Abel Janszoon Tasman (Verhandelingen en Berigten betrekkelijk het Zeewezen. Nieuwe Volgorde, 1843. p. 239). As regards Swart, cf. the pa- pers by H. DYSERINCK, in "Eigen Haard", 1896, pp. 454-456, 472-477.]

[5] Verhandelingen en Berigten betrekkelijk het Zeewezen. Nieuwe Vol- gorde, V, pp. 529 ff.]

[6] Geboorteplaats van Abel Jansz. Tasman (Algemeene Konst en Letter- bode 1846, I, pp. 66-68).]

[7] As late as 1891 SIR GEORGE BIRDWOOD (Report on the old re- cords of the India Office, second reprint. London, Allen, still gives the honour to Hoorn (p. 184, note).]

[8] Abel Janszoon Tasman (Bijdragen-tot de Taal, Land en Volkenkunde van Nederlandsch Indië, XXXVI, 1887, pp. 308-331).]

Nothing is known of Tasman's parents and other relations. The Lutjegast registers of baptisms, marriages and deaths that are still ex- tant, do not go higher up than the year 1684[1], so that no information is obtainable from these records, which then held the place now filled by the Public Registrar's books of our time. No family name at all resem- bling Tasman can now be traced in this part of the country[2]. One well- ascertained fact may, however, deserve passing notice. About the be- ginning of the seventeenth century there existed at Lutjegast a family of rather well-to-do farmers of the name of Tassema, settled on a ho- mestead bearing the same appellation, and conferring on its proprietor the right of taking a share in the administration of justice, and of membership of the assembly of the Groningen Provincial States. This circumstance must the more draw our attention, that in documents of the time the terminations man and ma of the family names in those parts, very often alternate with each other[3]. But in this case, too, common prudence prevents us from making confident inferences, nor do we at all feel at liberty to draw conclusions from certain data collected in an attempt[4] at accounting for the discoverer's family name, by deriving it from a word "tasch", which in the province of Groningen[5] designated a special kind of vessels.

No reminiscences of its world-renowned son have been preserved in his native village. Under these circumstances it is not wonderful that no particulars are forthcoming of our hero's youth and education. It deserves mention, however, that he did not grow up destitute of all education, as is clearly proved by the circumstance that not only he had learned the art of writing, but even showed no inconsiderable talent in committing his ideas and experiences to paper. Perhaps the latter circumstance, considered in connection with the deplorable condition of elementary education in the country districts of Groningen towards the beginning of the seventeenth century[6], and with the fact that numbers of those who like him served the Company in inferior positions, were innocent of any knowledge of the writing art, will justify the conclusion that Tasman was not born of a family belonging to the very lowest rank. But in the utter absence of positive data, no certain conclusions can be arrived at, since, also as regards education, he may have been subjected to influences which virtually neutralised the drawbacks in this respect incident to humble birth.

To us the whole of Tasmans's boyhood and youth is wrapped in profound obscurity. We catch no glimmer of light before we come to his years of maturity.

[1) Communicated by MR. J. A. FEITH, state-archivist for the province of Groningen.--Cf. PROF. LAUTS in Letterbode, 1846, I, p. 67.]

[2) Communicated by Mr. C. VAN NIJMEGEN SCHONEGEVEL, Burgomaster of the community of Grootegast, of which Lutjegast forms part.]

[3) Communicated by MR. J. A. FEITH, on the strength of various pieces of documentary evidence.]

[4) DOZY, 1. c., PP. 312-314.]

[5) Communicated by MR. J. A. FEITH, on the strength of certain old regulations for the inland navigation of Groningen.]

[6) Compare my paper: De Ommelander Schoolmeester in den goeden ouden tijd (Groningsche Volksalmanak for 1891, pp. 148-165), and the authorities there referred to.]

III

TASMAN'S SECOND MARRIAGE, 1632.--EXTERNAL CIRCUMSTANCES.-DEPARTURE FOR INDIA.

The light alluded to at the close of our last chapter, was obtained from the document already mentioned, which in 1887 Mr. Ch. M. Dozy discovered among the public records of the city of Amsterdam. It turned out to be a pre-contract of marriage, dated December 27, 1631[7], entered in the church registers of pre-contracts of Amsterdam, and is of paramount interest as regards our knowledge of Tasman's personal circumstances at the time. Besides, as we have mentioned in the preceding chapter, it enables us to fix the year of his birth with a certain degree of exactitude. We further learn from it that he was already a widower at the time when the document was drawn up. His first wife is in it referred to by the name of Claesgie Heyndrix, this being all that it tells us with regard to her or her wedded life with our hero. It should be added that in the church records of Amsterdam no mention has been found of his first marriage, so that most probably this was contracted somewhere else[1]. The will discovered at Batavia, however, throws some feeble light on this point. From it we are namely led to infer[2], that one of Tasman's daughters, whom we shall subsequently meet again at Batavia, had sprung from this first matrimonial union. Whatever may have been the social status of Tasman's parents at his birth, it is beyond doubt that he was himself in anything but thriving circumstances at the time, when he married his second wife. He is officially styled a "vaerentgesel," i.e. a common sailor, and consequently at twenty-eight years of age had by no means achieved a brilliant position in life; for we are led to conclude from this qualification that probably he had not attained any grade in transoceanic navigation[3]. His habitation at Amsterdam was in the Teerketelsteeg (i.e. Tar-kettle Lane), a narrow street of the humblest pretensions[4], a fact which certainly does not point to easy circumstances on his part. Nor in what we know of his second wife is there anything that would at all justify the conclusion that she was of higher middle class or even patrician descent. She could not write; the positions occupied by those who were most probably relations of hers by blood or marriage, are such as were generally held by persons belonging to the lower classes; the "Palmstraat" in which she lived, is not in any of the fashionable quarters and though a will made by her on December 18, 1636[5], afterwards shows that she was not destitute of means, in this case, too, the mention of her then place of abode, viz. "de Braak," corner of the "Palmdwarsstraat," a humble neighbourhood[6], goes a long way to prove that her social position was far from being an exalted one. It would seem likely that she, or at all events her family stock, belonged to the small town of Workum in Friesland[7].

However this may be, it is beyond doubt, that on the 27th of December, 1631, Abel Janszoon Tasman had officially registered his intention to marry Jannetie Tjaerss or Tjaerts, also known as Tjercx, Tiercse or Tjercks; i.e. Jannetje, daughter to Tjaerdt or Tjerck, this being the usual nominal designation in cases in which a family name was wanting. And on Sunday, January 1, 1632, the Amsterdam minister of religion, Henricus Geldorpius--the fact was till now unknown--definitely married the couple in the Old Church[8].

Connubial cohabitation was of no long duration in the case of our new-married couple; for shortly after the ceremony the husband must have sailed for India, the region that was destined to witness the great exploits to be achieved by him. The precise date of his departure for India is not known. The Old Colonial records[9], which from this point onward form the main source of our knowledge of Tasman's life and work, are quite silent on this point. Perhaps, however, also in this case we are enabled to fix an approximate date. We shall presently see, that on December 30, 1636, he set sail again on his home voyage from Batavia. He must accordingly at this period have finished his engagement with his masters, and have served what was styled his "verband," the term for which he had engaged his services to the East India Company. Now, according to the articles of indenture[10], which inter alia specified the terms of enlistment, this term was fixed at three years' residence in India for all "sea-faring persons" without distinction of rank, "without counting the time wanted for the voyages out and back." Tasman must therefore have arrived in India on December 29, 1633 at the latest, and consequently cannot have left the Netherlands later than in the course of the first half of the said year. He sailed probably in one of the ships fitted out by the Chamber of Amsterdam. At least in 1636 he went home in the ship "Banda," a vessel belonging to the said Chamber, and as a rule officers of the Company made the home voyage in ships belonging to the Chamber that had sent them out[1].

[1) DOZY, 1. c., p. 315.]

[2) DOZY, 1. c., p. 317 and pp. 327-330.]

[3) Cf. DOZY, 1. c., p. 310.]

[4) I here follow Dozy, 1. c., p. 315.]

[5) DOZY, 1. c., p. 317.]

[6) Communicated by MR. W. R. VEDER, municipal archivist of Amsterdam. Cf. J. TER GOUW, Geschiedenis van Amsterdam, V. Amsterdam, Holkema, 1886. pp. 94 f.]

[7) DOZY, 1. c., pp. 316-317.]

[8) Communicated by MR. W. R. VEDER, See Appendix B.]

[9) The documents to which I shall refer in the course of the present work, are all of them preserved in the State-Archives at the Hague, unless otherwise stated.]

[10) The articles of indenture, as drawn up in East India in 1634, have been published by J. A. VAN DER CHIJS in Nederlandsch-Indisch Plakaatboek, 1602-1811, I. Batavia, 's.Gravenhage, 1885, pp. 309-361.]

The earliest trace of his residence in the East Indies that has up to now been discovered[2], bears date February 18, 1634, on which day Tasman sailed from Batavia in a ship which was bound for the Amboyna seas.

IV

THE DUTCH IN AMBOYNA.--TASMAN APPOINTED SKIPPER, 1634.--FIRST VOYAGE OF DISCOVERY.-- SUBSEQUENT RESIDENCE IN THOSE PARTS.

The Dutch had come in contact with the natives of Amboyna for the first time in 1599. Wijbrandt Van Warwijck and Jacob Van Heemskerck, who had sailed from the Texel on May 1, 1598, in the fleet commanded by Jacob Van Neck, in March 1599 arrived with four vessels off Hitoe, the northernmost of the two peninsulas forming the island of Amboyna. They met with a very friendly reception. It seems not unlikely that this friendly attitude of the native population was largely due to their well-founded hope of finding in the new-comers efficient allies against the Portuguese, who had built a fortress in the southern peninsula of Leitimor, and were constantly at daggers drawn with the Hitoese. Next in power and influence in Amboyna and the neighbouring isles to these last mentioned European conquerors, and unfavourably disposed towards them, figured the Sultan of Ternate.

From this first meeting the connection of the Dutch with these regions was constantly kept up, at first with short interruptions, but soon continuously. It will hardly be wondered at that the Dutch, who from their first arrival in the East had been treated as enemies by the Portuguese[3], at that time the leading European power there, soon began to avail themselves of every opportunity that offered to pay these adversaries in the same coin. Always with the understanding, of course, that their commercial interests must not be allowed to suffer from so doing; for the promotion of these interests was quite naturally the main object with which these representatives of Dutch merchants carried their flag into Asia. If the two ends could be secured at the same time, so much the better. And in this way it was quite in the nature of things that Tasman's fellow-countrymen demanded payment for the aid they afforded to the Hitoese in their struggle against the common enemy, this payment taking the shape of advantageous terms in the purchase of cloves, the staple product of these parts, for which there was such a keen demand in Europe. Thus in September 1600, Admiral Steven Van der Haghen, concluded an exclusive contract with the Hitoese, and with their consent and cooperation built in their country a Dutch fortress, in which, pursuant to one of the clauses of the contract, a small garrison was stationed to repel the common enemy. Thus the first step had been taken on the road that was to lead to the sole sovereignty of the celebrated East India Company in the archipelago of Amboyna.

A far more important step was next taken in 1605. In the month of February of that year Van der Haghen took possession of the Portuguese fortress without a blow, thus putting a stop to all Portuguese authority in these islands. The blow was a heavy one, for Amboyna formed an intermediate station between the Moluccas and Malacca, the door which to the Portuguese opened the Malay Archipelago. From Amboyna, Banda was within easy reach; in short, Amboyna was the key to all those treasure-houses in which the spices of India were stapled. The conquest of the Portuguese fortress bore far-reaching results; for Van der Haghen looked upon that part of the Amboyna districts which the Portuguese had accounted their territory, as conquered land. Several village-chiefs, also in Hoewamohel or Little Ceram, took the oath of allegiance to the Dutch government. With the Hitoese, however, a treaty of alliance was concluded. The conquered fortress was named Victoria Castle and became the chief seat of the Dutch authority, now firmly established in these islands.

[1) Cf. Resolution of the "Heeren XVII", dd. 15 August, 1646.]

[2) See my paper on Abel Janszoon Tasman, in Groningsche Volksalmanak for 1893. Groningen, Van der Kamp, 1892, p. 122.]

[3) Cf. R. FRUIN, Een onuitgegeven werk van Hugo de Groot (De Gids, 1868, IV, especially pp. 7 ff.)]

It will easily be conceived that the representatives of the trading Company endeavoured to render the newly acquired political power subservient to their commercial interests. Thus, in the contracts and covenants, then and afterwards made with the magnates and the people of these regions, they constantly aimed at having clauses inserted that secured to their Company a monopoly of the clove-trade, to the exclusion of all foreigners, both Europeans and Asiatics. In these efforts they generally succeeded, thereby securing large profits to the Company. The contract of February 1615, especially, which put a fixed, but far too low a price on the cloves to be delivered in, was a very profitable one, at least from a point of view which took account of present profits exclusively, and disregarded ulterior contingencies. But, since the Company deprived the Amboynese of the advantages that might have accrued to them from the competition of other purchasers, this selfish policy, which besides was often applied in a bungling fashion, offensive to native feeling, and resulting from the slight regard in which Europeans of the seventeenth century held their dark-coloured brethren,--this purely mercantile and consequently selfish policy became at the same time one of the causes of the bad feeling which soon arose in the native mind against the Dutch government. And this bad feeling ultimately led to resistance and war against the hated intruders, who on their part used the victory which in the end always remained with them, for always tightening the reins, for pinioning the natives of these islands with increasing stringency as regarded their commercial connections, and for keeping them more and more from all contact with the foreign competitors who were so great a danger to the mercantile policy of a Company, that looked upon the monopoly system as its only haven of salvation. Again, this compulsory separation from the outer world forced the Amboynese to have recourse to the Dutch exclusively in the purchase of such foreign commodities, provisions and clothing materials as they stood in need of. And in the latter operations, too, the mercantile spirit of the Company's servants never ceased to show its real nature: they tried to obtain the highest prices for the articles of which they now had a monopoly. Thus the knife cut both ways, and always to the detriment of the native population.

But the commercial policy of the Dutch was by no means the only motive or the sole cause of the hostile spirit prevailing against them in the Amboyna archipelago, not only among their subjects there, but also among their allies, and even among a large section of those islanders who accounted themselves quite independent of the Company. Mohametanism was constantly gaining ground, and as it progressed, it became more and more hostile to the Christian foreigners. Then the Sultan of Ternate soon began to look with an evil eye on the increasing influence of the Company in these regions, because he understood to the full that every extension of its power was a danger to his own authority. Finally, the powerful Sultan of Macassr, too, cast greedy eyes towards Amboyna, since, to the advantage of his subjects and himself, he saw the European rivals of the Dutch gradually establish settlements in his dominions, attracted as they were by the scent of the Amboynese cloves, which, against the contractual stipulations, were smuggled into Macassar, where they found a ready market and fetched high prices[1].

It is in connection with these matters, and in these regions, that we find Tasman mentioned for the first time during his residence in India. On April 3, 1634 he signs a declaration in his capacity of first mate in the ship Weesp[2], then sailing in those seas. If, after his arrival in India, he should have happened to serve in this vessel for a longer time than can now be fixed with certainty, he must have seen a good deal of Asia before he set out for the Amboynese seas. From the month of September 1632 the Weesp had been knocking about all the Asiatic seas: she had touched at various places on the Coromandel coast, had been trading on the south-east coast of Borneo, had carried the Dutch flag into the Chinese waters, and had been cruising off Bantam[3]. But on the 18th of February, 1634, she again set sail from the roads of Batavia, this time with destination for Amboyna, with Tasman as first mate on board of her[1]. She carried on board the newly appointed Governor of Amboyna, Antonie Van den Heuvel

[1] Cf. on the points discussed in the text: P. A. TIELE en J. E. HEERES, Bouwstoffen voor de geschiedenis der Nederlanders in den Maleischen Archipel. I, II, 's-Gravenhage, Nijhoff, 1886, 1890. passim; P. A. TIELE, De Europeërs in den Maleischen Archipel, VI-IX (Bijdragen tot de taal, land en volkenkunde van Nederlandsch-Indië, Vierde Volgreeks, VI, VIII; Vijfde Volgreeks, I, II, passim); and the literature there referred to,]

[2] A copy of this "attestatie" is preserved in the State Archives at The Hague.]

[3] Resolutions of the Governor-General and Councillors, Sept. 1632-February 18, 1634.--Letters from the coast of Coromandel to the Governor-General and Councillors, and other documents relating to the said coast of the years 1632 and 1633. Daily journals of the Castle of Batavia, September 5, 1632-February 18, 1634.]

. The Governor had received orders, with two more ships, destined for Banda, to call at Macassar, which town was being blockaded by a Dutch fleet, since the conflicting interests of the Sultan of Macassar and those of the Company had by this time led to hostilities. The flotilla commanded by Van den Heuvel was expected to inspire at Macassar "greater respect and consideration for our power"[2]. The Weesp arrived there on March 2, and sailed from there for Boeton, with whose prince Van den Heuvel had various matters to settle. Their abode off Macassar made the Dutch aware that the blockade was a very ineffective one. Considerable reinforcements from Macassar, accordingly, shortly afterwards reached the Company's enemies in Amboyna, and on the whole, when on May 3[3] the Weesp cast anchor off the Castle of Victoria[4], matters there looked anything but promising for the Dutch; the resistance against their influence was constantly increasing, and the Company's forces were being more and more heavily taxed[5]. Now it appears that Tasman took an active share in whatever the Dutch undertook against their enemies and rebellious subjects in Amboyna in the course of the years immediately following.

As early as May 18, 1634 he was by Van den Heuvel appointed "skipper," in those days the title of the master of a ship. He was put in command of the ship Mocha[6]. It is not without interest here to point to the hitherto unknown fact, that the first voyage of any importance in which Tasman took a share as commander of a vessel, was a voyage of exploration and discovery, though on a small scale as yet. A cargo had to be transported from Amboyna to Banda, from which latter island the return-cargoes destined for the Netherlands had to be carried to Batavia by way of Amboyna. Shiproom was not wanting in Amboyna for both these objects, but the available vessels were of "so indifferent a constitution," and provided with "such poor sails and rigging," that fears were entertained that they might be "unable to reach their destination along the south coast of Ceram," the usual route especially during the western monsoon, "now that the eastern monsoon was raging furiously and blowing with cruel violence"[7]. They therefore endeavoured to direct their course through the sea north of Ceram, a track for the greater part still "unexplored," since there were reasons to suppose, that they would meet with fair weather in the course of this monsoon, while a higher shore, favourable winds, and a calm sea might reasonably be anticipated[8]. The Mocha formed part of the small squadron which was to undertake this voyage, and Tasman was ordered to take command under skipper Frans Leendertszoon Valck, who was put in charge of five small ships and a pinnace, and whose instructions expressly enjoined him to draw up a chart of the waters to be navigated, and of the north coast of Ceram. The object of this voyage, "never made hitherto," extending from June 5 to June 24, was completely attained, since it had now been made evident, that henceforth Banda could be safely reached from Amboyna, both during the eastern and the western monsoon[9]; and "pertinent charts" were drawn up[10].

The route lay through the narrow and shallow Nassau strait or Nassau Gut, between Poeloe Babi and Hoewamohel, and close inshore of the north coast of Ceram, of which a map was, attempted to be drawn up. A grievous obstacle to the voyage was experienced in the poor condition of the ships and the utter want of materials for caulking and repairing the vessels when necessary. They were literally in want of everything. "Thus," exclaims, somewhere in his diary, the Super-cargo De la Salle, who accompanied the expedition and kept a journal of it, "oftentimes the Company's precious capitals and crews are exposed to all hazards in the like insufficient and crazy yachts, without provisions beyond a handful of dry rice, with a bag of salt and nothing else; whoever cannot support life on such scanty sustenance, is free to starve.

[1] According to the declaration of April 3, 1634, mentioned supra.]

[2] Resolution of the G.G. and Counc., February 7, 1634.--Daily Journal of Batavia, February 18, 1634.]

[3] Not on May 4 (Groningsche Volksalmanak, 1893, p. 123).]

[4] Letter from Van den Heuvel to the G.-G., of May 30, 1634.]

[5] See TIELE-HEERES, Bouwstoffen, II, passim.]

[6] Letter from Van den Heuvel to the "Merchant" Pieter Chrestien, of May 18, 1634.]

[7] Letter from Van den Heuvel to the G.-G., of July 14-15, 1634.]

[8] Instructions for Commander Frans Leendertszoon Valck, bound to set sail for Banda along the north coast of Ceram, June 2, 1634.--Compare, as to the monsoon in these parts, G. W. W. C. VAN HOËVELL, Ambon en de Oeliasers. Dordrecht, Blussé en Van Braam, 1875, pp. 13-15.]

[9] Compare as regards this voyage: Dagh-register, gehouden bij den opper-Coopman Jacques De la Salle. The chart in this journal is now reproduced here.]

[10] Letter Van den Heuvel, 14-15 July.]

The search for new routes demands new ships, well fitted out and properly victualled." Fortunately there grew along the coast and in the neighbouring islets timber in abundance, sufficient to supply the most urgent wants. For the rest, the voyage passed smoothly enough, for the natives had fled to the interior almost everywhere, leaving their huts empty and abandoning their boats. The Mocha alone met with something of an adventure[1]. On June 15 she got separated from the other ships, and on the 18th next was near the native village of Rarakit, on the south-east coast of Ceram. Here Tasman landed, hoping to be able to procure supplies by barter with the natives. "Having spoken with the blacks," says De la Salle's journal, "and being amicably received by the same, at length at our departure, Fiscal Balthzar Wijntjes and Sub-merchant Abraham Van der Plasse were barbarously murdered, chopped into small pieces, and three persons very grievously wounded." Tasman succeeded in transporting the three wounded persons to the boat, which was rowed back to the ship, he and his companions being "in great peril of being all of them killed together." According to the Governor of Amboyna[2] the crew of the Mocha "had landed all too inconsiderately after the honest Dutch fashion of credulity and over-confidence." "It seemeth," exclaimed the Governor of Banda on learning these tidings[3], "it seemeth in very truth, as if the chronicles of light-hearted over-confidence, commonly full of instances of unsuspecting carelessness, in spite of thousands of witnesses to the contrary, were now fated to be deeply stained with the blood of Dutchmen."

On June 20 the Mocha again rejoined the rest of the squadron, and now the question was discussed, whether it would be in their power to chastise the natives for this murderous attack. But the small number of "able-bodied men" in the vessels compelled the commanders to give up all plans for taking signal revenge. The voyage was now continued; Banda was reached on June 24, and not long afterwards Tasman again found himself in the Amboynese waters.

We meet with him again there on July 16, still as commander of the Mocha[4]. From this date forward we can from day to day trace his career in these parts, bound up as it constantly was with the destinies of the said vessel during all the time he was knocking about there. His life is a monotonous one, however: cruising against enemies, or in search of smugglers, bringing in provisions for other ships, transmitting intelligence or commands, these form the staple of his occupations, very rarely varied by his taking a share in important military operations, or by occasional independent action of greater weight on his own part. We can here refer to the leading incidents only of this hitherto almost wholly unknown period in Tasman's career.

In the month of August 1634 he is sent to the south-east coast of Ceram, that the presence of his ship may add weight to negotiations then being carried on with the chiefs of certain native villages in those parts[5]. Somewhat later the Governor of Amboyna commands him to chastise the inhabitants of the island of Boeroe for a treacherous attack on the Dutch, a task of which he acquitted himself as efficiently as was possible with the means at his disposal[6]. He has hardly returned from this expedition, when he takes part in the blockade and investment of Lessiëla or Luciëla[7], on the east coast of Hoewamohel, one of the centres of the resistance against the Company, the said siege being undertaken by express command of the Supreme Board at Batavia. The enterprise proved abortive, the Dutch being afflicted with various maladies, especially beri-beri, to such an extent that after a more than two months' investment the vessels and troops were forced to abandon the place. Tasman was fortunate enough at the time to prevent the escape of the emprisoned native magnate Kakiali, a ringleader in the resistance, and one of the most dangerous adversaries that have ever opposed the Company in Amboyna. Almost immediately after the raising of the siege, on April 5, he acquits himself of the charge laid upon him of going on a cruise between the west coast of Hoewamohel and the islands of Manipa and Kelang, at the head of a small squadron; "in order to prevent the landing and departure of foreigners." For a few months in succession Tasman's place was there, and though now and then, when a superior officer paid an occasional visit to his squadron, or was temporarily attached to it with his ship, he was second in command only, yet he usually acted as "commandeur," a term that does not denote here a definite grade, but only, generally indicates the captain of a number of vessels, sent out under one command.

[1] Not the Anjelier, as related by FRANCOIS VALENTIJN, Beschrijving van Amboina, II, Dordrecht, Amsterdam, 1724. B. p. 102.]

[2] Letter, 14-15 July.]

[3] Letter to the G.-G., of Sept. 10, 1634.]

[4] As appears from An "attestatie" of that date, signed by him.]

[5] Resolution, taken at the Castle of Victoria, August 14, 1634.]

[6] For this exploit and other points referred to supra, see especially "Journaal ofte Dagh-Register over 't gepasseerde...in Amboyna", from December 1634 to January 31, 1637.]

[7] Cf. TIELEHEERES, Bouwstoffen, II, p. LX, and the "Bouwstoffen" there referred to.]

Immediately on arrival at his new station, he came to close quarters with some thirty well-manned and armed vessels, most of them belonging to Macassar, steering their course for the forbidden land; "firing at each other with large cannon, swivels and muskets;" but Tasman's vigorous action could not prevent the great majority of the native vessels from reaching their destination[1]. And in this way things went on during the whole of this time: smugglers were always plying their illegitimate trade, and Tasman very rarely succeeded in capturing and destroying any of them, and seizing their cargoes. The forces over which he had command were not nearly sufficient to secure the object of his presence in these waters, viz. keeping off the smugglers who tried to carry the cloves to other places, especially Macassar. He often had reinforcements sent him, but as often, contrary to Tasman's expectation, also these proved insufficient. On the whole the ships were in wretched condition, while the crews were harassed by disease. The results obtained were accordingly far from satisfactory, and Tasman was once upbraided by his superiors with want of self-confidence and consequent disobedience to their far-reaching commands.

In August he is directed to another station. With a small squadron he is sent to the north coast of Hitoe; again with orders to keep cruising, always cruising, a monotonous existence, only on one occasion diversified by a voyage to the east coast of Ceram. Although in this case again he had to put up with poorly equipped ships, and his crews were cruelly afflicted with illness--in February 1636, for instance, the sick on board the Mocha more than twice outnumbered the valid men--Tasman met with greater success on the coast of Hitoe than on the shores of Hoewamohel. Besides, his services were now more highly valued than when he was cruising in the latter locality. The authorities were not wanting now in giving him proofs of their being pleased with his management, and of their approval of his actions. In April he left Hitoe, and the few months more which he spent in the Amboyna regions, offered more variety. He was once more despatched to Hoewamohel, Manipa and Kelang, where he fought with varying chances against the hostile natives themselves, and against the foreigners who traded there: some thirty Javanese were by him made prisoners, a native village in Manipa was chastised; but during his absence the inhabitants of Macassar, surveying vantage, captured a pinnace which had on her own responsibility attacked them, and killed the greater part of the crew. Tasman recaptured the vessel, and was fortunate enough to rescue the wounded in her. After this expedition he seems to have been especially in or near the Castle of Victoria, where he was actually staying on the 18th of June. His task in these parts, however, was now soon at an end.

[1) Cf. TIELE-HEERES, Bouwstoffen, II, pp. 273 f.]

V

TASMAN'S RETURN TO THE NETHERLANDS 1636.--HIS SECOND STAY IN INDIA 1638.

Though the thing is not absolutely certain, yet it is highly probable that on the second of July Tasman sailed from Amboyna for Batavia in the ship "De Zeeuwsche Nachtegaal." We may namely infer from a report dated July 18--of which more anon--that at that time he was no longer in those parts, and between the date last mentioned and the 18th of June, above referred to, no other ship than the Nachtegaal set sail from Amboyna for the capital of Netherlands-India.

However this may be, from a missive dated September. 20, 1636[2] it is evident that on that day he was no longer in Amboyna. No particulars are known of his stay at Batavia during the last months of 1636.

[2) From the then governor of Amboyna, Jochem Roelofszoon Van Deutecom to the G.-G. and Counc.]

If during that time he remained on board the Zeeuwsche Nachtegaal, which ship arrived at Batavia on July 25[1], he must have made a voyage still to the west coast of Sumatra, in order to take in the pepper purchased there, a trip which extended from August 9 to October 27[2].

Tasman had no sooner shaken the dust of Amboyna off his feet, than the crew of the Mocha, on July 18[3], lodged a complaint against their late skipper with the Governor of this district. They charged "commander Abel" with having sold part of the ship's victuals to the inhabitants of a friendly native village and to the representative officer of the Company, and with having kept from them their rations of arrack, oil, and vinegar during two months. From the Governor's observation that "in due time" it would no doubt become known, "in how far this was true," we may reasonably infer that at the time Tasman was unable to justify himself at once, and was consequently no longer staying at Amboyna. The Governor, however, had the matter inquired into, and it appeared that the said sale had taken place after reference to the authorities, but that Tasman had never accounted for the moneys received by him in this transaction. The matter was now referred for settlement to the Governor-General and Councillors[4]. The final decision is not found recorded. But we may assume as almost positively certain, that the thing was settled by administrative machinery, and that the supreme authorities at Batavia found no reasons for bringing a judicial action against skipper Tasman; since the proceedings of the Council of Justice of the time, which have been preserved in their integrity, do not contain a word touching this matter.

Tasman's stay at Batavia was not a long one this time; for on December 30, 1636 we find him embarked on board the Banda, which ship, together with certain other vessels, constituted the return-fleet, ready to carry home the rich Indian cargoes. Of the date just mentioned there are extant two declarations[5], both of them bearing Tasman's signature, and enabling us to determine with some precision his position on board the Banda. In the first document, being an undertaking to make the home voyage round the west of Ireland and the north of Scotland, in order to avoid as much as possible any dangerous contact with the enemy's men-of-war and with Dunkirk privateers[6], Tasman figures as fourth in the list of subscribers; the first of them being the ex-governor of Formosa, the well-known Hans Putmans, only just returned from there[7], now commander of the whole return-fleet, and embarked on board the flag-ship Banda; next comes the skipper-commander Thijs or Mathijs Hendrikszoon Quast, just returned to Batavia from Japan and Formosa, who was to play a more important part in Tasman's later life; the third subscriber is David De Solemne, who had likewise already made his mark as a functionary of the Company, and was a member of the Board of Aldermen at Batavia, and one of the captains of the garrison there[8]. Fourth in the series we at last find Tasman's signature, still followed by some hundred names and crosses, the marks of the totally illiterate. The second of the documents mentioned, being a declaration that none of them was engaged in any mercantile transaction for his private account, is not signed by Putmans, but the other three names just mentioned are likewise found here in the same order as above given. Accordingly, if in this connection we leave out the supreme commander of the whole fleet, Tasman figures as third in rank of the officers on board the Banda. Quast was "acting" or commanding skipper[9], De Solemne was supercargo, and Tasman must be classed in the categories of "mates" or "officers," which together with the "Governor, skipper" and "supercargo" are referred to in the preamble of the first declaration. This designation, at the first glance, would seem to point to a kind of degradation; on further consideration, however, it by no means necessitates such an inference. For it may readily be presumed that Tasman, who wanted to return home, was not inclined to do so without receiving pay, as a passenger or "doodeter," as the term was, and therefore was content to put up with an inferior position, since there was no vacancy of acting skipper. And indeed the notion of actual degradation utterly disappears, when we find him designated as "skipper Abel" in the daily journal of the voyage, kept on board the Banda[1]. He likewise signs the resolutions of the ship's Council, taken on board the said vessel.

[1] Dagregister van Batavia, at this date.]

[2] Dagregister van Batavia, at these dates.]

[3] See the Amboyna "journael" at this date.]

[4] Letter from Amboyna, of Sept. 20, 1636.]

[5] Cf. Groningsche Volksalmanak for 1893, p. 123 f.]

[6] Cf. Letter from the "Heeren VII" to the G-G. and Counc., of March 22, 1631.--Resolutions of the council of the ships Banda and Nieuw-Zeeland, of May, 15, 1637.]

[7] Resolution of the G.-G. and Counc., of December 11, 1636.]

[8] Resolutions of the G.-G. and Counc., of October 18 and November 26, 1636.]

[9] Resolution of the G.-G. and Counc., of December 16, 1636.]

Already in the very first days of January 1637 the fleet lost one of its ships in a violent storm in Soenda Straits. Apart from this calamity, the voyage, which was made via the Cape of Good Hope and St. Helena, and round the north of Scotland, offered no striking incidents. The difficulties, in those days attending a long ocean-voyage, were experienced also in this case: want of fresh ship's provisions and refreshments, in some cases unseaworthiness of the ships, in casu of the Banda[2], insufficiency of the magnetic and other nautical observations, in the taking of which Tasman's aid was called in and highly valued, all these drawbacks made themselves felt also this time, as appears from the daily journal and the Council's resolutions. Still, home was reached after all difficulties, and on August 1, 1637 the Banda cast anchor off Den Helder.

The few particulars that have come down to us of Tasman's subsequent brief stay in the Netherlands, convey an impression that he had only returned home for ordering his affairs, and taking his wife along with him to the country that was destined to become his second home. On March 25, 1638, he is desirous of selling a house in the "Palmdwarsstraat" at Amsterdam[3], and as early as April 15, the Engel, a ship of about 150 lasts' burden and bound for Batavia, set sail from the Texel, with Tasman as commissioned skipper on board of her. This vessel had been fitted out by the Amsterdam Chamber[4]. No particulars are known of the voyage itself. We are only informed that the Engel came to anchor at Batavia, October 11[5]. Tasman was now bound to serve the Company for a term of at least ten years, "seeing that he has brought out his wife along with him"[6]. The virtuous Jannetie Tjaers was, like her husband, destined to pass the remainder of her life between the tropics, though we may reasonably surmise that her life was less eventful than her husband's.

Tasman was not allowed much time to get acclimatised. Already on the 15th of October it was resolved in the Council of India, that the Engel should be despatched to the coast of the Indian main land and to Persia, a plan which, however, was modified on November 1, because the Engel was "urgently wanted elsewhere." The vessel turned out to be required for service in Macassar and Amboyna[7]. The supercargo Hendrik Kerckringh, namely, had to set out for Macassar, with whose sultan a peace had been concluded on the 26th of July[8], in consequence of which the commercial intercourse with him had been renewed. For this voyage now choice was made of the Engel. After landing Kerkringh, the vessel was to take in as much rice at Macassar as she could carry, with destination for Amboyna, to which latter locality she had also to transport reinforcements of the garrison, and intelligence respecting the smuggling-trade which still continued to be carried on between Amboyna and Macassar[9]. The instructions given clearly show how highly Tasman's skill and seamanship were even then valued by the G.-G. and Councillors: whereas namely instructions were duly issued for the voyage from Batavia to Macassar, i.e. for the period during which the said supercargo had the command as the highest in rank, the document goes on as follows: "we shall not by the present determine what course the aforesaid flute shall have to follow from Macassar to Amboyna, since in this matter we entirely rely on the skill and experience of skipper Abel Janszoon Tasman, whom we have instructed by word of mouth."

[1] Sub, dato March, 26, 1637.]

[2] Resolution of the ship's Council, of January 25, 1637.]

[3] DOZY, 1. C. p. 318.]

[4] Uitloop Boekie van Scheepen, and Memoriael van de schepen uit patria naer Indié vertrokken.--Cf. Missive from the "Heeren XVII" to the G.-G. and Counc., of April 12, 1638.]

[5] Resolutions of the G.-G. and Councillors, of October, 11 and 15, 1638.]

[6] Resolution of the G.-G. and Counc,, of January 17, 1642.--Cf. Groningsche Volksalmanak for 1893, p. 125 f.]

[7] Resolution of the G.-G. and Counc., of November 6, 1638.]

[8] Book of Contracts of the E. I. Cy.--Cf. TIELE-HEERES, Bouwstoffen, II, pp. LXIX, 323 f.]

[9] Missive from the G.-G. and Counc. to Amboyna, of November 15, 1638.--"Naeder ordre voor den oppercoopman Henricq Kerckringh," of November 15, 1638.]

The Engel having sailed from Batavia November 16, arrived at Macassar December 5, departed thence for the Castle of Victoria[1] on the sixteenth of the same month, and cast anchor before the place last named January 26, 1639[2]. Tasman was once more employed to cruise in search of smugglers with his ship, and was stationed off Lesidi in Hoewamohel, and afterwards off Larike in Hitoe. He attended certain military operations, without, however, taking an active part in them[3]. On the 15th of April he sailed for Batavia in the Engel, accompanied by the Zon, with a joint cargo of upwards of 100,000 pounds of cloves[4], and cast anchor at Batavia on May 3[5]. Not three weeks elapsed, before the Governor-General and Councillors of India resolved on the expedition that was destined to render the names of Quast and Tasman famous in the history of Netherlands-India.

VI

RICA DE ORO Y RICA DE PLATA--VOYAGE OF DISCOVERY EAST OF JAPAN, BY QUAST AND TASMAN, 1639--SOURCES--RESULTS--LITERATURE.

The sub-merchant Willem Verstegen had served the Company for some years in Japan[6], when in 1635 he set out on his return from there to Batavia: In the course of this voyage he drew up a "remonstrance or brief proposal for obtaining a great treasure or rather a fresh beginning of commerce with certain rich auriferous and argentiferous islands situate in the South Sea or Pacific Ocean in 37½° Northern Latitude from the line equinoctial." This report[7] was intended for the G.-G. and Councillors, and was sent in to the Council of India by Verstegen after his arrival at Batavia on December 12, 1635[8].

It appears from Verstegen's statements that his surmises were not without foundation. "A long time ago," he relates, a Spanish vessel had sailed for New Spain from Manilla, "and east of Japan in the South Sea, in pretty near 37½° Northern Latitude, about 380 to 390 miles from the land (or at the uttermost 400 miles from Japan)", had by a violent storm been driven towards "a large and high-rising island." When the crew went ashore, the island proved to be a country, "strange and unknown to anybody; the people being of handsome stature, white-skinned and of good proportion, very affable and amicably disposed." On arriving at their destination, they related many marvels about the wealth of the said island: "giving their hearers to understand that so to say gold and silver were almost to be picked up at discretion on the shore, nay, that the kettles and other cooking utensils of the natives were mad of these metals."[9] It goes without saying that in those days, when the gold-fever constantly stirred the blood of Europeans abroad, reports of this nature were eagerly listened to and not forgotten. According to Verstegen's report, the King of Spain was accordingly said to have given orders to the viceroy of New Spain, "residing in the capital of Mecxico," to send out an expedition to make inquiries touching this island. Verstegen places this expedition in the year 10 or 11, or the year after the capture of Mr. de Witter," a chrono-logical statement to which we shall revert lower down. The voyage was reported to have taken place under the command of "general Jan Bastiaen Buscaijne, an old, grey-headed man, well advanced in years."

[1] Letter from Kerckringh to the G.-G., of April 24, 1639.]

[2] Letter from Joan Ottens, Governor of Amboyna to Kerckringh, of May 29, 1639.]

[3] Letter from Ottens to the G.-G. and Counc., of April 15, 1639.]

[4] "Factura" (invoice) and "cognoissement" (bill of lading) of the said vessels, dated April 15, 1639.]

[5] Letter from the G.-G. and Counc. to the "Heeren XVII," of December 18, 5639.]

[6] Cf. Resolution of the G.-G. and Counc., of December 25, 1635.]

[7] It bears date December 5, and is found printed, not exempt from mis-prints or clerical errors, in P. A. LEUPE, Reize van Maarten Gerritsz. Vries in 1643 naar Japan. Amsterdam, Frederik Muller, 1858, pp. 35-40.]

[8] Resolution of the G.-G. and Counc., of that date.]

[9] Compare what stories are told about this in the Relation des isles Philipines faite par l'amirante D. Hieronimo de Banvelos y Carrillo, p. 5, in THÉVENOT'S Relations de divers voyages curieux. II. Paris, Mabre Cramoisy, MDCLXVI.]

The expedition, which started from Acapulco, was said to have utterly miscarried, the ships having merely sighted the island and nothing more. Among Verstegen's authorities there were not only cer-tain Jedo and Nangasaki people, contemporaries of those who had joined the expedition, but he had also obtained information from some who had themselves formed part of it, and among them all there were certain Dutchmen, whom he knew to be reliable persons. What they told him, accordingly made so deep an impression upon him, that he thought it his duty to impart it to his superiors, and to advise a voyage of discovery for the purpose, starting from Japan, on which occasion efforts could at the same time be made to form commercial connec-tions with Corea and the north of China. One unaccountable circumstance did not fail to strike Verstegen very forcibly: viz. the fact that the Spaniards had made no further attempts when this sole expedi-tion had miscarried, and had failed to renew their endeavours to get possessed of the treasures of this mysterious island[1]; and this in spite of the circumstance that other Spanish ships were reported to have re-peatedly sighted the island in navigating these seas. But the resources of Spain were no longer capable of removing many difficulties; perhaps, according to Verstegen, their "small power" in America and in Manilla may have prevented them from undertaking further expeditions. Nay, he inclines to the idea that "the Lord God, considering the wickedness of the Spanish projects, may have frustrated this plan, being unwilling to allow the poor natives to be robbed of their heritage and possessions."

Verstegen's authorities had by no means fabricated the story[2]. Undoubtedly in the days alluded to there were rumours current about auriferous and argentiferous regions east of Japan; and undoubtedly the Spanish government had endeavoured to bring these regions within the circle of the then known world. Verstegen assigns this event "to the year 10 or eleven, or the year after the capture of Mr. de Witter." Regard being had to the numerous slips of the pen to be found in the otherwise authentic copy of his report that has been preserved, and to the obscurity of the phrase "the capture of Mr. de Witter," we may reasonably suppose, that here too we have to do with clerical errors. We may further safely conjecture that Verstegen here has in view the miscarriage, so fatal to the Dutch, of the expedition to the Philippine Islands under Francois Witten, in which "on April 25, 1610 the admiral was killed, and the ships were captured by the Spaniards "[3]. If we assume this conjecture to be right, we come with considerable certainty to the result that the said voyage of discovery of "general Jan Bastiaen Buscaijne " must have taken place in 1611.

What notions, we may ask, were then current as to this so-called "rich auriferous and argentiferous island,"--elsewhere[4] also styled "a very large country "--which Verstegen was referring to? We find very positive data for answering this question in a rare Spanish book that first appeared in Mexico in 1609, under the title Sucesos de las Islas Philipinas. The author of it was Antonio de Morga, who at the close of the sixteenth and the beginning of the seventeenth century filled very high and important posts, both in the Philippines and Mexico[5]. Now this author, who was therefore in a position to be perfectly au fait of the matter, gives an account of the route to be taken by ships from Mexico to the Philippines and vice versa, and makes the following statements touching the return voyage[6]:

[1] JAMES BURNEY, A chronological history of the voyages and discoveries in the South Sea. vol. II. London, Luke Hansard, 1806, states on p. 262, that the Spaniards are said to have made a voyage of discovery to these islands in 1620. He takes his information from ENGELBERT KAEMPFER, De Beschrijving van Japan. Amsterdam, Arent van Huyssteen, 1733, p. 49. (As regards the various editions of this work, cf.

TIELE, Bibliographie van Land en Volkenkunde. Amsterdam, Fred. Muller, 1884, pp. 133 f.) The evidently erroneous date of 1620 has found its way into other books also.--In Voyage de La Pérouse autour du monde, publié par M. L. A. MILET-MUREAU. Paris, Imprimerie de la République. 1797, the chronology as regards the dates is all at sea. Compare together tome I, pp. 26, 150, and tome III, p. 166. In accordance with this, there is no mention of any expedition of the kind in 1620, in any Spanish archival documents known to me.]

[2] Such details in Verstegen's report as do not bear on the point in question, must naturally be left without further discussion; I must confine myself to the main point, the voyage of 1611, in so far as it is connected with my present purpose.]

[3] And not in 1609, as stated by LEUPE, 1. c., p. 36.--See J. K. J. Da JONGE, De opkomst van het Nederlandsch gezag in Oost-Indië. III, 's-Gravenhage, Amsterdam, MDCCCLXV, pp. 106 f. and 269.--Cf. P. A. TIELE, De Europeérs in den Maleischen Archipel, VII (Bijdragen tot de taal-, land- en volkenkunde van Nederlandsch Indié, Vierde Volgreeks, VIII, 1884, pp. 106-108; F. BLUMENTRITT, Holländische Angriffe auf die Philippinen im XVI, XVII and XVIII Jahrhunderte (Separatabdruck aus dem Jahresberichte der Communal-Ober-Realschule in Leitmeritz vom Jahre 1880), pp. 12-13. The last paper draws from Spanish sources.]

[4] Missive from the G.-G. and Counc. to the "Heeren XVII," of January 4, 1636.]

[5] See the English version of this work by H. E. J. STANLEY, brought out by the Hackluyt Society in 1868 under the title: The Philippine Islands, Moluccas, Siam, Cambodia, Japan, and China, at the close of the Sixteenth Century, pp. I, II, 41, 229, 397, etc. Regarding this book, cf. W. E. RETANA, Archivo del bibliofilo Filipino, I, Madrid. 1895, p. 6 of the Epitome de la bibliografia general de Filipinas, Parte Primera; TIELE, Europeérs, V (Bijdragen, Vierde Volgreeks, V, p. 153), and VI (Bijdragen, Vierde Volgreeks, VI, p. 141).]

[6] P. 356.]

At four hundred leagues from the Philippines, the volcanoes and ridges of the Ladrone isles are seen, which run towards the north, as far as twenty-four degrees; and the Cape of Sestos, the headland of Japan, lies to the, north, six hundred leagues from the Philippines. The ships pass between other islands which are rarely seen, in thirty-eight degrees, the temperature cold in the neighbourhood of the islands Rica de Oro and Rica de Plata, and which are seldom reconnoitred: having left these islands there is a wide open sea; this is traversed with the winds that are met with for many leagues, as far as forty-two degrees latitude, making for the coast of New Spain and looking for the usual winds which prevail in that latitude, and which in general are north westerly, and at the end of a long navigation the coast of New Spain is reached." De Morga's statement as to the latitude has by some[1] been considered as a mistake, and it has been proposed to substitute 28° for 38°, as more in accordance with the latitude in which in modern and older charts the islands of Rica de Oro (Lot's Wife) and Rica (Roca) de Plata (Crespo) are laid down[2]. But when we find that Verstegen's authorities, too, place the "rich auriferous and argentiferous island" in 37½°, and if we furthermore consider the evident vagueness of De Morga's and his contemporaries' information about the islands which ships sailing between the Philippines and Mexico, passed on their way, we may safely leave out of the account here the present location of the islands now bearing the names, and may be allowed to assume, that in the early years of the seventeenth century gold- and silver-bearing islands were supposed to be situated in about 38 degrees Northern Latitude. Nor can we allow much weight to the objection that Verstegen in his report mentions one island, or "a country": this wording may be due only to the vagueness of his information, or to an incorrect interpretation of it on his part. For there is no doubt--and this clearly shows that Verstegen's authorities were assuredly not speaking without book--that in 1611 a voyage of discovery to these supposed islands was actually undertaken. All this also shows the fallacy of the view[3], that Verstegen's "rich auriferous and argentiferous island" should perhaps be meant for California, whose geographical situation was, indeed, in those days too well-known to the Dutch[4], to render such a mistake at all likely.

As early as the last quarter of the sixteenth century, the Spaniards--the Japanese accounts are far too vague to require notice here[5]--had indications respecting these mysterious islands. There is extant a letter of 1584[6] from a Spanish priest, Andres de Aguirre, who in his time was known as an able and reliable cosmographer[7], addressed to the governor of New-Spain, in which letter the said dignitary is informed of the particulars following. A Portuguese ship, which had sailed from Malacca with destination for Japan, had, when she had come in sight of the latter country, been tossed about on the ocean for eight days in succession by a storm from the West, in dark weather, without having seen any sign of land. On the ninth day, when the storm had abated and the sky become clearer, the men had sighted two large islands, "muy rricas, muy pobladas de gente, de mucha policia." These islands, situated in 35° and 40° N.L., it being impossible to compute the distance east of Japan, were

[1) STANLEY, in his Note on p. 356 of the translation.]

[2) Cf. JAMES BURNEY, l. C., pp. 260-267. In a MS. atlas of GERRIT DE HAAN, "Captain-lieutenant in the navy," and "master-cartographer" at Batavia (Resolution of the G.-G. and Counc., of December 6, 1752), entitled, "Ligtende Zee Fakkel off de Geheele Oost Indische Water-Weereldt" (Hague State Arch.), I (1760), No. 12, Rica de Plata is in about 34°, Rica de Oro in about 30° N.L.; STIELER'S Handatlas puts them in about the same latitude.--See also Atlas du voyage de La Pérouse, Nos. 1, 2, 15, 67 and p. 177 of Vol. III of the 3rd edition of: A Voyage to the Pacific Ocean. Performed under the Direction of captains Cook, Clerke and Gore, in the years 1776, 1777, 1778 and 1780. London, Nicoll and Cadell, MDCCLXXXV.]

[3) DE JONGE, V (II), p. CXXX and Note.]

[4) See, for instance, GERARDI MERCATORIS atlas, auctus a JODOCO HONDIO. Editio Secunda. Dispensis Cornelii Nicolai Amstelreodami, Anno 1608), pp. 345-346; GERARDI MERCATORIS et F. (sic!) HONDII Atlas ofte Afbeeldinghe van de gantsche Wereldt nu eerst uyt het Latijn in onse nederlantse Tale getranslateert. Tot Amsterdam. Bij Jan Janssen (Joannes Jansonius). Ao. D. 1634, pp. 379-380.]

[5) KAEMPFER, l. c., p. 59.--See also no. 21 of the "Memorie van de boecken en pampieren," which Maarten Gerritszoon Vries kept with him on his well-known voyage of discovery east of Japan in 1643. (LEUPE, Reize van Vries, p. 33, and 26).]

[6) In the Archivo General de Indias at Sevilla. For an opportunity to become acquainted with this and certain other documents, preserved in the Archivo just mentioned, I am indebted to the great courtesy of Mr. W. E. Retana at Madrid, who placed at my disposal extracts from such archival documents, preserved at Sevilla, as mention the islands of Rica de Oro and Rica de Plata; Mr. Retana having applied for these extracts with a view to the requirements of my subject. This letter is printed in Vol. XIII of Coleccion de documentos inéditos relativos la conquista y organizacion de las antiguas posesiones Españoles en America y Oceanea. Madrid, Perez, 1870, pp. 545-549.]

[7) Carta del Virrey de Nueva Espana a S. M., October 21, 1609.--As concerns Aguirre, cf. M. J. DE NAVARRETE, Biblioteca maritima Espanola. Tomo I. Madrid, Calero. 1851, pp. 70-74.]

named "yslas de Harmenio," after an Armenian merchant[1], who was on board the Portuguese ship. The Spaniards took due note of the information thus imparted. As early as the year 1586, a ship was despatched with the object of further reconnoitring not only these islands, but also certain others that were reported to lie in the northern part of the South Sea[2]. In the report of this voyage, sent in the year after[3], it is stated that a search had been made, not only for the island del Armenio, which is now laid down in 34°-35°, but also for an island Rica de Oro, which figured in certain charts as situated in 29°-31° N.L., and for Rica de Plata. None of the said islands were found, and the naval captain Pedro de Unamunu, who had drawn up this report, accordingly thought himself justified in expressing as his opinion, that Rica de Oro and Rica de Plata, at least, were non-existent, and that they had most probably been introduced into the chart on mere hearsay evidence. De Unamunu himself had met with two uninhabited islands only, in about 25° N.L. The result of this voyage was reported to the king of Spain[4], but in Mexico also the matter was by no means lost sight of, although several years were suffered to elapse before the work was taken in hand. In a letter of May 24, 1607 the Viceroy set forth to his master in Europe that it was highly desirable to make further search for the islands of Rica de Oro and Rica de Plata, which this time--note the utter vagueness of the statements as to their latitude--are supposed to lie in 34°-35° N.L. He laid stress on the fact that these islands might become of great importance as intermediate stations for ships plying between Mexico and the Philippines. As a fitting person for such a task the Viceroy mentions Sebastian Vizcayno, who had already made his mark as leader of voyages of discovery[5], and was in this capacity highly valued by the king of Spain[6]. The voyage of discovery itself was to be undertaken from the Philippines as the starting-point[7]. This proposal met with a favourable reception at Madrid: the Junta de Guerra de Indias advised approvingly on the matter, September 18, 1607[8], and on September 28, 1608, the Viceroy was, by order of His Majesty, directed to despatch the said Vizcaino, with orders to seek a harbour in the islands before mentioned, while at the same time the governor of the Philippines was instructed to give every possible succour to this expedition. Various circumstances delayed the preparations for the voyage. The viceroy of New Spain thought himself bound first to collect additional information touching these islands from persofis familiar with the navigation in those parts[9], and these in their turn concluded that the islands should be looked for in about 31°-33° N.L., where, with other islands, they were reported to have been sighted by ships sailing from the Philippines to Mexico. But at length these discussions after all led to the conclusion that the exploratory expedition had better start, not from the Philippines, but from Mexico[10]. In accordance with this conclusion, the viceroy now sent fresh advices to Spain, where in his opinion the decision ought to be taken[11]. Numerous conferences were held in consequence, both in the motherland and in the colonies, in which conferences a leading part was taken by Antonio de Morga, and by the well-known nautical expert and historian of the Philippine Islands[12], Hernando de los Rios, Coronel[13], who asserted to have himself

[1) "Mercador Armenio."]

[2) Carta del Virrey de Na Espana a S. M., May 10, 1586.]

[3) Relation y derrotero del viaje y navegacion hecha desde Macau hasta Acapulco en la fregata Nuestra Senora de la Esperanza, 1587.]

[4) Cartas del Virrey de Na España a S. M., December 10, 1587, and November 29, 1588.]

[5) Cf. P. A. TIELE, De ontdekkingsreizen sedert de vijftiende eeuw, vrij bewerkt naar Vivien de Saint-Martin. Leiden, Van Doesburgh, 1874, p. 173; NAVARRETE, 1. c., I, pp. 86, 110, 282; BURNEY, 1. c., II, pp. 182 ff.; 237, ff.; etc. As regards Vizcaino's death, BURNEY, II, p. 259, is unintelligible or mistaken.]

[6) Cf. e.g. Real Cedula al Gobernador de Filipinas, of August 19, 1606.]

[7) Carta del Virrey de Na Espana á. S. M., May 24, 1607.]

[8) See its Consultaq of that date.]

[9) Carta del Virrey de Na Espana a. S. M., May 24, 1609.]

[10) Testimonio de la junta celebrada en Mexico por Orden del Virrey, July 12, 1609.--Id., October, 1609.]

[11) Carta del Virrey de Nueva Espana a S. M., October 21, 1609.]

[12) NAVARRETE, I, pp. 636-647.]

[13) See Cartas de Hernando de los Rios a. S. M., January 27 and December 31, 1610; Consulta del Consejo de Indias, April 23, 1610; Real Cedula al Virrey de Na España, 1610; Parecer de Hernando de los Rios sobre el descubrimiento de las Islas Ricas de Oro y Rica de Plata, que le fué pedido por el Virrey de Na España, 1610; id., respondiendo a los apuntamientos que se le dieron, 1610.]

seen the islands of Rica de Oro and Rica de Plata, of which the latter according to him was situated in 36°, the former in 29° N.L., also according to charts then in use, both 150 Spanish miles east of Japan. He could, however, not tell, whether they were inhabited. These consultations, however, gave rise to the drawing up of another route: it was namely resolved that the exploratory expedition should start from Japan. In March 1611 a ship sailed from Mexico, under command of Sebastian Vizcaino, who was at the same time deputed to the Japanese government, in order to discover the islands of Rica de Oro and Rica de Plata[1]. This enterprise, of which the results are laid down in Vizcaino's report, headed Relation del viaje y descubrimiento de las islas llamadas Ricas de Oro y plata[2], totally miscarried. It got to Japan, it is true[3], and Vizcaino mapped out part of the coast of this country[4], but the islands he was sent in search of, remained undiscovered[5]. We need not enter any further into the results of this expedition--undoubtedly to be identified with the one that, according to Verstegen, was said to have taken place under the leadership of "general Jan Bastiaen Buscayne"--the less so, because it is evident that these results had become no further known to Verstegen than so far as he had heard them spoken of in Japan, and had referred to them in his well-known report. Now it was on this report that the Governor-General and Councillors and the Board of Directors of the East India Company based their plans for the discovery of the gold- and silver-bearing countries so much in request. Immediately after taking cognizance of Verstegen's narrative the Supreme Government at Batavia informed the Board of Directors of the Company of its intention "to pay attention to it in future," because they thought the affair "of great moment, considering the climate and situation of the said country, in whose latitude were to be found the richest treasures of the world" (an opinion, which later on they further insist on in the terms following: "that the principal and richest treasures in the whole world are to be met with from 31°, 32° to 40°, 42° N.L.," as is proved by "the richly-yielding silver, gold, copper and other mines, found to the north of Japan"[6]; and because they expected that "European, Indian and Chinese goods would be in request there for clothing, and might find a ready sale"[7].

Just about this time an important change took place in the government at Batavia. The Governor-General Hendrik Brouwer, who--as will appear by-and-by--had himself also given a good deal of attention to the project of a voyage of discovery round by the east of Japan, was in his official capacity replaced by Antonio Van Diemen[8] in January 1636, and Van Diemen, too, was not a man to dawdle in matters in which he deemed the interests of the Company to be concerned. The gold- and silver-lands east of Japan strongly attracted his attention, and he lost no time before putting his hand to the plough. As early as May 26, 1636 it was resolved in a meeting of the Council of India that an exploratory voyage should be undertaken to those regions, which resolution was expanded in the instructions of May 31, by the Governor-General and Councillors given to Nicolaas Coeckebacker, who, only just returned from Japan, was ready to depart thither again in the capacity of "President and Head of the Company's trade and excellent commerce in the empire of Japan." He received orders, when arrived in Japan "to deliberate" on the plan "with Commander Matthijs Hendricxsen Quast, and the most experienced skippers and chief mates there present," and "to come to a conclusion and carry into effect the sailing for the said island," always provided that the Company's commercial interests would allow of two ships of the Company's fleet then present in Japan, being temporarily used for this purpose. Already at this stage of the undertaking the Supreme Government at Batavia designated Commander Quast, who was in Japan at the time, to be the leader of the intended expedition, while

[1] Cartas del Virrey de Na Espana a S. M., March 18 and April 7, 1611.]

[2] The "relacion" is printed in the Coleccion, before-mentioned, Vol. VIII, p. 101-109.--Cf. NAVARRETE, Bibliotheca, p. 710. On my application for a copy of the journal mentioned by NAVARRETE, I was informed on the part of the director of the Depósito Hidrografico at Madrid, that the said journal was not preserved there, and that NAVARRETE must have made a mistake.]

[3] Real Cedula al Virrey de Na Espana, December 2, 1613.]

[4] Carta del Virrey de Na Espana a S. M., May 22, 1614.]

[5] Cf. Carta del Capn Gral de Filipinas, sent to Spain, dated July 13, 1740; and Verstegen's report.]

[6] See the instructions for the expedition under command of Quast, dated June 1, 1639, to be discussed infra.]

[7] Letter from the G.-G. and Counc. to the "Heeren XVII," of January 4, 1636.]

[8] DE JONGE, Opkomst, V, p. CXII.]

Verstegen himself, who was then likewise staying there, would have to join the enterprise, "in order to take due minutes of all incidents and discoveries." Besides, Vincent Romeijn, a Dutchman residing at Nangasaki[1], who in Mexico had witnessed the preparations for Vizcaino's voyage, to whom Verstegen was mainly indebted for his information, and who had expressed his willingness to join an eventual Dutch expedition to the gold- and silver-lands[2], Vincent Romeijn was to be requested to put his services at the Company's disposal on this occasion.

But the expedition was destined not to take place this time. On September 24, 1636 Coeckebacker convened the Council of the Dutch factory at Firando, among them also Quast and certain expert sailors; and it was "unanimously" resolved that "the voyage of discovery should be put off until further orders, awaiting a better opportunity and more effectual means, and should not be undertaken during the present season"[3]. The leading motive of this resolution was the consideration that the Company's ships could be more profitably employed elsewhere. But there was also a weighty material obstacle. The Governor-General and Councillors, in deciding that the said enterprise should start from Japan, had placed themselves on the stand-point taken up by the Spaniards when they were arranging for Vizcaino's expedition. In Coeckebacker's instructions, the Governor-General and Councillors state, in greater detail than is found in Verstegen's report, which may have been supplemented by verbal information, that the expedition had started from Japan, "because this country cannot be reached or touched at, except by sailing from east to west(!) in about 36° Northern Latitude, thus utilising the westerly trade-winds, which in this latitude prevail during the greater part of the year." Quast and the other nautical experts did not share this view, and in a meeting of the council, held September 24, 1636, they expressed an opinion that the enterprise "would hardly be feasible, when starting from Japan," at least not at this time of year, because "it would be very difficult for the ships to reach the said latitude, on account of the easterly winds which were asserted to blow continually there about this season." Nay, even if the voyage should be successful, it would prove impossible, in returning, "to accomplish the passage to Firando, on account of the north-westerly winds." In their opinion it would be far better to take for starting-point either Formosa, or the Moluccas, or Cape Espiritu Santo, in the north-east of Samar, one of the Philippine Islands[4].

The Supreme Government at Batavia took due note of this advice, and in a letter to the Board of Directors of the East India Company, of December 28, 1636, expressed its intention to act up to it. It would seem, that, apart from this, less sanguine reports about the mysterious islands had reached Batavia[5], at least the Governor-General and Councillors further state in the said letter, that "this opportunity did not seem to be quite so promising as it had been represented by current report."

As in 1636, also in the following year the project was not yet carried into execution, owing to lack of fitting vessels. This obstacle once removed, the expedition could take place "without detriment to the customary trade, to which as a rule we give the preference," as we read in a letter from the Governor-General and Councillors of December 9, 1637[6] to the Board of Directors, whose interest in the matter had been roused[7]. The lukewarm tone which Van Diemen now adopts in speaking of the project, shows that his expectations were by no means sanguine. The stimulus to action had therefore to come from the mother-country this time.

For the Board of Directors of the East India Company were in hopes of great profits, profits so great indeed, that they might be expected to be sufficient to bear a large part in the defrayal of the

[1) Cf. pp. 189 and 180 of the Transactions of the Asiatic Society of Japan, XI. Yokohama, Meiklejohn, 1893; Het Begin ende Voortgangh der Vereenigde Nederlantsche Geoctroyeerde Oost-Indische Compagnie, II (1646), no. 21, p. 189.]

[2) According to Verstegen's "Remonstrance."]

[3) "Copia Resolutiën bij d' E. He. president Nicolaes Couckebacker ende den Raet t' sedert 3en Junii 1636 tot 29en October daervolgende gearresteert."]

[4) Cf. also a letter from Coeckebacker to Governor-General Van Diemen, of November 2, 1636.]

[5) My efforts to trace these have remained without success. But on p.32 of LEUPE'S Reize van Vries is mentioned not only Verstegen's "remonstrantie" (no. 5), but also (no. 4) a "vertoogh" of the same official "nopende 't ontdecken van de onbekende custen van Corea, Jeso en Japan, mitsgaders d' eylanden daer by Oosten gelegen." Perhaps this document would elucidate the question, But it is unknown to me.]

[6) The same motive for postponement is employed in their letter to the Board, of December 18, 1639.]

[7) Letter from the Board of Directors to the G.-G. and Counc., of September 24, 1636.]

steadily increasing administrative expenses, necessitated by the Dutch settlements in the East. "Your Worships have acted wisely"--we read in their letter to the Governor-General and Councillors, of September 16, 1638--"in giving your further attention to the discovery of the South(land), and the gold-bearing island, which would be of great use to the Company, in order in time to get over its heavy burdens, and come into the real enjoyment of the profits of the East India trade." Nor did they confine themselves merely to this declaration of their satisfaction. "We more and more find it to be desirable "--thus proceeds the said missive, in this way allowing us a glimpse into our ancestors' information about the north-east of Asia--"that efforts should be set on foot to explore especially the countries west and north of Japan, up to such longitude and latitude as shall be found to be at all feasible; to wit: the coasts and countries of "Choré"[1] and "Tartarien"--of which they had been urging the exploration at a much earlier period already[2]--to the end that, if, contrary to our hopes, the trade to Japan should prove less profitable in future, we might find some compensation in sending cargoes to Choré and to Tartary, these being large and thickly populated countries, which may be in want of many things. Corré likewise produces excellent and precious goods and commodities, which could take the place of the Chinese articles, and Tartary borders on the north of China, in 42 and 43°, where are to be found the best climates of the world, producing the most excellent and finest silks...and celebrated on this account among all Western merchants who of olden times were wont to visit these countries, and continue to frequent the same to this day; so that we entertain great hopes in respect of them. The coasts of Tartary are very wild and desolate to the eastward, and at a considerable distance from the wealthy provinces of the interior; but we make no doubt that a diligent investigation and cautious exploration, first of the sea-coasts, and afterwards of the state of affairs in the interior, will by degrees give us opportunities to attain our object. We hereby request Your Worships for this purpose to employ such serviceable yachts as you may have at hand, and particularly such persons as are intelligent and eager to make important discoveries, besides well-seen in navigation, in making soundings and in determining the exact height, longitude and latitude of all such places as they shall call at, and finally skilful in drawing up proper maps of the same."

This missive from the Board of Directors directly called forth the resolution of the Governor-General and Councillors of May 24, 1639, in which the expedition was decided upon. The dignitaries last mentioned state in this resolution, it is true, that they had "long been inclined to and bent on" the enterprise, "especially after the most recent information of the year 1635," when Verstegen's report had come to their knowledge; but they were now to carry it into execution, because the Board of Directors had given "urgent injunctions" about it, and ships could now be spared, "without detriment to more important interests." The flutes Engel and Graft--the latter most probably named after the well-known village in North-Holland[3]--were told off for the enterprise, as being best adapted for "those shallow seas." The command was entrusted to Commander Quast, who was ordered to take on board a cargo of sundry goods, viz. "various kinds of specie, and minerals of gold, silver, copper, tin, iron, spelter, together with divers woollens and silks, both European and Indian, etc., to be shown to the inhabitants of the lands to be discovered, in order to find out at first hand, whether they have any of the same in their own country, or are desirous of having them, thereby furthering the Company's object of lucrative commerce."

Quast, who was then cruising along the north-west coast of Java, in search of hostile Spanish and Portuguese ships, and of English and Danish vessels that might happen to have enemies or enemies' goods on board of them[4], was forthwith recalled[5], and on May 28 a resolution could be taken regarding the fitting-out of the two vessels, set apart for the voyage. Each of them was to be manned with "45 able-bodied and stout men, among them 5 soldiers, together 90 "eaters," and properly

[1] Here, and in subsequent quotations from old journals, etc. the names of places are left as spelled in the original.]

[2) Cf. their letter to the G.-G. and Counc., of December 18, 1628.]

[3) Cf. Letter from the "Heeren XVII" to the G.-G. and Counc., January 2, 1637, in which she is mentioned together with "de Rijp." If the conjecture in the text is right, it is plain that the English translation "Canal" is a mistake; this is found inter alia in JAMES BACKHOUSE WALKER, Abel Janszoon Tasman: His life and voyages. (Tasmania, Grahame, 1896), p. 12.]

[4) See the "ordre" given him, dated May 11, 1639, and the letters sent to him on May 16 and 18.]

[5) Resolution of the G.-G. and Counc., May 25, 1639.--Letter from the G.-G. and Counc. to Quast, May 26, 1639.]

victualled and armed for a period of 12 calendar months." Quast took "his official leave" on June 1, and got orders to put off to sea on the following morning[1]. The same date of June 1 is found on the "Instructions for Commander Matthijs Quast and the Ship's Council of the flutes Engel and Graft, destined for the discovery of the lands and islands east of Japan, together with the coasts and lands of Tartary and Corea, respectively situated north-west and south-west of the Japanese Empire aforesaid." Of this letter of instruction the rough copy was drawn up by Van Diemen himself[2], after repeated conferences "with the most noted and most expert skippers together with certain chief mates," then staying at Batavia. Van Diemen's cosignatories to this document were the members of the Council of India Philips Lucaszoon, Nicolaas Couckebacker, and Cornelis Van der Lijn. The first of these Councillors was director-general[3], i.e. the second in authority in the Council, and especially charged with the conduct of the Company's mercantile affairs[4]; Couckebacker was fully conversant with everything connected with our relations with Japan, and Cornelis Van der Lijn was afterwards to succeed Lucaszoon as director-general, and ultimately to become governor-general[5].

We may as well subjoin a few particulars about the men who constituted the council of the two ships. In the first place Quast was appointed "Commander and chief of the two flutes, and of the officers and men embarked in the same." He carried "the flag at the maintopmast" of the Engel, on board of which he made the voyage, while to him alone was reserved the right of convening the ship's council, in which he occupied the chair and had the casting vote in case of equality of votes. He was an excellent expert in navigation, and the confidence reposed in him by the Governor-General and Councillors was amply deserved. He was a native of Schiedam, and had served the Company for some years past, navigating the Japanese and Chinese seas. For those parts he had set out from Batavia in July 1635, as second in command of a fleet, and from the instructions he had received on this occasion[6], it is evident that Quast was " fully conversant" with those regions[7]; after his return he was, in May 1636, put at the head of a squadron with destination for Siam and Japan[8]. A second time returned to Batavia, he set sail for home, as we have seen higher up, in December 1636, together with Tasman, and with a recommendation to the Board of Directors from the Governor-General[9]; on October 1638, on the same day with Tasman, he again set foot on the soil of Java. After the termination of the voyage of discovery we are now discussing, he was, in 1640, appointed "equipage-master" at Batavia, in which capacity he had to supervise the wharves, and had the control of everything connected with the fitting-out of the Company's ships[10]. He was not to fill this important post for a long time: on the 12th of July 1641, he set sail for Goa in command of a fleet of ten sail, with orders to blockade this principal seat of the Portuguese power in the East. He died September 22 of the same year, of the consequences of a wound received in an action with a Portuguese vessel.

Abel Tasman, skipper in the Graft, was second in command. "In case of impotence or decease of commander Quast (which God in his mercy avert)"--we read in the instructions--"his place shall be taken by skipper Abel Jansen Tasman, whom we command in such case to be acknowledged and obeyed in the same way as his predecessor in office."

As skipper of the Engel we find Lucas Albertsen, who was already known as an expert sailor, and who in 1645 was to make a voyage of discovery to the north coast of Borneo[11]. The other

[1] Res. of the G.-G. and Counc., of June 1, 1639.]

[2] Res. of the G.-G. and Counc., of June 1, 1639.]

[3] Cf. Res. of the G.-G. and Counc., of September 25, 1635.]

[4] KLERK DE REUS, Überblick, pp. 96 ff.]

[5] Cf. Ress. of the G.-G. and Counc., Aug. 8, 1641-October 13, 1646.]

[6) Dated, July 26, 1635.]

[7) Cf. P. A. LEUPE, Mathijs Hendricksz. Quast voor Goa, 1641 (Bi-jdragen tot de taal-, land- en volkenkunde van Nederlandsch-Indie. Nieuwe Volgreeks, II; 1858), p. 313.]

[8) See the "instructions" of May 16, 1636.]

[9 By letter of December 28, 1636.]

[10 Cf. KLERK DE REUS, 1. c., pp. 106-107.]

[11) Cf. my Bouwstoffen, III, pp. 246 f.]

members of the Ship's Council were the sub-merchant Hendrik Steen, the chief mates Pieter Doedesen Cant, and Jan Minckessen, to-gether with "the Commander's secretary" Philips Schillemans, who was afterwards to serve the Company in Tonquin[1].

To us the chief interest of the instructions lies in what they teach us respecting the geographical knowledge of the Netherlanders in the middle of the seventeenth century, and in the indications they give regarding the course to be followed by the ships. The main point to be observed is, that "the courses will have to be directed in such wise," that "when arrived in 36 and 37° northern latitude," the ships "shall have fully reached the longitude of East-Japan (without coming upon Japan itself)." "In order to get into the South Sea, three routes" were open according to the notions of the time. One of these had still been suggested by Governor-General Hendrik Brouwer[2]. "In order to get so much the higher to windward," Brouwer had suggested the idea of taking the course north of Borneo, Celebes and Djilolo, in order in this way to get into the Pacific Ocean by sailing south of the Philip-pines. Apart from the danger of navigating these seas, which were little if at all known to the Dutch at that time, the season was now too far advanced for taking this course, and still covering "so great a dis-tance" from the north-western extremity of Borneo to the east of Celebes, and then reaching the Pacific in fitting time. The second plan, viz. to take the ships' course between Luzon and Formosa, was like-wise disapproved of, "because it was feared that it would be exceedingly difficult to double the eastern extremity of Japan, when starting from the north-east point of the island of Manilha or Luton, on account of the south-east winds prevailing in the South Sea." There only remained the third route, which was accordingly prescribed in the instructions. The ships were ordered to pass eastward of the islands of Oentoeng Djawa (Amsterdam, etc.), "sailing close to the wind," next to take their course east of Banka "to shorten the voyage," and thence to proceed on their way "until they had got to about ten miles east of

Pulo Capas" (near the peninsula of Malacca, in slightly more than 5° N.L.). From there they were ordered to cross north-east by east to the bay of Manila, and while so doing they were instructed to reconnoitre the partly unknown sea west of Paragoa (Palúan) and east of the Paracels, which latter appellation must at that time have had a wider meaning than it has in the charts of our days, since these islands and reefs are stated to extend much farther south[3] than they are found to do in modern charts. Before, however, coming to the bay of Manila the ships were to steer for the north-west point of Mindoro, then to take their course north of this island and south of Luzon, through the two straits of Santo Bernardino, in order to reach cape Espiritu Santo at the north-west point of Samar, and from there to "run" into the Pacific. This was the route--Spanish charts were accordingly provided--which the Spanish ships, in sailing from Manila to Acapulco, were accustomed to follow, "the which vessels, usually sailing from the bay of Manilha about the middle of August, turn to the north at Cabo de Spirito Santo, hauling close to the wind, keep to windward of Japan, and make their passage with the aid of the north-west winds prevailing there"[4]. Where the large and unwieldy ships of their enemies usually succeeded in making their passage, the lighter and faster Dutch sailers could hardly be expected to fail of their object. The ships were, however, seriously warned to be on their guard, and keep clear of the bay of Manila and Luzon itself, that hostile encounters with the Spaniards might be avoided.

The course subsequently to be taken, is also indicated with such precision as was possible in the absence of sufficient data..."Having without accidents got into the South Sea past Cape Spirito Sancto,"--the instructions go on to say--"you will cross, sailing close to the wind, keeping a north-east or north-east by north course, and when thus doing you shall have got unto 36° N.L.,...you will have to run on nearly 40 miles east of Japan. But before sailing into the said latitude, you will, while losing the south-east trade-wind, meet with variable western and north-western winds, which you

[1] Cf. Resolution of the G.-G. and Counc., of July 1650.]

[2] Cf. the MS. "Beschrijvinge van de Oost Indische Compagnie," by its "advocate" (secretary or clerk) P. VAN DAM (1701), II, 1, pp. 279-289; and letter from Brouwer to Van Diemen, March 31, 1636.]

[3] Cf., for instance, the map of "India Orientalis" (pp. 373-374) in the atlas of MERCATOR and HONDIUS, ed. 1634; a MS. map of the northern part of the South Sea, drawn by JOAN BLAEU, with the date 1687 (Hague State. Arch.); No. 9 of Vol. I of the MS. atlas by G. DE HAAN.]

[4) Cf. DE MORGA, P. 355, 356.]

will avail yourselves of as occasion shall serve, trying to get between 37 and 38° to the north of the line equinoctial...It would be a good thing if you could succeed in reconnoitring the eastern extremity of Japan, but you should be very careful not to fall off to the south side of the said country, unless, having got between 28 and 32° N.L., the winds should become so favourable that you could come within sight of Japan without risks or delay in your voyage, in which case you would have a better and surer chance of getting to a distance of from 380 to 400 miles, by steering due east...It would not be strange, if in these regions (before you shall have covered a hundred miles in an eastern direction) you should discover certain islands, the which you will not pass by or leave out of sight, before having visited and explored the same.

The distance to the island intended to be discovered, has been reported to us to be about four hundred, that is to say Spanish miles, so that, when according to your best estimation you shall have got to upwards of 400 miles east of the east coast of Japan, without perceiving land (which we trust will turn out otherwise), you will not on this account lose either your wonted patience or your courage, but will run on due east for another two hundred miles, over and above the 400 miles hereinbefore mentioned, in hopes of coming upon profitable and promising lands, which it may please God to grant. But if, contrary to expectation, you should not discover either land or islands within the distance above referred to, we hereby command Your Worships, wind and weather permitting, to return, taking your course round the north of Japan, in order to explore the coasts of Tartary and China, together with the country of 'Corera' (sic!), and to find out what sort of profitable traffic might in those parts be engaged in for the benefit of the General Company. But since we may assume almost with certainty, that such return will prove impracticable, owing to the western and north-western winds, which in the said climes blow with great violence for the greater part of the year, we shall not enter into any ampler discussion of this matter, at the same time recommending the said plan to Your Worships' better judgment and experience, and leaving the rest to the chances of wind and weather.

In case, then, of contrary winds preventing you, when you shall have got as far as 600 miles east of Japan, from returning to Batavia by way of the north of Japan, along the coasts of Tartary, Corea and China, and via Taijowan (Formosa); and of the health of your crews, together with your stock of fresh water and victuals, allowing of the same, Your Worships will be free to run on for two hundred miles more and upwards, even as far as the coast of West India, making such exploration along the coast of the last mentioned continent, as the condition of your men and ships shall admit of, and afterwards endeavouring to get south again into the region of the south-east trade-winds; by the aid of which you will sail due west, making heedful inspection of the lands you shall meet on your way, and taking your course by way of the Ladrones, or Thieves' Islands, with a view to reconnoitring and visiting the said lands and islands, more especially such as are situated between 11½ and 14° Northern Latitude, in order to find out the exact rendezvous place of the Spanish silver-ships going from the West-Indies to Manilha (which are wont to call at certain of the said islands)[1], to the end that, opportunity serving, the Company's ships may be enabled...to cruise with the more hope of success in search of that rich booty.

And seeing that it is impossible for us to make any well-founded conjecture as to the time and the season of the year, when you will arrive at the Ladrones by the route herein prescribed, we cannot therefore give Your Worships any precise orders, whether you had better return to Batavia either via Japan, Tayowan, between the Philippine Islands and along the Moluccas, or in the other case round the north of Celebes and Borneo...

... The object we have in view, is...the discovery of the lands or islands situated in 37½° Northern Latitude, in the longitude of the eastern coast of Japan, at about 400 miles' distance from the latter country; and Your Worships will accordingly endeavour to get into the said latitude to windward of Japan, so as to be able to reach the said countries with an easterly course.

Yet having taken this matter into further consideration, and having been apprized by persons who have been residing in Japan, and having gathered from Spanish books and the maps contained in the

[1) Cf. DE MORGA, pp. 353 f.]

same, that there are sundry islands situated to the east of Japan at a distance of 100, 150 and 200 miles from there, between 30 and 36 degrees north of the line equinoctial;

item, that it is likewise considered certain that Japanese sailors have in their ships brought silver to Japan from the said islands, as also, that the two islets which in the Spanish charts are laid down between 35 and 36°, are called by the name of Armeneti[1] and Rico de Plata, that is to say "rich in silver;" therefore, and to the end that no chances of profit may be neglected in this affair, we have thought fit to direct Your Worship and Council at the same time, so to shape your course from Spirito Sancto that the aforesaid islands may eventually be made, and if possible discovered; the rather since we assume that, having met with the said two islets, about 200 Spanish miles[2] to the east of Japan, between 35 and 36 degrees N.L., this will not prevent you from sailing about 2 degrees more to the north, and attaining our object in this latitude. In case this should be effected, and the large island (which in the said Spanish map is laid down in 30 (38?) degrees, about 50 miles more westward than Rico de Plata, and is a little more than thirty miles in length from south to north) should have been reached and explored, we opine that Your Worship will hardly be able from there to make the aforesaid two islands in 35 and 36 degrees; which you will have to take into proper consideration, regulating yourselves by wind and weather, always reflecting that we shall be pleased to have both these lands made by the ships, but that Rico de Plata should have the preference..."

The vague terms of these instructions leave room for a voyage of discovery through the whole of the north part of the Pacific. These vague indications at the same clearly show how very inaccurate, incomplete and fragmentary were the notions then entertained respecting this ocean and the islands with which it is studded. This is expressly admitted in the instructions: the "intention" of the Governor-General and Councillors is in them set forth only as regards "the main points." "As for the other points," these dignitaries confidently "recommended and entrusted" them to the "zeal, vigilance and good management" of Quast and his subalterns. In order to stimulate this zeal, this vigilance, this good management, they held out the promise of rewards, if the expedition should prove successful, while at the same time premiums (afterwards fixed at 6[3], and still later at 10[4] guilders) were promised to those "who should first descry unknown lands, shores, and shoals or shallows." Stress is besides laid on the expediency of " keeping the experience gained a strict secret," with an eye to the watchful rivalry of jealous competitors[5].

The expedition, then, set out on the second day of June 1639, and the particulars of its progress that have been preserved, enable us to follow from day to day the certainly monotonous and constantly repeated experiences of those who took part in it. Besides certain missives of the time, in which reference is made to the enterprise, the Dutch State Archives at the Hague preserve the hitherto unpublished "Journal or daily record of the Worshipful Commander Matthijs Quast, sailing by command of the Worshipful Lords Governor-General and Councillors of India with the flute-ships Engel and Graft, in order to discover and explore the gold- and silver-bearing islands situated to the east, in about 37½° Northern Latitude, on which undertaking we pray God Almighty to give his blessing, to the best advantage, benefit and furtherance of the General Company. Amen." This journal, extending from June 2 to November 24, 1639, and, with the annexed drawings of surveys and reconnoitrings of the coasts, numbering 72 folio pages[6], was kept "on board the flute-ship Engel." This plain statement is subversive of the surmise[7] that the journal should have been Tasman's work.

[1] Cf. supra, "Armenio."]

[2] Cf. the "relacion" of Vizcaino, 1. c., p. 190.]

[3] Resolution of the Plenary Council (joint council of the two ships), of June 6, 1639.]

[4] Id., August 31, 1639.]

[5] Cf. Resolution of the G.-G. and Counc., of May 24, 1639. The instructions as to the mode of proceeding when new lands were discovered, the manner of mapping them out, etc.; the regulations concerning the diet of the men, etc. etc., highly interesting as they are, are omitted here, since on the whole they are identical with those contained in Tasman's instructions for his voyages in 1642 and 1644, which will be found further on.]

[6] PH. VON SIEBOLD, in Journal de la Haye of December 30, 1842, is in error as regards the number of MS. pages.]

[7] VON SIEBOLD, l. c.]

Of course a journal was also kept on board the Graft[1], but this has not come down to us. The surveys and reconnoitrings appended to Quast's ship's journal are highly praised by the learned Japanist[2] PH. VON SIEBOLD, who was in a position to compare them with observations of his own[3]. We get a welcome complement to the information contained in the journal, in the resolutions of the Ship's Council, taken on board the Engel, and in those decided upon by the joint Council of the two ships, the so-called Plenary Council. Of these the State Archives at the Hague preserve a copy, extending to 31 folio pages, made on board the Breda, the vessel in which Quast returned from Formosa to Batavia after the termination of the expedition. The resolutions of the Ship's Council on board the Engel have not been preserved; which is also the case as regards the chart, drawn up in the course of the voyage, and sent over from Batavia to the Netherlands, January 8, 1640[4]. But on the other hand we possess another chart of a slightly later date. This chart has been prepared under Tasman's eyes in Japan at the close of the year last mentioned by Arend Dierckszoon, and was despatched to Batavia, November 20[5]. The heading of this chart mentions "two plane-charts "[6], one of which seems to be lost[7]. The other, which has been preserved, and of which a reproduction is subjoined, is highly noteworthy, because it sets forth, not only the results of the voyage itself, but also what the leaders of the expedition gathered from the chart put into their hands by the Batavia authorities; in other words, what the Netherlanders at Batavia knew about those regions at the time of its setting-out. We are thus enabled to see at a glance the corrections which the Dutch thought themselves justified in introducing into the charts as the result of this voyage[8]. The chart we are now discussing, was in 1842 penes Jacob Swart, next came into the possession of Prince Henry of the Netherlands[9], and finally, in 1880, rejoined the archival documents of which it forms part in the State Archives at the Hague[10]).

During the first weeks the voyage[11] did not follow the plan prescribed in the instructions. After passing east of Banka, it was resolved to steer for " Poulo Lauro," near the peninsula of Malacca, in about 2° 20' N.L.[12]. The motives which led to this decision[13], again show, how little care was in those days bestowed on the fitting-out of the Company's ships, even in cases in which they were about to start on an arduous and perillous enterprise. The said island had, namely, to be called at, "considering the necessities of our vessels, and principally of the flute "t Gracht,' the latter

[1] Cf. Missive of the G.-G. and Counc. to the "Heeren XVII," of January 8, 1640, and the "memorie" in LEUPE'S Reize van Vries p. 32, no. 8.--But the "register" of the papers sent over from Batavia to the Netherlands, January 8, 1640, only mentions the "copia journael (not journals) en resolutiën." Perhaps the journal of the Graft was never sent to the Netherlands. In the Inventaris van 's Lands Archief to Batavia, by J. A. VAN DER CHUS (Batavia, Landsdrukkery 1882), too, I have found no mention of documents relating to the Graft.]

[2] See Levensbericht van Jhr. Dr. Philip Franz Von Siebold door T. C. L. WUNMALEN (Levensberichten der afgestorvene medeleden van de Maatschappij der Nederlandsche Letterkunde. Bijlage tot de Handelingen van 1871, pp. 265-288).]

[3] VON SIEBOLD, Entdeckungen, p. 60.]

[4] "Register" of the papers, sent over from Batavia to the Netherlands, January 8, 1840, and the "Memorie" in LEUPE'S Reize van Vries, p. 32,. no. 20.--The Missive from the G.-G. and Counc. to the "Heeren XVII," of January 8, 1640, mentions "charts," the register only speaks of the "origi-

nal chart of the discovery made." VON SIEBOLD is in error as to the charts (Journal de la Haye, Dec. 3o, 1842; Entdeckungen, p. 61).]

[5] As appears from a "memorandum" of missives sent over, etc., of the said date.]

[6] So does the "memorandum."]

[7] Cf., however, VON SIEBOLD, Entdeckungen, p. 61. He says, that the other chart has been published in the atlas of Johannes Van Keulen and there entitled "Nieuwe Afteekening van de Philippynse eylanden geleegen in de Oost-Indische Zee, tusschen Formosa en Borneo." (Cf. note 9 on the following page). I believe this to be a mistake, and Van Keulen's map to have nothing to do wits the chart lost. For Van Keulen's chart contains a great many Dutch names of localities in the Philippines. But a chart to be discussed later on in this book, drawn by Tasman of September 8, 1644, on which part of the Philippines is found represented, does not show a single Dutch name. If Tasman had known any Dutch names in the Philippines, he would of course have made use of them, and not have inscribed Spanish names only in his chart. We must therefore needs conclude that in 1644 he was not acquainted with any Dutch names there. These must therefore be of later date, and cannot possibly figure in a chart which would belong to the year 1639.]

[8] VON SIEBOLD has utilised them in the charts, appended to his Entdeckungen (Cf. p. 61 of his book).]

[9] See Von SIEBOLD in Journal de la Haye, December 30, 1842.--Cf. JACOB SWART in Verhandelingen en berichten betrekkelijk het Zeewezen. Nieuwe Volgorde, III (1843), p. 239. The latter's conjecture as to the origin of the chart, thus turned out to be erroneous.]

[10] Report of the Principal Keeper of the State Archives for 1880, p. 4.]

[11] In the sequel I follow the journal, unless otherwise stated.]

[12] Poeloe Aour in J. BLABU (1687); Poeloe Laur in the map of Sumatra in VALENTIJN'S Volume V (1726); Poeloe Auor in in DE HAAN, I, No. 7; Aor in STIELER.]

[13] Resolution of the Plenary Council, June 6, 1639.]

vessel being poorly provided with firewood and water, and wholly destitute of ballast, deficiencies which will have to be supplied before we can carry into due execution our destined voyage with the best security and without imminent peril." The said recruiting-place was made on the 9th of June, the ships having passed east of the Riouw and Lingga groups. Water, firewood and ballast were taken on board, but there was little contact with the natives. The sailors, coming ashore, "found all the houses empty and the inmates fled." The few whom they conversed with, gave as reason of this conduct that the natives dreaded a hostile visit from the Acheenese "armada." On June 13

they weighed anchor, and bent their course for Poeloe Timon[1] in 3°
N.L. Contrary to the clause of the instructions which directed them to
make Poeloe Kapas, and thence to cross towards Manila, it was resolved thus early already, ("since the Governor-General and
Councillors had indeed left the decision about the course to be taken,
mainly to the experience and good management of the skippers and
mates") "in order to avoid needless sailing," to steer north-east in order
to make for the Philippines[2]. They reached the Philippines later than
they thought they had a right to expect "according to the logbook and
the computations of the skippers and Mates," who "in their charts already sailed past islands," which in reality they had not yet reached[3].

On the 24th of June, however, they had "the islets lying off
Manilla," to the north-east of them. Again the prescribed course was
departed from: for Quast and Tasman had each for himself come to the
conclusion, that, since owing to the south-west wind it was hardly
practicable to sail round the south of Luzon, the route north of Luzon,
between this island and Formosa, would be far preferable. The latter
course was accordingly decided on. Even thus early in the voyage the
"Gracht" was in so wretched a condition, that she could only with
great difficulty keep up with the Engel, while the frequent rains "began
to affect" the crews. Again the insufficiency of the charts they had got
along with them, was clearly proved: the position of Luzon turned out
to be wrongly indicated, and had to be corrected in the charts they had
on board, and on the "ruled paper this day[4] prepared for this express
purpose." They doubled Cape Bojeador and Cape Engano, and
mapped out the islands north of Luzon. This time also, it is constantly
seen that the voyagers are in a region that is as good as unknown to
them. Fortunately they reached the eastern coast of Luzon, not without
some risk of being found out by the natives who came alongside of
Tasman's ship, led by a Spanish priest, a danger from which they escaped only by passing themselves off as Englishmen, bound on a
voyage from Malacca to Manila. This priest, belonging to "the order of
St. John," resided in " the island of Babugynes[5], with us (then?) known
as the island of Amsterdam"[6]. Here the Spaniards had built two mo-
nasteries, whose only inmates were native Christians. The inhabitants
of this and the neighbouring islands traded in "all sorts of cottons and
other small wares," which they carried to Mexico themselves (in Spanish vessels?), or which the Chinese fetched from there in their ships.
The padre, who was the only Spaniard in the island, told the voyagers
that it was inhabited by about 3000 "mesticos and natives." The Spaniards had another settlement in one of the neighbouring islands, and

on this occasion the Dutch also came into contact with a Spaniard residing there[7]. After doubling Cape Engano the ships passed along the
east coast of Luzon as close inshore as they were able, and as they
ventured to do on account of the danger of being discovered by the
Spaniards. In a few places on the coast only, they tried to cast anchor
in order to take in water and refreshments, on which occasions they
came into little, if any contact with the natives, who on their part ti-
midly kept aloof, when the strangers landed on their coast. On the 9th
of July the ships came to anchor at a point, which must be between 17°
33' and 16° 54' according to the latitude computed on board the Engel[8], and in 17° 20'

[1] J. BLAEU (1687) has Timaon; VALENTIJN has Poeloe Tayman; DE
HAAN, Timahon; STIELER, Tioman.]

[2] Resolution of the Plenary Council, of June 13, 1639.]

[3] Resolution of the Ship's Council in the Engel, June 21, 1639.]

[4] June 26.]

[5] One of Babuyan Islands]

[6] Journal, July 1.

[7] Cf. these statements concerning the results of Spanish missionary work
with what DE MORGA (p. 287) had to write only a few decades earlier,
viz. that as yet no converts had been made in those islands.]

[8] I have in my text constantly employed these longitudes and latitudes to
facilitate reference to the chart.--Cf. especially the paper of W. VAN
BEMMELEN printed infra, and his inaugural dissertation, De Isogonen in
de XVIIde en XVIIde eeuw (Utrecht, Van Druten, 1893), pp. 25-26.]

according to the chart; this point is sometimes found mentioned by the name of Quast's watering-place[1]. Leaving this spot, the
ships weighed anchor on July 10, and set sail in a south-east by east
direction, with which the actual voyage of discovery in the Pacific
Ocean had begun.

In the chart that has come down to us, the courses followed are
marked day by day. The limits prescribed for the expedition in the instructions, were reached, even overstepped. Only that part of the
mandate, that bore on the further exploration of "Tartary, Coerea and
China," had to be left unfulfilled, owing to the unsatisfactory condition
of the ships as well as the crews. The voyage was an uninterrupted
roving about the ocean, covering hundreds of miles, for some twenty
long weeks: a weary sail without anything to relieve its dreary mono-
tony. In a few rare cases islands were called at, several times also

apparent signs of land were descried, which after all proved disappointments; the outfit of the ships was more and more found to be utterly insufficient; violent storms harassed the ill-equipped vessels, and especially from the month of August death went its rounds in the ships, and found a ready prey in the many sailors laid up with illness, for whom there were hardly any refreshments available. How great was the distress we learn from the resolution of the Plenary Council consisting of the ship's officers of the two vessels, dated October 25, 1639. On the 15th of the same month, when they became aware that the search for the far-famed islands would prove fruitless this time, it had been resolved "to sail to windward of Japan, and undertake the discovery and exploration of Tartary and Corea." Some ten days later, however, the further execution of this plan had to be given up, and the motives for this change are stated as follows in the resolution above mentioned:

"Whereas at this present both our ships and crews are in very bad and dangerous condition, viz. that owing to continuous rolling the ships have sprung dreadful leaks, and are sorely in need of fresh rigging and caulking; item that the Engel has her bowsprit broken, the 'Gracht' can hardly bear up with her 'fished' masts any longer, and both the ships are leaky all over, to such an extent that in dirty weather the pumps must be constantly kept going; while on the other hand all our carpenters are laid up with illness; in the Engel there have been up to now eleven deaths and 20 cases of illness, item in the 'Gracht' 11 deaths and 18 men ill, who would all of them seem to be at death's door; and those who can just keep on their legs, with whom with God's aid we contrive to manage the ship, are not free from sea disease (seeing that in four months and upwards they have not tasted any refreshments), but sorely suffer from every change of weather, and feel their forces decrease day by day."

It was resolved, if no other land was met with on the way, to seek at Formosa the means for recruiting crews and ships, which they were so urgently in want of.

Commanders and crews alike must therefore have breathed again, when on the 23rd of November Formosa was sighted, and on the next day the Dutch colours were seen floating from the fortress of Zeelandia, the chief Dutch settlement in this island.

It is well-known, that in spite of the greatest watchfulness possible, and the sturdy perseverance of officers and men, the real object of the expedition was not attained: the important discoveries that had been hoped for, were not made. So far the Governor-General and

Councillors could say with perfect justice that the enterprise had "remained fruitless"[2]. But it was by no means destitute of practical results. The instructions clearly show how slight in those days was the knowledge of the Netherlanders as regards the northern part of the Pacific; the daily journal and the resolutions of the Ship's Councils are constantly complaining of the great inaccuracy of the maps, and of the discrepancies between the Dutch maps and the Spanish ones[3]. Now the expedition under Quast and Tasman furnished data, so far as their crude instruments allowed of this, to introduce corrections as regards the true position of the continents and islands then known, and already mapped out. These corrections, like their other observations, may be called excellent, if the instruments and means then available for navigators are taken into proper consideration. To Quast and Tasman, therefore, fully applies what La Pérouse once declared of the Netherlanders of the middle of the seventeenth century: "Il parait

[1] "Nieuwe Afteekening van de Phillipynse eylanden" in De nieuwe groote lichtende Zee-fakkel door JAN DE MARRE en JOANNES VAN KEULEN. VI. t'. Amsterdam by Joannes Van Keulen, 1753.--Cf. also P. MELVILL, VAN CARNBÉE in Moniteur des Indes-Orientales et Occidentales, 1848-1849, p. 392.]

[2] Missive to "Heeren XVII," January 8, 1640.]

[3] See e.g. Ress. of July 25, and August 3, 1639.]

que les Hollandais cherchaient a compenser ce désavantage (des méthodes d'observation très grossières) par les soins les plus minutieux sur l'estime des routes et l'exactitude des relèvements"[1]. The share which Tasman had in all this, is shown inter alia by the note in the chart. While, therefore, the northern part of the Pacific and the regions bordering on it to westward, were surveyed with greater accuracy, the expedition also taught other things that were utterly unknown to the Dutch of those days.

As early as the beginning of the voyage, they were in a position to note in the chart "a round, high-lying island, and another somewhat lower, unknown to the charts," situated to the north of Banca. North of Luzon, where they were staying in the latter end of June, they had, as we have seen higher up, to reconnoitre a region as good as totally unknown to them. We read in the journal under date of July 17: "In the morning, we observed numerous birds, among others certain arrow-tailed ducks ("pylsteerten"), with arrow-shaped tails pointed like the quills of a porcupine, .which made great noise and emitted loud shrieks in flying. The wind gradually veered round to the Southwest. We still had [it had been very rough weather for a couple of days] very heavy seas from various quarters, but chiefly from the north-west and south-east, so that our ships rolled violently...About 3 o'clock in the afternoon, when we were engaged in reading a sermon, the outlook from the maintopmast called out that there was a shoal ahead, about a mile north-east of us, on which there were exceedingly violent breakers...As far as we could discern with the naked eye, we found the same to be situated East-south-east and West-north-west, 1½ mile in length, and tapering to a very narrow slip to the south and north; by estimation it lies in 20° 38' N.L. and in 31° 6' longitude, reckoning east of the meridian of the centre of Poulo Timon[2], or North-east + 1/8 more easterly of Cape Spirito Sancto, at about 178 miles' distance from the same; and we named it Engel's shoal." This was presumably a "shoal" which was evidently not marked in the charts known to the Dutch of those days: for it is not mentioned as then already known in the chart of this voyage, reproduced in this work. It has long been[3], and is still known by the name of Parece (Parede?) Vela, at the present day also by the name of Douglas, after the navigator who in 1789 again sighted and described it[4].

A few days later the Journal gives the information following: "On Wednesday, July 20...we kept our course due North-east, and on all sides observed numerous gulls, as also sundry arrow-tailed mergansers or didappers ("pylsteerten"), which squealed and shrieked a good deal. Towards noon...we took no latitude...At about 6 glasses in the afternoon we saw a high-lying island to luffward about 4 miles to North-east by east, and East-north-east, ahead of us, and another somewhat smaller about one mile to the west of the first, which from afar looked like the roof of a farm-barn...The larger island is very high and steep; we gave to it the name of High Gull-Island (Hooge Meeuwen-eiland), and estimated it to lie in 25° 3' N.L. and 36° Longitude.

On Thursday July 21...we kept our course North-east by north, and saw a great many birds; at about one glass after early breakfast we saw land North-east by east of us, at 6 or 7 miles' distance, tolerably high, the outline broken with many hills; on coming nearer we found many small islets scattered about it; at noon we took the latitude of 26° 26'...according to our estimation, these islands are situated in 26° 38' N.L. and in 37° 8' E. Long., and have thus been laid down in our charts; in the afternoon we descried to the North-east another and second country; to both of them we gave names, to wit, to the first the name of Engel's Island, and to the second that of Gracht's Island. At sunset Engel's Island lay South-east by east, at 4 miles, and Gracht's Island North-east and North-east, by-north, at 3 miles from us; we could not observe any current, or take any soundings, nor could we discern any fitting anchoring-place for ships; the said islands are situated at about 4¾ miles from each other, South by east + ½ point more easterly, and North by west + ½ point more westerly.

On Friday July 22 at daybreak we saw to the North-north-west at about a mile's distance, and again in the same direction at about 1½ mile more to the north of us, certain cliffs and reefs in two

[1] MILET-MUREAU, Voyage de La Pérouse, III (1797), p. 113; cf. p. 94.]

[2] A little more than 104° (104° 15' according to VON SIEBOLD, Journal de la Haye, January 9/10, 1843), E. Long. from Greenwich.]

[3] Cf. Chart 67 in La Pérouse's Atlas.]

[4] Cf. VON SIEBOLD, Journal de la Haye, January 9, 1843. This author erroneously places it in 137° 10' E. Long. Greenwich, instead of 136° 10'. See also his Geschichte der Entdeckungen, p. 147, Anmerkung II. Cf. also P. MELVILL VAN CARNBEE in Moniteur des Indes-Orientales et Occidentales, 1848-1849, pp. 392-393. The Atlas du voyage de La Pérouse (No. 43) places it more to the north than Quast (20° 38'), and Douglas (2o° 37').]

groups near each other, appearing above the water, to which we gave the name of Gracht's Cliffs. We had the northern extremity of Gracht's Island south by west of us, at 3 miles and upwards distance; so that the said island and the cliffs aforementioned are found to be situated North and North by west, item South and South by east, at about 4 or 5 miles' distance from each other. At noon we were in 27° 40' latitude, with Gracht's Island about 9 miles South-west by south, and the northernmost cliffs 5 miles, the southernmost 4½ do. West to South of us ..."

If we compare this part of the Journal with the chart reproduced here, and the note given on it, it would seem that Quast and Tasman took the High Gull's Island, Engel's and Graft's Island to be the same islands which in the "old map, put into their hands by the Company," were known by the names of "I. delarto, Des Colunos, and De Sierta," together with one unnamed island. They did not, therefore, look upon them as newly discovered. The difference in situation is, however, considerable enough to make us hesitate to unconditionally embrace this opinion also at the present day, if such an opinion should have at all found acceptance. For in the map here reproduced, the islands last mentioned are found between 24° and 20° 30', which agrees pretty closely with the latitudes in which in XVII and XVIII century charts Isla Desierta, Dos Colunas, Una Coluna, and a second Desierta are laid down. It is clear that the maker of the map was greatly puzzled by the Spanish names, and has consequently given them a wrong spelling, which for the matter of that is the case with the majority of the maps of the time. These islands bear the names of "I. decerto, Dos Colunes and Una Coluna"[1], in a highly interesting MS. chart[2], prepared by order of the "Heeren XVII," by the cartographer Isaac de Graaff[3] at the latter end of the seventeenth century. In this chart, which has been drawn up with the aid of data, furnished by older charts of the East India Company, and in which are laid down the results of the well-known voyage of discovery, made in 1643 under command of Maarten Gerritszoon Vries, who utilised the results of the voyage of Quast and Tasman, we find to the north-west of these islands, the "Quats" (sic) Islands, between 29° and the group above mentioned. Although , the latitudes do not precisely agree with those found in the chart, here reproduced, of Quast's voyage of 1639, yet there is no doubt that the name of "Quats Islands" is meant to denote the group seen by our voyagers from the 20th to the 22nd of July. Accordingly, the Company's cartographers of the XVII century did most decidedly distinguish the islands just mentioned from the Desiertas and the Colunas. It is not to be determined with absolute certainty what islands in the charts of our day are to be identified with the latter group. There is every likelihood that, at least as regards the three northernmost of these islands, we have to think of the group, at present[4] known by the name of the Volcano Islands. Next, the High Gull's Island, discovered by Quast and Tasman, is most probably the island known to modern charts[5] by the name of Arzobispo, a supposition which does not clash with the indubitable fact, that the Graft's and Engel's Islands together with the Graft Cliffs constitute the group, now styled the Bonin Islands (Bonin-Sima). We must leave undecided the question, whether these islands were likewise known to the Spaniards[6], though it may be assumed as highly probable that they were: at all events, if they were known to the Spaniards, Quast and Tasman were either unaware of this circumstance, or quite insufficiently acquainted with it, so that to these commanders belongs the unassailable honour of having assigned to the said group a place in the chart, which may be pronounced highly correct, if we consider the imperfect instruments at their disposal[7].

[1] The fourth islet is not found in the chart. There was, indeed, no room on it for the 20th degree N.L.]

[2] No. 285 in the Inventaris der verzameling kaarten, berustende in het Rijks-Archief, I ('s-Gravenhage, Nijhoff, 1867), by P. A. LEUPE --Printed in VON SIEBOLD'S Entdeckungen, V, D.]

[3) See LEUPE, Inventaris, pp. VI, VII, and No. 285.]

[4) See ADOLF STIELER'S Hand-atlas.]

[5) See ADOLF STIELER'S Hand-atlas.]

[6) Cf. TIELE-VIVIEN DE SAINT-MARTIN, p. 66; VON SIEBOLD in LEUPE'S edition of Reize van Maarten Gerritsz. Vries, p. 268.]

[7) Cf. with the above the elaborate discussion in VON SIEBOLD, Ent-deckungen, pp. 60, 65, 68, 92-96, 148, 160, etc.; here the author gives 141° 2' 30" as the longitude of the island of Arzobispo, which is more correct than the one given in Journal de la Haye, January 9/10, 1843, where he erroneously places the island in 140° 2' 30". See also Note 2 on p. 393 of MELVILL VAN CARNBÉE'S Moniteur, and further pp. 392-394 of the same publication; VON SIEBOLD in LEUPE'S edition of Reize van Maarten Gerritsz. Vries, pp. 268-269: I cannot possibly enter into all the conjectures thrown out by VON SIEBOLD, respecting the supposed identity of islands laid down in XVI and XVII century charts, with those marked in charts of more recent date. I should certainly hesitate to endorse all of them, but I am as little prepared to dispute them, considering the utter uncertainty and inexactitude of the geographical conceptions of former times. I have therefore confined myself to what I deem indispensable to a complete understanding of what the journal supplemented by the chart, tells us about Quast's expedition.]

Several weeks were now to elapse, before land was once more sighted. Down to August 4 the voyage was steadily continued in a nearly north-eastern and eastern direction. At this date--by estimation they were in 29° 10' N.L., and the day before they made out to be about 205 miles east of Japan[1]--"no land being as yet sighted," they resolved to continue the search in a nearly northwesterly direction, until they began to bend their course nearly due west, when they estimated themselves to have come to about 35° N.L. The voyage was now proceeded with in the latter direction up to August 24, without their descrying any sign of land.

At the date last mentioned the journal reads as follows: "On Wednesday, August 24, in the morning...we changed our course to West-north-west...we took no latitude at noon...At noon, as we were taking our dinner, we sighted the land which, according to the Dutch chart[2], must be Japan, ahead to west of us so far as our eyes reached, at about to or 11 miles' distance, but on account of the dense fog we were unable to ascertain whether this was the mainland of Japan or islands only...On Thursday, August 25, we found ourselves at about 4 or 5 miles' distance from the shore, but the dense fog again prevented us from discerning the exact outline, although we got a decided impression, that we had the mainland ahead of us...We now altered our course...to eastward...At noon we were in 37° 40' latitude "[3].

Prom Japan they now sailed into the Pacific again, during the first weeks following, chiefly in an eastern and south-eastern direction, down to September 3, on which day, being in 35° 30' N.L., and fancying themselves to be "at upwards of 200 miles' distance to the east of Japan,"they changed their course to north-west in order to get to 37½° N.L. After this they continued their voyage in an easterly direction, but with considerable deviations in the latitude, down to September 24[4], when on concluding their observations they believed themselves to be "in longitude reckoning from Japan at about 600 Dutch or 700 Spanish miles' distance to eastward, in the prescribed latitude," and this, "without having during all this time sighted land, or having descried any certain signs of land being near."

They now resolved to return and traverse the sea in a more westerly direction, a plan which was carried out, between the supposed latitudes of about 36½° and 39½°. After this the voyage was continued almost constantly in a westerly direction, but in varying latitudes, in the course of which cruise they got as high as 42° N.L. Next, on October 15, it was resolved to proceed with the expedition in a more southerly, but always westerly direction, until at length on October 25--they then believed themselves to be in 39° 10' N.L.--all further attempts at making discoveries were discontinued, and it was decided to steer for Formosa.

On October 31 they had got to 34° 45' N.L., and were sailing almost due west. On November 1 they were in 34° 40', but to "every one's astonishment" the land which they had expected by this time, had still always not been reached, until on this day "at the sixth glass of the dog-watch" it was at length "descried." It turned out to be once more the coast of Japan, and the journal at this date gives, about the things now seen by our voyagers, certain particulars which are noteworthy, because they throw additional light on our ancestors' notions about the position and "lie" of Japan. A look at the chart here reproduced amply suffices to convince us that this knowledge was very inaccurate. The journal now goes on as follows: "On Wednesday, November 2...we were steering West by South, and were at about two miles' distance from the shore; we found the northernmost part of the said land to be about 4 or 5 miles from us; so that, although we found the land to be larger than was shown in the chart, we could not but believe that it must necessarily be the islands at the South-eastern extremity of Japan, which islands are situated pretty well in the latitude indicated, but slightly more to the south than they are laid down in the chart. We now turned our course to the south-west, following the trend of the coast on our right hand. We found the land in question to be of medium height, at times appearing double or triple; we saw a very high mountain over-topping the land, which mountain must accordingly have its base on other land beyond, or more to the west...

[1] Resolution of the Plenary Council, August 3, 1639.]

[2] Resolution of the Plenary Council, August 24, 1639.]

[3] Cf. VON SIEBOLD in Journal de la Haye, January 9/10, 1843; Ent-deckungen, p. 60; LEUPE'S Reize van Vries, p. 276.]

[4] Resolution of the Plenary Council, of that date.--Cf. VAN BEMMELEN, Isogonen, p. 26.]

The land extended from South-west to North-east for about 6, and from North by east to South by west for 3 miles. Seen from the sea, the whole of it looks like broken country; by observation it was found to lie in 34° 54' N.L., and in 28(?)° 13' Longitude. At about 4 miles north of the southern extremity--having first become aware of it in the night-time--we descried, somewhat more to the west, two other islands, which were found to lie at 4 or 5 miles' distance, South-west by west and North-east by east of the island first mentioned...At night-fall we descried straight ahead of us, in the South-south-west, two other large, high-lying islands, and suspected that there would be still more land thereabouts, so that...we thought it advisable to tack about to the south ... In the early part of the dog-watch, we had the islands, which we had last night seen in the south-south-west, due west of us...

On Thursday, November 3, at early dawn we descried west-south-west of us a pretty large island with two or three high moun-tains, or they might perhaps be separate islands. After breakfast the wind turning to the north-east, we took a southern course, and shortly after became aware of another island, less high than the last, south-south-west of us. By estimation these islands were found to lie South by west and North by east, at about 6 or 7 miles' distance from each other. In order to run to windward of the land and seaward, we now held our course south-south-east. At noon we had got into 32° 33' N.L., and should thus have covered 24 miles in the last twenty-four hours. We found the last-mentioned island to bear west of us, and now shaped our course south-west "

Our friends were mistaken, when, following the example of the charts given them for their guidance, they continued to call by the name of islands, the land which they had sighted on the 2nd of No-vember. They themselves found "the same to be larger than shown in the charts," and there can be little doubt that in the present case they had to deal with a part of the mainland, viz. Cape Sirahama (Sirofama) (34° 54' N.L. and 139° 44' E. Long. from Greenwich), the south-eastern extremity of Nippon. The very high mountain, mentioned in the journal, was most probably Mount Foesijama, which they can have observed in a north-easterly direction. The islands which they afterwards circumnavigated, form the island-chain, extending in a southerly or slightly south-easterly direction; VON SIEBOLD has proposed to name them Tasman's Isles, in order by so doing to pay honour to Tasman's share in this expedition, as well as to Quast's[1]. The ships were observed at Jedo, and notice of this given to the Dutch authorities there[2].

On November 10 they were "in expectation of sighting the land of Cicoko." On the following day they steered west by north, but saw "no land as yet." At last, on November 13, land was descried. It proved to be the East-coast of Kioesioe, erroneously styled Cikoko in the chart reproduced in this work. But I shall again let the journal speak for itself: "On Sunday, November 13...we spied land to west of us. After prayers...we were at about 3 miles' distance from the shore. We now shaped our course south-west by south...We took no latitude at noon...At sunset we saw the south-eastern extremity of the land south-south-west and south-west by south, at about 5 miles' distance from us...We kept in sight of the land as much as possible. At the close of the first watch we passed the south-eastern extremity aforesaid. We found that the land fell off to westward..." It is to this bay, that Von Siebold proposed to give the name of "Tasmans. Baai"[3]. The voyagers were further on sailing in the strait, to which in 1643 De Vries has given the name of Van Diemen's Strait, from the Governor-General, an appellation by which it is known even in our days.

"On Monday, November 14, we found ourselves about two miles from shore. We descried Tanaxima (Tanega Sima) 3 miles to the south, and south-west of us, a round, tall, helmet-shaped mountain, from whose top rose up huge clouds of smoke [most probably, Mount Iwoga Sima], together with many different other islands. At noon...we took the latitude of 31° 14', and were found to have covered 15 miles in a south-west by south direction in the last twenty-four hours...

[1] Entdeckungen, p. 60; Reize van Vries, pp. 271, 275.]

[2] See Daily Register, kept at Firando, December 25, 1639.--Cf. VALENTIJN, V, 2, Japan, p. 81,--As regards the information given in the text supra et infra, respecting Quast and Tasman's surveys of the coasts of Japan, cf. VON SIEBOLD in Journal de la Haye, January 11, 1843; Id., Entdeckungen, passim, and LEUPE, Reize van Vries, pp. 27o ff.--As con-

cerns the modern maps of Japan, I have consulted ADOLF STIELER, Hand Atlas.]

[3) Atlas, No. 10, and Erklarung der Karten, p. 192.]

In the early part of the day-watch we saw the south-west point (Satano Misaki), where the land trends to the south-west, forming a large bay (the Bay of Kagosima), which seems to offer a good road-stead in all wind.

On Tuesday, November 15, at daybreak, we had the smoking mountain alongside of us to the south-west...We shaped our course westward. At noon the latitude taken was 31° 10'...During the night we passed the westernmost islands (Ingersoll or Morrison), and turned our course to west-south-west.

On Wednesday, November 16, in the morning we kept on our west-south-west course, and saw some more islands lying south-east of us (the Seven Sisters of the Linschoten or Cecille Archipelago). The latitude observed at noon proved to be 3o° 20'..."

After constantly sailing on in a nearly south-westerly direction, on November 21 they had reached 26° 56' N.L. and saw "north-west of us, at about 8 or 9 miles' distance, the islands of Nanquin." On the 22nd they sighted the island of Baboxin[1], and soon after reached Formosa. Here, they dropped anchor before the fortress of Zeelandia, November 24, "in very woeful plight, there having been 21 deaths in the Engel, and 20 in the Gracht, and the others being all (many)[2] of them down with illness"[3].

Quast very soon after embarked again for Batavia on board the ship Breda, which was ready to set sail, and departed from Formosa, December 1, 1639[4]. He arrived at the capital of Netherlands-India, January 2, 1640[5], and there sent in his report to his superiors. Concerning this report, the latter authorities wrote as follows to the Board of Directors, on January 10, 1640: "In the ship Breda has returned hither from the voyage for the discovery of the countries to the east of Japan, but without having attained his object, Commander Matthijs Quast, who has sailed over upwards of 600 miles to the east' of Japan, in the latitude prescribed, without finding land; after which the wind turned to such a quarter that he resolved to turn his ships westward, and, going round by the north of Japan, to explore the coasts of Tartary, Corea and China, so that, returning in the same longitude, between 42° and 38° Northern Latitude, on his way back, also, he has seen no land; but being greatly distressed by disease on board their ships, the commanders were compelled to discontinue the voyage of discovery to the north, and on November 24 arrived at Tayouan, eastward of Japan, in very bad plight and with great loss of men, having in the two flutes lost 38 men, that is nearly half of the number they had on board, when they started on their expedition.

"The Commander opines that the said lands will never be found in the latitude aforesaid; we intend to inquire further into this matter, when the skippers and chief-mates shall have arrived here. Meanwhile with the present we beg leave to hand Your Worships their journals and charts, from which you will be enabled to gather exact particulars of their voyage, and of the courses kept by them. It is not our intention to take this discovery in hand a second time, but we shall await Your Worships' advices touching this matter. It seems to us to be a matter of great importance, that in 38° and 34° N.L., they encountered so many variable winds, and Commander Quast aforesaid has declared to us that, if he had tried to do so, he might have succeeded in making the Ladrones Isles, starting from the island of Luçon. It can hardly be supposed that in those regions the winds regularly blow so variably, but we presume that in their case this was due to accident only."

The "advice" of the Board of Directors was not long in coming. In their letter to the Governor-General and Councillors, of September 11, 1640, they authorised the latter to resume the enterprise, if the circumstances of the Company allowed of their doing so, and able seafaring men were

[1] I have not found this island in any modern maps or charts. In XVII century maps "Babucsin," or "the islands of Babockzijn" are lying in about 26° 30' N.L. This agrees pretty closely with the latitude mentioned in Quast's journal, which has: "At noon (of November 22) we were in 36 (read: 26) ° 8' latitude, at which time we estimated the aforesaid island to lie west by north of us, at 2½ miles' distance." In the XVII century charts, inter alia in the above-mentioned chart, no. 285 of LEUPE'S Inventaris, Baboxin is situated north of Poeloe Crocodil (Qy. Alligator Island? In STIELER, Hand Atlas, in 26° 15') It is to be presumed that Baboxin is the island, now named Tung-ying (VON SIEBOLD, Erklarung, p. 201).]

[2] "Dachregister" of the Factory of Taijouhan, November 24, 1639.]

[3] Missive from the governor of Formosa to the G.-G. and Counc., December 10, 1639.]

[4] Do., December 11, 1639.]

[5] Resolution of the G.-G. and Counc., January 2, 1640.]

available, without, however, giving "express orders" on the subject. In their letter of April 11, 1642 they again referred to this matter. "We are still always greatly inclined," they write, "to fit out another enterprise for the northern coasts of Tartary...for the further exploration of the said regions, for which purpose able skippers and mates would have to be employed with proper instructions...We continue to recommend the matter to Your Worships' attention...and would have it carried into effect on the first opportunity offering for securing ships and crews...always, however, without detriment to the Company's business."

But the Supreme Government at Batavia, too, had soon got over their first feeling of disappointment. Already in their missive to the Board of Directors, bearing date November 30, 1640, they expressed themselves in this fashion: "We likewise continue inclined to have further search made for the lands eastward of Japan..."It is well-known that this plan got realised in 1643, when the ships Castricum and Breskens, commanded by Marten Gerritszoon Vries and Hendrik Corneliszoon Schaep were fitted out "for the exploration of the north coast of Tartary, and from there for a renewed search for the silver- and gold-bearing islands to the east of Japan"[1]. If in the opinion of Governor-General Antonio Van Diemen, the expedition of 1639 had remained without results, still it has become one of the bases for subsequent explorations of the highest importance for the science of geography in its widest sense: not only for the voyage of Vries, but, through the latter, also for expeditions of much more recent date. For the documents in which Quast and Tasman had laid down the results of their experiences and observations during the voyage of 1639, together with others, formed the groundwork of the instructions drawn up for the guidance of Vries on his memorable expedition[2]. The object, too, for which our chart of Quast's exploratory voyage was prepared, clearly shows that the experiences gathered in 1639, were not lost upon Vries and his companions. To prove this, we need only refer to the correspondence between the Governor-General and Councillors, and the Netherlands "president" in Japan. On June 13, 1640 the latter dignitary was informed from Batavia, how Quast and his companions "had returned to Tayouan in wretched condition, and without having effected their purpose. Had they called at Japan," the letter goes on to say, "and there taken in fresh provisions, they would have saved the lives of many of their men, but fearing the Japanese might take it ill, if they did so, they abstained from casting anchor at unusual places in the said country. They have not seen any land, but on the other hand observed numerous unmistakeable signs of the same. We purpose renewing the said enterprise in the course of next year. Skipper Abel Tasman, now on board the Oost Cappel, was a sharer in the said expedition, and is still very eager to undertake another with the same object. If applied to, he will give Your Worship every information you may wish to have. We request you to let us know, whether a voyage of discovery of the kind would be likely to cause ill feeling on the part of the Japanese authorities, and whether in case of urgent necessity the Company's ships could without risk come to anchor on the Japanese coast for the purpose of taking in refreshments." The reply[3] of the Dutch representative then residing at Firando, François Caron, ran as follows: "We have duly gathered from the advices and verbal communications of skipper Abel Tasman that Your Worships contemplate a resumption of the attempts to discover the islands to the east of Japan; we have also been informed of the result of the said expedition, and have accordingly, in order to facilitate a closer study and more thorough understanding of the matter in question, induced skipper Tasman to have two plane-charts drawn up, based on his own ship's journals and registered courses, and on those of the chief-mate of the ship Engel, of which we beg leave to inclose copies, which, with the descriptive account annexed, will fully enable Your Worships to obtain an idea of the discrepancies between the old chart and the results now obtained, as regards the position of the lands and islands; while they will at the same time make you acquainted with the new courses followed."

"We are well assured that the islands searched for to the eastward, do not form part of the empire of Japan, since we have been informed on the best authority that the Japanese emperor has

[1] Letter from the G.-G. and Counc. to the "Heeren XVII," of January 23, 1643.]

[2] Cf. LEUPE'S edition of Vries's voyage, pp. 13, 14, 24, 32, 33.]

[3] Bearing date November 20, 1640.]

no land over which he would claim any jurisdiction, situated 400 Dutch miles out to sea to the eastward; so that in our opinion it would be both needless and unadvisable to apprize the Japanese authorities of this enterprise, the more so, since the land of Japan must on no account and for no reason whatever be called at with empty vessels at unusual points on the coast; especially in these times of great strictness on the part of the Japanese authorities, in which such ships would undoubtedly be looked upon as spies upon the country, whereas loaded vessels with customary cargoes for Japan might with some appearance of truth shelter themselves under the plea of having been driven to these points by storms and stress of weather; even under such circumstances, however, the thing is not without considerable risk, since it has never been done before now; and it will hardly be believed, that such fresh mistakes might proceed from better motives; considering all which it is greatly to be feared, that the ship will be kept in embargo for a long time, during which the cargo would suffer great damage, and our countrymen might find seriously discredited the good repute in which they are now held here."

The first author who has made mention of Quast and Tasman's voyage in 1639, would seem to have been the well-known astronomer and mathematician Dirck Rembrantsz van Nierop[1], who in 1669, with Gerrit van Goedesbergh, "Boeckverkooper op 't Water, bij de Nieuwe-Brug," Amsterdam, published a now rare quarto volume, entitled "Eenige Oefeningen in God-lijcke, Wiskonstige, en Natuerlijcke ding-en" [Sundry Exercises in Godly, Mathematical, and Natural Matters]. In 1674 a sequel to this work appeared with Abel Symonsz. Van der Storck, "Boeckverkooper op 't Water bij de Nieuwe Brugh, in de Delfse Bijbel," with the slightly modified title, "Tweede deal Van enige Oefeningen, 't Welk is in Geographia ofte Aertkloots-beskrijvinge, Waer in dat gehandelt wort: Ten eersten, over het vroeg vertonen der Sonne op Nova Sembla int Jaer 1597. Ten tweden, enige aenmerkingen op de Raise benoorden om na Oost India. Ten derden, van Abel Tasman ontdekking na het onbekende Suid-lant. Ten vierden, van de Letterspelling, dat is hoe men de Letteren uitspreken en spellen sal" [Second part of Sundry Exercises, namely in Geographia or description of the terrestrial globe; in which the Author treats: Firstly, of the Sun's early appearance in Nova Zembla, in the year 1597. Secondly, certain observations touching the voyage to East India round by the North. Thirdly, of Abel Tasman's voyage of discovery in search of the unknown South Land. Fourthly, of Orthography, that is to say, how one should pronounce the Letters, and spell words]. In the second section of this latter volume, Van Nierop has printed an abstract[2] of the instructions drawn up by the Governor-General and Councillors, for the behoof of the expedition under Vries in 1643, and in this connection also refers to the voyage of Quast and Tasman, and to the gold- and silver-bearing islands to the east of Japan. In the very same year a free English translation of Van Nierop's statements appeared in the Philosophical Transactions of the Royal Society in London[3], which translation, in a French dress, almost a century later, found its way into the Collection Académique, partie étrangère[4]. In this manner, that which the Netherlanders did, or did not know about those mysterious islands, found its way into the "Mémoire du roi," of

June 26, 1785, which has done duty as a memorandum of instructions for the behoof of the famous voyage round the world of Jean François Galaup de la Pérouse during the years 1785-1788.

" Il viendra se mettre"--we read there[5]--"par la latitude de 37 degrés ½, Nord, sur le méridien de 180 degrés. Il fera route a l'Ouest, pour rechercher une terre ou ile qu'on dit avoir été découverte en 1610 par les Espagnols; iI poussera cette recherche jusqu'au 165e degré de longitude1

[1] As regards this author cf. LAUTS, in Verhandelingen Zeewezen, Nieuwe Volgorde, III, pp. 330-339; A. J. VAN DER AA, Biographisch Woordenboek der Nederlanden (1852-1878), s. v.]

[2] Pp. 29-36.]

[3] Vol. IX (London, Martyn, 1674), 197-207.]

[4] Vol. IV (Dijon, Paris, MDCCLVII), pp. 55-63.]

[1] L. A. MILET-MUREAU, Voyage de La Pérouse autour du monde, I (Paris, Imprimerie de la Republique, an V, 1797), p. 26.--Other discoverers, too, have known and utilised the instructions given to Vries; but I cannot, of course, discuss them all in this place.--The expedition under James Cook, Clerke and Gore (1776-1780) sought Rica de Plata in a lower latitude. See pp. 177 ff. of Vol. III of the 3rd edition of A Voyage to the Pacific Ocean, undertaken for making discoveries in tlie Northern Hemisphere. Performed under the direction of Captains Cook, Clerke, and Gore. (London, Flughs, MDCCLXXXV).]

orientale." From No. 48 of the Notes géographiques et historiques, p??ur étre jointes au Mémoire du Roi[1], it appears that these instructions were partly based on the English version of Van Nierop's statements[2]. La Pérouse himself thus delivers himself in his journal[3] under date of Ottober, 1787: "Je dirigeai ma route pour couper par les 165d de longitude, le parallèle de 37d 30' sur lequel quelques géographes ont placé une grande lie riche et bien peuplée, découverte, dit-on, en 1620[4], par les Espagnols. La recherche de cette terre avait fait partie de l'objet des instructions du capitaine Vriès; et Von trouve un mémoire qui contient quelques détails sur cette île, dans le quatrième volume de la Collection académique, partie étrangère. Il me paraissait que, parmi les différentes recherches qui m'étaient plutôt indiquées qu'ordonnées par mes instructions, celle-là méritait la préférence. Je n'atteignis le parallèle des 37d 30' que le 14, à minuit: nous avions vu, dans cette même journée, cinq ou six oiseaux de terre, de l'espèce des linots, se percher' sur nos manoeuvres; et nous aperçûmes, le même soir, deux vols de canards ou de cormorans, oiseaux qui ne s'écartent presque jamais du rivage. Le temps était fort clair, et sur l'une et l'autre frégate, des vigies furent constamment au haut des mats. Une récompense assez considérable était promise à celui qui le premier apercevrait la terre;"--how vividly all this reminds us of what we find noted in Quast's journal, and of the resolutions taken in the course of his expedition;--"ce motif d'émulation était peu nécessaire: chaque matelot enviait l'honneur de faire le premier une découverte qui, d'après ma promesse, devait porter son nom. Mais malgré les indices certains du voisinage d'une terre, nous ne découvrîmes rien, quoique l'horizon fiat très étendu: je supposai que cette île devait être au Sud, et que les vents violens qui avaient récemment soufflé de cette partie, avaient écarté vers le Nord les petits oiseaux que nous avions vus se poser sur nos agrès; en conséquence je fis route au Sud jusqu'à minuit. Étant alors précisément, comme je l'ai dit, par 37d 3o' de latitude Nord, j'ordonnai de gouverner à l'Est, à très petites voiles, attendant le jour avec la plus vive impatience. Il se fit, et nous vîmes encore deux petits oiseaux; je continuai la route à l'Est: une grosse tortue passa, le même soir, le long du bord. Le lendemain, en parcourant toujours le même parallèle vers l'Est, nous vîmes un oiseau plus petit qu'un roitelet de France, perché sur le bras du grand hunier, et un troisième vol de canards: ainsi, à chaque instant, nos espérances étaient soutenues; mais nous n'avions jamais le bonheur de les voir se réaliser."

Indeed, the belief in the existence of the gold- and silver-bearing regions in $37\frac{1}{2}°$ N.L. must have been a very deep-rooted one, if not only cartographers continued to mark them in their charts[5], but also La Pérouse received instructions to try a new effort for discovering them, in spite of the negative results of Quast's and Vries's voyages being generally known; and if La Pérouse himself preferred the search for them to other explorations, also suggested to him. Nay, the editor of La Pérouse's journal, Milet-Mureau, gently reproves him for having discontinued the search: "Quel que soit le motif"--he says--"qui l'a déterminé, les fréquens indices de terre qu'ont eus les navigateurs, doivent faire regretter que La Pérouse n'ait pas pris le part de suivre le 37e ou le 38e parallèle. Les terres anciennement découvertes s'étant presque toutes retrouvées de nos jours, cette Ile sera sûrement l'objet de nouvelles recherches, et il y a lieu d'espérer qu'on la trouvera en parcourant le parallèle de 36d 30'."[6]

Again, availing himself of the experience gained by Quast and Tasman, the celebrated Russian explorer Adam Johann Von Krusenstern, in his voyage round the world in the years 1803-1806, attempted to find the gold- and silver-bearing islands, but he, too, was unsuccessful[7].

Spain, on the contrary, had long given up all hopes of disco-vering the eagerly desired islands, and had accordingly ceased to make any efforts in this direction. After this matter had again formed

[1) MILET-MUREAU, 1. C., pp. 150-151.]

[2) VAN NIEROP, p. 34.]

[3) III, pp. 166-167.]

[4) A mistake, instead of 1610.]

[5) Cf. VON SIEBOLD, Journal de la Haye, January 11, 1843.]

[6) Cf. also BUACHE (premier hydrographe de la marine), Mémoires de l'Institut national des sciences et arts, pour l'an IV de la République. Sciences morales et politiques. I, p. 477, Note I; pp. 486 ff. Paris, Baudouin, Thermidor, An VI.]

[7) Reise um die Welt in den Jahren 1803, 1804, 1805 und 1806, auf den Schiffen Nadeshda und Newa. I. Berlin, Haude und Spener; 1811, pp. 293-299; II B (1812), pp. 60 ff.]

the subject of discussions between Spain and Manila[1] in 1730, 1732 and 1734, the King, on March 12, 1738, directed his governor of the Philippines[2] to ask the opinion of practised sailors. It was given[3], with the result[4] that the authorities thought themselves justified in con-cluding that the islands of Rica de Oro and Rica de Plata had never yet been seen by any one. Nor do we find any mention made of ulterior endeavours, set on foot by Spaniards[5].

Although therefore the expedition undertaken by Quast and Tasman did not remain altogether unknown--and in the same cursory way it is referred to by the Amsterdam burgomaster Mr. Nicolaas Wit-sen in his well-known book "Noord' en Oost Tartarijen"[6]--although some of the results obtained in it may have occasionally found their way into a few seventeenth century charts (most of them, however, utterly ignoring them), still fully two centuries had to elapse before this enterprise was to have full light thrown upon it. For this fresh light we are indebted to the well-known scholar and scientist Von Siebold, who, with the assistance of De Munnick, in 1842 discovered in the Old Colonial Archives Quast's journal, together with the resolutions of the Ship's council and the Plenary Council. He forthwith published the results of his researches[7] in Journal de la Haye, December 30, 1842, and January 9-11, 1843. Of these highly interesting papers, shortly afterwards a separate reprint in quarto[8], which has now become rare, was published with the title Documens importans, sur la découverte des îles de Bonin, par des navigateurs Néerlandais en 1639. At a later date Von Siebold's researches were substantially reproduced in Le

Moniteur des Indes-Orientates et Occidentales, 1848-1849[9], the editor, the able cartographer and hydrographer[10] P. Melvill van Carnbée, supplementing them by the instructions given to Vries--erroneously mentioned as "encore inédite"[11--and by an account of the latter's voyage in 1643. Von Siebold himself once more printed the results of his investigations in his celebrated work Nippon, Archiv zur Beschreibung von Japan, in the part entitled Geschichtliche Uebersicht der Entdeckungen der Europaeer in Seegebiete von Japan und dessen Neben- und Schutzlaendern[12], to which part various charts are appended[13].

If therefore, thanks mainly to Von Siebold, a good deal of fresh light has been thrown on the expedition in which Tasman bore so large a part, the journal itself still remains unprinted; but the chart, here reproduced, drawn up under Tasman's supervision and with his aid, is more convenient for consultation than Quast's monotonous notes, and furnishes us with an equally vivid picture of his and Tasman's peregrinations about the Pacific Ocean[14].

[1] Letters of June 28, 1730; June 30, 1732; June 10, 1734.]

[2] In Real Cedula al Gobr. de Filipines, of that date.]

[3] Testimonio de varios informes dados por pilotos y personas practicas de Filipinas sobre las Islas Rica de Oro y Rica de Plata, November, 1739.]

[4] Carta del Capn. Gral de Filipinas, July 13, 1740.]

[5] Cf. also BURNEY, II, pp. 263-265.]

[6] Vol. I, Second Edition, Reprint (Amsterdam, Schalekamp, MDCCLXXXV), p. 156. The first edition was brought out in 1692. As regards the different editions, cf. P. A. LEUPE, Nederlandsche bibliographic van land- en volkenkunde. Amsterdam, Frederik Muller, 1884, pp. 268-270; and. J. F. GEBHARD, Het leven van Mr. Nicolaas Cornelisz. Witsen, 1641-1717. I. Utrecht, J. W. Leeftang, 1881. pp. 417 ff.--See also BURNEY, III (1813), p. 55-58.]

[7] Cf. also LAUTS, in Algemeene Konst- en Letterbode for 1843, I, pp. 30-32.]

[8] La Haye, chez Léopold Loebenberg, 1843.]

[9] La Haye, Belinfante, 1849, I. PP. 389-407.]

[10] VAN DER AA, i. v.]

[11] Moniteur, p. 396.]

[12] Pp. 59 ff., and the Anmerkungen referring to them.--I have used the copy of Nippon in the Royal Library at The Hague. As regards this work, which appeared 1832-1852, cf. P. A. TIELE, Bibliographie Land- en Volkenkunde, p. 220. A new edition of it is at present in course of prepa-

ration. Part I is already published. (Wtirzburg and Leipzig, Woerl, 1897). But the Geschichte des Entdeckungen is not to be reprinted.]

[13) This part has been published separately (Leiden, 1852, with an atlas), entitled: Geschichte der Entdeckungen, etc. It moreover contains an Erklärung der Karten, which the Uebersicht lacks.]

[14) See also W. VAN BEMMELEN'S paper, infra. Such passages of Quast's journal as give an account of the discovering of land, or of the calling at land or islands, have all of them been given in my text.]

VII

THE DUTCH IN FORMOSA.--TASMAN'S RETURN TO BATAVIA (1640)--SIGNIFICANCE OF THE DUTCH TRADE IN EASTERN ASIA.--TASMAN'S VOYAGE TO FORMOSA AND JAPAN.--TASMAN CASTS ANCHOR OFF FIRANDO.-- CRITICAL POSITION OF THE DUTCH FACTORY THERE (1640).--DEPARTURE FOR CAMBODJA.

The island of Formosa, which Tasman now touched at, was one of the most recently acquired possessions of the Dutch East India Company. She was led to lay hands on this island also, by her desire to secure a larger share of the Chinese trade than she had hitherto been mistress of[1]. As early as 1620[2] the Board of Directors had laid stress on the expediency of using Formosa as a station for the trade with China. Jan Pieterszoon Coen, who was then Governor-General, was fully aware of the great importance of a point like this, but the information collected by the Dutch concerning an anchoring-place on the west-coast of the island, were unsatisfactory. Coen therefore cast his eye on the Pescadores Isles, where he hoped to find an excellent road-stead.

In the first half of 1622 a considerable squadron sailed from Batavia for the coast of China, commanded by Cornelis Reyerszoon. The main object of the expedition was a twofold one. If this was deemed feasible by the commander of the fleet, he had orders to try to seize Macao, the Portuguese island-town on the Chinese coast; should this prove impossible, or the attempt miscarry, he was to induce the Chinese, bon gré mal gré, to cede to the Company a fitting sea-port, which might serve as a basis for her eventual mercantile operations with the Celestial Empire and its adjacent countries, and might enable the Dutch to prevent any commerce of their Spanish and Portuguese enemies with China In concise and forcible language Reyerszoon's instructions of April 9[3], 1622 thus set forth the views of his masters: "In order to get hold of the Chinese trade we deem it to be needful that with the Lord's help we take Maccaw, or erect a fortress somewhere in one of the most fitting places about Canton or Chincheu[4], maintain a garrison there, and constantly keep a sufficient fleet on the coast of China." The idea last mentioned was further developed as follows: "Should it be thought unadvisable to attack Maccau, or should the attempt against it miscarry, which God avert, Your Worship...will pass on with the main part of the fleet to the islands of Chincheu, called in the chart the Piscadores, situated in 23½° N. Latitude...The islands, called the Piscadores...would seem to be most excellently situated for enabling us to prevent the Chinese trade with Manilha, and to bend the Chinese to our will." The islands, it is true, were "sandy, barren, without either timber or stone," but this was made up for by "an excellent road-stead," which they were said to afford. Nor was Formosa lost sight of on this occasion. The Spaniards of Manila, from fear of the Dutch plans in the Chinese Sea, contemplated "erecting a fortress at the Southern extremity of Lequeo Pequeno, called Lamangh "which must have been meant for Formosa[5]"--where they hoped to find a convenient port." This Spanish project, too, Reyerszoon's expedition was intended to baffle. "The main part of the fleet"--the instructions go on to say--"having arrived at the Piscadores, whether having captured Maccau or not, whichever may be the case, Your Worship will forthwith despatch some yachts, pinnaces, or tingans to Lequeo Pequeno and all circumjacent islands, directing them to make diligent search for the best road-stead, and for the most fitting site for erecting a fortress, and for establishing a rendez-vous station. Your Worship will immediately occupy the place that shall be deemed most suitable for this purpose, have a fort built there and the same garrisoned, always on the understanding that this has not already been done at Maccau or thereabouts. And in case a fort should already have been built at Maccau or thereabouts, it is our express desire, that notwithstanding, should a suitable place for anchorage and rendezvousing be met with about Chincheu, in the Piscadores, in Lequeo Pequeno Isla Formosa, or elsewhere, yet the most fitting place there should be occupied and garrisoned...since by so doing

[1] For the details following, see especially TIELE, Europeers, IX (Bijdragen Taal-, land- en volkenkunde, XXX pp. 291-296.]

[2] In their missive to the G.-G. and Counc., September 9.]

[3] Not April 4, as stated by TIELE, l. c., p. 293, Note 2).]

[4] Tsuen-tschou.]

[5] Cf. VON SIEBOLD, Entdeckungen, pp. 72-73; TIELE, Europeers, IX, p. 291, Note 2).]

we shall be better enabled to prevent the Chinese from trading with Manilha and all other places, and compel them to conform to our will." And in the sequel the chief object of the new settlement is thus set forth without any mincing of the matter: "It is our desire and fixed intention, not to allow in future any Chinese junks to sail to any other port than Batavia, as soon as we shall be definitely settled on the coast of China." The Chinese were to be officially informed that for twenty years past the Dutch had requested permission. to establish a commercial connection with them, "without having obtained anything up to now"; it was now their plain duty to afford the Dutch opportunities for trade, and to give up their commerce with nations at war with the Dutch, "on pain of being declared our enemies, and treated as such."

This is not the place to enter into further particulars as to Coen's plans with respect to China. A word or two will suffice to tell the result of the expedition. The attempt against Macao on June 24, 1622, failed miserably; Reyerszoon got wounded, and he and his men had to beat a retreat with heavy losses and bloodied pates. A part of the Dutch fleet now set sail for the Pescadores under command of the admiral, and on July 11 came to anchor off the largest of the isles, Pehoe or Ponghoe, which afforded a good road-stead. Formosa and the surrounding islands were explored, but found less suitable, so that it was ultimately resolved to build a fortress at the south-western extremity of Pehoe.

But the Dutch found they had reckoned without the Chinese. On October 1 the Dutch got formal notice that the Chinese government would never suffer them to establish a settlement in the Pescadores isles, which China accounted to form part of her dominions; they might, so far as China was concerned, do so in Formosa, which was outside the Chinese jurisdiction. Upon this it came to open hostilities, which ultimately led to all plans for a settlement in the Pescadores being abandoned.

The first and foremost demand of the Chinese authorities was, that the Dutch should quit "Pehou within the jurisdiction of China"[1]. If they complied with this demand, and established themselves in Formosa (also called "Tayowan", and "Packan"), or in any other place of the vicinity, "if only outside the jurisdiction of China", the Chinese government would not refuse to come and trade there with the Dutch, and altogether to give up the commerce with Manila. Meanwhile Reyerszoon was not only engaged in causing a "fortress" to be built in Pehoe, but by order of the Supreme Government at Batavia, "had also begun to run up a fastness of bamboo and earth-works" at the west coast of Formosa, in 23° N. L., "at the southern corner of the entrance to the bay of Tayowan (this being the most suitable place he had found up to then)". On December 9, 1624 Reyerszoon returned to Batavia with the intelligence, "that our countrymen had quitted the fortress in Pehou, and had established themselves at Tayowan, every day expecting the opening of the coveted Chinese trade, of which there were already very fair prospects". Pehoe had been quitted, August 26, 1624. Martinus Sonck, who had been ordered to the coasts of China to replace Reyerszoon, had become aware that he must quit the island bon gré mal gré, since the superior numbers of the Chinese who were there investing the Dutch garrison, seemed to render a longer stay impossible. After some negotiation, in which the giving up of the trade to Manila on the part of the Chinese was not so much as alluded to, the Dutch withdrew "from Pehou with bag and baggage and set sail for Teyouwan ". Here the fortress which Reyerszoon had begun to build, was finished, and thus the foundation laid of one of the most important possessions which the Company has ever owned in the East; important chiefly as a staple of Chinese commodities and of home products as well, besides being one of the most successful missionary stations[2]. Sad to say, the Dutch occupation extended over a few decades only[3].

Before this fortress, then, bearing the name of Zeelandia, anchored Quast and Tasman after their weary wanderings over the ocean. Whereas Quast sailed for Batavia already on December 11, 1639, Tasman's services were turned to account for some time longer by the then governor of Formosa, Johan Van der Burch. Thus, at the request of the said governor, and with a view to the risks1

[1] For the facts stated in the sequel, see Dagh-Register gehouden int Casteel Batavia Anno 1624-1629. Uitgegeven door het Departement van Koloniën onder toezicht van J. E. HEEBES. ('s Gravenhage, Nijhoff, 1896), passim.]

[2] Cf. J. A. GROTHE, Archief voor de geschiedenis der oude Hollandsche Zending, III, IV: Formosa. Utrecht, Van Bentum, 1886-1887; J. J. VAN TOORENENBERGEN, De Nederlandsche Zending op Formosa, 1624-1661 (De Gids, 1892, III, pp. 31-68); W. CAMPBELL, An account of missionary success in the island of Formosa, I. London, Trübner, 1889.]

[3] As regards Formosa, cf. also VALENTIJN, IV, 2 (1726).]

threatening Dutch ships in these waters, in conjunction with skipper Maarten Gerritszoon Vries, then also staying in Formosa, he gave a professional opinion in writing, concerning the courses to be kept by Dutch ships in the sea between China and Formosa[1]; which written opinion also gained the approval of the Supreme Government at Batavia, and was consequently made to form the basis of the instructions and directions as to the courses to be kept, drawn up for the behoof of the captains of vessels ordered to navigate those waters[2].

On January 29, 1640, Tasman, too, set sail as captain of the Graft with a cargo worth at cost-price 139537 Dutch guilders, 11 stivers, 13 dolts. The significance of Formosa as a trade-centre may to a certain extent be gathered from the bill of cargo of the said ship, enumerating the different commodities which were delivered to the Dutch factory there, chiefly by Chinese dealers. Tasman, then, carried on board his ship "preserved ginger ", "spelter", "powdered sugar", alum, silks and damasks, chinaware, gold- and silver-wire, Chinese gold, etc.[3]

But of far greater importance than the exports to Batavia, was the mercantile intercourse of the time, in which Formosa bore a large share as the centre of the trade between Japan on the one hand, and on the other, China in the first place, but also Cambodja, Tonquin and Siam. Millions of money were by the Dutch in Japan exchanged for Chinese products: in 1639 they brought to Japan from Formosa goods amounting to 3 millions of Dutch guilders at cost-price, on which they made a profit of 60 pct.; in 1640 these imports rose to upwards of 5 millions, being nearly 5/6 of the aggregate imports by the Dutch into Japan[4]. The cargo of the Graft, indeed, like the whole of the cargoes brought by the ships from Formosa to Batavia (thence destined for the Netherlands and certain parts of Asia), formed but a small part of what the Chinese imported into Taywan. Thus in one day, January 12, 1640, one Chinese dealer brought to Formosa a quantity of silks worth one million and a half of guilders, while other parcels worth upwards of half a million were to follow this; almost the whole of this treasure being destined for Japan[5].

Formosa was furthermore the starting-point for the trade of the Dutch with Cambodja, Tonquin, and Siam, in all of which countries they turned over hundreds of thousands of guilders chiefly in the purchase of products in demand in Japan, while the articles they imported into those countries were for the greater part Japanese commodities.

Chinese and Japanese goods, especially precious metals, were from Formosa sent directly to the coasts of Coromandel and Surat--in December 1639, for instance, for more than one million and a half of guilders cost-price[6]. From Formosa Persia drew Chinese articles; sugar from both China and Formosa was carried to Persian markets; "deer-skins" from Formosa itself were inquired for in Japan[7]. Of a surety, the Governor-General and Councillors, who already deemed the cargo brought by the Graft "an excellent Chinese return-freight", had a right to speak "of the opulent Chinese trade" with Formosa, when the reports[8] brought over by Tasman acquainted them with this highly favourable state of affairs[9].

On February 19 the Graft cast anchor before Batavia, and for some time longer Tasman continued in command of this ship[10], which, after undergoing the needful repairs, was by decree of

[1] Missive from the governor of Formosa to the G.-G. and Counc., of January 28, 1640.]

[2] An "ordre ende seynbrieff" [letter of instructions and signals], resolved upon in the Council of India, and drawn up with the aid of this written opinion, is found inserted in the Resolution of the G.-G. and Counc., of June 5, 1640.--Cf. also their resolution of May 26, 1640, and their missive to the "president" in Formosa, Paulus Traudenius, of June 3, 1640.]

[3] According to the "facture" (invoice) of the Graft, of January 28, 1640.--See also "Daghregister des Comptoirs Tayouan," January29.]

[4] Missive from "President" Traudenius in Formosa to the Dutch "President" in Japan, Francois Caron, August 4, 1640.--"Extract uijt de Negotie boecken des Comptrs. Firando," for 1639 and 1640.--Cf. "Daghregister gehouden int Casteel Batavia anno 1640-1641," edited by J. A. VAN DER CHIJS (Batavia, The Hague, 1887), pp. 111, 146.]

[5] Missive from the governor of Formosa Van der Burch to the G.-G. and Counc., January 28, 1640.]

[6] As appears from the bills of lading of the ships. As regards Formosa, see also "Rappordt aen den Ed. Hr. Gouverneur elide de E. Raeden van India nopende...(de) gedaene visite des Comptoirs ende vorderen ommeslach tot Taijouan, gelegen opt Eylant Formosa door Nikolaas Coeckebacker," dated December 8, 1639; and furthermore the missives, invoices, etc. sent to Batavia from the said factory, in 1639.]

[7] Missive from the G.-G. and Counc. to "President" Traudenius in Formosa, of June 13, 1640.]

[8] Under date January 28, 1640.]

[9] Res. of the G.-G. and Counc., February 20, 1640.]

[10] Ress. of the G.-G. and Counc., March 10, 24, and 27, 1640,]

the Governor-General and Councillors of March 19, 1640, destined for Djambi, thence to sail for the north-east of Asia. Until the Graft should reach Djambi, the command remained in the hands of Tasman, who after arriving at the latter place was to hand it over to one of his colleagues, and to return to Batavia with the pepper laid up at Djambi, because his services were required elsewhere[1]. He was once more to be sent tb Formosa and Japan.

On May 26, 1640, indeed, it was resolved in the Council of India that three ships, the Meerman, the Oostcappel, and the Otter, should be despatched to those parts with merchandise, among which there were "curiosities...destined to secure the good will of his Imperial Majesty of Japan"; and on June 5 the ship Broeckoort was further added to the squadron.

The command of the four vessels, having on board "European and Batavian commodities" to an amount of upwards of 170,000 guilders[2], was entrusted to Tasman, who had returned from Djambi on the 1st of June, and was to continue commander until the ships should arrive at Formosa, when he had to put himself under the orders of the "president" or governor ad interim of this island, Paulus Traudenius[3], Van der Burch having died some time before, and no definite successor to him having yet been appointed; the instructions expressly stating that the said command was confided to him, because he was well-known to be "a painstaking, heedful and highly experienced skipper." Among the captains we further meet with Maarten Gerritszoon Vries and Jacob Jacobszoon Van der Meulen. The Oostcappel was to act as flag-ship[4]. The Broeckoort had on board 55 men, the three other vessels 50 men each, "all of them being provided with all necessaries for the period of ten months"[5]. On June 13 everything was in readiness for the expedition, and it was resolved to let the ships set sail "in the name of God" on the following morning "after due muster."

The instructions drawn up for the purpose of this voyage, afford us another glimpse of the knowledge of the Dutch of that time as regards the seas to be navigated on this occasion, and these data must not be omitted from a biography of the famous navigator, the less so since he had a large share in the drawing up of the directions for the courses to be kept. Their route was to lie by Lucipara and through the strait of Banca, then eastward of Lingga and Bintang, in order to make Poeloe Aor "with the object of surveying and reconnoitring the same". From there they were to try to run in sight of Poeloe Condor, next to pass between Poeloe Cecir de Mar and Cecir de Terra, and then to keep in sight of the shore as much as possible, "in order to keep clear of the Pracels; seeing that owing to the western winds the eastward current from the gulf of Cotchinchina is so strong, that in calm weather, and still more so in case of storm, it would throw the ships on the Pracels". Hainan being passed, it would be best to follow the example of the Portuguese "by standing off to sea, lest being overtaken by storms, the ships should be thrown on a lee-shore, seeing that the ty-phoons ("tuffons") usually come up with winds veering from north to east, so that it is highly perillous to seek the shore or an anchorage in bad weather".

As regards the making of Formosa itself, the commanders were referred to a separate "letter of directions and signals ", also dated June 13, drawn up pursuant to the advices and opinions deli-vered by Tasman and Vries, when they were staying in Formosa[6], especially with a view to the perils threatening our ships "on the shoals of the Piscadores". The instructions chiefly impress on the command-ers the expediency of surveying and reconnoitring the Lema Islands, to the south-east of Macao, when coming from the south, and of thence making for the Pescadores and Formosa in an

[2] LAUTS (Verhandeling Zeewezen, Nieuwe Volgorde, IV, p. 281), is not quite exhaustive as regards the cargo of the Oostcappel. The cargo to which he alludes (951,527 guilders) was put on board the Oostcappel in Formosa, with destination for Japan. Nor is he always quite correctly in-formed as regards other points also, and he now and then draws erroneous or not always legitimate conclusions respecting the period of Tasman's life treated in this chapter, and other periods. Other authors, too, naturally go wrong so far as they rely on Lauts; e.g. G. R. VOORMEULEN VAN BOEKEREN, Reizen en ontdekkingstochten van Abel Jansz. Tasman, van Lutkegast (Groningen, Scholtens, 1849), pp. 29 ff.; DOZY, 1. c., pp. 320 f.; the present writer in Groningsche Volksalmanak, pp. 528 f.; WALKER, 1. c., pp. 53 f. I have not thought it necessary to refer to all these inaccura-cies in detail: a comparison with the results of my renewed search through the archives will sufficiently point them out to the reader.]

[3] "Instructie ende Courswijsingh voor d' opperhooffden van de fluytschepen Oostcappel" (enz.), June 13, 1640.]

[4] Res. of the G.-G. and Counc., June 5, 1640.]

[5] Res. of the G.-G. and Counc., June 9, 1640.]

[6] "Ordre ende Instructie voor...de overigheijt van de fluijte Gracht," is-sued by the G.-G. and Counc., March 27, 1640.]

eastward direction. If the inverse route had to be followed, viz. by ships coming from Japan, they were to sail "as far as the well ascer-tained estimated northern latitude of 26 1/3°, in the neighbourhood of the islets of Baboxin and Crocodil (the Alligator Island), which lie at 7 or 8 miles' distance from the coast of China", and from there to make for the castle of Zeelandia in a southerly direction.

[1] The "letter" is a copy of the "ordre," inserted into the resolution of June 5.]

But Formosa was not to be the ultimate destination of the vessels. They were bound for Japan, and touched at Zeelandia chiefly to take in goods there, destined for the Japanese market[1]. Tasman having come to anchor before Zeelandia, July 2[2], the goods destined for Formosa were unloaded from the ships. As early as the beginning of August they were ready to sail for their new destination, for which they set out on the 6th and 7th of that month, with cargoes chiefly consisting of Chinese commodities to a value of about 3 million guilders[3]; among them the Oostcappel herself with 951,527 guilders, 13 stivers,1i doit; the total amount imported into Japan in 1640 representing a capital of 6.295.367 guilders, 8 stivers, 10 doits at cost-price[4]. On August 26 and following days the ships arrived safe[5] before Firando, or Hirado, on the north-east coast of Kioesioe, where the Dutch factory in Japan was established.

The Dutch in Japan were living through a crisis at this time. Since in 1609 the first official relations between the East India Company and Japan had been entered into[6]--leaving out of consideration the earlier more or less accidental and transient contacts[7], which had begun in 1600, and with which are associated the names of Jacob Quaeckernaeck, Melchior Van Santvoort and William Adams--her trade with Japan had in course of time gradually become a matter of more than ordinary importance to the Company. One especially among the Japanese export-articles, viz. silver, was, during the period of which we are treating, of paramount importance for the commerce carried on by the Dutch in the other parts of Asia. In 1639, for instance, the Dutch imported into Formosa from Japan silver to an amount of upwards of 4 million guilders, of which, though more than one million found its way to the Coast of Coromandel, Surat, etc., yet the greater portion was set apart for the trade in Chinese commodities[8]. The profits accruing to the Company were proportionately large. In 1638 she had made in Japan a net profit of upwards of two million guilders[9], and the year 1639 left a margin of 1.700.000 guilders[10].

Among the competitors whom the Company met with in Japan, the Portuguese again occupied a foremost place. The latter had, however, especially in the period of their subjection to Spain, maintained a very ill-advised policy with respect to Japan, by an injudicious proselytism in favour of the Roman Catholic Church. Here, as in many other parts of Asia, the Jesuits succeeded in making a large number of converts. They thus roused the suspicions of the Japanese government, which began to spy danger to itself in this rapid progress of proselytism. A few years before the Dutch had first come into contact with the

Japanese, there had been an outburst: bloody persecutions had harassed the Christian converts and their teachers, which ultimately, in 1639, were to result in the total expulsion of the Portuguese from Japan.

[1] Missive from the G.-G. and Counc. to Traudenius, June 13, 1640.]

[2] Daily journal of Formosa, of that date. See also "Dagh-Register gehouden int Casteel Batavia. Anno 1640-1641," edited by J. A. VAN DER CHIJS (Batavia, The Hague, 1887) p 111..]

[3] Daily journal of Formosa.--Missives from Traudenius to President Caron at Firando, August 4, 6, and 16, 1640; Missive from Francois Caron to the G.-G., Nov. 20, 1640; Extract from the trade-books of Firando, 1640.]

[4] Missive from the G.-G. and Counc., to the Board of Directors, January 8, 1641.--Resolution of the G.-G. and Counc., January 2, 1641.]

[5] "Dachregister gehouden op ons kantoor te Firando," February 3-November 19, 1640; August 25 and 26, etc.]

[6] See DE JONGE, Opkomst, III. 's Hage, Amsterdam, 1865, pp. 84-87; L. C. D. VAN DIJK, Zes jaren uit het leven van Wemmer van Berchem, gevolgd door Iets over onze vroegste betrekkingen met Japan. Amsterdam, Scheltema, 1858, B. pp. 21-31.]

[7] See DE JONGE, Opkomst, II. 's Hage, Amsterdam, 1864, p. 220; III, p. 83; VAN DIJK, Japan, B, pp. 1-26.]

[8] The above figures are taken from "Dachregister des Comptoirs Taijouhan."--See also G. LAUTS, Japan in zijne staatkunkundige en burgerlijke inrigtingen en het verkeer met Europesche natiën (Amsterdam, Beijerinck, 1847), pp. 195 ff.]

[9] Missive from the G.-G. and Counc. to the Board of Directors, December 18, 1639.]

[10] Missive from the G.-G. and Counc. to President Caron in Japan, June 13, 1640. As regards the trade with Japan see VALENTIJN, V, 2. Dordrecht, Amsterdam, 1736. Japan, especially pp. 105 ff.; OSCAR MUNSTERBERG, Japans auswärtiger Handel von 1542 bis 1854 (Münchener Volkswirthschaftliche Studien, X), Stuttgart, Cotta, 1896. The last named author has not made any independent study of documentary evidence in the archives, and is not acquainted with the latest Dutch publications of historical sources, though he had access to an extensive collection of literature on the subject. Cf. also a review by Oskar Nachod, who made studies in the Old Colonial Archives at the Hague (Export, March 5 and 12, 1896).]

Up to the period under review these persecutions had not yet been extended to the few Dutchmen who served the Company in Japan: they took good care to impress the Japanese authorities with a sense of the marked difference between the Protestant and the Roman-Catholic faith[1], and likewise to lay due stress on the distinction between themselves and their Portuguese enemies. Indeed, it was mainly their warnings that stirred distrust of the Roman-Catholics in the Japanese mind: a point on which the letters of the time written by Dutchmen, leave no room for doubt[2].

"It was our efforts," said Francois Caron, then president of the Dutch factory at Firando, "in burning words" to a Japanese statesman in a private interview held in 1639; "it was our efforts and repeated warnings addressed to the Japanese Court, that their Highnesses might be on their guard against the Spaniards and the brood of Romish Papists, that have mainly brought about the utter downfall of the Spanish and Portuguese power" in Japan. In this case, too, the question was one of self-preservation: in Japan also, the Dutch had constantly been thwarted by these rivals and enemies of theirs, but they now more than repaid their foes for the injury previously inflicted. "Our traffic with Japan," Caron went on to say to his Japanese host, "has long been a thorn in the side of the Spanish Portuguese, and had they been, able to destroy it, they would long ago have done so."

Much more so now, when they might be aware that their impending fall was in a great measure attributable to the hated enemy. In his missive of October 26, 1639, in which Caron gives an account of this interview to the Governor-General Antonio Van Diemen, he further writes: "Nor have we omitted, whenever opportunities have offered, constantly to apprize the councillors, regents, noblemen and commanders of the evil practices of the Jesuits and their confederates, of the assassination of the King of France, and of the Prince of Orange, telling them how the King of England and his Parliament have been in imminent peril of being blown up by gunpowder; how the King of Sweden has been in danger of losing his life by reading a petition imbued with a virulent poison; what bloody wars the Jesuits have kindled and urged on, and are still planning every day; in brief, how they are the prime movers of all disasters and overthrows of kings, countries and cities; which statements the Japanese have seen confirmed, and our predictions duly verified by the bloody tragedy of Arima."

The bloody tragedy of Arima[3]...The profound impression this sanguinary drama had left in the minds of contemporaries, is proved by the fact that it still lives in Japanese folk-tales. Arima is a village on the south-coast of the small peninsula of Simabara, at a short distance east of Nangasaki. A narrow strait separates it from the island-group of Amakoesa, a little more to the south. The immediate proximity of

Nangasaki, the harbour set apart for the dealings of European merchants, and the friendly attitude of the more or less independent lords of Simabara and Amakoesa, rendered the latter localities a promising field of labour for the Jesuit missionaries. And when in the last decades of the sixteenth century the Imperial government of Japan assumed a hostile attitude towards the Christian religion, it was precisely the somewhat isolated position of these places, that, in spite of their proximity to the capital, formed an additional motive for securing a still firmer footing to the Christian faith, already deeply rooted in the native soil, especially when the Roman-Catholic priests had found an asylum there, after having been expelled from Nangasaki. A Jesuit college and a seminary for the training of priests were established at Arima, and the two institutions constituted the starting-point for missionary labour in the first decades of the seventeenth century. But the times soon changed. This is not the place to enter into the details of this process; suffice it to say that after a time these parts of Japan

[1] Thus must accordingly be understood what YAMAGATA styles "anti-religious feelings which they (the Dutch) had represented themselves as possessing."--See this author's paper (based on Japanese evidence) The political relations of Japan and Holland under the Tokugawa regime (Notulen van de algemeene en bestuursvergaderingen van het Bataviaasch Genootschap van Kunsten en Wetenschappen, XXX, 1892), p. LXXXVII.--Cf. also ENGELBERT KAEMPFER, De Beschrijving van Japan, in' t Hoogduytsch beschreven, in het Engelsch overgezet, en uyt het Engelsch in 't Nederduytsch vertaalt. Amsterdam, Van Huyssteen, 1733, p. 252-254. [On this work see TIELE, Bibliographie Land- en Volkenkunde, pp. 133 f.); VALENTIJN, Japan, pp. 34-35; G. F. MEYLAN, Geschiedkundig Overzigt van den handel der Europezen op Japan (Verhandelingen van het Bataviaasch Genootschap van Kunsten en Wetenschappen, XIV, Batavia, Lands Drukkerij, 1833), p. 95; Von SIEBOLD, Nippon, VI, Vom Japanischen Handel, pp. 6 ff.; VON SIEBOLD, Essai historique, statistique et politique sur le commerce du Japon (Moniteur des Indes Orientales et Occidentales, 1847-1848, p. 32); G. LAUTS, Japan, p. 208; MUNSTERBERG, pp. 78-79, etc.]

[2] Cf. also MEYLAN, p. 16.]

[3] On this incident see MEYLAN, pp. 97 ff.; GEERTS, The Arima rebellion and the conduct of Koeckebacker in Transactions of the Asiatic Society of Japan, XI (1883), pp. 51-117; LUDWIG RIESS, Der Aufstand von Shimabara, 1637-1638, in Mittheilungen der Deutschen Gesellschaft für Natur- and Völkerkunde Ost-Asiens in Tokio, V, 45 (1891), pp. 191-214; MÜNSTERBERG, pp. 78-82.]

were placed under the rule of lords or governors, who tried to eradicate Christianity, and that social discontent began to put up its head there at the same time. Thus prepared, a rebellion broke out there in November and December 1637, which in a short time took alarming proportions, and may be assumed to have had a decisive influence on the views of the Japanese government with regard to the Christian missionary propaganda, and to the Portuguese who were the promoters of it. Christianity itself threatened to become a danger to the persons in power in Japan: the converts "conspire together, swerve from the path of duty and strike into cross-roads, infringe the ordinances, pronounce their sovereign lord their foe, against whom they stake their lives, at the risk of losing the same," thus runs the edict that forbade the Spaniards and Portuguese to reside within the empire[1]; and in an imperial edict of August, 1640[2] the "Christian doctrine" is branded as "the most pernicious and most injurious danger to the well-being of the Japanese empire". This, then, was the chief motive that led the Japanese authorities to destroy it, root and branch[3]. The Dutch, who in this saw their way to getting rid of opponents whom they detested, did not fail to point out the danger, and hasten the downfall of their hated rivals. And although their remonstrances were not directed against Christianity itself, or against the Japanese Christians, but against Jesuitism and the Spaniards and Portuguese, its representatives in Japan, yet this Christianity and these Christians also became the victims of the effect wrought by the Dutch denunciations. And when the rebellion of Arima afforded a very plausible pretext for stringent measures, the fate of the Christian faith and the Portuguese intruders alike was sealed. In April 1638 the rebellion was quelled and stamped out in blood: and with it Christianity in Japan received its death-blow. The expulsion of the Portuguese was only a question of time after this.

The decree expelling the Portuguese was issued in 1639, but not before "the Emperor"--we again quote Caron's words-"had closely scrutinised and perfectly understood all the questions and answers exchanged in the assembly between the councillors and ourselves," and before the Japanese authorities had received a reassuring answer to the question repeatedly put by them, whether, in case of the Portuguese being banished from Japan, the Dutch and the Chinese would be in a position to provide the empire of Japan with silk and silk stuffs, medicines, drugs and drysaltery, as the Portuguese had done up to now"[4]. On August 31 a government commissioner arrived at Nangasaki to see the edict put in force, and on the 2nd of September the decree was read out to the Portuguese.

" We find," thus ran the document as cited in Caron's letter[5], "that you and your countrymen are continually and down to the present day, bringing Popish priests into Japan, in direct contravention

of our strict regulations touching this matter. The which priests together with their disciples are seconded by you and your countrymen in the
attainment of their object. Whence proceeds that our subjects change
their allegiance, and many persons come to a miserable end. For the
which reason you all of you deserve death, and His Imperial Majesty
would but conform to justice by putting you all to death; yet, of his
great mercy, he will spare your lives and hereby commands you to
leave this country and never to return to the same. If on the contrary
you should disobey this command, you shall fare no better than you
deserve even now."

The blow was a mortal one to the Portuguese, and a period of
still greater commercial activity now seemed likely to open to the
Dutch merchants. There were loud jubilations at the castle of Batavia.
"Thanks be sent up to Almighty God for the blessing conferred on us!
may it bring on the utter overthrow of our enemies and promote the
Company's well-being over there!"

But the weapon which the Dutch had wielded against their opponents, proved to be a two-edged one. The suspicions of the Japanese
government had been aroused not only against the form of Christianity
which had established a footing in their country, but also against
Christianity in general; not only against those foreigners who bore the
name of Portuguese, but against all foreigners who

[1] See "Dachregister van 't gheene opt Comptoir Firando voorgevallen
is," August 22, 1639. An extract from this daily journal for 1635 and some
years following, is given in VALENTIJN, 1. c., pp. 76 ff.]

[2] Daily Journal of Firando, August 5, 1640. Cf. also VAN DER CHIJS'
edition of "Dagregister van Batavia 1640-1641," p. 259]

[3] Cf. also G. LAUTS, Japan, pp. 23, 30, 108 ff.; PH. F. VON SIEBOLD,
Urkundliche Darstellung der Bestrebungen von Niederland und Russland
zur Eröffnung Japan's für die Schiffahrt und den Seehandel aller Nationen.
Bonn, 1854, pp. 7-8.]

[4] As regards these interviews and palavers, see "Daghregister Firando,"
May 20-22, and 27, 1639.--Cf. also Missive from the G.-G. and Counc. to
our President in Japan, June 13, 1640.]

[5] 5) It is also cited in "Daghregister Firando," September 2, 1639.]

visited their ports. The Dutch were soon to learn it to their
cost. Directly after the edict that banished the Portuguese had been put
in force, the Chinese and the Netherlanders, who now chiefly en-
grossed the trade with Japan, although certain countries of Eastern
Asia continued to enjoy the same privilege [1], had read out to them an
Imperial admonition warning them against introducing into Japan any

priests or other persons who might be willing or able to spread the Christian doctrine, and against making attempts at christianisation on their own account. Caron foresaw that still stronger signs of distrust were to be expected[2], and the authorities at Batavia, on receiving these tidings, gave vent to their apprehensions in the anxious wish: "May the Lord preserve us from further restrictions!"[3]

These further restrictions were bound to come notwithstanding: the distrust against the Christian foreigners had not disappeared after the expulsion of the Portuguese. Caron did not disguise the fact from himself and his superiors, and we have his letter to Van Diemen of November 20, 1640, to prove it. "In the meantime," thus he unburdens himself to his superiors, "we find that all things here are falling from bad into worse, and that our well-founded reasons and excuses on the subject of religion are indeed heard, but noways accepted for truth. It would seem that some of our jealous detractors have misled the Regents of Nangasaque (who, settled in that hot-bed of Portuguese intrigue, are also far from being our friends), and made them believe that the duty of a Christian forbids him from suffering his faith and doctrine to remain stationary, and that consequently (seeing that the Portuguese power has been annihilated) the Dutch remain bound to prosecute the matter, not in this period of stringency to be sure, but in after-times, when they shall have reason to believe that the Japanese have been lulled to sleep by the seeming sincerity of the Netherlanders. To this our envious defamers add, that no Christians (whether Portuguese, Dutchmen, Englishmen, or any other nations of the said faith, and coming from those quarters) are under any circumstances to be trusted...In this and similar manners our state is attacked; thus do venomous serpents attempt to suck our blood...The Lord be "praised for the blessing that at present the Company's interests are in great favour, consideration and esteem with the Emperor and with almost all the Magnates as well, as has well appeared in all that has lately happened, but matters might be a great deal better yet, if the name of Christians did not go sorely against the grain with them. They know full well that we are Christians, and keep up our religion; nor are we prohibited or dissuaded from continuing to do so. Still this our Christian profession is the only reason why our doings, dealings and goings-on are so narrowly watched and supervised, a state of things which we fear and almost make bold to predict, will not improve but become more grievous every day; so that it is to be apprehended that (as matters now stand) they will more and more draw in the string which up to now has allowed us to fly about at will, and shorten it to such a degree, that there is no more room for suspicion and we are utterly delivered into their hands."

Such was the position of affairs when Tasman arrived in Japan, and cast anchor before Firando. Pursuant to the practice of the time, which gave to the commander of a ship a seat in the Council of the factory before which his vessel was lying at anchor, he became a temporary member of the council of this factory, of whose resolutions[4] he figures as cosignatory.

The impression conveyed by these resolutions is an anything but cheering one; on the contrary, the Councillors are found to allude to the "feeling of depression at the Company's miserable condition and ruinous losses." What had happened?

Although the Dutch felt far from easy as to what the future had in store for them, yet the blow fell quite unexpectedly. While Caron was engaged in drafting his letter to Batavia of November 20[5]

[1] The ordinary assumption that the Dutch and the Chinese had an exclusive privilege of the trade with Japan is erroneous, so far at least as concerns the period under review. Ships also from Tonquin, Siam and Cambodia were allowed to enter Japanese harbours, although in this case too, restrictions became more frequent as time went on. (Cf. Missive from the G.-G. and Counc. to the Board of Directors, December 12, 1642).]

[2] Missive to the G.-G., Oct. 26, 1639.]

[3] Missive to the Board of Directors, December 18, 1639.--Cf. also the missive from the G.-G. and Counc. to the President in Japan, June 13, 1640.]

[4] Under date September 11-December 29, 1640.]

[5] I have followed this letter and the Daily Journal of Firando.--See also VAN DER CHIJS' edition of Dagregister Nan Batavia, 1640-1641, pp. 130-157.--Cf. MEYLAN, pp. 109-117; VON SIEBOLD in Moniteur, pp. 33 ff.; LAUTS, Japan, pp. 203 ff.]

there arrived at Firando on the 8th of that month a government commissioner, seemingly for the purpose of inspecting and searching, before they weighed anchor, the Dutch ships that were ready to set sail. Caron felt no shadow of suspicion, so that he was utterly unprepared for the imperial edict[1] of which the commissioner apprized him on the very next day, and which ran as follows:

"His Imperial Majesty has been informed on the best authority, that you are all of you Christians no less than the Portuguese. You keep the Sunday holy, you inscribe the date of Christ's birth on the roofs and fronts of your houses, in the sight and before the eyes of our entire population; you have the Ten Commandments, the Lord's

Prayer, the Creed, Baptism, the Holy Communion, the Bible, the Testament, Moses, the Prophets, and the Apostles. In brief, you are at one with the Portuguese in the main points; the differences between you we hold to be slight; we have long known that you are Christians, but thought you worshipped another Christ; in consequence of all which His Majesty through my mouth lays upon you his positive command, that you shall pull down all your dwelling-houses (having the aforesaid date inscribed in their fronts, excepting none)...

"We will not allow you to keep your Sunday publicly, to the end that the memory of that name may perish for ever.

"The captain or chief of your nation shall not henceforth be allowed to remain in Japan for a longer term than one year, and shall be yearly replaced by another, as used to be the practice with the Maccauw people [i.e. with the Portuguese, when they were staying in Japan], lest the Christian doctrine should be propagated by a longer intercourse on his part with our nation."

The emperor's change of front was owing to his aversion to the Christian faith and his dread of Christianity, whose professors were all of them undeserving of his confidence, because they tried to conspire against his empire.

The government commissioner openly took up the position "of our declared enemy, as if he had come to destroy us all, at first threatening to have the heads of 8 or 10 of the most notable Netherlanders chopped off, if the command was not forthwith acted up to."

The Dutch forthwith set about the demolition of the newly erected warehouse, and had to bless their stars that they were suffered to put off the pulling down of their other dwellings, until the goods stored in them should have been disposed of. "Besides," Caron goes on to say, "we have received notice that our trade and mode of life shall have to be regulated in conformity with this new statute. Time will show how our trade and our life will shape themselves. We cannot but conclude that the Japanese mean to subject us to the same vexations with which they used to harass the Portuguese. Up to now we have with God's help borne everything with long-suffering patience;"-- Caron had quietly submitted to the commands laid upon him-- "whether we shall be able to persist in this submissive attitude, time will show. The vexations to which we are exposed, are getting worse, and they are likely to become more and more intolerable instead of being relaxed. The glory of our nation, only lately shining with radiant lustre in the eyes of the Japanese magnates, has been sadly eclipsed by the Christian name." "Meanwhile"--Caron concludes--"they are trying experiments to find out whether they will be able to get on and maintain themselves on their own country's supplies of food and clothing, to which end their efforts are more and more directed every day."

The latter circumstance especially entailed great dangers to Dutch commerce. In proportion as the Japanese tried to realise this idea, the Dutch imports into Japan, especially of silk-stuffs (a branch in which the Dutch had all along had to keep up a keen competition with the Chinese) must needs fall off, and the exports of precious metals could not but follow suit. Decrees had already been promulgated, prohibiting "the servants of the lesser nobility, of merchants and commoners, from henceforth wearing silk garments or the like habiliments, the which persons, numbering many thousands, consume large quantities of the same, since every one is desirous of dressing out his servants with great splendour; moreover enacting that actors and prostitutes shall henceforward not be allowed to use any brocades or stuffs, embroidered or printed with gold, either for clothing or bedding, which classes of persons, owing to their great numbers, were wont to purchase enormous quantities of the precious stuffs aforesaid."[2]

[1) Also printed in VALENTIJN, Japan, p. 101.]

[2) Missive from Caron to the G.-G., November 20, 1640.]

The working of two silver-mines had already been suspended by order of the government. Nor were the disastrous effects of these measures long in making themselves felt. "It is a fine fleet," that is lying ready to sail for Formosa--Caron writes on November 30, "but only a very modest capital;" the value of the cargoes was seven hundred thousand guilders only.

Besides, the edicts already issued by the Japanese authorities, who kept always insisting on the evacuation and demolition of the remaining houses, and the utter uncertainty in which the Netherlanders were as to the ultimate plans of the Japanese, made it advisable for the Dutch to dispose of the commodities stored at their factory, the more so as the stock on hand was very large, and the Chinese continued to send in fresh supplies in large quantities[1].

These sales were actually effected at ruinously low rates, to the grievous loss of the Company and the heart-felt sorrow of her servants. Not only had most of the goods to be given away at cost-price, but it even became necessary to put up with still lower figures in order to get rid of the stock on hand. "We must grin and bear it!" Caron wrote; but, as he delivered himself in a letter to Governor Traudenius of Formosa, dated December 18, 1640, he remained "in great dread and affliction, never having expected" that he should live to see "such disastrous times" in Japan.

Meanwhile things went on from bad to worse. The stringent measures taken in November had been followed by an absolute prohibition of the exportation of gold. Another decree now forbade "the killing and eating of cattle, since the Japanese have now been informed on unimpeachable authority that the Dutch are likewise Christians; the Japanese fancy that the eating of butcher's meat is a Christian ceremony, since of old no cattle used to be killed, but the practice has been introduced by the Portuguese." The Dutch were further enjoined to restore all the moneys they had borrowed of Japanese subjects. In order to be able to do so, they were compelled to procure ready money, again by the sale at any price of the goods in their warehouses. None of the Japanese capitalists or merchants any longer ventured as of old to advance to the Dutch the sums they needed for their trade.

"What all this is to end in," Caron complained to Traudenius on the same occasion[2], "who can guess! It is reported that new ordinances regulating our position are being prepared by the Japanese authorities; our name of being Christians is a particular eyesore to them; they charge us with converting the inhabitants of Formosa to the Christian faith; in sum, they say that we are not a whit better than the Portuguese, who are also constantly plotting such doings."

The critical position of the Company's affairs during Tasman's stay in Japan--a position which was destined to be further endangered by still more harassing restrictions, and finally led to the removal of the Dutch factory from Firando to Decima, in the immediate vicinity of Nangasaki--compelled Tasman to make a longer stay in Japan than he could possibly have foreseen: with the other servants of the Company he witnessed the evil times that had come upon them. On the 25th of September the Dutch Council at Firando had resolved to despatch to Cambodja the ship Oostcappel, with the goods purchased in Japan with destination for the former country. After discharging her cargo the said vessel was to carry the Cambodja merchandise to Batavia. But circumstances prevented the despatch of the this ship and of the other vessels, and it was not until December 29 that the Oostcappel weighed anchor under command of Tasman. She carried a cargo, worth a little less than a hundred thousand guilders, and set off for Cambodja via Formosa[3].

On the 6th of January, 1641, she cast anchor before the fortress of Zeelandia; here the goods destined for Formosa were unloaded, other "commodities inquired for in Cambodja" were put on board of her, and she very soon performed the rest of her voyage[4]. Only a week later she departed from the island with a cargo worth up-upwards of nineteen thousand guilders[5], and on the 3Ist of January Tasman and his ship reached their new destination[6].

[1] See Resolution Firando, December 29, 1640; Resolution of the G.-G. and Counc., January 2 and May 4, 1641]

[2] Cf. Missive from Caron to Traudenius, December 29, 1640; Daily journal of Firando, and VAN DER CHIJS' "Dagregister van Batavia, 1640-1641," pp. 176, 181, 182, 257-263.--As regards the incidents here related, see also Missive from the G.-G. and Counc. to the Board of Directors, January 8, 1641.]

[3] Daily Journal of Firando, December 29, 1640.--Missive from the Governor and Council of Formosa to the Dutch "President" in Japan, July 3, 1641.]

[4] Daily Journal of Formosa.--Missive from the Governor and Council of Formosa to the G.-G., January 10, 1641.]

[5] Daily Journal of Formosa.--Missive from the Governor and Council of Formosa to the "President" in Japan, July 3, 1641]

[6] VAN DER CHIJS' edition of "Dagregister van Batavia, 1640-1641" p. 242.]

VIII

RELATIONS BETWEEN THE DUTCH EAST INDIA COMPANY AND CAMBODJA.--INTERCOURSE OF THE DUTCH WITH LAOS.--TASMAN ONCE MORE IN CAMBODJA AND FORMOSA (1641)

The history of the relations of the Dutch East India Company with Cambodja, as indeed with the whole of Indo-China, is little known. The Dutch came into contact with Cambodja for the first time in 1601, when two vessels that had sailed from Bantam to form mercantile connections with China, visited the former country[1].

This visit, however, remained without results. In subsequent years, too, the Dutch occasionally did business with Cambodja. Thus, in 1616, 1617, and 1620, attempts at forming a permanent connection with this country were made by the Dutch factory at Patani[2], while, conversely, merchants of Cambodja visited Batavia[3].

But no really flourishing trade seemed likely to spring up with this new market, and efforts in this direction were threatened with utter frustration especially, when the plans of Governor-General Jan Pieterszoon Coen for concentrating the Company's trade in some of its most important settlements, already in 1622 caused the quite recently established factory in Cambodja to be abrogated[4]. Friendly relations, as a rule, continued to subsist, it is true[5], but the trade with this country was reduced to a minimum.

The Company's position in Japan made its influence felt here also. In 1635 the Supreme Government at Batavia was informed by its representatives in Japan that "for various reasons"--it would seem that the fear of Japanese contact with the Europeans, and of Christian proselytism were mainly instrumental in this case--"the Emperor had strictly prohibited all Japanese from undertaking any voyages to countries beyond the sea, to Cochinchyna, as far as Quinam or Tonquyn; nor were they allowed to visit Champa, Cambodja, Patane, Taijouan or any other places; moreover the Emperor had at very short notice sent orders for returning to all Japanese then residing abroad." This news coincided with another piece of intelligence, this time from Siam, viz. that the merchants of the northern districts, especially of Laos, who were in the habit of bringing their goods to market there, were in those days deterred from continuing to do so, by the rough treatment they had met with in Siam, and were reported to have transferred to Cambodja "the staple for benzoin and shellac." Lastly, the circumstance that Cambodja produced large quantities of rice, which everywhere in India was wanted for the Dutch factories and garrisons, was a powerful factor[6] among the motives that induced the resolution of the Governor-General and Councillors of April 9, 1636, to despatch a vessel with destination for Cambodja.

Hopes were entertained that, besides procuring what was wanted for Batavia and Europe, the Dutch would succeed there in buying up goods, for instance, deer-skins, for the Japan market among others[7], while, conversely, Japanese silver was sure to meet with a ready sale there. The Dutch merchants were received with great courtesy, and obtained the king's permission to build a factory and to export rice from his dominions. Nor were they long in beginning mercantile operations, which besides export business also comprised the importation of large quantities of cotton prints from the Coast of Coromandel. In spite of keen competition, chiefly on the part of the Portuguese and Chinese,

[1] DE JONGE, Opkomst, II, pp. 245-247.]

[2] J. A. B. WISELIUS (Geschiedenis en reizen der Nederlanders in Kambodja in de 17e en 18e eeuw) says erroneously that in the documents of the State-Archives in The Hague no mention is made of the Dutch relations with Cambodja before 1636. (De Gids, 1878, III, p. 73). Cf. my paper "Hendrik Jansen, een zeventiende-eeuwsche Groninger in Indië" (Indische Gids, 1896, p. 118)--See letters from the Dutch factory at Patani to Batavia, October 25, 1617; November 4, 1620; October 15, 1621.]

[3] Missives from the G.-G. to the Board of Directors, January 8, 1621 and March 18, 1629; Daily Journal of Batavia, 1631, 1632, passim, etc.]

[4] TIELE-HEERES, Bouwstoffen, II, p. XXXII.--Missive from the G.-G. to the Board of Directors, September 6, 1622.]

[5] See, for instance, Missives from the G.-G. and Counc. to the King of Cambodja, July 28, 1626 and June 8, 1633.--Daily Journal of Batavia, March 21 and May 25, 1631, etc.]

[6] Missive from the G.-G. and Counc. to the Board of Directors, January 4, 1636.]

[7) Cf. also "Verthooninge der gelegentheyt des Coninckrijx van Cambodia," in Kroniek van het Historisch Genootschap, gevestigd to Utrecht,
1871, pp. 304 ff.]

business went on to mutual satisfaction: in 1640 " the Company's trade and position were quite satisfactory there"[1].

Tasman himself, however, was once more unfortunate here[2].
Not only had he to bring the news that the critical situation in Japan
would prevent Cambodja goods from finding buyers there[3], but in
Cambodja itself also the outlook had become less favourable. Business
kept increasing, it is true, and a cargo worth twenty-five thousand
guilders could be put on board Tasman's ship, but the king of Cambodja refused to allow the exportation of rice, and seemed for the moment
more favourably disposed towards the Portuguese than towards the
Dutch[4], while "the people of Cambodja were daily becoming more
insolent and haughty"[5]. Fortunately they had thrown no obstacles in
the way of certain merchants of Laos, who had expressed a wish to
visit Batavia in order to confer with the Dutch authorities about the
interests of trade. These merchants, accordingly, on the 2nd of March
set sail for Batavia in the Oostcappel, taking a quantity of mercantile
articles along with them, and on April 11 next, the vessel arrived in the
road-stead of Batavia, bringing from the ruler of Cambodja a letter and
a present for the Governor-General and his Councillors[6].

The Governor-General and his Council resolved to receive the
letter and the merchants with "due ceremony"[7]. The pomp and circumstance of their reception was such that ". the heathen man (the
chief of the merchants) found it impossible to describe the honour and
amity shown them at Batavia"[8]. That the Company continued to attach
high importance to their trade relations with Cambodja and Laos--they
also hoped to draw gold from there[9]--they showed not only by treating
at Batavia with the strangers who had come there[10], but still more
markedly by resolving, on April 19 already, that the Oostcappel should
once more be despatched to Cambodja, and next to Japan via Formosa.

On their own part the merchants of Laos also seemed to see,
they were interested in maintaining the mercantile connection with the
Dutch. They requested, at all events, that some deputies from Batavia
might be sent to Laos along with them in the Oostcappel, which was to
carry them back, or that such persons might be deputed from the factory in Cambodja itself, "in order to accompany them to the Laos
country, conclude a closer alliance with their king, and confer with
him about matters of commerce." This proposal tallied exactly with
advices to the same effect, given to the Governor-General and Coun-

cillors by the supercargos Pieter Van Regemortes and Harmen Broeckmans, who represented the Company in Cambodja. They, too, had warmly advocated the expediency of buying up directly in Laos itself the products[11] of this "strange country never before visited by the Dutch"[12], of which the inhabitants "would seem to be civilised people and enterprising merchants." The Supreme Government, however, deemed it "unadvisable to establish a regular trade with the said country, but thought it more profitable to attract the Laos merchants to Cambodja and Batavia; the way thither is long and difficult, and consequently subject to heavy expense and numerous obstacles." They, however resolved, "in order to obtain reliable information as to what could be done in that

[1] Missive from the G--G. and Counc. to the Board of Directors, January 8, 1641.--See also VAN DER CHIJS, "Dagregister, 1640-1641," pp, 124-129.]

[2] LAUTS, and the writers who base themselves on his labours, do not allude to this stay of Tasman in Cambodja, though they do refer to a later voyage of his thither, undertaken from Batavia.]

[3] VAN DER CHIJS, "Dagregister, 1640-1641," pp. 242, 262; Missive from the ex-president in Japan to the Dutch supercargos in Cambodja, December 13, 1641.]

[4] Cf. Missive from the G.-G. to the King of Cambodja, May 14, 1641.]

[5] Cf. also VAN DER CHIJS, "Dagregister 1640-1641," p. 128.]

[6] VAN DER CHIJS, "Dagregister 1640-1641," pp. 242-247--Resolution of the G.-G. and Counc., April 11, 1641.]

[7] Cf. their Resolutions of April 11 and 18, 1641.--VAN DER CHIJS, "Dagregister 1640-1641," p. 246.]

[8] "Verbael ofte t' summier van d'advijsen, die sedert vltmo. October Anno 1641 uijt...Cambodia...en 't eijlandt Fermosa...in Batavia ontvangen zijn."--Cf. VALENTIJN, III, 2, Cambodia, p. 50.]

[9] Missive from the G.-G. and Counc. to the Board of Directors, December 12, 1641.]

[10] Resolutions of the G.-G. and Counc., April 18 and May 7, 1641.]

[11] Resolution of the G.-G. and Counc., May 7, 1641; Missive from the G.-G. and Counc. to the Board of Directors, Dec. 12, 1641; idem to supercargos Van Regemortes and Broeckmans, May 14, 1641. LAUTS has the erroneous spelling "Regemortel" (Verhandelingen Zeewezen, p. 284).]

[12] "Verbael van d' advijsen uijt...Cambodia...en 't eijlandt Fermosa."]

notable country, to authorise and enjoin" their representatives in Cambodja "to despatch to the Laos country by way of trial, two or more expert persons with a small quantity of sundry goods, that these persons might find out what business could be done there." Letters were drafted to the princes of Cambodja and Laos alike, and presents selected. "The king of Cambodia" was to be presented with "a silver telescope, handsomely engraved, two swords, two globular mirrors, and a string of amber beads weighing 12 oz."; while to the "King of Laos" were to be offered "an emerald set in gold, a brace of fire-lock pistols, a crooked sabre, a pair of embroidered gloves and a pair of plain ones." On May 14 everything was in readiness for departure, and on the next day the Oostcappel set sail with a crew of forty men, having on board the merchants of Laos and a cargo worth about twenty-five thousand guilders. She was commanded by Tasman, and made the voyage in company with six other vessels, all of them destined for the trade with Eastern Asia[1].

The course to be followed by the Oostcappel was, as far as Poeloe Condor, the same with her former route to Formosa; from this island she was to shape her course for "the Cambodja river," more especially for "the mouth of the Bassack river." They were accordingly to sail up the eastern mouth of the river Mekong, still known by the name of Bassak (Bathak)[2]. They reached the river at the latter end of May[3], but owing to the shallowness of the water, they did not succeed in visiting the Dutch factory before the 8th of June. In accordance with his instructions Tasman hastened to take in his cargo, chiefly destined for Japan, and representing a value of about 23.000 guilders, and sailed from the Mekong on the 27th of the same month.

Although the Portuguese had been expelled from Japan, they had by no means given up the hope of getting their share of the profits which the trade with that empire was able to yield. With the inhabitants of those few countries of Eastern Asia, which, like the Chinese and the Dutch, were still allowed access to Japan, or with Chinamen residing in the said countries, they concluded contracts by which these Asiatics engaged themselves to carry goods to Japan in their own vessels and under cover of their own flag. They did so, also in Cambodja. While Tasman was lying at anchor in the Mekong river, three "junks" were there fitted out by Cambodja subjects, for the purpose of carrying in them to Japan certain mercantile commodities, the property of Portuguese residents in Cambodja. Apprehensions were, however, entertained lest the Dutch ships might refuse to let pass the goods of their enemies, if they should meet with them out at sea, and the managers of the Dutch factory were therefore requested to grant passes of safe-conduct, "seeing that the said junks belong to this place, and navigate the sea for gain and profit," in order that these vessels might not be seized merely because they carried goods belonging to Portuguese merchants. The Dutch authorities, however, looked at the matter from another point of view, and opined that vessels "carrying Portuguese goods for freight," ought to be "seized no less than Portuguese ships." They further positively refused to grant passes, on the ground that they were not competent to do so, since the Governor-General and Councillors had expressly forbidden such actions on their part[4], and finally referred the petitioners to the Supreme Government at Batavia. After some hesitation the junks were loaded notwithstanding this answer, and they left the river on the 2 th of June. "In 10° 35' Northern Latitude, about 6 miles west of Poeloe Cicier de Terra," the junks were overtaken by the Oostcappel, on the 3rd of July. Although not expressly directed to do so by his instructions, Tasman was well aware that he would conform to the views of his superiors by boarding the vessels. One of the junks made her escape, but from another of them Tasman seized the goods destined for Japan to a value of about 15000 guilders, with which booty he arrived at Formosa on the 20th of July. There[5], however, the authorities were so little satisfied with his proceedings in this matter, that they cast him in a forfeit

[1] Resolutions of the G.-G. and Counc., May 14 and 22, 1641.--VAN DER CHIJS, "Dagregister 1640-1641," p. 304.]

[2] "Instructions for the officers of the flute-ship Oostcappel," May 14, 1641.]

[3] As regards what follows, see "Verbael" and Missive from Van Regemortes and Broeckmans to Governor Traudenius in Formosa, June 24, 1641.--"Journael ofte dachregister des Casteels Zeelandia," July 20, 1641.--Cf. VALENTIJN, III, 2 (1726), Cambodia, pp. 46-47; VOORMEULEN VAN BOEKEREN, pp. 32-33 (and, taking his information from him, WALKER, pp. 14-15) is mistaken in his account of the disputes between the Dutch and the Portuguese in Cambodja. VALENTIJN, whom he copied, has confounded different things. The said disputes began in February 1642, after Tasman's departure (see "Verbael").]

[4] In their Missive, dated May 14, 1641.]

[5] Not at Batavia, as LAUT, l. c., p. 285 has it.]

of two months' pay. One of the native vessels, namely-, had already been in his possession, and her captain was already on board the Oostcappel, when "in the evening[1] a heavy squall, with sudden gusts of wind, lightning and rain," loosened the rope with which the junk was fastened to Tasman's ship, and no Dutch sailors having been put on board of her as guards, "the prize had run inshore again and escaped."

Tasman made no long inactive stay in Formosa. As early as July 29, his cargo for Japan, worth about 32000 guilders, had been put on board, and in the beginning of August the Oostcappel again weighed anchor[2]. The vessel was not to reach her destination this time. On August 7, in about 26° N. L. she was befallen "by so violent a storm, that she lost all her masts, excepting none, and her rudder besides; they had 6 or 7 feet water in the hold, so that she was in imminent peril of going down, but it has pleased God Almighty to save and preserve her. After being driven hither and thither about the northern extremity of the coast of Formosa for 20 days together," the Oostcappel was sighted by certain other Dutch ships, which took her in tow, and tugged her to the road-stead before Zeelandia[3]. She remained at anchor here till November 17, when she departed for Batavia in company with the Gulden Buys and the Koninginne Marie. The three ships carried cargoes, worth nearly 500.000 guilders together, and chiefly consisting of sugar and silks[4]. Unfortunately only the Oostcappel was to come to port in safety, having on board only a small part of the whole cargo, namely a value of a little more than 36000 guilders, almost entirely in powdered sugar[5]: the two other ships, carrying goods to an amount of 450.000 guilders, went down with all hands on board. That Tasman's vessel came off safe, may almost be called a miracle. She was intended to be again despatched to Cambodja, but the skipper requested that this plan might be given up, "since he hardly saw his way to getting to Cambodja with his ship, unless at great risk." They had not, indeed, succeeded in getting her properly repaired: she had lost her masts, and could not possibly be "put into the required seaworthy condition again"[6]. Near Hainan, before the gulf of Tonquin, the ships had been overtaken by "a most extraordinary storm, in which they had got separated from each other." On December 20, the Oostcappel arrived in the road-stead of Batavia, "carrying a jury-mast or stump instead of her main-mast, which had gone by the board in the unsuccessful voyage to Japan[7]." The other ships were never seen or heard of again[8].

IX

PERSONALIA.--TASMAN'S VOYAGE TO PALEMBANG
(1642.)

Meanwhile, on October 11, 1641, the term had expired, for which Tasman had engaged his services to the Company in his grade of skipper, though not in his general capacity of functionary. The said term had therefore to be lengthened with three years. This was done by the resolution already mentioned, of the Governor-General and Councillors, dated January 17, 1642[9], by which Tasman was "continued as skipper for a further term of three years," counting from October 11, 1641. His monthly pay was raised from sixty to eighty guilders. It would seem that for some weeks he was suffered to remain quietly ashore: at all events no traces are discoverable of his having taken part in any undertaking. But there are found in the Company's archives certain hitherto unknown indications respecting his stay at Batavia. On the 23rd of January, for example, he was summoned before the

[1] Missive from the Governor and Council of Formosa to the Dutch Supercargos in Cambodja, December 14, 1641.]

[2] See bill of lading of the Oostcappel, dated July 29, 1641; Missive from the Governor and Council in Formosa to the Dutch President in Japan, August 9, 1641.]

[3] Missive from the Governor and Council of Formosa to the Dutch President in Japan, September 10, 1641.]

[4] "Verbael...Cambodia...en Formosa, 1641-1642."]

[5] Bill of lading of the Oostcappel, November 17, 1641; Missive from the Governor and Council of Formosa to the G.-G. and Counc., December 22, 1641.]

[6] Missive from the Governor and Council of Formosa to the G-G. and Counc., November 17, 1641.]

[7] "Verbael Cambodia, 1641-1642."]

[8] Missive from the G.-G. and Counc. to the Board of Directors, December 12, 1642,]

[9) See Appendix C.]

Council of Justice of the Castle of Batavia[1]; a civil action was brought against him and one of his assistants, "to require of him the restitution of such legacies as the defendants cum sociis have unlawfully enjoyed" out of the capital left at his death by a person deceased. The defendants "maintained the lawfulness of the legacies that had accrued to them," and made appeal to certain high functionaries who were shortly expected at Batavia from Formosa. Their plea proved insufficient, the Council of Justice "deciding that the defendants, until further proofs being forthcoming, shall provisionally restore the amount of the said legacies, at the same time casting them in the costs and expenses of the present action." We further find noted that by resolution of the Governor-General and Councillors of March 12, 1642, Tasman was charged with the valuation of a Portuguese ship, still captured by Quast. Apart from these scanty indications nothing is heard of him before the month of April, when he was charged with a mission to Palembang.

For many years relations of a mercantile character had been kept up between the Dutch East India Company and the state of Palembang on the east coast of Sumatra. The Dutch had originally established this connection chiefly with the object of procuring pepper, one of the spices most in demand in the European markets. In this case, too, it was simply self-interest that formed the foundation of the mutual relations, which were more or less amicable according as the interests of the two parties coincided or clashed. One of the most important factors affecting. these relations at the time of which we are treating, was the influence which the Soesoehoenan of Mataram, one of the Company's powerful enemies in Central Java[2], was able to exercise on the ruler of Palembang. Now as it happened, it was precisely at this time that the said influence assumed proportions so alarming to the Company[3], that the Governor-General and Councillors came to the conclusion that they on their part ought also to have their say in the matter.

On the 19th of April it was resolved that a small fleet should be despatched to Palembang, to consist of three ships, the Ruttem as flag-ship, Punte de Gale, and the Jager, together with the "chaloup" Johor, manned with 84 sailors and 30 soldiers. The squadron was put under command of skipper[4] Tasman, and, especially when we consider the importance and the difficulty of the expedition, his appointment to this responsible post furnishes abundant proof that the Supreme Government at Batavia had not been very deeply impressed by the

sentence pronounced in Formosa against the skipper of the Oostcappel. A few days later--on April 23--the instructions for this voyage
were drawn up[5]. Its object was mainly twofold. In the first place Tasman got orders to cause to be put on board his ships at Palembang, a
cargo lying ready there. Over and above this, however, he had a task
of a more weighty nature confided to him.

There were namely apprehensions entertained at Batavia that
events of an alarming nature had taken place on the East-coast of Sumatra. Supercargo Adriaan Van Liesveld, who supervised the
Company's interests there, had announced his return to Batavia; but,
although he might long before have arrived there, "his return had
against all expectation been in vain looked forward to." Now this gentleman's "tarriance" caused to the Supreme Government, "serious
alarms, lest to him with his ship, crew and cargo should have happened what we," the Governor-General and Councillors go on to say in
the instructions, "have long apprehended and conjectured from the
unexpected departure of the King of Palimbangh for Mataram, the
country of our enemy; to wit, that he may have been arrested, or.
worse still, his ship, crew and cargo, under pretence of friendship and
good will, have been plundered and seized by the people of Mataram,
the which God in his mercy avert."

In this case still another Dutch vessel, recently departed for
Palembang, would be in danger. Tasman was now to feel his way, and
to act according to circumstances and to the information, which he
might eventually be able to collect. If he found all safe at Palembang,
he had nothing to do beyond taking the goods on board. It was most
earnestly impressed on him that, also in this favourable case,

[1] "Civile Rolle van den Achtbaren Raet van Justitie des Casteels Batavia
van den Jare 1642."]

[2] See DE JONGE, Opkomst, IV, (1869) passim.]

[3] Cf. TIELE-HEERES, Bouwstoffen, II,, pp. LXXIV f., 361-363; III,
pp. XLII, 21, 118; DE JONGE, Opkomst, V, p. 256; Missives from Supercargo Adriaan Van Liesveld at Palembang to the G--G., January 17 and
February 23, 1642.]

[4] Not "commander," as given in LAUTS, Verhandelingen, p. 287, and in
writers following his lead.]

[5] "Ordre voor den E. Abel Janszoon Tasman, ende de verdere officieren
van [de schepen] gedestineert naer de riviere van Palembangh," April 23,
1642.]

not only the success of the expedition itself, but perhaps also the safety of many precious human lives and of costly merchandise would be dependent on his vigilance and good management, as well as on his seamanship and military skill. In case matters were found to wear a favourable aspect at Palembang, one more ticklish business was confided to his charge: also in this case, if at least the representatives of the Company at Palembang had no objection to such a course, he was to keep cruising before the river with two of his ships for some weeks together, with the object of heaving out the pepper on board all such "junks" as were engaged in carrying the said article from Palembang to ports other than Batavia--always granting receipts for the quantities seized, and referring the owners to Batavia. "for obtaining payment for the same." The Company's right to such proceedings they based on the "license to this effect granted us by the King of Palimbangh"[1]. If on the other hand the dreaded hostilities against the Dutch at Palembang had actually taken place, Tasman had orders forthwith to despatch to Batavia with this intelligence the "chaloupe" which formed part of the squadron. Then he was himself "cautiously to sail up the river," with the other vessels under his command, try to collect information there, and if necessary begin negotiations, all the time avoiding as much as possible "any bloodshed and extreme measures." If the Dutch residents at Palembang were still alive, but emprisoned, Tasman was to "signify" to the Palembang native authorities, that "unless within six hours"--here he was expressly prohibited from exceeding this term--"after notice given they released and set free the persons arrested with ship and goods, he had orders to declare war against them, and to proceed forthwith down the river, in order to meet the King,"--who was expected back from Mataram--"and not only to lodge with him a complaint of their doings, but also to take him into custody, until justice should have been done us." Furthermore the river was to be barred as closely as possibly, that no one "except by consent" of the Dutch captains might be able to come near it. If contrary to their hopes, the Dutch residents or some of them should have been killed, he need not have any further scruples, but "when encountering the native forces was enjoined to slay without delay all those who refused to give themselves up prisoners."

In the uncertainty prevailing at Batavia as to the state of affairs at Palembang, the authorities at head-quarters could hardly give minutely specified orders to skipper Tasman. This could only be done after exact reports had come in. But under the present circumstances, in this "dubious affair" a good deal had to be left to the skill of the leader of the expedition, and the Governor-General and Councillors seem to have felt they could do so with safety, for they conclude, thereby entirely obliterating the stigma of the sentence passed on him in Formosa: "for the rest relying on your good management and painstaking activity." And these two qualities also stood him in good stead in discharging himself of the additional duty laid upon him, of boarding "all the foreign Indian craft," and all the Spanish and Portuguese ships he should meet with in the course of his expedition, removing all the men and goods out of the same, drawing up an inventory of them," and taking them with him to Batavia.

Just as the instructions had been drawn up, Van Liesvelt came to anchor at Batavia, on the 21st of April[2]. The tidings he brought "concerning the affair of Palimbangh, and the perfidious minds of the natives there," did not reassure the Supreme Government on the subject of the fate of the Netherlanders still left there, and of the ship departed thither, and it was resolved that the expedition under Tasman should take place in the manner decided upon. In case he should find that all had remained quiet there, he was now directed to proceed against the magnates with diplomatic caution, and to make them believe that the Supreme Government at Batavia, having as yet had no tidings about Van Liesveld, had sent the ships to Palembang to protect this town against her enemies!

Instructions like these are calculated to bring out the versatility of the functionaries who served the Company in India at the time. They were employed literally for every thing. One day merchants, the next soldiers; now sailors, now diplomatists! It is true that the nature of the missions with which they were charged as negotiators with the native Princes, Magnates and peoples, would not always bear close scrutiny on the score of morality--the "- ordre- " given to Tasman on the 23rd of April puts the point beyond a doubt--but this circumstance throws no blame on the Company's servants themselves,

[1] This also appears from a missive from the G.-G. and Counc. to Van Liesveld, dated March 19, 1642.]

[2] Cf. Resolution of the G.-G. and Counc., April 23, 1642.]

who had merely to obey the commands laid upon them by their masters. Thus it cannot cast any slur on Tasman's fair fame if he acquitted himself of still another charge, not until now inserted in his instructions[1], viz. to lay his hands on, alive if possible, and carry to Batavia as a prisoner, a certain Chinaman who in the Company's archives is invariably styled "nachoda" [skipper] Benki or Binki, and who after quitting Batavia over head and ears in debt, was now living at Palembang in high favour with the native authorities, "putting great affronts upon us," and thwarting the Dutch wherever he could. This was to be done "either by violence or stratagem," capture by violence, however, being preferred. The Governor-General and Councillors engaged themselves afterwards to account for this indefensible proceeding to the King of Palembang. Tasman did not see his way to laying hold of him, "except," we read[2], "by trying to lure him on board a Dutch ship under pretence of friendship." The stratagem was successful, and the Chinaman was carried to Batavia in irons. Even admitting the truth of the statement that Binki had threatened to assassinate all the Netherlanders residing at Palembang[3], this piece of treachery cannot be palliated, though we cannot put the blame of it on Tasman: we can only say that this circumstance taken in connection with what had otherwise become known of Binki's interference with the Dutch interests, may help to account for the resolution of the Supreme Government that led to this breach of faith; an act that gave rise to no end of negotiations with Palembang, and even with its neighbour Djambi[4].

Apart from these indications in his instructions, it does not appear how Tasman acquitted himself of his task, about which he probably reported by word of mouth. It is not unlikely that on arriving at Palembang, for which destination he set out on April 24, he found matters in a more favourable position than had been presumed. Perhaps also the forces at his disposal may have overawed the enemy. At all events he took in his cargo, though he must have been cruising before the river for some considerable time, since he did not return to Batavia before the 10th of June[5].

X

GENERAL VIEW OF THE COMPANY'S POSITION IN THE EAST.

In this way in Eastern Asia and Sumatra Tasman amply deserved his share of the glory which the seventeenth century Netherlanders reaped in India. Nor has this glory been illegitimately obtained, also in the eyes of those who are by no means blind to the numerous shortcomings of which the Dutch were guilty in these regions, and who do not from partial prepossession endeavour to palliate these shortcomings with the cloak of charity, or at least to gloss them over, but on the contrary account it their duty to cast on them the white light of impartial historical research. Impartial research: that is to say, that those shortcomings are not explained away, but also, that they are, if possible, accounted for from the position in which the actors in them were placed, so that they can therefore be understood, and consequently perhaps be excused and condoned.

The history of the Netherlanders in India, any more than any other section of the history of mankind, can never be really understood, never be satisfactorily written, until the whole of the milieu in which those who have made that history, lived, moved and had their being, has been completely realised, fully understood, and on all points elucidated.

[1] LAUTS, 1. c., p. 287, has evidently failed to notice this; hence, this author and those who follow his lead, consider the emprisonment of Benki as the main object of Tasman's mission, and make erroneous inferences from it.]

[2*) Resolution of the G.-G. and Counc., July 2, 1642.]

[3) Ibidem.]

[4) Cf. HEERES, Bouwstoffen, III, pp. 118, 123, etc.]

[5) Resolution of the G.-G. and Counc., July 2, 1642.--What LAUTS (p. 288) says about the restoration of the friendly understanding with Palembang after Tasman's expedition, should be compared with the information on this point given in DE JONGE, Opkomst, V, pp. 256 and 257, from which it appears that LAUTS' way of representing the facts will not stand criticism. Of the "high praise" given to Tasman by Van Diemen, I have not found a trace in any of the documents I have consulted. VOORMEULEN VAN BOEKEREN, 1. c., p. 44 f., indulges in further embroidery on Lauts' statements. Thus he makes Tasman request an interview and have a conversation with the Sultan, who...was absent from his empire.]

Now the very first thing to be considered in this connection is, that when the Dutch turned their ships' heads to the East, they did not do so, because they believed they had a mission to fulfil there, or that they ought to appear there as the bearers of their own form of civilisation. To be sure, it was not long before they became conscious of an incipient feeling within them, gently reminding them that in the far East there were still other things to be attended to, besides the affairs of this world they then began to think it their duty to make attempts at transplanting to this new soil their religious ideas, and leading the blinded and erring sheep into Christ's fold[1]. But this consciousness of a higher mission was simply something adventitious. The object for which on the borders of the Amstel the first Company for transmarine trade ("Compagnie van Verre") was formed, was the most selfish of all possible ends, money-making. What the Dutch merchants had their eye on, was the profit-bringing trade in Indian spices: not the spreading of civilisation or the obtaining of political power in the East. And the succeeding associations that were destined to coalesce into the one great Chartered Company, started from the very same principle, and this identical principle has presided over the counsels of the Company's directors in the Netherlands down to the termination of its existence. It is true that in course of time other interests besides this have demanded and obtained a hearing: the propagation of Christianity, and the political position which the Company was gradually taking up in the East; but we repeat, these were unessentials, and unessentials they remained till the end; the main thing was always the making of trade-profits. No doubt missionary work has not been utterly neglected by the Directors of the Company, and when once complete light shall have been let in on its history, it will almost certainly appear that the trading corporation has to this subject devoted fully as much care as could in reason be demanded of a man of business. And how about its political position? it may be asked. By what we have narrated higher up about the Amboyna affairs, the way in which political influence was obtained, has become sufficiently clear. Mutatis mutandis the history of the Dutch settlement in this island-group affords an example of what took place almost everywhere else in the East. Political power was, especially in the opinion of the Board of Directors, a means to get hold of trade, or to retain it when once got hold of. Whoever peruses their letters cannot fail to see that the Directors regarded the Company's political position as a burden, which must be borne, only because, and so far as it was indispensable for the interests and for the maintenance of commerce. From the very nature of the case the Supreme Government at Batavia looked on this political position with very different eyes, because it was they who had laid its foundations and now had to maintain it, because they deeply felt and clearly saw that they were the rulers of a state. But the Directors at home, who looked at all this from afar, who as a rule understood from the figures sent them or drawn up by themselves, what exorbitant costs the maintenance of this position entailed--another drawback to the Company's sovereignty--; but who, apart from this, perceived but little of the gigantic empire which their "servants" had founded in the East; the Directors at home, had they been able to do so, would not improbably have been glad to turn the course of events, which had given rise to their political position in India--at least, if without the latter the profits of trade had also flowed into their pockets.

Had they been able to work their will, the history of the Dutch colonies in East India would no doubt have borne a very different character. Instead of giving a narrative of peaceable trade relations, which might in that case have constituted the Company's history, instead of setting forth the details of friendly or amicable intercourse with the native population, that history has become the account of an almost unparalleled struggle for life. And unfortunately many a page of the ample volume in which this history is recorded, is stained with spots of blood that can never be blotted out.

To excuse this blood-shed there is one extenuating circumstance only--fortunately it is a circumstance that is likely to weigh heavily in the balance of justice in exculpation of the perpetrators--to wit, that this blood was shed, because those who then presided over the colonial policy of the Dutch must have been aware of the fact, that without such deeds of violence the Dutch colonial empire in the East could not be upheld. If it was intended to retain the position once taken up, there was to be no hesitancy as regarded the removal of the obstacles to its progress which the Company found in its

[1] See, for example, Articles 10, 13, 42 of "Instructie voor Pieter Both, Gouverneur-Generaal, en die van den Raad van Indiën," November 14/27, 1609 (P. MIJER, Verzameling van instructies, ordonnancies en reglemen-

ten voor de regering van Nederlandsch-Indië. Batavia, Landsdrukkerij, 1848, pp. 8, 10, 20).]

forward march. Politics can never be a task for angels; colonial politics least of all. And emphatically least of all in the seventeenth century, when very different, far less humane ideas than at present, were prevalent on this subject, especially again as concerned the non-Christian Asiatics, almost universally looked down on with contempt. Of this feeling the Dutch were by no means a solitary example; it was shared by all the other colonial powers of Europe, who certainly were none of them their superiors in this respect. Where there is question of comparing Dutch colonial history with that of other nations, Spaniards, Portuguese, Englishmen or whomever else, the Netherlands may boldly open their historical records; they will triumphantly stand the test of comparison with the colonial annals of other nations. Their history will not reveal more and not greater shortcomings than those which may be laid at the door of other nations; will have in store not fewer and not less brilliant deeds of glory than others have achieved.

Many of those grand and glorious exploits were accomplished even in the first half of the seventeenth century. Even when we take a bird's eye view only of the condition of the Dutch East India Company in 1642, remembering at the same time that not half a century had then elapsed, since the first ships sailed from the low-lying lands by the sea, with their heads turned to the East; not half a century since the Netherlanders--a small band that could almost safely be disregarded and insulted by the Lusitanian rival, then still so powerful outwardly--reached Asia's shores; not half a century since they returned to the borders of Y and Amstel without any results beyond hopes for the future, and confidence in the success of fresh, efforts; when we institute these and the like comparisons, we cannot but receive the immediate impression that the founders of the Dutch power in the East have developed an amount of strength, given proofs of a degree of skill, exhibited a measure of energy that cannot fail to command our respectful admiration. That the results obtained by them were mainly the work of their leaders, among whom the Governors-General Jan Pieterszoon Coen and Antonio Van Diemen hold the foremost places, may be readily granted. But all the energy of the leading men, their skill and their strength, would have failed in the task, if in the execution of what they deemed necessary for the success of the great cause, they had not been in a position to rely on the hearts, the heads and the powerful arms of so many of their companions; and it is noteworthy that the majority of those who have contributed, to establish the Dutch colonial empire in the East, did not belong to those social layers that excel by culture, birth or wealth, but had sprung, if not from the very lowest class, at least from the humbler ranks of society. The glory achieved by them did not in the first place enhance the lustre of names already known, established or celebrated; it usually served to confer fame on the bearer's cognomen--often his by-name, or even his sobriquet--as well as on the bearer himself, far and wide over the vast extent of territory, where the Dutch had taken up their position in the East. The career of a Tasman may safely be considered typical of what the best among his countrymen have wrought and aspired to, of what glorious deeds they have done, and what reprehensible, or at all events mistaken actions they have been led into.

The vast extent of territory...From Madagascar to Japan, from New Guinea to the Red Sea! One part of it, the Dutch had conquered, sword in hand, another was by them regarded as a "sphere of influence," but by far the greatest portion of it was used by them simply as a field for their commercial operations[1].

The first Dutch possession which at the period under review was touched at in the voyage from the Netherlands to Java's garden of wonders, was the island of St. Helena, of which in 1633 the ex-Governor-General Jacques Specx on his home-voyage had taken possession on behalf of the States-General of the United Provinces [2]--St. Helena lying outside the lines of demarcation, laid down for its operations in the Company's charter--, and which, like the Cape of Good Hope, where, a short time after, the Company itself was to establish a Dutch settlement, was only used as a station for refreshments on the long voyage. Until a few years before, this had also been the case with the Mauritius, but in 1638 this island, too, had been declared a possession of the powerful mercantile association: it produced ebony, and formed the starting-point for the Dutch trade with Madagascar,

[1] As regards the field of the Company's operations, compare the list, drawn up after the conclusion of the truce between the Dutch republic and Portugal, entitled, "Namen van de plaatzen die in Orienten bij de Portugiesen en Nederlanders werden beaten en gefrequenteert," and printed in HEERES, Bouwstoffen, III, pp. 51-56. A bad translation of this list is given in [THÉVENOT'S] Relations de divers voyages curieux. II, Paris, Mabre-Cramoisy, 1666.]

[1] Report on the State Archives at the Hague for 1894, p, 12.]

which furnished slaves[1]. The South-western and Southern coasts of Arabia were visited by Dutch ships: Mocha, Aden, Fartak, and other places on the coast, together with the island of Socotra, saw the Princely standard floating from the Dutch top-masts. Already the attention of the Board of Directors had been drawn by the most cele-brated product of Mocha, its world-famed coffee[2], and since in 1638 the mercantile relations with Mocha had been renewed, after having lain dormant for a time[3], considerable quantities were from there car-ried to Persia in Dutch vessels[4].

In the latter country the Company had mercantile offices at Gamron (Bender Abbas), Lar, Shiraz, and Ispahan, in which localities in the first place silks, were bought up, which article was accounted one of the most important commodities dealt in by the Company. Of vast importance was also the Dutch factory at Surat. With this factory for their point of departure, the Dutch mercantile connections extended over the whole of Gujerat and the districts north of it. There were fac-tories at Bharotsch, Baroda, Cambay, Ahmadabad, nay, even at Agra and Jalalpur. The principal exports from these places were, for in-stance, saltpetre and indigo, but especially "all sorts of cotton goods," which the Company disposed of in the first place in the Malay Archi-pelago, a branch of its business which at one time was styled "the soul of the large body "[5]. More to the south, north of Goa, the Company possessed "a fortified factory" at Wingurla (Vengurlem), at that time the starting-point for the Dutch trade with the coast of Malabar (Tschaul, Calicut, Ponnani), and through these places, with the dis-tricts of the interior: pepper, especially, being bought up here. Cinnamon was the chief product of Ceylon, an island that had attracted the particular attention of the supreme Government at Batavia espe-cially of late years. The Dutch had there been fighting against the Portuguese, as a rule, though not invariably, with success. They had now established a firm footing there: Gale (Point de Galle) had been in their possession since 1640[6], and from there they extended their trade along the entire coast of the island, especially visiting Batticaloa and Trinconomale. As in Ceylon, the Company owned also on the coast of Coromandel a fortified place, which might serve as a basis for her op-erations. It was the castle of Geldria at Paliacatta (Palikat), within whose jurisdiction were the Dutch mercantile offices at Masulipatam, and certain other inferior ones, which carried on the highly important trade in diamonds, saltpetre, indigo, but especially in "divers assort-ments of cotton stuffs," with the entire eastern half of Hither-India, including Orissa. Bengal, in which country the Company had an office at the mouth of the Hoogly, furnished saltpetre, sugar, and above all silks; the trade with Arracan afforded rice and slaves, the commerce with Pegu and Tenasserim, small goods of various descriptions. Malacca, not conquered until 1641, constituted the key to the Malay Archipelago, and was the centre of the tin-trade of the Malay Peninsula; the Dutch factory in Siam furnished rice and goods for the Japan market; the Tonquin one, silks, and the latter two thus served to strengthen the prosperous trade of the Company with Eastern Asia, to which allusion has been made before.

But the real strength of the Company lay in the Malay Archipelago. Batavia had been made the chief seat of the Supreme Government, and here was the centre of the net-work that spread over that vast territory. Java itself was to the whole of Netherlands-India a rice-granary, to which access was not entirely barred even in times of war with the powerful empire of Mattaram. The West-coast of Sumatra and Acheen, Djambi and Palembang, with all of which an active intercourse was kept up, yielded huge quantities of pepper; Banda, which was a regular conquest of the Company, produced a greater quantity of nutmegs than the world was able to consume; Amboyna and the Moluccas, where Dutch influence was paramount, abounded with cloves; Solor, where the Dutch had a fortress, furnished odoriferous sandal-wood.

[1] See K. HEERINGA, De Nederlanders op Mauritius en Madagascar (Indische Gids, 1895, pp. 864-892, 1005-1036).]

[2] Cf. P. A. LEUPE in Bijdragen tot de taal-, land-, en volkenkunde van Nederlandsch-Indië. Fourth Series, II (1878), pp. 376-378. The author is, however, mistaken in stating that as early as 1640 Mocha coffee was sent to the Netherlands. Apart from this, his dates, too, are not quite reliable. The letter from the Amsterdam Chamber, in which a request is made for the sending over of coffee, bears date April 16, 1640, and not 163? But long before, coffee was known to the Dutch. Cf. Begin ende Voortgang, II, E E E E E (sic), p. 33.]

[3] Cf. "Instructie voor Pieter van den Broeck ende...den Raeth vant fluijtschip Rarob, gedestint (van Batavia) naar Mocha," August 2, 1638; "Rapport bij den oppercoopman Pieter van den Broeke aan dHr Generael gedaen," May 26, 1639.]

[4] "Schriftelijck Rapport...consernerende 't succes van de...negotie op Mocha," by J. S. Wurffbeen, October 13, 1640.]

[5] "Poincten ende articulen in forme van Generale Instructie voor Gouverneur-Generael ende Raden," April 26, 1650, printed in P. MIJER, Verzameling van instructiën, p. 87.]

[6] See W. VAN GEER, De opkomst van het Nederlandsch gezag over Ceilon, I. Leiden, Sijthoff, 1895, especially pp. 21-73.]

A very considerable part of these Eastern products served for the commerce carried on by the Dutch in India itself, where they provided one country with those articles which it did not produce itself, and which were elsewhere bought up by the Company. The great profits, accruing from this carrying-trade, were partly swallowed up by the heavy expenses entailed by the administrative arrangements of the Company in the vast field of its operations. The surplus profit had to be employed in the purchase of the return-cargoes for the Netherlands, and the still unattained ideal of the Board of Directors and the Supreme Government alike, was, that this surplus profit might reach such an amount, that the whole cost-price of these return-cargoes, which from 1639-1649 averaged two millions and a half of guilders a year[1]-- the selling price at home averaging eight millions--with all the expenses and charges for transmission, etc. incident to them, could be defrayed out of it; so that not a single doit of ready money need be sent to India from the Netherlands.

The progress of the Dutch Company in Asia had gradually begun to go hand in hand with the ousting of its European competitors, or the frustration of the endeavours made by Europeans to become its rivals. With results which as a rule were favourable, the great mercantile association had, either of its own accord, or forced by circumstances, joined issue with the Portuguese, the Spaniards, the English, French and Danes, and was carrying on the struggle, now sword in hand, at other times with its purse-strings untied. The two nations last mentioned were "negligible quantities" in the East; for the time being at least, the English had been worsted in their struggle with the Company: their time had not yet arrived; the strength of Spain as a colonial power did not lie in Asia: the Philippine Isles and a settlement in an out-of-the-way corner of the Moluccas, in Ternate, were their sole possessions in this part of the world. With the Portuguese the struggle had been longest, hardest, and most violent, and still, in spite of the heavy blows inflicted on them by the Dutch, they continued, especially in trade, to be adversaries who had to be reckoned with. Chiefly of late years, however, they had met with losses, hardly if at all to be made good. That the Dutch had established a firm footing in Ceylon was a bitter pill to their antagonists; that Malacca had been conquered by the Netherlanders was a death-blow to Portugal's political position in the East. The conquest of Malacca became an accomplished fact on January 14, 1641, and shortly after, intelligence reached India that Portugal had thrown off the Spanish yoke in 1640, and declared itself independent. One of the first measures taken by the government of the resuscitated State was the making of peace overtures to the Republic of the United Netherlands. In Asia, too, negotiations on this subject were soon entered into. It must have been a source of great satisfaction to the leaders of the Dutch colonial policy at Batavia, when in January 1642 envoys arrived there, sent by the Portuguese viceroy at Goa, with the object of suing for a cessation Of hostilities. This is not the place to enlarge on this subject, nor can we enter into an account of the complications which arose, when on the 2nd of October 1642 the authorities at Batavia got notice of the treaty of armistice, concluded at the Hague June 12, 1641, but not ratified until a long time afterwards.

What we have advanced will suffice to show that the Netherlands had become the ruling European power in Asia, and that Van Diemen's day-dream, the Dutch supremacy in the East, need not by any means be called a castle in the air[2].

At this juncture it was that the Governor-General and Councillors took the resolution--and they could do so "without cutting down the means for customary trade and war"--of employing two ships to undertake the expedition that was to signalise to the whole civilised world the names of Abel Tasman and his coadjutor Frans Jacobszoon Visscher. For on the first day of August, 1642, the Supreme Government at Batavia resolved to despatch skipper Tasman, with Visscher as his adviser, "in order to navigate to the Southern and Eastern Countries, which were only partially known, and had not hitherto been explored." The ships Heemskerck and de Zeehaen were designated for this new undertaking.

[1] See KLERK DE REUS, Uberblick, Beilage V.]

[1] As regards these various points, cf. VAN DAM, MS. Beschrijvinge; VALENTIJN; DE JONGE, Opkomst; TIELE-HEERES, Bouwstoffen; VAN GEER, Ceilon; etc.]

XI

SOURCES OF OUR KNOWLEDGE OF TASMAN'S EXPLORATORY VOYAGES TO THE SOUTH-LAND (1642-1644)--MAPS AND LITERATURE CONCERNING THE LATTER.

Between the amount of our knowledge respecting Tasman's famous voyage of discovery, begun in 1642, and the measure of our information touching the expedition undertaken by him in 1644, there is a great difference. Whereas the former can be known with full completeness and great exactitude of detail, our information as to the second voyage is of a sadly fragmentary nature. In the following we shall give a survey of the available authorities for the history of the two expeditions, and subjoin observations respecting the more important items of the literature bearing on the subject of these exploratory voyages.

The immediate inducement to the first voyage may be learned from various so-called General Missives, i.e. missives from the Governor-General and Councillors to the "Heeren XVII," of which missives those belonging to the said years have been preserved in originali. Next, from resolutions of the Supreme Government at Batavia, and from the instructions given to Tasman: of all these documents there are extant copies, drawn up and sent to the Board of Directors of the Company by order of the Governor-General and Councillors, of which copies the authenticity is accordingly beyond all reasonable doubt. The results of the first voyage can be inferred from the General Missives, and from certain other archival documents: all of them either originals, or authentic copies. The main authorities, however, for the history of this voyage are journals[1], kept in the course of it on board the Heemskerck, which journals have come down to us. It is highly probable that one or more journals were kept also on board the Zeehaen, but these have not been handed down to posterity. Nor, in the General Missive of December 22, 1643, in which the result of the voyage is given, is there question of any journal kept on board the

Zeehaen being sent to Europe; the missive only mentions that to the Netherlands are sent "the 'daily registers' of Tasman, and of 'Pilot Major' ' Francois Jacobszoon Visscher, in which the winds, the courses, the 'lie' of lands, the outward form of the peoples, etc. are pertinently indicated and delineated." From the instructions it is evident that Tasman and Visscher were both of them on board the Heemskerck. In the same way, in the missive from the "Heeren XVII" to the Governor-General and Councillors, bearing date September 21 1644, and written in answer to the General Missive last mentioned, there is question only of "the Journal of Skipper Commander Tasman and 'Pilot-Major' Visscher." The resolutions of the Ship's Council and of the Plenary Council are wanting.

Of the daily journal kept by Tasman we give a reproduction of an original copy. It is just possible that still other copies, drawn up in the same way and also signed by him, at one time existed[2], but so far as at present known, such copies have not been preserved.

In 1854 Jacob Swart had in his possession an "original narrative" [reisverhaal], also styled "a copy of the original journal," and "a journal signed by him [Tasman] with his own hand."[3] The various terms in which Swart describes his copy, already show that this manuscript has the same value as the one now reproduced, for the latter is also a "copy" in so far as it is copied fair from minutes, and it is signed with the famous navigator's own hand. If we go on to compare, page for page, the text printed by Swart with the journal here reproduced, we are more and more driven to the conclusion, that the copy used by Swart, which was not found among the papers left by him at his death[4], must have been the identical one used for the present reproduction. In various places, indications of longitude are missing in Swart's copy, which are also wanting in ours in the very same places In a few

[1] Here and elsewhere I make use of this general term, but I shall presently explain its precise meaning in this connection.]

[2] It was e.g. customary--though it was not always practised--that of important documents six copies were sent to patria: one for each Chamber of the Company. Cf. Resolution of the "Heeren XVII," November 12, 1611; General missive, December 12, 1642]

[1] See JACOB SWART'S introduction to the reprint of 1860, of his edition of the Journal, pp. VI, 1 and 3.]

[2] See P. A. LEUPE, De handschriften der ontdekkingsreis, in Bijdragen voor vaderlandsche geschiedenis en oudheidkunde, Nieuwe Reeks, VII (1872), p. 267.--The copy used by Swart accordingly is not mentioned in the Catalogus der bibliotheken nagelaten

door....Jacob Swart, alsmede van het...boeken-, kaarten- en instrumenten-magazijn van de firma wed. Gerard Hulst van Keulen te Amsterdam, waarvan de verkooping zal plaats hebben 7 September 1885 (bij) H. G. Bom, Amsterdam. (bij) H G. Born, Amsterdam]

{Page: Life.60}

cases discrepancies of spelling, observed by Swart, e.g. on p. 144 Garde Neys (April 4) and Gardenys (April 5), are also, found in our copy. The No. after Le Maire on p. 104 (January 22) is also wanting in our manuscript. The slip of the pen in our copy "Roolol" (February 14) instead of "Roobol," is found in Swart's edition (p. 128). We shall presently see that in our copy certain lines are missing on January 21, February 6, April 21, which lines are equally omitted in Swart's print. It is quite true that Swart does not mention certain surveyings of land, which are met with in our[1] copy, but in the description of these drawings Swart's edition, which, indeed, shows want of care and accuracy throughout[2], is not always so exact as to justify any conclusions from this circumstance, which for aught we know may be due to negligence or inadvertence. It is further to be noted that certain marginal notes, which according to Swart were found in his copy, in a different hand from that in which the journal itself was written, are also met with in our copy, likewise almost certainly written by another hand than the one that wrote the journal. These marginal jottings are referred to in note 1) on p. 96 of Swart's edition, and in note 2) on p. 108. At the first reference Swart says: "A note in the manuscript has: Dit sal mogelick 31[3] gr. moeten syn [This in perhaps a mistake, instead of 31°]. This note, however, is not in the hand of the writer of the journal;" and at the second reference: "In a marginal note we read: N.B. did moet West zijn [NB. this should be West], written in the same hand as the note on January 9." Now, in our copy we find noted in margine under date January 9, 1643: "NB sal moghelick 31 g. moeten zijn," and on January 24: "NB dit moet west zijn," likewise written probably by the same hand that wrote the marginal note of January 9, as also certain "NB"'s to October 7, 20, 22, 23, and November 14, 1642, and a few indications of longitude and latitude in the map of "Staete landt." There are differences of spelling, to be sure, and in one case the words are different ("NB" and "dit"); but then Swart did not always diplomatically adhere to the text of the original to be reproduced: now and then he thought it his duty to introduce corrections[4], and he was not always quite accurate himself[5]. The slight discrepancies referred to cannot therefore constitute a difficulty. It would indeed be highly remarkable, if the two corrections, one of which at least is erroneous[6], and, as appears from its wording ("sal mogelick"), cannot have originated with Tasman himself, who would undoubtedly have made a more correct and less hesitating conjecture[7];--it would, I say, be highly remarkable indeed, that both corrections should have been made in two different copies of a manuscript, which copies would have been likely to have got into quite different hands immediately after completion. For all these reasons it is highly probable, if not absolutely sure, that Swart's copy and ours are one and the same.

We need not here expatiate on the distinguishing features of our manuscript, which no doubt once formed part of one of the collections of archives of the East India Company, and was in 1867 presented to the Hague State Archives by Mr. J. G. Gleichman, LL. D.[8], The Hague, into whose possession it had come from the books and papers left by Mr. F. A. Van Hall: the facsimile here given faithfully reproduces the document. On one side of the vellum binding are found the words " Commandeur Abel Tasman," an annotation without significance; on the other side, partly illegible: "Journael gehouden [door?] Commandeur Abel Jan[sen Tasman?] op de voijagie over M[auritius?] om de Z[uyt?] gedaen. [Ao. 1643?] No. 35." There can be little doubt that the note last mentioned has

[1) For briefness' sake I shall in the sequel thus refer to the journal here reproduced.]

[2 Cf. LEUPE in Bijdragen vaderlandsche geschiedenis, l. c., pp. 267 f., 289-29o--The collation with Valentijn, too, Swart has done in a perfunctory way. The note, for example, on p. 66 of his edition of 1860 is incorrect. Both the surveyings, marked 5 E by Valentijn, are taken from the one dated December 19, 1642, and not, one of them from that of November 25. Indeed, in the note on p. 86 Swart admits that both of them belong to the surveyings under date December 19. The charts in Valentijn, No 2 B (p. 50) and No. 3 C (p. 51), are in our copy found under date December 1.]

[3) LEUPE in Bijdragen vaderlandsche geschiedenis, l. c. p. 268, has a misprint which in this place is serious enough, viz. "21" instead of "31."]

[4) See p. 5 of the edition of 1860.]

[5) Cf. LEUPE in Bijdragen vaderlandsche geschiedenis, l. c., pp. 268, 282-290.]

[6) See Note 2, p. 96 of SWART'S edition of 1860.]

[7) It is noteworthy in this connection, that in the Huydecoper MS, to be presently discussed, which must have been made from a copy of about the same date with ours, the text on January 24 is on this point identical with that in our copy. This MS has on January 9 the more correct latitude of 32° 4': the copyist who drew up our copy must therefore have made a mistake in transcribing his model, but the person who introduced the correction "31 g." also made a mistake.]

[8) Report on the State Archives, 1867, p. 2.]

been made on the cover at Batavia, when the manuscript was forwarded to the Netherlands; No. 35 is most probably the number of the manuscript in the list of the documents sent over. From Certain documents preserved in the State Archives at The Hague, it is evident that the same hand which wrote this note, did also other copying-work at Batavia in 1643.

Most probably our manuscript is not an original diary kept up to date day after day: it may be more correctly described as a consecutive narrative, which was most likely digested from the regular ship's journal in the course of the voyage; which was afterwards copied fair by another hand than Tasman's, and finally signed by Tasman himself. It is impossible to decide with absolute certainty who has drawn up the charts, marine surveyings and drawings occurring in our copy; on this point we can only hazard certain conjectures, about which more anon. It is quite evident[1], however, that the explanatory legends accompanying the charts, etc. have been written by another hand than the text itself

Now it is highly remarkable, that in the sad remnant of another copy of the journal, there are found legends evidently written by the same hand that made the fair copy of the text of our manuscript: the very regular handwriting showing that the transcriber was most probably a clerk in some government office. If we assume this as true, we may perhaps further venture on the hypothesis that our copy bears a more original character than the one just mentioned. We may safely suppose that in our copy the transcriber left blanks for the marine surveyings, etc. together with the legends, which would have to be afterwards supplied by another person, who was more of an expert, and which were actually so supplied at a subsequent time. I feel strengthened in this supposition of mine by numerous indications of more or less weight. On January 19, 1643, for instance, the transcriber would seem to have left too small a blank space, so that the legend had to be crowded on to the drawing; on January 23, there was no room for the legend on the drawing itself, so that, contrary to his ordinary practice, the expert inserted the legend between the lines of the text, where there was room to spare; on March 28 and 29, the blank left was larger than was found to be required. In the subsequent copies these marine surveyings etc. could then be copied at the same time with the text of the journal. This would at once account for the fact that the legends in the fragmentary MS. which we are discussing, are in the same hand as the text of our copy. This fragment consists of one folio leaf only, on which is found the drawing, belonging to December 19, 1642, representing the "Moordenaarsbaai" [Murderers' Bay], in the foreground the boat with natives, one of them standing up; together with the surveying of the "Zant duijnen" [sand dunes], which surveying faces the said drawing in our copy. Between the legends, as well as the drawing and the surveying, of the fragment on the one hand; and on the other, those occurring in our manuscript, there are perceptible differences. The drawing is slightly more careful than in our copy. Here and there the drawing in the fragment shows colours--again not quite the same as those found in our copy--laid on, presumably (at least in one place), at a later period, which we have reason to surmise was also the case with the colours with which our copy is embellished. The drawing of the Moordenaarsbaai is the one which is found in Valentijn's well-known extract from the journal, there marked No. 6 F^2. As in various other instances, Valentijn has introduced slight alterations from the original drawing. In Valentijn the man who is standing up in the boat is pointing to the ships; on the drawing of the fragment, and on the one found in our copy, the same man is pointing his finger exactly in the opposite direction. The drawing of the fragment bears the following note written in an antique hand: "No. 6 F. Samen half blad met 7 G." [No 6 F, together with 7 G to form a half-leaf]. This agrees with Valentijn, where 6 F and 7 G occur on one page[3], and the words "Samen half blad met" are in Valentijn's own handwriting[4]. Most certainly, therefore, the fragment is something of a relic: a fragment of a document used by Valentijn in the composition of his celebrated book. At all events this supposition is more probable than the view[5]

[1) See, for instance, on January 23 and 24, 1643.]

[2) Volume III, part 2, section Banda, facing p. 50.]

[3) Page 51.]

[4) I have been in a position to compare them with a letter of Valentijn of Aug. 16, 1723 in the municipal archives of Dordrecht. I am indebted for my knowledge of it to the kindness of the municipal archivist, Mr. J. C. OVERVOORDE.]

[5) LEUPE, l. c., p. 262; TIELE, Bibliographie land- en volkenkunde, p. 236.]

that our copy should have been utilised by him for this purpose. It will, indeed, become quite clear in the sequel, that Valentijn must have had still other data at his disposal than those with which our

124

copy could have furnished him. A somewhat minute circumstance proves this beyond a doubt. The natives in the boat on the drawing of the Moordenaarsbaai in our copy are represented with small tufts of hair at the back of their heads. In Valentijn these tufts of hair have been turned into feathers or plumes. Now this change is not owing to any flight of fancy on the part of the honest preacher: the same plumes or feathers figure on the drawing of the fragment. One more support to the theory that our copy stands nearer to the archetype than the copy of which the fragment once formed part; at all events this circumstance clearly proves that our copy cannot have been a replica of the one just mentioned. Nor has the maker of the drawing of the fragment unduly indulged in fanciful embellishment. Tasman himself, referring to the natives here alluded to, thus delivers himself in his journal: "They had black hair right on the top of their heads, tied up at the back of their heads after the Japanese fashion, but the hair being somewhat longer and thicker; the whole surmounted by a large thick feather." These feathers do not figure in the drawing in our copy, but the draughtsman of the fragment, as in duty bound, has reinstated them on the heads of the natives, and from this picture they have no doubt found their way to Valentijn's book.

The fragment is now preserved in the State Archives at The Hague, to which it was presented by Mr. D. Blok of Amsterdam, between the years 1872 and 1881[1].

In the Hague State Archives also reposes another journal of the famous voyage. This journal differs widely from those hitherto discussed. It forms part of a collection of documents referring to the Netherlands East and West India Companies, bearing dates ranging between 1602 and 1702. This Collection, at least the main part of it, was most probably left at his death by Salomon Swears, who was a member of the Council of India in the years in which Tasman's voyage to the South-land took place[2]. The documents were most likely made up, by a certain Cornelis Sweers, into bundles, all of them marked with the initials C. S. In 1859 the State Archives purchased a large part of this important Collection, then forming part of the property left at his death by Mr. J. C. De Jonge, LL. D., Principal Keeper of the Netherlands State Archives. The journal extends to 35[3] folio leaves in one of the volumes in which the various items of which the collection is made up, are united; of these leaves a few are left blank. It is easy to see that the journal at one time formed a separate volume. On its first page are the following words: "1643. Journaal, om de Zuijd"; this note is written in a later hand quite different from the one in which the journal itself is written; this same later hand is in other cases also met with in the Sweers collection, and has interspersed it with various brief notes respecting dates and other minutiae. The note on the first page has afterwards had its writing refreshed in other ink, and the words "en Nova Guinea" added to it, evidently by the same hand which has also supplied the running paging of this and other volumes of this collection, has written the titling on the backs, and added various tables of contents. The person who inserted the tables of contents and other additional matter, must have been alive in 1702, since a note in his hand bears this date[4]. Under the words above mentioned the same hand has written the word "dubbeld" [duplicate], which may be a hint to the effect that more copies of this journal existed at one time, but which may also mean that more journals of Tasman's voyage belonged to this collection, which we shall presently find to have actually been the case. The journal bears marginal notes and a few other annotations, all of them by the same hand which also wrote the tables of contents, etc. It opens as follows: "Jornael gehovden op de nieuwe voeijagie om de Zuijt in Indien gedaen door Commandeur Abel int jaer 1643 in Augusto." The same hand that wrote the marginal notes, etc., has after "Commandeur Abel" inserted the words "Jansz Tasman," and changed into "2" the figure "3" in 1643; it has besides written in the margin the words "met 't Jagt Heemskerk," and added a few more jottings of different

[1] The fragment must have found its way to the State Archives between 1872, the year in which Leupe wrote his paper on the manuscripts, when he evidently was not aware of the existence of this fragment, and 1881, the year in which Leupe died. For a note in Leupe's hand, deposited with the fragment, shows that he must have been acquainted with it.]

[2] See my Bouwstoffen, III, pp. 24, 50, 143, 201.]

[3] LEUPE, in Bijdragen vaderlandsche geschiedenis, 1. c., p. 260, speaks of 28 leaves, because he is referring to the written ones only.]

[4] Cf. LEUPE in Bijdragen voor geschiedenis, 1. c., p. 261.]

nature. This journal too has been kept on board the Heemskerck. Certain expressions would seem to raise a suspicion whether in this case we may not have to deal with a daily register kept by a member of the crew of the Zeehaen; but when on the other hand under November (December) 28, 1642, for example, we read: "Des smiddachs is onse Commandeur aen de Zeehaen gevaeren" [In the afternoon our Commander went on board the Zeehaen]; on February (March) 11, 1643: "van dage quam de Coopman van de Zeehaen aen ons boort" [this day the Supercargo of the Zeehaen came on board of us]; or on February (March) 13: "des voormiddachs quam de Schipper vande Zeehaen aen ons boort" [in the forenoon the Skipper of the Zeehaen came on board of us]; then we may take for granted that the writer of the journal must have been on board the Heemskerck. This by itself is quite sufficient to prove that this journal cannot be the journal kept by Visscher, referred to in the General Missive of December 22, 1643. Nor, indeed, does it contain any of the charts, marine surveyings and drawings, which according to the missive just mentioned were found in Visscher's daily register. Who actually wrote this journal, cannot now be ascertained: perhaps the writer was a sailor in a subordinate position. We may infer this, for example, from such an entry as the following on November (December) 26, 1642: "Des nachts hebben wij[1] een halffken arack minder gecregen" [We[1] got half a glass of arrack less at night]. However all this may be, it is absolutely sure that the writer was not the skipper of the Heemskerk; for on April (May) 5, 1643 the journal says: "smiddachs gingh de Commandeur met onse Schipper ande Zeehaen" [in the afternoon the Commander went on board the Zeehaen with our Skipper]. At all events the writer's penmanship was decidedly poor, and his command of the Dutch language a very restricted one. His longitudes and latitudes are utterly at variance with those found in the journal kept by Tasman himself. The whole of the form in which the journal is kept, conveys the impression that we have here to do with a draft-journal, kept up to date day by day. It is, however, difficult to bring this conclusion into harmony with a very singular mistake, which the writer has not only committed but to which he has also stuck to the end. The two vessels arrived in the road-stead of Mauritius on September 5, 1642, and remained lying there for more than a month. Now the writer, who does not even allude to the stay at Mauritius, omits changing the name of the month, and represents the ships as leaving Mauritius on September 8, instead of October 8. To this error, involving a difference of a whole month, he adheres to the end, so that according to him the voyagers returned to Batavia on May 15, 1643, instead of June 15. A slip like this is rather to be expected of a mechanical transcriber than of a person who is keeping a diary day by day, and who would be likely to have his attention drawn to his mistake at least on the first day of a new month. Compared with this error, other mistakes become as nothing, e.g. the substitution of 1641 or 1643 for 1642, etc. Now that we possess the journal reproduced in the present work, the manuscript we have just been discussing is not, indeed, of paramount interest for the history of Tasman's celebrated expedition. Still, it may be of some service for purposes of comparison, the more so as it gives a few particulars which are not contained in the journal kept by Tasman himself[2].

Among the annotations, few in number and of little importance, made in the manuscript by the writer of the marginal notes, one commands our attention. Between November (December) 18 and 19, namely, the annotator has added the following memorandum, again cancelled at a later time: "November en vervolgens tot 18 December inclusive hier overgeslagen. Ziet in 't accurater Journaal bij A. J. Tasmansz (sic!) aengehouden, in't boek met 't opschrift: Tasmans (sic!) ontdekte Nova Hollandia ofte Zuidland" [the rest of November and up to December 18 inclusive have been omitted here. See the more accurate Journal kept by A. J. Tasmansz in the book labelled: Tasmans ontdekte Nova Hollandia or Zuidland.] Can it be, that the writer of this memorandum felt that there was something wrong with the months, but immediately afterwards became aware that this remark was out of place there, so that he accordingly thought it better to cancel it again? However this may be, the warning memorandum is not without interest for the filiation of the manuscripts of Tasman's voyage; inasmuch as it proves the existence of a "journaal," about which it furnishes certain details. What journal now is meant here? To this question a very positive answer can be given. In 1872 there was in the

[1) The italics are my own.]

[2) Cf. LEUPE in Bijdragen voor geschiedenis, 1. c., pp. 279-281.]

possession of Mr. J. Huydecoper van Maarsseveen[1], now in that of his son, Jhr. J. E. Huydecoper van Maarsseveen en Nigtevegt, at Utrecht[2], a folio volume, like the other volumes of the Sweers collection, marked with the initials "C. S.," and containing notes in the same hand that wrote the marginal annotations in the journal which we have already discussed, and which also at one time formed part of the Sweers collection. There can therefore be no doubt that the Huydecoper MS. at one time belonged to the same Sweers collection which included the journal we have just described. The Huydecoper MS. extends to 190 pages, of which a great many are left blank; the journal itself, including the title, covers 113 pages. The hand repeatedly referred to, has appended to it an alphabetical "register." On the back of the binding is written the title as follows: "Tasmans ontdekte Nova Hollandia ofte Zuidland 1642, 43 met zijne Reyse na Nova Guinea." The first words of this title agree with the annotation between November (December) 18 and 19, referred to higher up, so that it can hardly be deemed a hazardous supposition to assume that in the Huydecoper MS., which evidently formed part of the same collection, we have re-discovered the "accurater journaal." We feel strengthened in this pre-presumption, if we take into consideration the fact that whereas the note repeatedly referred to mentions the "accurater Journaal bij A. J. Tasmansz gehouden," the Huydecoper MS. is entitled: "Extract wttet Journaal vanden Schipper Command, Abel Janssen Tasman bij hem selffs[3] in't ontdecken vant onbekende Zuijdlant gehouden" [Extract from the Journal of Skipper Commandeur Abel Janssen Tasman, kept by himself[3] in discovering the unknown South-land]. The following additional particulars may here be given respecting this manuscript. The title qualifies it as an "extract," and on the cover we likewise find written: "Extract. Zuijdland 1642, 1643." Quite at the end of the manuscript there are the words: " Onderstont[3]. Actum jnt schip Heemskercke," etc. We accordingly find that there is no question of an original document, not even of a duplicate. And in addition to all this, we find that it bears no signature at the end. Now it may be asked, what manuscript bearing a more original character, underlies this "extract?" It is quite impossible to assume that this more original manuscript has been our copy; the differences are too conspicuous to justify such a conclusion: thus, the extract contains items of information which are wanting in our manuscript[4]. Besides leaving out a number of indications of longitude which are found in the Huydecoper MS., the clerk who made the fair copy of our manuscript is guilty of certain other omissions. On November 8, for instance, between "werkelijk" and "datt alhier" our copy leaves out the words "met mottich, regenachtich mistich weer" [in drizzly, rainy, foggy weather], which are duly met with in the Huydecoper MS. Our copy has a serious oversight under date January 21, 1643. At this place we read as follows in the Huydecoper MS.: "...Deden onsen cours naer het noordelijcste eijlandt, om dat het grooste (sic!) van beijde eijlanden waar; dit zuijdelijckste eijlant leijt op de zuyderbreette van 21 graden 50 minuijten," etc. [We bent our course to the northernmost island, because it was the larger of the two islands; this southernmost island is in 21° 50' Southern Latitude, etc.]. The italicised words are not in our copy, and this omission materially affects the sense of the passage. Something like this is found on February 6. There the Huydecoper MS. has: "Deze eijlanden leggen op de zuijderbreette van 17 graden, de zuijdelijckste leggen op 17½ gra: off daer onttrent" [These islands are in 17 degrees S. L., the southernmost ones in 17½ degrees, or thereabouts]. Our copy omits the words in italics. On April 21, our copy, between

"1¾ mijl van ons," and "zagen als doen," leaves out[5] the words: "dit eijlandt is naer gissinge lanck 4 a 4½ mijl" (this island by guess has a length of from 4 to 4½ miles], which we have to supply from the Huydecoper MS. There are still more points of difference between the two manuscripts, but what we have just adduced decisively proves that the copyist who drew up the Huydecoper MS. did not use our copy as his model. What copy then, we may ask, did he actually use? There can be no doubt that he used a copy which differed from ours only in subordinate points: certain mistakes and obscurities (inter alia on September 11 and December 2)

[1] LEUPE, Bijdragen voor geschiedenis, 1. c., p. 260; cf. also pp. 263-266. I have observed a few slight errors in Leupe's account.]

[2] This gentleman kindly sent me the manuscript for purposes of comparison.]

[3] The italics are my own.]

[4] See LEUPE in Bijdragen voor geschiedenis, 1. c., pp. 273-275. Leupe has overlooked various discrepancies between the two journals, at least failed to register them: even certain important ones are left unnoticed by him.]

[5] This is not mentioned by Leupe.]

being even met with in both manuscripts. If now we further bear in mind that the Huydecoper MS. bears very probably a middle of XVII century character, and almost certainly formed part of the property left at his decease by Salomon Sweers, who was a member of the Council of India in the years in which Tasman's voyage took place --if we bear this in mind, two possibilities readily offer themselves. The copyist may have had before him either the minutes drawn up by Tasman, or another fair copy made on the basis of the said minutes, for example, the identical fair copy which he must have sent in to the Governor-General and Councillors. The first supposition becomes the less probable one, if we consider the subscription: "Onderstont Actum jnt schip Heemskercke. datum als booven laagers(ton)t"[1] etc., since the minutes are likely to have been without signature. Perhaps, therefore, we may assume with a fair degree of probability that the Huydecoper MS. was transcribed from the copy at the time presented by Tasman to the Governor-General and Councillors[2], which copy is no longer extant. However this may be, the Huydecoper MS. has an unmistakeable value for purposes of comparison. For the rest its intrinsic value is far inferior to that of our copy. It is a slovenly transcript, which is a better term to describe it than the designation "extract," used in the title-page; a number of omissions and many mistakes (e.g. regularly Gissemans instead of Gilsemans, Mullunus or Mollunos instead of Moluccos, "woor pausker," on September 17, instead of "worpancker," etc.) are to be observed. But it is especially the utter absence of charts, marine surveyings, and drawings[3], that characterises the Huydecoper MS. as decidedly inferior in value to the copy reproduced in the present work.

Lauts[4] refers to a journal of Tasman's voyage of 1642, which in July 1835 was sold by Mr. Bom, bookseller at Amsterdam, to a Dutch scholar residing in the Netherlands. In Catalogus van eene buitengewoon belangrijke verzameling...boeken...voorts eenige manuscripten...gedeeltelijk nagelaten door een Leeraar der Hervormde Gemeente en door den Heer L. Groenewoud, in leven Boekverkooper alhier: Al hetwelk verkocht zal worden op Maandag 27 Julij 1835 en volgende dagen...door den Boekhandelaar G. D. Bom...te Amsterdam" [Catalogue of a highly important collection of...books...together with a number of manuscripts...partly left by a Minister of the Reformed Church, and by Mr. L. Groenewoud, some time bookseller of this town: the whole to be sold by auction on Monday July 27, 1835 and subsequent days...by G. D. Bom, bookseller...at Amsterdam]--in this Catalogue the journal figures under the following title[5]: "Journaal door Abel Tasman van een voyagie van de stad Batavia in O. I. aangaande de ontdekking van het onbekende Zuidland in6 1642 m. zeer fr. teekeningen h. b." [Journal kept by Abel Tasman concerning a voyage from the City of Batavia in East India for the discovery of the unknown South-land, in 1642; with very fine drawings, half-bound].

In a MS. note in his own hand, written not before 1844, at present in the possession of Messrs. Fred. Muller and Co., of Amsterdam, Lauts writes as follows: "I have said on p. 296[4], that in 1835 I had erroneously referred to two MSS. of the voyage of 1642. I now find that I was not mistaken at the time. The MS. used by me is preserved in the family-archives of Messrs. Huydecoper van Maarsseveen; the other MS. then being the property of the book-selling firm of Hulst van Keulen, who had it sold in auction by Mr. Bom, the book-seller.--Ni fallor it fetched 90 guilders, and thus found its way to the Library of the Netherlands Institute of Sciences and Letters." The library just mentioned was afterwards transferred to the Amsterdam Royal Academy of Sciences. Investigations made there

[1] The italics are mine.]

[2] According to the inventory drawn up in 1882, the State Archives at Batavia no longer possess a copy of the journal. J. P. GELL, in his paper "On the first discovery of Tasmania," to be again referred to in the sequel, states that in the English interregnum from 1811 to 1816 "the journal of Captain Abel Jansen Tasman" was found at Batavia in "the archives of the

Company." Whence did Gell derive this information? We shall presently see that Gell himself most probably based his investigations on the manuscript in the British Museum, and on Burney's extract from it.]

[3] Those which are now found in it, to which we shall presently return again, did not originally form part of the MS., and have evidently been pasted into it at some subsequent period.]

[4] Algemeene Konst- en Letterbode for the year 1835, II, 262, and Verhandelingen en berigten Zeewezen, Nieuwe Volgorde, IV, 1844, p. 296, note 18.]

[5] At p. 92.--A copy of this rare catalogue is preserved in the library of the Vereeniging ter bevordering van de Belangen des Boekhandels [Association for the promotion of the interests of the book-trade]. I am indebted for my knowledge of it to the kindness of its librarian, Mr. R. W. P. De Vries.]

on my behalf remained without result, and no information respecting this alleged purchase could be gathered from the files of correspondence or the registers kept at the institution just mentioned. Messrs. Bom, though quite ready to oblige me, could not give me any positive information, since their day-books for the year 1835 were destroyed in a fire on their premises. Lauts does not say how he had come to the knowledge that the manuscript had previously belonged to the firm of Hulst van Keulen. Now, may not the reverse have taken place, and may not the copy sold in July 1835 have been purchased by that very firm, so that in that case the manuscript referred to would have been our copy?

One more copy of the journal is left me for discussion, viz. the one preserved in the British Museum[1], on which is based Burney's edition of the "journal," to be referred to in the sequel. Of the outward history of this manuscript certain particulars are known[2]. Prefixed to the text of the manuscript, namely, there are two letters from H. J. (Henry) Norris to Dr. Solander. In the first, dated Woodford, Monday 26 Aug. 1776, the writer states that at that time the manuscript was in the possession of Mr. Banks (Sir Joseph Banks), who had bought it of Sir James W.... "Some time before," the latter had acquired it for "but half a Guinea," when it was sold "at the late Mr. Lloyds house on Friday hill (just beyond Woodford)," where Norris himself had inspected it. So far the information furnished by Norris. In 1776 Mr. Banks had the manuscript translated from Dutch into English by the Rev. Charles Godfrey Woide, "then Chaplain to His Majesty's Dutch Chapel at St. James's Palace, and afterwards Under Librarian to the British Museum"[3], and this translation is preserved along with the Dutch manuscript itself. Sir Joseph afterwards bequeathed the two manuscripts to the British Museum, and on the cover of the Dutch MS. is accordingly found the inscription: "Tasman's Journal. Mus. Brit. ex legato J. Banks. Bart." The manuscript is bound in calf; it is a small-sized folio, and numbers 101 pages, inclusive of the prolegomena.

What place now in the whole series are we to assign to this manuscript? Woide already was aware of the fact that in this case he had not to deal with a manuscript bearing the character of an original. "I dont think," he writes inter alia--we may leave his other grounds undiscussed--in a sort of prefatory notice to his translation, "I dont think, that this copy is Tasman's his own handwritting. I find, when Tasman's name is signed, it is allways said: undersigned Tasman, which expression was superfluous, if Tasman had written it with his own hand." The cogency of this argument to prove the non-original character of the manuscript, was disputed by Burney[4], who thus delivered himself as regards this "objection": "The word Onderstout (sic!) accompanying the signatures, was a formality not unusually practised by those who subscribed their names; as appears by an example in this same Journal, where the opinion of one of the steersmen being demanded, is delivered in writing, 'Onderstout (sic!) by my, Pieter N. Duytz.' i.e. Undersigned: by me, Pieter N. Duytz. (MS. Journal. February the 14th 1643)." Woide as well as Burney were both of them mistaken. There cannot be the least doubt that the word onderstont (= below was written), which accompanies the various signatures, occurring in various places in the journal, is a quite unmistakeable indication that in those places we have to deal with copies, and not with originals. It is quite out of the question that this phrase should be "a formality not unusually practised by those who subscribed their names." But it does not follow that on this account a character of originality should necessarily be denied to a document containing signatures accompanied by this phrase. What, for example, is actually the case here? Tasman, when he drew up his journal such as we know it, had at his disposal the original written opinions and advices of himself, of the skippers and other ship's officers. These he utilised by inserting them in his journal, and for this purpose he had to transcribe them: he accordingly had then to affix the word onderstont to the signatures, in order to denote that in this case what the reader had before him, were copies.

[1) 8946, Plut. CLXXII D. I have not myself seen this MS., but the kindness of Mr. C. G. Luzac, of London, has furnished me with all the information I deemed necessary to enable me to determine as accurately as possible the place to be assigned to this document in the series of the manuscripts of Tasman's voyage.]

[2) Cf. also BURNEY, III (1813), p. 60.--T. M. HOCKER, Some Account of the Earliest Literature and Maps relating to New Zealand (Transactions of the New Zealand Institute, 1894, pp. 620-621).]

[3) BURNEY, l. c., p. 60.]

[4) Pp. 60-61.--Cf. also MATTHEW FLINDERS, Ontdekkingsreis naar het Groote Zuidland anders Nieuw-Holland;...in 1801, 1802 en 1803. Uit het Engelsch. IV. Haarlem, Loosjes, 1816, p. 224. See also the original edition, A voyage to Terra Australis; undertaken for the purpose of completing the discovery of that vast country, and prosecuted in the years 1801, 1802, and 1803, in his Mayesty's ship the Investigator...By Matthew Flinders, Commander. Vol. I, London, G. and W. Nicol, 1814. Introduction, p. LXXVI.]

But this insertion of transcripts of course need not in any way impair the original character of a manuscript. Woide's argument that the manuscript now preserved in the British. Museum should necessarily be a transcript, because "when Tasman's name is signed, it is allways said: undersigned Tasman," is accordingly without foundation. There is other internal evidence, however, to prove that in this case we have to do with a copy, viz. the signature at the close of the manuscript. This closing

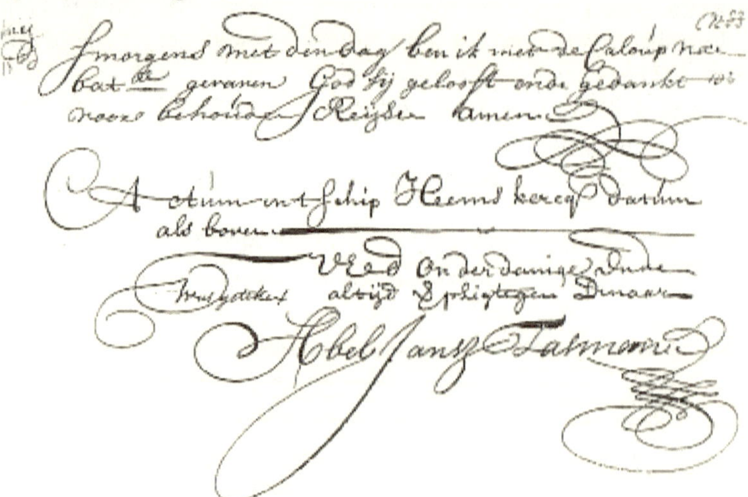

formula, of which we give a facsimile, runs as follows: "Actum in t schip Heems kercq datum als boven. VEd. onderdanige ende altijd verpligtigen Dinaar Was getekent[1] Abel Jansz Tasman" [Actum in the ship Heemskercq; date as above. Your Worships' obedient and for ever obliged Servant signed[1] Abel Jansz Tasman]. Now this phrase "was getekent" cannot mean anything else than that the whole journal is a copy, a fact which the transcriber has certified by prefixing to the signature the words "was getekent" (= was found signed).

Are there any data to determine the age of this transcript? Concerning this point Woide says "It is an old copy of Tasman's original. The manner of spelling proves in the most convincing manner that this copy was written a century ago." This would land us in the third quarter of the seventeenth century, roughly speaking. I should have hesitated to give so positive an opinion. I am even inclined to think that we may safely put the date of the copy somewhat later still, and take the earlier part of the eighteenth century as the terminus a quo.

We have now to consider the question, on what manuscript nearer to the archetype, then, this not always accurate, sometimes even slovenly[2] copy has been based. It is always ticklish to attempt to answer such a question with absolute certainty; but we may say with the highest possible degree of probability that the writer of the British Museum manuscript has transcribed either our copy or a transcript of the latter. Of course the difference in spelling cannot be alleged against this supposition; nor is this supposition affected by certain liberties in which the writer has indulged, and certain mistakes he has made in reproducing the text. Among these mistakes and oversights there are, however, some that bear a more serious character. The dates of September 22, 23, and 24, for example, have been left out. On December 2 further on, our copy reads. "Dat voor aen om geseyden hoeck, meenichten van meeuwen, wilde endtvogels ende ganzen...gezien hadden." [That in front of

[1] The italics are mine.]

[1] Cf. Woide apud BURNEY, c., pp. 60-61. The scribal errors are more numerous than there enumerated.]

the cape aforesaid, (they) had seen numbers of gulls, wild ducks and geese]. The British Museum copy corrupts this into "menigte van menschen wilden ent vogels en gansen" [a number of men, wild ducks and geese], and this, when it has just before been observed, that the Netherlanders "niemant to zien gekregen hadden" [had not got sight of any one]. Burney accordingly translates "They could see nobody," but later on "they saw people; and some wild ducks, and geese." In the map of Van Diemen's Land, in our copy facing December 2, the name Frederick Hendricx Bay is omitted. On January 9, 1643, the latitude noted is 35° 4', which is still more erroneous than the latitude given in our copy, nor is this the only mistake as regards longitudes and latitudes, committed by the scribe of the British Museum copy. On the other hand various interesting indications may be adduced in support of the supposition advanced by me. All the drawings, surveyings, and charts, occurring in our copy, are also found in the British Museum copy; nor does the latter contain any others[1]. Thus it is, for example, clearly observable in the chart of Van Diemen's Land (Tasmania), which in our copy faces December 2, 1642, that originally the degrees of longitude in it were given wrongly, and that these errors have been rectified from the data furnished on this point by the text of the journal. In the first instance, the degrees of longitude had been marked 164°-172°[2], which figures have afterwards been corrected to 162°-169°; 172° alone has been left unchanged. And now it is highly curious to notice that in the British Museum copy all the degrees of longitude have been altered in exactly the same way, while only 172° has remained as it was, thereby perpetuating the error. The copy also shows the exceptional length of the 169th degree of longitude, which is 1½ times the length of the others. It would be a most extraordinary coincidence, if the peculiarities just detailed should occur in two or more copies independent of each other. Something very like this is exemplified in the chart of Statenland. It is directly seen in the chart in our copy that it must have been the original intention of the draughtsman to mark the degrees of longitude on the left hand side of the chart only (from the beholder's point of view). Accordingly, on the right hand side only the 190th degree of longitude is found marked, and there can be little doubt that this isolated number was inserted at a subsequent time. And now it is really surprising to find this one degree marked in the chart in the British Museum copy. Near the anchoring-place on the Moordenaarsbaai we find the longitude of 191° 30', and the latitude of 40° 50' marked in the same hand which has marked the 190°. These indications are at variance with the general arrangement of the chart, in which originally no longitudes or latitudes were noted at the various parts of the coast touched at by the Netherlanders[3]. Also in this case it is highly remarkable that these very indications are also given in the British Museum copy[4]. The marginal note in our copy on January 24 "dit moet west zijn" [this should be west] has been utilised by the maker of the British Museum copy; he says: "'s midd: hadden de twe Eylandekens regt oost/west van ons 4 mijlen" (at noon we had the two islets due east/west of us at 4 miles' distance]. We further miss in the British Museum copy the degrees of longitude between May 21 and 27, which are left blank also in our copy. All these peculiarities are readily accounted for by assuming that it was our copy that served as the model for the London one, and they utterly exclude the possibility of any of the other copies known to us having formed the basis of the transcriber's work.

We now pass on to discuss the charts that formed part of the journals. We are dispensed from offering any observations on those charts which occur in our copy of the journal kept by Tasman: the facsimile we give faithfully reproduces them. Some of the others, however, demand a brief notice.

In the first place the Huydecoper MS. contains certain surveyings, taken on December 4 and 5,

[1] At first sight the numbers of these adjuncts in the two copies seem to disagree, but a closer scrutiny shows that the copyist has brought together on one sheet sometimes more, sometimes fewer items than he found in his model.]

[2] The erroneous longitudes on November 24 and December 1 agree with those found in the journal from the Sweers collection, preserved in the Netherlands State Archives.--VALENTIJN has other longitudes than our copy; but they do not tally with the text of our journal, nor do they correspond to the longitudes which he himself gives in his text.--Besides being found in BURNEY, this chart is also reproduced by A. MAULT, on an old manuscript chart of Tasmania in the records of the India Office (Australasian Association for the advancement of science. Hobart, 1892, Section E, p. 2). This copy is "taken from one made by Mr. Bonwick." That the copyist who made the British Museum copy, must have studied the journal, when he was reproducing the chart, is proved by the circumstance that he has marked the reckonings in the chart. The word Cool (Corael?) 60 (MAULT) on the west coast is not found in the chart itself in the British Museum, nor does it occur in Burney.]

[3] The figures at the "Klippige Hoek" are also clearly of later date.]

[4] These indications have not been reproduced by Burney.]

which do not agree with those found in our copy. These surveyings have the following legends appended to them: "Aldus verthoont hem t Landt op 4 Desember 1642 op de Zuyder Breete van 42 gradn 38 Menuyten als het 2 Mijlen van U js.--Maria Eylant.-- Aldus veithoont hem t lant op 4 December 1642 op de Zuyder Breete van 42 graden 40 Menuyten als het vastelandt 4 a 4½ Mijlen ende D'Eylanden 2½ a 3 Mijlen van U js.--d'E.Hr: Schoutens Eylant.-- Verthooningh op 5en December 1642 Als het 8 Mijlen van U js.--dE Hr. van der Lyns Eylant." [Thus appears the land on December 4, 1642 in 42° 38, S.L., at 2 miles' distance from the observer.--Maria Island.--Thus appears the land on December 4, 1642 in 42° 40' S.L., the main land being at from 4 to 41½ miles', and the islands at from 2½ to 3 miles' distance from the observer.--Schoutens Island.--

Appearance on December 5, 1642 at 8 miles' distance from the observer.--Van der Lyn's Island]. Besides, certain parts of the surveyings are indicated with some further detail.

Of greater importance, however, in this manuscript are two charts[1], referring to our voyage, which charts did not originally form part of the manuscript, but were inserted at some subsequent period. One of them fairly well corresponds to the chart of "Staete landt," found in our copy between January[2] 4 and 5, 1643. Fairly well...but not in all points. Leaving aside minute differences, I mention that in the chart of the Huydecoper MS. are not found the names "Abel Tasmans Passagie," and " Mordenaers Bay," which do appear in the chart in our copy. Furthermore the Huydecoper MS. has the words "Duijnich lant" [dune-like lands, where our chart reads: "Sant duiningen dick" [broad sandy dunes]. Another important difference[3] is, that in the chart in the Huydecoper MS. in about 193° 30' E. Long. and nearly 41° 20' S. Lat., the coast shows a break clearly intended to denote a "passage," whereas in the chart in our copy the coast-line is uninterrupted. Besides, there are certain differences in the delineation of the anchoring-places; the chart in our copy shows a larger number of islands along the coast; the chart in the Huydecoper MS. bears indications of the ship's reckonings between December 15, 1642 and January 6, 1643, which reckonings are not noted in the chart in our copy; and, what is of the greatest importance, the chart itself bears the information, that it has "been drawn with great diligence and assiduity by Franchoijs Jacobszoon, steersman" [met groot vlijt seer neerstig ontworpen (is) door Franchoijs Jacobszoon stierman]. We have therefore to do here with a product of the cartographic labours of Tasman's skilful coadjutor. This is also the case as regards the other chart in the Huydecoper MS., that claims notice here. This chart, like the one just referred to, gives the impression of being an original, and bears the following inscription: "Ontworp gedaen door Franchoys Jacobszoon stierman, de naemen gestelt naer ordre vanden Commandr. Tasman" [Draft made by Franchoys Jacobszoon, steersman, the names having been inserted according to directions given by Commander Tasman]. This chart is found to bear a strong resemblance to the one which in our copy is inserted at February[4] 7, 1643. But, as regards the names there given to the islands, etc., there is found so wide a difference from those which the same islands, etc. bear in Visscher's chart, that the words of the inscription just referred to: " the names having been inserted according to directions given by Commander Tasman," are calculated to create surprise at first sight. Some of these discrepancies between the names in the two charts demand our attention. The " Pijlstert Eylandt " [Arrow-tail Island] of our copy, in Visscher's chart bears the name of "Vrouwen borsten" [women's breasts], an appellation which our copy of the journal accounts for, by stating on January 19: "This island appears like two women's breasts, as seen east by north, at 6 miles' distance from the beholder"[5]. On the next day it got the name of "hooge pylstaerts eijlandt [high Arrow-tail Island], because there were so many arrow-tailed ducks observed about it." Instead of "t' Eijlandt Mijddelborch," Visscher's chart has "Hooch eylant" [High Island], a designation which is also found explained in the journal at January 21. "t' Eijlandt Amsterdam," also, is not called by this name in the chart of the Huydecoper MS., where we read the following account of it: "taemelick hooch [pretty high], als Gout-Staert jn Engelant ofte Strijssaert jn Normandie;" and this is not cleared up by what we read

[1] Cf. LEUPE in Bijdragen voor geschiedenis, 1. c., pp. 263-265.--I do not know Leupe's reasons for characterising the charts in our manuscript as copies from the two charts discussed in the text as found in the Huydecoper MS. (p. 265).]

[2] Not February, as given in Leupe.]

[3] This difference is not referred to by Leupe.]

[4] Not January, as LEUPE erroneously has it in Bijdragen voor geschiedenis, 1. c., p. 264.]

[5] Cf. also the surveying under the said date.]

in our copy and in the Huydecoper MS., which both of them on January 21 describe Amsterdam itself as "een laech eylandt, even als Hollandt is" [a low-lying island, just as Holland is]. One of the islets south of the island of Rotterdam, left without a name in the chart in our copy, bears in Visscher's chart the name of Amockakij, which agrees with the appellation of Namocaki in the surveying between January 24 and 25, and in the first drawing, which in our copy is found between January 25 and 26. Rotterdam itself is by Visscher called "Annakooka laech, dit is onse waeter plaets geweest" [low-lying, where we took in fresh water]; Tasman, besides naming it after the well-known Dutch mercantile town, in the drawing January 25/26, just mentioned, also styles it Anamocka. The two islands north-west of Rotterdam are in Visscher designated as follows: "Amtafoe, wel gelijckende in de hoochte Crakatouw in de Straedt Sunda" [Amtafoe, in height resembling Crakatouw in Sunda Straits], and "Kaij Baij." In the chart in our copy the two islands are left nameless, but in the drawing

January 25/26, repeatedly mentioned, they also figure as Amatafoa and Kaij Baij. But also on this point there are differences. Our copy states on January 24, that it is Kaij Baij, and not Amatafoa, which "in height and extent resembles Cracatouw in Zunda Straits." The island which in our chart lies in longitude 206° 20' E. and latitude 18° 50' S., is in Visscher's chart denominated "Hooch eijlandeken" [High Islet], which appellation is to some extent supported by statements in the journal. We further miss in the chart last mentioned the names of Van Diemens Reede, Vanderlins Reede, Justus Schoutens Bay, and Abel Tasmans Passagie, all of which names duly figure in the chart in our copy. The two charts show certain discrepancies in the grouping of the islands and shallows. It should besides be observed that the longitudes differ considerably[1]: the Huydecoper chart locates everything about 1½° less to the eastward, and less in accordance with the text of our copy, and that of the Huydecoper MS. Finally attention should be drawn to the circumstance that Visscher's chart notes the ship's reckonings between January 18 and February 7, which are wanting in the chart in our copy.

In the India Office there is preserved a chart of Tasmania which must not be left undiscussed in this place. The Report on the old records in the India Office, by George Birdwood[2], describes it as "a rough sketch, much damaged, and only kept together by being backed with goldbeater's skin." The chart[3] itself is drawn on paper, and in a seventeenth century hand entitled "A draught of the South land lately discovered 1643." It is impossible to say how this chart has come by its English title[4], nor are there any particulars forthcoming of its ulterior history. It fully impresses the observer as bearing the character of an original[5]. Was this chart drawn on board the Heemskerk or on board the Zeehaen?, we may ask. This question also is not likely to be ever satisfactorily answered[6]; nor shall we in this place attempt to solve the problem. We shall only have to draw attention to certain differences which strike the observer on comparing the chart in our copy with the "draught." The longitude degrees in the "draught" differ from those in our chart[7], as well as from the degrees marked in Valentijn's chart; but in the case of the latter the difference is much smaller. From this we may safely conclude that the "draught" does not bear what I should wish to call an official character. For on November 26, 1642 Tasman gave orders that "the charts (of the newly discovered land) drawn up by any person should lay down this land in the medium longitude of 163 degrees 50 minutes." In the "draught" we find it lying in 164° 40'. It is probable, therefore, that the "draught " had already been prepared, when this order was issued; the alternative being that the draughtsman

[1) LEUPE does not refer to this.]

[2) Second reprint (London, Allen, 1891), p. 77.]

[3) A facsimile 0f it is given by MAULT, l. c., who has kindly enabled me to take cognizance of it.]

[4) Cf., however, MAULT, 1. c., pp. 3, 4.]

[5) Cf. MAULT, 1. c., p. 4.--I have even been under a transient impression that it might have been drawn by the very person who has written our copy; an impression derived from a comparison of a single letter and various figures found in the chart, with those occurring in our copy.]

[6) MAULT, l. c., pp. 3, 4, inclines to the opinion, that it has been drawn on board the Zeehaen. One of his grounds for this opinion is, that the island to the north of Maria Island is found in the "draught," but not in the chart in our copy. The reason of this difference would then be that this island had not been seen by the sailors on board the Heemskerk, but only by the crew of the Zeehaen, which latter ship would then have been "much further inshore than her consort while sailing northward from the anchorage." But how then are we to explain the circumstance that the islet, situated hard by the anchorage in front of Frederik Hendrik Bay is also wanting in the chart in our copy, while it duly appears in the "draught"?]

[7) Cf. MAULT, 1. c., pp. 1 ff.]

has acted entirely on his personal responsibility. Still, the "draught" is not without interest for us, because it gives more than the chart in our copy. This additional matter is also found in the chart in Valentijn, who accordingly must have had before him a model with these addita, while it must remain a moot point whether he took these supplementary details from the chart in the copy, of which only the one folio leaf above described, now preserved in the Hague State Archives, has come down to us.--which chart must then have been more complete than any of the others known to us, since we shall presently see that it must then have included also those particulars which are not found in the "draught," but which do appear in the chart in our copy-- or whether by the side of those just referred to, he had still other data to work from. The "draught" shows both the islets near the anchorage in front of Frederik Hendrik Bay, and the one north of Maria Island, while neither of these are found in the chart in our copy. Valentijn has both of them. But Valentijn has also availed himself of what is not found in the "draught," but does appear in the chart in our copy, and in the charts resembling the latter, actually existing or no longer forthcoming. What Tasman has designated as the "Wits-eilanden", forms a group of three islands in the "draught," and of four in the chart in our copy: Valentijn, too, has four of them. The configurations of Tasman Island and of the islands east of Tasmania, which in the "draught" differ from those in our chart, in Valentijn agree with the latter. In the "draught" Cape Frederik Hendrik has become an island, while the chart gives it as a projecting point: Valentijn has the projecting point.

Recapitulating the results obtained, we may enumerate the following MS. sources for the history of Tasman's voyage of 1642-1643[1], of which sources we can at the same time approximately fix the chronological order. First in the order of time comes the draft journal, preserved in the State Archives at the Hague, most probably written by a sailor of inferior rank, and probably drawn up in the course of the voyage. The qualification last mentioned probably also applies to the "draught" of Tasmania in the India Office. Next in the series comes a class of copies, which, with varying intervals in each case, are all of them derivable from Tasman's own notes drawn up in the form of a journal during the voyage: among the extant copies belonging to this class, the original fair copy, reproduced in the present work (our copy) bears the most pronounced original character. Then follows the copy, of which the Hague State Archives preserve the one folio leaf, and which is most probably slightly younger, though on the whole it bears a coeval character. Finally we have the Huydecoper van Maarsseveen copy, closely related to the class of copies above described, and bearing probably a coeval, though not an original character. The British Museum copy is a transcript of our copy. Nothing certain can be predicated of the copy which is reported to have at one time existed at Batavia, and of the one which in 1835 was sold by Mr. Bom the Amsterdam bookseller: it is therefore quite impossible to determine the places which ought to be assigned to them in the chronological series.

Another source of information concerning this voyage is the chart made after the second expedition to the South-land, undertaken by Tasman in 1644. This chart was at one time in the possession of the Amsterdam firm of Hulst van Keulen, and at present belongs to Prince Roland Bonaparte at Paris. Swart appended a copy of it to his edition of the journal of 1642/3. This copy is[2] negligently made, but failing the original[3], it would appear to be sufficiently serviceable to enable us to determine the value of the original for our purpose; especially if we bear in mind, what is known about this chart from other sources[4], and remember Swart's statement that he has copied it

[1) I shall discuss one of the most important sources, viz. the chart registering the results of both this voyage and the 1644 one, when treating of the latter expedition.]

[2] My impression derived from a study of Swart's copy only, is that of slovenliness. Leupe, who was in a position to compare it with the original, judges more favourably of it. See Bijdragen voor vaderlandsche geschiedenis, 1. c., p. 269. But cf. also LEUPE'S remark in his book: De reizen der Nederlanders naar Nieuw-Guinea en de Papoesche eilanden in de 17de en 18de eeuw. 's Gravenhage, Nijhoff, 1875, p. 189. Mr. A. Mensing, of the publishing firm of Frederik Muller & Co, who has seen the chart, and accurately compared it with the Swart copy states that the chart itself is magnificently made and that Swart's copy is very inaccurate.]

[3] We must regret that Prince Bonaparte has elected to refuse our request for permission to append to the present work a reproduction of the chart in question.]

[4] SWART'S edition of 1860, pp. 2, 4-5, 182-189; LEUPE, Bijdragen vaderlandsche geschiedenis, 1. c., pp. 268-272.--The chart given in the present work, has been drawn up on the basis of the data at our disposal. It gives a good idea of the chart referred to in our text; but does not include a separate diagram, found in the original and representing the ship's courses from Jaya to Mauritius.]

"without alterations." The separate edition of 1860 gives emendations, and is more accurate than the one in Swart's well-known review, but there are still mistakes. That in this case we should have to do with a chart drawn in the course of the voyage itself, is out of the question. The truth is, that it was made immediately after the expedition, before the close of the year 1644, by order of Van Diemen, and under the eye of Tasman himself. On this point the wording of the superscription leaves no room for doubt. "Dit warck"--we are informed in seventeenth-century diction--"aldus by mallecanderen gevoecht ut verscheyden schriften als mede ut eygen bevinding by abel Jansen tasman Año 1644, dat door order van de E.d. hr. gouverneur general Anthonio Van diemens." [This work has thus been brought together out of divers writings, together with personal observations by Abel Jansen Tasman, A. D. 1644, by order of the worshipful lord governor-general Anthonio Van Diemen]. The superscription further informs us that all[1] the countries represented in the chart "have been discovered by the Company's explorers, excepting the north part of New Guinea and the western extremity of Java." We now see for what purpose the chart was drawn up: its object was to give a survey of what in 1644 was known to the Netherlanders respecting the South-land, if we may be allowed to retain this vague but generally accepted appellation.

What, we may ask, was the use of a survey like this? It seems by no means improbable that Van Diemen, who was always on the look-out for new discoveries, and who also, as we shall see further on, kept his eye on the regions already visited by Tasman, that Van Diemen, I say, caused this survey to be drawn up, precisely with a view to projects of this nature. The copy known to us is probably one that was sent over to the Netherlands: at least the back of the chart bears the words: "[Caert?][2] van de nieuwe ontdeckte Ooster en Zuyder Landen," together with a number (3): most probably the number of the chart in the register, unfortunately no longer extant, of the documents transmitted to the mother-country, December 23, 1644, and the brief description as usually found on the documents sent from India to the Board of Directors. The chart is drawn on Japanese paper[4], like the one which embodies the results of Quast and Tasman's expedition eastward of Japan in 1639, and that made by Tasman 8 September 1644, to be discussed infra. As regards the spelling of the names the chart seems to have been made up with great carelessness. In the copy made for his edition Swart has endeavoured to introduce corrections on this point, but elsewhere he has not always shown himself so accurate and exact as to justify us in accepting his emendations without due reserve. All this of course discounts the value of Swart's copy. Fortunately, however, it is sufficient for our purpose as regards the main points, for it clearly indicates the courses followed by Tasman in his two voyages, and consequently the results of his exploratory expeditions.

To some slight extent the copy admits of being checked and pieced out by what we know about another chart[5], most probably drawn by Visscher, which is likely to have borne a more original character[6]. This chart itself would seem to be no longer extant, but there exists of it an English copy, presumably made still in the seventeenth century[7], and probably drawn up with very

[1] It is therefore going slightly too far, to assert that Frans Jacobszoon Visscher must have been the maker of it, as we find affirmed by C. H. COOTE, Remarkable Maps of the XV, XVI, and XVIII centuries reproduced in their original size, p. 11 of the Introduction and Notes of part II, and p. 11 of the Introduction and Notes of part III (Amsterdam, Frederik Muller and Co., 1895). Why, indeed, could not Tasman have been its maker, seeing that he also drew the chart of September 8, 1644, to be mentioned infra? Cf. also LEUPE (Bijdragen tot de taal-, land- en volkenkunde van Neêrlandsch-Indië, IV, p. 131, Navorscher, 1862, p. 304, and Bijdragen vaderlandsche geschiedenis en oudheidkunde, l. c., p. 272). But he does not go so far as Coote does. He only assumes that Visscher must have been the author of the chart or a collaborator in its preparation.]

[2) Mr. Mensing tells me, that in the Bonaparte chart it says "Alle dese landen zin ontdeckt by de compangie ondeckers behalve het norder deell van noua Guina ende het west eynde van Java; dit warck," enz. Both legends are full of clerical errors and mistakes. Here Swart has read "Carten dese landen," etc. which is of course a mere blunder.]

[3) A corner torn off here. See LEUPE, Bijdragen vaderlandsche geschiedenis, 1. c., p. 268, Notes 2 and *.]

[4) See Leupe contra Swart in Bijdragen vaderlandsche geschiedenis, 1. c., p. 268.]

[5) See also LEUPE, Reizen Nieuw-Guinea, pp. 43, 171; P. A. LEUPE, De reizen der Nederlanders naar het Zuidland of Nieuw-Holland in de 17de en 18de eeuw. (Amsterdam, Hulst van Keulen, 1868) pp. 86-89.]

[6) Cf. also COOTE, Remarkable Maps, III, Introduction, p. II.]

[7) See R. H. MAJOR, Early voyages to Terra Australis, now called Australia (London. Hakluyt Society, 1859), pp. XCVI f. Mr. Mensing, however, assigns a much later date to this copy. His supposition is founded on the quality of the paper of this copy. That in the XVII century a chart or charts of Tasman's 1644 voyage were known in England, is proved by the circumstance that Dampier in his voyage of 1699 had with him a "draught" of the west coast of Australia, "which was Tasman's." See A voyage to New-Holland, etc. In the Year 1699. By Captain William Dampier. Volume III of A collection of voyages. The Third edition. (London, Knapton, MDCCXXIX, p. 94.)]

little care[1], which copy is at present preserved in the British Museum[2]. If we may rely on a reproduction of this copy[3], we may assume with a very fair degree of certainty that its original must have been a draft which is likely to have been used in the drawing-up[4] of Tasman's compilatory chart just discussed. At all events this is more probable than the reverse supposition, that the British Museum copy has been made from the Bonaparte chart, or from another resembling the latter: the discrepancies are too marked for such a supposition. We may surmise that Visscher had made a more or less rough draft; that the Bonaparte chart had transferred to it this rough draft, rendered more accurate on the one hand, but with the omission of certain details, which Tasman either considered as mistakes, or for other reasons thought it unadvisable to take over. In this way we might then account for the fact that Visscher's draft contains certain notes which are not found in Tasman's chart; thus there would be nothing strange in the fact that, where Tasman's chart, for instance, reads: "Compagnies Nieuw Nederland. In het Oosten het groote landt van Nova Guinea met het eerste bekende Zuidland, wezende één land en altezamen aan elkander vast, als bij deze gestippelde passage bij d'jachten Limmen, Zeemeeuw en de quel de Brak [gezien] kan worden. Ano 1644." [The

Company's Nieuw Nederland. In the east the large country of Nova Guinea with the first discovered South-land, forming all one continent together, as may be seen from this dotted line near the yachts Limmen and Zeemeeuw, and the 'quel' (galiot) de Brak, A.D. 1644], Visscher's draft--supposing that the English translation faithfully reproduces the original Dutch text--should have contained the following explanation: "This large land of New Guinea was first discovered to joyne to ye South land by ye Yot Lemmen as by this chart Ffrancois Jacobus Vis: Pilot Maior Anno 1643"[5]; especially if we bear in mind that, as appears from the "Instructions," Visscher was skipper of the Limmen in the expedition of 1644, and is therefore likely to have been inclined to give the place of honour to the ship which he himself commanded; thus it would become easy to account for the circumstance that a large number of local names appearing in Tasman's chart, are not found in Visscher's draft, and likewise that the soundings in the two charts strikingly differ from each other[6]; all which discrepancies can be readily accounted for, if we suppose Visscher's chart to have constituted one of the data for Tasman's work, but are utterly inexplicable on the supposition that Visscher's chart has been copied from Tasman's or from one resembling it. However this may be, now that we know Tasman's chart, the British Museum copy is not of sufficient importance to necessitate a more detailed discussion of the discrepancies referred to: the only service required of it being, that in a few cases it has to do duty to determine the results of Tasman and Visscher's two voyages slightly more circumstantially than would be possible without the copy in question.

A certain interest as a "check" also attaches to a chart, to be further discussed infra, made by Tasman himself a very short time after the termination of his second voyage, viz. on September 8, 1644. The names of places appearing in this chart "along the coast of Nova Guinea" are a highly welcome means of control, and a very serviceable complement to what we learn from the Bonaparte chart[7].

[1] On the coast of Van Diemensland, for example, are found the Boreels Islands, and slightly more to westward there is an island which on November 29 "showed like a high stumpy steeple." The English copy mixes up these different islands and has: "Borells Iland is like a steeple." "Van der Lijn's Island" becomes "Sanderlins Iland;" Drommeltjes van eylanden benoorden Nieuw-Guinea" [small island-groups north of New-Guinea] becomes "Dromel: loco Islands;" "met een riff" [with a reef), or something to that effect: "meeter nies;" Cabo St. Maria: "Abo St. Maria," etc. etc. Cf. LEUPE, Bijdragen vaderlandsche geschiedenis, 1. c., p. 271. I have not thought it necessary to record all these mistakes here.]

[2) Sloane MSS. No. 5222, Art. 12.]

[3) For this reproduction I am indebted to the great courtesy of Mr. A. Mault, who made of the copy a facsimile which has been photolithographed for the Royal Society of Tasmania. MAJOR gives a copy on a reduced scale in his book referred to higher up. RAINAUD, Le Continent Austral (Paris, Colin, 1893) gives (p. 363) a "Carte-esquisse des voyages de Tasman autour de l' Australie (d'après une carte hollandaise, Bibl. nation. Reg C. 6789)." This "carte" gives no details, and seems to be of no interest whatever.]

[4) Cf. LEUPE in Bijdragen vaderl. gesch. 1. c., pp. 271, 272.]

[5) A slip of the pen, of course, either by Visscher himself, or, what is more likely, by the seventeenth-century English copyist.--MAJOR, 1. c., p. XCVII, here refers to a "twofold blunder, both as to fact and date." The date is certainly wrong, but as regards the "fact" ("to joyne to the South land") there can be no question of a mistake. Tasman and Visscher really supposed that New Guinea and the "South-land" formed one whole. They were mistaken, but from their point of view they could only certify that they had discovered that New Guinea was joined to the "South-land." If the draughtsman (or the copyist?) had put the phrase cited in the text: "This large land... Anno 1643," more to the north in the chart, it would have been exactly in its place. Cf. also LEUPE, 1. c, pp. 270-271.]

[6) I fail to understand why LEUPE, Bijdragen vaderlandsche geschiedenis, 1. c., p. 271, says that "the soundings made in the course of the second voyage, generally" agree with each other in the chart of Tasman and in Visscher's draft.]

[7) Cf. LEUPE, Reizen Nieuw-Guinea, pp. 173-174, who is, however, mistaken as to the date of its being completed. This date was not September 1, but September 8, 1644]

Besides the charts hitherto discussed, there are at our disposal certain other authentic documents bearing on the voyage of 1644. The object for which the expedition was undertaken may be especially inferred from the instructions drawn up for the guidance of its leaders, and besides, from certain resolutions of the Governor-General and Councillors, and from certain letters written by these dignitaries. Its result is briefly stated in general terms, inter alia in the General missive of December 23, 1644. This missive refers to "the Chart and Journals inclosed" and to the "Batavian diary, in which are noted the courses and particulars of the voyage, under date August 4, 5 and 10 last past." This diary is no longer extant. The "chart" of which there is question here, may possibly be the one now in the possession of Prince Bonaparte. There can be no doubt that a journal of this voyage was sent over to Europe. In 1854 Leupe hit on a cover bearing the superscription: "Journaal ofte dachregister van de voyagie gedaen door den

Commandeur Abel Jansz. Tasman, met de Jachten Limmen, Zee-meeuw ende 't Galjoot de Haesewint, langs de custe van Nova Guinea ende 't onbekende Suyt-lant 1644, geannoteert door Crijn Hendrixen de Ratte, opperstierman op 't Jacht de Zeemeeuw"[1]) [Journal or daily register of the voyage made by Commander Abel Jansz. Tasman, with the Yachts Limmen, Zeemeeuw and the Galiot of de Hasewint, along the coast of Nova Guinea and the unknown South-land in the year 1644, written by Crijn Hendrixen de Ratte, first mate in the Yacht Zeemeeuw]. Furthermore, about the year 1859[2], Mr. Frederik Muller, the founder of the publishing firm of Fred. Muller and Co., discovered the binding which had once contained the account of the results of this voyage, not indeed as momentous as the one made in 1642/3, but still decidedly important enough to make us deeply regret that the narrative detailing the faits et gestes of our hardy navigators in the course of this expedition, has not come down to us[3]. Fortunately we need not give up all hope of once recovering it: many a lucky find quite unexpectedly made in cases when all hope had long been given up, may serve to buoy up our confidence. For the present, however, we are fain to put up with the fragmentary data touching this voyage, furnished by the Old Colonial Archives, and found scattered elsewhere.

Some years were to elapse before the results of the exploratory voyages were made public property. It was in the very nature of things that for the Board of Directors of the East India Company, who considered its very existence to be indissolubly bound up with the strict maintenance of its monopoly, and with the exclusion as far as possible of countrymen and foreigners alike from the commercial territory which they themselves occupied; it was, I say, in the very nature of things that for the Board of Directors there was not a single motive that could have prompted them to publish to the world at large the results of voyages of discovery undertaken at their command, at all events by functionaries in the service of the Company. In arranging for these expeditions their first and foremost object was, the obtaining of new commercial advantages, and they were far from deeming it their duty to draw the attention of others to these new markets. It were to be wished--thus they once unbosomed themselves[4] on hearing of rumours concerning fruit-bearing islands in the eastern part of the Malay Archipelago--"that the said land continued still unknown and never explored, so as not to tell foreigners the way to the Company's overthrow." These words gave characteristic utterance to the serious apprehensions entertained by the Directors at the idea of even the bare possibility of their once acquired and conquered mercantile privileges being infringed. A petty shopkeeper's policy this, no doubt, when

[1] See LABORANTER (pseudonym of P. A. Lam) in Navorscher, Vierde Jaargang (1854), pp. 161 f.--Cf. also LEUPE, Reizen Nieuw Guinea, p. 41.--A somewhat striking circumstance is the deviation in the names of the ships, a point to which I shall revert in the sequel.]

[2] See FREDERIK MULLER'S paper entitled "Ervaringen in Nederlandsche Archieven", in Nederlandsche Spectator, 1874, p. 226 or 227. Leupe, however, at the time assistant in the Netherlands State Archives, wrote in 1875: "We do not know anything about this binding" (Nieuw Guinea, p. 41, Note 2). My search for it has been equally fruitless.]

[3] No journal of it has been found either in the State Archives at the Hague, or in the Government Archives at Batavia. As regards the latter repository, see Tijdschrift voor Indische taal-, land- en volkenkunde, uitgegeven door het Bataviaasch Genootschap van Kunsten en Wetenschappen. Batavia, 's Hage, 1862, XII p. 544--About the year 1825, too, a search for it seems to have been made in India. See J. VAN WIJK ROELANDSZOON in Nouvelles Annales des Voyages, de la géographie et de l'histoire...publiées par J. B. Eyriès et Malte-Brun. Paris, XXVII, Gide, 1825, p. 144.--LAUTS (Konst- en Letterbode, 1835, p. 263) writes that he had heard it said, "that in England a MS. of Tasman's first voyage and another of his second ditto were reported to be preserved," but unfortunately, as a rule, Lauts is not prodigal of particulars respecting the sources from which he drew his information.]

[4] In their missive to the G.-G. and Counc. of September 9, 1645. Cf. my Bouwstoffen, III, pp. XXXIX--XL.]

judged from the far more liberal point of view so common in our days; still a policy that can be better accounted for, understood, and defended, when we see it put in practice by men who reaped ample profits from the application of their narrow system; at a time too, when mercantile competition was well-nigh equivalent to open hostility, a time, whose "commercial spirit had a general character of narrowness"[1]. It was not wonderful therefore that the Company's archives were not always accessible to such as were desirous of utilising the documents there preserved, for purposes utterly foreign, nay in the opinion of the Directors quite contrary, to the interests of the association whose management was entrusted to their care. Still, it is noteworthy that the results, for instance of Tasman's exploratory voyages, and for the matter of that, of other expeditions also, can have been given to the world at so comparatively early a date. This circumstance sufficiently proves that the desire of the Directors to make a secret of new discoveries did not assuredly go so far as to prompt them efficiently and systematically to thwart any attempts at publication, though on the other hand they are not likely to have afforded them any cordial and substantial support. For the matter of that, indeed, they cannot but have been aware that concealment on their part alone could not have the effect intended, unless such secrecy was equally observed by their subordinates. And among the latter there were numerous foreigners, more especially among the sailors of inferior rank. However all this may be, it is quite sure that as early as the middle of the seventeenth century the printing-press had published to the world at large a good deal of what the Netherlanders had been doing during the fifty years of their presence in the East[2].

A few years already before the text of any of the journals kept in the course of either voyage was published, certain results obtained by these expeditions had--in the Netherlands first--become known from charts.

Our attention is in the first place[3] claimed by a large map of India quae Orientalis dicitur, et insulae adiacenles, t' Amsterdam, Gedruckt bij Huych Allardt, inde Kalverstraat inde Werell-kaart[4]. It was engraved by Pieter Nolpe[5], who died in 1652 or 1653[6], and was dedicated by Allardt "nobilissimis, amplissimis atque prudentissimis viris domino Cornelio De Graaf[7], Haereditario in Suit Polsbroek,

[1] MAJOR, Early Voyages, p. IX. Cf. also FRUIN, Tien Jaren, p. 216. Cf. Major's temperate remarks concerning the uncommunicativeness of the Directors, pp. VI--XI. This secretiveness on the part of the Directors was animadverted upon already at an early period. Perhaps this was in the mind of the compiler of Begin ende Voortgang, where he says (II, Nnn 3, p. 90): "That in publishing the voyages now given to the world we have been fain to make shift with these and the like pieces (lacking well-nigh all arrangement), we earnestly request the reader not to impute to us, but to the lack 0f Documents ["Documenten"]; for, had we been provided with the same in manner as we were led to hope at the outset, you may rest assured that the work would have turned out briefer and more succinct, and would have been drawn up in a very different style." P. A. TIELE, in his Mémoire Bibliographique sur les journaux des navigateurs Néerlandais ré-imprimés dans les collections de De Bry et de Hulsius et dans les collections Hollandaises du XVIIe siècle. Amsterdam, Frederik Muller, 1867, p. 246, Note 1, translates--correctly perhaps--"Documenten" by the phrase "pièces officielles," and adds: "Cette demi-accusation regarde probablement les Directeurs de la Compagnie des I. 0."--Cf. also e.g. THÉVENOT in Voyages curieux in his "Avis," prefixed to the first edition (1663), and in the dedication "Au Roy," prefixed to the edition of 1696; Nouvelles Annales, publiées par Eyriès et Malte-Brun, II, p. 44-46, where a similar charge is copied from another French work dated 1663. As for the secretiveness on the part of the Directors see Res. of the States-General, Febr. 12, 1619; Ress. of the XVII, Jan. 29 and May 25, 1619; April 27, 1623; July 11, 1628; Aug. 21, 1629 etc.; missive of the XVII to

G.-G. and Counc. Oct. 25, 1628. Comp. also P. A. LEUPE, *De reizen der Nederlanders naar het Zuidland*. Amsterdam, Hulst van Keulen, 1868, p. 47.]

[2) The space at my disposal of course prevents me from giving the titles of these publications: I can only refer the reader to the well-known bibliographies of TIELE and others.]

[3) MAJOR, *Early Voyages*, pp. XCV and XCVI, is in error. The map of the world of Louis Mayerne Turquet, brought out in Paris in 1648, a copy of which is in the British Museum, does not give the results of Tasman's voyages. (Communicated by Messrs. C. H. Coote and Anton Mensing]. Major, indeed, refers to this map only as "mentioned" elsewhere. (Cf. EYRIES in *Nouvelles Annales*, II, p. 22. This author says, but erroneously: "La premiere carte que j'ai vue, oil les decouvertes faites a la côte occidentale de la Nouvelle-Hollande et celles du premier voyage de Tasman soient marquees, est la mappemonde de Louis Mayerne Turquet, publiée a Paris en 1648. La projection en est très bizarre." Presumably Major has taken his erroneous information from this utterance of Eyries). Major is equally mistaken where he says: "This outline (of Tasman's voyage or voyages) was also given in the map entitled Mar di India in the 1650 (Cf. Eyries, 1. c.) edition of Janssen's Atlas." The map last referred to, of which a reproduction is given in *Remarkable Maps*. Amsterdam, Frederik Muller & Cy, 1895, II, No. 12 and p. II of the Introduction and Notes, exhibits the results only of the discoveries anterior to Tasman's.]

[4) In the possession of Mr. C. M. DOZY, Leyden. Cf. what COOTE (*Remarkable Maps*, III, p. I) says about Hugo Allardt's map in Klencke's atlas.]

[5) According to the opinion of Mr. DOZY and Mr. J. Ph. VAN DER KELLEN, ex-director of the Museum of Engravings at Amsterdam.]

[6) See Mr. Doze's paper in the review "Oud-Holland," XV (1897), pp. 24 and 27.]

[7) De Graaf was a director of the Amsterdam Chamber of the East India Company [VALENTIJN, I (MDCCXXIV), a, p. 302, compared by me with the resolutions of the said Chamber]. The fact that Allard dedicates his map to him proves once more, that the secretiveness on the part of the Directors was not a very strict one.]

domino dri. Gerardo Schaap, domino in Kortenhouf, domino Nicolao Corver, domino dri. Franconi Vander Meer, Praetori Supremo, nec non Consulibus inclytae Rei publicae Amsterodamensis." Only in the year 1652 these four Amsterdam citizens were together burgomasters (consules) of the town[1]. The map accordingly dates between 1652 and 1653[2]. On this map the results of Tasman's two voyages of 1642/3 and 1644 are indicated. Whilst those of the latter are drawn on the map itself, the former are given on a small world-map in one of the corners, where Hollandia Nova and Ant. van Diemens Land are found. It should, however, be noted that, as regards the subject in hand, it bears a hybrid character. Whereas, namely, the discovery in 1642 of Van Diemensland (Tasmania)[3] is duly noted on it, together with results of the expedition of 1644, yet it does not contain the names given by Tasman in his first voyage to various points of the north-coast of his New Guinea. Allard and Nolpe show here the whole of that coast, as it was known in the pre-Tasmanic era[4]. The Bonaparte chart actually exhibits the results of Tasman's surveyings on the north-coast of his New-Guinea; nay, and this is indeed very remarkable, the Visscher draft in the British Museum, otherwise chary enough of place-names, is lavish of them precisely as regards the surveyings in question. This marked difference between Allardt's map and the two charts just referred to, clearly shows that Allardt was not acquainted with them. But on the other hand the question, what charts have formed the groundwork for his map, can not be answered in the absence of positive indications[5].

Nor can the charts last mentioned have been used by Nicolaus Joannes Visscher for the purposes of his map of the world[6], dating from 1657[7]. This map altogether ignores the 1644 voyage, and of the 1642/3 expedition it only notes the discovery of Van Diemens-land. All the place-names in the latter country occurring in this map of the world, are also found in the chart in our copy, excepting one, viz. the word "Zeehaen" on the west-coast, which exception clearly proves that our copy cannot

[1] JAN WAGENAAR, Amsterdam in zijne opkomst... Gebouwen...en Regeeringe. Derde stuk. Amsterdam, Yntema en Tieboel, 1767, p. 302.]

[2] That there should have been emendations made in the engraving after its first publication, is, in the opinion of Mr. VAN DER KELLEN, not admissible.]

[3] There was no room on it for Statenland (New Zealand) and the islands of Amsterdam, etc.]

[4] A comparison of this chart with those in Remarkable Maps, (e.g. II, no. 10) will show this at a glance.]

[5] Mr. COOTE (Remarkable Maps, III, p. I) assigns the dates 1647 and 1656 to a large terrestrial globe of uncertain date--hence my treating it in a note--still bearing the name of Guiljelmus Blaeu. (As regards the Blaeu's see especially P. J. H. BAUDET, Leven en werken van Willem Jansz. Blaeu. Uitgegeven door het Provinciaal Utrechtsch Genootschap van Kunsten en Wetenschappen. Utrecht, Van der Post, 1871; a "Naschrift," 1872; and Notice sur la part prise par Willem Jansz. Blaeu (1571-1638) dans la détermination des longitudes terrestres. Utrecht, Manssen, 1875). Only two exemplars of this globe would seem to have been preserved: one of

them being in the library of Trinity House in London, the other in the British Museum.

So far as Australia and New Guinea are concerned, a reproduction of it is given in Remarkable Maps, III, no. 1. It gives an idea of the results of the two voyages of discovery. It should however be noted that as regards the subject in hand, it bears the same hybrid character as the map referred to in the text. Whereas, namely, the discovery in 1642 and 1643 of Van Diemensland (Tasmania), of Statenland (New Zealand), of the islands of Amsterdam, Rotterdam, etc. is duly marked also on it, together with results 0f the expedition of 1644, yet it shows the whole of New Guinea, as it was known in the pre-Tasmanic era, as will appear from a comparison of it with the charts in Remarkable Maps, II. The presumption that the person who made Blaeu's globe was not acquainted with the Bonaparte chart and the Visscher draft, gains strength from a few other details. The globe shows the names Pedra Branca south of Van Diemens-land and Frederik Hendrik-baai on the south-coast of the latter, together with the name Moordenaars-baai on the west-coast of Statenland, all of them appellations unknown to the Bonaparte chart and the Visscher draft alike. The question now rises: What charts have formed the groundwork for this globe of Blaeu's? Presumably, the draft of Van Diemens-land, of which a copy is preserved in the India Office, was not among them, since it exhibits certain details not given by Blaeu. Nor can the Huydecoper copy have been one of Blaeu's sources, since it gives no map of Van Diemens-land, and its map of Statenland does not contain the name Moordenaars-baai. If on the 0ther hand we suppose Blaeu to have had before him the charts of our copy or of one corresponding to it, all these difficulties vanish: Pedra Branca, Frederik Hendrik-baai and Moordenaars-baai are all of them found in these charts; another chart gives Amsterdam, etc., while charts of New Guinea do not occur in this copy. We conclude then that Blaeu has most probably used the charts of our copy or of a copy in all respects equivalent to it, in all cases in which he registers the results of the voyage of 1642/3. Besides, he must have been cognisant of the results of the 1644 expedition. How he obtained this knowledge cannot now be determined; the Bonaparte chart and the Visscher draft, however, must be altogether excluded. I cannot therefore and after comparison with other maps of the time, agree with Mr. Coote, where (Remarkable Maps, Introduction and notes to Part II, p. I) he mentions the Bonaparte chart as one of the "main sources from which the Dutch cartographers of the latter half of the 17th century have drawn."]

[6] Reproduced in Remarkable Maps, III, 2. This reproduction is taken from a Staten-Bijbel 0f 1657, in the possession of Mr. A. Mensing. It is always very risky to assign the date that figures as the date of publicationo on the title-pages of Staten-Bijbels, also to the maps contained in them. It is a fact, that after the publication maps of a later date were often bound up with these Bibles. But there is no reason to believe this to have been the case in this instance; the less so, because the world-map in the 1661 edition of this Bible, also made by N. Visscher (Orbis terrarum tabula recens emendata et in lucem edita per N. Visscher) gives not only Van Diemens-land, but also Statenland; the latter at the spot where the map

discussed in the text has the legend about discoveries from the age of Columbus down to Le Maire.]

[7) COOTE, in Introduction to Remarkable Maps, III, p. I.]

alone have done duty in the drawing of the map in question. From another chart (to which we shall refer lower down), it appears that this word is intended to mark the spot where the Zeehaan was supposed to have first sighted land. None of the sources known up to the present goes to show that it was this ship and not the Heemskerk, that first made the discovery of Van Diemens-land. Perhaps the reason why, notwithstanding the silence of all the authorities, this name is found in Visscher's map of the world, may be sought in the circumstance that the draughtsman used a chart no longer extant, drawn up on board the Zeehaan, and expressly recording the fact that the discovery had been made on board the said vessel. One of the maps[1] in Joannes Janssonius'[2] Atlantis Majoris 5a pars...Orbis Maritimus, which atlas appeared at Amsterdam, 1658-1659[3], has the same note, slightly enlarged: "t' Landt bij de Zeehaen eerst gesien" [Land first sighted on board the Zeehaen]. For the rest, this map also shows names that are not found in the Bonaparte chart and in the Visscher draft in the British Museum; while at the same time, excepting the note concerning the Zeehaan just referred to, all the names occurring in it are also found in the charts in our copy of the journal. As regards the sources from which it was derived, we are led to about the same conclusion at which we arrived in the case of the map of the world of 1657. Janssonius, however, gives more than Visscher: his map exhibits not only Van Diemensland, but also Statenland, and besides we find in it evidence that also the 1644 voyage had not remained quite unknown to him, in the words: "Nova Hollandia detect(a) Anno 1644." The north-coast of New Guinea is not delineated in this map, but it is shown in a map[4], entitled Indiae Orientalis nec non insularum adiacentium Nova Descriptio Per Nicolaum Visscher, and comprised inter alia in J. Janssonius' Novus Atlas, das is Welt Beschreibung[5], brought out at Amsterdam, 1657-1658[6]. It is remarkable enough that, as regards this north-coast, this map also shows no traces of any acquaintance with the results of Tasman's 1642/3 voyage, so that we are led to conclude that the draughtsman must have been unacquainted with the Bonaparte chart or the Visscher draft. On the other hand, however, the maker of this map of India Orientalis must needs have been cognisant of the results of the second voyage, since he duly outlines the north-coast of New Holland. Nova totius terrarum orbis tabula auctore F. de Wit, published t' Amsterdam bij Frederick de Wit inde Calverstraet inde

Witte Paskaert, 1660[7], gives a tolerably complete survey of the results of both voyages: only the islets of Amsterdam, etc. are wanting; wanting also in this map again, is the new delineation of the north-coast of New Guinea. Nor is this delineation met with in a map[8] of 1660[9], entitled 't Ooster Deel van Oost Indien, streckende van Ceylon tot Japan en Hollandia Nova, published t Amsterdam bij Hendrick Doncker, Boekverkooper en Graadboogh maker In de Nieuw brug steegh in't Stuurmans gerèschap, which map again does give names, fixed upon in the (second) voyage of 1644.[10]

In the course of the next year the results of the exploratory voyages were, partly at least, spread abroad by means of the press in a very different manner. For in 1661 was brought out, Tot Amsterdam, Bij Danker Danckerts, in de Calverstraet in de Danckbaerheyt, a folio volume, entitled Afbeelding van't Stadt huys van Amsterdam, In dartigh coopere Plaaten, geordineert door Jacob van Campen; en Geteeckent door Jacob Vennekool [A delineation of the Town-hall of Amsterdam, on thirty

[1] Reproduced in Remarkable Maps, III, 3.]

[2] As regards Janssonius, cf. TIELE, Mémoire, pp. 10, 44, 365 etc.]

[3] It is still possible, that, although the title-page of this atlas bears this date, as Mr. COOTE told me (cf. Remarkable Maps, III, pp. I-II), the map referred to dates from another year; but there is no evidence either way. Cf. also TIELE, Bibliographie Land- en Volkenkunde, pp. 121 f.]

[4] Reproduced in Remarkable Maps, III, 4.]

[5] COOTE, in Remarkable Maps, III, p. II.]

[6] Cf. TIELE, Bibliographie Land- en Volkenkunde, p. 122. But what is said in note 3 supra, applies mutatis mutandis also to this atlas.]

[7] Reproduced in Remarkable Maps, III, 5.--It is also contained in Doncker's Atlas, to be mentioned by and by, preserved in the Hague State Archives.]

[8] Reproduced in Remarkable Maps, III, 6.]

[9] Cf. COOTE, in Remarkable Maps, III, p. II, and TIELE, Bibliographie Land. en Volkenkunde, p. 78. I only know an undated copy of this map contained in an atlas (State Archives) entitled Nieuw en Groote Lootsmans Zeespicgel, t' Amsterdam, Bij Hendrick Doncker, Boeckverkooper en Graedbooghmaker, in de Nieuwenbrugs-steeg, in't Stuermans Gereetschap. 1661.--In spite of the date of 1661 in the title, this atlas contains maps which themselves bear the dates of 1658-1665.]

[10] In describing the earliest charts in which Tasman's voyages are noted, I have especially dwelt on such of them as are found reproduced in "Remarkable Maps," discussing them in the order in which they occur there. I

have been led to adopt this plan by the consideration that such readers as wish to follow my disquisition, will find it easier to do so, if I refer them to this interesting collection, than if I should cite the authority of atlases dispersed in various places, and many of them difficult of access.]

copper plates, made by order of Jacob van Campen, and designed by Jacob Vennekool]. Plate O. 1. of this collection represents "De Grondt en Vloer van de Groote Burger Sael" [Floor of the great Civic Hall] of the said edifice. This floor was, oddly enough, inlaid inter alia with two hemispheres. In one of these are shown Van Diemensland (Tasmania) and the lands, surveyed in the 1644 expedition (Hollandia Nova); Statenland (New Zealand) is wanting. A reprint of this pictorial publication was issued Tot Amsterdam Bij Frederick de Widt, in de Witte Pascaert. This reprint bears no date, but has bound up with it another work on the Town-hall, published by De Witt, of which the first part[1] bears the date 1665. The erection of the Town-hall was begun in 1648, and the Municipality took possession of it in 1655[2]. December 9, 1656 is the date[3] of a short poem by the famous Dutch statesman and poet Constantijn Huygens[4], in which he celebrates this "terrestrial globe in two hemispheres represented on the floor." It would be difficult to give more convincing evidence than this public panegyric, that the secretiveness as regards the results of Tasman's voyages of discovery, was not very seriously meant. Wagenaar, "historiographer of the city" of Amsterdam, gives the following description of the hemispheres in the floor of the Civic Hall[5]: In the inlaid floor of the hall...was represented, in the centre, a transverse section of the celestial globe, in which was shown the Arctic pole; while the constellations in the manner in which they are usually pictured, together with the celestial circles made in brass, were inlaid in the marble floor. But in this plane celestial globe the pictures have greatly suffered from the ravages of time and wear and tear. On both sides of the celestial globe, towards the two extremities of the hall, were found two plane hemispheres: the eastern one represented Europe, Asia and Africa[6]; the western one, America. The coasts were marked out by coloured stones. The line equinoctial, the ecliptic and the other circles were made of brass. Time and wear and tear had partly shorn also these pieces of art of their pristine beauty. Therefore, a few years ago, they had begun to renovate the said hemispheres. But the material[7] by which the land and water were to be marked off from each other, being found to be too perishable, the space taken up by the hemispheres was cunningly filled up with marble, without again introducing the pictures formerly comprised in them: in which condition the work has continued down to the present time. Each of the three circles is about twenty-two feet in circumference." We see then that about the year 1765[8], when Wagenaar published the passage just given, the two hemispheres had disappeared from the floor

[1] Prima pars Praecipuarum effigierum ac ornamentorum, amplissimae Curiae Amstelrodamensis, maiori ex parte, in candido marmore effectorum, per Artum Quellinium, eiusdem civitatis Statuarium. [The title-page also gives a Dutch and a French translation of this title].]

[2] JAN WAGENAAR, Amsterdam in zijne opkomst,...gebouwen...en regeeringe. II. (Amsterdam, Tirion, 1765), p. 5.]

[3] De gedichten van Constantijn Huygens, uitgegeven door Dr. J. A. WORP, VI (Groningen, Wolters, 1896), pp. 82 f.]

[4] The poem runs as follows:

"Die op dit vloeren let, En op dit heerlijk welven, Moet zeggen bij hem selven, Voorseker dese Wet Bestaat in al haar leeden Uyt hoogh vernufte Lien; Zij leeren ons met reeden De Wereldt te vertreeden En opwaarts te aansien."

[Whosoever marks this floor and these gorgeous vaultings must think within himself: Verily, this corporation is in all its branches made up of exceedingly ingenious persons; they teach us in reason to trample upon the world, and to look up aloft.]

The Dutch poet Joost Van den Vondel also speaks of these hemispheres in his poem "Inwydinge van 't Stadthuis t'Amsterdam." (1655) Cf. p. 224 of De werken van J. Van den Vondel uitgegeven door J. VAN LENNEP en J. H. W. UNGER. 1654-1655. (Leiden, Silthoff).]

[5] Amsterdam, II, p. 53.]

[6] CASPARUS COMMELIN, Beschrijvinge van Amsterdam. Amsterdam, Oossaan, MDCXCIV, p, 271, has: "the 'omtrekken of uyterste grenzen' of the three parts of the ancient world, Europe, Asia and Africa...and a part of New Holland."]

[7] Presumably these are meant on p. 26, where Wagenaar speaks about "the 'gebeelde' stones that were 'geschikt tot' the two plane hemispheres in the floor of the Great (Civic) Hall, but not made use of." These stones where then (1765) preserved in one of the rooms of the T0wn-hall.]

[8] Le guide ou nouvelle description d'Amsterdam. Amsterdam, Covens & Monier, MDCCLXXII, has the following (p. 316): "Comme la Sale a été beaucoup battu, ces chefs d'oeuvre furent privés, de tems en tems, de leur premier ornement; du moins en partie. Pour cette raison on avoit entrepris, it y a quelques années, de renouveller les Hémispheres Terrestres; mais la matière, dont on devoit distinguer les Terres et les Eaux, ne se trouvant pas assez durable, on remplit la place des Hemisphères Terrestres tres artistement de marbre, sans que les premières figures y fussent dépeintes."-- Cf. also Wagenaar's Beschryving van Amsterdam gevolgd, in eene gere-

gelde aanwijzing van de sieraaden der publieke gebouwen dier stad. Amsterdam, Elwe, MDCCXC, p. 10.]

of the Civic Hall[1]; but it is worth noting in this connection that as late as 1743 hemispheres "cunningly made of brass and coloured stone, skilfully inlaid" are found described as lying in that floor[2]. In 1746 the renovation was begun[3], but did not succeed.

In our time, however, but not in Wagenaar's days[4], not in 1772[5], not in 1773[6], not in 1793[7], nor in 1807[8], the floor of the Groote Krijgsraad-zaal (great Court-martial Hall) is found inlaid with two hemispheres. Could these have been transferred thither from the Civic Hall? The very circumstance that the delineations do not agree with each other--in the map in the Court-martial Hall, for instance, Van Diemensland, now called Tasmania, forms a whole with New Holland, which was not the case in the hemisphere found in the Civic Hall; besides, there are differences between the names given in the maps[9]--this circumstance, I say, suggests a negative answer to the question. It appears from a document, covering the period from October 8 to November 12, 1806[10] in the Town-archives at Amsterdam, that in that time it was resolved to lay into the floor of the Groote Krijgsraadzaal two hemispheres of white marble within two circles of brass.

Between the years 1650 and 1660, then, Tasman's two exploratory voyages to what is now known as Australia, were already so well-known in the discoverer's native country, that they were duly reckoned with, when it was thought expedient to represent the surface of the globe within the walls of the "eighth wonder of the world."

As already mentioned higher up, from this time forward we regularly find the results of the voyages duly registered in the maps of the best-known atlases. To Tasman's native country, therefore--and not, as has been asserted[11], to foreigners--are we indebted for the promulgation of whatever new discoveries were made in the course of these voyages, which transferred from the terrae incognitae to the known world, the whole of a part of the earth's surface, which up to that time had either been only vaguely talked of, or been altogether unknown. Still, it was long supposed that on this point foreigners had had the start of Tasman's countrymen. In 1663, namely, there appeared at Paris[12] the first edition of the premiere partie of Melchisedec Thévenot's Relations de divers voyages cvrievx, qvi n'ont point esté ov qvi ont esté tradvits d' Hacluyt, de Purchas, & d'autres Voyageurs Anglois, Hollandois,...,enrichies...de Cartes Géographiques de Pays dont on n'a point encore donné de Cartes. Among these maps in the first part of the first edition of Thévenot's well-known work, there is one of what is now called Australia, "vne Carte de cette cinquième Partie du Monde"[13]. What data, we may ask, can have been at this Frenchman's disposal in the preparation of his work? His own statement on this point runs as follows: "Presque toutes les costes de ce Pays-la, ont esté découuertes, & la Carte que l'on en a mise icy, tire sa premiere origine de celle que l'on a fait tailler de pieces rapportées, sur le paué de la nouvelle Maison-de-Ville d'Amsterdam." From this the inference is, that Thévenot claims to have seen the Chart which was reported to have formed the basis of the two terrestrial hemispheres in the

[1] Cf. also BURNEY, III, p. 182.]

[2] See the well-known work: Tegenwoordige Staat der Vereenigde Nederlanden. Amsterdam, Tirion, 1743, V p. 35 ja, 38.]

[3] As appears from documents in the Town-Archives at Amsterdam, dated May 6 and 10, 1746, published in Bouwkundige Bijdragen, XII (1862), pp. 219 f.]

[4] WAGENAAR, 1. C., pp. 26-27.]

[5] Guide d'Amsterdam, pp. 325 f.]

[6] Cf. also BURNEY, III, p. 182.]

[7] Le guide d'Amsterdam Amsterdam, Cóvens, MDCCXCIII, pp. 159 f.]

[8] JAN FOKKE, Geschiedkundige beschrijving van het vermaarde stadhuis van Amsterdam. Amsterdam, Johannes Allart, MDCCCVIII, pp. 128 f. He says (p. IV), that he describes the building, just as he had seen it the year before.]

[9] Communicated by Mr. E. W. Moss, assist-librarian of the University-library at Amsterdam, who saw the floor of the Great Court-martial Hall (now invisible) in 1895.]

[10] Communicated by Mr. VEDER, Town-archivist.]

[11] For instance by EYRIES, Nouvelles Annales, II, pp. 13, 24.--See also COOTE in Remarkable Maps, Introduction and Notes to part III, p. I.]

[12] Imprimerie de Jacques Langlois, etc.--Cf. A. G. CAMUS, Mémoire sur la collection des grands et petits voyages et sur la collection des voyages de Melchisedech Thévenot. Paris, Baudouin, 1802, p. 281.]

[13] A reproduction of this map will be found in Remarkable Maps, III, 7.--This map also occurs in Receuil de voyages de Mr. Thévenot (A Paris, Chez Estienne Michallet, 1681.--Cf. CAMUS, p. 282), of which there is a copy in the Leiden University Library. But this map, though, excepting a slight correction, it is for the rest quite conformable to the 1663 one, shows the line of the "Route d'Abel Tazman," with various dates near Van Diemensland (Tasmania) and Nova Zelandia (Statenland). It is hard to see how Thévenot came by these dates. They do not quite correspond to the extract--to be discussed by and by--from Tasman's journal, published in

[1696 in the nouvelle édition of his "Relations." This edition also contains
the map, as given in the Receuil of 1681.]

floor of the Civic Hall in the town-hall of the famous trading-
city; from this chart, the map published by him had, according to his
statement, "tiré sa premiere origine." On the face of it, this is by no
means impossible: We have no reason to doubt that Thévenot was in a
position to utilise documents not till then elsewhere published, regarding what the Netherlanders had done in Tasman's time. The Relation
de l'estat present dv Commerce des Hollandois & des Portugais dans
les Indes Orientales, for instance, which opens Volume II, is not likely
to have been elsewhere printed before him[1], and we may safely admit
that in this case Thévenot's good faith is entirely above suspicion,
where he says: "Je la donne traduite fidelement sur l'Original manuscrit qui m'a esté enuoyé d'Hollande." If this is true, we have certainly
no reason to doubt the possibility of his having seen the chart from
which the hemispheres in the Town-hall had been modelled, and of
this chart having formed the groundwork for his map. But he must
have had other data besides: the map is far more elaborate, and the
legenda are much more in number. In this case too, the Bonaparte
chart and the British Museum draft are out of the question, regard being had to what Thévenot's map tells us about the north-coast of New
Guinea. Apart from this, his statements correspond to those made in
the charts above discussed[2]. The name "Vater (water) plaats" in Van
Diemensland (Tasmania), only, is not found in any of these[3]. That of
the 1642/3 expedition, charts--no longer available--must have existed,
in which this name was actually given, may perhaps be inferred from
the circumstance that this appellation is found, for instance[4], in the
Nieuwe Wassende Graade Paskaert van't Zuydelyckste deel van Asia,
contained in the Niew Zee Atlas of Water Weerelt, published Tot Rotterdam. By Pieter van Alphen, Boeck-verkooper by de Roo-Brugge in
de vierige Colom. 1660, dedicated to the Heeren Gecommitteerde Raden ter Admiraliteyt tot Rotterdam den 5 December 1659; a
cartographic compilation[5], of which the first map (of the world)[6] utterly ignores Tasman's discoveries, while the map above referred to,
being the last of the whole work, gives both Van Diemensland and the
results of the 1644 voyage, but at the same time leaves the north-coast
of New Guinea as it used to be represented in previous charts. Statenland (New Zealand) is not given in this map, nor, indeed, could it be
included, since the map does not extend so far eastward.

This map in Van Alphen's atlas bears a close resemblance to
Thévenot's map[7], but on the other hand there are certain slight discre-

pancies, which seem to show that Thévenot has not copied Van Alphen. What source, then, have they most probably drawn from? Here, too, no positive answer can be given: we can only, for the reason above mentioned, lay down as an undoubted fact, that the Bonaparte chart and the Visscher draft in the British Museum cannot have done duty as models; nor is it at all likely that the text of the journal has been utilised in their preparation. These two negative conclusions also apply to most, perhaps[8] to all of the printed charts and atlases, brought out in the Netherlands down to about the year 1660.

[1] The Dutch orginal I have included in Vol. III of my Bouwstoffen, pp. 51-56, because I had not found it printed anywhere else.]

[2] [5] I cannot endorse Coote's theory (Remarkable Maps, III), that Thévenot must have consulted Blaeu's maps in the first place. The name "Timorr Laut", for instance, is also found in the map, to be referred to by and by, in Van Alphen's work and Clippige Hoek in different other charts (Remarkable Maps, III, 3, 5). May not Thévenot have compiled his map from various others? The following circumstance would seem decidedly to point that way. On the coast near Zelandia Nova, beside "Het eijlandt drij Koningen," Thévenot places another island(?) "Koningen." Now it is highly probable that in this case he had before him two different Dutch readings, one with the name "Drie Koningen," the other with the name "Koningen," or with an indication of which only the word "Kon(m)ingen" was at all clèar to him. Not knowing that the two expressions were meant for the same thing, he transferred both of them to his map. Still, Thévenot's mistake here may also be due to sheer inadvertence. However this may be, this small slip has been perpetuated in subsequent French charts, e.g. in Hydrographie francoise. Receuil des cartes marines, dressées au dépôt des cartes, plans et journaux. Par ordre des Ministres de la Marine, depuis 1737 jusques en 1772. Par feu M. BELLIN, Ingénieur-Hydrographe du Dépôt et autres, II, No. 100 (1742-1756).]

[3] Nor is the name, to be discussed infra, Jacob Remens riuiere, on Nova Hollandia's west coast.]

[4] Also in Blaeu's Archipelagus of 1659 in Klencke's atlas (Remarkable Maps, III, Introduction, p. I), as Mr. Coote has informed me. This chart also has Jacob Remens Revier.]

[5] A copy of it is preserved in the State Archives at the Hague.]

[6] Nova totius terrarum geographica ac hydrographica tabvla. Auct. JACOBUS COLOM.]

[7] Van Alphen has also the Jacob Remens rivier.]

[8] Of course I have no absolute certainty on this point, since I have not been in a position to inspect all of them without exception. But the conclusions apply to all such maps and charts as I have been able to examine. Mr. Coote informs me that also the maps, mentioned on p. I, col. I of his

Introduction to part III of Remarkable Maps, bear the ante-Tasmanian character of the north-coast of Nova-Guinea.]

A few years later already, ampler information must, however, have been generally available. This appears from the Zee-atlas, in 1666 Gedruckt tot Amsterdam, Bij Pieter Goos, Waater in De Vergulde Zee-spiegel[1]. The information is evidently now more clearly defined, but not absolutely accurate. Whereas the Paskaerle zijnde l' Oosterdeel van Oost Indien contained in it, does give some names on the north-coast of Australia, fixed upon in Tasman's second voyage, and gives the shape of the north-coast of New Guinea, as it is found delineated in the Bonaparte chart, but has no traces of Tasman's visiting in 1644 a part of the south-coast of this island and the east-coast of the gulf of Carpentaria, north of Van Diemens rivier; whereas therefore this chart has not wholly lost the hybrid character to which I have referred above, Goos's Pascaerte vande Zvyd-Zee tusschen California, en Ilhas de Ladrones, which records the discoveries of 1642/3, also offers a good deal that is quite new. The names "De Eylanden van Onthong Java"[2], "Koens (read "Caens-") Eyl.," "Denys (Gardenijs-) Eyl.," "Visscher Eylanden," and "De bocht van Goede Hope" all of them owe their existence to Tasman's exploratory voyage northward of New Guinea[3]. It is hard to say what data Goos had at his disposal. His sources probably did not include the Bonaparte chart and the Visscher draft in the British Museum, since the shape of New Guinea in Goos's chart differs from that given to this island in the charts just referred to, while besides in them a few names are wanting which do occur in Goos's chart; inter alia "Sant duynen" in Statenland (New Zealand). Perhaps, besides the charts contained in the journal, also the land-surveyings occurring in it may this time have done duty; perhaps this has also been the case with the journal itself[4].

However this may be, after a very few years more we come upon proof incontrovertible that a journal of the voyage of 1642/3 must have been known and accessible. But before turning to this proof, we shall have to refer to an account of the said voyage based on information totally unconnected with the sources above discussed, or with the literature[5] to be referred to in the sequel. The year 1671 is the date of a compilation[6], put together by Arnoldus Montanus, and published t' Amsterdam, By Jacob Meurs Boek-verkooper en Plaetsnijder, op de Kaisarsgraft, schuin over de Wester-markt in de stad Meurs. The title runs as follows: De Nieuwe en Onbekende Weereld: of beschrijving van America en 't Zuid-land. The eleventh chapter of the third book of this folio[7] is superscribed "Onbekende Zuid-land,"

and contains a narrative of Tasman's voyage of 1642-1643. The narrative is not cast in the form of a journal, and though not presenting any great interest, still, as regards the history of this voyage of discovery, it is of some importance in that it gives certain details not mentioned anywhere else[8]. It may therefore do duty as a kind of supplement to Tasman's own journal. The narrative is based on information supplied by the "ship's surgeon Hendrik Haelbos," who formed part of the expedition, and plays a somewhat conspicuous part in the account given by Montanus. His name is expressly mentioned in the list of "the Names of the writers cited in the present Work," figuring at the end of Montanus'

[1] A copy of it is preserved in the Hague State Archives.]

[2] This name is also found in the Pascaerte van de Zvyd-Zee, 'tAmsterdam By JOHANNES VAN LOON Plaet-snyder en Zee-caert-maecker buyten de S. Anthonis-Poort, aen 't Kerck-hof, in 't Lelystraetje, contained in his Klaer-Lichtende Noort-Star ofte Zee-atlas, at least in the new edition of 1666 (Hague State Archives). The older edition of 1661 (TIELE, Bibliography, p. 156), I have not seen.]

[3] Precisely this part of Australia is wanting in Goos's (Joannus van Keulen's) chart, reproduced in GEORGE COLLINGRIDGE, The Discovery of Australia (Sydney, Hayes, 1895), facing p. 286.--The name "De bocht van Goede hoope" occurs also on Goos's "Oosterdeel van Oost Indien." On both Goos's charts is found the name "Strus hoeck" or "Struys hoeck" at the place where the Bonaparte chart has "(Salomon) Sweers hock." This is probably a mere slip, but it is perpetuated in different maps of later date. The names "Hoog landt" and "Een hoog eyl(and)" also owe their existence to Tasman's voyage of 1642/3.]

[4] I abstain from discussing such charts as have been prepared subsequent to the publications of the journal, unless they should happen to show deviations worth referring to.]

[1] Mr. Coote (Remarkable Maps, III, Introduction, p. II) prints the following extract from the text of the first English edition of DONCKER'S Sea atlas or the Watter World 1660, of which there is a copy in the British Museum: "We will call Terra Australis, those Countreys in the South of Nova Guinea, whether (sic) the Hollanders most zayled (sic) in the year 1644, and in these our Maps are called Hollandia Nova and Nova Zeelandia. Notwithstanding sith the coasts are but partly discovered, and that we have no knowledge of the inward Countreys, wee shall as yet let them rest under Asia, til further discovery; and commend such a division to our Posterity, if wee by our life gaine no more knowledg" (sic). The same passage is found in Dutch in de "Korte verklaringh der afdeelingh, gestaltenis, ende eigenschappen des Aerdtbodems" in Doncker's Atlas, with the year 1661 on the title-page, preserved in the State-Archives at the Hague, in Doncker's edition of 1666, and in other atlases, e.g. that of Goos (1666).]

[2] Cf. TIELE, Bibliographie Land- en Volkenkunde, pp. 171 f.]

[3) Pp. 577-585.]

[4) I do not, so far, agree with Tide's dictum: "The text is a mere compilation from the works of other authors, and is accordingly [the italics are
mine) of small value."]

folio. Haelbos's narrative, which would seem to have gone out
in print[1], since Montanus expressly contrasts the names of the writers
who were his authorities, with "several Journals not printed," is therefore probably, together with the charts already mentioned, the oldest
work in which Tasman's voyage is found described[2].

In the following year 1674 there at length appeared a work, of
which the author had had access to a copy of the journal of the 1642/3
voyage, kept by Tasman himself[3]. True, in a few places[4] in the first
volume of his exceedingly rare Eenige Oefeningen, to which we have
referred higher up, brought out in 1669, the author shows that he was
acquainted with the results of Tasman's two voyages of 1642/3 and
1644, but it was only in the second volume of this work[5], published in
1674, that Dirk Rembrantszoon Van Nierop gave to the world "Een
kort Verhael uyt het Journael van den Kommandeur Abel Jansen Tasman, int ontdekken van 't onbekende Suit-Lant"[6] [A brief abstract from
the journal kept by Commander A. J. Tasman in discovering the unknown South Land]. Now, which manuscript can Dirk
Rembrandtszoon have drawn from? We may at the outset put aside the
sailor's journal from the Sweers collection, now preserved in the Hague Archives, since it was not kept by Tasman himself, and because,
besides, Van Nierop gives particulars not contained in it. Next, our
copy is excluded also: the mere fact that Rembrandtszoon has recorded
the longitude on May 18, 1643, which our copy fails to do at the said
date, would make us doubt the possibility of our mathematician having
made use of the latter, at least to the exclusion of other copies. But
there is more to be said, to which we shall revert by and by.

Subsequent to Van Nierop, Nicolaas Witsen, himself a notable
promoter of ulterior voyages of discovery to the South-land[7], would
seem to have been the first to utilise for his geographical studies the
results of the 1642/3 expedition, making use of a ship's journal. The
first edition, now become exeedingly rare[8], of his well-known work
Noord en Oost Tartarye bears the date of 1692[9]. In its first volume[10]
certain parts of the journal are discussed, and some of them printed at
length. The most interesting feature, however, of Witsen's remarks
about this expedition, are certain cuts, copied from drawings in the
journal used by him, which cuts we may assume to have been the first
reproductions of the said drawings spread abroad by the printing-press.

Which journal, we may ask, has Witsen made use of? This is very hard to determine. The cuts may have been derived from our copy, or from one resembling it: the feathers on the heads of the New-Zealanders, found in the copy used by Valentijn, are not shown in the cuts given in Witsen's book, and, perhaps to prevent his text from clashing too much with the picture, he inserted the word " sometimes," so that his text reads as follows: "Black hair right atop of the head...on which there is sometimes[11] a large thick white feather." Besides, Witsen has certain turns of phrase, which are almost or absolutely identical with

[1) I have not succeeded in hunting up any copy of it.]

[2) Of Montanus' compilation there appeared, in the same year still, an English version by John Ogilby (TIELE, Bibliographie, p. 172). I have not seen this version. The year 1673 is the date of a German translation, also in folio, and now become very rare [see G. M. ASHER, A bibliographical and historical essay on the Dutch books and pamphlets relating to New-Netherland...Amsterdam, Frederik Muller, 1854-67, p. 23), entitled: Die Unbekante Neue Welt, oder Besthreibung des Welt-teils Amerika, and des Sud-Landes...Durch Dr. 0. D...Zu Amsterdam, Bey Jacob von Meurs, auf der Keysersgraft, in der Stadt Meurs; this translation also contains the information above mentioned concerning Tasman's first voyage (pp. 649-658).]

[3) TIELE, Bibliographie Land- en Volkenkunde, p. 178, is, however, too sweeping where he says that Van Nierop's work is "the first to mention Tasman's voyage of discovery." Van Nierop seems, indeed, to have been the first to use Tasman's own journal, but otherwise Montanus (and Haelbos?) have had the start of him. To be sure, Tiele had not seen Van Nierop's booklet (of which there is a copy in the Royal Library at the Hague), when he mentioned it in his bibliography. This also accounts for the fact that with reference to Montanus' work, Tiele could say (p. 172): "The description of the 'Unknown South Land' takes up 9 pages only" (the italics are mine], and that he does not refer to the number of pages taken up by this description in Rembrantszoon's publication, where it also covers 9 pages only, and these much smaller ones too.]

[4) Pp. 15, 19.]

[5) Pp. 56-64.]

[6) A contemporary(?) manuscript copy of this exceedingly rare tract is in the possession of Messrs Frederik Muller & Co. This proves its being scarce already in the XVII(?) century.]

[7) J. F. GEBHARD JR., Het leven van Mr. Nicolaas Comelisz. Witsen (1641-1717)--Utrecht, Leeflang, 1881, I, pp. 444, note 1), 481; II (1882), pp. 293-295.]

[8) I have used the edition of 1785.]

[9) See TIELE, Bibliographie Land- en Volkenkunde, pp. 268-270.--
GEBHARD, Witsen, I, pp. 425-426.]

[10) Pp. 173 ff.]

[11) The italics are mine.]

the corresponding passages in our copy; for example, certain expressions between January 21 and April 6 are by him used on pp. 178 and 179. On the other hand, however, Witsen's longitudes and latitudes do not always correspond to those in our journal, in some cases even showing enormous differences. Since Witsen does not profess to give any regular narrative of the voyage, but only selects certain episodes pretty much at random, without mentioning dates, it is quite impossible to control these longitudes and latitudes to any practical purpose, and this method of his prevents us from making any inferences at all reliable touching the sources from which he derived his knowledge. In one place he himself volunteers the information, that his statements are partly based on a "written account drawn up by one of the steersmen who with Tasman had made the voyage to the South in the year 1643"[1], and this goes a long way to prove that he cannot have used our journal, which as we know was signed by Tasman himself. The Sweers sailor's journal in the Hague State Archives is out of the question on account of its divergent purport; so is the Huydecoper copy, since it contains no drawings. We are left to grope in utter darkness as regards this point: Witsen may have used a journal which is no longer extant, or he may have compiled his account from various copies[2].

More than half a century after the appearance of Van Nierop's little book, viz. in 1726, the well-known Francois Valentijn, "sometime Minister of the Word of God in Amboyna, Banda, etc.", brought out[3] the second part of the third volume of his celebrated work Oud en Nieuw Oost-Indien, vervattende Een Naaukeurige en Uitvoerige Verhandelinge van Nederlands Mogendheyd In die Gewesten [Old and New East India, comprising a full and exact account of the Dutch power in the said regions], of which the first volume had appeared in 1724. The second part of the third volume, bearing the separate title of Verhandeling der Zee-horenkens en Zee-gewassen In en omtrent Amboina En de naby gelegene Eylanden, Mitsgaders een naaukeurige Beschrijving van Banda en de Eylanden onder die Landvoogdy begrepen. Als ook der Eylanden Timor en Solor, Celebes ofte Macassar, Borneo en Bali. Mitsgaders van de Koningryken Tonkin, Cambodia, en Siam. Benevens een Verhaal der Zaaken in de voornoemde Eylanden en Koningryken tot nu toe voorgevallen [A dissertation on the sea-shells, conchs, and marine plants found in and about Amboyna and the islands circumjacent; together with an exact account of Banda and the islands belonging to the said presidency; also of the islands of Timor and Solor, Celebes or Macassar, Borneo and Bali; moreover of the kingdoms of Tonquin, Cambodja, and Siam. To which is added a narrative of what has taken place in the islands and kingdoms aforesaid up to the present time]; this second part, I say, contains a narrative of Tasman's voyage of 1642-1643[4]. This account is more circumstantial than the one given in Van Nierop's book, and besides contains a "Chart of the Voyage of Abel Tasman according to his own directions," and several other charts, land-surveyings and drawings. The chart first mentioned contains names not fixed upon in Tasman's voyage: the names of Barnevelds Eiland[5], near Van Diemens-land (Tasmania), Baey van Philippus en Jacobus (in Statenland)[6], and 't eiland Uiterdam near Rotterdam and Amsterdam, are not mentioned in the journal[7]. Besides using the data furnished to him by the copy of the journal which he consulted, Valentijn has most probably compiled this chart from other charts, also of a later date, and not forming part of the copy of the journal of which he availed himself; with the exclusion always of the Bonaparte chart and the Visscher draft in the British Museum, on account of the divergent shape therein given to New Guinea. For, although he reproduces various charts that formed part of his copy of the journal, none of these reproductions affords information as regards the names above referred to. As I have already observed, the reproductions just mentioned, together with the land-surveyings and drawings, given by Valentijn, in a few cases differ from those in our copy; but Valentijn does not give more

[1) pp. 178, 179.]

[2) I must not, however, omit to mention that Witsen was on friendly terms with Van Nierop. See GEBHARD, 1. c., I, pp. 501 ff.]

[3) At Dordrecht, with Joannes Van Braam; at Amsterdam, with Gerard Onder de Linden.]

[4) Section Banda, pp. 47-58.]

[5) This name also occurs in other charts. I have noticed it in the Wassende Graade kaart van alle bekende Zeekusten op den geheelen Aardbodem door C. J. VOOGT, Geometra, contained in the atlas, entitled De nieuwe Groote Lichtende Zeefackel door Jan van Loon, en Claes Jansz. Vooght. t'Amsterdam, Gedruckt by Johannes van Keulen, 1706. Cf. TIELE, Bibliographie, p. 256.]

[6) This name is also met with in other charts; e.g. in the map of the world by Carel Allard in Atlas nouveau par le Sr. SANSON Geographe ordinaire du Roy. Paris, Hubert Jaillot, 1692.]

[7) VALENTIJN, 1. c., p. 54, also mentions Uiterdam in his text, but the chart he gives on p. 55 has no such name.]

than what our copy contains. That, however, he did not base his account on the latter, is made evident by various small details contained in his narrative, but not found in our copy: e.g. the longitude taken on May 18, 1643, which is also mentioned by Van Nierop. The latitude taken on February 6 differs in our copy from the one given in Valentijn, which in its turn agrees with the statement in Van Nierop[1]. What copy Valentijn used, we have already seen higher up: it was the one of which a fragment--one leaf with drawings--is now preserved in the State Archives at the Hague: If, however, we institute a close comparison between Valentijn's statements and those in Rembrandtszoon's work, it becomes perfectly evident, that either must Valentijn in various passages have simply copied Rembrandtszoon, or both have drawn from the same source. Valentijn is far more circumstantial, but at certain dates (e.g. on October 8, 1642) he sometimes agrees word for word with his predecessor. In some few cases (e.g. on January 21 and March 25, 1643) Valentijn first gives the condensed abstract, just as it is found in Van Nierop, and afterwards goes on to treat the same subject once more at great length. Next, we meet with passages (for instance, on November 18, 1642) in which Valentijn relates nearly the same things which are told in Van Nierop; only that Valentijn's account is less exact and more perfunctory. Then, both the authors sometimes make the very same mistakes, e.g. in marking the longitude and latitude of the landing-place in Frederik-Hendriksbaai[2]. There can therefore be no doubt that the two accounts are in some way related to each other. Can it be, that Valentijn first copied Van Nierop's account, and supplemented the latter by information derived from a copy of the journal. This is no doubt possible, though it is hardly likely. It is clear that Valentijn must have studied the whole of the journal: why then, now that this laborious task had at all events to be faced, instead, of drawing directly from the source nearest to his hand, should he have been at the increased trouble of studying the two sources and comparing them at the same time? It is therefore far more probable that Valentijn and Van Nierop both of them made use of the same copy of the journal, or at all events of two identical copies. If this was the case, and we can hardly escape from this conclusion, the nature of these copies can no longer be a mystery: they must have been copies that in various passages gave only a condensed abstract of Tasman's narrative: they cannot have been duplicates of the original copy. A small circumstance, quite insignificant in itself, must not pass unnoticed in this connection. The fragment still extant of the copy which Valentijn probably made use of, bears the paging 21, while the drawings found on it, occur on folios 32 and 33 of our copy: an indication that the first, which we know to have been written by the same hand as the second, has been a more condensed one. This circumstance materially strengthens the presumption which we have expressed higher up, that the Blok copy is likely to have borne a less original character than our copy, though at the same time the two may well have been coeval with each other. If Valentijn's account is carefully studied, it furthermore becomes evident that in those cases in which his copy goes into greater detail, it contains information due to Tasman himself. Thus he says, for instance[3]: "The quartermaster and two other men swam to our (i.e. Abel Tasman's) ship." And in certain passages (e.g. on February 20 and 26, March 14, 1643) Van Nierop uses the very same words that are employed in our copy. Taking everything into account, therefore, we may safely venture the hypothesis that Van Nierop and Valentijn both of them made use of an abstract of the narrative account of the voyage drawn up by Tasman himself, and that either this abstract was made from our copy, supplemented by a number of separate items of information; or the abstract was based on a copy closely agreeing with ours.

Van Nierop's Kort Verhael (brief narrative) has been translated more than once, and into various languages[4]; which has also been the case with Valentijn's abstract. The best known translation of

[1] The longitudes taken on Febr. 6 and May 18 are the same as those given in the Huydecoper copy.]

[2] VAN NIEROP, p. 57; VALENTIJN, 1. C., p. 48, jo our copy on December 1 and 4, 1642.]

[3] On p. 51.]

[4] I only know the French adaptation, entitled "Voyage d'Abel Tasman," in the Nouvelle Edition of MELCHISEDEC THÉVENOT'S Voyages curieux, II (Paris, Moette, 1694.--Cf. CAMUS, pp. 283-284, 292, 334), with which I have been made acquainted through the courtesy of Mr. Martinus Niijhoff, publisher at the Hague; and the French translation, made from an English version of 1711 (Cf. DALRYMPLE, Historical Collection, II, p. 65), and entitled: "Relation d'un voyage aux Terres Australes inconnues, Tirée du Journal du Capitaine Abel Jansen Tasman," in Voyages de François Coreal aux Indes Occidentales...Traduits de l'Espagnol. Avec une relation...(du) voyage de Narborough a la Mer du Sud, etc. Traduits de l'

Anglois. a Amsterdam, Chez J. Frederic Bernard, 1722, III, pp. 201-223.
The translator speaks in the first person, and not in the third, as Van
Nierop does [An abridgment of this translation is found in (De Brosses)
Histoire des navigations aux Terres Australes. Paris, Durand, MDCCLVI,
I, pp. 456-463]. In (A. F. PRÉVOST) Histoire générale des voyages.
Paris, Didot, MDCCLIII, XI, pp. 209-214, this French translation has been
followed. Also in Histoire Generale des voyages. Nouvelle Edition. La
Haye, Pierre De Hondt, MDCCLVIII, VI, Pp. 68-74, based on Prevost. To
"Le Routier manuscrit," to which De Hondt's edition refers, I cannot as-
sign a place among the manuscript journals of this voyage. The degrees of
longitude and latitude, therein mentioned, do not at all agree with any one
of the manuscript journals known to me. De Hondt has most probably
taken his engravings from Valentijn. Of De Hondt's edition there exists a
Dutch translation: Historische Beschrijving der reizen, about which see
Tiele in his Bibliographie land- en volkenkunde, pp. 25 f. In part XVIII
(Amsterdam, Hayman and others, MDCCLIX) the Reise van Abel Jansen
Tasman naar de onbekende Zuidlanden, in 1642, is found on pp. 361-368,
with the same engravings given in De Hondt.--Cf. also CAMUS, Mémoire, p. 334; EYRIES in Nouvelles Annales, II, p. 41; TIELE in
Bibliographische Adversaria, vol. I, pp. 200 f; etc. The English version of
1711 is perhaps meant on p. 345, Tome VI of the very inaccurate Biblio-
thèque universelle des voyages par G. BOUCHER DE LA
RICHARDERIE. Paris, Strasbourg, 1808. He speaks there of the voyages
of James (Jacques) Tasman!]

the latter work appeared in 1771, in the second volume[1] of the
well-known compilation of Alexander Dalrymple: An historical collection of the several voyages and discoveries in the South Pacific
Ocean, containing the Dutch Voyages[2]. The editor "used Valentijn as
the text, but collated" this text with the data otherwise at his disposal:
translations of Van Nierop's brief narrative. Part of the drawings and
land-surveyings given in Valentijn, Dalrymple has transferred to his
pages.

Additional light was thrown on the subject in 1813. In this
year appeared[3] the third volume of James Burney's well-known work:
A chronological history of the voyages and discoveries in the South
Sea or Pacific Ocean, which volume inter alia contained an abridgment[4]) of Woide's English translation of the copy of Tasman's journal
preserved in the British Museum, Burney having simply omitted from
his text such parts of it as he deemed unimportant[5]. All the charts contained in the British Museum copy of Tasman's Journal, Burney
transferred to his work; of "the Views of Land and other Drawings [6],
only a small portion has been taken."[7].

In the year in which Burney's translation was given to the
world, the Netherlands stood a fair chance of shaking off the yoke im-
posed upon them by the usurping genius who during a couple of

decades had been sapping the foundations of the European political system: the Netherlands vindicated and recovered their place among the free nations, and the greater part of the Dutch colonies and possessions were restored to them. With their new-born independence revived the desire of the Netherlanders to open the annals which held the record of the history of their nation; to study that glorious history, to learn to know it better, to supply its deficiencies, to rewrite it in the light of renewed research. The history of the Dutch colonies also soon got an ample share of this revived interest, which equally embraced the part which the Netherlanders had had in the discovery of the terra incognita. In 1825, for instance, was published the little book already mentioned, of the Utrecht professor G. Moll, entitled Verhandeling over eenige vroegere zeetogten der Nederlanders [An essay on

[1) On pp. 65-84.]

[2) London, Nourse, Payne & Elmsly. There exists also a French version of Dalrymple's work. Cf. BOUCHER, VI, p. 348.--D'Entrecasteaux has also drawn from Valentijn. See MATTHEW FLINDERS, Ontdekkingsreis naar het Groote Zuidland anders Nieuw-Holland...in 1801, 1802 en 1803. Haarlem, Loosjes, 1816. IV p. 231, Note.]

[3) London, Luke Hansard.]

[4) Pp. 63-110--MATTHEW FLINDERS also incorporated with his own work, certain parts of Woide's translation of the London manuscript. See his Ontdekkingreis naar het Groote Zuidland, IV, p. 224.--So did J. P. GELL, with or without the assistance of Burney's work, in his paper on the first discovery of Tasmania of November and December 1642 (Tasmanian Journal of Natural Science, Agriculture, Statistics, etc. II, 1846, pp. 321-327). I have not seen the publication last mentioned, but Mr. J. Backhouse Walker, of Hobart, has been kind enough to oblige me with a written copy of Gell's paper. This written copy I have compared with Burney and with what I knew about the London copy, and the comparison removed any doubts I might have entertained respecting the origin of Gell's statements. The latter, however, are not important enough to necessitate publication of the results of the comparison instituted by me.]

[5) Pp. 59-62. Besides, there are numerous mistakes in Burney's edition. These mistakes are in part clearly imputable to Burney himself, while others of them originated with Woide, who made the translation into English. I cannot of course enumerate them all here, but would draw attention to a few of them, well worth notice. On February 24, Burney gives the longitude taken, as 192° 58'. The London Manuscript, in accordance with our copy, has: 192° 28'. On April 4 and 5, Burney has Gerrit de Nys Island; the London MS. and our copy have: Gar(-)denys eiland. On April 22 bleek (water) is found translated by "black." On May 11, Burney gives: 6° 30' declination of the compass, while the London MS. and our copy both of them have: 6° 50'. On May 18, Burney has: "we believed them to be pirates;" the London MS. and our copy reading: "Tydoorezen." On May 19,

Burney has: "cultivated land," while the British Museum copy and ours
agree in reading: "gebroocken landt."]

[6) A few discrepancies will be noticed between the drawings figuring in
Burney, and those found in our copy. This circumstance, however, does
not make against our presumption that the British Museum exemplar is a
copy of ours. For Burney has not adhered closely to the British Museum
copy. Facing p. 85, for instance, there is a drawing which is not found in
our copy; but this drawing is also wanting in the London copy. It is evidently a blending of Tab. XIX and Tab. XX of the latter manuscript (in
our copy placed between January 23 and 24). The foreground with two
large boats is taken from Tab. XIX, the whole of the background with the
three small boats, from Tab. XX. Burney has put two men in the boat
shown in the drawing facing p. 99; the London MS. and our copy have
three men here.]

[7) P. 112.]

certain early voyages made by the Dutch]; in 1827 this example was followed by the ex-lieutenant of the navy R. G. Bennet, and
the Hattem boarding-school master J. Van Wijk Roelandsz., who in
the said year published their Verhandeling ter beantwoording der
vrage over de Nederlandsche ontdekkingen in Amerika, Australië, de
Indën en de Poollanden, en de namen, welke weleer aan dezelve door
Nederlanders zijn gegeven [A dissertation answering the question as to
the Dutch discoveries in America, Australia, the Indies, and the Polar
regions, and as to the names originally given to them by the Dutch][1],
an essay to which the Utrecht Society of Arts and Sciences had
awarded its first prize. Like Moll, the writers of course gave to Tasman the honour he so amply deserved; but as they did not make any
renewed investigations as to Tasman's life and labours, and do not
seem to have been completely acquainted with the literature concerning these points, then available, their work does not offer any new
points of view at all important for our purpose. A somewhat dubious
or hybrid place must be assigned to the well-known work, already alluded to, of the Amsterdam professor N. G. Van Kampen, published
1831-1833, under the title Geschiedenis der Nederlanders buiten Europa [History of the Netherlanders outside Europe]. In the Preface to
his first volume, which embraces the period of Tasman's activity, the
learned author expresses his regret that only printed sources and literature were available for his purpose. "How gladly," he says, "should we
give up a large portion of this printed matter, in exchange for a circumstantial narrative by Tasman himself, especially of his second
voyage, of which next to nothing is authoritatively known up to the
present time!"--"I am well aware," he goes on to say, "that in spite of

the numerous sources I have enumerated, there remains a great deal still to be unearthed and investigated, concerning which full information could be derived only from the records of the late Company, for whose secrecy[2], at this time of day at least, there would not seem to be any well-founded reason. The present Author can only express the fervent wish that the courteous kindness of those scholars and distinguished persons who have control over these records, may at some future time put at his disposal such unedited documents as might enable him to throw fresh light on the course of events, and maintain the honour of the Dutch name." His wish did not remain unfulfilled. In the Preface to the first part of the third volume of his work he was in a position to state that "he had been allowed to make use of the treasures of that rich storehouse of information, the Colonial Archives," at that time still preserved at Amsterdam. For this permission he was indebted to the then Secretary-General of the Colonial Department, Mr. J. C. Baud, LL. D., who afterwards became Governor-General of Netherlands India a. i. and Colonial Minister, and whose name must always be honourably mentioned whenever there is question of the scholarlike study of Dutch colonial history[3]. Van Kampen was fortunate enough to enter upon this task at a time when the care of the colonial archives was entrusted to the man whom we have already repeatedly referred to in the course of the present work, to P. L. De Munnick, then officially known as "Warehouse-master"--a designation that might well have galled any man who was apt to consider archival documents as historical treasures, and not as warehouse articles. Van Kampen gratefully alludes to De Munnick's "courteous assistance."

From that time dates the opening of the colonial archives for the purposes of scholarly research, and of investigations in the cause of historical science. But the colonial archives became far more generally useful after having been transferred to the State Archives at the Hague, in 1856[4]. And the light they were calculated to shed into the less known recesses of history, threw a part of its lustre on the history of the celebrated Dutch voyages of discovery, not least so on Tasman's expeditions[5]; a lustre still enhanced by the upshot of searches in other archives and private collections of documents. Such aids to investigation were at the disposal of Lauts, who besides having access to documents preserved in the colonial archives, could also avail himself inter alia of the Huydecoper van Maarsseveen

[1] Utrecht, J. Altheer. The Atlas, forming part of this dissertation, did not appear until 1829, with J. De Vos at Dordrecht.]

[2] Cf. also MOLL, Zeetogten, p. 220.]

XI

[3) See also DE MUNNICK in Verhandelingen Zeewezen, Nieuwe Volgorde, IV (1844), p. 67.]

[4) See P. F. HUBRECHT, De Onderwijswetten in Nederland en hare uitvoering. Vijfde Afdeeling. Wetenschap en Kunst. II. ('s Gravenhage, Sternberg, 1882), pp. 202 f.]

[5) Attempts have been made to popularise the results of these researches in books destined for the rising generation. Of such books I am acquainted with: P. WEEDA, Geschiedenis van de togten en ontdekkingen der Nederlanders, in Azien, Africa, America en Australië, Van het laatst der 16e eeuw tot op onzen tijd. Een leesboek voor de jeugd. Dordrecht, Blussé en Van Braam, 1840; and with VOORMEULEN VAN BOEKEREN, 1. c.]

journal[1]; of De Munnick himself, whom we afterwards meet with in the capacity of "archivist" of the colonial collections while they were still at Amsterdam; of Jacob Swart, who was in a position to derive a wealth of informations from the treasures in the possession of the bookselling firm of Hulst van Keulen; of P. A. Leupe, afterwards appointed to an official position in the State Archives; of Ch. M. Dozy[2]. Among all these contributions to historical knowledge it is the special merit of Swart to have first edited the original journal of Tasman, then in the possession of his firm; he brought out this text, from 1854 to 186o, in the periodical publication, of which he was editor, entitled Verhandelingen en mededeelingen betrekkelijk het Zeewezen en de Zeevaartkunde, and appended to it a reproduction without the colours, of the chart now in the possession of Prince Bonaparte. A separate reprint of this text of the journal, with a coloured and corrected reproduction of the chart, appeared in 1860, bearing the title Journaal van de reis naar het onbekende Zuidland, in den Jare 1642, door Abel Jansz. Tasman, met de schepen Heemskerck en de Zeehaen[3]. True, Swart's method of editing is a slovenly[4] one, and is far from coming up to the requirements to which a publication of the kind may be justly expected to answer; still, it cannot be denied that Swart must be fully credited with the undying honour of having first rendered accessible to scholars and to the general public, the complete text of the journal of this memorable voyage. The text, I say...for Swart has, strangely enough, not seen his way to appending to it the charts, land-surveyings and drawings: for these, students had still to recur to what Valentijn and Burney had thought fit to give.

The authors just mentioned have especially treated the voyage of 1642-1643, adding biographical particulars about Tasman and his coadjutor Visscher. As regards the expedition of 1644, it is true, the information that had been made available, was not withheld from the public: the interesting "Instructions," for instance, were printed[5]; but the light thus spread was far from clear. The journal, the main source of information, remained unprinted. Witsen most probably was acquainted with a journal kept in the course of the 1644 voyage[6], and the particulars published by him found their way throughout the civilized world[7].

The discussion of the literature bearing on Tasman's voyages to what is now known as Australia, must not be closed, before we have drawn particular attention to the interest shown in the history of the discovery, for the half century last past, by the present dwellers in the lands discovered by Tasman--the inhabitants of Tasmania and New Zealand. This interest is evinced by a number of essays and papers on the subject, brought out by them[8], among them the results of endeavours to ascertain more definitely the points touched at by Tasman in his voyages[9].

Let us now return to the resolution of the Governor-General and Councillors, dated August 1, 1642.

[1] As is shown by a manuscript note of his, now in the possession of Messrs. Frederik Muller & Co.]

[2] Of course I cannot undertake here to give a complete list of the works dealing with these voyages of discovery, a list which for the matter of that would not present any great interest. I have therefore confined myself to mentioning such writings as for some reason or other I thought of more than ordinary importance, and as I was in the occasion to see and read. For other books I would refer readers to the well-known bibliographical works.]

[3] Amsterdam, Hulst van Keulen.]

[4] I find it impossible to enumerate all the mistakes committed by Swart. A few curious slips may, however, be briefly referred to. On p. 22 (my references are to the edition as a separate publication) Swart prints: "Vocabulair fingerwoorden," for which read: "Vocabulair eeniger woorden"; on January 11, the journal has: "tegens malcander": this, Swart (p. 97) corrupts into "tegens macanan," which latter word he took to be Malay, and rendered by "het eten" (dinner-time); on May 29, the journal reads: "Deden onzen cours dicht langhs het land van meyninge (= with the intention) door de Straat," etc. Swart oddly enough mistakes meyninge for the name of a country, and on p. 175 speaks of a "land van Meyninge."]

[5] In part already in Dalrymple's Collection concerning Papua in the British Museum; see MATTHEW FLINDERS, Ontdekkings-reis, p. 146.-- Swart published the whole of the Instructions in 1844 in Verhandelingen Zeewezen, 1844, pp. 65-90---See also MAJOR, l. c., pp. 43-58.]

[6] E.g. p. 175.]

[7] Cf. EYRIES in Nouvelles Annales, II, pp. 37-38; FLINDERS (who bases himself on Dalrymple), l. c., pp. 208-210; MAJOR, Early Voyages,

pp. XCIV, XCVIII-XCIX--WALKER, Tasman (1896), is in error, where (on p. 36, Note +) he designates the translation in Major, pp. 91-98, as "notices" of the 1644 voyage.]

[8] As regards Tasmania, see the list of "Printed Works" in WALKER, Tasman (1896), pp. 46-48--As concerns New Zealand, I have taken cognisance, inter alia, of T. M. HOCKEN, Some Account of the Earliest Literature and Maps relating to New Zealand, in Transactions of the New Zealand Institute, 1894, pp. 616-634; Id. Abel Tasman and his Journal. A paper read before the Otago Institute, 10th September, 1895. (The part of the journal translated by Hocken, is taken from Swart's edition).]

[9] For instance by GELL, l. c.; J. BACKHOUSE WALKER, The discovery of Van Diemen's land in 1642; with notes on the localities mentioned in Tasman's journal of the voyage. Strutt, Hobart, 1891; T. M. HOCKEN, Abel Tasman, p. 7.]

XII

WHAT THE DUTCH KNEW ABOUT THE SOUTH-LAND IN 1642.

The resolution[1] referred to at the close of the preceding chapter provided for the sending out of certain ships bound "to navigate to the partially known and hitherto untouched South- and East-land, and eventually to explore the same," or--to adopt the more concise wording of the Instructions of August 13--for "the often attempted discovery of the unknown South-land."

Although this South-land is thus referred to as "unknown," the epithet "partially known," which is applied to it in the resolution above mentioned, proves that the Batavia authorities undoubtedly had some notion of the regions now by Tasman "to be navigated and eventually explored." If we wish to do full justice to the value and importance of the exploratory voyages made by Tasman from 1642 to 1644, we shall first have to answer the question, what the Dutch of that time actually knew about the portions of the world now to be explored. The Dutch, I say; for it will readily be conceded that, as regards the importance of these expeditions and the glory of the Dutch having made them, it is of very little moment to know whether other nations too had vague notions about those parts of our globe that extend east and south of the Malay Archipelago; whether they too had endeavoured to light up the obscurity prevailing on the point.

For indeed, if to other nations the darkness had been dissipated to any degree worth mentioning, the light thus spread had not shone to any distance[2], and nothing beyond the merest glimmer of it had reached the Dutch of that time. In fact, the instructions drawn up by the Governor-General and Councillors of India for the guidance of Tasman's voyages of discovery of 1642 and 1644, show hardly any traces of even vague knowledge on their part respecting previous discoveries in those regions by other Europeans. We may therefore safely take for granted that what they knew about this point amounted to next to nothing; for, had they had any precise information on this subject, we may rest assured, that the instructions would not have omitted to refer to such knowledge, just as the instructions handed to Quast and Tasman in 1639 had done, since, to be sure, every indication of the kind could not have failed to be welcome to the leaders of the expeditions now to be engaged in.

What then, we may ask, was the extent of Dutch[3] information regarding the South-land in the year 1642? In the course of time their knowledge on this point had been considerably enlarged by explorations undertaken by themselves. This is most clearly seen, if beside the pre-Tasmanic charts dated about 1640, we place the charts to be found in the well-known work of Jan Huyghen van Linschoten, of Haarlem, which was brought out in 1595/6[4] under the title "Itinerario, voyage ofte schipvaert...naer Oost ofte Portugaels Indien," but the contents of which must already have been known to the first Netherlanders who undertook the voyage to India in 1595[5]. It therefore records what, at

[1) Appendix D.]

[2) Compare A. RAINAUD, Le Continent Austral. Hypothèses et découvertes. Paris, Colin, 1893; e.g. pp. 268 f., 275, note 1, 276 ff., 350 ff. Mutatis mutandis, some of his utterances exactly apply to the Dutch of 1642; e.g. p. 107: "De telles découvertes non enregistrées par l'histoire ne sont d'aucun profit pour la science;" and p. 255: "Ces devanciers inconnus (a supposer qu'ils aient existè) n'ont laissè aucune trace authentique de leurs explorations"; and what he says about Magalhaes's discovery of the strait, named after him, might have been written of the discovery of Australia by the Dutch: "C'est grace a [leur] énergie, a [leur] perseverance, a (leur) audace que ce qui n'etait qu'une conjecture devint une certitude."-- Compare also TIELE, Europeers, VII (Bijdragen taal-, land- en volkenkunde Neêrlands Indië, vierde volgreeks, VIII, p. 49; MAJOR, Early voyages, p. IV, XII ff.]

[3) For the reason above given, I think it needless to make other than incidental mention of the information on this point, possessed by other European nations of the time.]

[4) T'Amsterdam. By Cornelis Claesz. op 't Water, in 't Schrijfboeck, by de Oude Brugghe.--As regards this remarkable book, see especially TIELE, Mémoire bibliographique, pp. 83-103; and the same writer's Bibliographie land- en volkenkunde, pp. 152-155.]

[5) Compare, for example, the statements made in the journal of Frank Van der Does, kept during the first voyage (DE JONGE, Opkomst, II, p. 297, alin. 5 at the end; p. 298, alin. 1), with Van Linschoten's Itinerario, 138, second column, at top; DE JONGE, II, pp. 318, 319, with the chart, entitled "Affbeeldinghe der custen des landts genaempt Terra de Natal," etc.--The letters-patent of the States-General authorizing the publication of this book are, indeed, dated October 8, 1594.]

the beginning of their navigation to Asia, the Dutch knew about the Eastern countries, including the South-land. Referring to

Java (Mayor)[1], the author, who, besides drawing on experiences of his own, based his statements on information furnished by Portuguese writers, delivers himself as follows[2]: "This Island begins in 7 degrees on the south side, and extends east by south for a length of 150 miles: but as to its breadth nothing is known up to now, since it has not yet been explored, nor has any information on this point been obtained from the natives; some hold it to be part of the continent named Terra incognita, which is believed to extend in this direction all the way from C. de boa Esperança: but as to this no certainty has been got up to the present time, so that it is by the generality held to be an island"[3. We see, then, that at the period in question opinions were divided as to the real nature of Java: the prevailing opinion setting it down as an island[4], while others looked upon it as the north coast of a vast continent. This continent, which with an irregular outline extends to the southward of the whole then know world, is the Terra Australis (Magallanica or incognita)[5]. As regards the part of it lying between the same degrees of longitude that comprise the Dutch Malay Archipelago, it is characterised by two projecting parts jutting out on the north: of one of these, the mysterious Beach, Prouincia aurifera, Java, supposing it to have formed part of this terra, would have constituted the northern portion[6]; the other is marked with the name of Noua Guinea[7], as to the true nature of which--whether island or the northern part of Terra Australis--the same uncertainty prevails[8]. Between Java and New Guinea the chart places a string of islands, occupying the site of the Minor Sunda, the South-western, and the South-eastern Isles, with Aroe as the easternmost point known. East of New Guinea[9], we observe, among others, the Insulae Salomonis[10]. The Fretum Magallanicum divides the southern extremity of South America from the north point of Terra Australis (Magallanica): Tierra del Fuego, Terra de Fogo[11].

Java was circumnavigated by the Dutch in their first voyage to the East Indies[12]. The doubts still entertained by Van Linschoten were thereby accordingly removed[13]. It could therefore now be taken for granted that the belt of islands extending between Sumatra and New Guinea was totally unconnected with the so-called South-(antarctic)land. To the Dutch of the early years of the seventeenth century, doubt and uncertainty, however, began with the island or continent of New Guinea. They honestly tried to remove this uncertainty. When in the early part of 1602, Admiral Wolphert Hermanszoon was lying at anchor before Banda With a number of ships, and on the loth of April "the Assembly of

[1] RAINAUD (p. 308, note 2) is quite at sea, where he identifies with Australia, the Jave le Grande (Jave Mayor) of which Van Linschoten speaks in this connection. Van Linschoten doubtless means here the island of Java, as appears from the whole description of the island and a glance at the maps in Van Linschoten's work. Rainaud himself elsewhere (p. 316) identifies this Java Major with the island of Java.]

[2] P. 25.]

[3] Cf. DE JONGE, Opkomst, II, p. 165.]

[4] See, for instance, the journal of Frank Van der Does (DE JONGE, Opkomst, II, pp. 318, 321, 325, 333, 351, 352, 354) where there is always question of the island of Java, whereas on pp. 341, 344, 349 mention is made of the "continent of Java." The Dutch of the time also did not know, that Francis Drake had sailed south of Java in 1580.]

[5] See as regards this presumed continent the work of RAINAUD, Le Continent Austral.]

[6] With this compare the mode of presentment in the chart reproduced as No. 1 in Part II of the Remarkable Maps, with the title "BENEDICT. ARIAS MONTANUS sacrae geographiae tabulam...Antvverpiae...describebat 1571."]

[7] Compare RAINAUD, pp. 274, 276, 307 f.]

[8] See, for example, Orbis terrae compendiosa descriptio, of 1587, in MERCATOR-HONDIUS' atlas of 1608.]

[9] At the North-East point of Tasman's Nova Guinea Swart's copy of the Bonaparte chart has Cabo de Santa Maria. Tasman's journal mentions on April 1, that this cape was thus called by the Spaniards.]

[10] Compare, for instance, the charts in Remarkable Maps, II, 2, 3, which in the main give the same impression of uncertainty.]

[11] Compare RAINAUD, pp. 264, 270 ff.]

[12] Cf. DE JONGE, Opkomst, I, p. 98; II, pp. 165, 202, 364.]

[13] Doubt on this point, however, continued to be occasionally expressed in charts also after that time. See, for instance, Remarkable Maps, II, Nos. 2, 3. Indeed, although in Van Linschoten the southern coasts of the string of islands east of Java are tacitly supposed to have been circumnavigated, or at least known in outline, charts of later date sometimes leave undefined the south-coast of one or the other of these islands; e.g. as regards Soembawa in the Allard-Nolpe-Dozy chart of c.1652. It may, however, be safely taken for granted, that on coming to the East the Netherlanders did not look upon this string of islands as connected with the South-land. We need not, therefore, go any farther into this question.]

the plenary Council" had resolved to send out the ship Duifken to Ceram, for the purpose of forming trade-connections, the captains of the ships received orders to inquire of the natives of the said island, "whether they have any knowledge of Nova Guinea, whether ships from there have ever arrived at Ceram, or any been sent out from the latter place to Nova Guinea." In a "Brief Relation touching certain islands with which the inhabitants of Ceran and Banda carry on trade," drawn up after the return of the ship Duifken, nothing is said concerning New Guinea that can in any way be of interest for the purposes of the present investigation: mere hearsay reports, of the less importance, since the vague information possessed by the Dutch, regarding the object of their inquiries, must needs have given to the questions put by them to the natives, a want of definiteness which cannot have led to any reliable correctness in the answers received by them[1].

The earliest account now known of any contact of the Dutch with New Guinea and with what is now called Australia, is the one concerning the voyage thither, undertaken again by the celebrated ship Duifken, under the command of Willem Jansz. or Janszoon, of Amsterdam, and Jan Lodewijkszoon Rosengeyn. The Duif ken sailed from Bantam on November 28[2], 1605, and on her voyage to New Guinea touched at the Key and Aroe Isles. She must have struck New Guinea in about 5° S. Lat. She next sailed along the south coast of it, past the narrows, now called Torres Strait, without realising its real nature, and surveyed the east coast of the Gulf of Carpentaria up to a point, then christened Cape Keerweer[3] (Turn-again)[4], which was ascertained to be in 13° 45' S. Lat.[5]. In the course of this part of the Duifken's voyage, she inter alia sailed up, in 11 ° 48', the river afterwards named Carpentier (Batavia) by Carstensz[6]. From Cape Keerweer she must have gone back the same way, surveying in the course of her return voyage the south coast of New Guinea as far as its south-western extremity, from where she sailed for the Banda group, which she must have reached before June 15, 1606, the date on which an account of the whole voyage was received at Bantam[7]. Besides

[1] See P. A. LEUPE, De reizen der Nederlanders naar Nieuw-Guinea en de Papoesche eilanden in de 17de en 18de eeuw. 's-Gravenhage, Nijhoff, 1875, p. 3. The information there given is derived from the journal kept on board the ship Gelderland. (Hague State Archives.--Cf. also DE JONGE, Opkomst. II, p. 534). This work of Leupe's and his study on De reizen der Nederlanders naar het Zuidland of Nieuw-Holland in de 17de en 18de eeuw. Amsterdam, Hulst van Keulen, 1868, have been mainly used by me in the disquisition that follows in the text. I have, however, been careful in every instance to compare the data furnished by him and others, with the original documents.]

[2] Not November 18, as given by RAINAUD, p. 357. The English captain John Saris, who puts the departure of the Duyfken on November 18, uses the Old Style. Whence Rainaud derives his precise knowledge of the

object with which the ship sailed from Bantam, I fail to understand--As regards the priority of the Dutch in the discovery of Australia, see also A. PELTZER in his paper Les colonies Australes (Bulletin de la Société de Géographie d'Anvers, IV, 1879, pp. 444, 448-456). He concludes: Taut donc laisser aux Hollandais, et aux Hollandais seuls, l'honneur d'avoir découvert le continent Austral en l'année 1606."]

[3] I give in italics such place-names as are also found in the chart appended to the present work, which chart is mainly based on Swart's copy of the Bonaparte chart.]

[4] For the modern names I use STIELER'S Hand-atlas, the charts in LEUPE'S Nieuw-Guinea, in P. J. B. C. ROBIDÉ VAN DER AA, Reizen naar Nederlandsch Nieuw-Guinea in 1871, 1872, 1875-1876. 's-Gravenhage, Nijhoff, 1879, and in Atlas der Nederlandsche Bezittingen in Oost-Indië door J. W. STEMFOORT en J. J. TEN SIETHOFF (1883-1885); etc.]

[5] MAJOR, Early Voyages, p. LXXIX, has 19¾°, which is a mistake.--I need hardly say, that the latitudes I give in the test, are taken from the journals and the other documents, exactly as they stand there. COOTE (Remarkable Maps, Introduction) calls the Cape Keerweer in the Gulf of Carpentaria "the spurious second Keerweer", and speaks of "the true (Carstensz, 1623) and false (Duyfken, 1606) Keerweers." This is a mistake. The Keerweer of the Duyfken in 13¾° is as true as the Keerweer of Carstensz in 7° S. L. That the Duifken sailed along the East coast of the Gulf of Carpentaria at least as far as 11° 48', appears from the journal kept by Carstensz on his voyage of 1623 (May 11th); and there is no reason at all to disbelieve e.g. the Instructions of January 29th 1644 for Tasman's second exploratory voyage, which say: "the name Cape Keerweer in their chart"; i.e. the chart of the voyage of the Duyfken. The positive manner, in which the Instructions speak here is the more to be trusted, because the same Instructions, when speaking about the different voyages, mention in each particular instance, whether there were journals and maps, or not. Of the voyage of the Duyfken (1605/6) there existed a chart in 1644, and this chart has Cape Keerweer in 13¾°. (Compare also RAINAUD, p. 358, note I). Both the Keerweers are found on a manuscript map of 1699 in the State Archives, no. 344 of Leupe's inventory, the work of the cartographer of the Dutch East India Company, and in G. de Haan's manuscript atlas of 1760.]

[6] See the journal of Carstensz, on May 1, in VAN DIJK, Mededeelingen uit het Oud-Indisch Archief. Amsterdam, Scheltema, 1859, B, p. 47.]

[7] Her explorations are therefore anterior to those of Luiz Vaez de Torres, who at the end of June 1606 was still in the neighbourhood of the islands, now known as the New Hebrides, which he and De Queiros had discovered some weeks before, and had christened Land of Espiritu Santo. From there De Torres was driven to the west (Torres-Strait and the South coast of New Guinea). As regards De Torres' discoveries see his letter of July 12, 1607 in STANLEY'S translation of De Morga's Philippine Islands, pp. 402-419; ROBIDÉ VAN DER AA, Reizen naar Nieuw-Guinea,

p. 352 and note; etc.--It is curious enough, that in Tasman's instructions of 1642 nothing is said about De Queiros' discoveries (New Hebrides) We must therefore take for granted that this discovery was not known to G.-G. & Council, and yet, as early as 1612 it was found referred to in printed Dutch books (TIELE, Bibliograhie Land- en Volkenkunde, pp. 87 f.).-- COLLINGRIDGE'S opinion (Discovery, p. 236, note *), that the Dutch sent out the expedition of 1606 after having heard of De Torres' discoveries, is far from being a well-founded one, I believe.]

giving a name to Cape Keerweer, the commanders of this expedition christened various points, seen or called at by the crew. We must leave undecided, whether all these names were given in the voyage home; part of them may well have originated on the voyage out. Of these names the following have come down to us[1]: Tyuri(?)[2] and Modder-Eylandt (the island of Prins Frederik Hendrik of our time, with the coast opposite to it), "which those on board the yacht Duyfken mistook for islands"[3], Duyfkens Eylant (the coast of Kapia) with Goenong Api[4] (Mount Lakahia), and Nieu Zeelandt (Koemawa)[5].

There are reasons to assume that the same yacht Duifken made another exploratory voyage to New Guinea at the close of 1606 and the beginning of 1607; at least on March 4 of the year last named, the supercargo Paulus Van Soldt, who on that date arrived before the Dutch Castle in Amboyna, and found the said yacht at anchor there, when referring to this ship, thought it necessary to note respecting her that she had just "returned from Nova Guinea"[6]. Van Soldt had left Bantam on January 27, and as long ago as June 15, 1606, news had reached the latter place of the Duifken having returned to Banda from her voyage in 1605/6, which we have just discussed. It is therefore difficult to believe[7], that as late as March 4, 1607 Van Soldt would have alluded to this voyage in the terms we have just seen him use. But, however this may be, nothing whatever is known as to the results of this second voyage.

Nor is anything known about the results of another project, for the carrying out of which certain steps were taken a few years later, in 1615/6. This plan did not originate with the East India Company, and to give the reader a clear idea of it, it will be necessary first to recall to his mind one of the articles of the Charter granted to this trading-association in 1602. The thirty-fourth article of the said Charter laid down the limits of the Company's privilege. It ran as follows: "And to the end that the intentions of the said united Company may be realised with the greater success, to the well-being of the United Provinces, the preservation and progress of transmarine traffic, as well as to the benefit and advantage of the Company aforesaid; We have granted and accorded to the Company aforesaid, in form as we also grant and accord by these presents, that no person, of what quality or condition soever, unless forming part of the said Company, shall be permitted to sail from these United Provinces, within a term of one and twenty years to come, beginning with and including this present year 1602, eastward of Cape de Bonne Esperance, or through the Straits of Magellanes[8], on pain of confiscation of both ships and goods in the same; due and complete reservation being made as regards the concessions heretofore granted to certain Companies for the navigation through the said Straits of Magellanes, on express condition that they shall send out their ships from this country within the space of four years from the date of the present, on pain of altogether losing the benefit of the concessions aforesaid.

"According to the spirit[8] of this article, therefore, every Netherlander outside the Company was utterly excluded from any chance of ever obtaining a share in the trade of the East. The letter[1], however, of the statute just made it possible to slip through the meshes. There was a prohibition, to be sure, against navigation eastward of the Cape of Good Hope, and through[8] the Straits of Magalhaes;

[1] Thanks to the chart (also contained in the Mercator-Hondius atlas, ed. 1634), entitled *Indiae Orientalis descriptio*, of 1633, by Joannes Janssonius (Remarkable Maps, II, 7 and Introduction). COOTE (Remarkable Maps, II, Introduction) is in error where he says that also the chart Remarkable Maps, II, 6 "represents the discovery of William Jansz. in the Jagt Duyfken on the S. W. coast of New Guinea 1605-6."]

[2] ROBIDÉ VAN DER AA, 1. c. p. 424 is wrong, I think, in reading here Tynri. The instructions of January 29, 1644 for Tasman's second exploratory voyage have "Ture."]

[3] Carstensz' words (VAN DIJK, Mededeelingen, B, p. 21, Note I).]

[4] Gouvongapy, in Janssonius' chart.]

[5] LAUTS'S observations on this voyage (see LEUPE, Zuidland, pp. 8-10; Niew-Guinea, pp. 4-5) are utterly void of solid foundation, just as are his longitudes and latitudes. Not to put too fine a point upon it, we might say that he mixes up the results of various voyages. Cf. also TIELE, De Europeërs in den Maleischen Archipel, VII (Bijdragen land- en volkenkunde Nederlandsch Indië, 4th series, VIII, pp. 49-51). On this voyage, also see DE JONGE, Opkomst, III, pp. 42-46; COLLINGRIDGE, Discovery, pp. 238-245. He does not understand Dutch, as appears from the mistakes he has made in copying the Dutch passage on p. 241. This "lack of knowledge of the Dutch language" (p. 238) has prevented his studying Dutch sources and literature. If he had done so, Collingridge would have become aware, that he is far too incredulous (e.g. pp. 265, 266, 268 f.) as regards the Dutch discoveries of Australia.]

[6) Begin ende Voortgang, II, J 3, p. 78.]

[7) Not, it appears, for DE JONGE, 1. c., p. 46; and COLLINGRIDGE. pp. 243 f.]

[8) The italics are mine.]

there was none against attempts to find a passage, hitherto unknown, south of those Straits[1]; why not, then, make the attempt at all hazards?

Now, it would appear that as early as 1615, certainly before January 30, 1616[2], a vessel, named Mauritius de Nassau, sailed from a Dutch port, under the command of Jan Remmetszoon, of Purmerend. The ship was ostensibly destined for Angola, but from there she was ordered to direct her course for "Terra Australe, called Terra del Fuego." The plan, therefore, was, from the west coast of Africa to sail southward, until the supposed South-land should have been reached, and then "to explore the whole of the coast of Terra Australi as far as the Straits of Magellanes, on the chance of finding an opening that might allow a passage to the South-sea; and on such opening being found, to run into and through the same, in order to discover whether they could in such manner get into the South-sea; should such passage to the South-sea have been found, they had orders to return home forthwith, but in case adverse circumstances should prevent them from doing so, they were to run on for the East Indies."

Nothing is known of the result of this expedition, which might possibly have led to fresh discoveries.

A great many more particulars, however, have come down to us concerning another voyage of slightly earlier date, which also aimed at evading the Company's exclusive privilege. I mean the well-known voyage of the ships Eendracht and Hoorn, commanded by Jacques Le Maire and Willem Corneliszoon Schouten, and fitted out by an association of merchants, formed at Hoorn, the master-spirit of which was Isaac Le Maire, Jacques Le Maire's father[3]; the avowed object of the expedition being the search for a passage south of the Straits of Magelhães, from the Atlantic into the Pacific Ocean.

If they should happen to discover rich regions adapted for trade, in the South-land westward of Tierra del Fuego, the object of the voyage would be held to be attained; in the opposite case they, were to turn their ships' heads to India[4].

On June 14, 1615 the anchors were weighed in the Texel roads, and not before January 20, 1616 did they reach the Straits of Magelhaes. On January 24 they sighted the passage which on February 12 had the name of Le Maire Straits conferred on it. The land--it was not then perceived to be an island--then seen east of the ships, was christened Statenland, and of course again duly looked upon as one of the projecting points of the so-called South-land, which by the discovery of this strait had therefore another, if only a comparatively small portion, viz. Tierra del Fuego, taken off it[5]. On the 31st of January there was no longer any land in sight, and the crew were now firmly convinced that "they had the vast South Sea ahead of them, without any land." Of course, in this memorable expedition, too, the long-expected, vast Terra Australis or South-land was not discovered, although various islands in the Pacific were touched at. Some of these places of call require more special notice in connection with our subject. On May 1, the discoverers came near an island which according to them was in 16° 10' S. Lat., and to which they gave the name of Kokos-eiland (Cocoa-Island): our charts now have it as Tafahi or Boscawen.

Slightly more to the south they sighted the island on which they bestowed the appellation of Verraders-eiland (Traitors' Island), now Niutabutabu or Keppel. They afterwards sighted the (Goede) Hope island (Nina-fu), and next arrived at the island-group to which they gave the name of Hoornsche

[1] It would seem, therefore, that at that time nothing was known of discoveries of Dirk Gerritszoon, in 1599 (the South shetland Group?). Compare RINAUD, p. 341.]

[2] This being the date of the "deposition made by Master Samuel Bloemaert" (one of the joint owners), in answer to the "interrogatory" to which he was subjected by certain Directors of the E. I. C. There is a copy of this deposition in the Hague State Archives. Cf. also TIELE, Bouwstoffen, I (1886), pp. LVIII f.]

[3] See R. C. BAKHUIZEN VAN DEN BRINK, Studiën en Schetsen over Vaderlandsche Geschiedenis. 's-Gravenhage, Nijhoff, 1877, IV, pp. 274 ff.]

[4] As regards the different editions of the journals of this expedition, see TIELE, Mémoire bibliographique, pp. 40 ff., and TIELE, Bibliographie land- en volkenkunde, sub voce Le Maire and Schouten. The editions often differ considerably as to their contents. Hence, I do not agree with e.g. Leupe on every point. In some of the editions there is a highly interesting small-scale map of Nova Guinea, which has evidently done duty in the preparation of various maps that profess to represent New Guinea previous to Tasman. There is a curious error in Thévenot's well-known chart. The small-scale map just referred to shows on the north coast of New Guinea the three islands of Arimoa, Moa and Insou. Now the last of these has in Thévenot's chart been transferred to the south coast, where it bears the name of "I(nsula) Sou." Van Alphen, one of the few cartographers who have taken over Insou, puts it in the right place. But the fact that In-

sou appears in Thévenot's chart as well as in Van Alphen's, again shows that the two charts must be closely related.]

[5] As regards the voyage in this part of the world by Francis Drake, in 1578 compare RAINAUD, pp. 271-273; TIELE-- VIVIEN DE SAINT-MARTIN, De ontdekkingsreizen sedert de vijftiende eeuw (Leiden, Van Doesburgh, 1874), p. 169.]

Eilanden (Hoorn Isles), now Fotuna and Alofi. On the 21st and 22nd of June, when they estimated themselves to be between 4° 50' and 4° 45' S. Lat., they surveyed a number of islands of which one received the name of Marken[1]. Shortly after, the Groene-eilanden (Green Islands) and Sint-Jans-eiland (St. John's Isle) were passed, after which they sailed round the north of what is now known as New Ireland or New-Mecklenburg, which, they suspected, might be the north coast of New Guinea. On this coast they inter alia gave a name to the Claes Pietersz baai[2], then sailed north of what is now New Hannover, and next between the island last mentioned and those at present known as Admiralty Isles, and finally struck the north coast of New Guinea, near Vulcanus Island[3], which also got its name in this expedition. This coast was now further skirted, and on it a name given to the Cornelis Kniersz Bay; the islands of Arimoa (with Moa and Insou) were touched at, and on July 24 names were bestowed on the Willem Schouten Isles and the Kaap de Goede Hoop (Cape of Good Hope): which shows that they had now got north of Geelvinkbaai. The north coast of New Guinea having thus been left, was, however, soon after approached again. They were tossed about for some time in what is now called Dampier Straits[4], which was held to be a bay land-locked on every side, and then held their course north of Waigeoe, until Gilolo was reached.

The expeditions of Remmetszoon, and of Schouten and Le Maire had not originated with the Company. Still, the latter had at no time lost sight of the advantages promised by a further exploration of the South-land. On the 8th and 21st of October 1616, the Governor-General and Councillors, staying in Ternate for the time being, resolved to fit out two ships under the command of Mr. Cornelis Dedel "for the better discovery of the South-land, Nova Guinea and the dependencies thereof"; and Dedel had already for this purpose arrived in Amboyna from Ternate, when unexpected circumstances made it expedient to employ the ships elsewhere[5].

But while this exploratory expedition was being discussed, while in the mother-country itself the Directors were seriously addressing their minds to "the discovery of the Southern Land" "[6], an accidental circumstance had already carried the Dutch a step further on the road that was destined to lead them to ampler and better knowledge of the mysterious regions which it was generally deemed desira-desirable to explore. In the course of January 1616 certain ships, among others the Eendracht, under the command of Skipper Dirk Hartogszoon of Amsterdam and Supercargo Gilles Mibais(e) of Liege, had sailed from the Netherlands. After leaving the Cape of Good Hope, in order to seek a more convenient route to Java than the one hitherto followed, the Eendracht--in accordance with orders given by the Directors[7]--sailed "far more south than was customary." In the month of October of the said year she unexpectedly struck the South-land, and on the 25th of that month cast anchor in a road-stead, to which the name of Dirk Hartogs-reede was given. This road-stead was first thought to form part of a continent, but a long time afterwards[8] turned out to belong to an island, which even now is known to the charts as Dirk Hartogs Island (25° 30'-26° 10' S. L.). October 27 they set sail again, this time in a northerly direction, in order to reach Bantam, and continued to survey the coast, which soon became known to the charts[9] by the name of Land van de Eendracht or Eenacrachtsland. In December Sapi Strait east of Soembawa was made[10].

[1] LEUPE, Nieuw Guinea, p. 164, is not quite correct here, I think.]

[2] The appellations Hoog land, Laag land, Hoog land, 25 eilanden en Hoog land, which are found in the charts (see Remarkable Maps, II, III) also originated in the course of this voyage.]

[3] The name Hoop berg (land), found in the charts, also dates from this expedition. The phrase "Terra d'os Papous, a Jacobo le Maire dicta Nova Guinea," is a blunder, of course. This name was given to the island by Yñigo Ortiz de Retes in 1545. Cf. TIELE, Europeërs, III, in Bijdragen taal-, land- en volkenkunde Neêrlandsch Indië, Vierde volgreeks, IV, p. 279; compare RAINAUD, pp. 275 f.]

[4] LEUPE, Nieuw-Guinea, p. 165, opines that the voyagers must have been between Salawati and the west coast of New Guinea. I do not think this at all probable.]

[5] See also LEUPE, Nieuw Guinea, p. 7.]

[6] Res. XVII, October 1616.]

[7] See LEUPE, Zuidland, pp. 10-14, 16-19.]

[8] LEUPE, Zuidland, pp. 170-178.]

[9] As regards the old charts, see especially Remarkable Maps, II, 4, entitled Caert van 't Landt van d' Eendracht uyt de Journalen ende afteykeningen der Stierluyden t' samengestelt, Ao. 1627. Bij HESSEL GERRITSZ. Not Eessel Gerrit, as the name is given by

COLLINGRIDGE, Discovery, p. 265). It is a pity, that this author has not seen this chart. His opinion of the discoveries made by the Eendraght, the Leeuwin, etc. would in that case have been a different one.]

[10) Cf. LEUPE, Zuidland, pp. 14-18, 28, 30.]

A year after this, the ship Zeewolf, commanded by Skipper Haevick Claaszoon of Hillegom, and Supercargo Pieter Dirxcsoon of Amsterdam, set sail from the Texel. Aftet leaving the Cape of Good Hope--this time also in conformity with orders given them by the Directors--they sailed mainly in a south-easterly and easterly direction, even as far as 39° S. Lat., whence they next tried to navigate to Java by holding on to the north. Authentic documents have come down to us[1], regarding the adventures of the crew on this expedition[2]. On June 24, 1618, the skipper writes to the Directors on this point as follows: "On April 29 we had run on upwards of a thousand miles to the east...we then changed our ship's course to the north-east. On May 5[3], we got to 28 degrees 26 minutes S. Lat...On May 11 we sighted land in 21 degrees 20 minutes S. Lat...it lay mainly South and West...We could not get to it; whether it is a continent or islands is known to God only, but I suspect it to be firm land, since I have in succession seen all the signs of it...Down to the 16th degree we have seen a good deal of sea-weed floating and land-birds flying about, which are also signs of firm land. This land is especially fit to be touched at by ships that come here with the eastern monsoon, in order to obtain a fixed course for Java or the Straits [of Sunda]; for when you see this land in 21, 22 or 23 degrees, and then hold your course N.N.W. and N. by W., you will get to the Western extremity of Java. And since we have been holding a fixed course all the time, I write this as an undoubted truth." So far Skipper Haevick Claeszoon.

Pieter Dircxzoon, in his turn, writes to the Directors as follows: "On the 24th [of March we set sail] from Table Bay... with destination for Bantam. In such manner that, thanks to God, we in a short time got into 37, 38 and 39 degrees S. Lat., whence we held on due east for upwards of a thousand miles, before turning to the north...After this, having got into 21" 15' S. Lat. on May 11...we discovered and sighted land. It lay to windward about 5 or 6 miles east of us...from the look-out we could discern still other land at both ends, to wit at the southern and northern extremities, but we could not without great difficulty get any higher, so that we do not know whether the whole of it is firm land, or composed of separate islands. There seems every probability that is a mainland coast, for it was very long. But the truth of it is known to the Lord God only. At all events it seems that it has never been touched at or discovered by any one, seeing that we have never heard of any such discovery, and the chart shows nothing but open sea here...Holding on a N.N.E. course we came in sight of land eastward of Bali, so that this land extends N.N.W. of Sunda Straits, and we cannot fail, with a North by West or Northern course, to make the island of Java east of the Straits."

At the same time with the Zeewolf, the Company had fitted out certain other ships, among them the ship Mauritius, commanded by Skipper Lenaert Jacobszoon. We get some information as to the goings-on of this vessel from a missive written by Willem Janszoon, who made the voyage in her as head of trading-matters. On October 6, 1618, he writes as follows to the Directors: "The present only serves to inform you, that on June 8 last in the ship Mauritius we passed the Cape de bon esperance with strong western winds, and found it unadvisable to touch at any land; we held on to eastward the distance of a thousand miles"--again, we see, pursuant to the orders given by the Directors--"though we had wished to run farther eastward still, in 38 degrees Southern Latitude. On July 31 we discovered an island, on which we landed...it was found to extend for 15 miles, N.N.E. to S.S.W., to the west side. Its northern extremity is in 22° S.L., S.S.E. and N.N.W., 240 miles from the south point of Sunda. From here, with a fair wind we by God's mercy safely arrived before Bantam on the 22nd day of August." A little more light is thrown on this surveying of the Southland[4] by a chart made in 1627 by Hessel Gerritsz, official "cartographer" to the East India Company[5], "from the Journals and drawings

[1] I need hardly reiterate here that, unless otherwise stated, all these documents are preserved in the State Archives at the Hague.]

[2] Not mentioned by RAINAUD.]

[3] LEUPE, Zuidland, p. 21, is mistaken as to the dates.]

[4] Not mentioned by RAINAUD.]

[5] Resolutions of the "Heeren XVII," dated March 21, 1619 and August 21, 1629. Gerritsz was presumably a collaborator in the map, entitled Typus Orbis terrarum in GERARDI MERCATORIS Atlas de novo multis in locis emendatus novisque tabulis auctus studio JUDOCI HONDIJ. Amsterodami, sumptibus Johannis Cloppenburgij, 1632. Of this atlas there exists an earlier edition with the same world-map. Compare TIELE, Bibliographie, no. 749; Catalogue Géographie, Cartographic, Voyages, Amsterdam, Frederik Muller & Cie., MDCCCXCV, No. 2476), but this I have not seen. This map of the world, together with the map of Keppler (Remarkable Maps, II, 6), is perhaps the first world-map, that gives the land of Eendracht. Keppler is more accurate however.]

of the steersmen"[1]. This map has the following legend at the South-land, in 21° 45' S. Lat.: Willems revier[2], besocht bij 't volck van 't schip Mauritius in Julius A° 1618"[3] [Willems River, visited by the crew of the ship Mauritius, in July, 1618]. The chart here referred to is one representing "'t Landt van d'Eendracht"; a direct proof that this name must at an early period have figured in the charts. The name had, indeed, been officially adopted by the Company, as soon as the result of Dirk Hartog's accidental surveyings had become known in the Netherlands. This is proved by the fact now to be stated. It frequently happened that certain marginal notes were made on the letters received from India by the Directors, especially in the case of matters which had more than was usual drawn the attention of the Company's managers. Marginal notes of the kind now are also found on the missive of Willem Janszoon, and this in a hand which regularly appears in the official documents of the Company, drawn up in this country at the time. Among these notes we find the word "Eendrachtsland" written in margine at the passage of the letter referring to the surveyings at the South-land made by the Mauritius[4]. Accordingly, the newly discovered coast was known in the mother-country by this celebrated name already in 1619, the very year in which the missive we are discussing must have arrived in the Netherlands.

In the same year 1619 the information at the disposal of the Netherlanders touching the outline of the west coast of what is now known as New Holland, was again enlarged[5], this time by the experience gained, and the observations taken on board the ship Dordrecht, commanded by Skipper Reyer Janszoon of Buiksloot, which had on board Frederik [De] Houtman as commander of a large fleet of eleven vessels of the East India Company, and the ship Amsterdam, under the command, probably, of Maarten Corneliszoon[6], which had on board Jacob Dedel as supercargo. These two ships got separated from the rest, and sailed together from the Cape of Good Hope, on June 8, 1619. Both [De] Houtman and Dedel have given an account of their adventures subsequent to that date, in three letters, all of them dated October 7. [De] Houtman writes as follows to the Stadtholder Prince Maurice:..."on June 8 we sailed with a fair wind from Table Bay with the ships Dordrecht and Amsterdam, and on the 19th of July we suddenly came upon the South-land Beach in 32 degrees 20 minutes, where we spent a few days in trying to survey and reconnoitre the same, but the impossibility of getting ashore,

[1] Remarkable Maps, II, 4.]

[2] Willems River cannot, of course, have been named after the Willem Jansz. of 1606 (LEUPE, Zuidland, p. 58). It may have got its name from Willem Janszoon, supercargo in the ship Mauritius. Some writers, however, derive this name from William I of Orange (MOLL, Zeetogten, p. 211), or give to this river the name "la rivière du roi Guillaume" (F. PÈRON, Voyage de découvertes aux Terres Australes 1800-1804, I, Paris, 1807, p. 126). I do not know why.]

[3] In Thévenot's chart (Remarkable Maps, III, 7) we find a little south of Willems River, a Jacob Remens River, which occurs also in other charts (for example, in Keppler's chart of 1630, No. II, 8 of Remarkable Maps, under the name of Jac. Rommer rivier). As LEUPE (Zuidland, p. 58) has observed already, this name was known as early as 1629. In Francois Pelsaert's "Droevige daghaenteijkeningh int verliesen van ons schip Batavia, verseijlt zijnde op de Abrolhos oft Clippen van Frederick Houtman, gelegen op de hoochte van 28 1/3 graden 9 mijlen van Zuidtlandt" [A mournful diurnal account of the loss of our ship Batavia, run aground on the Abrolhos or Frederick Houtman Cliffs, situated in 28 1/3 degrees, 9 miles from the South-land), the writer states, that when on June 16,15629 going on in a northerly direction, he estimated himself to be in 22° 17' S. Lat.: "I intended to run on for Jacob Remmessens River, but the wind turned to the North-east, so that we could not keep near the shore." It is unknown when this river had this name bestowed on it. Perhaps the name may have been derived from a steersman, one Jacob Remmetsz, whom Leupe has met with in the archives of the E. I. C.]

[4] LEUPE'S remark: "I am inclined to believe, however, that this note is of later date" (Zuidland, p. 26, Note 1) should by no means lead us to think that the note belongs to a later period: it certainly bears a quite undoubted contemporary character.]

[5] LEUPE, Zuidland, p. 35, cites a letter sent by the Directors to the Gov.-Gen. and Councillors, of Sept. 9, 1620. In this letter there is question of the discoveries made by "d' Eendracht, Zeewolff, 't Wapen van Amsterdam, and quite recently by Commanders Houtman and D'Edel." When, we may ask, did the ship 't Wapen van Amsterdam survey the South-land? There certainly was a ship of that name by the side of another vessel, named Amsterdam pur et simple. According to the Register of departures of vessels of the E. I. C., preserved in the State Archives at the Hague, this ship set sail from the Netherlands on May 11, 1613. I have not found any reliable trace of later date of this vessel, and the documents know nothing of any exploration of the South-land by her. I am inclined to think that Leupe is mistaken here. The letter itself, which is contained in the copying-book of letters, preserved in the State Archives, has suffered much from the ravages of time. Between the words "Zeewolff" and "Amsterdam" the paper has suffered so much, that nothing is left of the intervening letters. L. C. D. VAN DIJK, in his Mededeelingen uit het Oud-Indisch Archief. Amsterdam, Scheltema, 1859, p. 2, Note 2, has also printed the letter in question. He puts the words "'t Wapen van" in parentheses, in order to denote that they are merely conjectural. Leupe may have inadvertently omitted these parentheses. Perhaps the orginal text read: "Amsterdam ende." In this case there would have been two times

question of Dedel's voyage: once by a reference to the ship Amsterdam; and afterwards by mentioning Dedel's name itself. I must not, however, omit to make mention here of what the Instructions for Tasman's second voyage, dated January 29, 1644, say about an unsuccessful expedition undertaken by the ship 't Wapen van Amsterdam to the south coast of New Guinea in 1619.]

[6] I conclude this from Dedel's letter of October 7, 1619, to be referred to by and by.]

together with the strong wind then prevailing, prevented us from carrying out our plan, after which we held our course towards Java, which we sighted August 19." This account, although the briefest of the three that have come down to us, is of special importance, because in it [De] Houtman, who, as we shall presently see, was acquainted with the discovery made by the ship Eendracht, speaks of the "South-land Beach." We may conclude from this that the discoveries of the last few years were identified with the mysterious "Beach "[1].

To the Directors [De] Houtman writes with greater detail. After leaving the Cape of Good Hope, he says, "we ran on with a fair north-west wind as far as 36 degrees 30 minutes, whence we kept this steady breeze up to July 17th, when we calculated to have sailed due east in a straight line a distance of a thousand miles from the Cape de bonne esperance; we found the diminishing north-western variation of the compass to be 16 degrees, and resolved to change our course...to north-east and north-east by north, being then in 35 degrees 25 minutes southern latitude. And having kept the course aforesaid for about 60 miles, in the evening of the 19th we unexpectedly sighted land, which we held off from. On the l0th [we] found it to be a mainland coast, lying south and north...We could find no convenient landing-place owing to the heavy breakers, and the violence of the waves...[We] next sailed along the coast until July 28...and sighted a projecting point of the land on the same day...On the 29th ditto, thinking ourselves clear of all land, we changed our course to North by East. At noon we found ourselves in 29° 32' S. Lat. In the night, about three hours before daybreak, we again unexpectedly came upon land, which we observed to be a low-lying broken land with reefs all round it; we could see no high or firm land, so that it will be advisable to keep clear of the said reefs which might grievously endanger any vessels that might wish to touch at this land; we estimated it to be upwards of ten miles long, its latitude being 28° 46'. On the second of August, the wind turning contrary, we changed our course to eastward. At noon we again observed a long stretch of mainland, in 27° 40' S.

Lat. Here we became firmly convinced that this must be the land, which the ship d'Eendracht must have seen and sailed alongside of...nor do we at all doubt that all the land which (they?) saw in 22, 23 and 25°, and ourselves observed as far as 33°, must be one continuous mainland coast without a break. Sailing in 26° 20' [we were] in full sight of the land...--This South-land had need to be further surveyed and explored. On August 25 we got into Sonda Strait."

Jacob Dedel's letter to the Directors supplements [De] Houtman's account by furnishing additional particulars. "After many westerly, south-westerly and southerly winds, which we had in 35, 36 and 37° Southern Latitude, with occasional stiff breezes, (we) successfully got so far east, and on July 19 came upon the South-lands lying beyond Java; here we cast anchor in latitude 32½ degrees...We did our utmost to effect a landing which proved impracticable owing to the steep cliffs...but [we had to] be content with having seen the land, which when occasion shall serve, ought to be further surveyed and explored with fitting vessels or smaller craft. We did not always...keep close inshore, seeing that the coast was indented with large bays, but saw the land by fragments here and there; going on in this fashion in 27 degrees we also came upon the land discovered by the ship Eendracht[2]...From latitude 27° S. we next held a north and north by west course," for the isle of Java.

[1] Visscher in his memorial about the South-land of January 22, 1642, afterwards to be discussed, also speaks of the "unknown provinces of Beach."]

[2] Eendrachtsland was further surveyed--RAINAUD and COLLINGRIDGE hardly refer to any of the voyagers, to be discussed in this note--by the ship Leyden commanded by Skipper Claes Hermansz, the said ship striking the South-land in her voyage from the Cape to Java, July 21, 1623, "in latitude 27° S.", and surveying the same as far as 25° 48'.--In another voyage from the Cape to Java, this time under command of Skipper Daniel Janssen Cock, the same ship sighted "the Southland" on April 28, 1626 The ship's journal does not register any latitude on that day, but on the 27th she was in 27 2/3° S. L., and in "just short of" 26° on the 29th.--Two of the seven ships also, which sailed from the Texel, March 19, 1627, under the command of Governor-General Jan Pieterszoon Coen, saw the west coast of Australia. Coen himself gives the following particulars--not referred to by LEUPE--of his experiences on this occasion, in his letter to the Directors, dated October 30, 1627: "On the twenty-second day of July we left Table Bay with the ships Galias, Wttrecht and Texel...we got cut off from the other two, and continuing our voyage in the Galias, we came in sight of the land of Eendracht in 28½ S. L-, on September 5 in the afternoon..." The other vessel of this squadron, that surveyed the Southland was the ship het Wapen van Hoorn. A letter

and the journal of Supercargo J. Van Roosenbergh, who was on board, the former addressed to the Directors at Amsterdam, and dated November 8, 1627, furnish us with the following particulars of this ship's voyage: "On the 17th (of September] we saw the land of d'Eendracht in the vicinity of Dirck Hartochs roads..." In June 1629, Francois Pelszrt, who was wrecked on the Houtmans Abrolhos with the ship Batavia, surveyed the west coast of Australia from 28° 13 to 22° 17', after which he tried to reach Batavia. When he had got there, he returned thence to the Abrolhos, in order to rescue those men of his crew who had been left behind there. In the course of this return-voyage, in September, he surveyed the coast from about 29° 16' as far as the Abrolhos. This shipwreck, together with the horrible occurrences, which followed it, is so generally known that it is needless to go into detail about it here (see TIELE, Mémoire bibliographique, pp. 262-268; Bibliographie Land- en Volkenkunde, pp. 190-191; MAJOR, Early Voyages, pp. LXXXIX--XCII, 59-74, etc.). As regards Pelsaert's expedition in September, and his subsequent return to Batavia, I extract the following particulars from his "Dach aenteykeningh " [daily journal): "On the 3rd ditto...at noon we sighted the mainland of the Southland, lying N. N. W. and S. S. E. being in Latitude south 29° 16' [Pelsaert had then passed the Abrolhos, and was sailing on a northerly course)...On the 4th ditto...at noon we were in 28° 50' S. L. Here the land began to trend outward one point, to wit North by West and South by East...In the evening we became aware of a shallow straight ahead or to westward of us...on the 5th ditto...we saw ahead of us and skirting our course more breakers, shoals and strips of land...This reef or shoal extended S. S. W. and N. N. E....at eleven in the forenoon we had lost sight of the mainland, at noon we were in 28° 59' S. L., the extremity of the reef being W. S. West of us...On the 6th ditto...at noon we were in 28° 44' S. L...In the evening we again turned our course from the rocks to the open, sounded 40 fathom, but were surrounded by dangerous cliffs. These reefs here extend out to sea S. East and N. West...On the 13th ditto, at three o'clock in the morning we again observed breakers ahead...This was the northernmost point of the Abrolhos...at noon we were in 28° Latitude South. Shortly after, we again sighted the mainland of the South-land...On the 16th ditto...towards evening we saw the rocks on which our ship Batavia had been wrecked, and I was recognised from the Hooge Eylandt...On the 17th ditto...in the forenoon, coming near the island, we saw smoke rising up from a long island, two miles to westward of the wreck, and also from another small islet close to the wreck...(one of these islands in about 28½° S. L. was named Batavia's Churchyard)...On November 15...we weighed anchor in the name of God, and sailed away from these luckless Abrolhos to the mainland [of the Southland), keeping an E. N. East course...in order from there to continue our voyage to Batavia as expeditiously as possible...about noon we got close inshore...on the 16th ditto...towards noon we sighted a bay situated in 27° 51'."

Meanwhile Jacques Specx, member of the Council of India, had with certain vessels, in the night between the 26th and 27th of August, 1629, "struck the South-land, and had landed near the corner of Dirck Hartogs roads," after which the Plenary Council had resolved "from that time to direct the ships' course along the coast, lying in the chart East North East, going on to 22° S. Latitude." Of this expedition, which was specially intended to discover and further explore the coast, nothing more is now known.--We have better information, on the other hand, respecting an exploratory voyage, undertaken in 1635 by the ship Amsterdam, on board of which was Wollebrant Geleynszoon De Jongh, the commander of a fleet on its way from the mother-country to India. The following particulars are taken from De Jongh's account: On May 25th..."one hour after day-break...we sighted the South-land...we found our latitude to be 25 degrees 16 minutes South, but were not quite sure of our observation...item in the morning about two hours after day-break, morning-prayers being over, we saw straight ahead of us...the South-land; it lay east of us, about 4 or 5 miles by estimation, when we got sight of it; we found it to be low-lying land, its lie being pretty much as shown in the chart, N. N. E. and S. S: W., so far as we could make out...The land we saw, from which at noon we were at no more than 1½ or two miles' distance by estimation, we held to be the land of d' Eendracht, and the land we got near to at noon Dirck Hartochsz. road, for we had a great bay or bight between two projecting points..."]

In this voyage, accordingly, the coast which was soon to be known by the name of Dedelsland was skirted, and the Houtmans Abrolhos[1] discovered. Another couple of years later, the south-western extremity of what is now called Australia was to be reached by a Dutch ship. This was the vessel Leeuwin, which, after leaving the Netherlands in the spring of 1621, after a very long passage, in March[2], 1622, reached the South-land between about 33° 45' and 35° S.L., and conferred her name on the coast, then surveyed (Land van de Leeuwin), the name Cape Leeuwin keeping the memory of the said vessel alive to the present day. Although very little is known about this voyage, it would seem that on this occasion were discovered[3] " Laegh ghelyck verdroncken landt" [low-lying land usually under water] on the west coast, and "Laegh duynich landt " [low-lying dunes more to the south-east.

Of very great importance for the knowledge possessed by the Netherlanders concerning the south coast of what is now known as Australia, must have been the exploratory voyage, made along this coast in January 1627 by the ship Het Gulden Zeepaard. As regards this expedition, too, we are without sufficient data. The Gulden Zeepaard, fitted out by the Middelburg Chamber, was commanded by Skipper Francois Thijszoon, and had also on board the member of the Council of India Pieter Nuyts. In June or July 1626, she found herself totally deserted by the other ships[4], with which she had sailed

[1] Abrolhos, a Portuguese word for cliffs, rocky projections rising from the sea. COLLINGRIDGE, p. 192, believes the word arencs, designating an island on the western-coast of the so-called Australian continent, found

on a chart of 1550 in the British Museum, to be a corruption of "Abrolhos, the name it has preserved to this day"!! Here also took also place the shipwreck of the vessel Batavia, commanded by Pelsart, from whom in the present century the Pelsart group got its name (MAJOR, Early Voyages, p. 178).--Slightly more to the south (29° 10') is a cliff, called Tortelduif (Turtle-dove), which already occurs in the chart of HESSEL GERRITSZ, of 1627. The name almost certainly owes its origin to the ship Tortelduif, which sailed from the Texel, Nov. 16, 1623, and arrived at Batavia, June 21, 1624---See HEERES, Dagregister Batavia, 1624-1629, p. 55. Cf. LEUPE, Zuidland, p. 48.]

[2) See HESSEL GERRITSZ'S chart (Remarkable Maps, 4).]

[3) Remarkable Maps, II, 4. In Hydrographie françoise par BELLIN, II, no. 91 (MDCCLVII) this is translated as follows: "Terres de Diuning(!!) qui sons très basses et noyées," and in this manner changed the wording of the description of the land in the name of the land. On the chart of HESSEL GERRITSZ there are also found more to the North the words "Duynich landt boven met boomen ende boscage." Accordingly, COLLINGRIDGE'S note on p. 287 which derives the legend on Goos'map "from some notes on a chart by Captain Volkersen of the Waeikende Boey, who was in those parts in 1658", seems not well-founded. It is no doubt a mutilated transcript of the wording of Hessel Gerritsz.--Curiously enough, Collingridge (pp. 184 f., 191) derives the name Cape Lioness or Leeuwin from "the peculiar shape of the Australian continent" or from this part of Australia having been the abode of lions!! And yet he pretends (p. 241) to have himself cleared up in his book "for the first time, as far as the English-speaking world is concerned," the doubt "on the authenticity of that part of the south-west coast of Australia" having been first discovered by the Dutch vessel Leeuwin!]

[1) I gather this from the ship's council's resolutions of one of these ships, viz. of the yacht Domburg, dated June 21, 1627 and following days.]

from the Netherlands. On April 10, 1627 she arrived at Batavia[1]. When now, we may ask, has the South coast been surveyed by this vessel? Nearly[2] all the charts--and these are our only sources to ascertain the date--give it as January 26, 1627. There is no reason to prevent us from taking for granted that on this day the ship Zeepaard was lying on the south coast of Australia. Nuyts gave his name to the whole region then surveyed (Nuytsland or land van P. Nuyts), which extended as far as Longitude 133° 30' East of Greenwich, where even in our days the islands of St. Pieter and St. Francois[3] preserve the memory of the termination of this voyage, which islands, it would seem, were then also looked upon as the eastern extremity of the Southland[4].

Finally, another portion of the western coast-line of Australia was discovered in the early part of 1628, by the ship Vianen[5], which, having on board Gerrit Frederikszoon De Witt as commander, left Java for the Netherlands on January 14 of the said year, and "owing to head-winds," ran so far to the south, that she "came upon the South-land beyond Java"[6]. The name G. F. De Witt's land still indicates the region, then surveyed: about 21° S.L., north of the Willems River[7].

Thus, in the course of about a decade--between 1616 and 1628--, the west coast of what is now known as Australia, from a point north of 21° S.L. to its southern extremity, and from there the south coast had been surveyed as far as about Latitude 133° 30' East of Greenwich. But no more than surveyed only: they were very far from being thoroughly known at the date at which we have arrived. Few, if any attempts were made to explore any part beyond the coast-line itself; at many points even the coast-line had not come in sight, so that there the problem remained unsolved, whether it was a mainland with an unbroken coast-line, or a number of islands, that one had to do with.

The discoveries made in the course of those years bore a more or less accidental character. True, both in the mother-country and in India the discovery of Eendrachtsland had drawn considerable attention, and the skippers, who, in consequence of the recently appointed route from the Cape to Java, before referred to, were likely to come in sight of the South-land, received positive instructions[8], to make an accurate surveying of the coast-line they should see, but none of the ships which had hitherto carried the Dutch flag from De Witt's land to the islands of St. Francois and St. Pieter, had done so in the course of voyages specially destined for the discovery and exploration of the South-land. Yet, this was not owing to any want of interest in such discoveries: witness the projects for exploratory voyages formed soon after the results of the Eendracht expedition had become known[9], and the realisation of two of these projects, which were destined to enlarge the amount of Dutch knowledge concerning New Guinea and the north coast of what is now called Australia. The expeditions referred

[1] HEERES, Dagregister, p. 307.]

[2] Swart's reproduction of the Bonaparte chart has February. There is no reason to uphold this testimony against the others. I place especial confidence in a chart of HESSEL GERRITSZ in the Huydecoper van Maarsseveen copy, which also has January 26, 1627. This is also the case, indeed, with the copy of Visscher's draught, in the British Museum. The instructions of Pool in 1636, also mention January (LEUPE, Zuidland, p. 69).]

[3] Can these islands have been thus named after the skipper and the member of the Council of India, on board the Zeepaard?]

[4) See the Instructions given to Pool (LEUPE, Zuidland, p. 69.--Cf. General Missive, of December 12, 1642, Appendix E.]

[5) Also called Viane or Viana.]

[6) General Missive of November 3, 1628.]

[7) The name De Witt's Land is already found on a map of Blaeu's in an atlas of 1640 (Remarkable Maps, II, No. 10 and Introduction). COOTE is mistaken where in the Introduction he says that this map also gives the results of the voyage of the Duifken in 1605-1606. These results are, indeed, given in the map II, No. 7; which, being a great exception, renders this map (by Janssonius) a highly remarkable one.--In e.g. Atlas van Zeevaert en Koophandel voorheen in de Fransche taele uytgegeven door LOUIS RENARD en nu door Reinier en Josua Ottens (Amsterdam, R. en J. Ottens, MDCCXLV), De Witt's Land is translated as Terre Blanche!! (Carte nouvelle de la mer du Sud).--In NORDENSKIÖLD'S Facsimile-atlas to the early history of cartography. Stockholm, MDCCCLXXXIX, there is reproduced (no. 61) a map, with the suscription "Chart on Mercator's projection: Navigatio ac Itinerarium Johannis Hugonis Linscotani. Hagae-Comitis 1599." Nordenskiöld has made a mistake in assigning this map to the year 1599. In this map occur the discoveries of Schouten and Lemaire (1616), Eendrachtsland (1616), the Trialls (1622), the discoveries of Carstensz (1623), De Wittsland (1628)!!--Cf. COLLINGRIDGE, Discovery, p. 221; S. RUGE, Das unbekannte Südland (Deutsche Geographische Blätter, XVIII, 1895, p. 324 f.).]

[8) See LEUPE, Zuidland, p. 37, Note 1).]

[9) What was done in this matter in the Netherlands and in India from 1618 to 1623, is related by LEUPE, Zuidland, pp. 36-43; and by L. C. D. VAN DIJK, Mededeelingen uit het Oost-Indisch Archief. Amsterdam, Scheltema, 1859, A, pp. 2-7.--As regards subsequent years, see, for example, Missive from the "Heeren XVII" to the G.-G. and Counc., December 18, 1628.--One of the inducements to renewed voyages was the narrative of the wreck, in June 1622, of the English ship Trial "on certain cliffs, lying in Latitude 20° 10' south, and in the longitude of the western extremity of Java." From this shipwreck the rocks in question were in the charts named the Trial's rocks. (Compare the chart of Hessel Gerritsz, Remarkable Maps, II, 7).]

to are those of Jan Carstensz (Carstenszoon) in 1623, and of Gerrit Thomaszoon Pool and Pieter Pieterszoon in 1636.

On the 21st of January 1623 Supercargo Jan Carstenszoon of Emden, by order of Herman Van Speult, governor of Amboyna, sailed from the Amboyna group, with the ships Arnhem, commanded by Dirk Meliszoon, and Pera, of which Jan Van Sluys was master, the head of the expedition being on board the latter vessel[1]. By way of Banda he reached the Key-, and afterwards the Aroe Islands, whence, after running on chiefly in a north-westerly direction, on February 9, he got sight of the south-coast of New Guinea, the ships then being in

XII

4° 17' S. Lat. They tried to survey the coast in an easterly direction, on which occasion two days later a number of Netherlanders were killed by natives in 4° 20' and about 136° Long. E. of Greenwich[2]. Among these was the skipper of the Arnhem, who was replaced by Willem Joosten Van Colster or Van Coolsteerdt. On the 15th they were in Latitude 137° East[3]. On the 16th, in about 137° 30'[3], in the morning, when they...were "about 1½ mile from the low-lying coast...they saw, by estimation about 10 miles land-inward, a number of very high mountains which in many places were white with snow (the 'Snow-mountain,' or 'Snow-mountains'), from which the rivers take their sources." They sailed, mainly in a south-easterly direction, chiefly along "overflown land," and a few days after also along "leech landt" [low-lying land], and cast anchor at various points on the coast. On the 7th of March they again came in hostile contact with the natives in the latitude of 7°; "to this place or the land where the aforesaid has taken place (which heretofore in the year 1606 the crew of the yacht Duyfken made out to be islands), we have in the new chart[4] given the name of Keerweer [Turn-again], forasmuch as from this point the land is trending south-west and west." It is therefore highly probable that they had got near what is now known as Princess Marianne Strait, which divides Prince Frederik Hendrik island from New Guinea, but, unlike Willem Janszoon in 1607, Carstenszoon mistook Prince Frederik Hendrik island for a part of New Guinea. Skirting "Modder groundt" [mud-ground], the south-western extremity of Prince Frederik Hendrik island was doubled (Valsche Caep or Cape Valsch, 8° 15'), but here also attempts to get more knowledge of the coast were frustrated by the hostile attitude taken up by the natives. In the evening of the 21st of March, after sailing in an easterly direction for some time, they cast anchor "near an island, lying upward of a mile South and North from the mainland; a quarter of a mile North by East and South by West of the island, there is still a rock on which there are two dry trees." They found the island to be in Latitude 8° 8' South, and bestowed on it the name of Vleer muysen eylandt [Bats' Island], "from the large numbers of bats, that people the trees," while the opposite coast of New Guinea was christened[5] Clapper-kust [Cocoa-tree coast]. On March 28, they anchored in about 9° 6'. The land here "lay E.N E.", or East and East by North. They found here "divers shoals and reefs lying dry," the land was "low-lying and muddy, overgrown with low coppice and wild trees." They resolved not to try to press on farther east: "the reports aforesaid concerning the shallow soundings to eastward" led the ships' commanders to conclude "that it was impossible to go on skirting the land [they had] for so long followed to eastward." They accordingly resolved "to try back by tacking the same way they had come"--they had meanwhile proceeded some distance up the shallows--and to continue their voyage in a southerly direction. This plan was carried into effect; they sailed past the narrows, now called Torres Strait, but which they mistook for a bay (Drooge bocht = dry bight), indenting the land; and accordingly fancied New Guinea to form a whole with the north-eastern peninsula of what is now known as Australia. Carstenszoon, indeed, specifically called the land hitherto skirted by the ships "the western extremity of Nova Guinea."

[1] As regards this voyage, see VAN DIJK, Mededeelingen, A, pp., 9-38, and B, pp. 1-60, where the journal etc. are printed; LEUPE, Nieuw-Guinea, pp. 8-10; LEUPE, Zuidland, pp. 44-46, and above all, the very remarkable chart, made on this occasion, entitled "Caerte van Arent Martenszoon de Leeuw, opperstierman, die deze Westcust beseijlt heeft" (Remarkable Maps, II, 6).]

[2] See VAN BEMMELEN, Isogonen, p. 23; near the Dootslagers-rivier (Man-queller's River) in De Leeuw's chart. That Thévenot (as, indeed, also other charts; see Remarkable Maps, II) has here "Dootslagers-rivier," once more proves that he did not consult the Bonaparte-chart, but had other data at his disposal. Lauts's contention (LEUPE, Nieuw-Guinea, p. 38), that this name should have been derived from Willem Janszoon (1606), will not hold water.]

[3] VAN BEMMELEN, l. c.]

[4] That they had with them a chart of an earlier voyage (the one undertaken by Willem Janszoon in 1606) is evident from several passages in the journal, and also from contemporary letters, inter alia, one from the governor of Banda to the G.-G., dated May 16, 1623.]

[5] Although this name does not occur in De Leeuw's chart (LEUPE, Nieuw-Guinea, p. 44), it was first conferred in the course of Carstensz's voyage.]

Having thus on April 4, "with exceeding difficulty and great peril, got clear of the shallows aforementioned," on the 8th in 10° 15' they again came upon dangerous shoals, where they clearly saw several stones lying at the bottom." They had then probably got near the present Cook's Reef. On the 12th, being in 11° 45', they sighted "at sunrise the land of Nova Guinea (being quite bare, without either mountains or hills)," and had therefore got in sight of the peninsula of York[1], which they coasted along in a southerly direction, now and then trying to come in contact with the natives, without, however, thereby obtaining any results worth mentioning. Thus proceeding, on the 24th of April they got into 17° 8', where they resolved "to go back[2] and sail due north along the coast of Nova Guinea as long as practicable, to touch at sundry points on the said coast, and to investigate the same as closely as possible." In the latitude just referred to, a river discovered there was named Staten rivier, after Their High Mightinesses the States-General of the United Netherlands, a name still in use in the charts of our time. On the return-voyage the Pera got separated from the Arnhem, and Carstensz's ship continued her voyage alone. On April 29, in 16° 10', she discovered and christened the Nassau river; on May 3, in 15° 20' or 15° 30', the "Water-plaets" (Mitchell River); on May 4, in slightly northward of 15° 12', the Vereenichde Rivier [United River]; on May 8, in 13° 7' the Coen River[3]. On the 9th of May, in 12° 33', they again found a "Waeterplaets" (i.e. a river); on the 11th, in 11° 48', the river (de) Carpentier (Batavia)[4]; on the 13th, in 11° 16', the river Van Speult[5]; on the 14th , in 10° 50', a third "waeterplaets," this time near "an exceeding beautiful soete rivier [fresh-water river]," where the land was found to be "high, covered with dunes and reefy near the shore" (the 'Hooge Landt[6], now Cape York); they were then in sight of the Prince of Wales isles. From there they bent their course in a westerly, later in a north-westerly direction, and on the 23rd of May reached the Aroe islands.

In default of a journal of her voyage, the adventures of the ship Arnhem, after her separation from the Pera, are not nearly so well known as those of her companion. Only a few scattered memoranda concerning them are available[7]. On June 5, 1623 the governor of Amboyna, Herman Van Speult, writes to Governor-General Pieter De Carpentier: "The ship Eenhoorn arrived here from Banda on the sixteenth of May. She reports that the Yacht Aernhem had arrived there without her rudder, having been in 17 degrees S. Lat...[8] It would seem that the Aernhem and the Pera have got separated from each other. We hope that erelong the Pera will also turn up ("opdonderen"), which in that case at the close of the monsoon we shall send to your place, that she may give Your Worship thorough information regarding all that has happened." Not a word, then, as to the ship Arnhem's doings after her parting company with the Pera. On June 17th this letter is continued as follows: "Commander Carstens arrived here with the Yacht Pera on the 8th; he is going to your place in the Eenhoorn, together with the first mate, in order to give a report of his experiences, so that I think it needless to expatiate further on this point." This, too, does not carry us any further. Nor can we derive any light from a missive from the governor of Banda to the Governor-General, dated May 16, 1623, which

[1] RAINAUD is in error, when he says (p. 361), that Carstensz "touchait (le 12 Avril 1623)...par 11° 45' sud a la Terre d'Arnhem qu'il considéra comme le prolongement des côtes de la Nouvelle-Guinée." His statement: "En 1626 des navigateurs néerlandais découvrirent les rives méridionales de ce grand golfe (de Carpentarie) encore inconnues " is also a mistake, I believe.]

[2] SWART, Journaal, p. 183, places a second "Keer or Keergewrogt" in 17° and odd minutes S. L. This is a strange blunder. He has utterly misunderstood the legend of the Bonaparte chart, and reads there: "Hier toe hebbe der somig ende Keergewrogt." This is sheer nonsense. The reading means: "Up to here (Staten river) the previous discoverers have been." (Compare LEUPE, Handschriften, p. 269, the manuscript map in the State Archives, no, 344 of Leupe's inventory, and DE HAAN'S manuscript Atlas).]

[3] Named, of course, after the Governor-General.]

[4] In the journal itself the river is called Carpentier, as is also the case, for example, in the Bonaparte chart. In most of the other charts, however, the river bears the name of Batavia (see Remarkable Maps). Thévenot also has Batavia, thus again differing from the Bonaparte chart, also on this point. It is certainly worth noting that in a "Sommarie Extract van t' Journael," drawn up by Carstenszoon himself, the name (de) Carpentier, which figured there, has been struck out. Valentijn's compilation chart, already discussed, has both names.]

[5] So called from the governor of Amboyna, Herman Van Speult, who had fitted out the expedition.]

[6] In the Instructions for Tasman, January 29, 1644, there is question of the "Hoge eijlant-"]

[7] I have gone into greater detail concerning this voyage than as regards the other, because, strange to say, neither Van Dijk nor Leupe seem to have properly investigated this matter, about which they were in doubt and uncertainty, and which would therefore have required more light to be thrown upon it. TIELE-VIVIEN DE SAINT MARTIN. p. 190, is not quite correct as regards this matter.]

[8] Here follows a succinct account of what had happened on the voyage before the separation of the two ships, an account that it is not necessary to reproduce.]

states that the Arnhem was picked up rudderless, and gives certain particulars, without telling anything about what had happened after the separation of the two vessels. The Governor-General and Councillors in their General Missive of January 3, 1624, reported to the Directors on this matter, and here, too, we again learn that the ships had got as far as 17° 18' S. Lat., but absolutely nothing concerning what had happened either to the Pera or to the Arnhem, subsequent to their parting company in this latitude. They refer their correspondents to the "journal and abstract," which accompanied the missive. A few years later, however, a desire for further particulars was felt: it was in 1636, when a fresh expedition to those regions (the one commanded by Pool and Pieterszoon, of which more anon) was being arranged for. In the remarkable instructions for this voyage, issued by the G.-G. and Counc. on February 19, 1636, we read as follows: "In case no further information should be obtained (from the governor of Banda), it is our desire that you shall as speedily as possible navigate from Banda for Arnhems- and Speultsland, lying between 9 and thirteen degrees Southern Latitude[1], discovered A. D. 1623, as you will more particularly gather from the accompanying chart. These are vast lands...Sailing from the islands aforementioned[2], you will cross to eastward, in order to make the land of Nova Guinea, also[3] discovered A. D. 1623 by the yachts Pera and Arnhem as far as 17 degrees 8 minutes Southern Latitude; which we hold to be the South-land, extending to westward from the said latitude as far as 26 degrees or as far as the land of the Eendracht...From the farthest point discovered, being, as beforementioned, in 17 degrees 8 minutes Southern Latitude, you will follow the coastline down to Houtmans Abrolhos in 28 and 29 degrees [or down to] 33 and 34 degrees..." What can be meant by "the accompanying chart"? we naturally ask. An answer to this question is furnished by a missive from Anthonio Van Diemen to Pool, dated February 19, 1636, in which the latter is appointed leader of the expedition. We read there: "[We] herewith send [you] a chart of the lands A.D. 1623 surveyed by the yachts Pera and Arnhem; item a small chart of the South-land, coasted along by divers ships coming from the Netherlands, which charts may be of use to you." The words "the accompanying chart" cannot refer to the "small chart of the South-land," because this small chart contained that part only of the South-land which had been "coasted along by divers ships coming from the Netherlands," a description which cannot therefore refer to regions between 9° and 13° S. Lat. The "accompanying chart" can therefore only be the "chart of the lands A.D. 1623 surveyed by the yachts Pera and Arnhem". That chart accordingly showed. "Arnhems- and Speultsland, lying between 9 and 13 degrees Southern Latitude." The Pera did not discover the lands (islands)46], as is evident from her journal; they must accordingly have been discovered by the Arnhem. This tallies exactly with what we find stated in Tasman's instructions for the expedition of 1644, viz. that "on account of untimely separation (from the Pera], the ship Arnhem, after discovering the large islands of Aernhem and Speult, returned to Amboyna without any result worth mentioning"[5]. Here, too, we find the discovery of Arnhems- and Speults-lands (islands), attributed to the ship Arnhem.

Where, we may ask, are these lands (islands) to be sought? Between 9° and 13° S. Lat., say Pool's instructions. If we knew nothing beyond this, we might ask, whether, in the said latitude, they are situated on the east- or on the west-coast of the present gulf of Carpentaria[6]. But the description

[1] This latitude utterly disagrees with that of Prince Frederik Hendrik Island, on the south-coast of New Guinea, with which island VAN DIJK (Mededeelingen, p. 26) wants to identify Arnhems- and Speults-land.--We may pass over in silence what COLLINGRIDGE (pp. 268 f.) says about Speriet and Arnim. His conjecture Speult = Spu St. = Spiritu Santo is very ingenious, but devoid of foundation.]

[2] This may refer either to Arnhems- and Speults-lands, which are also called islands (see infra); or to the "lands and islands lying east of Banda," of which there is question in a paragraph of the instructions preceding the passage quoted in the text; or to both.]

[3] The italics are my own.]

[4] See Note 2 supra.]

[5] VAN DIJK, Mededeelingen, A, p. 25 has misunderstood the wording of the Instructions.]

[6] G. LAUTS, Geschiedenis van de vestiging, uitbreiding, bloei en verval van de magt der Nederlanders in Indië. Groningen, Van Boekeren, 1852, I, p. 167, says that Carstenszoon "has given its present name to the Gulf of Carpentaria." As is so often the case, Lauts here too gives no authority for his surmise. VAN DIJK. p. 23, has already pointed out its improbability, but it is still maintained, e.g. by BIRDWOOD, Report India Office, p. 188, where are found more mistakes. He erroneously places the discovery of Carpentaria in 1628, as does JAMES COOK in his chart of the Southern Hemisphere (A voyage towards the South Pole and round the world, I, London, Strahan and Cadell, 1777), which chart has other mistakes besides. When Carstenszoon set out on his expedition, it was not De Carpentier, but Coen who was Governor-General (Coen resigned February 1, 1623). He had therefore little reason to christen the coast after De Carpentier. It is not unlikely that the name of Carpentaria, which occurs in very early charts (inter alia in the Nolpe-Dozy chart of 1652/3, and in Thévenot's chart, but not in Swart's reproduction of the Bonaparte one), was given to the coast at a somewhat later period, when, regard being had to the dates of the DISCOVERIES only, which took place within De Carpentier's term of office, it was deemed fitting to make the latter dignitary stand sponsor. Most probably the gulf was afterwards named after the east-coast. RAINAUD, p. 361, is not quite clear, when he says: "Quant au nom de golfe de Carpentarie, il n'apparut que plus tard, sur les cartes du deuxième voyage de Tasman." What maps does he mean here?--Of course I can not dwell upon the mistakes and blunders of THÉVENOT (I, Avis)

and others, where, for example, they consider De Carpentier and Van Diemen, not as the promoters of voyages of discovery, but as the discoverers themselves.]

"large lands or islands" can hardly refer to the east-coast. It should further be considered that during the days following the separation of the Arnhem from the Pera, the wind was constantly in the east, so that it is quite possible that the Arnhem was driven to the west-coast of the gulf[1]. These various circumstances would in themselves lead us to surmise that the said lands or islands must be sought in the west part of the gulf, and this supposition is materially strengthened by a remark which the G.-G. and Counc. were led to make by the results of the 1636 expedition under Pool and Pieterszoon. In their General Missive of December 28, 1636, they say that Pieterszoon and those with him "(had) in 11 degrees Southern Latitude discovered great lands, to which they had given the names of Van Diemens- and Marias land, but which we (scil. Governor-General and Councillors) conjecture to be Arnhems- or Speults-islands[2], although the lie of the latter is different. The Council of these Yachts, finding it impossible to proceed eastward, after discovering Arnhems land 20 miles to westward, resolved to take their course to the north again, past the islands of Timor(laut) and Tenimber, and to return to Banda." We know, as will appear by-and-by, that the land discovered by Pieterszoon, and referred to in the General Missive, just quoted from (Van Diemen's- and Maria's land), is situated pretty well due south of Trangan, the southernmost of the Aroe isles, i.e. in about Lat. 134° East of Greenwich. It was conjectured[3], that this land might be the "Arnhems or Speults islands," in other words, Pieterszoon and those with him had not positively identified it with these islands in any of their charts, but they had been sailing in a westerly direction, when they fancied to have discovered Arnhems land: in their estimation, therefore, Arnhems land lay east of Van Diemen's and Maria's land, and this exactly agrees with the place invariably assigned to Arnhems land in the charts both of Tasman's time and our own[4]. Its shape also accounts for the circumstance that it was by turns looked upon as an island and as a land. Any doubt as to this name having been justly given to it, is therefore groundless[5]: the ship Arnhem must needs have been the discoverer of the land called after her.

Where, however, are we to locate Van Speultsland? There are few, if any direct data to answer this question[6]. The following facts should, however, be duly noted. The G.-G. and Counc. state that Pieterszoon "had discovered Arnhems (not Van Speult's) land 20 miles to westward "[7], and that he had then resolved to continue his voyage in a northerly direction in order to reach the Tenimber or Timor Laut islands. Now, if Van Speult's land had been situated west of Arnhems-land, there are two a priori possibilities: either the G.G. and Counc. would have mentioned the discovery of Van Speult's (not Anthems) land, so many miles to westward--which they did not do in their missive; or Van Speult's land lay so far to westward that Pieterszoon did not reach it. But we may take for granted, that, when he resolved to sail in a northerly direction, he had reached the present Van Diemen Cape in Melville Island. Therefore there is no room for Van Speult's land west of Arnhems-land: it must accordingly be sought east of it. Could it be the island in the gulf of Carpentaria still in our time[8] known as "Groote Eylandt?"

[1] This has already been observed by LEUPE, Zuidland, p. 45. See Carstenszoon's journal on April 8, and subsequent days.]

[2] "The newly found Van Diemen's land, also called Arnhems- or Speults land" (Daily Register, Batavia, October 6, 1636).]

[3] The italics are mine.]

[4] For example, in the Bonaparte chart, and in the Nolpe-Dozy one.]

[5] VAN DIJK, p. 24, is in doubt; LEUPE, Zuidland, pp. 45 f., admits the possibility, but makes no attempt at proving it.]

[6] I must, however, remind the reader that the Batavia Daily Register speaks of Arnhems- or Speultsland.--I do not understand whence Valentijn in his "chart of the south-eastern Banda isles" has taken the name "Riv. van Speult," east of Aernhems land.]

[7] "About 20 miles' distance from east to west" (Batavia Daily Register, October 6, 1636).]

[8] In Stieler's Atlas. In M. J. C. MEIKLEJOHN, Australasia (London, Holden, 1897) p. 71, the discovery of the "Groote Eylandt" is attributed to the Duyfken in 1606. There are more mistakes is this little book, which I mention here, only because it is one of the most recent books about Australia]

Turning to Pool's expedition, we find that Gerrit Thomaszoon Pool, on April 17, 1636, sailed from Banda with the ships Cleen Amsterdam and Cleen Wesel for the Goram group, whence, running on in a mainly eastern direction, on April 24 he struck the west-coast of New Guinea in 3° 32' S. Lat.[1] (Cape Baaik?). This coast is by him called "De lange hooge berch "[2]. They now went south, and "about two o'clock in the afternoon passed the eijlanden Amsterdam" (Sangala, Katoemin and Woelan?), next Kaap Amsterdam (Van den Bosch

Cape?), and on the 25th reached Poeloe Adi, by them called Wesels eylant." They anchored between this island and another, more to the south, which they christened "'t Vogelseijlant" [Bird Island]. After doubling the eastern extremity of Weselseiland, they held a northward course "in order to make the mainland coast again." They had in sight the Kamrau Bay, one of the eastern extremities of which they named "de N.O. hoecq"[3, and from there ran on along the coast [Steile hoek (Cape Boeroe), Goenong Api (Mount Lakahia), Vlakke hoek (Cape Debelle)]. On April 28, they saw a river "slightly east of the Vlacke hoeck; having got about half a mile further east they again saw a river," near which they dropt anchor. Here (Moordenaers revier), Pool with certain men of his crew were murdered by the natives[4]. He was succeeded in the command by Pieter Pieterszoon, who, always skirting the coast, on the 6th of May estimated himself to be in 5° 52', whence they held their course to the Aroe and Key Islands.

Near these island-groups Pieterszoon remained until June 9, on which day the ships "set sail from before Taranga (Trangan)", and continued their way in a mainly southerly direction. On the 13th at noon they were 10° 50'[5]. Here the journal goes on to say: "At four glasses after noon we saw land South-east by South...At about 6 miles' distance from there to westward we also saw land, not connected with the other land, but upwards of 3 miles distant from it..." On the 141h they skirted the coast in a southerly and South-by-East direction, but "finding they could not make the eastern land, ran on the westernmost land." In the night they were in 11° 8' S. Lat.[6]. They now coasted the land in a mainly westerly direction, until on the 21st they resolved to turn to the north, hoping to "make" Timor Laut[7]. The land, they had been surveying from the 13th to the 21st of June, the commanders named Vain Diemens (ende Marias)[8] lant. Most probably, Pieterszoon skirted the coast in a westerly direction as far as Cape Van Diemen, the north-eastern extremity of Melville Island, without perceiving that it was an island that he had here to do with, since he mistook the Dundas Strait of modern charts for a "bight or inlet"[9].

Recapitulating the results of the intentional or accidental exploratory expeditions of the Netherlanders down to Tasman's time[10], and adding to these the scanty items of information they had derived

[1] As regards this voyage, see VAN DIJK, 1. c., pp. 27-36; LEUPE, Nieuw Guinea, pp. 11-38; Id., Zuidland, pp. 67-82.--Besides these, I have of course also consulted the journal kept on this expedition. I have taken the latitudes from the latter, although, in this case too, they would now and then seem to be erroneous. Cf. also LEUPE, Nieuw-Guinea, p. 37.]

[2) Can this name have got corrupted to "large hoeck" (lang hoog) in Swart's reproduction of the Bonaparte chart?]

[3) I believe, that ROBIDÉ VAN DER AA, Reizen Nieuw-Guinea, p. 435 puts the N. 0. hoek too far towards the east. Can Aernorshoeck in Swart's reproduction of the Bonaparte chart be a corruption of this appellation? I am at a. loss to account for the name "Aernors." Or can it be a corruption of Aememshoeck?]

[4) "This disaster, we observe (in a missive dated December 24, 1636, to the governor of Banda, the writers say "we learn"), occurred in the same place and near the same river, where A. D. 1623 Commander Jan Carstensz. lost nine men who were grievously murdered when out fishing." Thus the G.-G. and Counc. in their General Missive of December, 28, 1636. This view is shared by ROBIDÉ VAN DER AA (Nieuw-Guinea, pp. 425 f.), and by LEUPE, Nieuw-Guinea, p. 38. VAN DIJK, Mededeelingen, in his map puts the scene of the 1623 slaughter more to westward. So does the manuscript chart of 1669 in the Hague State Archives, made by the Company's cartographer (No. 344 of LEUPE'S Inventory), which chart carefully distinguishes between the Dootslagers rivier (1623) and the Moordenaars rivier (1636). Near the latter (as does the manuscript atlas of De Haan of 1760) it places the Poolshoek, of which Polleshoeck or Pelleshoeck in Swart's reproduction of the Bonaparte chart is most probably a corruption. (At one time I fancied this might be a mutilation of Melishoeck).]

[5) I repeat that the latitudes in this journal are apt to be incorrect.]

[6) Not 12° 8', as LEUPE, Zuidland, p. 77, has it.]

[7) In this group, on July 1, he gave its name to the Oester-rivier, which is found in Swart's reproduction of the Bonaparte chart.]

[8) General Missive of December 28, 1636. Maria's land was most probably named after Van Diemen's wife Maria Van Aelst.]

[9) In close accordance with this are the place occupied by Van Diemensland in the Bonaparte chart, and the entire shape there given to this part of Northern Australia.]

[10) I would remind the reader that the treatment of all the items dealt with in this chapter is based on the study of authentic documents. Some time hence I hope to bring out with the publishers of the present work an English translation of the documents themselves, from which I drew in preparing this chapter; i.e. the documents on which rests our knowledge of the Dutch pre-Tasmanian discoveries of Australia and New-Guinea. To these I shall add the archivalia respecting the Dutch post-Tasmanian discoveries in those regions down to the extinction of the Dutch East India Company.]

from the investigations of other European nations, we arrive at the following amount of knowledge concerning the so-called Southland, then at the disposal of the Dutch navigators. They had surveyed various islands north-west of the Solomon islands[1], but had no certitude concerning the east-coast of New Guinea[2]; they were inclined to consider New Ireland (New-Mecklenburg) and New Hannover as parts of the north-coast of New Guinea; Geelvink Bay had not been surveyed, since they had remained north of Schoutens Island; Dampier Strait had been entered. North of New-Guinea therefore the ground had been pretty well, though not accurately reconnoitred. Some uncertainty prevailed respecting the farthest (north) west-coast of the said island and its position with regard to the islands to westward.[3] On the other hand, the coast had been skirted starting from the south-western extremity. Strange to say, Torres Strait was mistaken for an inlet instead of a strait, and this down to 1642, although the Spaniards had duly recognised it as such in 1606[4]. For the rest the peninsula of York (Carpentaria) had been coasted along as far as 17°. Here fresh uncertainty began, which was again replaced by a certain measure of knowledge regarding (perhaps the Groote Eylandt, but certainly) Arnhemsland, and the coast then following down to Cape Van Diemen in Melville Island, which was not looked upon as an island, because Dundas Strait was mistaken for an inlet. Utter ignorance again prevailed concerning the coast from there as far as 21°. Starting from this latitude, however, the Dutch had surveyed the whole West and South coast of Australia as far as the islands of Saint Francois and Saint Peter. But there is a wide difference between having surveyed a coast and being thoroughly acquainted with it: great uncertainty still prevailed respecting the real nature of the coast-line. No answer could as yet be given to the question, whether the coast-line was an uninterrupted one, or perhaps here and there broken into by straits; in other words, whether that part of the South-land which had been discovered up to now, was one vast mainland or an archipelago.

XIII

FRANS JACOBSZOON VISSCHER.--EXPLORATORY VOYAGES OF 1642 AND 1644.

After the specification given in our last chapter, of what was in 1642 known to the Netherlanders concerning the South-land[5], the aim of the voyage of 1642/3 will be readily understood. The Directors of the East India Company and the Supreme Government at Batavia were--at all events at the period

[1] Their notion of the site of the Solomon Islands was not very precise, as appears from the journal of Tasman's voyage of 1642/3 on February 8 and 14, 1643. Tasman had Portuguese chart(s) with him. Journal, February 14.]

[2] Tasman's journal, February 8, 1643.]

[3] Compare the instructions for Tasman, August 13, 1642.]

[4] It is well-known, that the details, at least, of De Torres's discovery continued unknown until 1762, when his report was found in the archives of Manila (RAINAUD, p. 329, note 4; TIELE, Europëers, VII, p. 52, note 1).--But compare also E. T. HAMY in his paper entitled Commentaires sur quelques cartes anciennes de la Nouvelle Guinée (Extrait du Bulletin de la Société de Géographie de Paris, 1877, p. 30, note 1).--However, in some maps of the first half of the 18th century the strait is drawn, e.g. in Carte Nouvelle de la mer du sud in RENARD-OTTENS' atlas of 1745. But this map is far from accurate.--In the latter part of the XVII century, however, the possibility of New Guinea and "the other Southland" being separated by a strait, was admitted by the Dutch (WITSEN, Tartarije, I, pp. 164-167; LEUPE, Nieuw-Guinea, p. 86).]

[5] The following charge brought by COLLINGRIDGE, Discovery, p. 219, I cannot, of course, let pass unchallenged: "It is a known fact that the Dutch appropriated to themselves Portuguese and Spanish documents and charts, which, when altered to serve their purpose, made them appear to be the actual discoverers, whereas, in reality, the countries described in such documents and charts had at the time never been visited by them." This charge is utterly baseless, and has not a leg to stand upon, nor is it by any means "a curious fact that in all the works--and they are legion--in which the history of early Australian maritime discovery has been treated, these

frauds have never been noticed." It was quite impossiblc that these "frauds" should have been "noticed", because they never existed. What Netherlander, for example, has ever seriously applied to Dutch discoveries the paragraph from Wytfliet, which Collingridge reproduces on pp. 219 f? Nor can we admit as evidence what Collingridge himself says about Terra del Zur (pp. 275 f.). The Netherlanders simply put into their maps this foreign name for South-land, just as they did with the appellation "Mar di India". Nor have they ever laid claim to the discovery of the South-land which did not exist. When they discovered what is now known as Australia, they thought this to be the supposed South-land (Terra del Zur); and therefore they transferred this name to what in their charts was afterwards to bear the name of Nieuw Holland (New Holland) (Cf. Swart's reproduction of the Bonaparte chart; Remarkable Maps, III, 1, 5, etc.).--Or are we to accept as a proof what Collingridge says on p. 299. "The great bay in question is Van Diemen's Gulf, which retained on old Dutch charts the term Baya (Bahia), given to it, no doubt, by the Portuguese who must have been there before"? The name is sometimes given as "Baya van Diemen" (e.g. Remarkable Maps, III, 1), but also, and this is the original Dutch form, "Van Diemen's BAY" (Swart's reproduction of the Bonaparte chart; Remarkable Maps, III, 4, 6, 7); and the translation of this name into a foreign language is merely a would-be ornamentation.--If, on p. 304 of his book, Collingridge refers to the Abrolhos question as "an example of the marvellous sagacity of the Hollanders for netherlandising expressions that otherwise would not be Dutch to any one," he clearly proves that the history of this name is utterly unknown to him. In this way we might multiply instances, but we forbear.]

under review[1]--surprisingly unanimous in desiring to extend and deepen the knowledge which, in the thirty years that had elapsed since 1606, the Dutch had obtained on the point referred to. Of their zeal on this point their letters[2] furnish the most undeniable evidence. Of course, the general objects for which voyages of discovery were undertaken, were first and foremost the extension of the Company's field for mercantile operations, and the enlargement of her commercial profits, and next to these, "the best way of using the sea and of finding out the winds that would enable ships to navigate it all the year round"[3]. But also the extension of the Dutch power, of Dutch supremacy in the East[4], was earnestly kept in view, especially by the far-seeing Van Diemen, whose commercial talents did not prevent him from being a statesman at the same time[5]. Nor can any doubt be entertained, that the thirst for knowledge of what had hitherto been a profound secret, was a powerful incentive actuating him and his coadjutors, when we see how eager were men like Tasman and Visscher for being entrusted with the task of making new discoveries.

The good intentions entertained in high quarters had, however, up to now hung fire, chiefly in consequence of the want of vessels. As late as December 12, 1641, the Governor-General and Councillors wrote as follows to the Directors: "We feel earnestly inclined to the discovery of the South-land. The flute-ship, Zeehaen was told off for this service, but the unexampled delay in the arrival of the ships from Persia and Surat has compelled us to employ the said Zeehaen for the latest voyage to Taijouan and Japan. In consequence of which we have been forced, sorely against his wish and our own, to detain in this road-stead for the space of 9 months, the celebrated Frans Visscher (whom we intend to employ in the discovery of the South-lands). We trust, however, that the thing will be effected in good time." The answer from the Netherlands, dated September 25, 1642 ran as follows: "We trust that the intended further discovery of the South-land, which we have urged in divers letters, has by this time been carried into effect, in consequence of the opportune arrival of fitting vessels for the purpose; but if this should not be the case, we hereby once more recommend the project to your serious attention; seeing that many are of opinion that great profits for the Company might accrue thereby, as perhaps time will show."

When this answer was being indited in the Netherlands, the expedition of 1642 had already left the port of Batavia. As we have already seen, the obstacle which had so long delayed the matter, had for a time at least been removed, and the Governor-General and Councillors were now in a position "to set apart and fit out two strong and able vessels, now at hand"[6], for the end proposed. This object is now briefly and clearly defined as follows[6]: "In the first place to navigate from here to the island of Mauritius, and thence to shape their course for the south about the middle of October, as far as 52 or at most 54 degrees Latitude South, in order to discover on an eastward course such lands as they shall come upon in this latitude or previously...without running farther southward than the 54th degree, even in case they should not meet with any land there; then to sail as far as the longitude of Nova Guinea and the Salomonis islands[7] or slightly more to eastward; in order to ascertain whether between

[1] The Directors, it is true, very soon after began to flag in their zeal (Cf. my Bouwstoffen, III,. pp. LXXVII-LXXXVI), although more liberal notions once more prevailed in later days.]

[2] General Missives of December 28, 1636; December 9, 1637; Dec. 22, 1638; Dec. 18, 1639; Nov. 30, 1640; Letters from the Directors to the Gov.-Gen. and Counc., Sept. 16, 1638 and April 11, 1642; Letter from the outgoing Gov.-Gen. H. Brouwer to his successor Van Diemen, of March 31, 1636.]

[3) General Missive, Dec. 27, 1634-January 8, 1635.]

[4) Cf. the opening sentences of the Instructions of January 29, 1644 for Tasman's second voyage for the discovery of the South-land.]

[5) Cf. my Bouwstoffen, l.c.]

[6) Resolution of the G.-G. and C., dated August 1, 1642.]

[7) Rainaud, p. 365, erroneously states that Tasman's instructions enjoined him "de revenir a Batavia par les Iles de Hoorn, de Schouten et de Le Maire, ou l'on croyait retrouver les Salomon d'Alvaro de Mendaña." Nor can I agree with the words I have italicised in the following extract from S. RUGE'S paper "Des unbekannte Südland" (Deutsche Geographische Blätter, XVIII, 1895, p. 331): "Da die Salomonsinseln und das Heiligegeistland des Quiros auch sum Südland gehörten, so musste Tasman auf alle Falle bis zum Meridian der Salomonsinseln vorgehen."]

those lands, the land of d'Eendracht [by which is meant[1] the whole of the west- and south-coast of the present Australia, then known to the Netherlanders], and the unknown South-land, there is any passage into, the great South Sea or Pacific; next[2], after making investigations east and north of the Salomonis islands and Nova Guinea, to steer for the South--'to Cape Keer-weer'[3]--through the narrows near Gilolo, in order to find out whether the discovered west-coast of Nova Guinea[4] is connected with the land of d'Eendracht, or separated from the same by channels and passages; after this to sail along the whole of this unknown north-coast as far as the 21st degree near Willems river, in order from there to return hither through the strait of Sunda with the Eastern monsoon in the month of June or July of the year following"[5]. The hoped-for "passage into the great South Sea", would, if found, "of which there can be hardly any doubt," furnish a "short and convenient route to Chily." Now this last "would be a matter of the utmost importance and of great advantage to the Company." For in that case it would become possible "to form trade connections with the vast and renowned country of Chily," and "for the Company to enter upon important dealings with the Chilese, and by means of this route to snatch rich booty from the Castilian, who would never dream of our ships coming that way"[6]. What consciousness of strength there must have been in the minds of the directors in India of the Company's affairs, if, in preparing an expedition like this, they at the very same moment were contemplating the extension to South-America of their operations of trade and war alike! Nor was it a mere project they were revolving in their minds. "Meanwhile," they further wrote to the Managers, their masters, in their letter of December 12,

1642, "in case of success, we shall use every opportunity to utilise the route thus discovered for sending a cargo thither by way of trial."

The ships set apart for the expedition were the yacht Heemskerk--the flag-ship--and the flute[7] Zeehaen[8]. The former, a "small war-yacht"[9], had sailed from the Netherlands for India for the first time in 1638, and was of 60 tons or lasts' burden, the latter had first been put in commission in 1640[10] and measured 100 lasts[11]. The Heemskerk was manned with 60, the Zeehaen with 50, "of the ablest-bodied sea-faring men" that were to be found at Batavia. The ships were victualled for the space of from 12 to 18 months, and further provided with "divers commodities and minerals," for which it was hoped to find a market in the countries to be discovered[12].

The, command of the undertaking was entrusted to Tasman, as "skipper-commander"[13]. The master of the Heemskerk was Skipper Yde T'Jercxzoon Holman or Holleman. This navigator, a native of Jever, in what is now known as the Grand-Duchy of Oldenburg[14], had come out to India in 1640

[1] This is evident from the instructions.]

[2] This part of the instructions was not executed by Tasman. For this reason the expedition of 1644 was undertaken.]

[3] Instructions.--These instructions are of course mistaken in laying down Cape Keerweer in 18° S. L. "Cape Keerweer" here can only be meant for what is now known as Cape Turnagain, the Cape Keerweer of the ship Duifken in 1606, in about 13° 45'. This is abundantly proved by comparing with these instructions, those drawn up for Tasman's second voyage, dated January 29, 1644.]

[4] i.e. the east-coast of the Gulf of Carpentaria.]

[5] The object of the expedition is of course more fully set forth in the Instructions of August 13, 3642 (Appendix E.). This object is also described in the General-Missive of December 12, 1642, of which an extract is given Appendix F. It appears to me that the said object is. in the briefest and clearest way stated in the Resolution of the G.-G. and C. of Aug. 1, 1642, which resolution I have made use of in the text.]

[6] The Gov.-Gen. and Councillors, however, felt that there was a technical difficulty. They were not quite sure that Chili did not come under the charter of the Dutch West India Company, and if it did, they would not be free to trade with that country. Nor was this difficulty removed by the Managers in their letter of August 31, 1643. Cf. also A. TELTING. De Nederlanders in Chili, 1643 (Indische Gids, i893, pp. 2013 ff-).]

[7] Flutes are long, narrow ships, "quick sailers, of comparatively small draught with a good deal of ship-room" (Cf. FRUIN, Tien jaren, 4th Edition, p. 203).]

[8) This name has got corrupted to Zeachan or Zeachen, and has given rise to all sorts of mistakes, into which it is impossible to enter here. Cf. inter alia RAINAUD, pp. 358 f.]

[9) Resolution of the "Heeren XVII," August-September, 1638.]

[10) According to the "Register of out-going Ships" (Uitloop Boekie).]

[11) Resolution of the "Heeren XVII," September 6, 1640.]

[12) I transcribe from the General Daybook of Batavia the highly curious inventory of these articles, never before printed (Appendix G.]

[13) Here, too, "Commander" is not indicative of a definite grade, but merely denotes the head of the whole expedition, as against the two skippers, each of whom only had command of his particular vessel.]

[14) This would seem definitely to dispose of the hesitating conjecture brought forward as to a possible relationship between this skipper and Tasman's wife (Dozy, in Bijdragen taal-, land- en volkenkunde, XXXVI, p. 323).]

as a second mate, and must soon after have been promoted to the rank of skipper, since as early as August 8, 1642, his pay in this grade was, by resolution of the Governor-General and Councillors, raised "in consideration of his ability and good services rendered." The instructions accordingly appointed him Tasman's successor in office, in case the latter should unfortunately come to die in the course of the voyage. His colleague on board the Zeehaen, Gerrit Janszoon, likewise an "experienced sailor"[1], was a native of Leiden [2]. He died in the course of this expedition, on the 6th of June, 1643[3]. As "supercargo" in the Zeehaen we find Isaack Gilsemans. He was most probably[4] the "draughtsman" mentioned in the Instructions, who had been directed to join the expedition in order to "make exact drawings of the appearance and shape of the lands, islands, capes, bights, inlets, bays, rivers, shoals, sand-banks, reefs, cliffs and rocks, etc.," which they should fall in with. Gilsemans was a native of Rotterdam, and shortly before, May 17, 1642, had risen from "subcargo" to the rank of "supercargo"[5], having come out to India "as corporal" in 1634. "Subcargo" on board the Heemskerck was Abraham Coomans[6]. These persons together with the first mates constituted the Plenary Council[7] (Breede Raad) of the expedition, Tasman being "permanent president," and Coomans, secretary. First mate on board the Zeehaen was Hendrik Pietersen[8], while in the Heemskerk this place was held by the "pilot-major" or "steersman-major" Frans Jacobszoon Visscher.

This highly remarkable man certainly deserves to be briefly noticed here. He was born at Flushing[9], and for many years in succession rendered important services to the East India Company, whose archives contain references to him as early as 1632.

Already in 1623 he had sailed for India as a steersman in one of the ships forming part of a flotilla that set out for the Indies from the Netherlands under the command of Jacques L'Hermite and Gheen Huygen Schapenham[10]. In 1632, "one Francoys Jacopsen, steersman" is found in Cambodja. He had "arrived there with certain Japanese junks, belonging to the lord of Firando," and utilises this opportunity for transmitting to the Governor-General information concerning the situation in Cambodja, by means of a couple of Cambodja ships bound for Batavia[11]. At that time, then, Visscher was already in full action. He had already seen Japan, when as a steersman he was staying in Cambodja[12]. In the following year, 1633, we find Visscher in Tonquin, again on board of a Japanese vessel: here, too, he seems to have looked about him to some purpose, for we find him sending a report of his observations to the Dutch authorities in Japan[13]. In those days he seems either to have temporarily left the company's service, or at all events to have had a furlough, for we find him designated also as a "free or uncovenanted steersman." About the middle of 1634 he is found staying at Nangasaki, having just returned from Tonquin, and the representatives of the Company at Firando take immediate

[1) Res. of the G.-G. and C., Aug. 1, 1642.]

[2) See Appendix G. I have not met with any particulars of his official career in the service of the E. I. C.]

[3) According to the steersman's journal in the Sweers collection.]

[4) Cf. Res. of the G.-G. and C., Aug. 1, 1642, and the Journal, Sept. 25, 1642.]

[5) Res. G.-G. and C., May 17, 1642.]

[6) I have found no particulars concerning him.]

[7) The "Breede Raad" was the Council of the two ships, as distinguished from the Ship's Council on board each of the vessels separately. Besides those mentioned in the text as members of the Plenary Council, the following names of persons belonging to the crews have been handed down to us. On boord the Heemskerk: the (under-)steersmen Crijn Hendrikszoon de Ratte or de Radde, born at Middelburg, and Carsten Jurriaenszoon; the master-gunner Eldert Luytiens, who died November 1; the master-carpenter Pieter Jacobszoon, and the carpenter Jan Joppen, the steward's mate Jan Pieterszoon van Meldorp, who died June 5; the sailor Joris Claesen van Bahuys. On board the Zeehaen: the (under-)steersmen Pieter Nanninghszoon Duijts and Cornelis Ijsbrantszoon Roobol; the quartermaster Cornelis Joppen, and the sailors Pieter Pieterszoon van Kopenhage, who died January 18, Jan Tijssen, Tobias Pieterszoon, of

Delft, and Jan Isbrandtszoon [The last three were murdered near New-Zealand, December 19 (Steersman's Journal--Sweers Collection)]; and the skipper's boy Gerrit Gerritszoon. The surgeon or barber Hendrik Haalbos was probably on board the Heemskerk.]

[8) In the Instructions his christian name only is given. See, however, the Journal under Oct. 4; 1642. I have met with no particulars concerning him.]

[9) See the Res. of the G.-G. and C. of January 12, 1641 apud LEUPE, Abel Jansz. Tasman en Franchoys Jacobsz Visscher (Bijdragen taal-, land- en volkenkunde Neêrlandsch Indië, IV, p. 134).]

[10) LEUPE in Bijdragen Geschiedenis en Oudheidkunde, New Series, VII, p. 290.]

[11) Daily Register of Batavia, April 14, 1632.]

[12) In the Daily Register of Firando, October 1, 1634, for example, he is mentioned as "having full knowledge of the bay and islands about Nan-gasaki."]

[13) Daily Register kept at the office of the factory of Firando, September 13, 1633; August 8, 1634.]

steps to secure his services- Up to that time the Netherlanders had not succeeded in obtaining sufficient information concerning the coast-lines of the Japanese islands, and of course it was to them a matter of the highest importance to possess accurate and reliable data respecting coasts, which their ships had to pass with the most precious of cargoes. Already at an earlier period, accordingly, attempts had been made to make land-surveyings; on the present occasion Visscher was entrusted with the task in question. On the 11th of August 1634, namely, it was resolved "to give precedence to the surveying and exploration of the coasts of Gotto, Zatsuma and Arrima (seeing that incoming ships and yachts are more interested in the same, in order to enable them to make their ports in storms, fogs and the like) before the surveying etc. of Kijnokijnij, Osacca and Saccaija (although the steersman Hendrick Aertsen who [by order of the Governor-General], on the 26th of June last, partly surveyed the west-coast of the island of Gotto, had obstacles thrown in his way by the inhabitants or rulers of the same)," and to entrust this work "to the steersman Frans Jacobszoon Visscher, who has greater skill in the surveying of coasts and the mapping out of lands than any of the steersmen present in these parts"[1]. On this service he set out with two of his countrymen on August 19. This time again the project was frustrated by opposition on the part of the inhabitants and rulers of the coast to be surveyed; in spite of the "letters of recommendation" from the Japanese authorities at Firando, which Visscher and his coadjutors carried with them, the execution of their task proved altogether impossible. Though they were kindly received at Oetska ("up to which point Hendrick Aertsen had surveyed and explored Gotto to eastward," and where Visscher was now to begin his "explorations and soundings"), the authorities of the place would "by no means allow the Netherlanders to take soundings there and explore the coast, expressly charging them to betake themselves to Firando again with all possible expedition, and not to return." Visscher accordingly came back without having effected his purpose[2]. At first the Dutch representatives in Japan seemed unwilling to give the matter up, the orders from Batavia being too peremptory. On the 10th of September Visscher was again designated for a similar expedition, this time "to explore the coast and take soundings near and about Kijnokijnij, Saccaij and Osacca." This last resolution was, however, afterwards rescinded[3]. That also elsewhere in those parts[4] he had rendered, in the province of hydrography, important services which were duly appreciated at Batavia, is sufficiently evident from the circumstance, that when some time after Matthijs Quast, a skipper of great experience in those waters, sailed for Formosa and Japan, the Governor-General handed[5] him an "indication of the courses to be kept, drawn up by the steersman Frans Visscher, giving pertinent directions for safely passing through the bay between Chincheo and Japan."

In 1636 Visscher returned to the Netherlands in the fleet of the ex-Governor-General Hendrik Brouwer, "with whom he had important conversations touching the best manner of cruising for the Company's ships in order to harass the Spanish ships coming from New Spain, bound for Manilla "[6]. His stay in the Netherlands, however, was not of long duration, for on the 26th of April 1637 he returned to Batavia with the rank of first mate or upper-steersman[7]; in 1638 already we find him in Tonquin again [the ex-Governor-General Brouwer calls him "an expert navigator in Tonquin waters"[8]], where he is charged with the task of drawing up a chart of the bay of Tonquin[9]; and in the same year "the island of Aijnan was thoroughly surveyed, explored and accurately mapped out" by the 'pilot' Frans Visscher": a matter of great moment to "our navigators in Tonquin waters"[10]. In July

[1) Daily Register Firando, Aug. 11, 1634.]

[2) Daily Register Firando, Aug. 22, 1634.]

[3) Ibid. Sept. 10 and Oct. 5, 1634.]

[4) In a missive to his successor in office Van Diemen, dated March 31, 1636, the outgoing Governor-General Hendrik Brouwer speaks highly of "the chart" of the bay of Firando, "made by our Frans Visser."]

[5) Instructions, July 26, 1635.]

[6) LEUPE, Tasman en Visscher, p. 135. Leupe evidently bases himself here on Visscher's Memoir ("Advijs") of January 23, 1642, touching the exploration of Japan.--See also the letter from Hendrik Brouwer to his successor Vin Diemen, dated March 31, 1636.]

[7) See Res. of the G.-G. and C., January 12, 1641.]

[8) Missive to Van Diemen, March 31, 1636.]

[9) LEUPE, Zuidland, p. 88, Note 1).]

[10) General Missive, December 22, 1638--Cf. LEUPE, Bijdragen Geschiedenis, l. c., p. 292; VALENTIJN, III, 2, Tonkin, pp. 27-29.]

1639 he is still found staying in Tonquin[1], and in August of the following year we meet with him again in Japan[2], whence he must very soon after have returned to Batavia. On the 12th of January 1641, at least, he was, by resolution of the Governor-General and Councillors, "in consideration of his good knowledge in navigation, for the space of three consecutive years, continued in his present capacity [of upper-steersman or 'pilot-major']," and his pay raised from 66 to 80 guilders per month.

At that time, as we have already seen, his superiors had pitched upon him to join the projected exploratory voyage to the Southland; the postponement of which compelled him to spend the greater part of the year ashore without definite employment. Still, he was by no means idle; and since he could not be practically employed, he busied himself in putting to paper his ideas touching the voyage about to be undertaken: his "Memoir concerning the discovery of the Southland"[3] dated January 22, 1642, was one of the results of his cogitations. This memoir undoubtedly formed the basis of the Instructions of August 13, and on the whole Visscher played an important part in all the preparations for this expedition[4]. The Instructions expressly recognise his cooperation, where they say: "In all matters pertaining to navigation, such as the courses to be kept, the discovery of coasts, etc. the steersman Francoys Jacobszoon is to have the second vote, and due weight is to be attached to his advice, this present voyage having been projected with his assistance and cooperation." The special place, held by Visscher on this voyage, is, indeed, directly apparent from the circumstance that the Instructions are specially addressed to him also: in the preamble he is assigned a place between Tasman as the leader, and the Plenary Council. That on the voyage itself he held a foremost place, is abundantly proved by the "Journal," kept by Tasman himself[5], and his skill as a cartographer showed to great advantage also this time.

Nor did Visscher at all remain idle during the time which still was to elapse between the drawing-up of the "Memoir" just referred to and the departure of the expeditionary ships. The 23rd of January is the date of an "Advice or Memoir touching the discovery of the northern quarters of Japan," also from his hand[6], which formed one of the bases for the celebrated voyage of Vries in 1643, which was been discussed higher up. On the 12th of March 1642 he was by the Governor-General and Councillors appointed on a special committee, which, as we have already seen, also numbered Tasman among its members, and was charged with appraising a conquered Portuguese ship. From the 1st of July dates a "Dissertation on the best use of the Variation Compass," written by him. The Supreme Government at Batavia spoke with high praise of this dissertation, in their missive to the Managers, of December 12, 1642: "For the benefit of navigation and the improvement of the nautical art," they say, "the pilot-major Franchoys Jacobszoon Visscher has presented to us a written discourse, in which with well-founded arguments he has set forth a method for rectifying and equalising the Company's variation compasses, thereby giving great and important aid to such as have to determine the varying longitude, this being a matter that may be of signal service in the mapping out of lands, and the correcting of charts, especially as regards the importance of making satisfactory and almost faultless estimations; in consideration whereof we would request Your Worships to have this noteworthy proposal (of which we beg leave to inclose a copy[7]) examined and tested by experts, since we are confident that the Company might be greatly benefited by the same."

Visscher had hardly returned from the exploratory voyage to the South-land, when he was again set to work by his superiors. From the 23rd of June, 1643 dates an "Instruction to sail from Batavia1

[1] See "Rappordt aen d'Ed. Hr. Gouverneur Generaal ende Raeden van India nopende mijne bezendinge naar Tonckin, etc. [Report made to the Honble Lord Gov.-Gen. and Counc. of India, touching my mission to Tonquin, etc.]; dated December 5, 1639, by Nicolaas Coeckebacker.]

[2] Daily Register Firando, Aug. 24, 1640.--From his stay in Eastern Asia probably date the maps of China, Formosa and the Pescadores, made with Visscher's assistance, which in 1642 were handed to a commander who

had orders to cruise on the coast of China to watch for hostile vessels (LEUPE, Zuidland, p. 88, Note 1).]

[3] Appendix H. This memoir is very interesting, and shows the great designs of Visscher as regards the discovery of the South-land. Compare S. RUGE, Südland, 1. c., p. 322; WALKER, Tasman, pp. 26 ff.]

[4] Cf. also the Resolution of the G.-G. and C., August 1, 1642.]

[5] To which I would beg to refer the reader as regards the point referred to in the text.]

[6] Cf. LEUPE, Tasman en Visscher, pp. 130 f., 136; Id., Reize van Vries, pp. 53 f.; 33, N. 12; 241. An abstract of the Japan memoir is preserved in the Hague State-Archives, Sweers Collection.]

[7] Still extant in the Hague State Archives.]

to the Piscadores, and from Taijouan or the Piscadores to Batavia; drawn up by the Pilot-major Francois Jacobszoon Visscher," which Instruction served as "Letter of orders and signals" for a vessel then ready to sail for those parts. The Dutch "president" of Formosa, then holding office, got positive orders from the Governor-General and Councillors[1], to cause these instructions "to be transcribed and copies of the same to be handed to the commanders of all vessels coming hither, that they may regulate themselves accordingly." In still another manner were Visscher's services recognised by the Supreme Government at Batavia, when by their resolution of October 26, 1643, they increased his monthly pay as a "skipper and pilot-major" to 95 guilders "in consideration of his great knowledge and eminent services to navigation."

Very soon after this preparations were again set on foot at Batavia for the new voyage of discovery to the South-land. Visscher played an important part also in these preparatory measures and in the enterprise itself. Directly after the return of the second expedition, we again find traces of Visscher's restless activity. In a resolution namely of the Governor-General and Councillors, dated October 17, 1644, it is stated that Visscher and Tasman[2] had pointed out a "new route and passage" for waylaying the Spanish silver-ships between Acapulco and Manila. These memoirs or advices formed the basis for an important expedition of which Visscher formed part, but of which the leadership was entrusted to Commander Maarten Gerritszoon Vries, who was expressly directed constantly to confer with the "pilot-major as regards the determination of the courses to be held"[3].

The ships which formed part of this expedition, were ordered to proceed to the Moluccas, whence they were to be dispatched on a cruise to watch for the silver-ships. For several years past flotillas had been sent out for this purpose, but hitherto always without result. The Supreme Government, therefore, had "time and again contemplated other methods of action": thus "the experienced pilot-major Francois Jacobszoon Visscher had proposed a certain manner of cruising near and about the Ladrones isles, departing from the latter between fourteen and twelve degrees Northern Latitude to run for the channels of the Holy Ghost and Sta. Clara, for the purpose of meeting the enemy's ships at sea, and cutting them off from the land for the time being." But the execution of this plan had hitherto been frustrated by the circumstance that "the rendezvous assigned, being the Ladrones isles, is not be reached owing to the constant south-easterly winds prevailing in the great South Sea." At present, however--we see that "the recent discovery of the South-land" was already bearing fruit--"the discovery of the unknown South-land and of the north-coast of Nova Guinea, made by Abel Tasman," had opened up "a convenient route;" and according to the said navigator the Ladrones islands "could without much difficulty be successfully fetched up by running eastward along the said north-coast of Guinea." Tasman's proposal was, "with Visscher's advice, duly ventilated, discussed and deliberated on" by the Governor-General and Councillors, and the upshot of this discussion was the instruction for the expedition. The ships were ordered in the beginning of February to navigate from Ternate to the cape of Maba[4], through Patientie Strait along the coast of Weda, following Abel Tasman's course along the north-coast of New Guinea[5], "sailing on the said course until you estimate yourselves to have come to 50 or 60 miles east of the Ladrones islands, which point it is assumed you will be able to reach in a short time with the land-and sea-winds, together with the westerly or north-westerly winds (which are held to prevail on the said coast from the month of December down to the end of March, and to constitute the monsoon). If then you should find this to be practicable, we should deem it advisable for you to further survey the coast about 40 miles more to eastward[6], until you shall have got into the longitude of 168 degrees, this being the longitude of Salomon Sweers cape"[7], in order to run "as far as possible eastward

[1] Missive, June 23, 1643. Visscher's Instruction (a copy of which is still extant in the Hague State Archives) did duty even at a later period. See "Copying-Book of letters dispatched, instructions issued, and orders sent from Batavia to different parts" [Copie Boeck van affgesonden brieven, verleende jnstructien ende Commissien uijt Batavia naer verscheijde Quartieren gesonden]; from 1645 to 1653 passim.]

[2] Tasman's advice is contained in the chart, dated September 8, 1644, reproduced in the present work.]

[3] Instructions, October 31, 1644.--As regards this expedition, see also L. C. D. VAN DIJK, Neerlands vroegste betrekkingen met Borneo. Amsterdam, Scheltema, 1862, pp. 289-299; LEUPE, Nieuw-Guinea, pp. 172-175.]

[4] Poeloe Gebeh? Cp. the chart, dated September 8, 1644.]

[5] The Tasman chart of Sept. 8, 1644 clearly shows the route.]

[6] Farther to eastward than indicated in Tasman's chart.]

[7] The eastern extremity of what is now called New Hanover. The name in the text was conferred on Tasman's 1642/3 voyage.]

of the Ladrones islands." From Salomon Sweers cape they were directed to sail in a northerly direction as far as 13½° N. Lat., and then to run for the Ladrones on a western course. Should the plan to seize the silver-ships miscarry, the Plenary Council was authorised to decide on an attempt against the Philippines, if they should deem such attempt feasible, the Instructions here setting forth the information concerning the Babuyan islands, obtained by Tasman in 1639. If, on the other hand, the rich booty should fall into their hands, they were to take it to the Pescadores and Formosa.

The voyage was unsuccessful so far as its main object was concerned, and the results of the coup de main upon the Philippines were nothing to speak of. The only thing that needs mention here, is that Vries sailed "along the ('barren') coast of Nova Guinea (about as far as Salomon Sweers cape), he having, as much as time and circumstances would allow, explored and surveyed the said coast by making occasional landings, and having found the inhabitants of it to be a wild, robust and warlike people"--he got into hostile contact with them--"of whom in the way of refreshments he could obtain nothing but cocoa-nuts, while he utterly failed to find any traces or collect information as to any precious metals, stones or other valuable commodities obtainable in those parts."

Visscher's fortunes subsequent to this last expedition are as yet unknown.

Such, then, were the ship's officers who attended Tasman on his renowned expedition[1]. The voyage was begun on the 14th of August [2]. In the island of Mauritius, where they arrived September 5, the ships were provided with necessaries by order of the Governor-General and Councillors[3]. Here it became once more apparent, how very little care the Supreme Government at Batavia bestowed on the fitting-out of ships dispatched on such perillous voyages. Commander Van der Stel vividly represents to his masters[4] "how hopelessly unsatisfactory was the outfit of the ships for a voyage of such a nature, so that we have been compelled to provide them with firewood, canvass, cordage and various other necessaries"[5]. The Zeehaen, for example, "had put to sea with her upper work half-rotten, so that a great part of it had to be repaired and renewed." Tasman, who, pending his stay in Mauritius, as the higher in rank, took precedence of Commander Van der Stel, was by the latter presented with "a printed journal (containing certain small charts), kept on divers voyages through the straits of Lamair and Magellanes, to the Salmonis islands and other parts. The whole bearing the title of De nieuwe werelt[6]. To which is added a vocabulary of certain words from the languages of the Slamonis islands, of Nova Guinea, and certain other lands situated in the said parts, which vocabulary might happen to be of use on their voyage." The voyage (Abel Tasman's course or "passagie")[7] was resumed on the 8th of October "with our men strong and in good liking"[8], at which date the ships again put to sea, in order to seek the South-land on an easterly course[9]. The latitude ordained in the Instructions was not reached:

[1] As regards the further outfit of the ships, etc. I would refer the reader to the Instructions.]

[2] Cf. also Res- G.-G. and C., Aug. 13, 1642 (Appendix I.)--The Governor-General and Councilors anticipated the result of the discoveries, when, as early as 1642, they wrote: "The whole of the newly discovered South-land, situated under the longitude from 55 to 220 degrees inclusive, i.e. between the meridians of Cabo Bona Spei and of the easternmost of the Salomonis islands, from the Equinoctial Line to the Antarctic Pole, or between the farthest coasts and islands of the whole Southland on both sides, has lately been first discovered by the Netherlanders, and the whole of it been legally taken possession of. No Portuguese ship ever visited that part of the world." This passage occurs in the list of "Names and places in the East, possessed and frequented by the Portuguese and the Netherlanders," drawn up in consequence of the truce between the Netherlands and Portugal, concluded in 1641/2; (See my Bouwstoffen, III, pp. 51-56).]

[3] In their missive to Commander Van der Stel, dated Aug. 13, 1642.]

[4] In his letter to the G.-G. and C., October 13, 1642.]

[5] The "Journal" conveys a more modest impression of the assistance given. See also the missive of G.-G. and Council to the Commander of Mauritius, Sept. 2, 1642. Cf., however, also K. HEERINGA, De Nederlanders op Mauritius en Madagascar (Indische Gids, 1895, p. 1007) and the missive of the Commander of Mauritius to G.-G. and C., June 11, 1644.]

[6) Probably the book discussed in TIELE, Bibliographie Land- en Volkenkunde, pp. 108 f.]

[7) I have italicised such names of localities as are found in our chart, which has been drawn mainly from Swart's reproduction of the Bonaparte chart.]

[8) General Missive of Dec. 12, 1642.]

[9) I fail to understand RAINAUD'S (p. 365) reasons for stating that on leaving Mauritius Tasman "fit voile au sud a la recherche de la grande ile tracée sur d'anciennes cartes portugaises et espagnoles, l'ile de Zanzibar ou pays des 'Géants', laquelle semble répondre a l'ile désolée de Kerguelen."--As regards the voyage itself I beg leave to refer the reader to the "Journal," with the notes appended by me, and to Dr. VAN BEMMELEN'S paper. In the text I refer to a few points only.]

the southernmost latitude they got into was 49° 4'[1], according to the estimation of the commanders; it was made on the 6th of November, after which date it was resolved to "run north again."

About 4 o'clock in the afternoon of the 24th of November land was sighted. On this "first land by them met with in the South Sea, and not as yet known to any European nation," they conferred[2] the name of "Anthoonij van Diemen's landt" (the present Tasmania), in honour of the Governor-General, the prime mover or auctor intellectualis of the expedition; while "the islands circumjacent, as many as they got knowledge of, were named after the Honble Councillors of India." They continued to survey the coast discovered until December 5, when they resolved to continue the voyage, and "hold an eastward course (again)." On the 13th they sighted "a large and high land about noon." As they were lying off this land, on the 19th a hostile attack was made by the natives on the Dutch sailors (Moordenaarsbaai)[3]. To this land was given the name of Staten landt (now New Zealand), in honour of Their High Mightinesses the States-General, seeing that this land might quite possibly[4] form part of, and be joined to the State landt." So firmly rooted in the minds of Tasman and his associates was the notion of a vast South-land, that, when by their exploratory voyage they cut off from this supposed South-land a large part of the hitherto unknown world, yet, when they discovered a country of which they only surveyed the west-coast, and of which they failed to ascertain the insular nature, they forthwith in their minds connected this country with the Statenland[5], south of South America, which since Schouten and Lemaire's voyage had been looked upon as one of the northern extremities of the South-land in question [6] It was "confidently believed"[7], that the newly-discovered Staten land was "the mainland coast of the unknown South-land." At first they "entertained little doubt"--they were then at anchor in the Zeehaensbocht--"that they should there find a passage into the vast South Sea," but to their "profound regret" they failed to discover any such passage, though they kept hoping, "seeing that the tide runs from the south-east"[8]; they evidently thought that the bay was

[1] The steersman's journal in the Sweers Collection has a higher degree of Southern Latitude here. I follow the journal by Tasman himself in "our" copy.]

[2] Dr. HOCKER, Abel Tasman and his journal (p. 7), is mistaken where he says: "I may here remark, that in all probability the interesting process of name-giving did not take place until after Tasman's return to Batavia." The names were conferred immediately after each discovery.]

[3] Compare the native story about "two large vessels, much larger than theirs, which some time or other came here, and were totally destroyed by the inhabitants, and all the people belonging to them killed" in Journal of Joseph Banks during Captain Cook's first voyage in H. M. S. Endeavour in 1768-71; edited by JOSEPH D. HOOKER (London, Macmillan, 1896), pp. 215 f.]

[4] "Though this is uncertain" is the reading of the Huydecoper copy.]

[5] Compare RAINAUD, p. 373.]

[6] Cp. also Visscher's Memoir about the Southland. In this same year the ex-Governor-General Hendrik Brouwer ascertained the insular nature of the Statenland south of South America, in consequence of which the notion of a supposed South-land was again shaken. Cf. A. TELTING, De Nederlanders in Chili 1643 (Indische Gids, 1893, pp. 2020 f.); RAINAUD, pp. 347 ff.]

[7] The Huydecoper copy reads "supposed."]

[8] Journal on Dec. 24, 1642. RAINAUD erroneously puts this on Dec. 25. He is mistaken where he says (p. 368), that the Dutch on this voyage did not "soupçonner l'existence de ce canal." Compare also RUGE, Südland, 1. c. p. 333: "Tasman war nahe Baran, die Natur des Landes richtig zu beurteilen." It is highly remarkable that in the Visscher chart of Statenland, of which a part is reproduced here, and which is contained in the Huydecoper journal, the Zeehaensbocht is not so completely closed, as it is in the chart of Statenland in our copy, but, in about 41° 20' S. Lat. and 193° 30' E. Long., shows an opening as the place for a "passage through." IN THIS CHART, THEREFORE, THE PRESENT COOK'S STRAIT, IS UNMISTAKABLY MARKED.--Cf. Journal of Joseph Banks during Captain Cook's first voyage in H. M. S. Endeavour in 1768-71] London, Macmillan, 1896. p. 213.]

land-locked on the east side, and consequently did not discover what is now known as Cook's Strait. On the 4th of January 1643[1] they had come "off a cape" (Cabo Maria van Diemen), and had "an island north-west by north" of them (they named it Drie coninghen Eylant, "because we came to anchor there on the eve of Epiphany or Twelfthnight"). "Here," the Journal goes on to say, "we found ourselves in a very strong current, which set us to eastward, while at the same time a strong sea came running from the north-east, which not a little rejoiced us, because we hoped thus to find a passage [into the South Sea]. [Near the cape] the land trends to eastward." No attempts were, however, made to get certitude on this point, and on January 6 they proceeded on their way. Still there was a firm conviction on the subject: "The sea runs very strongly from the eastward, so that there is no ground for us to suppose any great mainland to lie east of us...The heavy swells are now running from the south-east. This water-route from Batavia to Chyly is a very smooth one, so that there is no objection to making use of it..."[2].

Sailing on in a mainly northerly direction, on January 19 and subsequent days, they discovered various islands forming part of the Tonga Archipelago, or Friendship Isles[3], after which on February 6 and following days the Fiji islands were fallen in with. Running on chiefly in a north-western direction, it was not before the 22nd of March[4] and following days that they discovered or saw back divers islands north of the Salomon isles[5]: the Ontongh Java group, now also known by the name of Njoea isles; Marken; the Groene- (Green) or Sir Ch. Hardy., and the St. Jans islands[6]. On the 1st of April they got "the coast of Nova Guinea alongside," as they thought, "which by the Spaniards is called Cabo Santa Maria;" they were then near the north-eastern extremity of New Ireland or New Mecklenburg. Always fancying themselves sailing along the north-coast of New Guinea, they now skirted the north-coast of New Ireland or New Mecklenburg and of New Hanover, which was not recognised as a separate island; and christened various islands which they sighted to the northward of the said coasts: Anthony Caens-, Gardenijs- and Visschers islands, until on April 8, "the land began gradually to trend more to the south," and they had reached the north-western extremity of the present New Hanover (Salomon Sweershoek). On the 9th of April the cape just mentioned was doubled, and the voyage continued on a southern course "both for purposes of discovery, and in order to find a passage to the south as quickly as possible": it was namely hoped that here "a passage through to Cape Keerweer might be found." This hope remained unfulfilled; the voyagers soon became aware[7] that they had got "into a large bay," and "that towards the west the land formed an uninterrupted coast-line." Sailing nearly due south, they had traversed from north to south the bay formed by New Hanover, New Ireland and New Britain or New Pomerania, without observing the strait between the two last-mentioned islands (St- George's Channel), and had accordingly fallen into the mistake that the eastern side of the bay formed one unbroken coast-line.

The north-coast of New Britain was now skirted, after which they reached the north-coast of New Guinea, without, however, discovering the present Dampier Strait. On the 12th of May they passed the north-coast of Willem Schoutens island, which rendered it impossible for them to discover what is now called Great Geelvink bay. Just as Lemaire had done, Tasman also looked upon Gemien or Dampier Strait as a landlocked bay. The consequence was that they continued to mistake for the

[1) RAINAUD erroneously has "February 4."]

[2) Journal, January 7, 8, 1643.]

[3) As to the natives of the Tonga Archipelago keeping remembrance of Tasman's visit there, see BASIL THOMSON, The diversions of a prime minister. Edinburgh and London, Blackwood, MDCCCXCIV, pp. 311 f.: "On January 27, 1643, Abel Tasman (the great countryman of Schouten) anchored off Hitufo in Tongatabu...Tasman sailed away, and the Tongans saw no more of the foreigners for 124 years. The priceless iron tools they had given them had long been worn out and disappeared, but the memory of their coming, embalmed by one of the native poets, remained fresh to its smallest details..."I feel greatly indebted to the author's courtesy in drawing my attention to his interesting work.]

[4) The sailor's journal in the Sweers Collection has here the date March (February) 20.]

[5) "On their way they fell in with some more islands and shoals, which they (we?) firmly believe to belong to the Insulis Salomonis." Res- G.-G. and C., June 19, 1643 (Appendix J.) Whether this "firm belief" originated with Tasman and his coadjutors, or with the G.-G. and C., is left a moot point by the wording of the resolution.]

[6) The Sweers sailor's journal puts the discovery of these islands on March (February) 26; our journal on March 28.]

[7) Journal, April 13, 14. The sailor's journal has: "we presumed."--As for the ante-Tasmanic opinions cp. Remarkable Maps, II, III. Tasman's mistake had not been made before him.]

north-coast of New Guinea the island of Waigeoe, of which they next passed the north-coast. Between what they took to be the west-coast of New Guinea (Waigeoe), and what was by them looked upon as one of the eastern extremities of Celebes (Poeloe Gebeh), they subsequently found "a convenient passage through, which in future may be of great use to the Company's (ships)[1], coming from Peru or Chyly at the time of the eastern monsoon"[2]. The ships next passed, eastward of Poeloe Gagi, the western opening of Gemien or Dampier Strait, again without becoming aware of its real nature. On the 25th of May Poeloe Koffian was passed, and on the 26th Misool[3], after which the ships soon found themselves in well-known waters. On the 15th of June, 1643 Tasman and his companions landed at Batavia[4].

When returned to Batavia Tasman and his coadjutors, "the South-Land navigators"[5], received a reward in money, the customary mode of remuneration in those days. The terms[6] in which the Supreme Government awards this recompense are highly characteristic: "And inasmuch as by the Instructions given to the said Commander Tasman and his Council, we have assured and promised the leaders of the expedition and the common sailors to give them a handsome reward on their return, for extraordinary pains taken and diligence shown by them, in case in the course of this voyage any rich lands or islands profitable to the Company, or any serviceable passages should be discovered: therefore, although in fact no treasures or profitable commodities, but only the lands aforementioned and a promising passage have as yet been discovered (whose real situation will have to be ascertained by further investigation[7]), yet we have unanimously resolved to award recompenses to the said discoverers on behalf of the Company for the reasons aforesaid, and in fulfilment of our promise; to wit, to the Commander, skippers, supercargoes and subcargoes, steersmen, inclusive of the book-keeper, two months' pay each, and to the common sailors one month's pay each." The reasons assigned for the recompense exactly convey the impression made on the Supreme Government at Batavia by the result of Tasman's expedition. The undertaking was by them looked upon as a "remarkable voyag,"e[8] but according to them, Tasman "had been to some extent remiss in investigating the situation, conformation and nature of the lands and peoples discovered, and left the main part of this task to be executed by by some more inquisitive successor." In the eyes of Van Diemen and the Councillors of India, then, the fact that on this voyage new lands, and perhaps a "passage to the South Sea" had been discovered, was indeed a very important one, but according to them Tasman had committed a mistake in neglecting to make his investigation a more thorough one; in other words, in having failed to ascertain whether the regions discovered might become of importance for the Company's trade[9].

But before the "more inquisitive successor" above alluded to had been appointed, Tasman and Visscher had a fresh task assigned to them. "To prevent their being idle inthe meantime," the Governor-General and Councillors forthwith resolved "to dispatch" Tasman and Visscher "with two yachts to the north coast of Nova Guinea by way of Banda, about the month of February, for the

[1*) Huydecoper Journal.]

[2*) Journal, May 20.]

[3*) Described in the Sweers sailor's journal as "a long island eastward of the eastern extremity of the coast of Zeram." Cf. Swart's reproduction of the Bonaparte chart.]

[4*) RAINAUD, l. c. p. 368, says: "Dans cette longue traversée Tasman avait été constamment favorisé par la direction des courants de l'Océan Indien et de l'Océan Pacifique; ce qui explique la rapidité de sa marche." The journal does not show so much contentment with wind and weather. Compare, for instance, the journal on March 5, 1643.]

[5) The phrase occurs in the General Missive of Dec. 12, 1642.]

[6) See Res. of the G.-G. and Counc., of June 19, 1643.]

[7) The italics are my own. In the Res. of the G.-G. and Counc. of Sept 4, 1643 we also read: "As regards the new short passage to the South Sea and the coast of New Spain, which commander Tasman is supposed to have discovered, we consider the same as yet a matter of uncertainty, inasmuch as we do not positively know whether the said passage is quite free, or may still have more large lands lying across and in front of it, a point which we intend to have more pertinently inquired into on further discovery of the newly found South-land." See also General Missive of December 22, 1643 (Appendix K.) The Managers of the E. I. C. (as appears from their letters to the G.-G. and C., dated Sept. 21, 1644 and Sept. 9, 1645) refused to countenance any further investigations extending to Chili, chiefly because they deemed such investigations to clash with the provisions of the West India Company's charter.</]

[8) Instructions for the voyage of 1644.]

[9) The Managers thought it needless to refer to the results of this expedition at all!]

purpose of discovering the said land from Cabo Keerweer in 17[1] degrees Latitude, and farther to westward, and of ascertaining whether the known South-land is connected with the same or separated from it, seeing that certainty as to his point will be of great use in future explorations"[2].

This resolution gave rise to the expedition undertaken by Tasman and Visscher in 1644. We "intend," thus runs the General Missive of January 4, 1644, "to have the unknown land situated between Nova Guinea and the unknown South-land discovered and surveyed by way of Banda by Commander Tasman and Pilot-major

Frans Visscher with two yachts and a pinnace, in February next; the said exploration to begin from Cape Keer-weer (being the farthest point of Nova Guinea discovered by Commander Carstens in the year 1623[3]), and with God's aid to end at Willems River (being the northernmost extremity of the known South-land), in which intervening region (extending to a length of fully 400 miles) there are likely to be found sundry lands and islands, not far distant from Java; this expedition being also charged with the task of ascertaining whether the two large lands aforementioned are connected with each other, or are separated by channels; certainty about this point being highly desirable with a view to the further exploration of the newly discovered South-lands, and of the passage to the South Sea and to Chili; on which account it is expedient that the said point should be investigated as soon as possible, the more so since such investigation can be conveniently completed within the space of five or six months."

"By September next, when the projected discovery of the north coast of the South-land is likely to have been successfully effected, we also intend to dispatch two or three yachts for the further exploration of the newly discovered South-lands, with express orders to ascertain what advantages for the Company may be obtained there. They will especially have to inquire whether in these vast regions there are any silver-, gold-, or copper-mines, which we deem very likely, seeing they are situated under a climate especially adapted for such mines, and resembling that of the silver- and gold-bearing regions of Peru, Chili, China and Japan"[4].

On the 13th of January next the new expedition was definitely resolved upon in the Council of India[5]. Three ships were to be fitted out under the command of Tasman, "assisted by" Visscher, "and other able steersmen," for the purpose "of further and more exact discovery, and of clearly ascertaining whether the coast of Nova Guinea and the unknown South-land are connected together, or are divided from each other by channels...item of deciding the question whether or not the newly discovered Van Diemens land[6]...forms one whole with the two great lands just mentioned, or with either of them; item of finding out what other unknown islands may be situated between Nova Guinea and the South-land, and what treasures, advantages, profitable trade-connections and convenient passages may there be available for the benefit of the General Company."

The object of this expedition is more amply set forth in the Instructions of January 29[7], which

[1) An inaccurate statement, of course.]

[2) Missive of December 22, 1643.]

[3] This is incorrect of course, for Carstensz got beyond Keerweer; the mistake does not occur in the Instructions of January 29, 1644.]

[4] I leave out what the Missive further states as to the plans of the G.-G. and C. for harassing Spain in South-America through the "new passage," and for forming trade-connections with Chili. As appears from their missive to the Supreme Government at Batavia, of Sept. 9, 1645, the Managers of the Company flatly refused to countenance any such plans. The missive just mentioned also contains some characteristic utterances referring to the plans for supplementing and completing Tasman and Visscher's discoveries. "We have also gathered from your letter," the Managers say, "that your Worships have again taken in hand the further discovery of the coast of Nova Guinea, in the hope of finding silver- and gold-mines there. We cannot anticipate any great results from the continuation of such discoveries, which besides entail further expenditure for the Company, since they require more yachts and an increase of sailors. The Company has now made a sufficient number of discoveries for maintaining its trade, provided the latter be carried on with success. We do not think it part of our task to seek out gold- and silver-mines for the Company, and having found such, to try to derive profit from the same; such things involve a good deal more, demanding excessive expenditure and large numbers of hands; it is clearly seen in the West Indies, what numbers of persons and quantities of necessaries are required to work the King's mines, so that gold and silver are not extracted from the earth without excessive outlay, as some would seem to imagine. These plans of Your Worships somewhat aim beyond our mark. The gold- and silver-mines that will best serve the Company's turn, have already been found, which we deem to be our trade over the whole of India, and especially in Taijouan and Japan, if only God be graciously pleased to continue the same to us."]

[5] Appendix L.]

[6] i.e. the present Tasmania.]

[7] Appendix M. I cannot conveniently discuss the whole of these Instructions in the text, but for particulars would refer the reader to this Appendix.]

were drawn up with "the advice and concurrence" of Tasman and Visscher. The vessels told off for this expedition "for the true and complete discovery of the South-land"[1], were the yacht Limmen, carrying 45 seamen and 11 soldiers, the yacht Zeemeeuw or Meeuw, having on board 35 seamen and 6 soldiers, and the "quel"[2] or galiot Bracq with 14 seamen. The Limmen had probably first come out in 1639, and measured 60 lasts[3]; the Zeemeeuw, of 50 lasts, in 1643; and the Bracq, in 1640. The ships were victualled for 8 months, and took on board various commodities that might prove needful for forming commercial connections[4]. On the 29th of January it was resolved that the ships should "put off to sea in the name of God, early to-morrow, after due muster."

For this expedition also Tasman was appointed "commander of the three yachts and of the men on board of the same," and "permanent president" of the Plenary Council. He carried the "flag floating from the topmast of the yacht Limmen." Among the members of the Plenary Council were Visscher, who in his capacity of "skipper pilot-major" had command of the Limmen, which was the flag-ship; next, the skipper of the Zeemeeuw, Dirk Corneliszoon Haen[1], who in case of Tasman dying was appointed to succeed him as commander; the "supercargo" of the latter vessel, Isaac Gilsemans, already known to us; the skipper of the Bracq, Jaspar Janszoon Koos[5]; the first mate in the Limmen, Crijn Hendrickszoon (De Ratte), of Middelburg, who had come out to India on "half-pay" in 1641, had formed part of the 1642/3 expedition, and been appointed master-steersman in 1644[6]; his colleagues, Carsten Jurriaenszoon on board the Zeemeeuw, and Cornelis Roobol in the Bracq, all of them known to us. Secretary of the Council, and full member at the same time, was the Subcargo Anthonij Blauw[7]. Besides, there was a "draughtsman" appointed to join the expedition, whose duty it was to map out the coasts, etc. touched at.

Tasman had got orders first to call at Macassar[8], where the plan was to he kept secret[9], next at Amboyna, and ultimately at Banda. In these islands he was to take in refreshments, and try to provide himself with all necessaries; at the same time he was enjoined to ask the governors of those parts "for written memoranda setting forth the special information they might possess touching the lands and islands east of Banda. Thence, in the month of February, he was to continue his voyage" on an eastward course between and in sight of the islands of Tenimber, Key and Arouw, to Cape Ture or Valsche Caep, situated in 8 degrees on the south coast of Nova Guinea." From there he was to skirt the said coast to eastward as far as 9°, next "cautiously cross the shallow bay situated there, and seek a road-stead near the Hoge Eijlant or Speults River...meanwhile sending off the galiot Brack into the bay (i.e. Torres Strait) for the space of two or three days, with the object of finding out within this vast bay any eventual passage to the South sea." They were next to run southward as far as 17° ("the farthest point discovered"), in order to ascertain "whether this land is divided from the large known South-land." Should this prove to be the case, then Tasman was ordered to run on southward "as far as the newly discovered Van Diemens land" (Tasmania), and from there towards the islands of St. Pieter and St. Francois, whence he was to sail along "the east coast of the, in that case known, South-land" as far as De Witsland and Willems River. If no passage was found south of 17°, Tasman was to skirt the land in a westerly direction as far as Willems River, and then, if practicable[10], to sail along Eendrachtsland as far as Houtmans

[1] Ress. of G.-G. and C., of January 13 and 25, 1644.]

[2] "Quel" is another name for a galiot (General Missive, Dec. 12, 1642; Dagh Register gehouden int Casteel Batavia Anno 1640-1641, uitgegeven onder toezicht van J. A. VAN DER ,CHIJS. Batavia, 's Hage, 1887, pp. 233, 234; Cf. Swart's reproduction of the Bonaparte chart).]

[3] Uitloopboekie [Memorandum of outgoing ships].--LEUPE'S suggestion (Navorscher, i854, p. 161), that the names of Brack and Hasewind, "being closely allied in meaning, may not unlikely have been interchangeable," is shown to be a mistake by the fact that the E. I. C. owned not only a quel or galiot bearing the name of Brack, but also a galiot of the name of Hasewind. (Uitloopboekie for the year 1642; General Missive, Dec. 23, 1642).]

[4] See the specification in Appendix N.]

[5] I have not come across any particulars of his career as a servant of the E. I. C.]

[6] Res. G.-G. and C. Aug. 22, 1644--Perhaps he was afterwards appointed first mate in the Zeemeeuw (LEUPE, Navorscher, i854, p. 160.]

[7] See Note 5) supra.]

[8] As far as Macassar, Supercargo Adriaan Van Zuidwijk accompanied the expedition, and as being highest in official rank, held command of the ships up to there.]

[9] Instructions of the G.-G. and C. for Van Zuidwijk, Jan. 29, 1644.]

[10] What A. F. CALVERT, The Discovery of Australia, London, Philip, 1893, states, viz. that Tasman was ordered "to follow the coast, despite adverse winds," is not quite correct. His note, accordingly, ought to be cancelled.]

Abrolhos; or otherwise to run eastward again from Willems River "in order to further explore Aernhems- and Van Diemens land, and ascertain once for all whether or not the said lands constitute one and the same island...and also, what other islands may be situated between Balij, Cumbawa, Timor and the South-land."

As no journal of this voyage is forthcoming, we are forced to put up with notices scattered here and there, apart from what we learn from the well-known chart[1].

On the 22nd of February the ships arrived off Amboyna[2], on the 27th of the same month they got near Banda. The Governor of Banda, Cornelis Witsen, ordered "the quartermaster Jan Jorisse (alias capteyntge)," who in Banda "acted as interpreter (when men of Eastern nations appear here)", to join Tasman's expedition. The adjunction to the expedition of this quartermaster was intended "to procure for Tasman in Arouw[3] the services of an interpreter conversant with the language of Nova Guinea, since Jorisse is of opinion that there will be plenty of such interpreters available there[4]." Aroe was accordingly called at by the ships[5], and from there (Abel Tasman passagie)[6] the ships ran eastward, until they reached the west (north) coast of what is now known as Prince Frederick Hendrik Island. They next doubled Cape Tyuri (Ture) or Valsche Kaap, sailed along the east (south) coast of the island just mentioned, and after this again reached the coast of New Guinea[7], which they skirted as far as the Torres Strait of modern maps. Tasman and his men failed to recognise the real nature of this channel; in this case, too, the strait was taken to be a land-locked bay (Droog hoeck or bocht?).

We see, then, that Tasman did not give a satisfactory solution of this part of the problem set him: in his estimation New Guinea and the present Australia formed one whole. Tasman next sailed along the east coast of the present Gulf of Carpentaria[8], until he got to about 17°, this being the farthest point reached by previous Dutch explorers (Carstenszoon; Tot hier toe hebben sommige ontdekkers geweest = certain discoverers have been up to here). From there he skirted this coast in a southerly direction[9], then sailed along the south-coast of the Gulf of Carpentaria[10], where he wrongly supposed the present island of Mornington to be connected with the mainland, doubled the said island[11], and then ran on a westward course along the south coast just mentioned[12]. He mistook the present Van der Lijns Island and Observation Island for parts of the main-land[13], doubled them, made the same mistake as regards Maria-eiland[14], came to anchor in what he called Limmens bocht, and in this way got to the west coast of the Gulf of Carpentaria (Laegh landt). He now held his course between the present Groote Eylandt and the mainland coast, until he reached Arnhems land. Accordingly, he had duly

[1] Viz. Swart's reproduction of the Bonaparte chart. What WITSEN, Noord- en Oost-Tartarije, I, i.a. p. 175 etc. says about this expedition, seems to me not accurate and certain enough to be made use of. It is found reproduced in the works of Major, Calvert and others.]

[2] Missive of the Governor and Council of Amboyna to G.-G. and C., of April 25, 1644--WALKER, Tasman pp. 36 is incorrect as regards the course taken by Tasman.]

[3] Aroe.]

[4) That Jorissen accompanied the expedition is made evident by a letter of the G.-G. and C. to the Governor and Council of Banda, dated Nov. 29, 1644, in which it is stated that he "has assisted skipper-commander Tasman in the discovery of the South-land."]

[5) Missive of the Governor and Council of Banda to the G.-G. and C. dated April 17, 1645.]

[6) I italicise such names as are found in Swart's reproduction of the Bonaparte chart, and were conferred by Tasman in the course of this voyage.]

[7) Here Tasman most probably gave names to the Mannen(?)rivier (most probably Meeuwen rivier, from the yacht Zeemeeuw or Meeuw), the Clappers rivier (or did this name originate with Carstenszoon? Cf. ROBIDÉ VAN DER AA, Reizen Nieuw Guinea, pp. 426 f.), and the Rivier d'Orange.]

[8) He probably christened here the Staatenrivier? or Soete Rivier?, Prince-rivier, Rivier met tbosch, Vliegen baij; Visschen(Versche?)rivier, Laeghlant, Rivier Pera, Rivier Arnhem. That Tasman did not find Torres Strait, is in so many words stated in a letter from G.-G. and C. to the governor of Banda, Nov. 29, 1644: he had found no channel between Nova Guinea and the Southland.]

[9) Here he gave names to Van Diemens rivier, Van der Lijns rivier (now Norman River?), and rivier Caron (now Flinders River?)]

[10) Rivier Maetsuycker (Leichhardt River?), Sweers-rivier, Laegh land.]

[11) Can this be meant by Cabo Van Diemen?]

[12) Demmers-rivier (from the name of the member of the C. of I., Gerard Demmer.--In some maps this river is also called Van Diemens rivier), Witsen-rivier, Rivier Croock (from Paulus Croock, member of the C. of I.), Van Alphen's rivier (from Simon Van Alphen, member of the C. of I.), Abel Tasmans rivier or baij (?), Waterplaets, Vlakke bocht (?).]

[13) Cabo Van der Lijn? In some maps: C. Van der Laits.]

[14) Cabo de Marie? In some maps it is called C. Maire, e.g. on the map in COLLINGRIDGE, p. 286.]

resolved the question whether there was any passage to the south between 17° South. Lat. and Arnhems land[1]. He now doubled the present Wessels-island and the islands south of it, without recognising the insular character of all of them, then discovered Crocodils eiland(en), and continued his way eastward[2]. He sighted Maria-land, which had already been discovered by the ship Arnhem, visited Van Diemen baay[3], but fancied this to be land-locked on every side except the northern one, and mistook Melville island (Van Diemens land) for a part of the mainland. Tasman next sailed along the west coast of Australia as far as Eendrachtsland, after which he returned to Batavia, where he arrived in the month of August[4], after having once more touched at the Key and Aroe Islands[5].

The western part of the present Australia, which part had now been completely skirted, was in Tasman's chart christened Compagnies Nieuw Nederland[6], a name which in Dutch charts was, however, soon replaced by the Latin appellation Nova Hollandia[7], which afterwards gave rise to the Duch name Nieuw-Holland, the latter term being ultimately employed to designate the whole of the circumnavigated continent[8]. To distinguish it from Nova Hollandia, the Statenland, discovered by Tasman, had afterwards conferred on it the name[9] of Nova-Zeelandia or Nieuw Zeeland. That part of the present Australia which was still thought to be connected with New Guinea, continued to be called by Tasman by its old name of South-land. The eastern coast-line had not yet been discovered, no more than the southern one east of Nuytsland[10].

Thus--and the words succinctly describe Tasman's achievements--the "vast and hitherto unknown South-land had by Tasman been sailed round in two voyages," as the Governor-General and Councillors stated in their General Missive of December 23, 1644. But this time, too, they were not completely satisfied: true, the results also of the voyage of 1644 were highly important, but the question whether the discovered regions would yield profit to the Company's commerce, once more remained unanswered. This time again the explorers "had found nothing that could be turned to profit, but had only come across naked beach-roving wretches, destitute even of rice, and not possessed of any fruits worth mentioning, miserably poor, and in many places of a very bad disposition...We are left quite ignorant what the soil of this South-land produces or contains, since the men have done nothing but sail along the coast; he who wants to find out what the land yields, must walk over it in every direction; the voyagers pretend this to have been out of their power, which may to some extent be true." The Governor-General and Councillors accordingly intended "to have everything more closely investigated by more vigilant and courageous persons than had hitherto been employed on this service; for the exploration of unknown regions can by no means be entrusted to the first comer..."

These then were the thanks reaped by Tasman, Visscher and their coadjutors[11] for the all but

[1] Cf. General Missive of Dec. 23, 1644. Appendix O. And yet this continued to be believed after Tasman. Cp. RAINAUD, p. 387 and note 5).--

The present Groote Eylandt is called Van der Lijns eiland on manuscript maps (17th and 18th centuries) of the Dutch East India Company.]

[2] Moeilijke bocht, vuile hoek (can this have got corrupted to I. Foule in BELLIN, Hydrographie Française?), Laeg land.--In the manuscript map of De Haan (1760) the present Wessels-island is called Droog eijland, and the passage between the main-land and Crocodils-islands: 't Jagt Limmens-passage.]

[3] Witte water? or rivier (?), Alhier leggen drie bergen.]

[4] General Missive of Dec. 23, 1644.]

[5] As appears from a missive of the G.-G. and C. to the Governor and Council of Banda, dated Nov. 29, 1644.]

[6] See Swart's reproduction of the Bonaparte chart.]

[7] Already in the map of the Amsterdam Town-hall, as reproduced in the first edition of Danckerts, and in the Nolpe-Dozy chart. I do not quite understand the observation of COLLINGRIDGE, Discovery, p. 280, that the name "Nova Hollandia and Nieuw Holland (was) transferred by (the Dutch) to the southern continent from the icy regions they had explored in the Arctic seas, when attempting to reach India and the Spice Islands by a north-east passage."--BURNEY, Chronological History, III, p. 181, and others are mistaken on this point.]

[8] I do not know the authority for RAINAUD'S statement (pp. 370 f.): "Un décret des Etats-Généraux des ProvincesUnies imposa a la plus grande partie des terres nouvellement découvertes le nom de Nouvelle Hollande." For the rest, this page of Rainaud's book contains other statements which it would be hard or impossible to prove.]

[9] See, for instance, Remarkable Maps, III, various charts. The name was most probably given, after the voyage of Hendrik Brouwer in 1643 had removed all doubt as regards the insular character of the Statenland south of South America. Of course, "l'appellation de Nouvelle Zélande (est) bien anterieure au premier voyage de Cook" (RAINAUD, p. 425, Note 2).]

[10] Still, the roughly marked outline of these parts of the coast in Swart's reproduction of the Bonaparte chart, which shows that there was a vague presumption of the real state of affairs, is worth notice.]

[11] The Managers did not allude to their achievements with even a single word!]

completed discovery of the fifth part of the world[1]. Posterity has judged otherwise: foreigners and Tasman's countrymen have vied with each other in magnifying the exceptional importance of these expeditions of which the one undertaken in 1642/3 must rank with the most renowned exploratory voyages of Europeans outside Europe. Tasman's countrymen, and foreigners no less, have recognised the merits of himself and those with him: many a geographical appellation

bestowed on the discovered regions by foreigners[2], furnishes incidental proof of this.

And that such recognition was amply deserved[3], is triumphantly proved even by the fact alone that the results of these two
expeditions have furnished the basis for subsequent voyages, not by
Netherlanders only, but by foreigners as well. When in after days the
latter began to feel inclined and called to penetrate farther into those
regions, they founded their plans on the basis laid by Tasman's voyages between 1642 and 1644[4]. It is the unfading and undying glory of
our fellow-countryman, that others have availed themselves of the out-
come of his exertions.

XIV

PERSONALIA (1644-1659).--TASMAN'S MISSIONS TO DJAMBI (1646), TO SIAM (1647), AND TO THE PHILIPPINES (1648).--CONCLUSION[5].

During some time after his second voyage Tasman remained ashore at Batavia, without, however, being idle. On the 29th of August, 1644, we find him appointed on a committee of inquiry respecting merchandise in a vessel that had suffered shipwreck[6]. On the 4th of October[7], he was promoted to

[1] To Tasman, indeed, especially applies what RAINAUD says pp. 356 f.: "Les anciennes navigations des Hollandais la côte d'Australie...ont une grande importance, car ils nous ont révélé une cinquiéme partie du monde. Pendant près de quarante ans (1606-1644) les marins des Pays-Bas ont fréquenté ces côtes que l'on croyait appartenir au continent austral et contribué plus que personne depuis Magellan k modifier l'idée que se faisaient les théoriciens de cette terre mystérieuse."--Cf. what BURNEY, Chronological History, III, p. 59, says about the expedition of 1642/3: "One of the most importance to geography of any which had been undertaken since the first circumnavigation of the globe."]

[2] E.g. Tasman-land (Kimberley), Tasman-island (one of the Salomon-islands) etc. The name of Tasmania is a striking instance. In Mémoires de la Société royale de Géographie d'Anvers, II, 1883, p. 9, the writer pointedly observes, that "la justice des siècles a converti (le nom de terre de Van Diemen) en celui de Tasmanie." But E. DE HARVEN, the writer in question of the paper just quoted from, entitled "La Nouvelle Zélande," is hopelessly at sea where he says that Van Diemensland was thus christened by Tasman "du nom de sa femme."]

[3] It has rather an odd sound, therefore, when CALVERT, The Discovery of Australia (p. 35), says: These self-explanatory and highly congratulatory remarks [in a chart named "Tasman's map"] show what the Dutch thought of their new acquisition, now for the first time called New Holland; and that while they are disposed to admit some remote Spanish pretensions, they take to themselves the main credit of the discovery." Of course they did, and do. The exploratory voyages of De Queiros, for instance (of which there is question in the map referred to), have never been denied by the Dutch. Nor is there any reason why they should have done

so. But in importance these discoveries will not bear comparison with those made by Tasman and Visscher. Besides, the chart in reference to which Calvert delivers himself as above, is of much younger date than Tasman's voyages. The "N B" at the place where Pieter Nuytsland is marked ("This is the. countrey seated according to Coll. Porry (the italics are mine) in the best climate of the world") convincingly proves that the chart must be younger than the first quarter of the eighteenth century. As regards Purrey, see VALENTIJN, III, 2, Banda, p. 71; MAJOR, Early Voyages, p. CXV; COLLINGRIDGE, p. 303; Resolutions of the Lords XVII, October 3, 1718 and March II, 1719.--The chart reproduced in Calvert's book most probably did duty in an English expedition. However this may be, the mistakes in the place-names in New Zealand sufficiently prove that it was copied from the chart in Thévenot's work.]

[4) RAINAUD, l.c., p. 370: "Pendant plus de cent ans, de 1644 a 1770, date de l'arrivée de Cook a la côte orientale, on ne connut de l'Australie que les parties du littoral explorées par Tasman et ses prédécesseurs"; and on p. 366, Note 4: "Li comme sur d'autres points Cook n'eut qu'a suivre les traces de Tasman." And James Cook himself says: "To the Dutch we must...ascribe the merit of being our harbingers, though we afterward went beyond them in the road they had first ventured to tread" (A voyage to the Pacific Ocean, performed under the Direction of Captains Cook, Clerke and Gore. I, Third edition, London, Nicol and Cadell, 1785, p. XII).

In his expeditions to New Guinea and Australia, William Dampier made use of charts giving the discoveries made by Tasman. See A Voyage to New-Holland etc. in the year 1699 by Captain William Dampier, III (Third edition, London, Knapton, 1729), p. 94; the title-page of A continuation of a voyage to New-Holland, and the chart facing this title-page, etc. etc. Perhaps Dampier also used the Visscher draught, now preserved in the British Museum. The spelling of certain place-names would seem greatly to favour this view.--James Cook availed himself of the results obtained in Tasman's voyages. See, for instance, Journal of Joseph Banks during Captain Cook's first voyage in H. M. S. Endeavour in 1768-71; edited by JOSEPH D. HOOKER (London, Macmillan, 1896), passim; etc. etc. The same thing was done by Marion du Fresne, D'Entrecasteaux, Baudin, Flinders and others, as appears from their instructions or their accounts of their voyages. Of course it would be impossible to cite all this evidence here in extenso.]

[5) I have in this chapter made use of various particulars of Tasman's career that were unknown hitherto.]

[6) Resolutions of the G.-G. and C., Aug. 29 and Sept. 14, 1644. I have mentioned higher up the chart drawn by him in 1644, and reproduced in the present work, which chart indicates the courses to be kept in cruising to watch for the Spanish silver-ships.]

[7) By resolution of the G.-G. and C. of that date. Appendix P.]

a higher grade: he now got the rank of skipper-commander, of which he had repeatedly borne the title, and been invested with the authority. The pay of 100 guilders per month attached to it, was by the resolution even reckoned to have come into force on the 14th of August 1642, at which date he had first been "employed in the said capacity." The terms in which this promotion was awarded to him, mention the "reasonable contentment" of the Governor-General and Councillors with what he had performed in his two voyages of discovery, and the "courage found in him to render additional good service to the General Company on similar occasions, in seeking rich countries or profitable trade-connections;" a clear proof that the gratitude he had deserved, went beyond the official recognition vouchsafed to him immediately after his voyages.

On November 2 he was by the Governor-General and Councillors appointed member of the Council of Justice of Batavia[1] in the room of Marten Gerritszoon Vries, Tasman being specially charged with examining the ships' journals sent in[2]. In this capacity he inter alia formed part of the committee which by resolution of the Governor-General and Councillors of April 18, 1645 was appointed to have solemnly "proclaimed from the steps of the Town-hall of the city of Batavia," the treaty of "trefues" (truce), concluded between the Dutch East India Company and the viceroy of Portuguese India[3]. By the side of these functions he was also engaged in other occupations. Thus, February 1, 1646 is the date of an "Indication of the courses to be kept in navigating from Batavia to Punte Gale in Ceylon, in the months of January and February," drawn up by Tasman[4]; in this document we find him alluding to his "own observations" touching this route, which shows that at one time he had served the Company also to westward of the Malay Archipelago. On the 5th of February he has the task assigned to him of accompanying along Bali Strait certain ships destined for Ceylon, with orders to navigate to Ceylon by the south of Java route[5]. On the 24th of July he is found to have drawn us an "Indication of the courses to be kept by the ships that are to navigate from Batavia to Manilha"[6].

Soon after this, however, his services were again required away from Batavia. The Supreme Government had been informed that the English intended to send to Djambi a considerable amount of specie for the purchase of pepper. Now, in order to "steal a march on our English friends, and prevent them from obtaining a full return-cargo to England," it was resolved to dispatch Tasman to Djambi with the ship Hasewint and 12000 reals in cash, with orders for the Dutch representative there, to "purchase pepper for the amount mentioned, and in the way of business to take as much advantage of the English as possible, even if he should have to pay ¾, or a whole real more per picol than the customary market-rate"[7]. Tasman being the higher in official rank, was to take precedence of the Company's representative during his stay at Djambi[8]. After acquitting hemself of his mission, he returned to Batavia on the 22nd of September, with the report that there was "every appearance of obtaining a considerable quantity of pepper and of taking advantage of the English"[9].

From this date we again find Tasman residing at Batavia for a considerable period, and employed by the Governor-General and Councillors in various transactions, inter alia in matters connected with the fitting-out of ships[10], until about the middle of 1647 he was again charged with the command of a more important expedition. On the 17th of August of that year the Supreme Government resolved to

[1] This council had been instituted in 1620. As regards its jurisdiction, see KLERK DE REDS, Ueberblick, pp. 146 ff.]

[2] Res. of the G.-G. and C., November 2, 1644 ((Appendix Q.)]

[3] He is further mentioned as a member of the Council of Justice in the Resolutions of the G.-G. and C., dated Nov. 12 and Dec. 23, 1644; January 20 and Dec. 17, 1645; and in various court-minutes of 1646.]

[4] Preserved in the State Archives at the Hague.]

[5] Missive of the G.-G. and C. to the commander of the said ships, dated February 5, 1646.]

[6] Preserved in the Hague State Archives. Cf. also the Book of outgoing letters of the G.-G. and C., on April 12, 1647. A few weeks before the date mentioned in the text, Tasman with two of his colleagues "in the church of God" at Batavia had a dispute with a dismissed member of the Council of Justice, who in spite of his dismissal insisted on taking his former seat in the pew reserved for members of the Council. The matter was brought before the court, but I have not found any record of the decision given. Cf. Res. of the G.-G. and C., May 12, 1646.]

[7] Res. of the G.-G. and C., Sept. 4, 1646.]

[8] Missive of the G.-G. and C. to the Dutch supercargo at Djambi, Sept. 6, 1646.]

[9] Res. of the G.-G. and C., Sept. 22, 1646.]

[10] Res. of the G.-G. and C., March 9, 1647.]

send three ships to Siam "for the purpose of fetching from there with all convenient speed the required quantity of sappan-wood and other necessary commodities mentioned in the requisition from the

Netherlands, together with a sufficient supply of timber and of rice for the use of the interior; also to provide to the full the required quantity of benzoin, tin and sappan-wood for the districts of Surat and Persia." The command of the ships was entrusted to Tasman, who at the same time had orders to deliver various presents to the King of Siam and the Magnates of the kingdom. During his stay in Siam Tasman took precedence of all the Netherlanders residing there[2]. According to his instructions, dated August 24, he was to weigh anchor on the following day.

Tasman returned to Batavia on the 20tb of November. This time, it is true, Siam had not yielded so much merchandise as had been looked for, but for the rest the reports he brought back were of a highly satisfactory nature[2]. The letters and presents were "with due solemnity and in accordance with the Siamese ceremonial handed to his Majesty and his Berckelangh"[3] by Tasman himself and the head of the Dutch factory. "The King showed himself much pleased with the same, and by word of mouth promised to assist them in whatever they should have to ask for." The general state of affairs was such that the Governor-General and Councillors, in reporting Tasman's mission to the Managers[4], could state "that the Company's affairs in Siam were in a thriving way."

After his return from Siam we find Tasman again at Batavia, where in January 1648 he was charged with the muster of the return-fleet then ready to sail[5]. In the same month the Supreme Government considered the expediency of once more attempting to inflict a blow on the Spaniards in the Philippines. Since at that juncture they were "abundantly provided with ships," the Governor-General then in office, Cornelis Van der Lijn, Van Diemen's[6] successor, on January 18, besides suggesting certain expeditions of a commercial character, submitted the following proposal to the Council of India: "Inasmuch as now, in two consecutive years[7], each time powerful armaments, both as regards ships and men, have been dispatched to Manilha for the purpose of harassing our common enemy the Spaniard, of utterly crippling the said Spaniard there by continual attacks, by cutting him off from the Chinese trade and by intercepting his silver-ships, and of even expelling him from the Moluccas[8] in course of time, to the end that we may the more securely for the Company possess the said parts and consequently also Amboyna and Banda; as also of thereby increasing the trade of Taijouan[9]; these desired objects, however, having been left unattained up to the present, owing to divers obstacles and intervening circumstances"; therefore the Governor-General deemed it advisable "again" to fit out a like expedition "on the same errand." The Council "unanimously" considered "the proposed further attempt against the enemy highly necessary and calculated to further the well-being of the Company, and at the same to do serious damage and notable prejudice to this our general enemy the Spaniard, on account of all which the proposal was carried nem. con." The command of this expedition was given to Jacob Jacobszoon Van der Meulen[10], who, however, fell ill while unforeseen circumstances were causing delay in the dispatching of the expedition[11], so that it became necessary to look about for a substitute. The choice of the Governor-General and Councillors then fell on Tasman[12], and the terms in which

[1] Missive of the G.-G. and C. to the Dutch supercargo in Siam, Aug. 24, 1647, and other documents referring to this voyage.]

[2 Missive of the G.-G. and C. to the Dutch "chief" and his Council in Siam, April 22, 1648.]

[3] Or Phra-Klang, a Siamese minister, who managed the foreign affairs.]

[4] General Missive, Dec. 31, 1647.]

[5] Daily Register of Batavia, 8-15 January, 1648.]

[6] Van Diemen had died, April 19, 1645.]

[7] As concerns these expeditions, see L. C. D. VAN DIJK, Neêrlands vroegste betrekkingen met Borneo, den Solo-Archipel,...Siam,...enz. (Amsterdam, Scheltema, 1862), pp. 288 ff.]

[8] The Spaniards were still holding their own there.]

[9] In their General Missive of January 18, 1649, the G.-G. and C. state that the repeated "attempts against Manilha" have given an extraordinary impulse to the trade of the Chinese with the Dutch in Formosa. These attempts also prevented the Spaniards from trading with Cambodja.]

[10] Res. of the G.-G. and C., January 27, 1648.]

[11] Res. of the G.-G. and C., April 11 and 21, 1648.]

[12] Res. of the G.-G. and C., April 27, 1648.]

the command was entrusted to him are highly flattering[1]: "Mature deliberations," the Supreme Government writes, "were held on the question, which of the Company's available servants of sufficient rank had best be appointed and nominated to the charge aforesaid, in consequence of which it was unanimously determined and resolved to employ on the said service in the capacity of Commander, Skipper-commander Abel Tasman (of whose ability and experience we are likewise fully assured)." At the same time, April 27, 1648, Tasman was honourably discharged of his membership of the Council of Justice.

The 14th of May is the date of the "Instructions for Commander Abel Jansen Tasman and the Plenary and Privy Councils of the eight ships and yachts, destined to set sail from (Batavia) for the coast of Manilha, for the purpose of harassing and injuring our general enemy the Spaniard, and obstructing his trade with China, as also of preventing him from sending ships to Nova Hispania this year." Of these eight ships the Banda was to be the "flag-ship or admiral"; the vice-commander of the fleet, Dirk Ogel, was ordered on board the Jonge Prins, and Rear-admiral Johan Truytman on board the ship Reijnsburch. The ships were manned with 900 seafaring men, and 250 soldiers, forming 5 companies, commanded by 2 captains, 3 lieutenants, 5 ancients and 12 sergeants, all of them chosen from the "ablest" military men to be found at Batavia. The ships carried 226 pieces of cannon, "to wit, 44 of gun-metal and 182 iron ones." To the expedition also belonged "a number of Mestizos and a Chinaman, well acquainted and experienced in those parts, in order to supply Tasman with reliable information touching several bays and inlets unknown to him up to now." No instructions were given as to the route to be followed: it was left to the "experience" of Tasman and his Council, "to perform" the voyage as quickly as possible " between Mindora and the mainland of Luconia, towards the Inbocadero[2] as far as Cabo de Spiritu Sancto[3]." Here they were directed to endeavour to intercept the silver-ships coming from Mexico, and at the same time to try to prevent the Spaniards from conversely sending out ships to Mexico. The Governor-General and Councillors hoped that Tasman would not meet with any great resistance, since, they thought, the succours of ships and other necessaries received by the Spaniards in Manilha must have been inconsiderable of late years. The admiral was to " keep up the blockade of Manilha down to the first of October, at which time the season is past for making the voyage to Nova Hispania, the more so as there is no other practicable passage than that through the Embocadero." After cruising in these waters till October 1, he was to "run straight for Sangora[4], which is being invested by the fleet of the king of Siam, and in the taking of which," the Governor-General and Councillors wrote, "(this prince) has requested our aid[5], in order to assist in taking possession of the town for the said Majesty, unless this has been effected before your arrival; if not, you will use your best endeavours in the work, seeing that by so doing we shall render the said King an important service, in consequence of which we may expect to obtain great advantages and benefits for the Company." In furtherance of the object last mentioned, Tasman himself was directed to go back to Siam after the capture of Sangora, in order to strengthen the interest of the Company also in that-country. In order to stimulate the zeal of the men, rewards were promised, e.g. to every one who should first discover any silver-ship that was afterwards captured or destroyed. Tasman was at the same time instructed "to note down in the chart all such corrections as experience should prove necessary, likewise to map out all islands, reefs, rocks, sand-banks and shoals, and finally to have sufficient plans and drawings made of all fortresses, fortified places, towers and other considerable buildings."

On the 13th of May everything was ready for departure and the next day "at noon a festive leave-dinner took place at the residence of the Lord Governor-General, at which dinner the Commander and the chief officers of the Manilha armament, together with certain of the Company's qualified servants, attended by special invitation." On May 15 "at early morning," the Governor-General, "attended by certain of the Lords Councillors and other qualified persons," went on board the Banda for the purpose of formally installing Tasman, and at noon the fleet put to sea[6].

[1] Cf. also Tasman's Commission, dated May 14, 1648. Appendix R.]

[2] Bernardino Strait.]

[3] The north-eastern extremity of Samar.]

[4] On the east coast of the Malay peninsula.]

[5] See the letter of the Phra-Klang of Siam in the Daily Register of Batavia, April 30, 1648; Missive of the G.-G. to "Oija Berckelangh," dated April 22, 1648.]

[6] Daily Register Batavia, May i3-15, 1648.]

On June 6 Mindoro was reached. They first tried to make prisoners of war, and obtain "reliable information concerning the enemy's position." They sailed along the north coast of Mindoro, through Bernardino Strait (the Embocadero), and obtained information from prisoners who had fallen into their hands near the island of "Thijgauw" (Ticao). The information supplied disappointed Tasman, for it taught him that he had come too late to prevent the sailing of the ship destined from Manila to Mexico. He immediately proceeded on his way to Cape Espiritu Santo at the north-eastern extremity of Samar[1], "in order to watch for and intercept the Spanish silver-ship"; on the way "divers harbours, bays and inlets were visited," but no enemy's ships seen. The Dutch vessels kept cruising there for some time, but without any success: no ships came in sight. The fleet was, however, overtaken by a violent storm, in which the Rijnsburch went down with part of her crew, and another ship, "utterly helpless and having lost her masts and yards," got separated from the rest of the fleet[2]. The remaining ships re-assembled and once more took to cruising north of Samar, after first taking in refreshments at the island of Catanduanes.

On July 28 it was resolved to make an attempt against the bay of Albay on the south-east coast of Luzon, with a view to landing, and trying to get possession of the Spanish fortress and magazines there. The attempt was successful: the enemy at first prepared for defence, but on the 30th of July, when Tasman was proceeding to an attack on "the fortress of Albay," it was found that the Spaniards had abandoned it, and retreated to the interior. But the hope of capturing a large stock of ammunition here was frustrated. The Dutch occupied the conquered fortress, and on August I undertook an "expedition into the interior" of the province of Camarines with the object of pursuing the enemy. For this purpose the Dutch troops were formed into eight companies. They expelled the enemy from the village of "Cagsagua," which was laid in ashes. After this raid the Dutch returned, and quitted the bay of Albay after having likewise razed the fortress and the surrounding village-- "all of them notable feats" in the opinion of the Supreme Government. The resolution to quit Albay was hastened by the circumstance that a deserter from the enemy and certain prisoners reported that the Spanish silvership coming from Mexico had evaded the Dutch ships by sailing round the north of Luzon, in consequence of which information it was decided that an attempt should still be made to capture this ship. Two ships of the fleet having been dispatched to Formosa according to the Instructions, the Dutch commander went in pursuit of the Spanish vessel north of Luzon with the four remaining ships of the armament. In this way he arrived at the east-coast "in Lampon," opposite the island of Polillo. There they sighted the silvership of which they were in pursuit, "an opportunity as dear to us as our own life" writes Tasman. The Spaniards, however, set fire to the vessel, rather than give it up to the enemy. The crew and passengers had previously quitted the ship, and of her cargo nothing fell into the hands of the Dutch. Tasman had now executed what he had been enjoined to do by his Instructions, so far as it had been in his power--but the G.-G. and C. wrote that in this respect the undertaking had not "come up to their wish." The commander then resolved still to "harass the enemy also round by the north, and to make some show of our armed forces on the whole coast of Luconia, in order to reconnoitre the various ways of access to the island and impress the enemy with some wholesome terror." This time again the enemy remained in hiding; not a vessel was seen. First came the turn of the Babuyan isles, where Tasman knew his ground, having visited these parts in 1639 on the expedition commanded by Quast. Here also the Dutch laid waste and destroyed what they could lay hands on, not, however, without meeting with some resistance from the enemy. Thence they "navigated along the west-coast of Lucon, with the intention of running into Manilhas Bay, in order to ascertain the strength of the enemy's naval forces." But adverse circumstances, among the rest the disabled condition of one of the ships, prevented the execution of this bold project, and on September 29 the west-coast of Luzon was left behind. The expedition just described was the last important undertaking of the East India Company against the Spaniards in Asia, for soon after there was peace also in these parts. The ships next proceeded on their way to Siam, where, according to the Instructions given by the Governor-General and Councillors, they had to support the ruler of this country against his enemies.

They reached Siam after a difficult passage on the 11th and 12th of November. It was high

[1] On old Dutch charts this island is called Tandaya or Philippines. See e,g. VALENTIJNS chart of the Philippines. Tasman also gives the name "d'eijlanden van de Philipinas" or "Ignatios-eijlanden," to Samar and the islets lying near it.]

[2] This ship arrived safe at Formosa (Missive of the Governor and Council of Formosa to Tasman, dated October 8, 1648).]

time, the number of sick persons on board the ships being very large. The Banda alone had 90 of them, Tasman himself[1] among the number, and in all there had already been 70 deaths[2]. Refreshments were forthwith requested and obtained of the Dutch manager at Aiuthia[3].

On board the ships there were only 664 men left, among them 191 soldiers, "the greater part of them being ill and disabled." Nor was it wonderful if, whatever appearances were kept up before the King of Siam, and whatever confident statements were made to this potentate as to the strength of the Dutch, the Dutch felt sensibly relieved, when they were informed that the expedition of Siam against Sangora had been given up, since the King of Siam, who had once before met with a rebuff there[4], had now put it out of his head altogether[5]. Tasman was therefore at liberty to set sail for Batavia, which he did on the 16th of

December[6], and in January 1649 returned to the capital of the Dutch Indies.

For Tasman personally the voyage to the Philippines entailed very unpleasant consequences. In the course of this expedition, led on by passion, and perhaps heated by wine[7], he was guilty of an act which it is impossible to excuse, even if we make allowances for the coarser modes of thinking of the time. While he was anchored with his fleet off the Babuyan isles, and had gone into camp in one of them, on August 27 he issued an order forbidding the military on pain of death to go outside their quarters. In direct contravention of this order, on the evening of the following day Tasman, returning to the camp from a monastery where he had been "banqueting and carousing" with certain officers, found two sailors on forbidden ground. They had gone out on a foraging expedition by order of one of their officers, and pleaded ignorance of Tasman's order, while the sentinels had allowed them to pass out. Without any form of law, even without hearing the sailors, Tasman on the spot condemned them to be hanged on a tree. He hurriedly made a halter with his own hands, and put it round the neck of one of the delinquents, at the same time ordering vice-commander Ogel, in spite of the latter's energetic protest, to ascend a tree and hang the sailor in question by the neck. While Tasman was fitting a halter round the second sailor's neck, Ogel quietly allowed the first to drop on the ground, so that this time Tasman's passion and rage had no irretrievable consequences[8]. But on his return to Batavia the commander was indicted before the Council of Justice on account of this act of violence[9]. Tasman asserted that the sailors had made an attempt at desertion, that it was not true that he had been

[1] Report of the Commissioner to Siam, Pieter De Goyer, dated September 8, 1648.--De Goyer had been sent to Siam for the customary annual inspection. This time, among other things, he was directed to institute an inquiry respecting certain complaints, which Tasman, after his visit to Siam in 1647, had formulated against the Dutch manager there, Jan Van Muyden. The latter asserted that Tasman had played an anything but honourable part there, and had attempted to supplant Van Muyden in favour of a subaltern official of the East India Company, who had succeeded in getting round Tasman. To me it also seems that Tasman's mode of dealing was not quite correct. But on the other hand Van Muyden's reputation was none of the best. As regards this affair, see Instructions for De Goyer, dated September 7, 1648; missive of Van Muyden to the G.-G. and C., Dec. 18, 1648; De Goyer's Report; "Copia attestatiën," made in Siam, June 9, 1648; General Missive, January 1649; Criminal Rolls of the Council of Justice at Batavia, June 12, 1649; Res. G.-G. and C., April 23, 1650; General Missive, January 24, 1651.]

[2) The above particulars of this expedition are taken partly from a missive sent in by Tasman and his Council, dated Nov. 11, 1648, of which a very slovenly copy is found inserted in the Daily Register of Batavia for the year 1648; partly from a missive to Formosa, sent by Tasman in August, 1648, and from the General Missive of January 18, 1649. VAN DIJK, Borneo, pp. 300 f., also refers to it, but is often wrong in giving the names of places.--FERDINAND BLUMENTRITT, Holländische Angriffe auf die Philippinen im XVI, XVII and XVIII Jahrhunderte (Separatabdruck aus dem Jahresberichte der Communal-Ober-Realschule in Leitmeritz vom Jahre 1880), who has drawn his information almost exclusively from Spanish sources, does not speak about an expedition under Tasman's command. But presumably what is said on p. 35 about "einige Holländische Kreuzer" regards this expedition, though it does not tally as concerns the details with the more ample information given us by Tasman himself.]

[3) Missive from Siam to the G.-G. and C., Nov. 20, 1648.]

[4) Cf. my Bouwstoffen, pp. 345 f., 375 f.]

[5) "Still, by the readiness which we have shown to comply with their request, our honour has remained intact, while a good deal of expense has been spared, the King appearing so much pleased that he has provided our ships with too lasts of rice and a considerable quantity of refreshments, and besides made us a present of an exceptionally large elephant, measuring upwards of 10 feet, and presented three smaller ones to the Dutch representatives there" (General Missive, January 18, 1649).]

[6) De Goyer Report.]

[7) That Tasman was not averse to conviviality and feasting, was also asserted by commander Van der Stel in Mauritius, who in his letter of June 1, 1644 to the G.-G. and C. charged him with shouting, drinking and rioting (Cf. HEERINGA in Indische Gids 1895, p. 1007).]

[8) VAN DIJK Borneo, p. 301, is mistaken or obscure, since he fails to make it clear that the man was saved.]

[9) The matter was tried there from May 1 to November 23, 1649. I print the sentence below as Appendix S.]

"banqueting and carousing ", and that he had put the halter round the delinquent's neck only by way of "deterrent menace." In spite of this defence Tasman was, on the 23rd of November 1649, condemned to be deprived of his grade and pay "during the pleasure" of the Governor-General, and at the same time, "to declare in public court with uncovered head," that he had inflicted this shameful treatment on the said sailor" extra-judicially, of his own will, and against all form of law." He was also fined and condemned to pay an indemnity to the person molested.

But the affair had other consequences besides. In January 1648 Tasman had been appointed member of the church-vestry (elder) at Batavia[1]. His term of office expired in 1650, and he was not re-eligible. But on the same day on which Tasman's sentence was pronounced by the Council of Justice, delegates from the church-vestry appeared before the Council of India to give notice that the vestry had been compelled to hold the election of vestrymen at an earlier date than usual "on account of the untimely demise and resignation of certain deacons." On this occasion Tasman had not been re-elected elder. They had evidently wished to remove him from the vestry, and had no doubt preferred this more delicate way to a formal deprivation, such as was sometimes resorted to in other cases[2]. The measure was duly ratified by the Governor-General and Councillors[3].

Thus the circumnavigator of Australia found himself suspended from his rank and place of skipper-commander. The duration of his suspension was left to 'he Governor-General's discretion; the Council of Justice had negatived the demand of the advocate-fiscal of India to have Tasman pronounced "incapable of holding any public function whatever."

The suspension was not of long duration. As early as September 24, 1650 he virtually did duty in his old grade again[4], and on the 20th December of the same year he thinks himself justified in petitioning for promotion. But the Governor-General and Councillors opined that "as yet his abilities and services rendered do not deserve more" than what had been allowed him up to now, and did not comply with his request, the less so as there was no vacancy at the time[5]. Shortly after, however, on January 5, 1651, he was fully rehabilitated in due form, and "at his urgent request and seeing that in divers parts of the world he has rendered the Company good services, and may in time to come continue to do so, (was) relieved of his suspension and reinstated in his previous capacity and pay." This reinstatement was at the same time officially assumed to have come into force as early as September 24, 1650[6].

From this time, however, we learn little if anything more respecting his activity in the Company's service. It has been ascertained, however, that he did not long continue in it after this. In 1653 the archives of the East India Company refer to him as "ex-commander," so that he must have given up his place before this date[7].

Little is known of Tasman's life as a private citizen. He continued to reside at Batavia after his honourable discharge from the Company's service. It is highly probable that he was in affluent circumstances; he held considerable property in land, so much even that only a small number of the inhabitants of the capital of Netherlands India equalled him in this respect. He most probably[8] resided then in the most fashionable quarter of the town, on the Tijgersgracht[9]. Here he continued to reside

[1] VALENTIJN, IVb, p. 129.--As late as January 18, 1649, we find Tasman as cosignatory of a missive of the vestry to the "Heeren XVII."]

[2] Cf. e.g. Res. G.-G. and C., January 15, 1647.]

[3] Res. G.-G. and C., November 23, 1649.]

[4] See the list of "Persons promoted" on January 5, 1651. Appendix U. In the Res. of the G.-G. and C., dated Oct. 19, 1650, Tasman accordingly figures as doing actual duty again.]

[5] Res. G.-G. and C., Dec. 20, 1650. Appendix T.]

[6] List of "Persons promoted" on January 5, 1651 (not on January 1, as stated by VAN DIJK, Borneo, p. 301, Note 1).]

[7] I have also found the following note which is not quite clear: "Register of private letters as follows...No. 8. I (Letter) of Abel Jansz Tasman, to the Managers of the East India Company at Amsterdam. All which have by the Honbie Lords G.-G. and C. of India been handed to the undersigned in his capacity of Advocate-fiscal of India, that in virtue of the same he may bring such action as he shall deem proper and advisable. Accordingly ...find the same duly recapitulated...Abel Jansz Tasman has failed to prove his contention. Batavia, this last day of January, A. D. 1653. Herman Klencke van Odessen."--Perhaps this refers to a private letter from Tasman, received in Holland in 1651 (Res. XVII, October 3, 1651). The Lords XVII asked information about the matter from G.-G. and C. (Missive Oct. 14, 1651).]

[8] In his will, however, he describes himself as living outside Batavia.]

[9] I follow LAUTS here (Verhandelingen en berigten Zeewezen, New Series, IV, p. 290). Though at variance with what I have written in Groningsche Volksalmanak for 1893, p. 141, the following account which I transcribe in full, on mature consideration and on reading General Missive Dec. 10, 1650, appears to me to be well-founded. Lauts delivers himself as follows: "The well-to-do citizen (Tasman)...was among...the greatest landed proprietors of the town of Batavia. This becomes evident from the plan of Batavia, drawn up in 1650 in consequence of the constant extension and embellishment of the town (Note: The plan in my possession, a MS. one on a pretty large scale, I have not found anywhere reproduced)...According to the plan the whole area of the town, both west and east of the great river, covered 5,544 acres, of which about 288 acres belonged to Tasman (Note: Strictly speaking, Tasman's property was in two parts, 'one of which, known as No. 9, covering 5 acres (= 3 hectares) and 26 rods, was most probably a pleasure-garden. The second part, No. 26, covered 282 acres and 30 rods; it was in Block Q and had west of it the

Tijgersgracht, east of it the Malabargracht, afterwards known as Kaai-mansgracht, to the north was the Amsterdam gracht, and to the south the Stads-binnengracht). Only very few of the townsmen owned more property in the town...Tasman's property was in the best and most fashionable part of the town, where he himself resided on the Tijgersgracht." The place of "Block Q" can easily be found on plans of more recent date, e.g. on one of the year 1770, in the work, entitled Batavia, de hoofdstad van Neerlands 0. Indien, in derzelver gelegenheid, opkomst, etc. (Amsterdam, Harlingen, MDCCLXXXII) facing p. 114.--In missive G. and C. of Banda to the Councillors of India, April 20, 1646; in General missives, Jan. 15 and Dec. 31, 1647; in missive of G.-G. and C. to Banda, April 24, 1648, there are references to Tasman's financial affairs, but the details are without importance.]

with his second wife, to whom he had been married in 1632[1]. His daughter from his first marriage, Claesgen, had married at Batavia, first Master Philip Heylman, about whom we know little or nothing--he died about January 1656, an elder of the church-vestry of Batavia--(a son named Abel had been born of this marriage), and in second wedlock Mr. Jacob Bremer, who was still alive in 1672, and is found to have held various dignities[2].

Though during the closing years of his life Tasman no longer held any public function, he did not remain wholly inactive. He took part in what little trade for private account was permitted to such Netherlanders established in India as were not attached to the service of the Company. Thus in 1653 we find him referred to as joint-owner of "a private vessel," trading along the north-coast of Java. On the 10th of March of the same year the Governor-General and Councillors wrote to the Dutch "resident" at Djapara that the said vessel,--a "tingang," not a large ship--was ready to depart for his place, and that "Ex-commander" Tasman and his partner had paid into the Company's treasury 1000 pieces of eight "to be paid back to them in cash (at Djapara) for the furtherance of their trade, this republic being interested in the said trade." On the following day the vessel set sail from Batavia for her destination[3]. Tasman himself commanded the vessel, which reached Djapara on the 15th of March, and, after taking in cargo, returned to Batavia already on the 28th of the same month[4]. Similar expeditions were undertaken by Tasman also later in the same year. Thus in the month of August he lay with his vessel near Demak. In a letter, dated August 23, 1653, written by the functionary who at the time represented the Company's interests there, to the Governor-General and Councillors, we find inter alia the statement that he (the functionary in question) "(intended) to go to the coast in order to secure for the Company the Batavian vessels already loaded, and Mr.

Abel Tasman[5], who was about to return to Batavia with his tingangh and two rafts constructed for the occasion, on which he has put a large number of cattle." It would seem that these "rafts," or the use to which they were put, were an innovation introduced by Tasman. At least the writer of the letter goes on to say that "in case this invention of Tasman's should be found practicable, though in my opinion it may easily turn to his disadvantage, it will henceforth be no longer necessary to provide ship-room for the transport of this description of cargo; but I am inclined to share the opinion of the majority of experts who are afraid the whole thing will prove a failure." We do not know the result of this experiment for seeking a means to save ship-room in the transport of cattle by sea: a rather humble task for the first circumnavigator of Australia!

We now lose Tasman's track for a few years. Not until the 10th of April 1657 do we once more come upon a document from his hand, namely his last will and testament[6], which bears the

[1] On the 16th of August 1650, there was publicly sold at Amsterdam, also on behalf of Tasman, "for the time residing in East India," a house in the Palmdwarsstraat, of which house Tasman's wife was presumably joint-proprietress (Dozy, l.c. p. 318).]

[2] These particulars are derived from Tasman's will, printed by DOZY, (Bijdragen taal-, land- en volkenkunde, XXXVI, pp. 329-331; see Appendix V.--Cf. also Dozy l.C., pp. 327 f.;-VALENTIJN, IVA, pp. 396, 401, 407, 408, IVB, pp. 131, 132; Ress. G.-G. and C. Jan, 14, 1653, Jan. 20, 1656 (Heylman); June 1, 1658, etc. etc. (Bremer); Daily Register Batavia edited by VAN DER CHIJs, Anno 1661, 1663-1667, passim.]

[3] "Lists of the ships, both such as have arrived here (at Batavia) from other ports, and such as have left here for other places," on March 11, 1653.]

[4] "Copies of missives from the Residents at Japara," March 28, April 29, 30, 1653.--Daily Register Batavia, 1653, edited by VAN DER CHIJS (Batavia, The Hague, 1888), p. 39.]

[5] We may conclude from the Daily Register of Batavia 1653, pp. 122-124, that these ships near Demak had been prevented from setting sail by the Javanese, and were set free on this occasion.]

[6] Printed infra, Appendix V., from DOZY'S text l.c.]

date just given. On that day he was "in his dwelling-house outside the town of Batavia."Although" being able to stand and walk," he was "sick in body " then, but still enjoying "the use of his senses, memory and mental faculties." The expression that he "recommended his dead body for honest bestowal into the earth or the sea according to circumstances" allows us to conclude that he had no idea as yet of giving up his commercial undertakings by sea. In his will he divided his estate between his wife and his daughter and grand-children. First and foremost, however, he made a legacy: "In the first place," we read, "I give and bequeath to the poor people of the village named Luytgegast the lump sum of five-and-twenty guilders of forty half-stivers each..." Tasman did not forget his humble birth-place in the days of his prosperity.

From a note dated October 42, 1659, by the Secretary of the "Weeskamer" (Board for the management of orphans' estates) at Batavia[1], at foot of the authenticated copy of the will preserved in the Government Archives at Batavia, we may perhaps conclude that Tasman had died shortly before the date just mentioned, though it is impossible to fix the time of his decease with certainty[2]. However this may be, his death must have occurred about this time[3], for as early as the beginning of 1661 his relict had again signed a contract of marriage with Jan Meynderts Springer, an ex-functionary of the Company (he had been skipper), and afterwards a prominent burgess of Batavia[4], who had been established in the capital of Netherlands India as a private citizen for a few years past. There is a dash of romance about this union, for it took place by the bride's sick-bed: "In the evening, after prayers," we read in the Daily Register of the Castle of Batavia, February 5, 1661[5], "Jan Meynderts Springer, burgess of this town, was by Their Worships (the Governor-General and Councillors) at his request allowed to be married to-morrow to his betrothed bride, mistress Anna Tjerks, widow of the late Commander Abel Tasman, the customary banns having been published on three consecutive Sundays, and permission granted that on account of her grievous illness the ceremony shall take place by her sick-bed, on condition that the said Springer shall by way of consideration pay too pieces of eight to the deaconry of this town (Batavia)."

Tasman has by some been pronounced a genius[6]. No one who has endeavoured to obtain a full and comprehensive view of his life and labours, will readily endorse such a conclusion. It would be hard in his life and life's work to point to any flashes of genius or any acts indicating a superior mind. But he undoubtedly was a man of great talents, a man of far more than common ability. No great problems presented themselves to him for solution, while he felt in himself the power to solve them once for all; but he certainly used his best endeavours to further the solution of existing problems that had hitherto baffled the world. Once the question of the existence and whereabouts of the mysterious South-land having been asked, it had not left him at rest; and when the solution of the problem was to be attempted, when a man like Antonio Van Diemen above all, "a name which will ever rank among the greatest promotors of maritime discovery "[7], had undertaken the solution as his life's task, Tasman as well as Visscher were "earnestly inclined" to the exploratory expeditions required for the purpose. And few will be found to gainsay that he performed the task with great talent, with great ability, with great energy and with great care[8].

[1] The note bears the signature "Cornelis Mol. Secrets." That Mol was Secretary to the "Weeskamer," we know from the Daily Register of Batavia 1659, edited by VAN DER CHIJS (Batavia, The Hague, i889), pp. 2, 118.]

[2] It is worth noting that the Daily Register of Batavia for 1659 does not refer to his death.]

[3] The Pall Mall Magazine for March i896 brings on p. 354 a reproduction of a portrait alleged to represent Abel Janszoon Tasman. Mr. Walker, of Hobart, writes to me: "The original painting is a full-length." In the accompanying letter-press the portrait is attributed to Bartholomeus Van der Heist. Mr. C. HOFSTEDE DE GROOT, director of the Amsterdam Museum of Engravings, a competent authority on the history of Dutch painting, writes to me that he does not believe the picture to be a Van der Helst. It is highly improbable a priori, that the portrait should represent Tasman. When in 1637/8 Tasman was staying in the Netherlands, it is very unlikely that he should have indulged in the luxury of sitting for his portrait; and at a later time when he was better off and better known, he did not visit Europe again.]

[4] Ress. G.-G. and C. May 29, 1654, October 5, 1655, etc. etc.--Daily Register Batavia 1659, p. 113.]

[5] Edition VAN DER CHIJS (Batavia, The Hague, 1889), p. 31.]

[6] MALTE-BRUN in Nouvelles Annales des Voyages, I, p. 2; N. G. VAN KAMPEN, Vaderlandsche Karakterkunde, II, A (Haarlem, Bohn, MDCCCXXVI), p. 97.]

[7] BURNEY, Chronological History, III, p. 55.]

[8] BURNEY, l.c. III, p. 112, writes: "In conclusion, it must be allowed, that Abel Jansen Tasman was both a great and a fortunate discoverer, and his success (1642/3) is in part only to be attributed to Fortune. The track in which he sailed, and the careful Reckoning kept by him, which so nearly assigns the true situation to each of his discoveries, shew him to have been an enterprizing and an able navigator; and it is to be esteemed no small addition to his important discoveries, and indeed no slight evidence of his merit, that he explored a larger portion of Unknown Sea in a high latitude, and thereby restricted the limits of a supposed continent, more than any other navigator between the time of Magalhanes and the time of Captain

Cook."--In Notes géographiques et historiques in Voyage de La Pérouse autour du monde, rédigé par L. A. MILET-MUREAU (Paris, 1797), p. 109, we likewise read: "Toutes les terres et Iles vues dans ce voyage (1642/3) ont été reconnues de noire temps, et trouvées dans la position qui leur avait été asslgnee par Tasman." See also HOOKER, Journal Banks, pp. 221 f.; Krusenstern's opinion in MOLL, Verhandeling, pp. 191 f.]

And by the side of his nautical talents he displayed other qualifications of a high order throughout his chequered and deeply interesting career: "now a soldier, now a diplomatic agent; one day a trader, the next a member of council"[1]. It is to be regretted, no doubt, that we cannot feel for his character the same admiration with which his talents fill us: on more than one occasion his life shows shadows, where his moral qualities are concerned; shadows which are only partially accounted for by the coarse-grained surroundings among which he lived and had his being.

And yet Holland may be proud to number among her sons the man who once, by no less a judge than Adam Johann Von Krusenstern, was styled the greatest navigator of the seventeenth century[2]. "Holland, the land of dauntless mariners," it has once been said in daring metaphor, "Holland has written on the seas the epic of her glorious history, she has once made the ocean one of her tributary provinces"[3]. Of this grand epos Abel Janszoon Tasman and his helper Frans Jacobszoon Visscher have written one of the cantos; it was they who incorporated part of this province with the country of their birth.

[1] Eene Herinnering" by J. E. HEERES (Eigen Haard, 1892, p. 747).]

[2] Cf. MOLL, Verhandeling, p. 187.]

[3] Cp. Eigen Haard, 1893, p. 747.]

APPENDICES

Appendix A

December 27, 1631.

(Dirckie Jacobs, the bride's mother, gives her consent to the marriage aforesaid, as declared by Jan Jacobsz.) Item, appeared Abel Janszoon, of Luttiegast, sailor, aged 28 years, living in Teerketeisteech, widower of Claesgie Heyndrix; and Jannetie Tjaerss, of A(msterdam), aged 21 years, assisted by her sister Giertie Tjaers, living in Palmstraat;

Requesting that their banns may be published on three consecutive Sundays, etc.

Abel Jansen Tasman   X X
                         (Mark of Jannetie Tjaerss)

[Extracted from the Register of Banns of marriage.]

Appendix B.

On Sunday the eleventh do.[1] H. Geldorpius has joined in wedlock as below

Abel Jansz.   Jannetje Tjaerts.
[Extracted from the Register of Marriages.]
[1) January 1632.]

Appendix C.

Resolution of the Govemor-General and Councillors, dated January 17, 1642.

Abel Janssen Tasman, of Lutge gast, being recently returned to this country, having been appointed skipper in the flute den Engel ad 60 guilders on October 1, 1638, is by the present continued as such ad 80 guilders for a term of three years counting from October 11 last past, on condition, however, that he shall remain bound to complete his ten years' engagement entered into in the Netherlands (seeing that he has brought his wife along with him).

Appendix D.

Resolution of the Governor-General and Councillors, dated Friday, August the first, 1642.

Since our predecessors the Lords Governors-General Jan Pietersen Coen deceased, Pieter de Carpentier, Henrick Brouwer and ourselves, pending their administration and ours, have been greatly inclined to forward the navigation to the partly known and still unexplored South- and East-land, in order to the direct discovery of the same, and to the consequent opening up of important countries or leastwise of convenient routes to well-known opulent markets, in such fashion that the same might in due time be used for the improvement and increase of the Company's general prosperity, Our Worshipful Masters have not only highly approved of the said plan, but also by successive general missives strongly recommended the said Governors-General to carry the same into execution; but owing to the requirements of commerce and war in this country, together with the deficiency of fitting vessels, to our regret little has up to now been done towards the furthering of this good work, except that in the beginning of our administration, we have, pursuant to the resolution of February 13, 1636, dispatched via Banda along the coast of Nova Guinea, under the command of the Hon. Gerrit Thomassen Pool deceased, the yachts Cleen

Amsterdam and Wesel, which ships have by contrary winds been prevented from proceeding so far to the East and South as we could have wished and had instructed the said Hon. Pool to attempt; in such fashion that, having up to that time obtained scant knowledge of the matters aforesaid, we have since amply and fully conferred with divers persons known to be thoroughly conversant with the matter in hand, more especially with the renowned and highly experienced pilot Frans Jacobssen Visscher, touching discoveries eventually to be made, and the direction in which they had best be undertaken; and having received from him as also from other experts certain advices and opinions in writing concerning this matter, we now deem and consider it most expedient for an expedition to set out about this time from here for the island of Mauritius, and from there to navigate southward with the sun in the beginning of the month of October, thus endeavouring to make the discoveries aforementioned from the West to the East; which matter having been diligently weighed by us, and it having been found on due estimation of the Company's naval forces now available, that for the furtherance of this important work and useful undertaking we might, without detriment to the Company's ordinary trade and military interests, fit out and dispatch two able ships adapted for the purpose and at present available for the said enterprise;

Therefore, for the reasons above set forth, it has been unanimously determined and resolved, to dispatch for the discovery and exploration of the supposed rich Southern and Eastern lands, etcetera, the ship Heemskerck and the flute de Zeehaen, the first manned with 60, and the second with 50 of the most efficient able-bodied sailors available on the roadstead here, victualled at all points for twelve calendar months, but with rice for eighteen ditto; furthermore amply provided with all useful necessaries and with divers commodities and a quantity of precious and other metals for bartering purposes in the lands eventually to be touched at; the whole under the command of the Hon. Abel Janssen Tasman, who together with Commander Matthijs Quast deceased sailed east of Japan A.D. 1639, and is now strongly inclined to this discovery; seconded by the aforementioned Pilot Major Frans Visscher, together with Skippers Gerrit Janssen and Jde T'Jercksen, who have both of them approved themselves experienced navigators, and Merchant Jsaack Gilsemans, who is sufficiently versed in navigation and the drawing-up of land-surveyings: supported by such able steersmen as the said Tasman shall be able to select; instructing them, as before attempted, first to sail from here to Mauritius, and after taking in refreshments there, to sail due south about the middle of October as far as 52 or at most 54 degrees Southern Latitude, in order to discover and survey in an easterly direction such lands as they shall meet with in the latitude aforesaid or before it, to determine their proper longitudes and latitudes, and duly observe and note whatever requires observation for the purposes of this important voyage, without, however, running farther south than the 54th degree, even in case they should not find any land there; next to sail as far as the longitude of Nova Guinea and the Solomon Islands or somewhat farther east, in order to ascertain whether there is any passage into the great South-Sea between the said lands, the land of d'Eendracht and the unknown South-land; subsequently, after completion of this search, to steer east and north of the Solomon Islands and Nova Guinea through the narrows near Gilolo, in order to find out likewise whether the west-coast of Nova Guinea already discovered, is connected with the land of d'Eendracht, or divided from it by channels and straits; then to run along the whole length of the utterly unknown north-coast, as far as 21 degrees, near the Willems River; thence to return hither with the east monsoon through Sunda Straits, in the month of June or July of next year.

The Hon. Justus Schouten, Councillor-extraordinary of India, is by the present directed to draw up fitting Instructions with the advice of the parties concerned, and to submit the same for due examination to this Council by the time the said ships shall have completed their preparations; the Hon. Cornelis Vander Lijn being at the same time enjoined to put on board the ships bound for the South-land, over and above what they shall themselves require and what is embarked for bartering purposes, such necessaries for the island of Mauritius as Commander Adriaen vander Stel, who arrived here with the flute d'Eendracht on July 26 last, requires for the said island.

Actum in the Castle of Batavia, date ut supra, signed

Antonio van Diemen.	Salomon Sweers.
Cornelis van der Lijn.	Cornelis Witsen.
Joan Maetsuijker.	Pieter Boreel, and
Justus Schouten.	Pieter Mestdagh, Secretary.

Appendix E.

Instructions for Skipper Commander Abel Jansz. Tasman, Pilot-Major Franchoys Jacobsz. Visscher, and the Council of the Ship Heemskerck and the Flute de Zeehaen, destined for the discovery

and exploration of the unknown and known South-land, of the South-east coast of Nova Guinea, and of the islands circumjacent.

It is well-known that a hundred and fifty years ago only a third part of the globe (divided into Europe, Asia and Africa) was known, and that the Kings of Castile and Portugal (Ferdinandus Catholicus and Don Emanuel) caused the unknown part of the world, commonly called America or the New World (and by cosmographers divided into North and South America), to be discovered by the highly renowned naval heroes Christopher Colombus and Americus Vesputius, who thereby achieved immortal praise; likewise that about the same time the unexplored coasts and islands of Africa and East India were first reached and discovered by the famous Vasco de Gama and other Portuguese Captains. With what invaluable treasures, profitable trade-connections, useful trades, excellent territories, vast powers and dominions the said kings have by this discovery and its consequences enriched their kingdoms and crowns; what numberless multitudes of blind heathen have by the same been introduced to the blessed light of the Christian religion; all this is well-known to the expert, has always been held highly praiseworthy by all persons of good sense, and has consequently served other European Princes as an example for the discovery of many Northerly regions.

Nevertheless up to this time no Christian kings, princes or commonwealths have seriously endeavoured to make timely discovery of the remaining unknown part of the terrestrial globe (situated in the south, and presumably almost as large as the Old or New World), although there are good reasons to suppose that it contains many excellent and fertile regions, seeing that it lies in the frigid, the temperate and the torrid zones, so that it must needs comprise well-populated districts in favourable climates and under propitious shies. And seeing that in many countries north of the line Equinoctial (in from 15 to 40 degrees Latitude), there are found many rich mines of precious and other metals, and other treasures, there must be similar fertile and rich regions situated south of the Equator, of which matter we have conspicuous examples and clear proofs in the gold- and silver-bearing provinces of Peru, Chili, Monomotapa or Sofala (all of them situated south of the Equator), so that it may be confidently expected that the expense and trouble that must be bestowed in the eventual discovery of so large a portion of the world, will be rewarded with certain fruits of material profit and immortal fame.

This being the case, and no European colony being better fitted for initiating these promising discoveries than the city of Batavia (which is as it were the centre of East India, both known and unknown), therefore the Governors-General Jan Pietersz. Coen and Henrick Brouwer (our predecessors in office) were during their periods of office seriously inclined to send out expeditions for the discovery of the unknown Southern regions, although they were prevented from so doing by voyages of greater necessity. Likewise ourselves have, during the period of our office, been well disposed towards the same, our Lords and Masters equally recommending the said matter as a highly useful one. For all which reasons we, the Council of India, having made a proper estimate of the Company's naval forces now available, and having found that, without detriment to other more important expeditions, both warlike and mercantile, two able and fitting vessels may without inconvenience be set apart for this purpose, have determined no longer to postpone the long contemplated discovery of the unknown South-land, but to take the matter in hand forthwith, using for the purpose the ship Heemskerck together with the flute de Zeehaen (duly provided with all necessaries), placing the said vessels under the command of your persons, to whom, as well fitted and inclined to the same, we with full confidence commit this important voyage, trusting that you will ably and prudently manage the same with good judgment, necessary courage and the requisite patience, so that on your return you will be able to give us a full and satisfactory account of the execution of your mandate.

We shall not here enlarge on the various methods for discovering the South-land, submitted to us in writing by certain experienced pilots, but will rather refer you to the appended copies of the same, of which you can avail yourselves on occasion; while in the following we proceed to give you such rules and instructions as we think best adapted to meet your case, it being always understood, however, that you will be at liberty at all times to introduce such corrections as with the advice of your council you shall deem to be required by time, place and circumstances, with an eye to the advantage of the company and the attainment of our object; all which we confidently leave to your tried judgment and experience. Tomorrow morning, after due muster, you will then set sail together, and try to get out of Sunda Strait as quickly as possible, setting your course so as to fall in speedily with the South-east trade-wind, with which you will take your way westward to the island of Mauritius (running in sight of Diego Rodrigos), and come to anchor there in the South-east harbour before the fortress of Fredrick Henrick, where you will hand to Commander Adriaan Van der Stel our annexed letters together with the commodities you have taken on board for the said island; while you are there, you will quickly and properly provide your ships with water, firewood and refreshments, bestowing on this no more than 14 or 15 days, however, or till. the 12 or 15th of October at the latest, taking due care that during that time your crews be properly refreshed and dieted exclusively on fresh viands, to which end we have given the needful orders to Commander Van der Stel, to assist you to the extent of his power, and if necessary to allow you to go a-hunting for wild animals.

As before mentioned, your necessities having been provided for, you will about medio October, or earlier, set sail from the Mauritius, shaping your course with the trade-wind nearly southward, as high as wind and weather shall permit, until about the Southern Latitude of 36 or 38 degrees, when you have got out of the eastern trade-wind, you shall fall in with the variable winds, with which you will always put about on the best tack for getting to the southward, until you get into the western trade-wind, with which you will sail nearly southward until you come 'upon the unknown South-land, or as far as South Lat. 52 or 54 degr. inclusive; and if in this latitude you should not discover any land, you will set your course due east, and sail on until you get into the longitude of the eastern point of Nova Guinea, or of the Salomonis islands, situated in about 220 degr. longitude, or until you should meet with land; and when this is the case, whether in the beginning or afterwards when you have sailed more to eastward, you will sail eastward (as before mentioned) along the coasts or islands discovered, following the direction of the same.

All the lands, islands, points, turnings, inlets, bays, rivers, shoals, banks, sands, cliffs, rocks etc., which you may meet with and pass, you will duly map out and describe, and also have proper drawings made of their appearance and shape, for which purpose we have ordered an able draughtsman to join your expedition; you will likewise carefully note in what latitude they are situated; how the coasts, islands, capes, headlands or points, bays and rivers bear from each other and by what distances they are separated; what conspicuous landmarks such as mountains, hills, trees or buildings, by which they may be recognised, are visible on them; likewise what depths and shallows, sunken rocks, projecting shoals and reefs are situated about and near the points; how and by what marks these may most conveniently be avoided; item whether the grounds or bottoms are hard, rugged, soft, level, sloping or steep; whether one should come on sounding, or not;

by what land- and seamarks the best anchoring-grounds in road-steads and bays may be known; the bearings of the inlets, creeks and rivers, and how these may best be made and entered; what winds blow in these regions; the direction of the currents; whether the tides are regulated by the moon or by the winds; what changes of monsoons, rains and dry weather you observe; furthermore diligently observing and noting whatever requires the careful attention of experienced steersmen, and may in future be helpful to others who shall navigate to the countries discovered. The summer season being evidently the time best fitted for the intended voyage and for the observation of all the things mentioned, on account of the length of the days and the shortness of the nights at that time of year, you will take care not to neglect time nor waste any needlessly, but make the most of the summer season and the favourable weather, when you will be able to sail on by night and by day alike, which you cannot do when the days are drawing in and there is no moon; seeing that it is of the highest importance that you should get sight of everything, if you wish to discover a great deal soon and in a short time.

As already mentioned, you will explore the coast discovered on an eastward course, or if you should not meet with any land, you will continue your eastward course as far as the longitude of New Guinea or the Salomonis islands. Unless after mature consideration you should deem it better to sail no farther than the longitude of the eastern extremity of the known South-land or of the islands of St. Pieter and Franchoys, and then to direct your course due north, in order to run in sight of these islands; thence to follow the coast to eastward in order to ascertain how far it extends and whether this discovered South-land joins Nova Guinea near Cape Keerweer, or whether it is separated from the same by channels or passages; in which latter case, by passing through one of the channels as far as the Wilms river, the north-coast might be conveniently explored sailing westward; but since it is most likely to be supposed that these lands join each other without a break, and it is uncertain whether you would be able to follow its south-coast as far as Nova Guinea, owing to its north-east trend and your falling in with the eastern trade-wind, so that you might perhaps be compelled for that purpose to go southward in order to fall in with the westerly winds, or otherwise to return to Batavia by the westward route along the land of d'Eendracht; therefore we think the route first proposed to be the more eligible one, namely, to sail to eastward as far as the longitude of Nova Guinea, or of the -Salomonis islands.

We therefore, as aforesaid, give it as our opinion, that in case you should in sailing eastwards not come upon any land in 48, 52 or 54 degrees Southern Latitude, you should not seek any land farther to southward, but proceed on an easterly course as far as the longitude of the east side of Nova Guinea, and with the consent of the Council, from there to the Salomonis islands, or still 100, 150 or 200 miles more to eastward, in order to become the better assured of a passage from the Indian Ocean into the South-sea, and to prepare the way for afterwards conveniently finding a short route to Chili.

When on the course thus indicated you shall have reached the longitude of the Salomonis islands, or have got from 100 to 200 miles more to eastward, you will with the south-east trade-wind and keeping a westerly course explore the same, and otherwise sail northward and westward, south or north of the islands (if such they be), towards the east-coast of Nova-Guinea and along it, as far as the island of Gylolo, where we have no doubt you will discover certain passages or channels to the south, which, that you may conveniently and profitably pass through the same, you will endeavour to be near in the unsettled month of April, in order to get to Cape Keer-weer, with the variable winds, by interior passages (if practicable) east of Ceram, and the. islands of Cauwer, Quey and Arou; all which should be effected before the east monsoon begins to stiffen, as otherwise efforts to run to the south so far to eastward would be attended with great difficulty.

Now when you have fetched up Cape Keer-weer (in a degrees latitude) you will sail along the coast of this land to westward as far as Wilms river (situated in Eendraghts landt in 21 degrees), making use of the south-east trade-wind, and following the direction of the coast; observing, describing and noting what above has been enumerated as regards the discovery and exploration of the unknown South-land, more especially diligently endeavouring to ascertain whether between Nova Guinea and the land of d'Eendracht, particularly at the points just mentioned, Cape Keer-weer and the Wilms river, there are any channels or passages to southward, such channels or passages being of the utmost importance for getting speedily into the South Sea.

What instructions were in 1636 given to Commander Gerrit Pool for the discovery of this unknown region, you will be able to see from the copy of the same which we annex, and of which you can avail yourselves on occasion.

From Willems river, which we hope you will reach about the month of May or July or next year, you will shape your course straight for the middle of the isle of Java, then sail along its south-coast with the east-monsoon, and thus pass through Sunda Strait on your way to Batavia, between the western extremity of Java and the Prince islands.

That you may avoid running against unknown land, and being cast on shoals or cliffs, and prevent accidents thereby arising so far as human precaution may go, you will cause a a proper look-out to be kept without intermission, and promise a reasonable reward to the person who shall first see and become aware of unknown coasts or dangerous shoals.

The above is what we have deemed needful to enjoin you regarding courses and sailing-routes in order to the discovery of the unknown southern regions; what other things may be required according as circumstances shall present themselves, we herewith refer to your good management, experienced seamanship and the decision of the Ship's council.

Passing on to other matters which you will have diligently to observe, attend to and pursue in the voyage now by you to be undertaken, we urgently recommend you, in discovering new coasts, to come to anchor now and then when time and place shall serve, always seeking and selecting convenient and fitting bays or road-steads, where you may lie with least danger, for which purpose the two Tinganghs you take along with you, may be of great use, more especially in the discovery and exploration of bays, shoals, harbours, rivers, etc., what time you shall have come near Nova Guinea and the land of d'Eendracht, or got into smooth seas with the south-east trade-wind.

In landing with small craft extreme caution will everywhere have to be used, seeing that it is well-known that the southern regions are peopled by fierce savages, for which reason you will always have to be well armed and to use every prudent precaution, since experience has taught in all parts of the world that barbarian men are nowise to be trusted, because they commonly think that the foreigners who so unexpectedly appear before them, have come only to seize their land, which (owing to heedlessness and over-confidence) in the discovery of America occasioned many instances of treacherous slaughter. On which account, you will treat with amity and kindness such barbarian men as you shall meet and come to parley with, and connive at small affronts, thefts and the like which they should put upon or commit against our men, lest punishments inflicted should give them a grudge against us; and by shows of kindness gain them over to us, that you may the more readily from them obtain information touching themselves, their country, and their circumstances, thus learning whether there is anything profitable to be got or effected.

So far as time shall allow, you will diligently strive to gather information concerning the situation of their country, the fruits and cattle it produces, their method of building houses, the appearance and shape of the inhabitants, their dress, arms, manners, diet, means of livelihood, religion, mode of government, their wars and the like notable things, more especially whether they are kindly or cruelly disposed; showing them various specimens of the commodities you have taken with you for that purpose, so as to learn what commodities and materials are found in their country, and what things they are desirous of obtaining from us in return; all which matters you will carefully note, correctly describe and faithfully set forth in drawings; keeping for the purpose an ample and elaborate journal, in which you will set down an exact record of all that may befall you, that on your return you may be able to lay a proper report before us.

If, unlikely as it may be, you should happen to come to any country peopled by civilised men, you will give to them greater attention than to wild barbarians, endeavouring to come into contact and parley with its magistrates and subjects, letting them know that you have landed there for the sake of commerce, showing them specimens of the commodities which you have taken on board for the purpose, for which we refer you to the specified invoice; closely observing what things they set store by and are most inclined to; especially trying to find out what commodities their country yields, likewise inquiring after gold and silver whether the latter are by them held in high esteem; making them believe that you are by no means eager for precious metals, so as to leave them ignorant of the value of the same; and if they should offer you gold or silver in exchange for your articles, you will pretend to hold the same in slight regard, showing them copper, pewter or lead and giving them an impression as if the minerals last mentioned were by us set greater value on.

You will prudently prevent all manner of insolence and all arbitrary action on the part of our men against the nations discovered, and take due care that no injury be done them in their houses, gardens, vessels, or their property, their wives, etc.; nor shall you carry off any of the inhabitants from their country against their will; should, however, any of them be voluntarily disposed to accompany you, you are at full liberty to bring them hither.

If in the course of this voyage there should be discovered any rich countries or regions, islands, or passages, profitable to the Company, we shall not be found ungrateful towards the managers of the expedition and all the well-behaved men taking part in it, duly recompensing the pains and trouble they have been at, and honouring them with such rewards as their services done shall be found to have deserved; on all which all of you may rely to the fullest extent.

The ships are manned with no able-bodied men, to wit the Heemskerck with 60, and the Zeehaen with 50; they are victualled and provided with all necessaries for twelve, and with rice for 18 calendar months; out of these you will have the ordinary rations regularly and properly served out, with two meat-days and one bacon-day every week, and one mutchkin and a half of arrack every day; all which you will cause to be properly arranged and seen to. Of strong arrack each of the ships will take on board two hogsheads, to be in moderation served out in cold weather for the sake of the men's health. But above all you will carefully husband the fresh water, that you may not come to be in want of it, or be forced to delay your voyage in order to seek it, or return from such search unsuccessfully.

And to the end that this voyage may be well regulated and performed in accordance with these instructions and our good intentions, that proper order may be maintained among the men, law and justice be administered in conformity with the general regulations, and furthermore everything that in so long and dangerous an expedition shall occur and be required, be done and executed to the best advantage and service of the Company; therefore we have appointed the Honble Abel Jansz. Tasman Commander of the two ships, by the present authorising him to carry the flag on the main-topmast of the Heemskerck, to convene the council, and permanently to occupy the chair in the same; in consideration thereof commanding and enjoining all Officers and sailors, excepting none, who have been ordered on board the ships Heemskerck and Zeehaen, to acknowledge the aforesaid Abel Tasman as their Commander and Chief, to respect and obey him, and likewise on all occasions to assist him with their good advice and diligent service; for the furtherance of the voyage and the discovery of unknown lands, in such fashion as befits vigilant and faithful servants, and as on their return they can conscientiously answer for to ourselves.

The council of these ships will consist of the persons following, to wit:

The Commander Abel Jansz Tasman, permanent President,
The Skipper Yde T'jercxsz on board the Heemskerck.
The Pilot-Major Francois Jacobsz   do.
The Skipper Gerrit Jansz on board the Zeehaen.
The Supercargo Isaack Gilsemans   do.

The Subcargo Abraham Coomans, on board the Heemskerck who will also act as Secretary.

The first steersman Henrick...on board the Zeehaen.

In this Council all matters relating to the progress of this voyage and the execution of our instructions will have to be discussed and determined, the Commander to have a double vote in case of equality of votes; in matters touching the administration of justice the master-boatswains will also have to be summoned, according to the orders of Our Masters, but in matters relating to navigation, such as the courses to be held and the discoveries of lands to be made, the Pilot-major Francoys Jacobsz will give his vote immediately after the Commander, and his advice be duly attended to, the plan of this voyage having been drawn up in conjunction with him; in these cases the second mates will also have to be summoned to attend the Council, in which they will have an advisory vote; the Commander will have to collect these votes, and decisions to be determined by a majority of the same, the Commander taking due care that all resolutions taken be forthwith recorded, properly signed and efficiently executed for the service of the Company.

In case of decease of Commander Tasman (which God in His mercy avert), Skipper Yde T'jercksen shall succeed to his place, and command, in all points replacing his predecessor, according to these our instructions, and be obeyed like him.

As soon as you shall be at sea, you will with the advice of the Council, and in order the better to remain together, draw up a proper code of signals, such code being of the utmost importance for the execution of our plan, which code should also contain arrangements necessary for enabling you to come together again, if by storm (which God avert) you should get separated from each other.

Concluding these instructions, we cordially wish you the blessing of the Ruler of all things, praying that He may in His mercy endow you with manly courage in the execution of the intended discovery, and may grant you a safe return, to the increase of His glory, the greater reputation of our country, the benefit of the Company's service, and your own immortal honour.

Done in the Castle of Batavia, the 13th of August, A.D. 1642.

(Signed) Antonio van Diemen, Cornelis Vander Lijn, Joan Maet-suijcker, Justus Schouten, Salomon Sweers, Cornelis Witsen and Pieter Boreel.

All continents and islands, which you shall discover, touch at and set foot on, you will take possession of on behalf of Their High Mightinesses the States General of the United-Provinces, the which in uninhabited regions or in such countries as have no sovereign, may be done by erecting a memorial-stone or by planting our Prince-flag in sign of actual occupation, seeing that such lands justly belong to the discoverer and first occupier; but in populated regions or in such as have undoubted lards, the consent of the people or the king will be required before you can enter into possession of them, the which you should try to obtain by friendly persuasion' and by presenting them with some small tree planted in a little earth, by erecting some stone structure in conjunction with the people, or by setting up the Prince-flag in commemoration of their voluntary assent or submission; all which occurrences you will carefully note in your Journal, mentioning by name such persons as have been present at them, that such record may in future be of service to our republic.

Given at Batavia, date as above,

In the name of the Honble Governor-General and Councillors of India

(Signed) Justus Schouten.

A List of the Papers handed to Skipper Commander Abel Jansz. Tasman (with destination for the discovery of the South-land).

No. 1. Instructions for the Commander aforesaid.
"   2. Observations by Skipper Marten Gerritsz. Vries touching the discovery of the South-land[1].
"   3. Disquisition touching the same discovery by the Pilot-major Francoys Jacobsz.[1]
"   4. Memoir by the same on the same subject[2].
"   5. Spanish description of Nova Guinea and the Salomons islands[1]
"   6. Copy of the Instructions for Commander Gerrit Pool for the dis-covery   of the unknown lands east-ward of Banda, and of the South-land[3].

"   7. Vocabulary of certain words of the languages of the Salomonis islands, of Nova Guinea, and of the islands circumjacent.
"   8. Invoice of the cargoes of the Heemskerck and the Zeehaen[4].
"   9. Inventory of the Heemskerck[1].
" 10 Inventory of the Zeehaen[1].

[1) No longer extant.]

[2) Appendix H.]

[3) Discussed in my text.]

[4) Appendix G.]

Appendix F.

Missive of the Governor-General and Councillors to the Lords XVII.

Most Noble Wise Provident and very Discreet Gentlemen.

We are fully as much disposed as Your Worships to further the discovery of unknown lands; for the undertaking of which there is no want of able skippers and skilful steersmen, much less, thanks to God, of victuals and all sorts of necessaries required for such voyages; what we are in want of, is sailors and especially fitting yachts and flute-ships. We have, however, done our utmost, and have now engaged in making preparation for the further discovery and exploration of the South-land, both of what is as yet unknown and what has already been discovered, of the South and East coast of Nova Guinea, together with the islands situated in those parts; for this purpose, on August the 4th last, as hereinbefore mentioned, the yacht Heemskercken and the flute Zeehaen, under the command of Skipper Commander Abel Jansen Tasman, Frans Jacobszoon alias Visscher, in the capacity of Pilot-Major, and Skippers Yde t'Jercksen and Gerrit Janszoon, seconded by expert steersmen, manned with 110 heads, provided with victuals for twelve, and with rice for eighteen calendar months, navigated to the island of Mauritius; thence, after taking in fresh water and firewood, to turn their course to the south between 12 and 15 October, until they shall have fallen in with the western trade-wind; after which they have instructions to keep on their southerly course till they come upon the known South-land; and in case they do not find the same or other lands within 52 or 54 degrees Southern Latitude, they have orders to turn their course eastward as far as the latitude of the eastern extremity of Nova Guinea or the Salomon Islands, situated in about 220 degrees Eastern Latitude, or until they shall meet with land, in which case they are instructed to sail eastward, as before mentioned, along the coast or islands discovered, according to the lie of the same. Unless after mature deliberation the discoverers should deem it more expedient, not to navigate beyond the longitude of the eastern extremity of the known south-coast or the islands of St. Pieter and St. Francoys, but to skirt in an easterly direction the northern coast of the said land, in order to find out how far it extends, and whether it is connected with Nova Guinea near Cape Keerweer, or divided from it,by channels or straits, in which latter case, by running westward through one of the said channels as far as Willems River, the North-coast can readily be discovered.

But since it may reasonably be presumed that the said lands are connected with each other; if there are many obstacles and inconveniencies to be expected there, as we have more amply set forth in our instructions, we opine that it would be advisable to follow the manner and course first mentioned, videlicet to sail eastward as far as the longitude of Nova Guinea or the Salomon Isles; and should no land be made in thus sailing eastward in 48, 52 and 54 degrees Southern latitude, we leave the Ships' Council at liberty to run from 100 to 150, or even 200 miles east of the Salomon Isles, in order to get the better assured of any eventual passage from the Indian Ocean into the South Sea, and to prepare the way for ultimately discovering a better and shorter route from here to Chili, a point on which there arc hardly any doubts entertained, and which would prove to be a matter of high importance and great advantage to the Company.

Having thus set forth the main points touched upon in the instructions we have given to the discoverers, we shall not further enlarge on this matter here, but as regards the rest, scilicet what observations should be made during the voyage out and in returning; how they should comport themselves towards the natives; item what commodities, goods, precious and other metals, etc., these ships shall take on board, in order to enable the voyagers to find out and observe with the more certainty what goods are in demand with these southern nations, and what articles their countries produce, and the like points of importance, we beg leave to refer Your Worships to our instructions and other inclosed memoranda touching the discovery aforesaid, handed to the Commander and Council of these ships; trusting Your Worhips will derive satisfaction from the perusal of the same, a d will together with ourselves pray Almighty God to crown this enterprise with success, so that it may redound to the benefit and increase of God's church, to the conversion of many blinded heathen, to the profit of the company's shareholders, to the credit of our country, and especially to the honour of the discoverers, to whom in case of success we have promised honourable donations and due promotion in rank.

Hardly any serious doubts are entertained as to the possibility of finding a shorter and more commodious route from here to Chili; the safe return of this expedition will bring us certitude as regards this point. Should its result prove such a route practicable, which God in his mercy grant, the Company will be enabled to do great things with the Chilese, and have opportunities, owing to the said new route, to snatch rich booty from the Castilian in the West Indies, who will never dream of such a thing. We earnestly request Your Worships to give your serious attention to this project, and let us have your advice upon it, since we do not exactly know whether the charter of the West India Company extends to Chili, in which case Your Worships, and consequently ourselves also, would by the said charter be prevented from establishing factories in Chili and engaging in mercantile operations there. Meanwhile, in case of success and of the route proving practicable, we shall neglect no opportunity for dispatching a cargo to Chili by way of trial, that we may become assured what can be done for the Company's benefit in this vast and renowned region, for which purpose we shall require fitting ships, for which and other reasons our strength of seafaring men and sea-going craft cannot well be retrenched to such an extent as Your Worships deem advisable owing to the cessation of hostilities with the Portuguese. And since Your Worships have directed us in this matter most conscientiously to consider with how many ships the Company's commerce over the whole of India can be maintained, we would beg leave to state that last year Your Worships received from us special and ample information on this point, together with a statement of the manner in which, and the places where, the Company's ships were employed for the furtherance of customary commerce, both as to quantity and quality; to which we would now add, that up to the present for the due maintenance of the commerce aforesaid, the number of ships available here has proved too small rather than too large; so that we are sadly deficient in what would be required for the discovery of unknown countries and for the seeking of fresh trade-markets, on both which points, as aforesaid, a great deal more might be done, in which to our regret we have up to the present been unable to effect anything worth mentioning. We have therefore come to the conclusion that in the first time to follow our naval strength must not be reduced or curtailed, but contrariwise increased by the addition of able yachts of little draught, of flutes and small yachts.

We subjoin a detailed list of Your Worships' naval strength in these parts, from which you will readily gather that our application is not destitute of foundation; and we only add that, seeing that we are now at peace with the Portuguese (though, to be sure, for how long the good God only knows), we shall for the first time to come be able to dispense with the strong men-of-war previously applied for; and that, considering that no garrison need further be maintained at Goa, we have, as you will be-duly informed, conformably cut down the amount of our estimate of moneys required here, which we were the more willing to do since .in the course of this year we have been more efficiently seconded by Your Worships than has ever been the case before this.

Written in Your Worships' Castle of Batavia, this Twelfth day of December, A. D. 1642.

Your Worships' affectionate friends and devoted servants, the Governor-General and Councillors of India,

    Antonio Van Diemen.

Anth. Caen. Cornelis Vander Lijn.

Joan Maetsuycker.

J. Schouten. Salomon Sweers. 1642.

Cornelis Witsen.

Appendix G.

Voyage to the South-land debitor to the Office of Batavia f2965.16.12 for the following goods, merchandise etc., by order of the Worshipful Lord Governor-General and Councillors of India embarked and put on board the yacht Heemskerck and the flute Zeehaen, this day sailing from here for the Southland by way of the island of Mauritius, consigned into the hands of Skipper Commander Abel Janssen Tasman, to be by him employed and bartered there, by way of trial, to the best advantage of the. General Company, in case of successful discovery of Southern or Eastern lands, and to be in proper time duly proved and accounted for; the whole being packed, assorted and bought at such prices as may be more detailedly seen from the invoice-book, to wit:

In the yacht Heemskerck (Bill of Lading signed by Skipper Ide Tjercks Holleman) the articles following:

```
4 pieces of coloured cloth, measuring together
    110½ ells, ad 5¾ guilders an ell, .   makes  ƒ 635. 7. 8
5 pieces of silk patholen . . . . . .  „   „  45.—
10 pieces of coloured armozeen . . . . .  „   „  51.—
4 pieces of red beteela . . . . . . . .  „   „  30.—
4 pieces of Guinea linen . . . . . . .  „   „  24.—
10 Golconda blankets . . . . . . . . .  „   „  22.—
10 green Chinese cangans . . . . . . .  „   „  22.15
500 Chinese small mirrors . . . . . .  „   „  65.—
50 catties of Chinese coral . . . . . .  „   „  63.15
1 picol wax . . . . . . . . . . . .  „   „  56.02
2 picols of pepper . . . . . . . . .  „   „  51.—
20 book (?) mirrors ad 2 guilders . . . .  „   „  40.—
50 ordinary knives . . . . . . . . .  „   „  21. 7. 2
19 pounds of elephants' teeth . . . . .  „   „  19.—
2 packets of tinsel . . . . . . . . .  „   „  20.—
200 pounds of ironmongery . . . . . .  „   „  24.—
½ reals' weight of gold in a gold conbangh  „   „  20.14. 6
50 pounds of Dutch steel. . . . . . .  „   „  17.10
50 pounds of Sandal wood . . . . . .  „   „  18. 9.12
4 white narrow baftas . . . . . . .  „   „  20.—
4 yarn taffechelas . . . . . . . . .  „   „  16.—
1 picol sugar . . . . . . . . . . .  „   „  14. 0. 8
25 pounds of tin . . . . . . . . . .  „   „  11. 3. 2
50 pounds of pewter . . . . . . . .  „   „  11. 3. 2
25 pieces of assorted iron pots . . . .  „   „  11. 9. 8
```

20 pounds of cloves . . . . makes ƒ 10.—
200 small Chinese wooden combs . . . . „ „ 10. 4
50 parrangs ⎫
50 small hatchets⎭ *ad* 12ps. per real . . „ „ 21. 7. 2
1 picol cassia lignea . . . . „ „ 7.13
4 pounds of tortoise-shell . . . . . . „ „ 4.16
2 pieces of calitur wood. . . . . . . „ „ 4. 4
50 pounds of lead . . . . „ „ 4.—
50 Chinese needles . . . . „ „ 3. 8
4 blue chelas . . . . „ „ 16.16
20 single tapechindes . . . . „ „ 15.—
4 Sarasses leij de Coutchin . . . . . „ „ 14.—
4 broad Surate chintzes . . . . . . „ „ 12.—
4 poulangobars . . . . „ „ 8. 8
10 packets of Chinese gold-wire . . . . „ „ 1.19
10 pounds of mace . . . . „ „ 2.10
4/8 reals' weight of silver in one coupan . „ „ 1.11.14
10 pounds of nutmegs . . . . „ „ 1.—
50 pounds of various brass wares in a basket ⎫
   divers Nuremberg wares in a basket . . ⎪
50 pounds of sappan wood . . . . . . ⎬ ——
50 pounds of ebony . . . . ⎪
100 pieces of assorted china porcelain . . . ⎪
1 large brass basin . . . . ⎪
3 pearls . . . . ⎭
                                    ———— ƒ 1470. 4

In the flute-ship the Zeehaen (Bill of Lading signed by Super-cargo Isaacq Gilsemans and Skipper Gerrit Janssen, of Leyden) the articles following:

4 pieces of cloth, measuring together 114³/₄ ells,
   ad 5¹/₄ guilders . . . . makes ƒ 659.16. 4
500 small Chinese mirrors . . . . . . „ „ 65.—
50 catties of Chinese coral . . . . . „ „ 63.15
1 picol wax . . . . „ „ 56. 2
2 picols pepper *ad* 10 reals per picol. . „ „ 51.—
10 coloured armozeens . . . . „ „ 51.—
2 pieces of silk patholen . . . . . . „ „ 45.—
20 book(?) mirrors . . . . „ „ 40.—
4 red beteelas. . . . . „ „ 30.—
4 Guinea linens . . . . „ „ 24.—
10 Chinese cangans . . . . „ „ 22.15
10 Golconda blankets . . . . „ „ 22.—
4 white and black narrow baftas . . . „ „ 20.—
4 taffachelas gingham . . . . „ „ 16.—
4 blue chelas . . . . „ „ 16.16
20 single tapechindes . . . . „ „ 15.—
4 Sarasses leij de Coutchin. . . . . „ „ 14.—
4 broad Surate chintzes . . . . . . „ „ 12.—
4 poulangobars . . . . „ „ 8. 8
200 pounds of various ironmongery . . . „ „ 24.—
50 ordinary knives . . . . „ „ 21. 7. 2
20 pounds of elephants' teeth . . . . „ „ 20.—
2 packets of tinsel . . . . „ „ 20.—
50 parrangs ⎫
50 small hatchets⎭ *ad* 12 ps. per real . . „ „ 21. 7. 2
50 pounds of Sandal wood . . . . . . „ „ 18. 9.12
50 pounds of Dutch steel. . . . . . „ „ 17.10
1 picol powdered sugar . . . . . . „ „ 14. 0. 8
25 assorted iron pots . . . . „ „ 11. 9. 8
25 pounds of tin . . . . „ „ 11. 3. 2
50 pounds of pewter . . . . „ „ 11. 3. 2
200 small wooden combs . . . . „ „ 10. 4
20 pounds of cloves. . . . . „ „ 10.—
1 picol cassia lignea . . . . „ „ 7.13
2 pieces of calitur wood . . . . . . „ „ 4. 4
5000 Chinese needles . . . . „ „ 3.18
4 pounds of tortoise-shell . . . . . „ „ 4.16
50 pounds of lead . . . . „ „ 4.—
10 pounds of mace . . . . „ „ 2.10
10 pounds of nutmegs . . . . „ „ 1.—
10 packets of gold-wire . . . . . . „ „ 1.19
5/8 reals' weight of gold . . . . . . „ „ 20.14.06
5/8 reals' weight of silver in one coupan . „ „ 1.11.14
50 pounds of various brass wares in a basket . . „ —.—

<pre>
  50 pounds of sappan wood . . . . ƒ   —.—
  50 pounds of ebony . . . . ,,   —.—
 100 pieces of assorted fine and coarse china porcelain,,   —.—
   3 pearls . . . . ,,   —.—
                                                 ─────────────
                                                 ƒ 1495.12.12
</pre>

Together the cargoes per Heemskerck and
Zeehaen bound for the South-land amount to . ƒ 2965.16.12

Appendix H.

Memoir touching the discovery of the South-land.

In the first place it would appear to us most suitable to set out from Battavia about the middle of August or the first of September at the latest, for divers reasons; first, to use the main part of the summer season and the long days for making discoveries, since it is unknown to us what occurrences we may meet with that might take up our time; secondly, in order to take in fresh water, firewood, etc., at the island of Mauritius, to reach which we shall require at least a month under favourable circumstances, while we shall have to lie still there from 15 to 20 days; the sun then declines south of the equator, which is the best season for us to sail south with the sun as far as 52 or 54 degrees; by that time we shall have got to the beginning of November, when in those southern regions the longest days are approaching, together with the most favourable weather, and northern winds from time to time. It is therefore the best season both for getting southward quickest and for making discoveries, since about that time we may sail pretty fast by day and night alike, whereas on the other hand at the period of the short days one can never be without certain apprehensions, and is besides liable to be befallen by storms, with snow, hail and cold weather.

(Proposal touching the discovery, starting from Batavia via Mauritius, sailing south and eastward.)

But if we sail hence at the time aforesaid, we have from 3 to 3½ months' time to make this discovery with minute care, both as regards large rivers, bays, rocks, shoals, sands, shallows and depths, and the nature of the inhabitants; what commodities are obtainable and what others may be disposed of there in return; all which requires a good deal of time, since such people are shy, rude and savage, and can therefore hardly be treated with and pacified within a short period. Now, in case we should have got to the latitude aforesaid of 52 or 54 degrees, without coming upon land, we should, in accordance with the preceding instructions, have to shape our course to eastward, until we should meet with land, or as far as the longitude of the east side of Nova Guinea, and then sail north by west in order to fetch up Nova Guinea; or, if preferred, we might run so far to eastward till we had the Salomones islands north of us, and then keep a northward course in order to discover the said Islands, which lie spread over so vast an area that we could hardly miss them; this, considering everything, appears to us the best way of going to work, since we do not in the least doubt that divers strange things will be revealed to us in the Salomones islands; the return-voyage might take place along the north of Nova Guinea, then along Cheram-laeut, passing between Nova-Guinea and Cheram to reach Banda or Amboina.

(Respecting the discovery starting from Europe, sailing eastward from Capo de goods hoope.)

Further discoveries might be made by starting from the Netherlands, sailing for Cape de bonne Esperance, and from there running directly southward as far as the 54th degree aforesaid, or until land should be met with: by so doing one would begin the discovery fully 50o miles more to westward; and, should no land be found, one might, as before mentioned, sail eastward as far as the longitude of the Salomonis islands.

(To make the discovery, startingt from the Netherlands, via Brazil, and sailing eastward from the Strait of Lemaire.)

We shall now propose still another method for discovering the South-land still 700 or 800 miles farther westward, starting from the Netherlands.

After leaving the Netherlands one might set one's course for the Bay de todos los Sanctus or rio Janeiro in the Brazil, there take in refreshments and provisions of all necessaries, then run for the strait of Lameer, keeping in with the eastern side, to wit Staten landt, which is a high double jagged coast, always covered with snow; and since there is no want of westerly winds there, one might easily sail eastward along Staten landt, and in this way come to a perfect knowledge how far the said Staten landt extends; sailing on the said easterly course as far as the longitude of the Salomonis islands, in which way one would become acquainted with all the utterly unknown provinces of Beach, and could return to Amboina or Banda by the aforesaid route northward of Nova Guinea.

(Indications for the discovery, starting from Chili, of the Salomonis islands as far as the Strait of le Maire.)

In my opinion it would at present be impossible to discover the South-land referred to, between and starting from the Salomonis islands, eastward to the strait of la Meer.

Coming from the west the voyage would be too long and too difficult, nor, owing to the westerly winds, can it be done by coming from the east through the strait of la Meer; but if the Netherlanders possessed some fitting refreshing-station on the coast of Chili, for example Conseption or Chillewey, one might fit out an expedition from Chili, and run westward with the trade-wind in from 12 to 15 degrees Southern Latitude (this being the latitude in which the Salomonis islands are currently believed to lie), until one got sight of the Salomonis islands, or got into the longitude in which they are marked on the Globe. If in this case one could get refreshments there, it would be all the better. Starting from the Salomonis islands aforesaid, one would have to do one's best to get to the south, and to fall in with the western Inds, even if it were as far as the 50th degree or until land were met with. Then taking advantage of these western win one would have to sail eastward again as far as the strait of la Meer or the ancient strait of Maggellaen; by which method one will be enableII to discover the southern portion of the world all round the globe, and find out what it consists of, whether land, sea or icebergs, all that God has ordained there; excepting only the north side of the South-land already known: viz. from 22° S. L. or froth the Willems river, situated nearly south of the middle of Java, down to the Valsche hoecq, bearing from the island of Arnoy[1] east-south-east, 60 miles.

(Proposal for discovering the land between Nova Guinea and d'Eendrachtslandt.)

The only part undiscovered would then, as just said, extend from the cape in 22 degrees south of the middle of Java, to the Valsche Hoecq, tying 6o miles east-south-east of the south-side of Aru, in Latitude 8 degr. 10 min. South; but this coast forms a large bay here, and was partly discovered before as far as 17 degrees near Staten river, in the year 1623, April 24; still, there is a large part left undiscovered from there to the cape in 22 degrees, since the coast there trends chiefly to west and west by south.

Now in order to make a perfect chart of this remaining part, and further rectify certain parts imperfectly mapped before, it would be necessary to sail from Banda or Amboina eastward as far as Aru in the month of March; and from the southern extremity of Aru to shape one's course east-south-east in order to reach the Valsche Hoecq in April, which is a doubtful month as regards the wind; in which case one might easily by sounding get as near the land as time and circumstances will allow. According to the annotations of the previous discoverers, the sea is very shallow there, so that with the wind blowing hard from the west, which would make the coast there a lee shore, one would be exposed to many perils. But if one arrived in those parts in April, I think there would be no difficulty; and this could be done without much loss of time, since the discoverers sailing westward as far as 22 degr. S. Lat., and coming near or along the South-land, can fetch up the coast of Java on the south side, and thus could easily come back to Batavia in the month of June or July.

Written in the castle of Batavia this 22nd of January, 1642.

(Signed) Franchoijs Jacobsen.

    [1) Aroe.]

Appendix I.

Wednesday, August 13, 1642.

The ship Heemskerck and the flute Zeehaen, according to the resolution of the first of this month destined for the unknown South- and East-lands, via the island of Mauritius, being now ready for departure, having taken on board their victuals, provisions, necessaries and whatever more is wanted for this expedition, together' with the necessaries for Mauritius itself; item the instructions for the leaders of this voyage, drafted by the Honble Justus Schouten, Councillor-extraordinary of India, together with the missive addressed to Commander Adriaen vander Stel in the said island of Mauritius, and duly amplified by the Secretary of this assembly in accordance with the suggestions of the Governor-General, being drawn up in due form and now ready to be handed to the parties concerned; item the other documents required for the said voyage being also ready; all of them having been properly examined by this Council and ratified by our signatures,

It has been unanimously resolved to let the discoverers aforesaid set sail in the name of God early to-morrow after due muster, to take their course from here to Mauritius and thence to the southward. To this end the Honble Schouten and the Secretary aforesaid are hereby deputed to install on board the Honble Abel Janssen Tasman, as Commander of these two ships, and at the same time to make promise to the officers and the crews of the two ships alike, that we shall on their return honourably reward them all for their good services in discovering and exploring important coasts or useful routes or passages.

Thus resolved and determined in the Castle of Batavia, datum ut supra.
(Signed)

Antonio Van Diemen.
Cornelis Vander Lijn.
Joan Maetsuijcker.
Justus Schouten.
Salomon Sweers.
Cornelis Witsen.
Pieter Boreel, and
Pieter Mestdagh, Secretary.

Appendix J.

Friday, June XIX, A.D. XVICXLIII.

Inasmuch as on the 15th instant Commander Abel Janszoon Tasman has again come to anchor on this road-stead (for which God be praised) with the yacht Heemskerck and the flute Zeehaen, who on the 14th of August of last year had been dispatched from here by way of the island of Mauritius with orders to navigate to and discover the unknown Southern and Eastern lands; as shown by the journals kept on board the said vessels and the reckonings recorded by them, in sailing on an eastern course they found the wind very strong and the seas so high that they did not think it advisable to run farther southward, but thought it better gradually to deviate more to northward of the said course, until they came to 44° Lat. and 167° Long., where on the 24th of November last they sighted and discovered a certain great land surrounded by islands, which land they have christened Antonij van Diemens land, without, however, being aware how far it extends to north-west or north-east, and without communicating with any of the inhabitants, the ships having only sailed along the south-coast of it and onward as far as 189° Long., where in the Latitude of from 43 to 35 degrees, on December 13, they sighted and came upon another large land, to which they have given the name of Staten landt, of which latter land they found the natives to be of a malignant and murderous nature, seeing that in a certain large bay these natives came upon them with a number of strongly. manned prows, cut off one of our boats from the ships, and killed four of our men in her with wooden clubs, and wounded another who returned on board swimming; the said land was found to trend to Southward in Lat. 35° and Long. 192°, and consequently a passage from the Indian Ocean into the South Sea had been found, it having been ascertained that in this parallel, where the westerly trade-wind is blowing, there is a convenient passage to the gold-bearing coast of Chili; from there running on a north-east course they next in Lat. 21° and Long. 205° came upon certain islands apparently well-peopled by civilised and kindly disposed natives, who allowed them to land and take in fresh water, at the same time providing them with such refreshments as they stood in need of; thence they next turned their course to westward, passed a few more islands and shoals, which they strongly surmise to form part of the Insulis Salomonis, and then went on tacking about as far as between the 5th and 4th degree, where they got the coast of New Guinea alongside; they sailed on north of this coast, until they got between the western extremity of it and the island of Gilolo, then ran south towards the north coast of Ceram, and farther on through Buton strait, whence they arrived here as above stated;

And inasmuch as by the instructions handed to Commander Tasman aforesaid and his Council, we had assured and promised them that, in case in the course of this voyage any rich lands or islands profitable to the Company's commerce should be discovered, or serviceable passages for navigation be found, we should on their return award a handsome recompense to the leaders of the undertaking and the common sailors for extraordinary pains taken and diligence shown by them;

therefore, although in point of fact no treasures or matters of great profit have as yet been found, but only the lands aforesaid and the promising passage referred to been discovered, whose real situation and nature will have to be further ascertained by a subsequent investigation set on foot for the express purpose,

yet we have unanimously resolved for the reasons above cited to award a recompense to the said discoverers on behalf of the Honourable Company and in fulfilment oft our promise aforesaid; to wit, to the commander, skippers, super-, and sub-cargoes, steersmen and inclusive of the book-keeper, two month's pay each; and to the common sailors and soldiers one months' pay each; for which they shall each of them be credited in running account to the debit of the Company, and subsequently be debited again for the amount of the said recompenses, which shall be paid to them in cash.

Done and resolved in the Castle of Batavia, date as above,
(Signed)
Antonio Van Diemen.
Cornelis Van der Lijn.
Joan Maetsuijcker.
Justus Schouten.
Salomon Sweers, and
Pieter Mestdagh, Secretary.

Appendix K.

Noble, worshipful, wise, provident and very discreet gentlemen,

From our latest advices you will have seen that we had fitted our certain ships for the further discovery of the South-land both known and unknown, and what instructions we had given to the leaders for their guidance in the said expedition. The yacht Heemskerck and the flute-ship Zeehaen sent out for the purpose under the command of Skipper-commander Abel Tasman, returned safe to this roadstead on the 15th of June last, having made the home voyage between Halemachera and Nova Guinea through the narrows or passage of Maba along Ceram and through Bouton strait; in the course of their voyage they lost to men through illness, and four others besides that were slain by the savages on the coast of Staten land. Several new lands and islands have by them been discovered in the south, besides which they affirm that they have found an open passage into the South Sea to get to Chili. It would carry us too far to detail in this place the particulars of this voyage, nor would it be necessary since everything is most fully and amply set forth in the Batavia minutes, under the date of June 15, while for your Worships' further information we also send along with the present, the daily registers kept by the aforesaid Tasman and the Pilot-major Francois Jacobsen Visscher, the said registers pertinently showing the winds and the courses held, and faithfully delineating the aspect and trend of the coasts, and the outward figure of the natives, etc. We have, however, observed that the said commander has been somewhat remiss in investigating the situation, conformation and nature of the lands discovered, and of the natives inhabiting the same, and as regards the main point has left everything to be more closely inquired into by more industrious successors. It also appears that in running to southward from the island of Mauritius, they did not sight any land until they had come to the 49th degree; but thence going eastward they finally got into the South Sea to the south of the Southland. Now, that in this latitude there really is a passage to Chili and Peru, as the discoverers stoutly affirm, we are not prepared to take for granted, since, if they had run a few more degrees to the south, they might not unlikely have come upon land again, perhaps even upon the Statenland (thus named by them) which they had left south of them, and which may possibly extend as far as Le Maire Strait, or maybe even many more miles to eastward. All;this is mere guess-work, and nothing positive can be laid down respecting unknown matters.

In spite of all this, after the return of the discoverers aforesaid we did not give up our plan of having the same voyage undertaken a second time in October last with a fitting number of ships, yachts and men, with orders to further explore the passage to Chili, to form alliances and trade-connections with the Chilese, with God's aid to wrest from the Spaniards the island of Chily-Way, and to establish a permanent settlement there, and by the way endeavour to obtain some good booty in the South Sea; all which bade fair to be crowned with success and to result in considerable profit to the Company. But these plans of ours were frustrated by the machinations of the Portuguese over here (with whom we were compelled to renew hostilities, and to vindicate the company's right, to employ our forces against them, as we shall further show in the fitting place). Meanwhile the overbold Portuguese in these parts are bringing about their own destruction, but at the same time are doing the Spaniards such staunch service that for the moment we are forced to leave the latter unmolested in the South Sea and elsewhere. Besides this, they would probably have met the Lord General Brouwer in the waters of Chili (unless they should have been there before his Worship), which might have given rise to unexpected encounters on both sides. Still, we have resolved to stand by our plan of taking the matter in hand again towards September or October next (provided the Company's affairs will allow of it), this time arms in hand, and to have conveyed to Chili such goods as we know to be in request there, unless your Worships should send us counter-orders, to the effect that we are forbidden to navigate and trade thither in virtue of the West India Company's Charter, decision on which point on your part we look forward to receiving in March or April next.

At all events, about that time the further discovery of the South-lands will be vigorously taken in hand again, in the well-founded hope that something profitable will ultimately turn up there. And in order to prevent their being idle in the interim, we intend to dispatch the said Tasman and Pilot-major Frans Visscher with two yachts to the north coast of Nova Guinea by way of Banda about the month of February next; and to have the said land discovered and surveyed from Cabo Keerweer in 57 degrees to westward, in order to ascertain whether the known South-land is connected with the same or divided from it, which point if decided is likely to be of material assistance in the exploration subsequently to be undertaken. The result of which expedition shall in due time be reported to you.

Written in Your Worships' Castle of Batavia, Dec. 22, 1643...

Antonio van Diemen.
Anth. Caen.
Cornelis van der Lijn.
Joan Maetsuycker.
J. Schouten.
Salomon Sweers.

Appendix L.

Wednesday, January 13, 1644. (Resolution for expedition.)

Having besides made an estimate of the quantities of merchandise which, in furtherance of our trade and for the maintenance of the same, will shortly have to be sent off from here, and of the ships required for the said object, available in this country; and becoming aware that over and above the ship-room wanted for the proper attainment of the purpose just referred to, we are in a position to dispatch two or three yachts for the discovery of new lands, and the seeking of profitable markets; and having for a long time past been inclined to have certain knowledge whether the coast of Nova Guinea and the unknown Southland form one unbroken whole, or are divided from each other by channels or passages, as our predecessors in office as long ago as the years 1607, 1617, 1623 and 1627, and as ourselves during our term of office in the year 1636 sent an expedition thither consisting of the yachts Cleyn Amsterdam and Wesel, under the command of

Commander Gerrit Thomasz Pool; but having up to the present, owing to various intervening obstacles, obtained no absolute certainty as regards these points;

item, being desirous of ascertaining whether the new Van Diemens land discovered in the south in November 1642 by skipper-commander Abel Jansz. Tasman with the yacht Heemskerck and the flute Zeeheen, be connected with these two large lands or either of them, or utterly divided from both of them;

item, being anxious to know what other unknown islands may lie between Nova Guinea and the South-land; also, what treasures, advantages, profitable trade-connections or convenient channels or passages may be available there for the benefit of the General Company and for the extension of its trade and the improvement of its position in these parts;

therefore, for the reasons and considerations hereinbefore mentioned, it has been unanimously determined and resolved, that, for the purposes of further and more complete discovery, and of more detailed investigation of the points briefly touched upon in the above preamble, the yachts Limmen and Zeemeeuw, and the galiot Bracq, which are specially adapted for this service, shall be dispatched from Batavia, well fitted and properly victualled, under the command of skipper-commander Abel Jansz. Tasman aforesaid, assisted by skipper and pilot-major Francois Jacobsz Visscher and other able steersmen; the said vessels being directed to take their course by way of Macasaar, whither they will have to carry and conduct ashore the supercargo Adriaen van Zuijdwijck..., together with his attendants and cargasons, who, according to annual custom and in accordance with the contract entered into with the king of Macassar in the year 1632, will have to reside there until September next, and to observe what is going on there, giving advice of his arrival there to Governor Gerrard Demmer in Amboyna, with the said yachts, which after leaving Amboyna will, in furtherance of the discovery aforesaid, shape their course by way of Banda for the coast of Nova Guinea, and ultimately for the South-land, in such fashion that they will make sure to return to Batavia through the strait of Sunda by June or July next. The Honorable Justus Schouten, councillor-extraordinary to the present assembly, is by the present directed to draw up in its name the needful instructions for this expedition with the advice and concurrence of skipper-commander Tasman and Pilot-major Visser aforesaid, and to submit the same to our scrutiny, that after approval they may be ratified by us, and the ships be with them dispatched on their mission as speedily as possible; the Honorable Director-general Cornelis van der Lijn being at the same time assigned to make an estimate of the cargason which the said Suijdwijck shall require for Macassar, therein availing himself of the latter gentleman's advice, to have the same embarked on board the yacht Limmen, and besides, to make a rough draught of the instructions to be given him,

Done and resolved in the Castle of Batavia, date as above.
(Signed)
Antonio Van Diemen.
 Justus Schouten.
Cornelis Van der Lijn.
Salomon Sweers.
Joan Maetsuijcker.
Pieter Mestdagh, Secectary.

Appendix M.

Instructions for Skipper Commander Abel Jansen Tasman, Skipper Pilot-Major Frans Jacobsz Visscher, and the Council of the Yachts Limmen, Zee-Meeuw and the Quel the Brack, destined for the further discovery of Nova Guinea, and of the unknown coasts of the discovered East- and South-lands, together with the channels and islands presumably situated between and near the same.

Both by word of mouth and through the perusal of Journals, Charts and other writings, it is in the main well-known to you, how the successive Governors of India, at the express command of our Lords and Masters the "Heeren XVII", have, in order to the aggrandisement, enlargement and improvement of the Dutch East India Company's standing and trade in the East, divers times diligently endeavoured to make timely discovery of the vast country of Nova Guinea and of other unknown Eastern and Southern regions; to wit, that four several voyages have up to now with scant success been made for this desired discovery, of the which voyages

The first was undertaken in the year 1606 with the Yacht 't Duijffken, by order of President Jan Willemsz Verschoor (who then managed the Company's affairs in Bantham), on which voyage the islands of Key and Arouw were visited in passing, and the unknown south and west coasts of Nova Guinea were discovered over a length of 220 miles from 5 to 13¾° Southern Latitude, it being only ascertained that vast regions were for the greater part uncultivated, and certain parts inhabited by savage, cruel, black barbarians, who slew some of our sailors, so that no information was obtained touching the exact situation of the country and regarding the commodities obtainable and in demand there; our men having by want of provisions and other necessaries, been compelled to return and give up the discovery they had begun, only registering in their chart with the name of Cape Keer-weer the extreme point of the discovered land in 13¾° Southern Latitude.

The second voyage was made in the year 1617 with a certain Yacht, under the command of Treasurer d'Edel, but had scant success, while no trustworthy information is now available touching its progress, owing to the Journal kept of it being lost.

From that time until the year 1623, owing to want of available ships, further discovery of the unknown East- and South-lands was suspended, but in the interim in the year 1619 the ship 't Wapen van Amsterdam, passing Banda on her way thither, was cast on the south-coast of Nova Guinea, where also some of her crew were slain by the barbarian inhabitants, so that no certain information respecting the situation of the country was obtained; likewise, during the same period in the years 1616, 1618, 1619 and 1622, the west coast of the great unknown South-land from 35 to 22° was unexpectedly and accidentally discovered by the ships d'Eendracht, Mauritius, Amsterdam, Dordrecht and Leeuwin, coming from the Netherlands; for the further exploration of which discoveries, in September A. D. 1622, Governor-General Jan Pietersz. Coen of glorious memory sent out the Yachts Haringh and Hasewint, whose voyage was cut short by their meeting with the ship Mauritius, and their search for the ship Rotterdam, upon which by the Honourable Governor-General's orders

The third voyage was undertaken from Amboyna in the month of January 1623 with the Yachts Pera and Arnhem, commanded by Commander Jan Carstens, for the purpose of entering into friendly relations with the inhabitants of the islands of Key, Arou and Tenimber, and of exploring Nova Guinea and the South-lands, on which occasion alliances were made with the islands aforesaid, the south-coast of Nova Guinea was further discovered, the skipper of the Yacht Arnhem with eight men of her crew were traitorously slain by the naives, but owing to untimely separation the Yacht Arnhem, after discovering the large islands of Arnhem and Speult, returned to Amboyna unsuccessfully enough, while the Yacht Pera, continuing her voyage, navigated along the south coast of Nova Guinea as far as a shallow bay in 10°, and afterwards along the west coast of the same land as far as Cape Keer-Weer, whence she further explored the coast to southward as far as 17° near the Staten river, where she saw the land stretching farther to westward, after which she returned again to Amboyna; in which discovery shallow flat bottoms, wild coasts, and regions thinly peopled with divers wild, cruel, poor and savage nations were found almost everywhere, and in the main nothing profitable was effected for the Company; the Journal of this voyage being also missing at present, though the coasts and lands discovered in the course of it may be seen from the chart drawn up on this occasion.

The scanty result of the third voyage just referred to, together with want of available ships, prevented until the year 1636 the following up of the discovery thus begun. Meanwhile in the year 1627 the ship t' Gulde Zeepaert, coming from the Netherlands, accidentally discovered upwards of 250 miles of the south coast of the great Southland, and in the following year 1628 the ship Viana, homeward bound from Batavia, equally unexpectedly discovered the coast of the same land on the north side in the Southern Latitude of 21°, and sailed along it a distance of about 50 miles; none of these discoveries, however, resulting in the obtaining of any considerable information respecting the situation and condition of this vast land, it only having been found that it has barren and dangerous coasts, green, fertile fields and exceedingly savage, black, barbarian inhabitants, as has been sufficiently proved by the welt-known wrecking of the ship Batavia and the horrors and miseries consequent thereon, and by the experiences gone through by the crew of the Yacht Sardam in sailing along its coasts.

Finally the fourth voyage for the further discovery of Nova Guinea and the East- and South-lands was begun from Banda in the month of April of the year 1636 (pending our period of administration) with the Yachts Amsterdam and Wesel (under the management of Commander Gerrit Thomasz Pool), which expedition touched at the South Coast of Nova Guinea in 3½°, sailed along it a distance of about 60 miles eastward as far as the 5th degree, at which point (being the same place where A. D, 1623 the Skipper of the Yacht Arnhem had been slain) Commander Pool with three of his men were murdered by the barbarian inhabitants; in spite of which the voyage was diligently prosecuted under the leadership of Supercargo Pieter Pietersz., and the islands of Keij and Arouw visited, but since owing to their meeting with very stiff easterly gales, they could not fetch up the west coast of Nova Guinea, they next sailed nearly southward and in 11° discovered upwards of 30 miles of the coast of Aernhems or Van Diemens-land, without at any time seeing human beings, although they did observe signs of smoke; next turning northward they touched at the unknown islands of Timor-laut and the known islands of Tenimber, Kauwer, etc., although they never had any parley with the natives who were very shy and timorous; so that after three months' cruising they returned to Banda in July, without having discovered or effected anything notable in the course of this voyage, as may been seen and read in their chart, and Journal.

After this unsuccessful expedition no further dispatch of ships for the purpose of additional discoveries eastwards was taken in hand, until last year the exploration of the as yet unknown South lands was seriously resumed under your management, in the course of which memorable voyage the great unknown Staten and Van Diemens lands in 35 and 43° Southern Latitude were discovered, and a long-desired passage into the South-Sea was found; of all which, since it is fully known to you, no specified account is needful on the present occasion.

In order to attain to a full and perfect knowledge of so many new great lands of which the discovery has now been made, begun or is yet in contemplation, according to the Company's intentions and the recommendations of our Lords and Masters, it yet remains for the future to ascertain whether Nova Guinea joins the great South-land or is separated from the same by channels and intervening islands; and also, whether the newly discovered Van Diemens land does or does not form a connected whole with these two great countries, or with either of them; likewise, what unknown islands may be situated between Nova Guinea and the unknown South-land; after which investigation it will be easier and more expedient to try to obtain ampler information concerning the nature and situation of all the known and unknown lands referred to.

All the above matters having been ripely considered, a proper estimate having been made of the Company's naval forces now available, and it having been found that, without detriment to customary trade and the necessities of war, two or three yachts may without inconvenience be set apart for this purpose, therefore it has been resolved in the Council of India to destine and dispatch on the further discovery of the East and South-lands the Yachts Limmen and Zee-Meeuw, and the Quel the Brack, to provide the same with all necessaries, and to entrust to you the command of this expedition, convinced as we are that you will ably and prudently manage this important voyage with courage, vigilance, prudence, good judgment and the necessary patience, so that on your return you will be able to give us a satisfactory account of your execution of this mandate.

To begin with, you will, to-morrow morning after due muster, set sail together, shaping your course for Macassar, Amboyna and Banda in such fashion, and executing there such orders as have been enjoined you by separate instructions, to which you will have to conform in every point while sailing thither.

Being arrived in Amboyna and Banda you will amply provide your Yachts with water, firewood, and other things that should be needful, properly refresh your crews while there with fresh viands, and duly victual your ships for the voyage, to which end we by the present give the needful orders to the Lords Vice-Governors Gerrit Demmer and Cornelis Witsen, to whom you will communicate these your Instructions, and require them to give you a written account of the more detailed information they may possess concerning the lands and islands situated eastward of Banda, more especially the journal of Commander Carstens, copies of which we think likely to be still accessible there, and which may be of use to you in your journey; at the same time we nowise desire that any time should be uselessly wasted on this, but enjoin you, diligently to arrange everything in the shortest possible time in such fashion that you will be ready to begin your voyage to Banda towards the close of February with the regular western monsoon; drawing up beforehand, at the very beginning of your voyage and with the aid of the Council a proper code of signals, which code should also contain directions necessary for enabling you to come together again, if by storms or other accidents (which God in his mercy avert) the Yachts should get separated from each other, such measures being of the utmost importance for the successful termination of the intended voyage.

Having executed our orders in Amboyna and Banda, you will, as before mentioned, at the close of February, or earlier if possible, set out on your ordained voyage in the name of God, shaping your course eastward, between and in sight of Tenimber, Key and Arouw, towards the point of Ture or Valsche Caep, situated in the 8th degree on the south coast of Nova Guinea, thence follow the coast-line to eastward as far as the 9th degree, next cautiously cross the shallow bay situated there, and then come to anchor with the Yachts near the Hoge Eijlant or Speults river, where you will reconnoitre the situation of the land, sending in the meantime the Quel the Brack into the bay for two or three days for the purpose of ascertaining whether in this large bay there is any passage to the South Sea, a fact which may be in a short time investigated and settled either in this way, or by the direction of the current.

Starting from this bay you will skirt the west-coast of Nova Guinea as far as the farthest point discovered in 17°, and next follow its line either to westward or to southward. It is, however, to be feared that in those parts you may fall in with the south-east trade-wind, which would render it difficult for you to keep in with the coast, if the latter should trend south-eastward. Still, you will use your utmost endeavours to do so, that it may once for all be decided whether this land is separated from the great known South-land, a fact that might easily be ascertained from the heavy and slow swells of the sea, in which case you will, if at all feasible, try to sail to south-eastward as far as the new Van Diemens land, and from there to the islands of St. Pieter and Francois, in order that you may discover its extension to northward, and thereby also ascertain whether there is a passage through leading to the South Sea, a state of things that would be highly desirable. Having found these things such as we presume and fervently hope them to be, you will on your return through the passage discovered sail along the east-coast of the known South-land, and skirt its line to westward as far as de Wits land and Willems river in 22°; after which the whole of the known South-land would have been circumnavigated and found to be the largest island of the world.

But if, as seems likely enough, the land of Nova Guinea joins the South-land without any channels, and consequently forms a whole with it, you will be enabled by the south-east trade-wind conveniently to skirt the north-coast of it from 17 to 22°, and fully discover the same; from where, if wind and weather are at all favourable, you will further continue your course along the land of d'Eendracht as far as Houtmans Abrolhos, and come to anchor there at the most convenient place, in order to make efforts to bring up from the bottom the chest with eight thousand rixdollars, sunk with the lost ship Batavia in 1629, owing to a metal half-cannon having fallen upon it, and which the men of the Yacht Sardam dived for without success, and so save the same together with the said gun, which would be good service done to the Company, on which account you will not fail diligently to attend to this business. You will likewise make search on the mainland to ascertain whether the two Netherlanders who, having forfeited their lives, were put ashore here by Commander Francisco Pelsert at the same period, are still alive, in which case you will from them ask information touching the country, and, if they should wish it, allow them to take passage hither with you; on which occasion you will also, about

28 or 26°, seek for a convenient place for obtaining water and re-freshments, which would be a thing highly desirable for ships bound to India from the Netherlands..

But if the advanced season of the year and eventual storms should not allow of your sailing as far as Houtmans shoals, which we must leave to the discretion of yourself and your council, according as you shall find required by circumstances, you will have ripely to deliberate whether from Willems river you cannot sail back eastward along the coast of the Southland, and run across from the Witsland nearly in an eastward direction, with the south-east trade wind, in order to make further discovery of Aernhems and Van Diemens land, and clearly ascertain whether the said lands do not form one and the same island, and what commodities might be obtainable there; as likewise what other islands may be situated between Balij, Cumbava and Timor, and the South-land.

All which having with Gods help been successfully performed, which we trust may be the case before the end of the month of June, you will, whether you have made Houtmans Abrolbos or Van Diemens land, together shape your course for the south coast of Java, and skirting it, return through the Straits of Sunda to Batavia, where we shall expect your successful return by the month of July next.

All the lands, islands, points, turnings, inlets, bays, rivers, shoals, banks, sands, reefs, cliff; rocks, etc., which you may meet with and pass, both on the coasts of Nova Guinea and of the South-land; and in the Indian Ocean and the interior-sea, you will carefully map out and describe, and also have proper drawings made of their appearance and shape, for which purpose we have procured an able draughtsman to join your expedition; you will likewise carefully note in what latitude and longitude they are situated; how the coasts, islands, capes, headlands or points, bays and rivers bear from each other and by what distances they are separated; what conspicuous landmarks such as mountains, hills, trees or buildings, by which they may be recognised, are visible on them; likewise what depths and shallows, sunken rocks, projecting shoals and reefs are situated about and near the points; how and by what marks these may most conveniently be avoided; item whether the grounds or bottoms are hard, rugged, soft, level, sloping or steep; whether ships should come on sounding, or not; by what land- and sea-marks the best anchoring-grounds in road-steads and bays may be known; the bearings of the inlets, creeks and rivers, and how these may best be made and entered; what winds blow in these regions; the direction of the currents; whether the tides are regulated by the moon or by the winds; what changes of monsoons, rains and dry weather you observe; furthermore diligently noting and observing whatever requires the careful attention of experienced steerssteersmen, and may in future be helpful to others who shall navigate to the countries discovered. Owing to the drawing in of the days, the season of the year will nowise permit any waste of time or needless lingering anywhere, but you will on the contrary diligently make the most of the time at your disposal, it being of the highest importance that you should discover a great deal in the shortest compass of time.

But in order to properly discover and carefully reconnoitre the coasts of the East- and South-lands, it will be necessary for you to come to anchor now and then, when time and place shall serve, always seeking and selecting such bays or road steads as you may with least peril run into, lie at anchor in, depart from, and clear out of in case of favourable winds or for other reasons. In landing with your small craft great caution, circumspection and prudence will have to be used, since, as aforesaid, it has repeatedly been experienced that Nova Guinea is inhabited by cruel, bloodthirsty men, and it remains quite uncertain up to now, with what sort of men the South-lands are peopled, though it may well be presumed that, so far from being civilised or polite persons, they are rude, wild, fierce barbarians, for which reason you will always have to be well armed, and to use every prudent precaution, since experience has taught in all parts of the world that barbarians are nowise to be trusted, because they commonly think that the strange and unknown persons who so unexpectedly appear before them, have come only to seize their lands, which in the discovery of America and of the Eastern regions has well been proved by the surprise and slaughter of many heedless and over-confident discoverers, oftentimes to the utter ruin of their expeditions. On which account you will treat with amity and kindness such barbarians as you shall meet and come to parley with, and connive at slight affronts, thefts and the like which they should put upon or commit against our men, lest retaliation should give them a grudge against us; and by shows of kindness gain them over to you, that you may the more readily from them obtain information touching themselves, their country and their circumstances, more especially whether in their country there is anything profitable for the Company to be obtained, imported or effected.

So far as time shall allow you to do, you will diligently strive to gather information concerning the situation of their country, the fruits end cattle it produces, their method of building houses, the appearance and shape of the inhabitants, their dress, arms, manners, customs, diet, means of subsistence, religion, manner of government, their wars and the like notable things, more especially whether they are kindly or cruelly disposed; showing them divers specimens of the commodities you have taken on board for that purpose, so as to learn what commodities and materials are found in their country, and what things they are desirous of obtaining from us in return; all which matters you will carefully note, correctly describe, and faithfully set forth in drawings; keeping for the purpose an ample and elaborate journal, in which you will set down an exact record of all that may befall you, that on your return you may be able to lay a proper report before us.

If, unlikely as it may seem, you should happen to come to any country peopled by a civilised race of men, you will give to them greater attention than to savage barbarians, endeavouring to come into contact and parley with its magistrates and subjects, letting them know that you have come there for the sake of commerce, regularly showing them the goods and samples of the commodities you have taken on board for the purpose, distributed over the two Yachts and the Quel, as duly specified in the invoice amounting to a sum total of f2809:12:6, of which the subcargoes will keep account-books in the requisite form, that in due time they may give a full and exact account of the same, and hand the balance over to ourselves.

In showing to the natives the goods and samples of commodities aforesaid, you will, together with the subcargoes, closely observe what things these foreign natives set store by, and what commodities they arc eager to have; likewise trying to find out what commodities their country yields, especially inquiring after gold and silver, and whether the latter are by them held in high esteem; making them believe that you are by no means eager for the possession of precious metals, so as to leave them ignorant of the value of the same; and if they should offer you gold or silver in exchange for your articles, you will pretend to hold the same in slight regard, showing them copper, pewter, tin or lead, and giving them an impression as if the minerals last mentioned were by us set greater store by. And if you should find them inclined to negotiate with us, you will put upon our goods, especially on such as they are very eager for, so high a price, that they will not be sold or bartered except at a very large profit; not taking any thing in exchange for them, except such things as you certainly know to be profitable for the Company, which you will no doubt learn in the course of the negotiations; it being especially needful that you should bring hither samples of the rarest and most precious commodities there to be obtained, and elaborate descriptions of the others, that we may know what return-cargoes might be got from there, which might be of great use for future business.

You will prudently prevent all manner of insolence and all arbitrary action on the part of our men against the nations discovered, and take due care that no injury be done them in their houses, gardens, vessels, or to their property, their wives, etc.; nor shall you carry off any of the inhabitants out of their country against their will; should, however, a few of them be ready to go with you of their own accord, you are at liberty to bring them hither.

And since we have now set forth in the main our intentions with respect to the voyage by you to be undertaken, and no exact orders can be given touching all matters that might occur, we shall leave the rest and all other things that may present themselves, recommended to your zeal, vigilance and good judgment, together with the prudent disposition of the Council, with hopeful confidence that you will in this expedition so comport and exert yourselves that it will redound to the advantage of the General Company, in which case we shall not be niggardly in deservedly rewarding you for the due performance of your duties; for, if in the course of your voyage any lands, islands or passages, profitable for the Company, should be discovered, we herewith engage ourselves to honour the managers of the venture and all the well-behaved men taking part in it, with such rewards as their good services done shall be found to have deserved, and as will convince them of our gratitude for the same; on all which all of you may rely to the fullest extent. In the same way you will also promise a reasonable premium to those who shall first discover unknown lands, islands, shoals, rocks or dangerous shallows, that all accidents may as far as possible be prevented.

And to the end that for the future the fruits of the pains and expense bestowed on this undertaking may not eventually be taken from us by other European nations, you will in all cases, on behalf and in the name of the Chartered Dutch Company, take possession of such lands and islands as you have discovered, and as have only barbarian inhabitants or none at all; such taking into possession to be signalised by some fitting mark, such as the sowing of fruits, the planting of trees, the erecting of some stone, wooden or other structure, in which, together with the national or the Company's arms, you will cause to be chiselled or carved an inscription recording in what year and season each separate land has by you been reached and taken possession of, and declaring at the same time your fixed intention to send a body of men thither from here by the first opportunity, and thus duly secure to ourselves this property by founding a permanent colony there. But if, unlikely as it may seem, you should chance to discover any lands or islands, enjoying a civilised and regular government, you will endeavour in the best possible way, on behalf of the Company aforesaid, to conclude a treaty with the governors or regents of the same, to obtain of them a transfer of their dominions if they can be got to grant the same, or to get the right of visiting them to the exclusion of other nations, or other similar privileges for the General Company; of all which you will keep a careful record in your Journals, expressly mentioning the names and styles of those whom you have treated with, to be of service to the Company in case of need.

And to the end that this perillous voyage may be well regulated and performed in accordance with these instructions and our good intentions; that proper order may be maintained among the men, law and justice be administered in conformity with the general regulations, and furthermore everything that in so long and dangerous an expedition may occur and be required, be done and executed to the best advantage and service of the Company; therefore we have appointed the Honourable Abel Jansen Tasman Commander of the three Yachts and of the men on board of the same, by the present authorising him to carry the flag on the main-topmast of the Yacht Limmen, to convene the Council; and permanently to occupy the chair in the same; in consideration thereof commanding and enjoining all Officers, soldiers and sailors, excepting none, who have been ordered on board the Yachts Limmen and Zeemeeuw, and the Quel de Brack, to acknowledge the said Abel Tasnan as their Commander and chief, to respect and obey him, and likewise on all occasions to assist him with their good advice and diligent service, for the furtherance of the voyage and the ordained discovery of unknown lands, in such fashion as befits vigilant and faithful servants, and as on their return they can conscientiously answer for to ourselves.

The Council of these three Yachts will consist of the persons following, to wit:

The Commander Abel Jansz Tasman, permanent President.
The Skipper Pilot-Major Francois Jacobsz on board the Limmen.
The Skipper Dirck Cornelisz Haen)
The Supercargo Isaac Gilsemans   ) on board the Zee-meeuw.
The Skipper Jasper Jansz Koos, on board the Quel de Brac.
Crijn Hendricksz, Steersman on board the Limmen.

Carsten Jeuraensz, Steersman on board the Meeuw.
Cornelis Robol, Steersman on board the Brac.
And the Subcargo Anthonij Blauw, as Counsel and Secretary.

In this Plenary Council all matters relating to the progress of the voyage, the execution of our orders, and the administration of justice will have to be discussed, settled and determined, the Commander to have a double vote in case of equality of votes; but in matters relating to navigation and the discovery of lands the second mates will also attend the Council and have an advisory vote; the Commander will have to collect the votes, a majority of which will be decisive, the Commander taking due care that all resolutions taken be forthwith registered in triplo, signed, and executed for the service of the Company. And as regards the private ships councils of each of the Yachts, the subcargoes or book-keepers, and the master-boatswains will also be summoned to attend them, in accordance with the orders of our masters.

In case of decease of Commander Tasman (which God in his mercy avert) he shall in his place be succeeded by the person nominated in the deed inclosed by us, who shall command, in all points replacing his predecessor, according to these our instructions, and be duly obeyed like him.

The Yachts will be manned with 111 able-bodied men, among whom there are 16 soldiers and one officer, to wit:

On board the Limmen   45 sailors 11 soldiers together 56 men.
On board the Zeemeeuw   35 sailors 6 soldiers together 41 men.
On board the Quel de Brac 14 sailors   together 14 men.
----
facit 94 sailors 17 soldiers together 111 men.

They are provided with all needful ammunition, tools and provisions, and abundantly victualled for eight calendar months. Let everything be well and duly husbanded, and the customary rations of two meat-days and one bacon-day, one mutchkin of vinegar and ½ mutchkin of oil per week, and 1½ mutchkin of wrack per day, be regularly served out. Of strong arrack each of the Yachts will take on board one hogshead, 120 cans for the Brac to be provided out of the Zeemeeuw, the whole to be in moderation served out in cold "weather for the benefit of the men's health. But above all you will carefully husband the firewood and the fresh water, however amply you may be provided with water-casks, that you may not come to be in want of them, or be forced to delay your voyage in order to seek for them, or to return from such search unsuccessfully, which would redound to the serious detriment of the Company (which has been at great expense in fitting out these Yachts) and to the discredit of you all, and should accordingly with all diligent prudence be prevented.

What furthermore shall have to be done in the course of this voyage, being matters yet unknown, we shall not in this place prescribe, but leave the same recommended to your Council's trusted management, seriously enjoining all of you to use in everything such needful caution, that the Company's valuable ships and crews be as much as possible kept out of all presumed perils, in furtherance of which it is our express desire that the Commander shall never without good cause leave his ship, but shall always remain on board the Yachts, unless with the approval of the Council the Company's service should require the contrary, that the object of this important voyage may not by unforeseen fatal accidents be defeated. Finally and in conclusion of these our Instructions we cordially wish you the blessing of the Ruler of all things, praying that he may in His mercy endow you with manly courage in the execution of the intended discovery, and may grant you a safe return, to the increase of His glory, the greater reputation of our country, the benefit of the Company's service, the complete satisfaction of ourselves, and your own immortal honour.
Done in the Castle of Batavia this 29th of January 1644.

(Signed)
Antonio van Diemen, Cornelis Vanderlijn, Joan Maetsuijeker, Justus Schouten, and Salotnon Sweerts.

A sealed Commission for the Successor of Commander Abel Jansen Tasman, in the event of the latter's decease.

Regard being had to the mortality of men, and to the disorders which will often arise therefrom in consequence of the decease of the chiefs appointed by Commission, therefore for the possible prevention of such disorders we have thought fit to ordain, as we ordain by these presents, that in the event of Skipper Abel Jansz Tasman happening to depart this life in the course of this voyage of discovery(which God in His mercy avert), the Skipper of the Yacht the Zee-meeuw, Dirck Cornelisz Haen shall succeed to his place, and be acknowledged as leader; shall consider as destined for himself our Instructions to the said Tasman, and act in conformity with the same, this being our express desire, and in our opinion, in such a case, for the benefit of the general Company.

Done in the Castle of Batavia this 29th of January 1644.
(Signed)
Antonio Van Diemen, Cornelis VanderLijn, Joan Maetsuijcker, Justus Schouten and Salomon Sweers.

Appendix N.

The voyage to the Southland debitor to the Factory of Batavia f2809:12:6, for the goods and sundry articles hereunder mentioned [by order of the Hon. Lord Governor-General and Councillors of India, shipped and loaded on board the yachts Limmen and Zeemeeuw, and the quel-galiot Bracq, leaving here this day (under bill of lading signed by the respective supercargoes and skippers) by way of Maccassar, Amboijna and Banda, for the discovery of new lands], consigned with destination for the South-land into the hands of Skipper-Commander Abel Jansz Tasman, to be by him, after discovery of new lands, exhibited to the inhabitants of the same by way of sample or trial, the said Tasman being enjoined diligently to inquire what profit may in future be made on the said goods and articles for the General Company; he being bound in, due time to give in a proper reckoning and a specified and vouched account concerning the same goods; the whole of them being carefully . packed and well assorted, and bearing such prices as are specified in the invoice-book.

<pre>
 5 pieces of coloured cloths, measuring together
        130¼ ells ad ƒ 6.— per ell . . . . ƒ 781.10.
25 pieces of coloured armozeens ad 2 reals p. piece „ 127.10.

20 dº of black and white broad baftas . . „   95.—
</pre>

```
 10 pieces of red bethilles . . . . . . . . . ƒ  75.—
143 pounds of elephants' teeth, ad 25 stivers per
       pound . . . . . . . . . . . . . . . . „ 178.15
 20 pieces of copaiba gum, ad 18 guilders each. „ 360.—
  3 picols pepper ad 10 reals per picol . . . „  76.10
  3 pieces of caliteur-wood . . . . . . . . . „   6. 6
2½ picols wax . . . . . . . . . . . . . . . . „ 127.10.
 28 pieces of single negros cloths, ad 10 stivers
       each. . . . . . . . . . . . . . . . . . „  14.—
 20 pieces surate cotton-blankets, ad 3½ guilders
       each. . . . . . . . . . . . . . . . . . „  70.—
 10 pieces silk patols measuring 50 astas, 28 stivers
       per asta . . . . . . . . . . . . . . . „  70—
 10 pieces white Guinea linen, ad 6 guilders each „ 60.—
500 pounds of assorted iron, ad 9 guilders per
       hundredweight . . . . . . . . . . . . . „  45.—
  3 picols white powdered sugar, ad 5½ reals
       per picol . . . . . . . . . . . . . . . „  42. 1. 8
 80 catties sandal-wood, ad 10 stivers per cattie „ 40.—
 30 pieces Dutch shirts, ad ½ real each . . . „  38. 5.
  3 lasts of salt. . . . . . . . . . . . . . . „  38. 5.
 10 pieces Sarassa de Coutchin, ad 3 guilders 5
       stivers each . . . . . . . . . . . . . „  32.10.
100 pounds of Dutch steel and 50 pieces of
       "cust claver"(?). . . . . . . . . . . . „  33.—
 50 pieces gilded folding-mirrors, ad 10 stivers each „ 25.—
 10   d°  poulangh gobers, ad 2¼ guilders each „  22.10
 10   d°  cain goulonghs, ad 2 guilders 4 stivers
       each . . . . . . . . . . . . . . . . . „  22.—
 10   d°  tape grande, ad 2 guilders each . . . „ 20.—
 20   d°  canvass, ad 28 stivers each . . . . . „ 28.—
 10   d°  narrow chintz, ad 2 guilders 15 stivers
       each . . . . . . . . . . . . . . . . . „  27.10.
 10   d°  blue madaps, ad 2 guilders each . . „  20.—
 10   d°  yarn taffachelas, ad 2 guilders each. . „ 20.—
 40 catties of tin, ad 10 stivers per cattie . . . „ 20.—
 80   d°  of pewter, ad 9 reals per hundredweight „ 18. 3. 6
  4 parcels of tinsel . . . . . . . . . . . . . „ 22. 6. 4
 10 pieces tape quitel, ad 32 stivers each . . . „ 16.—
 10   d°  broad surate tapechindes, ad 17 stivers
       each . . . . . . . . . . . . . . . . . „  8.10.
 25   d°  captured cannabins(?), ad 4 stivers each „  5.—
 25 packets of Chinese gold-wire, ad 7 reals per
       hundredweight . . . . . . . . . . . . . „  4.11. 4
150 pounds of lead, ad 9 guilders per hundred-
       weight . . . . . . . . . . . . . . . . „  13.10.
 50 pieces of iron pans, ad 12 stivers each . . „  30.—
  8 pounds of tortoise-shell . . . . . . . . . „ 13. 4.
200 pieces of various assortments of china porcelain „ 19. 2. 8
1¼ reals' weight of gold, in two pieces. . . . . „ 41. 8.12
1¼ reals' weight of silver, in two pieces . . . „  3. 3.12
  A seine or fishing-net, value . . . . . . . . „ 40.—
 20 pieces Chinese blue cangans . . . . . . . „ 58.10.
500 pieces small Chinese mirrors           ⎫
1000   d°       d°    needles. .            ⎪
500    d°       d°  small pitchers          ⎪
 50    d°  narrow chisels . . .             ⎪
 60    d°  indifferent knives. .            ⎪
 50    pounds of cloves. . . .              ⎬ not appraised.
 10      d°   of mace, 10 pounds            ⎪
               of nutmegs . . .            ⎪
 10    d°    of cassia lignea .             ⎪
100    d°    of various copper              ⎪
             articles . . . . .            ⎭
  8 small pearls . . . . . . .
  3 pounds of ebony . . . .
  1 small lump of gold . . .
  1 small bar of silver. . . .
```

The cargoes on board the Limmen, Zeemeeuw
and Bracq, destined for the South-land, amounting to ƒ 2809.12. 6

Appendix O.

Noble, worshipful, wise, provident and very discreet Gentlemen,

We strongly incline to the further discovery of Tartary and the northern parts of America, together with the South-lands lately discovered in the East, and the Salomon's islands, of which we at the time transmitted charts to Your Worships, together with Our experiences and opinions touching this matter; but more urgent affairs and want of fitting yachts have up to now prevented our taking further steps It will, however, be necessary to further attend to this navigation, and to have the lands already discovered more completely explored, since we are firmly convinced they will be found to contain gold and silver; we are also becoming more and more persuaded that the discovery of some rich mines is certainly necessary for the company, and trust that the same will in due time be found. In case we should in these parts succeed in coming to an agreement and honourable peace with the Portuguese, without prejudice to the Company and saving its respect, we strongly incline to have an expedition to Chili set on foot, in order to ascertain whether goods in demand there can be exchanged for gold, and at the same time to attempt to capture some good booty in the West Indies by taking the enemy at unawares, which it is presumed we cannot fail with God's aid to succeed in; and since Your Worships are of opinion, that the Directors of the West India Company are sure to take their stand on their charter extending to Chili, we shall, unless otherwise directed by Your Worships, not make any attempts at settlement there, which, but for the said circumstance, could easily be effected on our part and also maintained afterwards. We are well aware of what has formerly been done there under the leadership of the Lord General Brouwer, now with God.

In conformity with our plan, intimated to Your Worships some time ago, touching the exploration and surveying of the inner coast of Nova Guinea, and the question of ascertaining whether in 17, 18 or 20 degrees Latitude there should be found any channel or passage into the South Sea, and whether the said coast should extend to the south-west as far as Willems River, we have dispatched thither, by way of Macassar, Amboina and Banda, the yachts Limmen and Zeemeeuw, and the galiot Bracq, and entrusted the leadership of this expedition to skipper-commander Abel Tasman, assisted by Pilot-major Frans Jacobsen Visscher. 'For briefness' sake we shall not repeat here the considerations that have led to this voyage, and the instructions we have given to these persons, but beg leave to refer Your Worships to the orders given them, registered in our letter.book, under the date of January 29 of the present year. The said yachts set sail from Banda on February an, and followed the coast-line, but found no open channel between the half-known Nova Guinea and the known land of d'Eendracht or Willems river in 22 2/3 degrees South Lat. and 119° Longitude; they, however, found a large, spacious bay or gulf, as shown in the annexed chart and journals. Nor did they make any profit by bartering transactions, having only met with naked, beach-roving wretches, destitute of rice, and not possessed of any fruits worth mentioning, excessively poor, and in many places of a very malignant nature, as Your Worships may in great detail gather from the Batavia minutes, in which the courses kept and the incidents of the voyage are recorded, under date 4, 5 and 10 August last, at which time the said Tasman returned to our port through Sunda Strait, from the latitude and longitude aforesaid of the South-land (having continually sailed in shallow water along the coast). What there is in this South-land, whether above or under the earth, continues unknown, since the men have done nothing beyond sailing along the coast; he who makes it his business to find out what the land produces, must walk all over it, which these discoverers pretend to have been out of their power, which may be true to some extent. Meanwhile, this vast and hitherto unknown South-land has by the said Tasman been sailed round in two voyages, and is computed to comprise 2000 miles of land, as shown by the delineations of the coasts which we subjoin for Your Worships' inspection. Now it can hardly be supposed that no profit of any kind should be obtainable in so vast a country, situated under various zones, the south-eastern part extending between 43½ and 2½ degrees Southern Latitude. The same reasoning will apply to the vast northern parts of America; such things should not be done in a hurry, to be sure, and we would request Your Worships to rest assured, that whenever opportunity serves we shall from time to time have everything diligently and closely investigated by persons, more vigilant and courageous than those who have hitherto been employed on this service. The thorough exploration of newly discovered lands is no work for the first comer; besides, it requires fitting and strong yachts and a great number of men, both of them points on which we firmly trust Your Worships will not leave us unprovided, but meet our requirements in the same way as has been the case up to now. May God grant that in the one or the other part of the world some prolific silver- or gold-mine be hit upon, to the solace of the general shareholders and the signal honour of the first discoverer...

Written in Your Worships' Castle of Batavia, December 23, 1644.
(Signed)
Antonio van Diemen, Cornelis van der Lijn, Salomon Sweers, Paulus Croocq, Simon van Alphen.

Appendix P.

Tuesday, October IV, A. D. 1644.

Abel Jansz Tasman, of Lutgegast in Friesland, last returned to these parts on the 11th of October 1638, in the flute Engel as skipper, at 60 guilders monthly pay; his pay having subsequently been raised to 8o guilders per month in the year 1642; having on August 4 of the same year been dispatched by way of the island of Mauritius, as skipper-commander, with the yacht Heemskercq and the flute Seehaen, for the purpose of discovering the surmised South-lands; and likewise on the 30th of January last, by way of Banda, with two yachts and a galiot for the purpose of making the same discovery on that side; he having, in the course of these two voyages, given us reasonable contentment by his duty done and service rendered; is, in consideration of this, at his request, and regard being had to his abilities, and to the fact that he has resided in these parts for another six years in succession, and that we find in him the courage required to do additional good service to the Company on similar occasions, in seeking rich lands or forming profitable trade-connections, by the present officially confirmed in his aforesaid capacity of skipper-commander, and admitted to a new engagement for three consecutive years, on a salary of 100 guilders per month, reckoned from the 24th of August 1642 aforesaid, when he has first been employed in the said capacity, and the engagement...of this current month...

Done and resolved at the Castle of Batavia, date as above.
(Signed) Antonio van Diemen, Cornelis van der Lijn, Salomon Sweers, Paulus Croocq, Simon van Alphen, and Pieter Mestdagh, Secretary.

Appendix Q.

Wednesday, November II, A. D. 1644.

Resolved, in the room of Commander Marten Gerritsz Vries, who left for the Moluccas yesterday with the ships Sutphen and Schiedam, again to employ in the Council of Justice, Skipper-commander Abel Jansz Tasman, who is to take his seat next to the youngest member of the said Council, provided he take the customary oath, to be administered to him to-morrow by the Hon. Simon van Alphen, president of the said Council, at the same time directing and authorising the said Tasman, in accordance with the resolution of the first of, February of the present year, to demand inspection of and examine all ships' journals submitted to the Council, and pertinently report on the same to us, in the same way as the said Vries has done up to his departure.

Done and resolved at the Castle of Batavia, date as above,
(Signed)
Antonio van Diemen, Cornelis van der Lijn, Salomon Sweers, Paulus Croocq, Simon van Alphen, and Pieter Mestdagh, Secretary.

Appendix R.

Manilha. Commission for Commander Abel Jansen Tasman.

Cornelis van der Lijn, Governor General, and the Councillors of India, on behalf of Their High Mightinesses the States-General of the Free United Netherlands, of His Highness and Princely Grace Wilhelm Frederick, by the grace of God Prince of Orange, Count of Nassau etc., and of the Worshipful Lords Managers of the Chartered Dutch Company here in East India, send greeting to all those who shall see these presents or hear the same read, and let them know what follows:

Inasmuch as lately in the Council of India we took in hand and resolved once more this year and now for the third time to dispatch from here to the waters of Manilha a strong and sufficient armament, for the purpose of harassing and injuring our hereditary enemy the Castilian, and more especially of eventually (with God's help) intercepting and capturing the silver.ship bound from Aqua Pulco to Manilha, as also of keeping the Spanish naval forces shut up and enclosed within their bays and harbours, in such wise as to prevent them from sending out this year any ships to Nova Hispania, Spanish Ternate or any other parts, to the end that the Honble Corn. pang may at last succeed in enjoying the long-desired, fruits of her long-borne heavy expenses;

Therefore, with this end in view, we have provided for the timely equipment and fitting.out of the following ships and war-yachts, to wit: Banda, Jonge Prins, Reijnsburgh, Snoucq, Arent, Arnemuijden, Luijpaert and Popkensburgh, item have duly fitted the same with all requisites for such an expedition, victualled and amply manned them with soldiers and seafaring men; which important fleet we deem sufficiently strong and powerful, with God's blessing, to execute the Company's designs in laudable fashion. But inasmuch as, to direct and execute everything with wisdom and good discretion, it is imperatively necessary that such armament should be provided with an Intelligent, experienced and courageous leader, who at all times and everywhere shall have and exercise the supreme command and direction by land and sea;

Therefore, being fully assured and satisfied of the requisite skill, courage, and many years' experience of Skipper-commander Abel Jansen Tasman, we have, in consequence, nominated, appointed and authorised the same, as we nominate, appoint and authorise him by these presents, to be our commander and leader of the eight war-ships aforesaid, and, in virtue of this our present commission, to command or rule over the said offensive fleet; permanently to carry the flag at the topmast-head; to convene the ship's council when found necessary, and permanently to take the chair in the same; to administer right and justice, with the advice of the council, both in civil and criminal matters; as also, as occasion shall be found to require, to have promptly effected, and furthermore properly to execute all that by explicit instructions shall be enjoined him; in such wise and fashion as shall become and befit an honourable, worthy and faithful leader and commander of so powerful an armament; on which account we enjoin and direct vice-commander Dirck Jansen Ogel, rear-admiral Johan Truijtman, and furthermore all supercargoes, skippers, captains, lieutenants, all subaltern officers, soldiers and sailors, who are now setting out for the coast of Manilha in the eight ships aforesaid or shall eventually afterwards join this expedition, to acknowledge and accept the said Abel Jansen Tasman as their leader and commander, and to respect and obey him in such wise as if ourselves were personally present there; item to render and give the said Tasman, in the discharge of his functions, all necessary advice, aid and assistance, in conformity with the oath of allegiance, by which each of them is pledged and bound to the republic of the United Netherlands and to the General Company:

inasmuch as we deem this to be behoveful for the better service and greater well-being of the Company aforementioned.

Granted at the Castle of Batavia in the island of Great Java, May 14, A. D. 1648.

(Signed)
Cornelis van der Lijn.

Appendix S.

Extract from the "Copia Criminal Calendar of the Worshipful Council of Justice of the Castle of Batavia" Dec. 12, 1648-Nov. 27, 1649.

Tuesday, this 23rd day of November, 1649. Presentibus omnibus.

In the action pendent before the Worshipful Council of Justice of the Castle of Batavia between Mr. Johan Cunaeus, LL. D, advocate-fiscal of India, nomine officii Plaintiff on one part, and Abel Jansen Tasman, Commander in the service of the Hon" Company, Defendant on the other part, in which action the Plaintiff had sent in a demand in writing, and set forth, that the Defendant had sailed from here for the Manilhas in the year 1648 as commander of a considerable naval force; that a camp having been pitched there in the Baviauw islands, the Defendant, on the 28th of August last, having during the whole of the said day been banqueting with certain of his officers in a certain monastery, and having on his way back at night-fall, at half a musket-shot's distance from the camp aforesaid, met with one Coenraet Janssen of Amsterdam, serving the Honble Company as ship-boy at 5 guilders a month, together with another common sailor, who had both of them on that day as well as the day before been out for the purpose of obtaining some cattle by order of their officers, and although the said persons by so doing had not been guilty of any misdemeanour, since they were ignorant of and wholly unacquainted with the order forbidding all men to go outside the camp on pain of death (which order the Defendant pretends to have had promulgated on the 27th of August aforesaid), seeing that (as before stated) they had at that time been in the interior, as also that they had passed the sentinels without being challenged by them, or informed of the order issued, yet the Defendant (although a few years before he had been a member of this Worshipful Council, and had from the Supreme Government of this town received ample and honourable instructions to which he would have had generally to conform himself in the maintenance or execution of justice) has taken upon him, without any complaint from the Lord-fiscal, without inquiring into the matter, without summoning his Council for the purpose, nay, without even hearing the delinquents, to seize hold of the said two young sailors, and to condemn them to be hanged on a tree, for which purpose the Defendant with many menaces has obtained a piece of tow-match from the soldiers there present, with which having made a halter, the Defendant has himself hastily put the said halter round the neck of the aforesaid Coenraet Jansen, and ordered his vice-commander named Dirck Oogel (who requested that this unlawful execution might be postponed until the Council should have been convened to decide upon it), to ascend a tree and to hang the said Coenraet on the same; which having been done, the Defendant has taken away from under the innocent man's feet the bench on which he had ordered him to stand up, and in this wise, to the eternal and inextinguishable ignominy of himself and his honest parents, suffered him to remain suspended, the Defendant himself making meanwhile another halter to inflict the same punishment on the second sailor, until at length the vice-commander aforesaid (who remained seated on the tree), becoming aware of the sufferer's exceeding agony, and perceiving that the man had almost passed from life unto death, without doubt finding his mind grievously burdened on this account, has let go the delinquent, and allowed him to drop down on the ground, where he remained lying like a dead man for a while, the wales caused by the pressure of the halter continuing visible on his neck for upwards of three weeks after the time; on account of which unlawful and tyrannous execution, in which the Defendant has been bold enough to appear as accuser, judge and executioner all at once and in one person, and by which accordingly law and justice have been most grievously violated, the Plaintiff has concluded that by Their Worships' definitive sentence the Defendant ought to be deprived of his honourable command and moreover pronounced incapable of holding any public functions; besides condemned, honourably and profitably to indemnify the sufferer for the grievous bodily injury and shameful treatment inflicted; honorably, by humbly craving God's and the Council's pardon, and by declaring that he has injudiciously and unlawfully inflicted such infamous treatment on the person injured; and profitably, by paying over to the person injured the sum of one thousand pieces of eight; the Defendant, over and above this, being cast in a fine of six hundred of the same pieces of eight, to be applied usu, cum expensis.

Against the which the Defendant in his written answer had alleged, that, on the day before the said execution, he had by public beat of drum caused it be openly proclaimed and announced, that on pain of being punished with death, no one should be allowed to go outside the place of encampment; the which public prohibition being made light of by many young sailors, and specially by the said Coenraet Jansen, who were daily loafing about like lawless persons in the enemy's territory, in imminent peril of losing their lives, the said Coenraet together with one of his comrades, on the day following the said public prohibition, ha impudently and faithlessly abandoned on the beach the boat of the ship to which they belonged, and fled into the interior outside the camp, where they have been found, without having any arms about them, by the Defendant and the vice-commander aforesaid; who having declared to them their deserved punishment, the said vice-commander has procured a length of tow-match from the soldiers, has put round the aforesaid Coenraet's neck a halter made of the same, and by means thereof caused him to be suspended from a tree for a short time, setting him free, however, immediately afterwards; the Defendant furthermore denying that he had been banqueting and carousing at the time, and also that the said Coenraet should have fainted in consequence of the treatment inflicted; finally, that the defendant should have made a halter for the other sailor's neck; the whole proving that his the Defendant's proceedings were intended to serve as a deterrent menace only to all other transgressors of the Commander's orders; the Defendant accordingly maintaining that the said execution has taken place lawfully in accordance with the articles of war, and in order to the prevention of more serious accidents; and in consideration of this, concluding contrariwise, that no action shall lie, and consequently the Plaintiff be nonsuited in his demand, and the Defendant acquitted, with costs to be charged on the Plaintiff.

Parties having furthermore submitted reply and rejoinder, waived the producing of further evidence, and sued for a decision hinc jude, the Council on the appointed day having recapitulated the documents and the evidence submitted by both parties, and having carefully weighed and pondered whatever was pertinent to the matter in hand, and might in any way affect their Worships' opinion, Administering justice on behalf and in the name of Their High Mightinesses the

States-General of the Free United Netherlands, suspend the Defendant from the exercise of his office and functions, and from the enjoyment of his pay during the pleasure of the Honourable Lord Governor-General of India, and condemn the same to declare with uncovered head in the public court that he has injudiciously and unlawfully, also extra-judicially against all form of law, and of his own will, personally inflicted the said infamous treatment on the aforesaid Coenraet Jansen; the defendant forfeiting moreover the sum of one thousand pieces of eight for the benefit of the said Coenraet, and being mulcted in a sum of one hundred and fifty pieces of eight, to be divided as customary, with costs.

Below was written: in my presence, and was signed Vincent van Moock, secretary.

Appendix T.

Tuesday, December XX, A.D. 1650.

As also the person of Abel Janszoon Tasman, of Littgegast in Friesland, skipper-commander in the service of the Honble. Company on a monthly pay of one hundred guilders, appearing before the Council aforesaid, requesting that, in consideration of the term of his engagement having expired some time before, he may be promoted in rank and his pay raised, the G.-G. &c., having taken into account his abilities and services rendered, and considered that as yet these do not deserve a higher reward, have accordingly resolved to refuse his request until such time as he shall be employed on more important service; determining and resolving moreover that, to avoid burdening Our Lords and Masters with unnecessary charges, no one, of what grade or rank soever, shall henceforth be promoted in rank or pay, unless, in case of vacancy and opening for immediate employment, circumstances should seem absolutely to require such promotion.

In the Castle of Batavia, date as above.
(Signed) Carel Reniersz., Joan Maetsuijcker, Gerard Demmer, Joan Cunaeus, Arnold de Vlamingh van Oudtshoorn, Willem van der Beecq, and Willem Verstegen.

Appendix U.

Persons promoted in rank and pay since December 13, A. D. 1650.

This 5th day of January, 1651.

Whereas Abel Janszoon, of Ltitgegast in Friesland, lately Skipper-Commander in the service of the Honble Company, on a monthly pay of one hundred guilders, was from this charge and pay suspended by the Worshipful Council of Justice of this Castle of Batavia, A. D. 1649, on account of misdemeanours committed by him on the last voyage to Manilha, the suspension from his rank and pay to continue during the pleasure of the Governor-General and Councillors of India; this day, at his urgent request, and seeing that in divers parts of the world he has rendered the Company good services, and may in time to come continue to do so, he is by the present relieved of the said suspension, and reinstated in his previous capacity and pay of Skipper-Commander, the present resolution being assumed to have come into force on the 24th of September of last year, being the date on which he has begun again to do active duty for the Company.

In the Castle of Batavia ...

Appendix V.

(Tasman's Will)

In the name of God Amen. I, Abel Tesman (sic), sometime commander in the Honble Company's service, residing outside the town of Batavia, being able to go and stand, but sick in body, though in the full enjoyment of my senses, memory and mental faculties, considering the frailty of life so that there is nothing surer than death and nothing less certain than the hour of the same, have therefore, before departing this world, of my own deliberation and free will resolved to make and conclude a private last will and testament, such as I make and conclude by the present in manner as described, to wit: imprimis, I commend my soul on departing this life into the special grace and mercy of Almighty God, and my dead body to an honest bestowal into the earth or the sea, according to circumstances; and before proceeding to a disposal of my worldly goods which I have received from God as a loan, and am to leave behind me, I hereby declare firstly to revoke, cancel and nullify by the present all testaments, codicils, legacies and bequests, excepting none, privately. or publicly passed, made and undersigned by me, wherever they may be found, it being my express will and desire that this my private testament shall solely come into force and effect, in such fashion as any one's last will and testament can stand in due form and have proper and legal force, even in case the formalities here required by the law had been omitted or left unobserved, notwithstanding any custom of town or country or any written statute in any way to the contrary, all the which I testator declare to be null and void in so far as they should interfere with this my will; proceeding to the disposal of my goods, estates and chattels, First I give and bequeath to the poor people of the village named Luytgegarst the lump sum of five-and-twenty guilders of forty half-stivers each; secondly I bequeath to Abel my daughter's son, born of her marriage with the late master Philip Heylman, in his lifetime first physician of the Castle of Batavia, a gold cup of 4 reals' weight, and a sword with silver hilt; all other goods, moveables and immoveables, excepting none of any description soever, wherever found or situated, I give and bequeath to my beloved wife Joanna Tiercx, to deal with and dispose of the same as her own free property, without contradiction from any one; save only that, in case she should happen to contract another marriage, she shall be bound and obliged, to the children of my daughter Claesjen, both those born of her second marriage with Mr. Jacob Breemer, and those she has borne to her first husband, to make cession of the just moiety of our whole estate; the said children shall likewise obtain the moiety in case my wife aforesaid should die a widow after me; besides it is my will and desire that my wife aforesaid shall not be held bound to deliver in any schedule, inventory, account, or balance-sheet of what she shall come into possession of out of our estate; and in case my daughter aforesaid should think fit to importune my wife, and force her to deliver in such schedule and inventory touching her child's portion or touching that which has been by me bequeathed and set apart for her children; or in case she should think fit to dispute and call in question this my will, either herself or through some other person on behalf of herself or her children, then it is my will and desire that my wife, instead of giving up the moiety of our estate, shall be bound and obliged to make cession of only a child's portion, id est a fourth part of the entire estate, without anything more, in which case the three other fourths shall fall wholly and fully without any deduction to my wife, therewith to deal and thereof to dispose as her own free property. Furthermore it is my will and desire that in case any of my aforesaid daughter's children should happen to die unmarried, the deceased's portion shall devolve on his surviving sisters and brothers as regards all that has been hereinbefore mentioned. I also institute and appoint my heirs my daughter Claesie's children, born in wedlock or to be born hereafter, an in case my private will and testament should be disputed or called in question as above, I institute and appoint my aforesaid wife Joanna joint-heir to my estate for a child's portion without anything more. The above I have caused to be written by Jan Keyser, of Breda, notary public, whom for the purpose I have requested to come to my dwelling-house outside the town of Batavia, on Monday the 10th of April, in the year of our Lord Jesus Christ XVIc and fifty-seven. The present signed with my own hand (signed) A. J. Tasman, Below this was written: in presence of-me, requested to witness the present (signed) Jan Keysers, Notary-public. To this testament was appended a half-sheet of paper, on which was imprinted the seal of the Company with four others of Notary Keyser, and on which was written what follows: In the name of God Amen. -This 10th day of April, 1657, appeared before me Jan Keyser, of Breda, Notary-public to the Honble Councillors of Brabant at The Hague, and admitted to practise and residing in the town of Batavia, and before the witnesses hereafter named, Mr. Abel Tesman, sometime commander in the service of the Honble Company, sick in body but able to go and stand, enjoying the full use of his senses, memory, and mental faculties, as openly appeared to myself Notary and to the witnesses, and declared that his last will and testament by himself signed with his own hand, was contained and written in this paper sealed in quadruplo with the seal of myself Notary public, it being his will and desire that whatever he has therein ordained shall take place and have effect, in such fashion as any one's last will and testament can stand in due form notwithstanding any custom of the country or written statutes to the contrary, and that certain requisite formalities had been omitted [four or five words illegible],...

to be null and void insofar as they should be found to interfere with this his will.

Thus done and passed at the dwelling-house of the declarant, outside this town on the tenth of the month and year aforesaid, about five o'clock in the afternoon, in the presence of Jacob Jacobsz van Dantsick, burgess of this town, living in the neighbourhood of the declarant, and Lambert van Dam, Notary's clerk, summoned to witness this as credible witnesses, who have signed their names to the present together with the declarant and me Notary (signed) A. J. Tasman (lower down was written quod attestor Jan Keyser, Notary (in margine was written) X (to which as added in writing) written by Jacob Jacobsz van Dansick and Lambert van Dam.

Collated and found conform in Batavia, this 22nd day of October, A. D. 1659.

in witness whereof

Cornelis Mol, Secretary.